CHILTON'S
REPAIR & TUNE-UP GUIDE
FORD MERCURY LINCOLN MID-SIZE 1971-85

All U.S. and Canadian models of FORD Elite, LTD 1983-85,
LTD II 1977-79, Ranchero, Torino, Gran Torino, Thunderbird 1977-85 •
MERCURY Cougar 1972-85, Marquis 1983-85, Montego, XR-7 1980-85 •
LINCOLN Continental 1982-85, Mark VII 1984-85, Versailles 1978-80

President LAWRENCE A. FORNASIERI
Vice President and General Manager JOHN P. KUSHNERICK
Editor-in-Chief KERRY A. FREEMAN, S.A.E.
Senior Editor RICHARD J. RIVELE, S.A.E.
Editor RON WEBB

CHILTON BOOK COMPANY
Radnor, Pennsylvania
19089

SAFETY NOTICE

Proper service and repair procedures are vital to the safe, reliable operation of all motor vehicles, as well as the personal safety of those performing repairs. This book outlines procedures for servicing and repairing vehicles using safe, effective methods. The procedures contain many NOTES, CAUTIONS and WARNINGS which should be followed along with standard safety procedures to eliminate the possibility of personal injury or improper service which could damage the vehicle or compromise its safety.

It is important to note that repair procedures and techniques, tools and parts for servicing motor vehicles, as well as the skill and experience of the individual performing the work vary widely. It is not possible to anticipate all of the conceivable ways or conditions under which vehicles may be serviced, or to provide cautions as to all of the possible hazards that may result. Standard and accepted safety precautions and equipment should be used when handling toxic or flammable fluids, and safety goggles or other protection should be used during cutting, grinding, chiseling, prying, or any other process that can cause material removal or projectiles.

Some procedures require the use of tools specially designed for a specific purpose. Before substituting another tool or procedure, you must be completely satisfied that neither your personal safety, nor the performance of the vehicle will be endangered.

Although information in this guide is based on industry sources and is as complete as possible at the time of publication, the possibility exists that the manufacturer made later changes which could not be included here. While striving for total accuracy, Chilton Book Company cannot assume responsibility for any errors, changes, or omissions that may occur in the compilation of this data.

PART NUMBERS

Part numbers listed in this reference are not recommendations by Chilton for any product by brand name. They are references that can be used with interchange manuals and aftermarket supplier catalogs to locate each brand supplier's discrete part number.

SPECIAL TOOLS

Special tools are recommended by the vehicle manufacturer to perform their specific job. Use has been kept to a minimum, but where absolutely necessary, are they referred to in the text by the part number of the tool manufacturer. These tools can be purchased, under the appropriate part number, from Owatonna Tool Company, Owatonna, MN 55060 or an equivalent tool can be purchased locally from a tool supplier or parts outlet. Before substituting any tool for the one recommended, read the SAFETY NOTICE at the top of this page.

ACKNOWLEDGMENTS

The Chilton Book Company expresses its appreciation to the Ford Motor Company for the technical information and illustrations contained within this manual.

Copyright © 1985 by Chilton Book Company
All Rights Reserved
Published in Radnor, Pennsylvania 19089, by Chilton Book Company

Manufactured in the United States of America
    890   4321098

Chilton's Repair & Tune-Up Guide: Ford/Mercury/Lincoln Mid-Size 1971–85
ISBN 0-8019-7566-2 pbk.
Library of Congress Catalog Card No. 84-45484

CONTENTS

Quick Reference Specifications For Your Vehicle

Fill in this chart with the most commonly used specifications for your vehicle. Specifications can be found in Chapters 1 through 3 or on the tune-up decal under the hood of the vehicle.

Tune-Up

Firing Order_____

Spark Plugs:

    Type_____

    Gap (in.)_____

Point Gap (in.)_____

Dwell Angle (°)_____

Ignition Timing (°)_____

    Vacuum (Connected/Disconnected)_____

Valve Clearance (in.)

    Intake_____   Exhaust_____

Capacities

Engine Oil (qts)

    With Filter Change_____

    Without Filter Change_____

Cooling System (qts)_____

Manual Transmission (pts)_____

    Type_____

Automatic Transmission (pts)_____

    Type_____

Front Differential (pts)_____

    Type_____

Rear Differential (pts)_____

    Type_____

Transfer Case (pts)_____

    Type_____

FREQUENTLY REPLACED PARTS

Use these spaces to record the part numbers of frequently replaced parts.

PCV VALVE	OIL FILTER	AIR FILTER
Manufacturer_____	Manufacturer_____	Manufacturer_____
Part No._____	Part No._____	Part No._____

General Information and Maintenance

1

HOW TO USE THIS BOOK

This Chilton's Repair & Tune-Up Guide is intended to teach you about the inner workings of your car and save you money on its upkeep. The first two chapters contain maintenance and tune-up information and procedures. The following chapters concern themselves with the more complex systems of your car. Operating systems from engine through brakes are covered to the extent that we feel the average do-it-yourselfer should get involved. This book will not explain, for example, such things as rebuilding the differential for the simple reason that the expertise required and the investment in special tools make this task uneconomical.

We will tell you how to do many jobs (using available tools) that can save you money, give you personal satisfaction and help you avoid problems.

This book will also serve as a reference for owners who want to understand their car and/or their mechanics better. In this case, no tools at all are required.

Before removing any parts, read through the entire procedure. This will give you the overall view of what tools and supplies will be required.

The sections begin with a brief discussion of the system and what it involves, followed by adjustments, maintenance, removal and installation procedures, and repair or overhaul procedures. When repair is not considered feasible, we tell you how to remove the part and then how to install the new or rebuilt replacement. In this way, you at least save the labor costs. Backyard repair of such components as the alternator is just not practical.

Two basic mechanic's rules should be mentioned here. One, whenever the left side of the car or engine is referred to, it is meant to specify the driver's side. Conversely, the right side of the car means the passenger's side. Secondly, most screws and bolts are removed by turning counterclockwise, and tightened by turning clockwise. Safety is always the most important rule. Constantly be aware of the dangers involved in working on an automobile and take the proper precautions. Use jackstands when working under a raised vehicle. Don't smoke or allow an exposed flame to come near the battery or any part of the fuel system. Always use the proper tool and use it correctly; bruised knuckles and skinned fingers aren't a mechanic's standard equipment. Always take your time and have patience. Once you have some experience, working on your car will become an enjoyable hobby.

TOOLS AND EQUIPMENT

It would be impossible to catalog each and every tool that you may need to perform all the operations included in this book. It would also not be wise for the amateur to rush out and buy an expensive set of tools on the theory that he may need one of them at some time. The best approach is to proceed slowly, gathering together a good quality set of those tools that are used most frequently. Don't be misled by the low cost of bargain tools. It is far better to spend a little more for quality, name brand tools. Forged wrenches, 6 or 12 point sockets and fine-tooth ratchets are by far preferable to their less expensive counterparts. As any good mechanic can tell you, there are few worse experiences than trying to work on a car or truck with bad tools. Your monetary savings will be far outweighed by frustration and mangled knuckles.

Begin accumulating those tools that are used most frequently; those associated with routine maintenance and tune-up. In addition to the normal assortment of screwdrivers and pliers, you should have the following tools for routine maintenance jobs:

1. SAE and metric wrenches, sockets and combination open end/box end wrenches.
2. Jackstands—for support;
3. Oil filter wrench;
4. Oil filler spout or funnel;
5. Grease gun—for chassis lubrication;
6. Hydrometer—for checking the battery;
7. A low flat pan for draining oil;
8. Lots of rags for wiping up the inevitable mess.

In addition to the above items, there are several others that are not absolutely necessary, but are handy to have around. These include oil drying compound, a transmission funnel, and the usual supply of lubricants, antifreeze and fluids, although these can be purchased as needed. This is a basic list for routine maintenance, but only your personal needs can accurately determine your list of tools.

The second list of tools is for tune-ups. While the tools involved here are slightly more sophisticated, they need not be outrageously expensive. There are several inexpensive tachometers on the market that are every bit as good for the average mechanic as an expensive professional model. Just be sure that it works on 4, 6, and 8 cylinder engines. A basic list of tune-up equipment could include:
1. Tachometer;
NOTE: *A combination dwell meter and tachometer (dwelltach) will be helpful for older models with contact point type ignition.*
2. Spark plug wrench;
3. Timing light (preferably a DC high voltage light that works from the car's battery);
4. A set of flat feeler gauges;
5. A set of round wire spark plug gauges.

In addition to these basic tools, there are several other tools and gauges you may find useful. These include:
1. A compression gauge. The screw-in type is slower to use, but eliminates the possibility of a faulty reading due to escaping pressure;
2. A manifold vacuum gauge;
3. A test light;
4. An induction meter. This is used for determining whether or not there is current in a wire. These are handy for use if a wire is broken somewhere in a wiring harness.

As a final note, you will probably find a torque wrench necessary for all but the most basic work. The beam type models are perfectly adequate, although the newer click type are more precise.

Special Tools

Normally, the use of special factory tools is avoided for repair procedures, since these are not readily available for the do-it-yourself mechanic. When it is possible to perform the job with more commonly available tools, it will be pointed out, but occasionally, a special tool was designed to perform a specific function and should be used. Before substituting another tool, you should be convinced that neither your safety nor the performance of the vehicle will be compromised.

Some special tools are available commercially from major tool manufacturers. Others for your car can be purchased from your dealer or from Owatonna Tool Co., Owatonna, Minnesota 55060.

SERVICING YOUR VEHICLE SAFELY

It is virtually impossible to anticipate all of the hazards involved with automotive maintenance and service but care and common sense will prevent most accidents.

The rules of safety for mechanics range from "don't smoke around gasoline," to "use the proper tool for the job." The trick to avoiding injuries is to develop safe work habits and take every possible precaution.

Do's

• Do keep a fire extinguisher and first aid kit within easy reach.
• Do wear safety glasses or goggles when cutting, drilling, grinding or prying. If you wear glasses for the sake of vision, then they should be made of hardened glass that can serve also as safety glasses, or wear safety goggles over your regular glasses.
• Do shield your eyes whenever you work around the battery. Batteries contain sulphuric acid; in case of contact with the eyes or skin, flush the area with water or a mixture of water and baking soda and get medical attention immediately.
• Do use safety stands for any under-car service. Jacks are for raising vehicles; safety stands are for making sure the vehicle stays raised until you want it to come down. Whenever the vehicle is raised, block the wheels remaining on the ground and set the parking brake.
• Do use adequate ventilation when working with any chemicals. Asbestos dust resulting from brake lining wear could cause cancer.
• Do disconnect the negative battery cable when working on the electrical system.
• Do follow manufacturer's directions whenever working with potentially hazardous

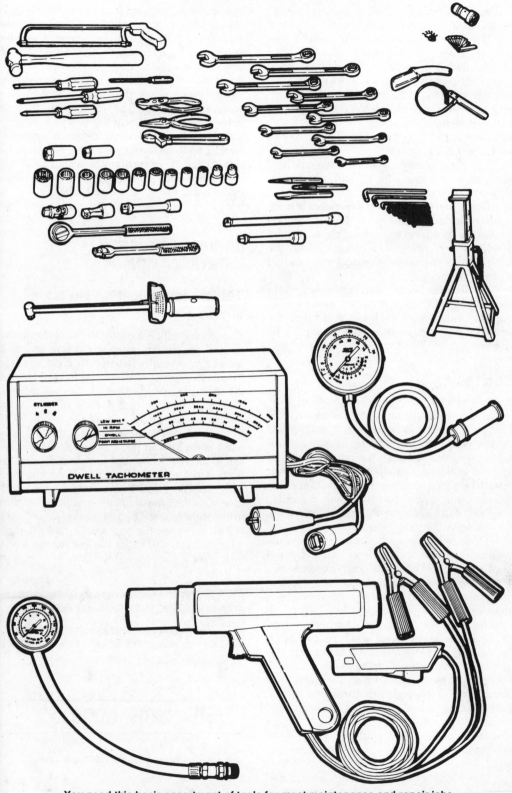

You need this basic assortment of tools for most maintenance and repair jobs

materials. Both brake fluid and antifreeze are poisonous if taken internally.

• Do properly maintain your tools. Loose hammerheads, mushroomed punches and chisels, frayed or poorly grounded electrical cords, excessively worn screwdrivers, spread wrenches (open end), cracked sockets, slipping ratchets, or faulty droplight sockets can cause accidents.

• Do use the proper size and type of tool for the job being done.

• Do when possible, pull on a wrench handle rather than push on it, and adjust your stance to prevent a fall.

• Do be sure that adjustable wrenches are tightly adjusted on the nut or bolt and pulled so that the face is on the side of the fixed jaw.

• Do select a wrench or socket that fits the nut or bolt. The wrench or socket should sit straight, not cocked.

• Do strike squarely with a hammer; avoid glancing blows.

• Do set the parking brake and block the wheels if the work requires that the engine be running.

Don't's

• Don't run an engine in a garage or anywhere else without proper ventilation—EVER! Carbon monoxide is poisonous; it is absorbed by the body 400 times faster than oxygen; it takes a long time to leave the human body and you can build up a deadly supply of it in your system by simply breathing in a little every day. You may not realize you are slowly poisoning yourself. Always use power vents, windows, fans or open the garage doors.

• Don't work around moving parts while wearing a necktie or other loose clothing. Short sleeves are much safer than long, loose sleeves. Hard-toed shoes with neoprene soles protect your toes and give a better grip on slippery surfaces. Jewelry such as watches, fancy belt buckles, beads or body adornment of any kind is not safe while working around a car. Long hair should be hidden under a hat or cap.

• Don't use pockets for toolboxes. A fall or bump can drive a screwdriver deep into your body. Even a wiping cloth hanging from the back pocket can wrap around a spinning shaft or fan.

• Don't smoke when working around gasoline, cleaning solvent or other flammable material.

• Don't smoke when working around the battery. When the battery is being charged, it gives off explosive hydrogen gas.

• Don't use gasoline to wash your hands; there are excellent soaps available. Gasoline may contain lead, and lead can enter the body through a cut, accumulating in the body until you are very ill. Gasoline also removes all the natural oils from the skin so that bone dry hands will suck up oil and grease.

• Don't service the air conditioning system unless you are equipped with the necessary tools and training. The refrigerant, R-12, is extremely cold and when exposed to the air, will instantly freeze any surface it comes in contact with, including your eyes. Although the refrigerant is normally non-toxic, R-12 becomes a deadly poisonous gas in the presence of an open flame. One good whiff of the vapors from burning refrigerant can be fatal.

SERIAL NUMBER IDENTIFICATION

Vehicle Identification Number
1971–80

The official vehicle identification number for title and registration purposes is stamped on a metal tag, which is fastened to the top of the instrument panel. The tag is located on the driver's side, visible through the windshield. The first digit in the vehicle identification number is the model year of the car (0–1970, 4–1974, etc.). The second digit is the assembly plant code for the plant in which the vehicle was built. The third and fourth digits are the body serial code designations (2-dr sdn, 4-dr sdn). The fifth digit is the engine code which identifies the type of engine originally installed in the vehicle (see "Engine Codes" chart). The last six digits are the consecutive unit numbers which start at 100,001 for the first car of a model year built at each assembly plant.

1S53F100001

Vehicle identification plate (1971 only)

(VEHICLE IDENTIFICATION NUMBER)

Vehicle identification plate, 1972 and later

From 1981

Beginning in 1981, the serial number contains seventeen or more digits or letters. The first three give the "world" manufacturer code; the fourth—the type of restraint system; the fifth will remain the letter "P"; the sixth and seventh—the car line, series and body type; the eighth—the engine type; the ninth—a check digit; the tenth—the model year; the elev-

Engine Identification Codes

Engine	Year	Code
4-140 Non-Turbo	1981–85	A
4-140 Turbo	1984–85	W(T)
6-200	1981–83	B
6-232	1982–85	3
6-250	1971–74	L
8-255	1980–82	D
8-302	1971–85	F
8-351C	1971–74	H
8-351C 4bbl	1971	M
8-351M	1975–79	Q
8-351W	1973–79	H
8-400	1972–78	S
8-429	1972–73	N
8-429CJ	1971	C
8-429CJ-RA	1971	J
8-460	1974–75	A
8-460PI	1973–76	C

C: Cleveland
M: Modified Cleveland
W: Windsor
CJ: Cobra Jet
RA: Ram Air
PI: Police Interceptor

Transmission Codes

Type	Year	Code
3 Speed Manual	1971–74	1
4 Speed Manual	1980–83	6
4 Speed Manual	1980–83	4
4 Speed Manual	1983–85	7
5 Speed Manual	1984–85	2
C3 Automatic	1983–85	V
C4 Automatic	1971–80	W
C5 Automatic	1982–85	C
AOD Auto Overdrive	1980–85	T
CW Automatic	1974–75	Y
FMX Automatic	1971–80	X
C6 Automatic	1971–80	U
C6 Auto Special	1971–79	Z

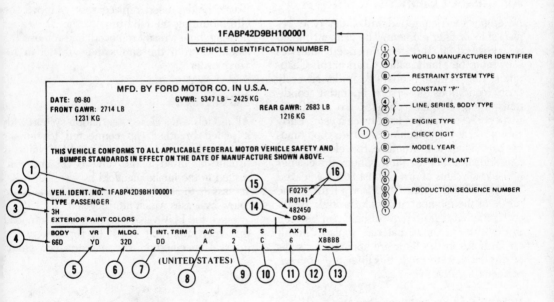

2. Vehicle type
3. Paint
4. Body type code
5. Vinyl roof
6. Body side moulding
7. Trim code—(First code letter = fabric and seat type. Second code = color)
8. Air conditioning
9. Radio
10. Sun/moon roof
11. Axle ratio
12. Transmission
13. Springs—Front l. and r., rear l. and r. (4 codes)
14. District sales office
15. PTO/SPL order number
16. Accessory reserve load

Vehicle identification—from 1981

Rear Axle Codes

Ratio	Year	Code
2.26	1979–80	G
2.47	1978, 82–83	B(C)
2.50	1978	1(J)
2.73	1979–85	8(H)(M)
2.75	1971–78	2(K)
3.00	1971–78	6(O)
3.07	1971, 74–75	B, 5(E)
3.08	1979–85	Y(Z)
3.25	1971–77	9(R)
3.27	1983–85	5(E)
3.42	1982–85	4(D)
3.45	1982–85	F(R)
3.55	1984–85	2(K)
3.63	1983	A
3.73	1984–85	(W)
3.85	1983	J

NOTE: *Figures in Parentheses Indicate locking differential.*

enth—the assembly plant; the remaining numbers are the production sequence.

ROUTINE MAINTENANCE

Air Cleaner Element

All engines are equipped with a dry type, replaceable air filter element. The element should be replaced at the recommended intervals shown on the Maintenance Chart in this Chapter. If your vehicle is operated under severely dusty conditions or severe operating conditions, more frequent changes are necessary. Inspect the element at least twice a year. Early spring and at the beginning of fall are good times for the inspection. Remove the element and check for holes in the filter. Check the cleaner housing for signs of dirt or dust that has leaked through the filter element. Place a light on the inside of the element and look through the filter at the light. If no glow of light can be seen through the element material, replace the filter. If holes in the filter are apparent or signs of dirt leakage through the filter are noticed, replace the filter.

REMOVAL AND INSTALLATION

Air Cleaner Assembly

1. Disconnect all hoses, ducts and vacuum tubes from the air cleaner assembly.
2. Remove the top cover wing nut and grommet (if equipped). Remove any side bracket mount retaining bolts (if equipped). Remove the air cleaner assembly from the top of the carburetor or intake assembly.
3. Remove the cover and the element, wipe clean all inside surfaces of the air cleaner housing and cover. Check the condition of the mounting gasket (cleaner base to carburetor). Replace the mounting gasket if it is worn or broken.
4. Reposition the cleaner assembly, element and cover on the carburetor or intake assembly.
5. Reconnect all hoses, duct and vacuum hoses removed. Tighten the wing nut finger tight.

Element

The element can, in most cases, be replaced by removing the wing nut and cleaner assembly cover. If the inside of the housing is dirty, however, remove the assembly for cleaning to prevent dirt from entering the carburetor.

CRANKCASE VENTILATION FILTER-IN AIR CLEANER

Replace or inspect cleaner mounted crankcase ventilation filter (on models equipped) at the same time the air cleaner filter element is serviced. To replace the filter, simply remove the air cleaner top cover and pull the filter from its housing. Push a new filter into the housing and install the air cleaner cover. If the filter and plastic holder need replacement, remove the clip mounting the feed tube to the air cleaner housing (hose already removed) and remove the assembly from the air cleaner. Install in reverse order.

PCV Valve

All models use a closed ventilation system with a sealed breather cap connected to the air cleaner by a rubber hose. The PCV valve is usually mounted in the valve cover and connected to the intake manifold by a rubber hose. Its task is to regulate the amount of crankcase (blow-by) gases which are recycled.

Since the PCV valve works under severe load it is very important that it be replaced at the interval specified in the maintenance chart.

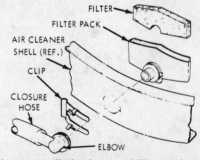

Crankcase ventilation hose and filter pack assembly

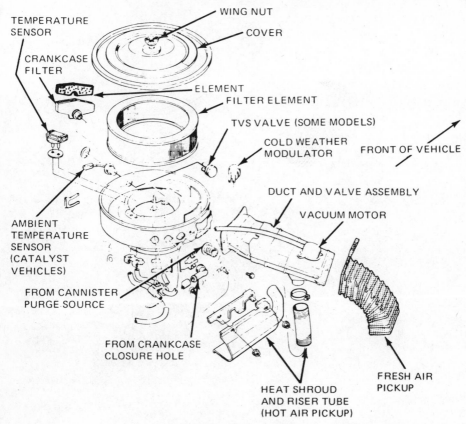

TEMPERATURE
SENSOR

WING NUT

COVER

CRANKCASE
FILTER

ELEMENT
FILTER ELEMENT

TVS VALVE (SOME MODELS)

COLD WEATHER
MODULATOR

FRONT OF VEHICLE

DUCT AND VALVE ASSEMBLY

VACUUM MOTOR

AMBIENT
TEMPERATURE
SENSOR
(CATALYST
VEHICLES)

FROM CANNISTER
PURGE SOURCE

FROM CRANKCASE
CLOSURE HOLE

HEAT SHROUD
AND RISER TUBE
(HOT AIR PICKUP)

FRESH AIR
PICKUP

Typical air cleaner assembly

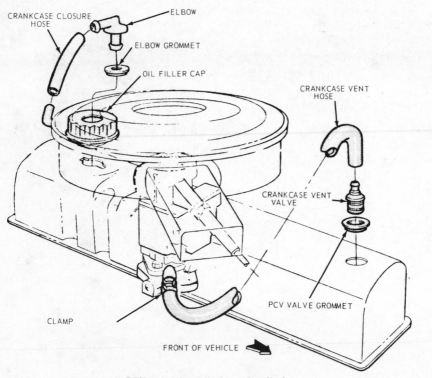

CRANKCASE CLOSURE
HOSE

ELBOW

ELBOW GROMMET

OIL FILLER CAP

CRANKCASE VENT
HOSE

CRANKCASE VENT
VALVE

PCV VALVE GROMMET

CLAMP

FRONT OF VEHICLE

PCV valve installation—6 cylinder

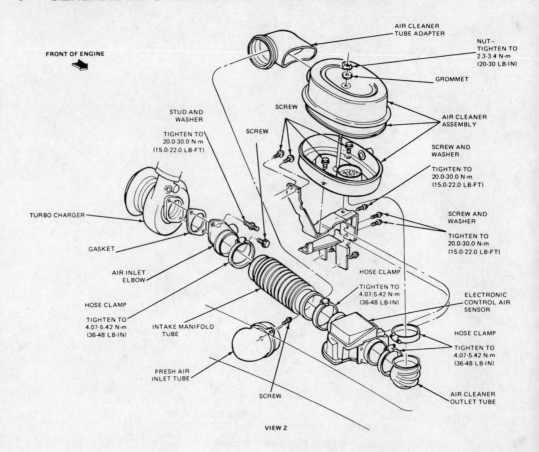

FRONT OF ENGINE

AIR CLEANER TUBE ADAPTER

NUT— TIGHTEN TO 2.3-3.4 N·m (20-30 LB-IN)

GROMMET

SCREW

AIR CLEANER ASSEMBLY

STUD AND WASHER

TIGHTEN TO 20.0-30.0 N·m (15.0-22.0 LB-FT)

SCREW

SCREW AND WASHER

TIGHTEN TO 20.0-30.0 N·m (15.0-22.0 LB-FT)

TURBO CHARGER

SCREW AND WASHER

TIGHTEN TO 20.0-30.0 N·m (15.0-22.0 LB-FT)

GASKET

HOSE CLAMP

AIR INLET ELBOW

TIGHTEN TO 4.07-5.42 N·m (36-48 LB-IN)

ELECTRONIC CONTROL AIR SENSOR

HOSE CLAMP

TIGHTEN TO 4.07-5.42 N·m (36-48 LB-IN)

INTAKE MANIFOLD TUBE

HOSE CLAMP

TIGHTEN TO 4.07-5.42 N·m (36-48 LB-IN)

FRESH AIR INLET TUBE

AIR CLEANER OUTLET TUBE

SCREW

VIEW Z

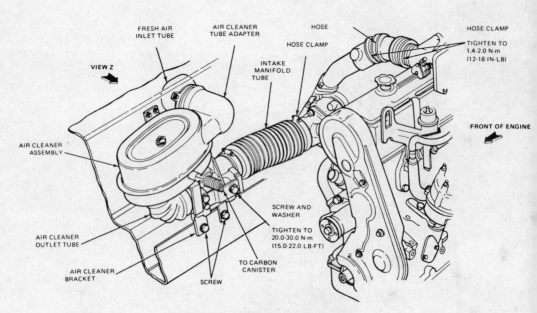

VIEW Z

FRESH AIR INLET TUBE

AIR CLEANER TUBE ADAPTER

HOSE

HOSE CLAMP

INTAKE MANIFOLD TUBE

HOSE CLAMP

HOSE CLAMP

TIGHTEN TO 1.4-2.0 N·m (12-18 IN·LB)

AIR CLEANER ASSEMBLY

FRONT OF ENGINE

AIR CLEANER OUTLET TUBE

SCREW AND WASHER

TIGHTEN TO 20.0-30.0 N·m (15.0-22.0 LB-FT)

AIR CLEANER BRACKET

TO CARBON CANISTER

SCREW

4-140 Turbo engine air cleaner assembly

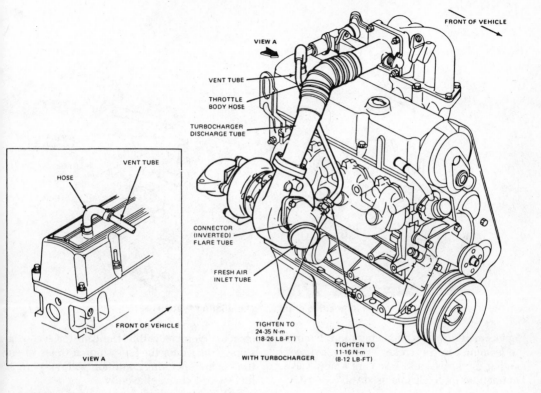

FRONT OF VEHICLE

VIEW A

VENT TUBE

THROTTLE
BODY HOSE

TURBOCHARGER
DISCHARGE TUBE

CONNECTOR
(INVERTED)
FLARE TUBE

FRESH AIR
INLET TUBE

TIGHTEN TO
24-35 N·m
(18-26 LB·FT)

TIGHTEN TO
11-16 N·m
(8-12 LB·FT)

WITH TURBOCHARGER

HOSE

VENT TUBE

FRONT OF VEHICLE

VIEW A

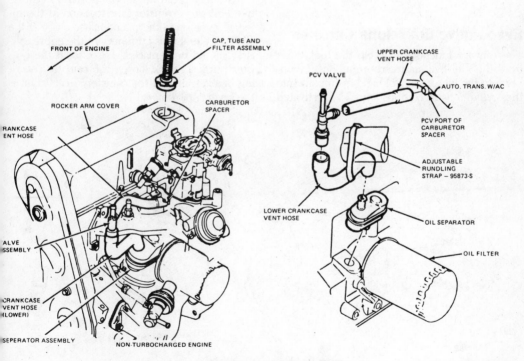

FRONT OF ENGINE

CAP, TUBE AND
FILTER ASSEMBLY

PCV VALVE

UPPER CRANKCASE
VENT HOSE

AUTO. TRANS. W/AC

ROCKER ARM COVER

CARBURETOR
SPACER

PCV PORT OF
CARBURETOR
SPACER

CRANKCASE
VENT HOSE

ADJUSTABLE
RUNDLING
STRAP – 95873-S

VALVE
ASSEMBLY

LOWER CRANKCASE
VENT HOSE

OIL SEPARATOR

OIL FILTER

CRANKCASE
VENT HOSE
(LOWER)

SEPERATOR ASSEMBLY

NON-TURBOCHARGED ENGINE

4-140 late model PCV system

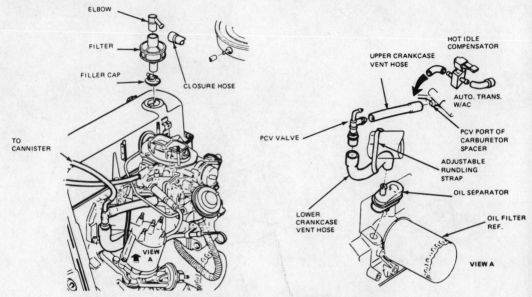

4-140 positive crankcase ventilation system

Replacement involves removing the valve from the grommet in the rocker arm cover disconnecting the hose(s) and installing a new valve. Do not attempt to clean a used valve.

Evaporative Emissions Canister

The canister functions to cycle the fuel vapor from the fuel tank and carburetor float chamber into the intake manifold and eventually into the cylinders for combustion. The activated charcoal element within the canister acts as a storage device for the fuel vapor at times when the engine operating condition will not permit fuel vapor to burn efficiently.

The only required service for the evaporative emissions canister is inspection at the interval specified in the maintenance chart. If the charcoal element is gummed up the entire canister should be replaced. Disconnect the canister purge hose(s); loosen the canister retaining bracket; lift out the canister. Installation is the reverse of removal.

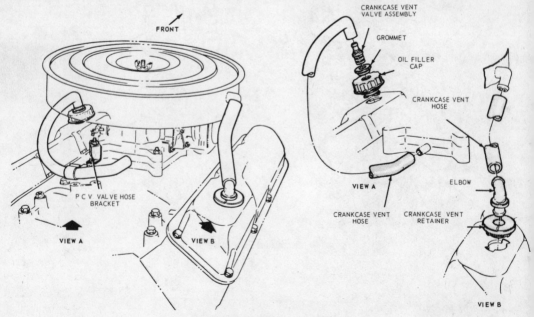

PCV valve installation—302 V8

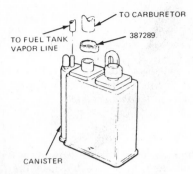

TO CARBURETOR

TO FUEL TANK
VAPOR LINE

387289

CANISTER

Typical carbon canister

Battery

FLUID LEVEL (EXCEPT "MAINTENANCE FREE" BATTERIES)

Check the battery electrolyte level at least once a month, or more often in hot weather or during periods of extended car operation. The level can be checked through the case on translucent polypropylene batteries; the cell caps must be removed on other models. The electrolyte level in each cell should be kept filled to the split ring inside, or the line marked on the outside of the case.

If the level is low, add only distilled water, or colorless, odorless drinking water, through the opening until the level is correct. Each cell is completely separate from the others, so each must be checked and filled individually.

If water is added in freezing weather, the car should be driven several miles to allow the water to mix with the electrolyte. Otherwise, the battery could freeze.

SPECIFIC GRAVITY (EXCEPT "MAINTENANCE FREE" BATTERIES)

At least once a year, check the specific gravity of the battery. It should be between 1.20 and 1.26 at room temperature.

The specific gravity can be checked with the use of an hydrometer, an inexpensive instrument available from many sources, including auto parts stores. The hydrometer has a squeeze bulb at one end and a nozzle at the other. Battery electrolyte is sucked into the hydrometer until the float is lifted from its seat. The specific gravity is then read by noting the position of the float. Generally, if after charging, the specific gravity between any two cells varies more than 50 points (.50), the battery is bad and should be replaced.

It is not possible to check the specific gravity in this manner on sealed ("maintenance free") batteries. Instead, the indicator built into the top of the case must be relied on to display any signs of battery deterioration. If the indicator is dark, the battery can be assumed to be OK.

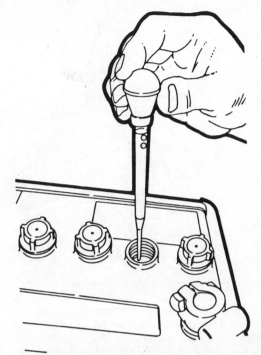

Checking the battery with a hydrometer

If the indicator is light, the specific gravity is low, and the battery should be charged or replaced.

CABLES AND CLAMPS

Once a year, the battery terminals and the cable clamps should be cleaned. Loosen the clamps and remove the cables, negative cable first. On batteries with posts on top, the use of a puller specially made for the purpose is recommended. These are inexpensive, and available in auto parts stores. Side terminal battery cables are secured with a bolt.

Clean the cable clamps and the battery terminal with a wire brush, until all corrosion, grease, etc. is removed and the metal is shiny. It is especially important to clean the inside of the clamp thoroughly, since a small deposit of foreign material or oxidation there will prevent a sound electrical connection and inhibit either starting or charging. Special tools are available for cleaning these parts, one type for conventional batteries and another type for side terminal batteries.

Before installing the cables, loosen the battery hold-down clamp or strap, remove the battery and check the battery tray. Clear it of any debris, and check it for soundness. Rust should be wire brushed away, and the metal given a coat of anti-rust paint. Replace the battery and tighten the hold-down clamp or strap securely, but be careful not to overtighten, which will crack the battery case.

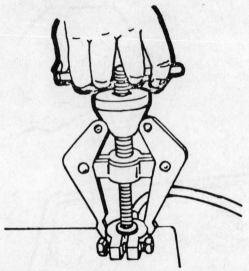

Use a puller to remove the battery cable

After the clamps and terminals are clean, reinstall the cables, negative cable last; do not hammer on the clamps to install. Tighten the clamps securely, but do not distort them. Give the clamps and terminals a thin external coat of grease after installation, to retard corrosion.

Check the cables at the same time that the terminals are cleaned. If the cable insulation is cracked or broken, or if the ends are frayed, the cable should be replaced with a new cable of the same length and gauge.

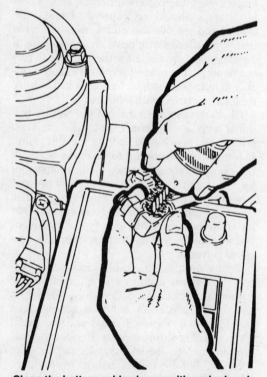

Clean the battery cable clamps with a wire brush

CAUTION: *Keep flame or sparks away from the battery; it gives off explosive hydrogen gas. Battery electrolyte contains sulphuric acid. If you should splash any on your skin or in your eyes, flush the affected area with plenty of clear water; if it lands in your eyes, get medical help immediately.*

Heat Riser

Some models are equipped with exhaust control (heat riser) valves located near the head pipe connection in the exhaust manifold. These valves aid initial warmup in cold weather by restricting exhaust gas flow slightly. The heat generated by this restriction is transferred to the intake manifold where it results in improved fuel vaporization.

The operation of the exhaust control valve should be checked every 6 months or 6,000

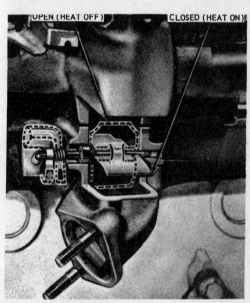

Six cylinder heat riser

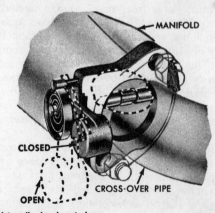

Eight cylinder heat riser

miles. Make sure that the thermostatic spring is hooked on the stop pin and that the tension holds the valve shut. Rotate the counterweight by hand and make sure that it moves freely through about 90° of rotation. A valve which is operating properly will open when light finger pressure is applied (cold engine). Lubricate the shaft bushings with a mixture of penetrating oil and graphite. Operate the valve manually a few times to work in the lubricant.

Belts

Once a year or at 12,000 mile intervals, the tension (and condition) of the alternator, power steering (if so equipped), air conditioning (if so equipped), and Thermactor air pump drive belts should be checked, and, if necessary, adjusted. Loose accessory drive belts can lead to poor engine cooling and diminish alternator, power steering pump, air conditioning compressor or Thermactor air pump output. A belt that is too tight places a severe strain on the water pump, alternator, power steering pump, compressor or air pump bearings.

Replace any belt that is so glazed, worn or stretched that it cannot be tightened sufficiently.

NOTE: *The material used in late model drive belts is such that the belts do not show wear. Replace belts at least every three years.*

On vehicles with matched belts, replace both belts. New belts are to be adjusted to a tension of 140 lbs (½ in., ⅜ in., and ¹⁵⁄₃₂ in. wide belts) or 80 lbs (¼ in. wide belts) measured on a belt tension gauge. Any belt that has been operating for a minimum of 10 minutes is considered a used belt. In the first 10 minutes, the belt should stretch to its maximum extent. After 10 minutes, stop the engine and recheck the belt tension. Belt tension for a used belt should be maintained at 110 lbs (all except ¼ in. wide belts) or 60 lbs (¼ in. wide belts). If a belt tension gauge is not available, the following procedures may be used.

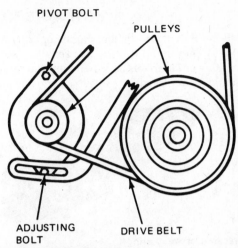

Alternator belt adjustment

ADJUSTMENTS

CAUTION: *On models equipped with an electric cooling fan, disconnect the negative battery cable or fan motor wiring harness connector before replacing or adjusting drive belts. The fan may come on, under certain circumstances, even though the ignition is off.*

ALTERNATOR (FAN DRIVE) BELT

All Except "Serpentine" (Single) Belt

1. Position a ruler perpendicular to the drive belt at its longest run. Test the tightness of the belt by pressing it firmly with your thumb. The deflection should not exceed ¼ in.

2. If the deflection exceeds ¼ in., loosen the alternator mounting and adjusting arm bolts.

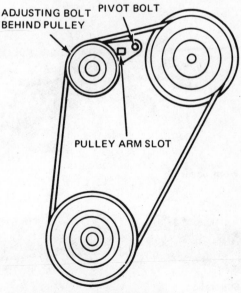

Air conditioning belt adjustment

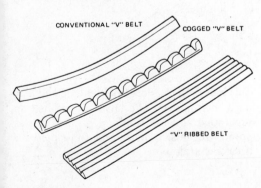

Drive belt types

HOW TO SPOT WORN V-BELTS

V-Belts are vital to efficient engine operation—they drive the fan, water pump and other accessories. They require little maintenance (occasional tightening) but they will not last forever. Slipping or failure of the V-belt will lead to overheating. If your V-belt looks like any of these, it should be replaced.

This belt has deep cracks, which cause it to flex. Too much flexing leads to heat build-up and premature failure. These cracks can be caused by using the belt on a pulley that is too small. Notched belts are available for small diameter pulleys.

Cracking or weathering

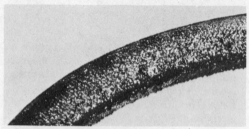

Oil and grease on a belt can cause the belt's rubber compounds to soften and separate from the reinforcing cords that hold the belt together. The belt will first slip, then finally fail altogether.

Softening (grease and oil)

Glazing is caused by a belt that is slipping. A slipping belt can cause a run-down battery, erratic power steering, overheating or poor accessory performance. The more the belt slips, the more glazing will be built up on the surface of the belt. The more the belt is glazed, the more it will slip. If the glazing is light, tighten the belt.

Glazing

The cover of this belt is worn off and is peeling away. The reinforcing cords will begin to wear and the belt will shortly break. When the belt cover wears in spots or has a rough jagged appearance, check the pulley grooves for roughness.

Worn cover

This belt is on the verge of breaking and leaving you stranded. The layers of the belt are separating and the reinforcing cords are exposed. It's just a matter of time before it breaks completely.

Separation

3a. On 1971–72 V8 and 6 cylinder models, use a pry bar or broom handle to move the alternator toward or away from the engine until the proper tension is reached.

CAUTION: *Apply tension to the front of the alternator only. Positioning the pry bar against the rear end housing will damage the alternator.*

3b. On 1973 and later models, place a 1 in. open-end or adjustable wrench on the adjusting ridge cast on the body, and pull on the wrench until the proper tension is achieved.

4. Holding the alternator in place to maintain tension, tighten the adjusting arm bolt. Recheck the belt tension. When the belt is properly tensioned, tighten the alternator mounting bolt.

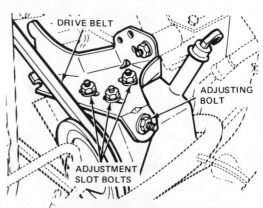
Power steering belt adjustment (slider type)

POWER STEERING DRIVE BELT

All In-Line Six-Cylinder and 1971–72 V8 Models

1. Holding a ruler perpendicular to the drive belt at its longest run, test the tightness of the belt by pressing it firmly with your thumb. The deflection should not exceed ¼ in.

2. To adjust the belt tension, loosen the adjusting and mounting bolts on the front face of the steering pump cover plate (hub side).

3. Using a pry bar or broom handle on the pump hub, move the power steering pump toward or away from the engine until the proper tension is reached. Do not pry against the reservoir as it is relatively soft and easily deformed.

4. Holding the pump in place, tighten the adjusting arm bolt and then recheck the belt tension. When the belt is properly tensioned tighten the mounting bolts.

1973 AND LATER V8 MODELS (EXCEPT SINGLE DRIVE BELT)

1. Position a ruler perpendicular to the drive belt at its longest run. Test the tightness of the belt by pressing it firmly with your thumb. The deflection should be about ¼ in.

2. To adjust the belt tension, loosen the three bolts in the three elongated adjusting slots at the power steering pump attaching bracket.

3. Turn the steering pump drive belt adjusting nut as required until the proper deflection is obtained. Turning the adjusting nut clockwise will increase tension and decrease deflection; counterclockwise will decrease tension and increase deflection.

4. Without disturbing the pump, tighten the three attaching bolts.

AIR CONDITIONING COMPRESSOR DRIVE BELT (EXCEPT SINGLE DRIVE BELT)

1. Position a ruler perpendicular to the drive belt at its longest run. Test the tightness of the belt by pressing it firmly with your thumb. The deflection should not exceed ¼ in.

2. If the engine is equipped with an idler pulley, loosen the idler pulley adjusting bolt, insert a pry bar between the pulley and the engine (or in the idler pulley adjusting slot), and adjust the tension accordingly. If the engine is not equipped with an idler pulley, the alternator must be moved to accomplish this adjustment, as outlined under "Alternator (Fan Drive) Belt."

3. When the proper tension is reached, tighten the idler pulley adjusting bolt (if so equipped) or the alternator adjusting and mounting bolts.

THERMACTOR AIR PUMP DRIVE BELT

1. Position a ruler perpendicular to the drive belt at its longest run. Test the tightness of the belt by pressing it firmly with your thumb. The deflection should be about ¼ in.

2. To adjust the belt tension, loosen the adjusting arm bolt slightly. If necessary, also loosen the mounting belt slightly.

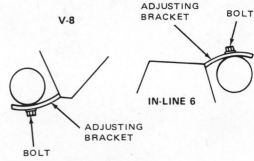
Air pump adjustment points

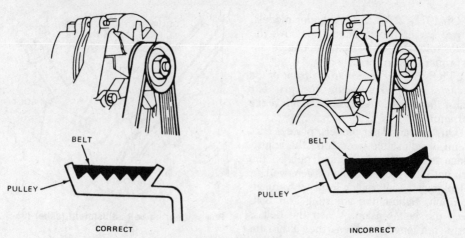

BELT

PULLEY

CORRECT

BELT

PULLEY

INCORRECT

Ribbed belt installation

3. Using a pry bar or broom handle, pry against the pump rear cover to move the pump toward or away from the engine as necessary.

CAUTION: *Do not pry against the pump housing itself, as damage to the housing may result.*

4. Holding the pump in place, tighten the adjusting arm bolt and recheck the tension. When the belt is properly tensioned, tighten the mounting bolt.

SINGLE DRIVE BELT MODELS

(Serpentine Drive Belt)

Most late models (starting in 1979) feature a single, wide, ribbed V-belt that drives the water pump, alternator, and (on some models) the air conditioner compressor. To install a new belt, loosen the bracket lock bolt; retract the belt tensioner with a pry bar and slide the old belt off of the pulleys. Slip on a new belt and re-

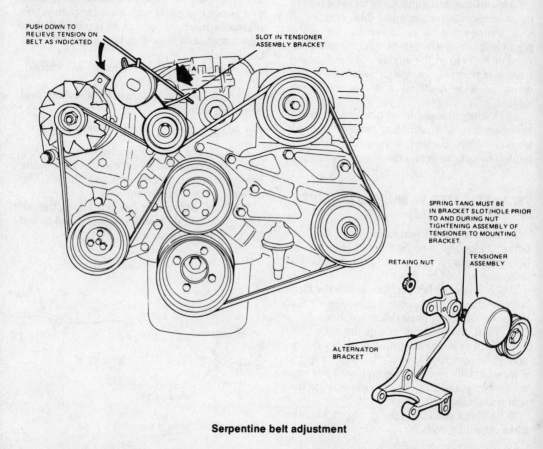

PUSH DOWN TO
RELIEVE TENSION ON
BELT AS INDICATED

SLOT IN TENSIONER
ASSEMBLY BRACKET

SPRING TANG MUST BE
IN BRACKET SLOT/HOLE PRIOR
TO AND DURING NUT
TIGHTENING ASSEMBLY OF
TENSIONER TO MOUNTING
BRACKET.

RETAING NUT

TENSIONER
ASSEMBLY

ALTERNATOR
BRACKET

Serpentine belt adjustment

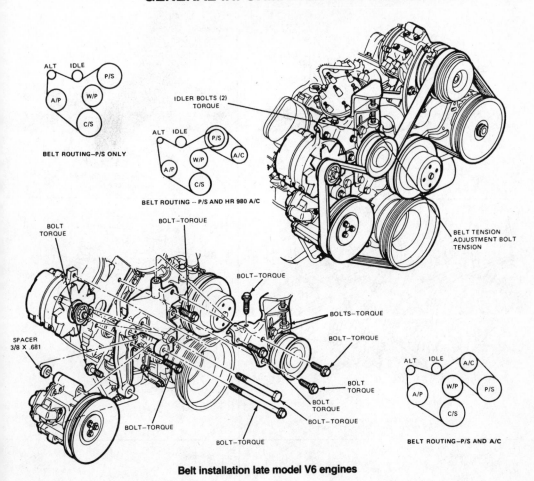

Belt installation late model V6 engines

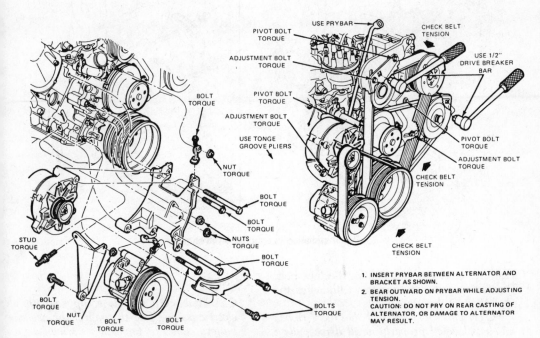

1. INSERT PRYBAR BETWEEN ALTERNATOR AND BRACKET AS SHOWN.
2. BEAR OUTWARD ON PRYBAR WHILE ADJUSTING TENSION.
   CAUTION: DO NOT PRY ON REAR CASTING OF ALTERNATOR, OR DAMAGE TO ALTERNATOR MAY RESULT.

Belt installation late model V8 engines

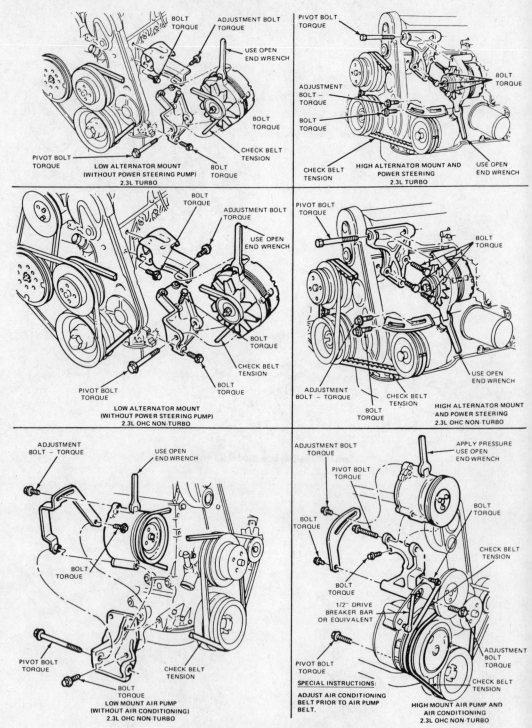

Belt installation late model 4-140 engines

lease the tensioner and tighten the lock bolt. The spring powered tensioner eliminates the need for periodic adjustments.

NOTE: *Check to make sure that the V-ribbed belt is located properly in all drive pulleys before applying tensioner pressure.*

Hoses

CAUTION: *On models equipped with an electric cooling fan, disconnect the negative battery cable, or fan motor wiring harness connector before replacing any radia-*

HOW TO SPOT BAD HOSES

Both the upper and lower radiator hoses are called upon to perform difficult jobs in an inhospitable environment. They are subject to nearly 18 psi at under hood temperatures often over 280°F., and must circulate nearly 7500 gallons of coolant an hour—3 good reasons to have good hoses.

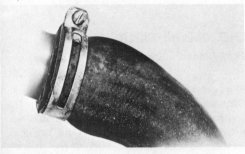

Swollen hose

A good test for any hose is to feel it for soft or spongy spots. Frequently these will appear as swollen areas of the hose. The most likely cause is oil soaking. This hose could burst at any time, when hot or under pressure.

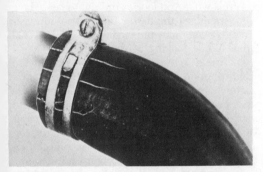

Cracked hose

Cracked hoses can usually be seen but feel the hoses to be sure they have not hardened; a prime cause of cracking. This hose has cracked down to the reinforcing cords and could split at any of the cracks.

Frayed hose end (due to weak clamp)

Weakened clamps frequently are the cause of hose and cooling system failure. The connection between the pipe and hose has deteriorated enough to allow coolant to escape when the engine is hot.

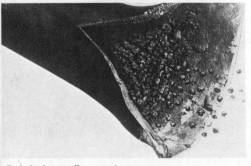

Debris in cooling system

Debris, rust and scale in the cooling system can cause the inside of a hose to weaken. This can usually be felt on the outside of the hose as soft or thinner areas.

tor/heater hose. The fan may come on, under certain circumstances, even though the ignition is Off.

REPLACEMENT

Inspect the condition of the radiator and heater hoses periodically. Early spring and at the beginning of the fall or winter, when you are performing other maintenance, are good times. Make sure the engine and cooling system are cold. Visually inspect for cracking, rotting or collapsed hoses, replace as necessary. Run your hand along the length of the hose. If a weak or swollen spot is noted when squeezing the hose wall, replace the hose.

Drain the cooling system into a suitable container (if the coolant is to be reused). Loosen the hose clamps at each end of the hose that requires replacement. Twist, pull and slide the hose off of the radiator, water pump, thermostat or heater connection. Clean the hose mounting connections. Position the hose clamps on the new hose. Coat the connection surfaces with a water resistant sealer and slide the hose into position. Make sure the hose clamps are located beyond the raised bead of the connector (if equipped) and centered in the clamping area of the connection. Tighten the clamps to between 20–30 inch lbs. Do not overtighten. Fill the cooling system. Start the engine and allow to reach normal operating temperature. Check for leaks.

Air Conditioning

CAUTION: *Do not loosen any lines or fittings on the air conditioning system. Refrigerant, when exposed to air, will instantly freeze anything it comes in contact with. When exposed to flame, it becomes highly toxic. Have repair work done by a professional.*

CHECKING REFRIGERANT LEVEL

Sight Glass Equipped

First, wipe the sight glass clean with a cloth wrapped around the eraser end of a pencil. Connect a tachometer to the engine with the positive line connected to the distributor side of the ignition coil and the negative line connected to a good ground, such as the steering box. Have a friend operate the air conditioner controls while you look at the sight glass. Have your friend set the dash panel control to maximum cooling. Start the engine and idle at 1,500 rpm. While looking at the sight glass, signal your friend to turn the blower switch to the High position. If a few bubbles appear immediately after the blower is turned on and then disappear, the system is sufficiently charged with refrigerant. If, on the other hand, a large amount of bubbles, foam or froth continue after the blower has operated for a few seconds, then the system is in need of additional refrigerant.

If no bubbles appear at all, then there is either sufficient refrigerant in the system or it is bone

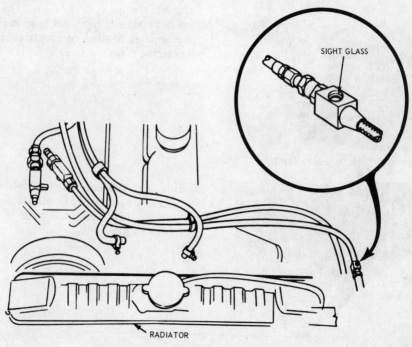

Typical air conditioning sight glass location

dry. To make a determination follow the procedure given below for models without a sight glass.

Models Without a Sight Glass

To determine if the refrigerant is at the proper level of charge, turn on the engine and run the air conditioner for a few minutes. Feel the temperature of the hose running from the receiver/dryer and of the hose running to the condensor. They should both be cold and approximately the same temperature. If they are both warm the system probably has no refrigerant. If they are different temperatures there is a malfunction in the system.

CAUTION: *Do not attempt to work on the air conditioning system yourself. Consult a professional garage with the proper testing equipment.*

Windshield Wipers

For maximum effectiveness and longest element life, the windshield and wiper blades should be kept clean. Dirt, tree sap, road tar and so on will cause streaking, smearing and blade deterioration if left on the glass. It is advisable to wash the windshield carefully with a commercial glass cleaner at least once a month. Wipe off the rubber blades with the wet rag afterwards. Do not attempt to move the wipers by hand; damage to the motor and drive mechanism will result.

If the blades are found to be cracked, broken or torn, they should be replaced immediately. Replacement intervals will vary with usage, although ozone deterioration usually limits blade life to about one year. If the wiper pattern is smeared or streaked, or if the blade chatters across the glass, the elements should be replaced. It is easiest and most sensible to replace the elements in pairs.

There are basically three different types of refills, which differ in their method of replacement. One type has two release buttons, approximately one-third of the way up from the ends of the blade frame. Pushing the buttons down releases a lock and allows the rubber filler to be removed from the frame. The new filler slides back into the frame and locks in place.

The second type of refill has two metal tabs which are unlocked by squeezing them together. The rubber filler can then be withdrawn from the frame jaws. A new refill is installed by inserting the refill into the front frame jaws and sliding it rearward to engage the remaining frame jaws. There are usually four jaws; be certain when installing that the refill is engaged in all of them. At the end of its travel,

the tabs will lock into place on the front jaws of the wiper blade frame.

The third type is a refill made from polycarbonate. The refill has a simple locking device at one end which flexes downward out of the groove into which the jaws of the holder fit, allowing easy release. By sliding the new refill through all the jaws and pushing through the slight resistance when it reaches the end of its travel, the refill will lock into position.

Regardless of the type of refill used, make sure that all of the frame jaws are engaged as the refill is pushed into place and locked. The metal blade holder and frame will scratch the glass if allowed to touch it.

ARM AND BLADE REPLACEMENT

A detailed description and procedures for replacing the wiper arm and blade is found in Chapter 5.

Tires and Wheels

Inspect the tires regularly for wear and damage. Remove stones or other foreign particles which may be lodged in the tread. If tread wear is excessive or irregular it could be a sign of front end problems, or simply improper inflation.

The inflation should be checked at least once per month and adjusted if necessary. The tires must be cold (driven less than one mile) or an inaccurate reading will result. Do not forget to check the spare.

The correct inflation pressure for your vehicle can be found on a decal mounted to the car. Depending upon model and year, the decal can be located at the driver's door, the passenger's door or the glove box. If you cannot find the decal a local automobile tire dealer can furnish you with the information.

TIRE ROTATION

Tires should be rotated periodically to get the maximum tread life available. A good time to do this is when changing over from regular tires to snow tires, or about once per year. If front end problems are suspected have them corrected before rotating the tires. Torque the lug nuts to 70–115 ft. lbs.

Fuel Filter

NOTE: *See Chapter 4 "Diesel Fuel System" for fuel filter instruction for the 2.4L Diesel Engine.*

Gasoline engines are equipped with a carburetor mounted gas filter. Externally mounted filters are of one piece construction and cannot be cleaned. Model 2700/7200VV carburetors use

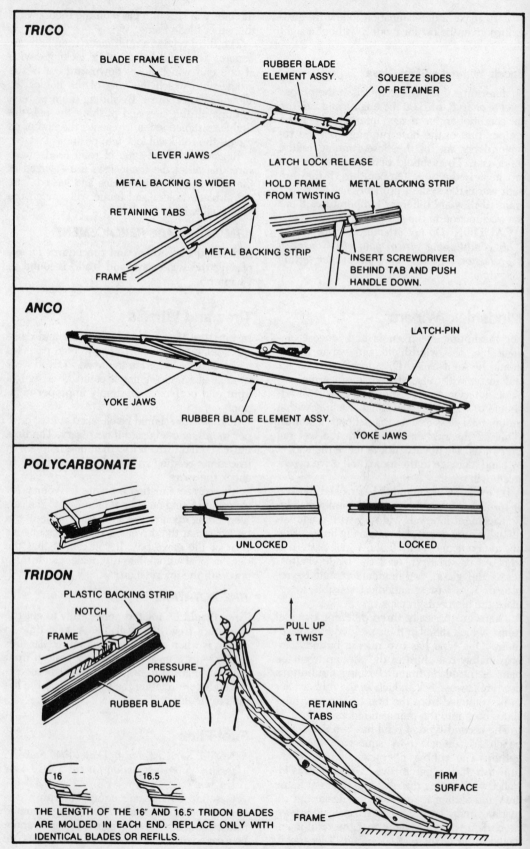

Wiper insert replacement

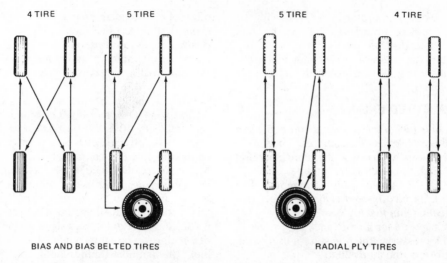

4 TIRE   5 TIRE   5 TIRE   4 TIRE

BIAS AND BIAS BELTED TIRES   RADIAL PLY TIRES

Tire rotation diagram

a replaceable filter located behind the carburetor inlet fitting. Replace the fuel filter at the same time the air cleaner element is changed. Replace the filter immediately if it becomes clogged or restricted. The diesel engine is equipped with a fuel filter/water separator. The filter is of spin-on cartridge-type design.

REPLACEMENT—GASOLINE ENGINES

Externally Mounted-Steel Line Connected

1. Remove the air cleaner assembly.
2. Place an ¹¹⁄₁₆ or suitable size open-end wrench on the filter hex nut to prevent the filter from turning, when loosening the fuel line.
3. Loosen the fuel line fitting nut with a proper size wrench (½ or ⅝ inch).
4. Remove the fuel line from the filter.
5. Remove the fuel filter from the carburetor by rotating it counterclockwise.
6. Apply one drop of Loctite Hydraulic Sealant No. 069 to the external threads of the new filter and install the filter. Tighten to 5–6 ft. lbs.
7. Apply a drop of oil to the threads of the fuel line fitting. Start the fuel line fitting into the filter by hand.
8. Hold the fuel filter with a suitable wrench and tighten the fuel line fitting to 15–18 ft. lbs.
9. Start the engine and check for fuel leaks. Shut off the engine and install the air cleaner assembly.

Externally Mounted-Hose Connected

1. Remove the air cleaner assembly.
2. Remove or slide the hose clamps from the rubber hose. Remove the hose connector from the fuel filter.

3. Unscrew the fuel filter from the carburetor.
4. Discard the fuel filter, hose and clamps.
5. Apply one drop of Loctite Hydraulic Sealant No. 069 on the external threads of the new fuel filter.
6. Hand start the filter into the carburetor inlet fitting, tighten the filter to 80–100 inch lbs.
7. Position the retaining clamps in the center of the connecting hose.
8. Slide the hose over the inlet fitting of the fuel filter, and over the steel gas line.
9. Slide the clamps into their proper position. Both the filter and steel supply line are equipped with a ridge, position the clamp behind the ridge and tighten the clamp (if worm drive).
10. Start the engine and check for fuel leaks. Shut off the engine and install the air cleaner.

Internally Mounted—2700/7200 VV Carburetors

1. Remove the air cleaner assembly.
2. Hold the carburetor inlet fitting with the proper size flare wrench. Loosen and remove the steel fuel supply line from the carburetor.
3. Unscrew the fuel inlet fitting from the carburetor.
4. Remove the fitting, gasket, filter and spring.
5. Install the spring, new filter, gasket and inlet fitting. Tighten the fitting to 90–125 inch lbs.
6. Lubricate the steel line fitting with a drop of light oil. Hand start the fitting into the carburetor inlet.

7. Hold the carburetor inlet fitting with the proper size flare wrench and tighten the steel line fitting to 15–18 ft. lbs.

8. Start the engine and check for fuel leaks. Shut off the engine and install the air cleaner assembly.

FUEL INJECTED ENGINES

The in-line fuel filter is located on a bracket under the vehicle near the right rear wheel well. The filter usually shares a common mounting bracket with the electric fuel pump.

CAUTION: *Always depressurize the fuel system, on fuel injected vehicles, before disconnecting any fuel lines.*

See Chapter 4 for instructions.

1. Depressurize the fuel system using Tool T80L9974A or the equivalent.

2. Raise the rear of the vehicle and support safely on jackstands.

3. Disconnect the quick connect fitting at both ends of the fuel filter. See Chapter 4 for fuel fitting disconnect instructions.

4. Remove the fuel filter and retainer from the mounting bracket.

5. Remove the filter and insulating (rubber) ring from the retainer. Note that the direction of the flow arrow points to the open end of the retainer. Discard the old filter.

6. Place the new filter into the retainer with the flow arrow pointing in the proper direction. (Toward the open end of the retainer).

7. Install the rubber insulating. If the filter moves freely in the retainer after installing the rubber insulating rings, replace the insulators.

8. Install the retainer on to the bracket. Tighten the mounting bolts to 51–60 inch lbs.

9. Push the quick connect fuel fittings onto the filter ends.

10. Start the engine and check for fuel leaks. Shut off the engine and lower the vehicle to the ground.

FLUIDS AND LUBRICANTS

Fuel Recommendations

It is important to use fuel of the proper octane rating in your car. Octane rating is based on the quantity of anti-knock compounds added to the fuel and it determines the speed at which the gas will burn. The lower the octane rating, the faster it burns. The higher the octane, the slower the fuel will burn and a greater percentage of compounds in the fuel prevent spark ping (knock), detonation and preignition (dieseling).

As the temperature of the engine increases, the air-fuel mixture exhibits a tendency to ig-

nite before the spark plug is fired. If fuel of an octane rating too low for the engine is used, this will allow combustion to occur before the piston has completed its compression stroke, thereby creating a very high pressure very rapidly.

Fuel of the proper octane rating, for the compression ratio and ignition timing of your car, will slow the combustion process sufficiently to allow the spark plug enough time to ignite the mixture completely and smoothly. Many non-catalyst models are designed to run on regular fuel. The use of some "super-premium" fuel is no substitution for a properly tuned and maintained engine. Chances are that if your engine exhibits any signs of spark ping, detonation or preignition when using regular fuel, the ignition timing should be checked against specifications or the cylinder head should be removed for decarbonizing.

Vehicles equipped with catalytic converters must use UNLEADED GASOLINE ONLY. Use of unleaded fuel shortens the life of spark plugs, exhaust systems and EGR valves and can damage the catalytic converter. Most converter equipped models are designed to operate using unleaded gasoline with a minimum rating of 87 octane. Use of unleaded gas with octane ratings lower than 87 can cause persistent spark knock which could lead to engine damage.

Light spark knock may be noticed when accelerating or driving up hills. The slight knocking may be considered normal (with 87 octane) because the maximum fuel economy is obtained under condition of occasional light spark knock. Gasoline with an octane rating higher than 87 may be used, but it is not necessary (in most cases) for proper operation.

If spark knock is constant, when using 87 octane, at cruising speeds on level ground, ignition timing adjustment may be required.

Engine

OIL RECOMMENDATION

When adding the oil to the crankcase or changing the oil or filter, it is important that oil of an equal quality to original be used in your car. The use of inferior oils may void your warranty. Generally speaking, oil that has been rated "SE"; "SF" for 1980 and later models; heavy-duty detergent by the American Petroleum Institute will prove satisfactory.

Oil of the SE/SF variety performs a multitude of functions in addition to its basic job of reducing friction of the engine's moving parts. Through a balanced formula of polymeric dispersants and metallic detergents, the oil prevents high temperature and low temperature

Capacities

Year	Engine No. Cyl Displacement (cu in.)	Engine Crankcase (Add 1 qt for new filter)	Transmission (pts to refill after draining)			Drive Axle (pts)	Gasoline Tank (gals)	Cooling System (qts)	
			Manual		Automatic (Total Capacity)			W/heater	W A/C
			3 spd	4/5 spd					
'71	6-250	3.5	3.5	—	18	4	20[3]	11	11
	8-302	4	3.5	—	18	4	20[3]	15	15.5
	8-351	4	3.5	4	22	5	20[3]	15.5	16.5
	8-429	6[2]	—	4	26	5	20[3]	19.5	19.5
'72–'73	6-250	3.5	3.5	—	18	4	22.5[3]	11.5	11.5
	8-302	4	3.5	—	18	4	22.5[3]	15	15
	8-351	4	—	4	20.5[4]	4	22.5[3]	15.5	16
	8-400	4	—	—	26	4	22.5[3]	17.5	17.5
	8-429	4	—	—	26	5	22.5	19	19
'74	6-250	4	—	—	[5]	4	26.5[6]	11.5	—
	8-302	4	3.5	—	[5]	4	26.5[6]	15.7	15.7
	8-351	4	—	—	[7]	4	26.5[6]	[8]	[8]
	8-400	4	—	—	25	5	26.5[6]	17.7	18.3
	8-460	6	—	—	25	5	26.5[6]	18.9	19.5
'75	8-351	4[11]	—	—	[9]	4	26.5[6]	[10]	[10]
	8-400	4[11]	—	—	[9]	5	26.5[6]	17.1	17.5
	8-460	4	—	—	[9]	5	26.5[6]	19.2	19.2
'76	8-351	4	—	—	[9]	5	26.5[6]	[10]	[10]
	8-400	4	—	—	[9]	5	26.5[6]	17.1	17.5[13]
	8-460	4[1]	—	—	24.4	5	26.5[6]	19.2	19.2[14]
'77–'78	8-302	4	—	—	22	4	26.0[6]	14.8	15.1
	8-351	4	—	—	[17]	5	26.0[6][12]	[15]	[15]
	8-400	4	—	—	[18]	5	26.0[6]	17.0[16]	17.0[16]
'78–'80	Versailles 8-302	4	—	—	20.5[17]	5.0	19.2	14.6	14.6
	8-351W	4	—	—	20.5	5.0	19.2	15.7	15.7
'78–'79	LTD II, Thunderbird, Cougar, Cougar XR-7 8-302	4	—	—	[18]	5.0	21.0[19]	14.3	14.6
	8-351W	4	—	—	[18]	5.0	21.0[19]	15.5	16.0
	8-351M	4	—	—	[18]	5.0	21.0[19]	16.5	16.5
	8-400	4	—	—	[18]	5.0	21.0[19]	16.5	16.5
'80–'81	Cougar XR-7, Thunderbird 6-200	4	—	—	16	3.5	17.5	13.0	13.2
	8-255	4	—	—	20[20]	3.5	17.5	13.2	13.3
	8-302	4	—	—	20[20]	3.5	17.5	12.7	12.8
'81	Cougar 4-140	4	—	2.8	16	3.5	14.7	8.6	8.6
	6-200	4	—	—	16	3.5	16.0	8.1	8.1
	8-255	4	—	—	19	3.5	16.0	13.4	13.5

Capacities (Cont.)

Year	Engine No. Cyl Displacement (cu in.)	Engine Crankcase (Add 1 qt for new filter)	Transmission (pts to refill after draining)			Drive Axle (pts)	Gasoline Tank (gals)	Cooling System (qts)	
			Manual		Automatic (Total Capacity)			W/heater	W A/C
			3 spd	4/5 spd					
'82	Cougar XR-7, Thunderbird, Lincoln Continental 6-200	4	—	—	22	3.25	21	8.4	8.4
	6-232	4	—	—	24	3.25	21 [21]	8.3	8.6
	8-255	4	—	—	24	3.25	21	14.9	15
	8-302	4	—	—	24	3.25	22.6	13.3	13.4
'82	Cougar 4-140	4	—	—	16	[23]	16.0 [23]	10.2	10.2
	6-200	4	—	—	22	3.25	16.0 [23]	8.4	8.4
	6-232	4	—	—	22	3.25	16.0 [23]	8.3	8.3
'83–'85	LTD/Marquis 4-140	4	—	2.8	16	3.25 [24]	16	8.6	9.4
	4-140P	4	—	—	16	3.25 [24]	24	8.6	9.4
	6-200	4	—	—	22	3.25 [24]	16	8.4	8.5
	6-232	4	—	—	22 [20]	3.25 [24]	16	10.7	10.8
'83–'85	Thunderbird, Cougar Continental 4-140 Turbo	4.5 [25]	—	4.75	—	3.25 [24]	18	8.4	8.7
	6-232	4	—	—	22 [20]	3.25 [24]	21	10.4	10.7
	8-302	4	—	—	22 [20]	3.25 [24]	20.7 [26]	13.3	13.4

T-Turbocharged
P-Propane
[1] 460 police is 4
[2] 429 4 bbl—4 qts
   429 CJ, SCJ—6 qts
   add 1 qt if equipped with oil cooler
[3] Less 2 gals—station wagon, Ranchero
[4] 26 pts for 351 CJ
[5] C4—18 or 20 pts: FMX—22 pts
[6] Station wagon—21.2 gallons
[7] 351 2V with C4—20 pts; 351 2V with FMX—22 pts; 351 2V with C6—25 pts; 351 4V with C6—21 pts
[8] 351W 2v—16.4 qts w/heater; 16.8 w/AC
   351C 2v—15.9 qts w/heater; 16.5 w/AC
   351C 4v—15.9 qts w/heater; 16.9 w/AC
[9] C4—20 pts; FMX—22 pts: C6—25 pts
[10] 351 Windsor—15.9 qts w/heater; 16.2 w/AC
   351 Modified—17.1 qts w/heater; 17.5 w/AC; 18.0 police

[11] Add only ½ qt of oil for new service filter
[12] T-bird w/351 for Calif.—22.0
[13] Police or heavy trailer tow—18.0
[14] Police or heavy trailer tow—19.7
[15] 351W—15.9 w/heater; 16.2 w/AC
   351M—17.0 w/heater or w/AC; 17.5 police and taxi
[16] 17.5 police
[17] 1979 and later; 20 pts
[18] C4: 20 pts. C6: 25 pts. FMX: 22 pts.
[19] 1979 optional tank; 27.5 gals.
[20] AOD transmission—24 pts.
[21] Continental: 20 gals std: 22.6 gals optional
[22] 6.75 in. axle—2.5 pts; 7.5 in. axle—3.5 pts.
[23] 20 gals optional
[24] Traction-Lok; 3.55 pts.
[25] Turbo: 4.5 qts, add ½ qt with filter
[26] 22.3 gal Continental

deposits and also keeps sludge and dirt particles in suspension. Acids, particularly sulphuric acid, as well as other products of combustion of sulphur fuels, are neutralized by the oil. These acids, if permitted to concentrate, may cause corrosion and rapid wear of the internal parts of the engine.

It is important to choose an oil of the proper viscosity for climatic and operational conditions. Viscosity in an index of the oil's thickness at different temperatures. A thicker oil (higher numerical rating) is needed for high temperature operation, whereas thinner oil (lower numerical rating) is required for cold weather operation. Due to the need for an oil that embodies both these characteristics in parts of the country where there is wide temperature variation within a small period of time, multigrade oils

Oil Viscosity—Temperature Chart

When Outside Temperature is Consistently	Use SAE Viscosity Number
SINGLE GRADE OILS	
−10°F to 32°F	10W
10°F to 60°F	20W-20
32°F to 90°F	30
Above 60°F	40
MULTIGRADE OILS	
Below 32°F	5W-30*
−10°F to 90°F	10W-30
Above—10°F	10W-40
Above 10°F	20W-40
Above 20°F	20W-50

*When sustained high-speed operation is anticipated, use the next higher grade.

have been developed. Basically a multigrade oil is thinner at low temperatures and thicker at high temperatures. For example, a 10W–40 oil exhibits the characteristics of a 10 weight oil when the car is first started and the oil is cold. Its lighter weight allows it to travel to the lubricating surfaces quicker and offer less resistance to starter motor cranking than, let's say, a straight 30 weight oil. But after the engine reaches operating temperature, the 10W–40 oil begins acting like a straight 40 weight oil, its heavier weight providing greater lubricating protection and less susceptibility to foaming than a straight 30 weight oil. Whatever your driving needs, the oil viscosity-temperature chart should prove useful in selecting the proper grade. The SAE viscosity rating is printed or stamped on the top of every oil container.

OIL LEVEL CHECK

The engine oil level should be checked frequently; for instance, at each refueling stop. Be sure that the vehicle is parked on a level surface with the engine off. Also, allow a few minutes after turning off the engine for the oil to drain into the pan or an inaccurate reading will result.

1. Open the hood and remove the engine oil dipstick.

2. Wipe the dipstick with a clean, lint-free rag and reinsert it. Be sure to insert it all the way.

3. Pull out the dipstick and note the oil level. It should be between the SAFE (MAX) mark and the ADD (MIN) mark.

4. If the level is below the lower mark, replace the dipstick and add fresh oil to bring the level within the proper range. Do not overfill.

5. Recheck the oil level and close the hood. NOTE: *Use a multi-grade oil with API classification SE, or SF.*

```
ADD 2  I ADD 1 →I SAFE I←  WARRANTY
```

```
ADD →I SAFE I←           WARRANTY
```

```
ADD I← SAFE→I  I←MAX. OVERFILL
```

(Note lubricant level should be within the safe range) typical engine oil dipstick

OIL AND FILTER CHANGE

The engine oil and oil filter should be changed at the recommended intervals on the maintenance schedule chart. After the engine has reached operating temperature, shut it off, firmly apply the parking brake, block the wheels, place a drip pan beneath the oil pan and remove the drain plug. Allow the engine to drain thoroughly before replacing the drain plug.

NOTE: *On some V8 engines a dual sump oil pan was used. When changing the oil both drain plugs (front and side) must be removed. Failure to remove both plugs can lead to an incorrect oil level reading.*

Place the drip pan beneath the oil filter. To remove the filter, turn it counterclockwise using a strap wrench. Wipe the contact surface of the new filter clean of all dirt and coat the rubber gasket with clean engine oil. Clean the mating surface of the adapter on the block. To install, hand turn the new filter clockwise until the gasket just contacts the cylinder block. Do not use a strap wrench to install. Then hand-turn the filter ½ additional turn. Unscrew the filler cap on the valve cover and fill the crankcase to the proper level on the dipstick with the recommended grade of oil. Install the cap, start the engine and operate at fast idle. Check the oil filter contact area and then drain plug for leaks.

Shut off the engine and allow enough time for the oil to drain back into the oil pan. Recheck the oil level with the dipstick. Add oil as necessary to proper level indicated by the dipstick.

Certain operating conditions may warrant more frequent oil changes. If the vehicle is used for short trips, where the engine does not have a chance to fully warm-up before it is shut off, water condensation and low temperature deposits may make it necessary to change the oil sooner. If the vehicle is used mostly in stop-and-go traffic, corrosive acids and high temperature deposits may necessitate shorter oil changing intervals. The shorter intervals also apply to industrial or rural areas where high concentrations of dust and other airborne particulate matter contaminate the oil. Finally, if the car is used for towing trailers, a severe load is placed on the engine causing the oil to "thin-out" sooner, making necessary the shorter oil changing intervals.

Transmission
FLUID RECOMMENDATION

Automatic Transmissions

• 1971–79	C3	Type F
	C4	Type F
	C6 (thru 76)	Type F
	C6 (77–79)	Dexron II
	CW/FMX	Type F
	JATCO	Dexron II
• 1980	C3	Type F
	C4	Dexron II
	C6	Dexron II
	FMX	Type F
	AOD	Dexron II
	JATCO	Dexron II
• 1981 and later	C3	Dexron II
	C4	Dexron II
	C5	Type H
	C6	Dexron II
	AOD	Dexron II

Manual Transmission

• Except 4 and 5 speed OD	SAE 85W/85/90*
• 4 and 5 speed OD	Dexron II*

*85W-90 gear oil may be used in OD transmissions in warm climates, or if gear/bearing noise is excessive. Dexron II may be used in non-OD transmissions if hard shifting is encountered in colder climates.

LEVEL CHECK
Automatic Transmissions

It is very important to maintain the proper fluid level in an automatic transmission. If the level is either too high or too low, poor shifting operation and internal damage are likely to occur. For this reason a regular check of the fluid level is essential.

1. Drive the vehicle for 15–20 minutes to allow the transmission to reach operating temperature.
2. Park the car on a level surface, apply the parking brake and leave the engine idling. Shift the transmission and engage each gear, then place the gear selector in P (PARK).

Typical automatic transmission dipstick

WARRANTY REQUIRES ESP M2C138 CJ OIL

C-6 automatic transmission dipstick (note the special fluid designation)

3. Wipe away any dirt in the area of the transmission dipstick to prevent it from falling into the filler tube. Withdraw the dipstick, wipe it with a clean, lint-free rag and reinsert it until it seats.
4. Withdraw the dipstick and note the fluid level. It should be between the upper (FULL) mark and the lower (ADD) mark.
5. If the level is below the lower mark, use a funnel and add fluid in small quantities through the dipstick filler neck. Keep the engine running while adding fluid and check the level after each small amount. Do not overfill.

Manual Transmission

The fluid level should be checked every 6 months/6,000 miles, whichever comes first.
1. Park the car on a level surface, turn off the engine, apply the parking brake and block the wheels.
2. Remove the filler plug from the side of the transmission case with a proper size wrench. The fluid level should be even with the bottom of the filler hole.
3. If additional fluid is necessary, add it through the filler hole using a syphon pump or squeeze bottle.
4. Replace the filler plug; do not over-tighten.

DRAIN AND REFILL
Automatic Transmission

Refer to Chapter 6 for fluid change procedures.

Manual Transmission

Place a suitable drain pan under the transmission. Remove the drain plug and allow the gear lube to drain out. Replace the drain plug, remove the filler plug and fill the transmission to the proper level with the required fluid. Reinstall the filler plug.

FILL AND FLUID SPECIFICATIONS (DIPSTICK INFORMATION)

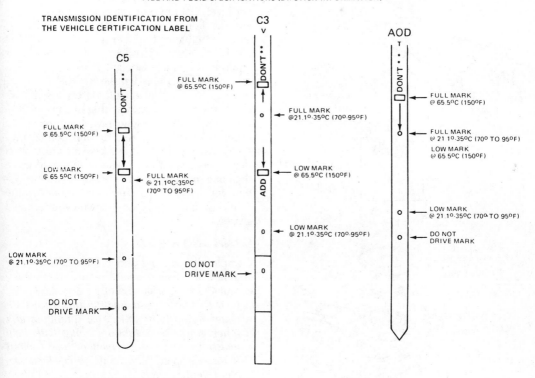

** DON'T ADD IF BETWEEN ARROWS

Automatic transmission dipstick markings for late models

Rear Axle (Differential)
FLUID LEVEL CHECK

Like the manual transmission, the rear axle fluid should be checked every six months/6,000 miles. A filler plug is provided near the center of the rear cover or on the upper (driveshaft) side of the gear case. Remove the plug and check to ensure that the fluid level is even with the bottom of the filler hole. Add SAE 85W/90/95 gear lube as required. If the vehicle is equipped with a limited slip rear axle, add the required special fluid. Install the filler plug but do not overtighten.

DRAIN AND REFILL

Normal maintenance does not require changing the rear axle fluid. However, to do so, remove the rear drain plug (models equipped), the lower two cover bolts, or the cover. Catch the drained fluid in a suitable container. If the rear cover was removed, clean the mounting surfaces of the cover and rear housing. Install a new gasket (early models) or (on late models) apply a continuous bead of Silicone Rubber Sealant (D6AZ19562A/B or the equivalent) around the rear housing face inside the circle

of bolt holes. Install the cover and tighten the bolts. Parts must be assembled within a half hour after the sealant is applied. If the fluid was drained by removing the two lower cover bolts, apply sealant to the bolts before reinstallation. Fill the rear axle through the filler hole with the proper lube. Add friction modifier to limited slip models if required.

Coolant
FLUID RECOMMENDATIONS

When additional coolant is required to maintain the proper level, always added a 50/50 mix of anti-freeze/coolant and water.

LEVEL CHECK

CAUTION: *Exercise extreme care when removing the cap from a hot radiator. Wait a few minutes until the engine has time to cool somewhat, then wrap a thick towel around the radiator cap and slowly turn it counterclockwise to the first stop. Step back and allow the pressure to release from the cooling system. Then, when the steam has stopped venting, press down on the cap, turn it one*

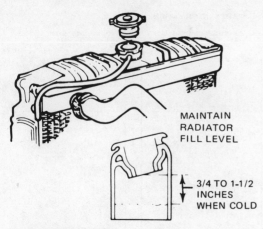

MAINTAIN
RADIATOR
FILL LEVEL

3/4 TO 1-1/2
INCHES
WHEN COLD

Vertical flow radiator

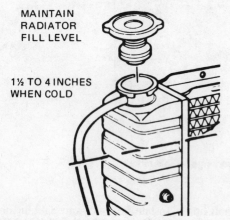

MAINTAIN
RADIATOR
FILL LEVEL

1½ TO 4 INCHES
WHEN COLD

Crossflow radiator

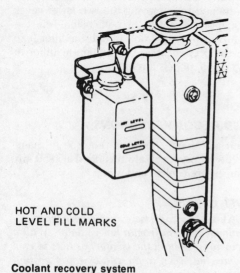

HOT AND COLD
LEVEL FILL MARKS

Coolant recovery system

more stop counterclockwise and remove the cap.

The coolant level in the radiator should be checked on a monthly basis, preferably when the engine is cold. On a cold engine, the coolant level should be maintained at one inch below the filler neck on vertical flow radiators, and 2½ in. below the filler neck at the "COLD FILL" mark on crossflow radiators. On cars equipped with the Coolant Recovery System, the level is maintained at the "COLD LEVEL" mark in the translucent plastic expansion bottle. Top up as necessary with a mixture of 50% water and 50% ethylene glycol antifreeze, to ensure proper rust, freezing and boiling protection. If you have to add coolant more often than once a month or if you have to add more than one quart at a time, check the cooling system for leaks. Also check for water in the crankcase oil, indicating a blown cylinder head gasket.

DRAIN AND REFILL

Completely draining and refilling the cooling system every two years at least will remove accumulated rust, scale and other deposits.

NOTE: *Use a good quality antifreeze with water pump lubricants, rust inhibitors and other corrosion inhibitors along with acid neutralizers. Use a permanent type coolant that meets specification ESE-M97B44A or the equivalent.*

1. Drain the existing antifreeze and coolant. Open the radiator and engine drain petcocks (models equipped), or disconnect the bottom radiator hose, at the radiator outlet. Set heater temperature controls to the full HOT position.

NOTE: *Before opening the radiator petcock, spray it with some penetrating lubricant.*

2. Close the petcock or re-connect the lower hose and fill the system with water.

3. Add a can of quality radiator flush. If equipped with a V6 or diesel engine, be sure flush is safe to use in engines having aluminum components.

4. Idle the engine until the upper radiator hose gets hot.

5. Drain the system again.

6. Repeat this process until the drained water is clear and free of scale.

7. Close all petcocks and connect all the hoses.

8. If equipped with a coolant recovery system, flush the reservoir with water and leave empty.

9. Determine the capacity of your cooling system (see capacities specifications). Add a 50/50 mix of quality antifreeze (ethylene glycol) and water to provide the desired protection.

SYSTEM INSPECTION

Most permanent anti-freeze/coolant have a colored dye added which makes the solution an

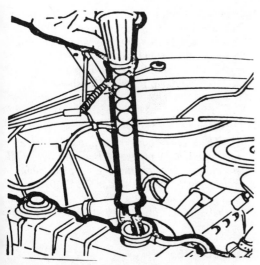

Testing coolant condition with a tester

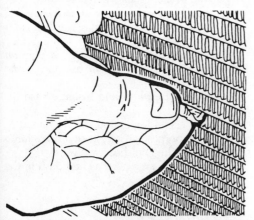

Clean debris from the radiator fins

excellent leak detector. When servicing the cooling system, check for leakage at;

- All hoses and hose connections
- Radiator seams, radiator core, and radiator draincock
- All engine block and cylinder head freeze (core) plugs, and drain plugs
- Edges of all cooling system gaskets (head gaskets, thermostat gasket)
- Transmission fluid cooler
- Heating system components, water pump
- Check the engine oil dipstick for signs of coolant in the engine oil
- Check the coolant in the radiator for signs of oil in the coolant

Investigate and correct any indication of coolant leakage.

Check the Radiator Cap

While you are checking the coolant level, check the radiator cap for a worn or cracked gasket.

If the cap doesn't seal properly, fluid will be lost and the engine will overheat.

Worn caps should be replaced with a new one.

Clean Radiator of Debris

Periodically clean any debris—leaves, paper, insects, etc.—from the radiator fins. Pick the large pieces off by hand. The smaller pieces can be washed away with water pressure from a hose.

Carefully straighten any bent radiator fins with a pair of needle nose pliers. Be careful—the fins are very soft. Don't wiggle the fins back and forth too much. Straighten them once and try not to move them again.

CHECKING SYSTEM PROTECTION

A 50/50 mix of coolant concentrate and water will usually provide protection to −35°F. Freeze protection may be checked by using a cooling system hydrometer. Inexpensive hydrometers (floating ball types) may be obtained from a local department store (automotive section) or an auto supply store. Follow the directions packaged with the coolant hydrometer when checking protection.

Master Cylinder

LEVEL CHECK

The brake fluid in the master cylinder should be checked every 6 months/6,000 miles.

Cast Iron Reservoir

1. Park the vehicle on a level surface and open the hood.
2. Pry the retaining spring bar holding the cover onto the master cylinder to one side.
3. Clean any dirt from the sides and top of the cover before removal. Remove the master cylinder cover and gasket.
4. Add fluid, if necessary, to within ⅜ths of an inch of the top of the reservoir, or to the full level indicator (on models equipped).
5. Push the gasket bellows back into the cover. Reinstall the gasket and cover and position the retainer spring bar.

Plastic Reservoir

Check fluid level on side of reservoir. If fluid is required, remove the screw on filler cap and gasket from the master cylinder. Fill the reservoir to the full line in the reservoir. Install the filler cap, making sure the gasket is properly seated in the cap.

FLUID RECOMMENDATION

Use only Heavy Duty Brake Fluid meeting DOT 3 specifications.

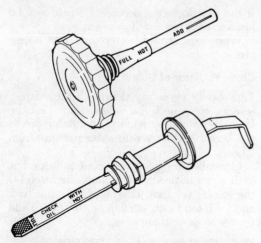

Typical power steering pump reservoir dipsticks

Power Steering

LEVEL CHECK

Check the power steering fluid level every 6 months/6,000 miles.

1. Park the vehicle on a level surface. Run the engine until normal operating temperature is reached.

2. Turn the steering all the way to the left and then all the way to the right several times. Center the steering wheel and shut off the engine.

3. Open the hood and check the power steering reservoir fluid level.

4. Remove the filler cap and wipe the dipstick attached clean.

5. Reinsert the dipstick and tighten the cap. Remove the dipstick and note the fluid level indicated on the dipstick.

6. The level should be at any point below the Full mark, but not below the Add mark.

7. Add fluid if necessary. Do not overfill.

FLUID RECOMMENDATION

Add Type F automatic transmission fluid, do not overfill the reservoir.

Steering Gear Lubricant

EXCEPT RACK AND PINION STEERING

If there is binding in the steering gear or if the wheels do not return to a straight-ahead position after a turn, the lubricant level of the steering gear should be checked. Remove the filler plug using a 11/16 in. open-end wrench and remove the lower cover bolt using a 9/16 in. wrench, to expose both holes. Slowly turn the steering wheel to the left until it stops. At this point, lubricant should be rising in the lower cover bolt hole. Then slowly turn the steering

wheel to the right until it stops. At this point, lubricant should be rising in the filler plug hole. If the lubricant does not rise when the wheel is turned, add a small amount of SAE 90 steering gear lubricant until it does. Replace the cover bolt and the filler plug when finished.

Chassis Greasing

NOTE: *Depending on year and model, vehicles may have plugs or grease fittings in all steering/suspension linkage or pivot points. Follow instructions under "Ball Joints" if equipped with plugs. Newer models have sealed "points" and lubrication is not necessary.*

BALL JOINTS

1. Park the vehicle on a level surface, set the parking brake, block the rear wheels, raise the front end and support it with jack stands.

2. Wipe away any dirt from the ball joint lubrication plugs.

NOTE: *The upper ball joint has a plug on the top; the lower ball joint has one on the bottom.*

3. Pull out the plugs and install grease fittings.

4. Using a hand-operated grease gun containing multi-purpose grease, force lubricant into the joint until the joint boot swells.

5. Remove the grease fitting and push in the lubrication plug.

6. Lower the vehicle.

STEERING ARM STOPS

The steering arm stops are attached to the lower control arm. They are located between each steering arm and the upturned end of the front suspension strut.

1. Park the vehicle on a level surface, set the parking brake, block the rear wheels, raise the front end and support it with jack stands.

2. Clean the friction points and apply multi-purpose grease.

3. Lower the vehicle.

MANUAL TRANSMISSION AND CLUTCH LINKAGE

On models so equipped, apply a small amount of chassis grease to the pivot points of the transmission and clutch linkage as per the chassis lubrication diagram.

AUTOMATIC TRANSMISSION LINKAGE

On models so equipped, apply a small amount of 10W engine oil to the kickdown and shift linkage at the pivot points.

JUMP STARTING A DEAD BATTERY

The chemical reaction in a battery produces explosive hydrogen gas. This is the safe way to jump start a dead battery, reducing the chances of an accidental spark that could cause an explosion.

Jump Starting Precautions

1. Be sure both batteries are of the same voltage.
2. Be sure both batteries are of the same polarity (have the same grounded terminal).
3. Be sure the vehicles are not touching.
4. Be sure the vent cap holes are not obstructed.
5. Do not smoke or allow sparks around the battery.
6. In cold weather, check for frozen electrolyte in the battery.
7. Do not allow electrolyte on your skin or clothing.
8. Be sure the electrolyte is not frozen.

Jump Starting Procedure

1. Determine voltages of the two batteries; they must be the same.
2. Bring the starting vehicle close (they must not touch) so that the batteries can be reached easily.
3. Turn off all accessories and both engines. Put both cars in Neutral or Park and set the handbrake.
4. Cover the cell caps with a rag—do not cover terminals.
5. If the terminals on the run-down battery are heavily corroded, clean them.
6. Identify the positive and negative posts on both batteries and connect the cables in the order shown.
7. Start the engine of the starting vehicle and run it at fast idle. Try to start the car with the dead battery. Crank it for no more than 10 seconds at a time and let it cool off for 20 seconds in between tries.
8. If it doesn't start in 3 tries, there is something else wrong.
9. Disconnect the cables in the reverse order.
10. Replace the cell covers and dispose of the rags.

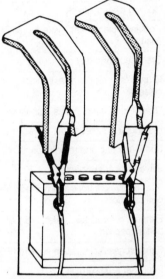

Side terminal batteries occasionally pose a problem when connecting jumper cables. There frequently isn't enough room to clamp the cables without touching sheet metal. Side terminal adaptors are available to alleviate this problem and should be removed after use.

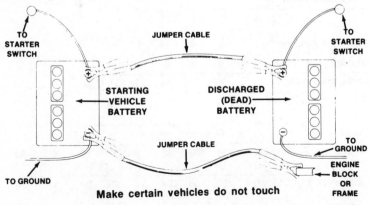

Make certain vehicles do not touch

This hook-up for negative ground cars only

Maintenance Interval Chart

Operation	'71	'72	'73	'74	'75	'76	'77–'79	'80–'82	'83–'85	See Chapter
				Thousand Miles						
ENGINE										
Air cleaner replacement—exc. V8	12	12	—	—	—	—	—	30	30	1
Air cleaner replacement—V8	24	12	12	24	20	20	30	30	30	1
Air intake temperature control system check	12	12	12	12	15	15	20	22.5	22.5	4
Carburetor idle speed and mixture, fast idle, throttle solenoid adj	12	12	12	24	15	15	22.5	30	30	2
Cooling system check	12	12	12	12	15	15	12	12	12	1
Coolant replacement; system draining and flushing	24	24	24	24	40	40	45	52.5	52.5	1
Crankcase breather cap cleaning	6	6	12	12	20	20	30	52.5	52.5	1
Crankcase breather filter replacement (in air cleaner)	6	6	8	24	20	20	30	52.5	52.5	1
Distributor breaker points inspection	12	12	12	6	—	—	—	—	—	2
Distributor breaker points replacement	12	12	24	24	—	—	—	—	—	2
Distributor cap and rotor inspection	12	12	24	①	15	15	22.5	22.5	22.5	2
Drive belts adjustment	12	12	12	12	15	15	22.5	30	30	1
Evaporative control system check; inspect carbon canister	12	12	12	24	20	20	30	52.5	52.5	1
Exhaust control valve (heat riser) lubrication and inspection	6	6	8	6	15	15	15	15	15	1
Exhaust gas recirculation system (EGR) check	—	—	12	12	15	15	15	15	15	4
Fuel filter replacement	12	12	12	6	15	10	10	12	12	1
Ignition timing adjustment	12	12	12	②	⑤	⑤	⑤	⑤	⑤	2
Intake manifold bold torque check (V8 only)	12	12	24	12	15	15	15	15	15	3
Oil change (Turbo—every 5,000 miles)	6	6	4	6	5	5	7.5	7.5	7.5	1
Oil filter replacement (Turbo—each oil change)	6	6	8	12	10	10	15	15	15	1
PCV system valve replacement, system cleaning	12	12	12	24	20	20	22.5	52.5	52.5	4
Spark plug replacement; plug wire check	12	12	12	③	15	15	22.5	30	30	2
Thermactor air injection system check	—	—	—	24	15	15	22.5	22.5	22.5	4
CHASSIS										
Automatic transmission band adjustment	④	④	④	④	④	④	④	④	④	6
Automatic transmission fluid level check	6	6	8	12	15	15	15	15	15	1
Brake system inspection, lining replacement	30	30	24	24	25	30	30	30	30	9
Brake master cylinder reservoir fluid level check	6	6	8	12	15	30	30	30	30	1
Clutch pedal free-play adjustment	6	—	—	—	—	—	—	—	—	6
Front suspension ball joints and steering linkage lubrication	36	36	36	36	30	30	30	30	30	1
Front wheel bearings cleaning, adjusting and repacking	30	30	24	24	25	30	30	30	30	9

Maintenance Interval Chart (Cont.)

Operation	Thousand Miles										See Chapter
	'71	'72	'73	'74	'75	'76	'77–'79	'80–'82	'83–'85		
Manual transmission fluid level check	6	—	—	—	—	—	—	15	15		1
Power steering pump reservoir fluid level check	6	6	4	6	15	15	15	15	15		1
Rear axle fluid level check	6	6	8	12	15	15	15	15	15		1
Steering arm stop lubrication; steering linkage inspection	12	12	12	12	15	15	15	15	15		1

① Conventional ignition—24; electronic ignition—18
② Conventional ignition—12; electronic ignition—18
③ Conventional ignition—12; electronic ignition—18
④ Normal service—12,000 mi. only; severe (fleet) service—6,000/18,000/30,000 mi. intervals
⑤ Periodic adjustment unnecessary

PARKING BRAKE LINKAGE

At yearly intervals or whenever binding is noticeable in the parking brake linkage, lubricate the cable guides, levers and linkages with a suitable chassis grease.

BODY LUBRICATION

At the intervals recommended in the maintenance schedule, door, hood and trunk hinges, checks and latches should be greased with a white grease such as Lubriplate®. Also, the lock cylinders should be lubricated with a few drops of graphite lubricant.

DRAIN HOLE CLEANING

The doors and rocker panels of your car are equipped with drain holes to allow water to drain out of the inside of the body panels. If the drain holes become clogged with dirt, leaves, pine needles, etc., the water will remain inside the panels, causing rust. To prevent this, open the drain holes with a screwdriver. If your car is equipped with rubber dust valves instead, simply open the dust valve with your finger.

Front Wheel Bearings

Refer to Chapter 9, "Brakes" for procedure.

PUSHING AND TOWING

NOTE: *Push starting is not recommended for cars equipped with a catalytic converter. Raw gas collecting in the converter may cause damage. Jump starting is recommended.*

To push start your manual transmission equipped car (automatic transmission models cannot be push started), make sure of bumper alignment. If the bumper of the car pushing does not match with your car's bumper, it would be wise to tie an old tire either on the back of your car, or on the front of the pushing car. Switch the ignition to "ON" and depress the clutch pedal. Shift the transmission to third gear and hold the accelerator pedal about halfway down. Signal the push car to proceed, when the car speed reaches about 10 mph, gradually release the clutch pedal. The car engine should start, if not have the car towed.

If the transmission and rear axle are in proper working order, the car can be towed with the rear wheels on the ground for distances under 15 miles at speeds no greater than 30 mph. If the transmission or rear is known to be damaged or if the car has to be towed over 15 miles or over 30 mph the car must be dollied or towed with the rear wheels raised and the steering wheel secured so that the front wheels remain in the straight-ahead position. Never use the key controlled steering wheel lock to hold the front wheels in position. The steering wheel must be clamped with a special clamping device designed for towing service. If the key controlled lock is used damage to the lock and steering column may occur.

JACKING

Your car is equipped with either a scissors type jack, or a bumper jack. The scissor-type jack is placed under the side of the car so that it fits into the notch in the vertical rocker panel flange nearest the wheel to be changed. These jacking notches are located approximately 8 inches from the wheel opening on the rocker panel flanges. Bumper jack slots or flats are provided on the front and rear bumper. Be sure the jack is inserted firmly and is straight before raising the vehicle.

When raising the car with a scissors or bumper jack follow these precautions: Park the car on a level spot, put the selector in P (PARK) with an automatic transmission or in reverse if your car has a manual transmission, apply the parking brake and block the front and the back of the wheel that is diagonally opposite the wheel being changed. These jacks are fine for changing a tire, but never crawl under the car when it is supported only by the scissors or bumper jack.

CAUTION: *If you're going to work beneath the vehicle, always support it on jackstands.*

TUNE-UP PROCEDURES

Spark Plugs

A typical spark plug consists of a metal shell surrounding a cereamic insulator. A metal electrode extends downward through the center of the insulator and protrudes a small distance. Located at the end of the plug and attached to the side of the outer metal shell is the side electrode. The side electrode bends in at a 90° angle so that its tip is even with, and parallel to, the tip of the center electrode. The distance between these two electrodes (measured in thousandths of an inch) is called the spark plug gap. The spark plug in no way produces a spark but merely provides a gap across which the current can arc. The coil produces anywhere from 20,000 to 40,000 volts or more, which travels to the distributor where it is distributed through the spark plug wires to the spark plugs. The current passes along the center electrode and jumps the gap to the side electrode, and, in so doing, ignites the air/fuel mixture in the combustion chamber.

SPARK PLUG HEAT RANGE

Spark plug heat range is the ability of the plug to dissipate heat. The longer the insulator (or the farther it extends into the engine), the hotter the plug will operate; the shorter the insulator the cooler it will operate. A plug that absorbs little heat and remains too cool will quickly accummulate deposits of oil and carbon since it is not hot enough to burn them off. This leads to plug fouling and consequently to misfiring. A plug that absorbs too much heat will have no deposits, but, due to the excessive heat, the electrodes will burn away quickly and in some instances, preignition may result. Preignition takes place when plug tips get so hot that they glow sufficiently to ignite the fuel/air mixture before the actual spark occurs. This early ignition will usually cause a pinging during low speeds and heavy loads.

The general rule of thumb for choosing the correct heat range when picking a spark plug is: if most of your driving is long distance, high speed travel, use a colder plug; if most of your driving is stop and go, use a hotter plug. Original equipment plugs are compromise plugs, but most people never have occasion to change their plugs from the factory-recommended heat range.

REPLACING SPARK PLUGS

A set of spark plugs usually requires replacement after about 10,000 miles on cars with conventional ignition systems and after about 20,000 to 30,000 miles on cars with electronic ignition, depending on your style of driving. In normal operation, plug gap increases about 0.001 in. for every 1,000–2,500 miles. As the gap increases, the plug's voltage requirement also increases. It requires a greater voltage to jump the wider gap and about two to three times as much voltage to fire a plug at high speeds than at idle.

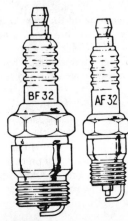

Typical spark plugs—left is $^{13}/_{16}$ in. (18 mm); right is $^5/_8$ in. (14 mm)

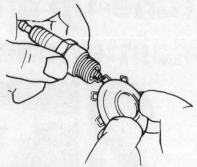

Checking spark plug gap

When you're removing spark plugs, you should work on one at a time. Don't start by removing the plug wires all at once, because unless you number them, they may become mixed up. Take a minute before you begin and number the wires with tape. The best location for numbering is near where the wires come out of the cap.

NOTE: *On models equipped with electronic ignition, apply a small amount of silicone dielectric compound (D7AZ19A331A or the equivalent) to the inside of the terminal boots whenever an ignition wire is disconnected from a plug, or coil/distributor cap connection.*

1. Twist the spark plug boot and remove the boot and wire from the plug. Do not pull on the wire itself as this will ruin the wire.

2. If possible, use a brush or rag to clean the area around the spark plug. Make sure that all the dirt is removed so that none will enter the cylinder after the plug is removed.

3. Remove the spark plug using the proper size socket. A 13/16″ size socket may be used on all models from 1971–72. 1974 and later models use either a 5/8″ or 13/16″ size socket depending on the engine. Turn the socket counterclockwise to remove the plug. Be sure to hold the socket straight on the plug to avoid breaking the plug, or rounding off the hex on the plug.

4. Once the plug is out, check it against the plugs shown in the "Color" section in this book to determine engine condition. This is crucial since plug readings are vital signs of engine condition.

5. Use a round wire feeler gauge to check the plug gap. The correct size gauge should pass through the electrode gap with a slight drag. If you're in doubt, try one size smaller and one larger. The smaller gauge should go through easily while the larger one shouldn't go through at all. If the gap is incorrect, use the electrode bending tool on the end of the gauge to adjust the gap. When adjusting the gap, always bend the side electrode. The center electrode is non-adjustable.

6. Squirt a drop of penetrating oil on the threads of the new plug and install it. Don't oil the threads too heavily. Turn the plug in clockwise by hand until it is snug.

7. When the plug is finger tight, tighten it with a wrench. Take care not to overtighten. Torque to 15 ft-lbs.

8. Install the plug boot firmly over the plug. Proceed to the next plug.

CHECKING AND REPLACING SPARK PLUG CABLES

Visually inspect the spark plug cables for burns, cuts, or breaks in the insulation. Check the spark plug boots and the nipples on the distributor cap and coil. Replace any damaged wiring. If no physical damage is obvious, the wires can be checked with an ohmmeter for excessive resistance. (See the tune-up and troubleshooting section.)

NOTE: *On models equipped with electronic ignition, apply a small amount of silicone dielectric compound (D7AZ19A331A or the equivalent) to the inside of the terminal boots whenever an ignition wire is disconnected from a plug, or coil/distributor cap connection.*

When installing a new set of spark plug cables, replace the cables one at a time so there will be no mixup. Start by replacing the longest cable first. Install the boot firmly over the spark plug. Route the wire exactly the same as the original. Insert the nipple firmly into the tower on the distributor cap. Repeat the process for each cable.

Breaker Points and Condenser

The points function as a circuit breaker for the primary circuit of the ignition system. The ignition coil must boost the 12 volts of electrical pressure supplied by the battery to as much as 25,000 volts in order to fire the spark plugs. To do this, the coil depends on the points and the condenser to make a clean break in the primary circuit.

NOTE: *Some 1974 and all 1975 and later models are equipped with a breakerless, solidstate ignition system. The breakerless system eliminates the points and condenser completely.*

The coil has both primary and secondary circuits. When the ignition is turned on, the battery supplies voltage through the coil and on to the points. The points are connected to ground, completing the primary circuit. As the current passes through the coil, a magnetic field is created in the iron center core of the coil. As the cam in the distributor turns, the points open and the primary circuit is interrupted. The

CONDITION	CAUSED BY
BURNED	ANY DISCOLORATION OTHER THAN A FROSTED SLATE GREY SHALL BE CONSIDERED AS BURNED POINTS.
EXCESSIVE METAL TRANSFER OR PITTING	INCORRECT ALIGNMENT. INCORRECT VOLTAGE REGULATOR SETTING. RADIO CONDENSER INSTALLED TO THE DISTRIBUTOR SIDE OF THE COIL. IGNITION CONDENSER OF IMPROPER CAPACITY. EXTENDED OPERATION OF THE ENGINE AT SPEEDS OTHER THAN NORMAL.

Breaker points diagnosis

magnetic field in the primary circuit of the coil collapses and cuts through the secondary circuit windings around the iron core. Because of the scientific phenomenon called "electromagnetic induction," the battery voltage is at this point increased to a level sufficient to fire the spark plugs.

When the points open, the electrical charge in the primary circuit jumps the gap created between the two open contacts of the points. If this electrical charge were not transferred elsewhere, the metal contacts of the points would melt and the gap between the points would start to change rapidly. If this gap is not maintained, the points will not break the primary circuit. If the primary circuit is not broken, the secondary circuit will not have enough voltage to fire the spark plugs.

The function of the condenser is to absorb excessive voltage from the points when they open and thus prevent the points from becoming pitted or burned.

The cycle must be completed by the ignition system every time a spark fires. In a V8 engine, all of the spark plugs fire once for every two revolutions of the crankshaft. That means that in one revolution, four spark plugs fire. So, when the engine is at an idle speed of 800 rpm, the points are opening and closing 3,200 times a minute.

There are two ways to check the breaker point gap: It can be done with a feeler gauge or a dwell meter. Either way you set the points, you are basically adjusting the amount of time that the points remain open. The time is measured in degrees of distributor rotation. When you measure the gap between the breaker points with a feeler gauge, you are setting the maximum amount the points will open when the rubbing block on the points is on a high point

of the distributor cam. When you adjust the points with a dwell meter, you are adjusting the number of degrees that the points will remain closed before they start to open as a high point of the distributor cam approaches the rubbing block of the points.

When you replace a set of points, always replace the condenser at the same time.

When you change the point gap or dwell, you will also have changed the ignition timing. So, if the point gap or dwell is changed, the ignition timing must be adjusted also. Changing the ignition timing, however, does not affect the dwell.

INSPECTION OF THE POINTS

1. Disconnect the high-tension wire from the top of the distributor and the coil.

2. Remove the distributor cap by prying the spring clips on the side of the distributor away from the cap. Lift the cap and wires from the top of the distributor.

3. Remove the rotor from the distributor shaft by pulling it straight up. Examine the condition of the rotor. If it is cracked or the metal

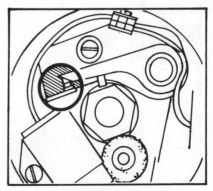

Checking point face alignment

Tune-Up Specifications

Year	Engine No. Cyl Displacement (cu. in.)	hp	Spark Plugs Orig. Type	Gap (in.)	Distributor Point Dwell* (deg)	Point Gap (in.)	Ignition Timing (deg)▲ Man Trans	Auto Trans	Intake Valve Opens ■(deg)	Fuel Pump Pressure (psi)	Idle Speed (rpm)▲● Man Trans	Auto Trans
'71	6-250	145	BRF-82	.034	36	.027/.025	6B	6B	10	4–6	750	600
	8-302	210	BRF-42	.034	27	.021	6B	6B	16	4–6	800/500	575 (600/500)
	8-351C	240	ARF-42	.034	27	.021	6B	6B	12	5–7	700/500	600
	8-351W	240	BRF-42	.034	27	.021	6B	6B	12	5–7	700/500	575 (600/500)
	8-351C	285	AFR-32	.034	27/29	.021/.017	6B	6B	18	5–7	800/500	600
	8-429	360	BRF-42	.034	27/29	.021/.017	4B	4B	16	5–7	700	600 (600/500)
	8-429CJ	370	ARF-42	.034	25	.020	10B	10B	32	4½–6½	700	650 (650/500)
	8-429SCJ	385	ARF-42	.034	28	.020	10B	10B	40½	4½–6½	650/500	700/500
'72	6-250	95	BRF-82	.034	37	.027	6B	6B	10(16)	4½–6½	750/500	600/500
	8-302	140	BRF-42	.034	28	.017	6B	6B	16	5½–6½	800/500	575 (600/500)
	8-351C	165	ARF-42	.034	28	.017	6B	6B	12	5½–6½	800/500	575/500 (625/500)
	8-351W	165	BRF-42	.034	28	.017	—	6B	12	5½–6½	—	575 (600/500)
	8-400	168	ARF-42	.034	28	.017	—	6B	17	4½–5½	—	625/500
	8-429	205	ARF-42	.034	28	.017	—	10B	8	5½–6½	—	600/500
'73	6-250	95	BRF-82	.034	37	.027/.025	6B	6B	16	4½–6½	750/500	600/500
	8-302	140	BRF-42	.034	28	.017	6B	6B	16	5½–6½	800/500	575 (600/500)

Year	Engine		Spark Plug	Gap	Dwell	Point Gap		Timing			Idle Speed
	8-351C	165	ARF-42	.034	28	.017	—	6B	12	5½–6½	—	625/500
	8-351W	165	BRF-42	.034	28	.017	—	6B	12	5½–6½	—	575 (600/500)
'74	8-400	168	ARF-42	.034	28	.017	—	6B	17	5½–6½	—	625–500
	8-429	205	ARF-42	.034	28	.017	—	10B	8	5½–6½	—	600/500
	8-460PI	269	ARF-42	.035	28	.017	—	10B	18	5½–6½	—	600
	6-260	91	BRF-82	.044	37⑩	.027	6B	6B	26	5½–6½	800/500	625/500
	8-302	140	BRF-42	.044	28⑩	.017	10B	6B	16⑦	5½–6½	800/500	625/500
	8-351W	162	BRF-42	.044	28⑩	.017	—	6B	15	5½–6½	—	600/500
	8-351C	163	ARF-42	.044	28⑩	.017	—	14B	11.5	5½–6½	—	600/500
	8-400	170	ARF-42	.044	Electronic		—	12B⑥	17	5½–6½	—	625/500
	8-460	195, 220, 260	ARF-42	.054	Electronic		—	14B	8	5½–6½	—	650/500
'75	8-351W	153, 154	ARF-42	.044	Electronic		—	6B	15	5½–6½	—	600/500
	8-351M	148, 150	ARF-42	.044	Electronic		—	6B	19½	5½–6½	—	700/500
	8-400	144, 158	ARF-42	.044	Electronic		—	6B	17	5½–6½	—	625/500
	8-460	216, 217	ARF-52	.044	Electronic		—	14B	8	5½–6½	—	650/500
	8-460PI	226	ARF-52	.044	Electronic		—	14B	18	5½–7	—	700/500
'76	8-351W	All	ARF-42/52⑧	.054	Electronic		—	⑧	15	5½–6½	—	650
	8-351M	All	ARF-42/52⑧	.044	Electronic		—	⑧	19½	5½–6½	—	650 (650/675⑧)
	8-400	All	ARF-42/52⑧	.044	Electronic		—	⑧	17	5½–6½	—	650(625)
	8-460	All	ARF-52	.044	Electronic		—	8/14B⑧⑨ @ 650	8	5½–6½	—	650
	8-460PI	226	ARF-52	.044	Electronic		—	14B⑨ @ 650	18	5½–7	—	650
'77	8-302	All	ARF-52④	.050	Electronic		—	8B⑬	16	5½–6½	—	650
	8-351W	All	ARF-52④	.050	Electronic		—	4B	23	4–6	—	650

Tune-Up Specifications (Cont.)

Year	Engine No. Cyl Displacement (cu. in.)	hp	Spark Plugs Orig. Type	Spark Plugs Gap (in.)	Distributor Point Dwell* (deg)	Distributor Point Gap (in.)	Ignition Timing (deg)▲ Man Trans	Ignition Timing (deg)▲ Auto Trans	Intake Valve Opens ■(deg)	Fuel Pump Pressure (psi)	Idle Speed (rpm)▲● Man Trans	Idle Speed (rpm)▲● Auto Trans
'77	8-351M	All	ARF-52 ④	.050	Electronic		—	8B⑭	19½	6½-7½	—	650
'78	8-400	All	ARF-54 ④	.050	Electronic		—	8B	17	7-8	—	650
	8-302	All	ARF-52 ⑮	.050	Electronic		—	14B	16	5½-6½	—	650
	8-351M	All	ARF-52 ⑮	.050	Electronic		—	14B	23	4-6	—	650
	8-351W	All	ARF-52 ⑮	.050	Electronic		—	14B⑯	19½	6½-7½	—	650
	8-400	All	ARF-5 ⑮	.050	Electronic		—	13B⑯	17	6½-7½	—	650
'79	8-302	All	ASF-52	.050	Electronic		—	8B	16	5½-6½	—	600
	8-351M	All	ASF-52	.050	Electronic		—	12B⑪	17⑫	7-8	—	600
	8-351W	All	ASF-52	.050	Electronic		—	15B	23	6½-8	—	600
'80	8-255	All	ASF-42	.050	Electronic		—	8B	16	5½-6	—	550
	8-255 Calif.	All	ASF-42	.050	Electronic		—	EEC	16	5½-6½	—	EEC
	8-302	All	ASF-52	.050	Electronic		—	8B	16	5½-6½	—	550
	8-302 Calif.	All	ASF-52	.050	Electronic		—	EEC	16	5½-6½	—	EEC
'81	4-140	All	AWSF-42	.034	Electronic		6B	6B	22	5½-6½	700	700
	6-200	All	BSF-92	.050	Electronic		10B	10B	20	6-8	900	900
	8-255	All	ASF-52	.050	Electronic		—	10B	16	6-8	—	800
	8-302	All	ASF-52	.050	Electronic		—	8B	16	6-8	—	800
'82-'85	4-140	All	AWSF-42 ⑱	.034	Electronic		—	⑧	22	6-8	850⑧	750⑧
	6-200	All	BSF-92	.050	Electronic		—	⑧	20	6-8	—	700⑧
	6-232	All	AGSF-52 ⑲	.044	Electronic		—	⑧	13	6-8⑳	—	500⑰⑧

8-255	All	ASF-52	.050	Electronic	—	16	⑧	6-8	—	700 ⑧
8-302	All	ASF-52 ⑧	.050 ②	Electronic	—	16	⑧	6-8 ㉒	—	500 ⑧

NOTE: The underhood specifications sticker often reflects tune-up specification changes made in production. Sticker figures must be used if they disagree with those in this chart.

*Where two dwell or point gap figures are separated by a slash, the first figure is for engines equipped with dual diaphragm distributors and the second figure is for engines equipped with single diaphragm distributors

▲ See text for procedure

● In all cases where two idle speed figures are separated by a slash, the first is for idle speed with solenoid energized and automatic transmission in Drive, while the second is for idle speed with solenoid disconnected and automatic transmission in Neutral. Figures in parentheses are for California

■ All figures are in degrees Before Top Dead Center

① For air conditioned vehicles, adjust idle speed to 600 rpm with A/C on
② For air conditioned vehicles, adjust idle speed to 800 rpm with A/C on
③ Figure is .020 for manual transmission with dual point distributor
④ ARF-52-6 for Calif. engines, gap is .060 in.
⑤ Figure is 32°–35° on manual transmission model with dual point distributor with both point sets combined
⑥ At 500 rpm
⑦ 20° BTC for 302 automatic
⑧ Depends on emission equipment; check underhood specifications sticker
⑨ In Drive
⑩ Electronic ignition used on all engines assembled after May, 1974
⑪ 14B in Calif.
⑫ Calif.: 19.5
⑬ Versailles: 12B
⑭ California: 9B
⑮ California: ARF-52-6; gap .060
⑯ California: 16B
⑰ California: T'bird & XR-7—700 w/TSP on
　　Cougar—650 w/TSP off
　　Continental—700 w/TSP on
⑱ Turbo models: AWSF-32C
⑲ CFI (injected) models: AWSF-54
⑳ CFI (injected) 40–45

㉑ .044, 83 and later
㉒ Injected models—39
B Before Top Dead Center
C Cleveland
M Modified Cleveland
CJ Cobra Jet
HO High Output
N.A. Not available
SCJ Super Cobra Jet
W Windsor
EEC: Electrical Engine Control; Adjustment is not possible.
— Not applicable

tip is excessively worn or burned, it should be replaced.

4. Pry open the contacts of the points with a screwdriver and check the condition of the contacts. If they are excessively worn, burned or pitted, they should be replaced.

5. If the points are in good condition, adjust them, and replace the rotor and the distributor cap. If the points need to be replaced, follow the replacement procedure given below.

REPLACEMENT OF THE BREAKER POINTS AND CONDENSER

1. Remove the coil high-tension wire from top of the distributor cap. Remove the distributor cap from the distributor and place it out of the way. Remove the rotor from the distributor shaft.

NOTE: *Refer to Step 2 in the following "Adjustment" procedure. It is far easier to have the rubbing block on cam prior to point assembly removal.*

2. Loosen the screw or nut which holds the condenser lead to the body of the breaker points and remove the condenser and coil leads from the points.

3. Remove the screw which holds and grounds the condenser to the distributor body. Remove the condenser from the distributor and discard it.

4. Remove the points assembly attaching

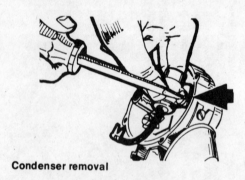

Condenser removal

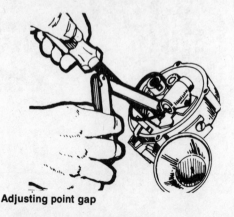

Adjusting point gap

screws and adjustment lockscrews. A screwdriver with a holding mechanism will come in handy here so that you don't drop a screw into the distributor and have to remove the entire distributor to retrieve it.

5. Remove the points by lifting them straight up and off the locating dowel on the plate. Wipe off the cam and apply new cam lubricant. Discard the old set of points.

6. Slip the new set of points onto the locating dowel and install the screws that hold the assembly onto the plate. Snug the screws against the points but do not tighten them all the way at this time.

NOTE: *Be sure the braided grounding strap is installed under one screw.*

7. Attach the new condenser to the plate with the ground screw.

8. Attach the condenser lead to the points at the proper place.

9. Apply a small amount of cam lubricant to the shaft where the rubbing block of the points touches.

ADJUSTMENT OF THE BREAKER POINTS WITH A FEELER GAUGE

1. If the contact points of the assembly are not parallel, bend the stationary contact so that they make contact across the entire surface of the contacts. Bend only the stationary bracket part of the point assembly; not the moveable contact.

2. Turn the engine until the rubbing block of the point is on one of the high points of the distributor cam. You can do this by either turning the ignition switch to the start position and releasing it quickly ("bumping" the engine) or by using a wrench on the bolt which holds the crankshaft pulley to the crankshaft.

3. Place the correct size feeler gauge between the contacts. Make sure that it is parallel with the contact surfaces.

4. With your free hand, insert a screwdriver into the notch provided for adjustment or into the eccentric adjusting screw, then twist the screwdriver to either increase or decrease the gap to the proper setting.

5. Tighten the adjustment lockscrew and recheck the contact gap to make sure that it didn't change when the lockscrew was tightened.

6. Replace the rotor and distributor cap, and the high-tension wire that connects the top of the distributor and the coil. Make sure that the rotor is firmly seated all the way onto the distributor shaft and that the tab of the rotor is aligned with the notch in the shaft. Align the tab in the base of the distributor cap with the notch in the distributor body. Make sure that the cap is firmly seated on the distributor and

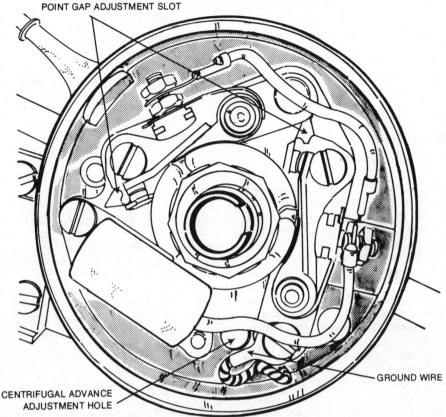

POINT GAP ADJUSTMENT SLOT

CENTRIFUGAL ADVANCE
ADJUSTMENT HOLE

GROUND WIRE

Dual point set used on Super Cobrajet engines

that the retainer clips are in place. Make sure that the end of the high tension wire is firmly placed in the top of the distributor and the coil.

NOTE: *1972–73 351M & CJ engines with manual transmissions have distributors equipped with dual points. On these models, set each gap to .020 in., then take a combined dwell reading.*

ADJUSTMENT OF THE BREAKER POINTS WITH A DWELL METER

1. Adjust the points with a feeler gauge as described earlier.

2. Connect the dwell meter to the ignition circuit according to the manufacturer's instructions. One lead of the meter is connected to a ground and the other lead is to be connected to the distributor post on the coil. An adapter is usually provided for this purpose.

3. If the dwell meter has a set line on it, adjust the meter to zero the indicator.

4. Start the engine.

NOTE: *Be careful when working on any vehicle while the engine is running. Make sure that the transmission is in Neutral or Park and that the parking brake is applied. Keep hands, clothing, tools, and the wires of the test instruments clear of the rotating fan blades.*

5. Observe the reading on the dwell meter. If the reading is within the specified range, turn off the engine and remove the dwell meter.

6. If the reading is above the specified range, the breaker point gap is too small. If the reading is below the specified range, the gap is too large. In either case, the engine must be stopped

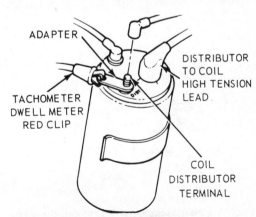

ADAPTER

DISTRIBUTOR
TO COIL
HIGH TENSION
LEAD

TACHOMETER
DWELL METER
RED CLIP

COIL
DISTRIBUTOR
TERMINAL

Attaching dwell/tachometer, with adaptor, on ignition coil (1971–74 models)

and the gap adjusted in the manner previously covered. After making the adjustment, start the engine and check the reading on the dwell meter. When the correct reading is obtained, disconnect the dwell meter.

7. Check the adjustment of the ignition timing.

Electronic Ignition Systems
SOLID STATE IGNITION

Some 1974 and all 1975–76 engines are equipped with the breakerless (solid state) electronic ignition system. The conventional contact breaker points and condenser in the distributor are replaced by a permanent magnet low-voltage generator. The generator consists of an armature with four, six or eight teeth mounted on the top of the distributor shaft, and a permanent magnet inside a small coil. The coil is riveted in place to provide a preset air gap with the armature. The distributor base, cap, rotor and vacuum and centrifugal spark advance are about the same as the conventional system.

The distributor is wired to a solid state module in the engine compartment. Inside the module is an electronic circuit board which consists of inner connecting resistors, capacitors, transistors and diodes. The module senses a signal from the magnetic generator to perform the switching function of conventional points and it senses and controls dwell.

Unless a malfunction occurs, or the distributor is moved or replaced, the initial ignition timing remains constant. Because the low voltage coil in the distributor is riveted in position, gap adjustment is not possible.

Troubleshootng

With the ignition switch "on," the primary circuit is on and the ignition coil is energized. When the armature "spokes" approach the

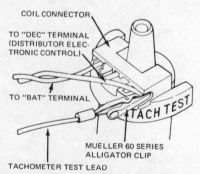

COIL CONNECTOR
TO "DEC" TERMINAL (DISTRIBUTOR ELECTRONIC CONTROL)
TO "BAT" TERMINAL
TACH TEST
MUELLER 60 SERIES ALLIGATOR CLIP
TACHOMETER TEST LEAD

Attaching dwell/tachometer lead to coil connector (electronic ignition)

magnetic pickup coil assembly, they induce a voltage which tells the amplifier to turn the coil primary current off. A timing circuit in the amplifier module will turn the current on again after the coil field has collapsed. When the current is "on," it flows from the battery through the ignition switch, the primary windings of the ignition coil, and through the amplifier module circuits to ground. When the current is off, the magnetic field built up in the ignition coil is allowed to collapse, inducing a high voltage into the secondary windings of the coil. High voltage is produced each time the field is thus built up and collapsed.

The high voltage flows through the coil high tension lead to the distributor cap where the rotor distributes it to one of the spark plug terminals in the distributor cap. This process is repeated for every power stroke of the engine.

Ignition system troubles are caused by a failure in the primary and/or the secondary circuit; incorrect ignition timing; or incorrect distributor advance. Circuit failures may be caused by shorts, corroded or dirty terminals, loose connections, defective wire insulation, cracked distributor cap or rotor, defective pick-up coil assembly or amplifier module, defective distributor points, fouled spark plugs, or by improper dwell angle.

If an engine starting or operating trouble is attributed to the ignition system, start the engine and verify the complaint. On engines that will not start, be sure there is gasoline in the fuel tank and that fuel is reaching the carburetor. Then locate the ignition system problem by an oscilloscope test or by a spark intensity test.

SPARK INTENSITY TEST

1. Connect auxiliary starter switch in the starting circuit.

2. Remove the coil high tension lead from the distributor cap.

3. Turn on the ignition switch.

4. While holding the high tension lead approximately 3/16 inch from the cylinder head or any other good ground, crank the engine with an auxiliary starter switch.

If the spark is good, the trouble lies in the secondary circuit.

A breakdown or energy loss in the secondary circuit can be caused by: fouled or improperly adjusted spark plugs; defective high tension wiring; or high tension leakage across the coil, distributor cap or rotor resulting from an accumulation of dirt.

To check the spark intensity at the spark plugs, thereby isolating an ignition problem to a particular cylinder, proceed as follows:

1. Disconnect a spark plug wire. When removing wires from spark plugs, twist the molded cap back and forth on the plug insulator to free cap. Do not pull directly on the wire, or it may become separated from the connector inside the cap.

Check the spark intensity of one wire at a time.

NOTE: *Use insulated pliers to hold the wire when cranking the engine.*

2. Install a terminal adapter in the terminal of the wire to be checked. Hold the adapter approximately ³⁄₁₆ inch from the exhaust manifold and crank the engine, using an auxiliary starter switch. The spark should jump the gap regularly.

3. If the spark intensity of all the wires is satisfactory, the coil, condenser, rotor, distributor cap and the secondary wires are probably satisfactory.

If the spark is good at only some wires, check the resistance of those particular leads.

If the spark is equal at all wires, but weak or intermittent, check the coil, distributor cap and the coil to distributor high tension wire. The wire should be clean and bright on the conducting ends, and on the coil tower and distributor sockets. the wire should fit snugly and be bottomed in the sockets.

If there is no spark or a weak spark, the trouble is in the primary circuit, coil to distributor high tension lead, or the coil.

PRIMARY CIRCUIT TEST

A breakdown or energy loss in the primary circuit can be caused by: defective primary wiring, loose or corroded connections, inoperative or defective magnetic pickup coil assembly, or defective amplifier module.

A complete test of the primary circuit consists of checking the circuits in the ignition coil, the magnetic pickup coil assembly and the amplifier module. Wiring harness checks will be included as a part of basic component circuit tests.

Always inspect connectors for dirt, corrosion or poor fit before assuming you have spotted a possible problem.

Make sure the battery is fully charged before beginning tests. Perform a Spark Intensity Test. If no spark is observed, make sure the high tension coil wire is good. Disconnect the three-way and four-way connectors at the electronic module.

The first trouble isolation tests will be conducted on the harness terminals, with the electronic module disconnected from the circuit.

Make the following tests using a sensitive volt-ohmmeter. These tests will direct you to the proper follow-up test to determine the actual problem.

If the circuit checks good at all these test points, connect a known good electronic module in place of the vehicle module and again

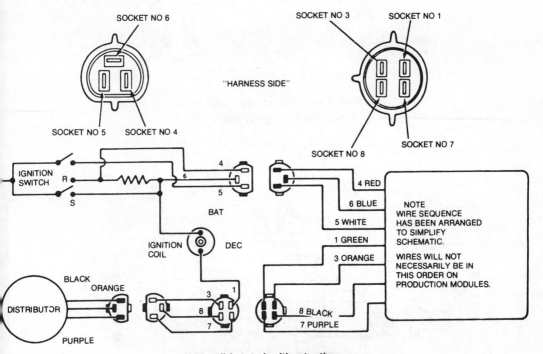

1975 solid state ignition testing

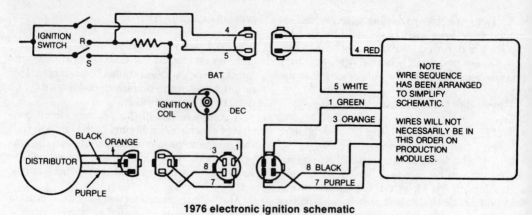

1976 electronic ignition schematic

NOTE
WIRE SEQUENCE
HAS BEEN ARRANGED
TO SIMPLIFY
SCHEMATIC.

WIRES WILL NOT
NECESSARILY BE IN
THIS ORDER ON
PRODUCTION
MODULES.

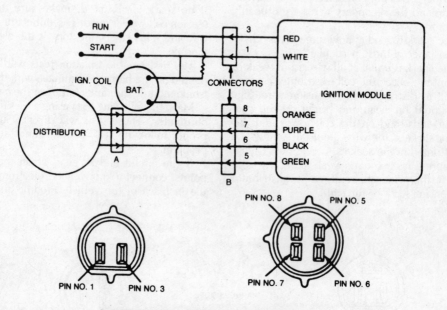

ELECTRONIC MODULE CONNECTORS – HARNESS SIDE

1977 Dura Spark II schematic

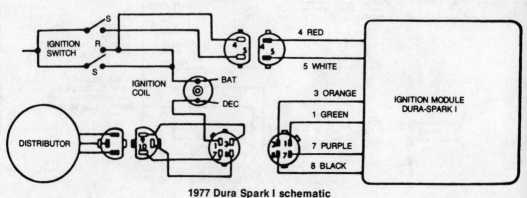

1977 Dura Spark I schematic

Test Sequence

	Test Voltage Between	Should Be	If Not, Conduct
1975			
Key On	Socket #4 and Engine Ground	Battery Voltage ±0.1 Volt	Module Bias Test
	Socket #1 and Engine Ground	Battery Voltage ±0.1 Volt	Battery Source Test
Cranking	Socket #5 and Engine Ground	8 to 12 volts	Cranking Test
	Jumper #1 to #8 Read #6	more than 6 volts	Starting Circuit Test
	Pin #7 and Pin #8	½ volt minimum AC or any DC volt wiggle	Distributor Hardware Test

	Test Voltage Between	Should Be	If Not, Conduct
Key Off	Socket #7 and #3 Socket #8 and Engine Ground Socket #7 and Engine Ground Socket #3 and Engine Ground	400 to 800 ohms 0 ohms more than 70,000 ohms	Magnetic Pick-up (Stator) Test
	Socket #4 and Coil Tower Socket #1 and Pin #6	7000 to 13000 ohms 1.0 to 2.0 ohms	Coil Test
	Socket #1 and Engine Ground	more than 4.0 ohms	Short Test
	Socket # 4 and Pin #6	1.0 to 2.0 ohms	Resistance Wire Test

	Test Voltage Between	Should Be	If Not, Conduct
1976			
Key On	Socket #4 and Engine Ground	Battery Voltage ±0.1 Volt	Battery Source Test
	Socket #1 and Engine Ground	Battery Voltage +0.1 Volt	Battery Source Test
Cranking	Socket #5 and Engine Ground	8 to 12 volts	Check Supply Circuit (starting) through Ignition Switch
	Jumper #1 to #8 Read #6	more than 6 volts	Starting Circuit Test
	Pin #3 and Pin #8	½ volt minimum AC or any DC volt wiggle	Distributor Hardware Test

	Test Voltage Between	Should Be	If Not, Conduct
Key Off	Socket #8 and #3 Socket #7 and Engine Ground Socket #8 and Engine Ground Socket #3 and Engine Ground	400 to 800 ohms 0 ohms more than 70,000 ohms more than 70,000 ohms	Magnetic Pick-up (Stator) Test
	Socket #4 and Coil Tower	7000 to 13,000 ohms	Coil Test
	Socket #1 and Engine Ground	more than 4.0 ohms	Short Test
		0.5 to 1.5 ohms Dura-Spark I	
	Socket #1 and Engine Ground	more than 4 ohms	Short Test
	Socket #4 and Coil "Bat" Term. (Except Dura-Spark I)	1.0 to 2.0 ohms Breakerless	Resistance Wire Test
		0.7 to 1.7 ohms Dura-Spark II	

	Test Voltage Between	Should Be	If Not, Conduct
1977			
Key On	Socket #4 and Engine Ground	Battery Voltage ±0.1 Volt	Module Bias Test
	Socket #1 and Engine Ground	Battery Voltage ±0.1 Volt	Battery Source Test

Test Sequence (Cont.)

	Test Voltage Between	Should Be	If Not, Conduct
Cranking	Socket #5 and Engine Ground	8 to 12 volts	Cranking Test
	Jumper #1 to #8—Read Coil "Bat" Term. & Engine Ground	more than 6 volts	Starting Circuit Test
	Sockets #7 and #3	½ volt minimum wiggle	Distributor Hardware Test

	Test Resistance Between	Should Be	If Not, Conduct
Key Off	Sockets #7 and #3 Socket #8 and Engine Ground Socket #7 and Engine Ground Socket #3 and Engine Ground	400 to 800 ohms 0 ohms more than 70,000 ohms more than 70,000 ohms	Magnetic Pick-up (Stator) Test
	Socket #4 and Coil Tower	7000 to 13,000 ohms	Coil Test
	Socket #1 and Coil "Bat" Term.	1.0 to 2.0 ohms Breakerless & Dura-Spark II	

1978–82

	Test Voltage Between	Should Be	If Not, Conduct
Key On	Socket #4 and Engine Ground	Battery Voltage ±0.1 Volt	Module Bias Test
	Socket #1 and Engine Ground	Battery Voltage ±0.1 Volt	Battery Source Test
Cranking	Socket #5 and Engine Ground	8 to 12 volts	Cranking Test
	Jumper #1 to #8—Read Coil "Bat" Term & Engine Ground	more than 6 volts	Starting Circuit Test
	Sockets #7 and #3	½ volt minimum wiggle	Distributor Hardware Test
Key Off	Sockets #7 and #3 Socket #8 and Engine Ground Socket #7 and Engine Ground Socket #3 and Engine Ground	400 to 800 ohms 0 ohms more than 70,000 ohms more than 70,000 ohms	Magnetic Pick-up (Stator) Test
	Socket #4 and Coil Tower	7000 to 13,000 ohms	Coil Test
	Socket #1 and Coil "Bat" Term	1.0 to 2.0 ohms Breakerless & Dura Spark II	
		0.5 to 1.5 ohms Dura-Spark I	
	Socket #1 and Engine Ground	more than 4.0 ohms	Short Test
	Socket #4 and Coil "Bat" Term (Except Dura-Spark I)	1.0 to 2.0 ohms Breakerless	Resistance Wire Test
		0.7 to 1.7 ohms Dura Spark II	

perform the spark intensity test. If the substitution corrects the malfunction, again reconnect the vehicle module and perform the spark intensity test. If the malfunction still exists, the problem is in the module and it must be replaced. If the problem is gone, it may be an intermittent fault or may be in the wiring connectors.

If the substitution module does not correct the problem, reconnect the original module and make the repairs elsewhere in the system.

MODULE BIAS TEST

Measure the voltage at the red wire socket to engine ground with the ignition key "on." If the voltage observed is less than battery voltage, repair the voltage feed wiring to the module for running conditions (red wire).

BATTERY SOURCE TEST

1. Connect the voltmeter leads from the battery terminal at the coil to engine ground,

without disconnecting the coil from the circuit.

2. Install a jumper wire from the DEC terminal of the coil to a good engine ground.

3. Turn the lights and all accessories off.

4. Turn the ignition switch "on."

5. If the voltmeter reading is between 4.9 and 7.9 volts, the primary circuit from the battery is satisfactory.

6. If the voltmeter reading is less than 4.9 volts, check the following:

    a. The primary wiring for worn insulation, broken strands, and loose or corroded terminals.

    b. The resistance wiring for defects.

7. If the voltmeter reading is greater than 7.9 volts, the resistance wire should be replaced after verifying defect.

CRANKING TEST

Measure the voltage at the white wire socket to engine ground with the engine cranking. If the voltage observed is not 8 to 12 volts, repair the voltage feed to the module for starting conditions (white wire).

STARTING CIRCUIT TEST

If the reading is not between 8 and 12 volts, the ignition by-pass circuit is open or grounded from either the starter solenoid or the ignition switch to the green wire socket. Check primary connections at the coil and the coil lead from the module to the coil.

DISTRIBUTOR HARDWARE TEST

1. Disconnect three-wire weatherproof connector at distributor pigtail.

2. Connect a D.C. voltmeter on a 2.5 volt scale to the two parallel blades. With the engine cranking, the meter needle should oscillate.

3. Remove the distributor cap and check for visual damage or misassembly.

    a. Sintered iron armature (6- or 8-toothed wheel) must be tight on sleeve, and the roll pin aligning the armature must be in position.

    b. Sintered iron stator must not be broken.

    c. Armature must rotate when engine is cranked.

4. If the hardware is all right, but the meter doesn't oscillate, replace the magnetic pick-up assembly.

MAGNETIC PICK-UP TESTS

1. Resistance of pickup coil measured between two parallel pins in the distributor connector must be 400–800 ohms.

2. Resistance between the third blade (ground) and the distributor bowl must be zero ohms.

3. Resistance between either parallel blade and engine ground must be greater than 70,000 ohms.

4. If any test fails, the distributor stator assembly is defective and must be replaced.

5. If above readings are not the same as measured in the original test, check for defective harness. If readings are the same, proceed.

6. If these tests check all right, the signal generator portion of the distributor is working properly.

IGNITION COIL TEST

The breakerless ignition coil must be diagnosed separately from the rest of the ignition system.

1. Primary resistance must be 1.0–2.0 ohms, measured from the BAT to the DEC terminals.

2. Secondary resistance must be 7,000–13,000 ohms, measured from the BAT or DEC terminal to the center tower of the coil.

3. If resistance tests are all right, but coil is still suspected, test on coil tester by following the test equipment manufacturer's instructions for a standard coil. If reading differs from the original test, check for defective harness.

SHORT TEST

If the resistance from Pin 5 (green wire) to ground is less than 10 ohms, check for short to ground at the DEC terminal of the ignition coil or in the connection wiring to that terminal.

Tachometer-To-Coil Connection—Electronic Ignition

The new solid state ignition coil connector allows a tachometer test lead with an alligator-type clip to be connected to the DEC (Distributor Electronic Control) terminal without removing the connector.

When engine rpm must be checked, install the tachometer alligator clip into the "TACH TEST" cavity as shown. If the coil connector must be removed, grasp the wires and pull horizontally until it disconnects from the terminals.

Dura Spark Ignition

Basically, four electronic ignition systems have been used in Ford Motor Company vehicles from 1978–85:

1. Dura Spark I

IGNITION SYSTEM
II. Primary (Low Voltage) Portion—A. Dura Spark II

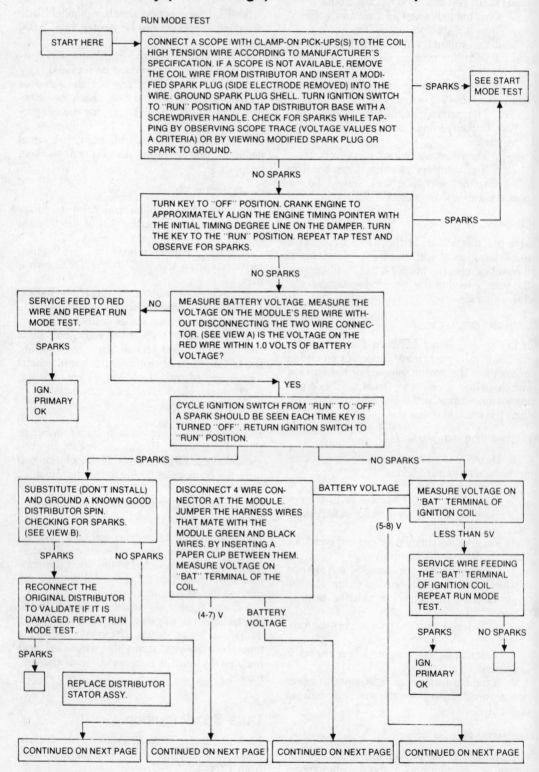

RUN MODE TEST

START HERE → CONNECT A SCOPE WITH CLAMP-ON PICK-UPS(S) TO THE COIL HIGH TENSION WIRE ACCORDING TO MANUFACTURER'S SPECIFICATION. IF A SCOPE IS NOT AVAILABLE, REMOVE THE COIL WIRE FROM DISTRIBUTOR AND INSERT A MODIFIED SPARK PLUG (SIDE ELECTRODE REMOVED) INTO THE WIRE. GROUND SPARK PLUG SHELL. TURN IGNITION SWITCH TO "RUN" POSITION AND TAP DISTRIBUTOR BASE WITH A SCREWDRIVER HANDLE. CHECK FOR SPARKS WHILE TAPPING BY OBSERVING SCOPE TRACE (VOLTAGE VALUES NOT A CRITERIA) OR BY VIEWING MODIFIED SPARK PLUG OR SPARK TO GROUND. — SPARKS → SEE START MODE TEST

NO SPARKS

TURN KEY TO "OFF" POSITION. CRANK ENGINE TO APPROXIMATELY ALIGN THE ENGINE TIMING POINTER WITH THE INITIAL TIMING DEGREE LINE ON THE DAMPER. TURN THE KEY TO THE "RUN" POSITION. REPEAT TAP TEST AND OBSERVE FOR SPARKS. — SPARKS

NO SPARKS

SERVICE FEED TO RED WIRE AND REPEAT RUN MODE TEST. ← NO — MEASURE BATTERY VOLTAGE. MEASURE THE VOLTAGE ON THE MODULE'S RED WIRE WITHOUT DISCONNECTING THE TWO WIRE CONNECTOR. (SEE VIEW A) IS THE VOLTAGE ON THE RED WIRE WITHIN 1.0 VOLTS OF BATTERY VOLTAGE?

SPARKS

IGN. PRIMARY OK

YES

CYCLE IGNITION SWITCH FROM "RUN" TO "OFF" A SPARK SHOULD BE SEEN EACH TIME KEY IS TURNED "OFF". RETURN IGNITION SWITCH TO "RUN" POSITION.

SPARKS — NO SPARKS

SUBSTITUTE (DON'T INSTALL) AND GROUND A KNOWN GOOD DISTRIBUTOR SPIN. CHECKING FOR SPARKS. (SEE VIEW B).

DISCONNECT 4 WIRE CONNECTOR AT THE MODULE. JUMPER THE HARNESS WIRES THAT MATE WITH THE MODULE GREEN AND BLACK WIRES. BY INSERTING A PAPER CLIP BETWEEN THEM. MEASURE VOLTAGE ON "BAT" TERMINAL OF THE COIL.

BATTERY VOLTAGE

MEASURE VOLTAGE ON "BAT" TERMINAL OF IGNITION COIL

(5-8) V

LESS THAN 5V

SPARKS — NO SPARKS

RECONNECT THE ORIGINAL DISTRIBUTOR TO VALIDATE IF IT IS DAMAGED. REPEAT RUN MODE TEST.

SERVICE WIRE FEEDING THE "BAT" TERMINAL OF IGNITION COIL. REPEAT RUN MODE TEST.

SPARKS

(4-7) V   BATTERY VOLTAGE

SPARKS — NO SPARKS

REPLACE DISTRIBUTOR STATOR ASSY.

IGN. PRIMARY OK

CONTINUED ON NEXT PAGE   CONTINUED ON NEXT PAGE   CONTINUED ON NEXT PAGE   CONTINUED ON NEXT PAGE

IGNITION SYSTEM (CONTINUED)
II. Primary (Low Voltage) Portion (continued)
A. Dura Spark II (continued)

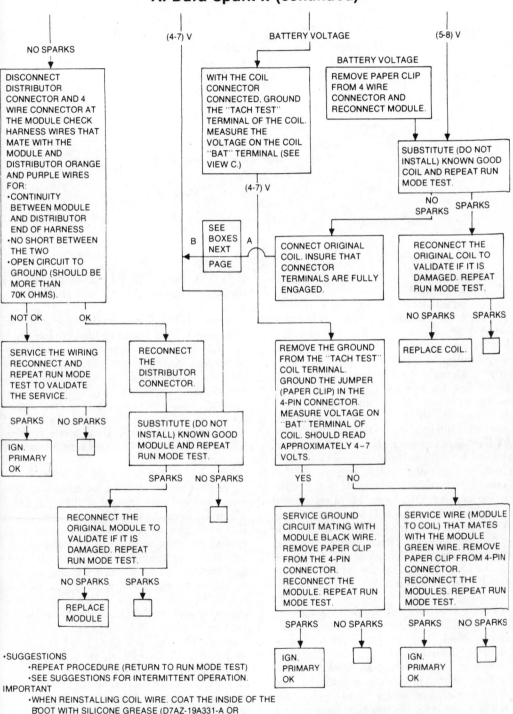

•SUGGESTIONS
•REPEAT PROCEDURE (RETURN TO RUN MODE TEST)
•SEE SUGGESTIONS FOR INTERMITTENT OPERATION.
IMPORTANT
•WHEN REINSTALLING COIL WIRE. COAT THE INSIDE OF THE
BOOT WITH SILICONE GREASE (D7AZ-19A331-A OR
EQUIVALENT) USING SMALL, CLEAN SCREWDRIVER BLADE.

IGNITION SYSTEM (CONTINUED)
II. Primary (Low Voltage) Portion (Continued)
A. Dura Spark II (continued)

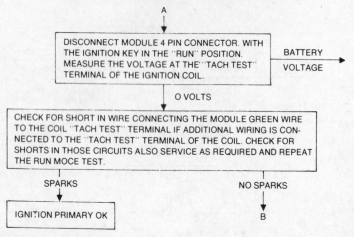

2. Dura Spark II
3. Dura Spark III
4. Universal Distributor-TFI (EECIV)

In 1977, the Dura Spark systems, were introduced. Dura Spark I and Dura Spark II systems are nearly identical in operation, and virtually identical in appearance. The Dura Spark I uses a special control module which senses current flow through the ignition coil and adjust the dwell, or coil "on" time for maximum spark intensity. If the Dura Spark I module senses that the ignition is ON, but the distributor shaft is not turning, the current to the coil is turned OFF by the module. The Dura Spark II system does not have this feature—the coil is energized for the full amount of time that the ignition switch is ON. Keep this in mind when servicing the Dura Spark II system, as the ignition system could inadvertently "fire" while performing ignition system services (such as distributor cap removal) while the ignition is ON. All Dura Spark II systems are easily identified by having a two-piece, flat topped distributor cap.

In 1980, the new Dura Spark III system was introduced. This version is based on the previous systems, but the input signal is controlled by the EEC system, rather than as a function of engine timing and distributor armature position. The distributor, rotor, cap, and control module are unique to this system; the spark plugs and plug wires are the same as those used with the Dura Spark II system. Although the Dura Spark II and III control modules are similar in appearance, they cannot be interchanged between systems.

The V series, with the modified Dura Spark II system, uses a special control module designed to function with the vehicles EEC system.

Some 1978 and later engines use a special Dura Spark Dual Mode ignition control module. The module is equipped with an altitude sensor, an economy modulator, or pressure switches (turbocharged engines only). This module, when combined with the additional switches and sensor, varies the base engine timing according to altitude and engine load conditions. Dura Spark Dual Mode ignition control modules have three wiring harness from the module.

1980–81 49-state and 1982 Canadian 2.3 liter engines with automatic transmissions have Dual Mode Crank Retard ignition module, which has the same function as the Dura Spark II module plus an ignition timing retard function which is operational during engine cranking. The spark timing retard feature eases engine starting, but allows normal timing advance as soon as the engine is running. This module can be identified by the presence of a white connector shell on the four-pin connector at the module.

Some 1981 and later Dura Spark II systems used with some 255 and 302 cu. in. engines are equipped with a Universal Ignition Module (UIM) which includes a run-retard function. The operation of the module is basically the same as the Dura Spark Dual Mode module.

The Universal Distributor (EEC-IV) has a die-cast base which incorporates an externally mounted TFI-IV ignition module, and contains a "Hall-Effect" vane switch stator assembly and provision for fixed octane adjustment. No dis-

IGNITION SYSTEM (CONTINUED)
II. Primary (Low Voltage) Portion (continued)
A. Dura Spark II (continued)

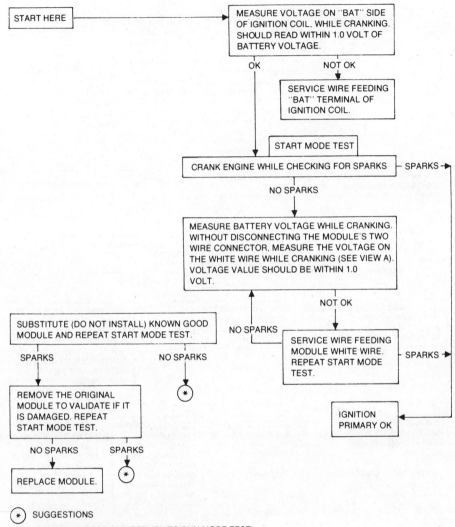

START HERE

MEASURE VOLTAGE ON "BAT" SIDE OF IGNITION COIL, WHILE CRANKING. SHOULD READ WITHIN 1.0 VOLT OF BATTERY VOLTAGE.

OK — NOT OK

SERVICE WIRE FEEDING "BAT" TERMINAL OF IGNITION COIL.

START MODE TEST

CRANK ENGINE WHILE CHECKING FOR SPARKS — SPARKS →

NO SPARKS

MEASURE BATTERY VOLTAGE WHILE CRANKING. WITHOUT DISCONNECTING THE MODULE'S TWO WIRE CONNECTOR, MEASURE THE VOLTAGE ON THE WHITE WIRE WHILE CRANKING (SEE VIEW A). VOLTAGE VALUE SHOULD BE WITHIN 1.0 VOLT.

NOT OK

SUBSTITUTE (DO NOT INSTALL) KNOWN GOOD MODULE AND REPEAT START MODE TEST.

NO SPARKS

SPARKS — NO SPARKS

SERVICE WIRE FEEDING MODULE WHITE WIRE. REPEAT START MODE TEST. — SPARKS →

REMOVE THE ORIGINAL MODULE TO VALIDATE IF IT IS DAMAGED. REPEAT START MODE TEST.

(*)

IGNITION PRIMARY OK

NO SPARKS — SPARKS

REPLACE MODULE.

(*)

(*) SUGGESTIONS

•REPEAT PROCEDURE (RETURN TO RUN MODE TEST)
•SEE SUGGESTIONS FOR INTERMITTENT OPERATION.

IMPORTANT

•WHEN REINSTALLING COIL WIRE, COAT THE INSIDE OF THE BOOT WITH SILICONE GREASE (D7AZ-19A331-A OR EQUIVALENT DOW 111 OR GE-G627) USING A SMALL, CLEAN SCREWDRIVER BLADE.

tributor calibration is required and initial timing adjustment is normally not required. The primary function of the EEC-IV Universal Distributor system is to direct high secondary voltage to the spark plugs. In addition, the distributor supplies crankshaft position and frequency information to a computer using a Profile Ignition Pickup. The "Hall-Effect" switch in the distributor consists of a Hall Effect device on one side and a magnet on the other side. A rotary cup which has windows and tabs rotates and passes through the space between the device and the magnet. When a window is between the sides of the switch the magnetic path is not completed and the switch is Off, sending no signal. When a tab passes between the switch the magnetic path is completed and the Hall Effect Device is turned On and a signal is sent. The voltage pulse (signal) is used by is EEC-IV system for sensing crankshaft position and computing the desired spark advance based on engine demand and calibration.

RUN MODE TEST

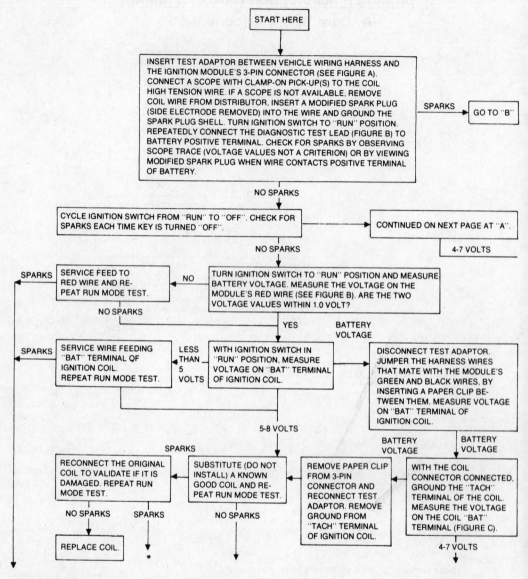

*SUGGESTIONS:

•REPEAT PROCEDURE (START AT RUN MODE TEST)

•SEE SUGGESTIONS FOR INTERMITTENT OPERATION

Dura Spark Operation

With the ignition switch "on," the primary circuit is on and the ignition coil is energized. When the armature "spokes" approach the magnetic pickup coil assembly, they induce a voltage which tells the amplifier to turn the coil primary current off. A timing circuit in the amplifier module will turn the current on again after the coil field has collapsed. When the current is "on," it flows from the battery through the ignition switch, the primary windings of the ignition coil, and through the amplifier module circuits to ground. When the current is off, the magnetic field built up in the ignition coil is allowed to collapse, inducing a high voltage into the secondary windings of the coil. High voltage is produced each time the field is thus built up and collapsed. When Dura Spark is used in

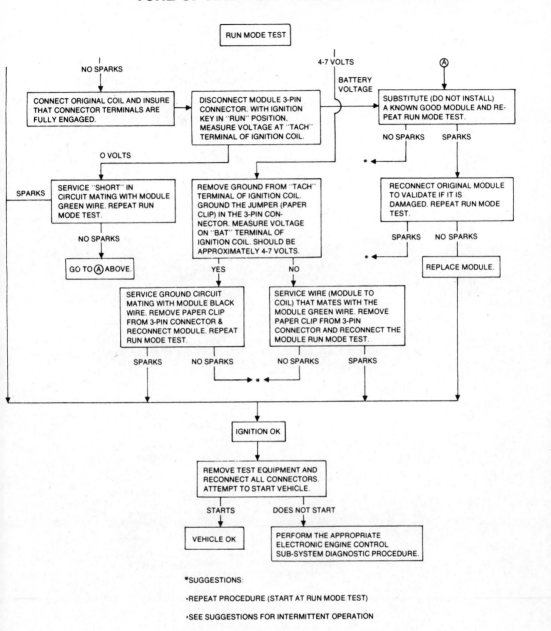

RUN MODE TEST

NO SPARKS | 4-7 VOLTS | BATTERY VOLTAGE | (A)

CONNECT ORIGINAL COIL AND INSURE THAT CONNECTOR TERMINALS ARE FULLY ENGAGED.

DISCONNECT MODULE 3-PIN CONNECTOR. WITH IGNITION KEY IN "RUN" POSITION, MEASURE VOLTAGE AT "TACH" TERMINAL OF IGNITION COIL.

SUBSTITUTE (DO NOT INSTALL) A KNOWN GOOD MODULE AND RE-PEAT RUN MODE TEST.

NO SPARKS   SPARKS

O VOLTS

SPARKS

SERVICE "SHORT" IN CIRCUIT MATING WITH MODULE GREEN WIRE. REPEAT RUN MODE TEST.

REMOVE GROUND FROM "TACH" TERMINAL OF IGNITION COIL. GROUND THE JUMPER (PAPER CLIP) IN THE 3-PIN CON-NECTOR. MEASURE VOLTAGE ON "BAT" TERMINAL OF IGNITION COIL. SHOULD BE APPROXIMATELY 4-7 VOLTS.

RECONNECT ORIGINAL MODULE TO VALIDATE IF IT IS DAMAGED. REPEAT RUN MODE TEST.

SPARKS   NO SPARKS

NO SPARKS

GO TO (A) ABOVE.

YES   NO

REPLACE MODULE.

SERVICE GROUND CIRCUIT MATING WITH MODULE BLACK WIRE. REMOVE PAPER CLIP FROM 3-PIN CONNECTOR & RECONNECT MODULE. REPEAT RUN MODE TEST.

SERVICE WIRE (MODULE TO COIL) THAT MATES WITH THE MODULE GREEN WIRE. REMOVE PAPER CLIP FROM 3-PIN CONNECTOR AND RECONNECT THE MODULE RUN MODE TEST.

SPARKS   NO SPARKS   NO SPARKS   SPARKS

IGNITION OK

REMOVE TEST EQUIPMENT AND RECONNECT ALL CONNECTORS. ATTEMPT TO START VEHICLE.

STARTS   DOES NOT START

VEHICLE OK

PERFORM THE APPROPRIATE ELECTRONIC ENGINE CONTROL SUB-SYSTEM DIAGNOSTIC PROCEDURE.

*SUGGESTIONS:

•REPEAT PROCEDURE (START AT RUN MODE TEST)

•SEE SUGGESTIONS FOR INTERMITTENT OPERATION

conjunction with EEC, the EEC computer tells the Dura Spark module when to turn the coil primary current off or on. In this case, the armature position is only a reference signal of engine timing, used by the EEC computer in combination with other reference signals to determine optimum ignition spark timing.

The high voltage flows through the coil high tension lead to the distributor cap where the rotor distributes it to one of the spark plug terminals in the distributor cap. This process is repeated for every power stroke of the engine.

Ignition system troubles are caused by a failure in the primary and/or the secondary circuit; incorrect ignition timing; or incorrect distributor advance. Circuit failures may be caused by shorts, corroded or dirty terminals, loose connections, defective wire insulation, cracked distributor cap or rotor, defective pick-up coil assembly or amplifier module, defective distributor points or fouled spark plugs.

If an engine starting or operating trouble is attributed to the ignition system, start the engine and verify the complaint. On engines that will not start, be sure that there is gasoline in the fuel tank and that fuel is reaching the carburetor. Then locate the ignition system problem using the following procedures.

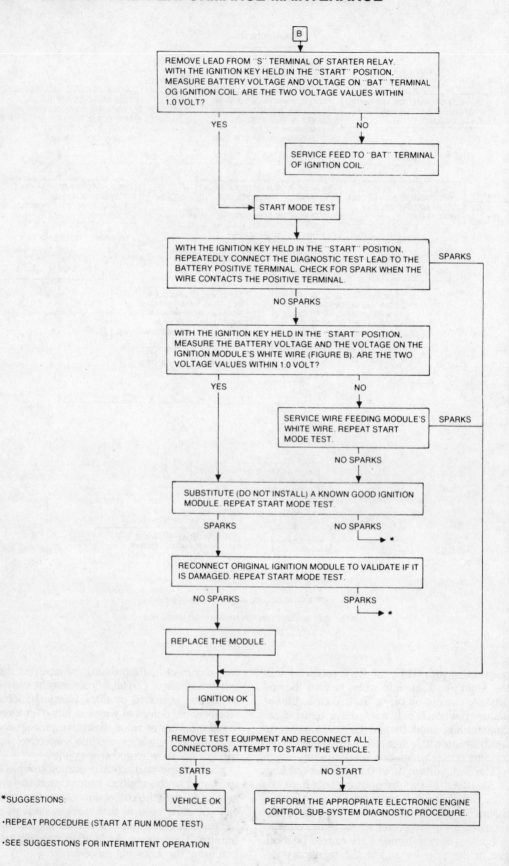

B

REMOVE LEAD FROM "S" TERMINAL OF STARTER RELAY. WITH THE IGNITION KEY HELD IN THE "START" POSITION, MEASURE BATTERY VOLTAGE AND VOLTAGE ON "BAT" TERMINAL OG IGNITION COIL. ARE THE TWO VOLTAGE VALUES WITHIN 1.0 VOLT?

YES   NO

SERVICE FEED TO "BAT" TERMINAL OF IGNITION COIL.

START MODE TEST

WITH THE IGNITION KEY HELD IN THE "START" POSITION, REPEATEDLY CONNECT THE DIAGNOSTIC TEST LEAD TO THE BATTERY POSITIVE TERMINAL. CHECK FOR SPARK WHEN THE WIRE CONTACTS THE POSITIVE TERMINAL.   SPARKS

NO SPARKS

WITH THE IGNITION KEY HELD IN THE "START" POSITION, MEASURE THE BATTERY VOLTAGE AND THE VOLTAGE ON THE IGNITION MODULE'S WHITE WIRE (FIGURE B). ARE THE TWO VOLTAGE VALUES WITHIN 1.0 VOLT?

YES   NO

SERVICE WIRE FEEDING MODULE'S WHITE WIRE. REPEAT START MODE TEST.   SPARKS

NO SPARKS

SUBSTITUTE (DO NOT INSTALL) A KNOWN GOOD IGNITION MODULE. REPEAT START MODE TEST.

SPARKS   NO SPARKS
                          *

RECONNECT ORIGINAL IGNITION MODULE TO VALIDATE IF IT IS DAMAGED. REPEAT START MODE TEST.

NO SPARKS   SPARKS
                             *

REPLACE THE MODULE.

IGNITION OK

REMOVE TEST EQUIPMENT AND RECONNECT ALL CONNECTORS. ATTEMPT TO START THE VEHICLE.

STARTS   NO START

VEHICLE OK

PERFORM THE APPROPRIATE ELECTRONIC ENGINE CONTROL SUB-SYSTEM DIAGNOSTIC PROCEDURE.

*SUGGESTIONS:

•REPEAT PROCEDURE (START AT RUN MODE TEST)

•SEE SUGGESTIONS FOR INTERMITTENT OPERATION

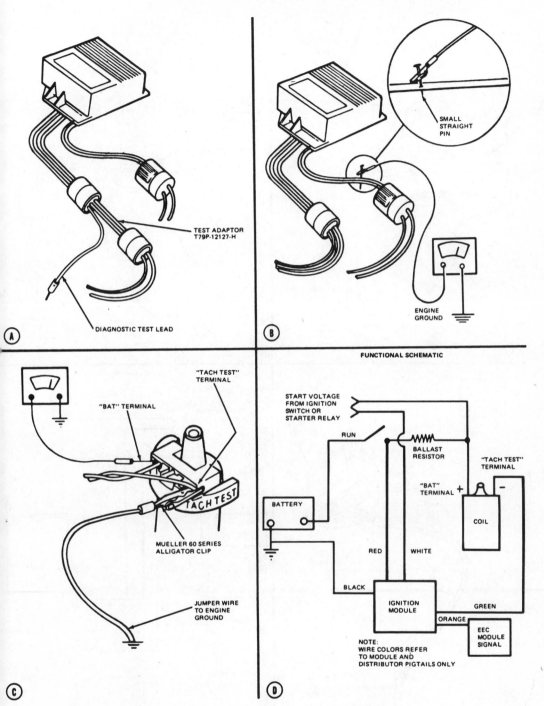

Testing the Dura Spark ignition on models with EEC

TROUBLESHOOTING DURA SPARK I

The following Dura Spark II troubleshooting procedures may be used on Dura Spark I systems with a few variations. The Dura Spark I module has internal connections which shut off the primary circuit in the run mode when the engine stalls. To perform the above trouble-shooting procedures, it is necessary to by-pass these connections. However, with these connections by-passed, the current flow in the primary becomes so great that it will damage both the ignition coil and module unless a ballast resistor is installed in series with the primary circuit at the BAT terminal of the ignition coil. Such a resistor is available from Ford (Motor-

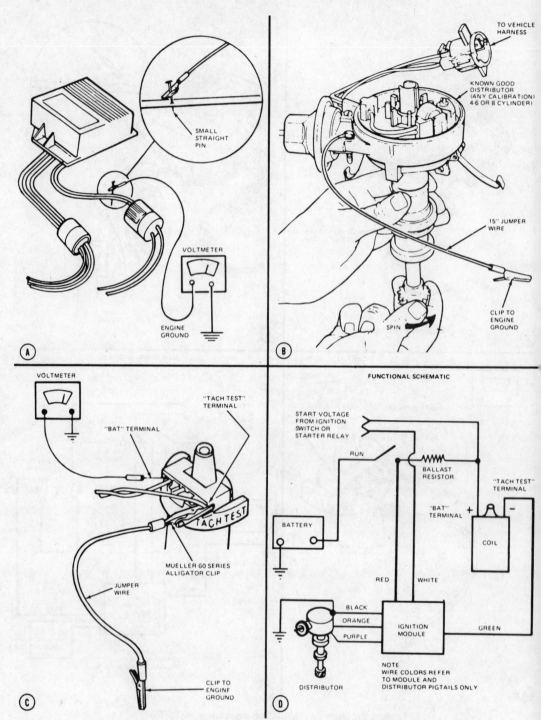

Testing the Dura Spark ignition on models without EEC

craft part number DY-36). A 1.3 ohm, 100 watt wire-wound power resistor can also be used.

To install the resistor, proceed as follows.

NOTE: *The resistor will become very hot during testing.*

1. Release the BAT terminal lead from the coil by inserting a paper clip through the hole in the rear of the horseshoe coil connector and manipulating it against the locking tab in the connector until the lead comes free.

2. Insert a paper clip in the BAT terminal of the connector on the coil. Using jumper leads, connect the ballast resistor as shown.

3. Using a straight pin, pierce both the red

and white leads of the module to short these two together. This will by-pass the internal connections of the module which turn off the ignition circuit when the engine is not running.

CAUTION: *Pierce the wires only AFTER the ballast resistor is in place or you could damage the ignition coil and module.*

4. With the ballast resistor and by-pass in place, proceed with the Dura Spark II troubleshooting procedures.

TROUBLESHOOTING DURA SPARK II

The following procedures can be used to determine whether the ignition system is working or not. If these procedures fail to correct the problem, a full troubleshooting procedure should be performed.

Preliminary Checks

1. Check the battery's state of charge and connections.

2. Inspect all wires and connections for breaks, cuts, abrasions, or burn spots. Repair as necessary.

3. Unplug all connectors one at a time and inspect for corroded or burned contacts. Repair and plug connectors back together. DO NOT remove the dielectric compound in the connectors.

4. Check for loose or damaged spark plug or coil wires. A wire resistance check is given at the end of this section. If the boots or nipples are removed on 8mm ignition wires, reline the inside of each with new silicone di-electric compound (Motorcraft WA 10).

Special Tools

To perform the following tests, two special tools are needed; the ignition test jumper shown in the illustration and a modified spark plug. Use the illustration to assemble the ignition test jumper. The test jumper must be used when performing the following tests. The modified spark plug is basically a spark plug with the side electrode removed. Ford makes a special tool called a Spark Tester for this purpose, which besides not having a side electrode is equipped

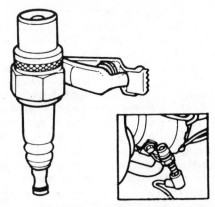

Spark plug tester; actually a modified spark plug (side electrode removed) with a spring for ground

with a spring clip so that it can be grounded to engine metal. It is recommended that the Spark Tester be used as there is less chance of being shocked.

Run Mode Spark Test

NOTE: *The wire colors given here are the main colors of the wires, not the dots or hashmarks.*

STEP 1

1. Remove the distributor cap and rotor from the distributor.

2. With the ignition off, turn the engine over by hand until one of the teeth on the distributor armature aligns with the magnet in the pickup coil.

3. Remove the coil wire from the distributor cap. On 1978 and later models, install the modified spark plug (see Special Tools, above) in the coil wire terminal and using heavy gloves and insulated pliers, hold the spark plug shell against the engine block.

4. Turn the ignition to RUN (not START) and tap the distributor body with a screwdriver handle. There should be a spark at the modified spark plug or at the coil wire terminal.

5. If a good spark is evident, the primary circuit is OK: perform Start Mode Spark Test. If there is no spark, proceed to Step 2.

STEP 2

1. Unplug the module connector(s) which contain(s) the green and black module leads.

2. In the harness side of the connector(s), connect the special test jumper (see Special Tools, above) between the leads which connect to the green and black leads of the module pig tails. Use paper clips on connector socket holes to make contact. Do not allow clips to ground.

3. Turn the ignition switch to RUN (not START) and close the test jumper switch. Leave

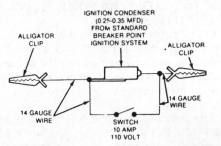

Test jumper wire switch used for testing Dura Spark ignition systems

closed for about 1 second, then open. Repeat several times. There should be a spark each time the switch is opened. On Dura Spark I systems, close the test switch for 10 seconds on the first cycle. After that, 1 second is adequate.

4. If there is no spark, the problem is probably in the primary circuit through the ignition switch, the coil, the green lead or the black lead, or the ground connection in the distributor: perform Step 3. If there is a spark, the primary circuit wiring and coil are probably OK. The problem is probably in the distributor pickup, the module red wire, or the module: perform Step 6.

STEP 3

1. Disconnect the test jumper lead from the black lead and connect it to a good ground. Turn the test jumper switch on and off several times as in Step 2.

2. If there is no spark, the problem is probably in the green lead, the coil, or the coil feed circuit: perform Step 5.

3. If there is spark, the problem is probably in the black lead or the distributor ground connection: perform Step 4.

STEP 4

1. Connect an ohmmeter between the black lead and ground. With the meter on its lowest scale, there should be no measureable resistance in the circuit. If there is resistance, check the distributor ground connection and the black lead from the module. Repair as necessary, remove the ohmmeter, plug in all connections and repeat step 1.

If there is no resistance, the primary ground wiring is OK: perform Step 6.

STEP 5

1. Disconnect the test jumper from the green lead and ground and connect it between the TACH-TEST terminal of the coil and a good ground on the engine.

2. With the ignition switch in the RUN position, turn the jumper switch on. Hold it on for about 1 second then turn it off as in Step 2. Repeat several times. There should be a spark each time the switch is turned off. If there is no spark, the problem is probably in the primary circuit running through the ignition switch to the coil BAT terminal, or in the coil itself. Check coil resistance (test given later in this section), and check the coil for internal shorts or opens. Check the coil feed circuit for opens, shorts or high resistance. Repair as necessary, reconnect all connectors and repeat Step 1. If there is spark, the coil and its feed circuit are OK. The problem could be in the green lead between the coil and the module. Check for

open or short, repair as necessary, reconnect all connectors and repeat Step 1.

STEP 6

To perform this step, a voltmeter which is not combined with a dwell meter is needed. The slight needle oscillations ($\frac{1}{2}$ V) you'll be looking for may not be detectable on the combined voltmeter/dwell meter unit.

1. Connect a voltmeter between the orange and purple leads on the harness side of the module connectors.

CAUTION: *On catalytic converter equipped cars, disconnect the air supply line between the Thermactor by-pass valve and the manifold before cranking the engine with the ignition off. This will prevent damage to the catalytic converter. After testing, run the engine for at least 3 minutes before reconnecting the by-pass valve, to clear excess fuel from the exhaust system.*

2. Set the voltmeter on its lowest scale and crank the engine. The meter needle should oscillate slightly (about $\frac{1}{2}$ volt). If the meter does not oscillate, check the circuit through the magnetic pick-up in the distributor for open, shorts, shorts to ground and resistance. Resistance between the orange and purple leads should be 400–1000 ohms, and between each lead and ground should be more than 70,000 ohms. Repair as necessary, reconnect all connectors and repeat Step 1.

If the meter oscillates, the problem is probably in the power feed to the module (red wire) or in the module itself: proceed to Step 7.

STEP 7

1. Remove all meters and jumpers and plug in all connectors.

2. Turn the ignition switch to the RUN position and measure voltage between the battery positive terminal and engine ground. It should be 12 volts.

3. Next, measure voltage between the red lead of the module and engine ground. To make this measurement, it will be necessary to pierce the red wire with a straight pin and connect the voltmeter to the straight pin and to ground. DO NOT ALLOW THE STRAIGHT PIN TO GROUND ITSELF.

4. The two readings should be within one volt of each other. If not within one volt, the problem is in the power feed to the red lead. Check for shorts, open, or high resistance and correct as necessary. After repairs, repeat Step 1.

If the readings are within one volt, the problem is probably in the module. Replace with a good module and repeat Step 1. If this corrects the problem, reconnect the old module and re-

eat Step 1. If problem returns, permanently
nstall the new module.

Start Mode Spark Test

NOTE: *The wire colors given here are the
main colors of the wires, not the dots or
hashmarks.*

1. Remove the coil wire from the distribu-
or cap. Install the modified spark plug men-
ioned under "Special Tools", above, in the coil
wire and ground it to engine metal either by
ts spring clip (Spark Tester) or by holding the
park plug shell against the engine block with
nsulated pliers.

NOTE: *See "CAUTION" under Step 6 of
"Run Mode Spark Test", above.*

2. Have an assistant crank the engine using
he ignition switch and check for spark. If there
s good spark, the problem is probably in the
distributor cap, rotor, ignition cables or spark
plugs. If there is no spark, proceed to Step 3.

3. Measure the battery voltage. Next, measure the voltage at the white wire of the module while cranking the engine. To make this
measurement, it will be necessary to pierce the
white wire with a straight pin and connect the
voltmeter to the straight pin and to ground.
DO NOT ALLOW THE STRAIGHT PIN TO
GROUND ITSELF. The battery voltage and
the voltage at the white wire should be within
1 volt of each other. If the readings are not
within 1 volt of each other, check and repair
the feed through the ignition switch to the white
wire. Recheck for spark (Step 1). If the readings are within 1 volt of each other, or if there
is still no spark after power feed to white wire
is repaired, proceed to Step 4.

4. Measure the coil BAT terminal voltage
while cranking the engine. The reading should
be within 1 volt of battery voltage. If the readings are not within 1 volt of each other, check
and repair the feed through the ignition switch
to the coil. If the readings are within 1 volt of
each other, the problem is probably in the ignition module. Substitute another module and
repeat test for spark (Step 1).

TFI SYSTEM TESTING

NOTE: *If the engine operates but has no
power, the problem could be in the EEC system. Check the initial timing, if the engine is
operating at a fixed 10° BTDC the system is
in fail-safe mode. Have the EEC system
checked with necessary diagnostic equipment.*

NOTE: *After performing any test which requires piercing a wire with a straight pin,
remove the straight pin and seal the holes in
the wire with silicone sealer.*

Ignition Coil Secondary Voltage

1. Disconnect the secondary (high voltage)
coil wire from the distributor cap and install a
spark tester (see Special Tools, located with the
Dura Spark Troubleshooting) between the coil
wire and ground.

2. Crank the engine—a good, strong spark
should be noted at the spark tester. If spark is
noted, but the engine will not start, check the
spark plugs, spark plug wiring, and fuel system. If there is no spark at the tester:

a. Check the ignition coil secondary wire
resistance; it should be no more than 5000
ohms per inch.

b. Inspect the ignition coil for damage
and/or carbon tracking.

c. With the distributor cap removed, verify
that the distributor shaft turns with the engine; if it does not, repair the engine as required.

d. If the fault was not found in a, b, or c,
proceed to the next test.

Ignition Coil Primary Circuit Switching

1. Insert a small straight pin in the wire which
runs from the coil negative (−) terminal to the
TFI module, about one inch from the module.

CAUTION: *The pin must not touch ground.*

2. Connect a 12VDC test lamp between the
straight pin and an engine ground.

3. Crank the engine, noting the operation of
the test lamp. If the test lamp flashes, proceed
to the next test. If the test lamp lights but does
not flash, proceed to the Wiring Harness test.
If the test lamp does not light at all, proceed to
the Primary Circuit Continuity test.

Ignition Coil Resistance

Replace the ignition coil if the resistance is out
of the specification range.

Wiring Harness

1. Disconnect the wiring harness connector
from the TFI module; the connector tabs must
be PUSHED to disengage the connector. Inspect the connector for damage, dirt, and corrosion.

2. Attach the negative lead of a voltmeter to
the base of the distributor. Attach the other
voltmeter lead to a small straight pin.

a. With the ignition switch in the RUN
position, insert the straight pin into the No.
1 terminal of the TFI module connector. Note
the voltage reading and proceed to b.

b. With the ignition switch in the RUN
position, move the straight pin to the No. 2
connector terminal. Again, note the voltage
reading, then proceed to c.

c. Move the straight pin to the No. 3 connector terminal, then turn the ignition switch to the START position. Note the voltage reading then turn the ignition OFF.

3. The voltage readings from a, b, and c should all be at least 90% of the available battery voltage. If the readings are okay, proceed to the Stator Assembly and Module test. If any reading is less than 90% of the battery voltage, inspect the wiring, connectors, and/or ignition switch for defects. If the voltage is low only at the No. 1 terminal, proceed to the ignition coil primary voltage test.

Stator Assembly and Module

1. Remove the distributor from the engine.
2. Remove the TFI module from the distributor.
3. Inspect the distributor terminals, ground screw, and stator wiring for damage. Repair as necessary.
4. Measure the resistance of the stator assembly, using an ohmmeter. If the ohmmeter reading is 800–975 ohms; the stator is okay, but the TFI module must be replaced. If the ohmmeter reading is less than 800 ohms or more than 975 ohms; the TFI module is okay, but the stator assembly must be replaced.
5. Reinstall the TFI module and the distributor.

Primary Circuit Continuity

This test is performed in the same manner as the previous Wiring Harness test, but only the No. 1 terminal conductor is tested (ignition switch in RUN position). If the voltage is less than 90% of the available battery voltage, proceed to the next test.

Ignition Coil Primary Voltage

1. Attach the negative lead of a voltmeter to the distributor base.
2. Turn the ignition switch ON and connect the positive voltmeter lead to the negative (−) ignition coil terminal. Note the voltage reading and turn the ignition OFF. If the voltmeter reading is less than 90% of the available battery voltage, inspect the wiring between the ignition module and the negative (−) coil terminal, then proceed to the last test, which follows.

Ignition Coil Supply Voltage

1. Attach the negative lead of a voltmeter to the distributor base.
2. Turn the ignition switch ON and connect the positive voltmeter lead to the positive (+) ignition coil terminal.
NOTE: *Note the voltage reading then turn the ignition OFF.*
If the voltage reading is at least 90% of the

battery voltage, yet the engine will still not run; check the ignition coil connector and terminals for corrosion, dirt, and/or damage. Replace the ignition switch if the connectors and terminals are okay.

3. Connect any remaining wiring.

GENERAL TESTING—ALL SYSTEMS

Ignition Coil Test

The ignition coil must be diagnosed separately from the rest of the ignition system.

1. Primary resistance is measured between the two primary (low voltage) coil terminals, with the coil connector disconnected and the ignition switch off. Primary resistance must be 0.71–0.77 ohms for Dura Spark I. For Dura Spark II, it must be 1.13–1.23 ohms. For TFI systems, the primary resistance should be 0.3–1.0 ohms.

2. On Dura Spark ignitions, the secondary resistance is measured between the BATT and high voltage (secondary) terminals of the ignition coil with the ignition off, and the wiring from the coil disconnected. Secondary resistance must be 7350–8250 ohms on Dura Spark I systems. Dura Spark II figure is 7700–9300 ohms. For TFI systems, the primary resistance should be 8000–11,500 ohms.

3. If resistance tests are alright, but the coil is still suspected, test the coil on a coil tester by following the test equipment manufacturer's instructions for a standard coil. If the reading differs from the original test, check for a defective harness.

Resistance Wire Test

Replace the resistance wire if it doesn't show a resistance of 1.05–1.15 for Dura Spark II. The resistance wire isn't used on Dura Spark I or TFI systems.

Spark Plug Wire Resistance

Resistance on these wires must not exceed 5,000 ohms per inch. To properly measure this, remove the wires from the plugs, and remove the distributor cap. Measure the resistance through the distributor cap at that end. Do not pierce any ignition wire for any reason. Measure only from the two ends.

NOTE: *Silicone grease must be reapplied to the spark plug wires whenever they are removed:*

When removing the wires from the spark plugs, a special tool such as the one pictured should be used. Do not pull on the wires. Grasp and twist the boot to remove the wire.

Whenever the high tension wires are removed from the plugs, coil, or distributor, silicone grease must be applied to the boot before reconnection. Use a clean small screwdriver blade to coat the entire interior surface with Ford silicone grease D7AZ-19A331-A, Dow Corning #111, or General Electric G-627.

Adjustments

The air gap between the armature and magnetic pick-up coil in the distributor is not adjustable, nor are there any adjustments for the amplifier module. Inoperative components are simply replaced. Any attempt to connect components outside the vehicle may result in component failure.

Ignition Timing

Ignition timing is the measurement, in degrees of crankshaft rotation, of the point at which the spark plugs fire in each of the cylinders. It is measured in degrees before or after Top Dead Center (TDC) of the compression stroke. Ignition timing is controlled by turning the distributor body in the engine.

Ideally, the air/fuel mixture in the cylinder will be ignited by the spark plug just as the piston passes TDC of the compression stroke. If this happens, the piston will be beginning the power stroke just as the compressed and ignited air/fuel mixture starts to expand. The expansion of the air/fuel mixture then forces the piston down on the power stroke and turns the crankshaft.

Because it takes a fraction of a second for the spark plug to ignite the mixture in the cylinder, the spark plug must fire a little before the piston reaches TDC. Otherwise, the mixture will not be completely ignited as the piston passes TDC and the full power of the explosion will not be used by the engine.

The timing measurement is given in degrees of crankshaft rotation before the piston reaches TDC (BTDC). If the setting for the ignition timing is 5° BTDC, each spark plug must fire 5° before each piston reaches TDC. This only holds true, however, when the engine is at idle speed.

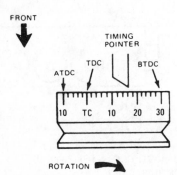

4-140 timing marks

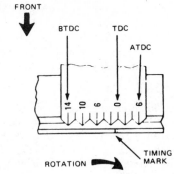

6-200, 250 timing marks

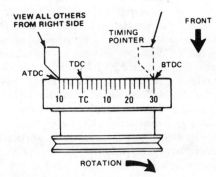

V6 and V8 timing marks

As the engine speed increases, the pistons go faster. The spark plugs have to ignite the fuel even sooner if it is to be completely ignited when the piston reaches TDC. To do this, the distributor has a means to advance the timing of the spark as the engine speed increases. This is accomplished by centrifugal weights within the distributor and a vacuum diaphragm mounted on the side of the distributor. It is necessary to disconnect the vacuum lines from the diaphragm when the ignition timing is being set.

If the ignition is set too far advanced (BTDC), the ignition and expansion of the fuel in the cylinder will occur too soon and tend to force the piston down while it is still traveling up. This causes engine ping. If the ignition spark is set too far retarded after TDC (ATDC), the piston will have already passed TDC and started on its way down when the fuel is ignited. This will cause the piston to be forced down for only a portion of its travel. This will result in poor engine performance and lack of power.

The timing is best checked with a timing light. This device is usually connected in series with the No. 1 spark plug. The current that fires the spark plug also causes the timing light to flash.

There is a notch on the crankshaft pulley on in-line 6 cyl. engines. A scale of degrees of crankshaft rotation is attached to the engine block in such a position that the notch will pass close by the scale. On the V6 and V8 engines, the scale is located on the crankshaft pulley and a pointer is attached to the engine block so that the scale will pass close by. When the engine is running, the timing light is aimed at the mark on the crankshaft pulley and the scale.

ADJUSTMENT

NOTE: *Some engines have monolithic timing set at the factory. The monolithic system uses a timing receptacle on the front of the engine which can be connected to digital readout equipment, which electronically determines timing. Timing can also be adjusted in the conventional way. Many 1980 and later models are equipped with EEC engine controls. All ignition timing is controlled by the EEC module. Initial ignition timing is not adjustable and no attempt at adjustment should be made on EECIII models, or models equipped with an indexed distributor base. For a description of EEC systems, refer to the Unit Repair sections on "Electronic Ignition Systems" and on "Engine Controls."*
NOTE: *Requirements vary from model to model. Always refer to the "Emissions Specification Sticker" for exact timing procedures.*

1. Locate the timing marks and pointer on the lower engine pulley and engine's front cover.
2. Clean the marks and apply chalk or bright-colored paint to the pointer.
3. On 1981 and later models, if the ignition module has (-12A244-) as a basic part number, disconnect the two wire connector (yellow and black wires). On engines equipped with the EECIV system, disconnect the single white (black on some models) wire connector near the distributor.
4. Attach a timing light and tachometer according to manufacturer's specifications.
5. Disconnect the plug all vacuum lines leading to the distributor.
6. Start the engine, allow it to warm to normal operating temperature, then set the idle to the specifications given on the underhood sticker (for timing).
7. On 1981 and later models equipped with the module mentioned in Step 3, jumper the pins in the module connector for the yellow and black wires.
8. Aim the timing light at the timing mark and pointer on the front of the engine. If the marks align when the timing light flashes, remove the timing light, set the idle to its proper specification, and connect the vacuum lines at the distributor. If the marks do not align when the light flashes, turn the engine off and loosen the distributor holddown clamp slightly.
9. Start the engine again, and observe the alignment of the timing marks. To advance the

timing, turn the distributor counterclockwise, on six cylinder engines except the 232 (3.8L) V6, or clockwise, for the 232 (3.8L) V6 and V8 engines. When altering the timing, it is wise to tap the distributor lightly with a wooden hammer handle to move it in the disired direction. Grasping the distributor with your hand may result in a painful electric shock. When the timing marks are aligned, turn the engine off and tighten the distributor hold-down clamp. Remove the test equipment, reconnect the vacuum hoses and white (black) single wire connector (EECIV).
10. On 1981 and later models equipped with the module mentioned in Step 3, remove the jumper connected in Step 7 and reconnect the two wire connector. Test the module operation as follows:
   a. Disconnect and plug the vaccum source hose to the ignition timing vacuum switch.
   b. Using an external vacuum source, apply vacuum greater than 12 in. Hg to the switch, and compare the ignition timing with the requirements below:
   - 4 cylinder—per specifications less 32°–40°
   - 6 cylinder—per specifications less 21°–27°
   - 8 cylinder—per specifications less 16°–20°

TACHOMETER CONNECTION

The coil connector used with DuraSpark is provided with a cavity for connection of a tachometer, so that the connector doesn't have to be removed to check engine rpm.

Install a tach lead with an alligator clip on its end into the cavity marked TACH TEST and connect the other lead to a good ground.

If the coil connector must be removed, pull it out horizontally until it is disengaged from the coil terminal.

FIRING ORDERS

To avoid confusion, replace spark plug wires one at a time.

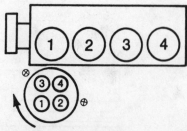

FORD MOTOR CO. 4-140 (2300cc)
Engine firing order: 1-3-4-2
Distributor rotation: clockwise

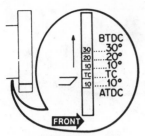

1971 timing mark (except 429 Hi-Perf.)

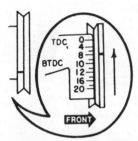

1971 429 V8 Hi-Perf.

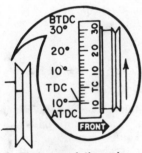

Timing mark through 1974 and 1971 429 Hi-Perf.

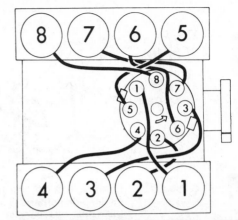

FORD MOTOR CO. 302, 429, 460 V8 (through 1974)
Engine firing order: 1-5-4-2-6-3-7-8
Distributor rotation: counterclockwise

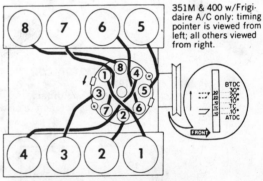

351M & 400 w/Frigidaire A/C only: timing pointer is viewed from left; all others viewed from right.

Ford Motor Co. H.O. 302, 351, 400 V8
Engine firing order; 1-3-7-2-6-5-4-8
Distributor rotation; counterclockwise

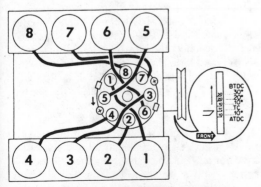

Ford Motor Co. 255, 302 (Exc. H.O.), 460 V8
Engine firing order; 1-5-4-2-6-3-7-8
Distribution rotation; counterclockwise

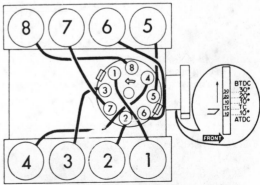

FORD MOTOR CO. 351, 400 V8 (through 1974)
Engine firing order: 1-3-7-2-6-5-4-8
Distributor rotation: counterclockwise

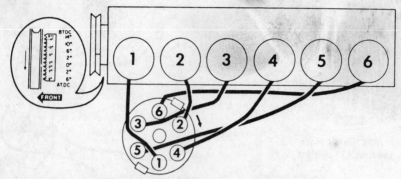

FORD MOTOR CO. 200, 250 6-cyl. (1977 and later)
Engine firing order: 1-5-3-6-2-4
Distributor rotation: clockwise

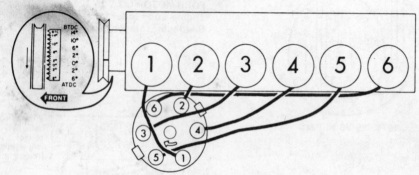

FORD MOTOR CO. 170, 200, 250 6-cyl. (through 1976)
Engine firing order: 1-5-3-6-2-4
Distributor rotation: clockwise

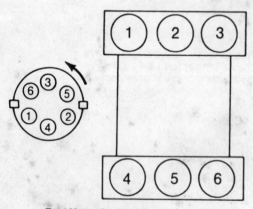

Ford Motor Co. 232 V6
Firing order; 1-4-2-5-3-6
Distributor rotation; counterclockwise

Valve Clearance Adjustment

NOTE: *Only engines with solid (mechanical) lifters require valve adjustments. All Ford engines covered in this book, except the 429 SCJ and 2.4L diesel have hydraulic lifters.*

429 SCJ ONLY

Preliminary (Cold)

If some component of the valve train has been replaced; i.e., rocker arm, push rod, camshaft, etc., it will be necessary to make a preliminary (cold) valve clearance adjustment before starting the engine. If the valve clearance adjustment is made for an engine tune-up, follow the final (hot) adjustment procedure.

The cylinders are numbered from front to rear-right bank, 1-2-3-4; left bank, 5-6-7-8.

The valves are arranged from front to rear, on the left bank E-I-E-I-E-I-E-I, and on the right bank I-E-I-E-I-E-I-E.

1. Disconnect the brown lead (I terminal) and the red and blue lead (S terminal) at the starter relay. Install an auxiliary starter switch between the battery and S terminals of the starter relay. Crank the engine with the ignition switch OFF.

2. With the crankshaft in the positions given in A, B and C in the illustration, loosen the lock nut and set the valve clearance to specifications with a step-type feeler gauge (go and no go). After adjusting each valve, torque the lock nut to specifications.

3. Rotate the crankshaft until No. 1 piston

With No. 1 at TDC at end of compression stroke make a chalk mark at points B and C approximately 90 degrees apart.

TIMING POINTER

POSITION A – No. 1 at TDC at end of compression stroke.
POSITION B – Rotate the crankshaft 180 degrees (one half revolution) clockwise from POSITION A.
POSITION C – Rotate the crankshaft 270 degrees (three quarter revolution) clockwise from POSITION B.

Crankshaft pulley indexing for valve adjustment on 429SCJ engine

is on TDC at the end of the compression stroke, POSITION A. Adjust the following valves:
- No. 1 Intake No. 1 Exhaust
- No. 7 Intake No. 5 Exhaust
- No. 8 Intake No. 4 Exhaust

4. Rotate the crankshaft to POSITION B. Adjust the following valves:
- No. 5 Intake No. 2 Exhaust
- No. 4 Intake No. 6 Exhaust

5. Rotate the crankshaft to POSITION C. Adjust the following valves:
- No. 2 Intake No. 7 Exhaust
- No. 3 Intake No. 3 Exhaust
- No. 6 Intake No. 8 Exhaust

Final (Hot)

It is very important that the valve clearance be held to the correct specifications because:

If the clearance is set too close, the valve will open too early and close too late, resulting in rough engine idle. Burning and warping of the valves will also occur because the valves cannot make firm contact with the seats long enough to cool properly. If the clearance is excessive, it will cause the valve to open too late and close too early causing valve bounce. In addition, damage to the camshaft lobes is likely because the tappet foot will not follow the pattern of the camshaft lobe causing a shock contact between these two parts.

1. Be sure the engine is at normal operating temperature before attempting to set the valve clearance.

2. With the engine idling, set the valve clearance using a step-type feeler gauge only (go and no go). The final (hot) intake and exhaust valve clearance settings are listed in the Specifications.

3. After adjusting each valve, torque the lock nut to specifications and recheck the valve clearance.

Mechanical Valve Lifter Clearance

Engine	Intake (Hot) in.	Exhaust (Hot) in.
429 SCJ	.019	.019

2.4L DIESEL ENGINE

NOTE: *Adjustment procedure is for cold engine only.*

1. Remove the valve cover.

2. Position the camshaft so that base circle of the lobe of the valve to be adjusted is facing the rocker arm.

3. Loosen the adjusting eccentric locknut using a valve clearance adjusting Wrench, Tool T84P-6575-A, or equivalent and a 12mm open end wrench.

4. Rotate the eccentric using a small punch until the valve clearance is adjusted to specification: Intake: 0.012 inch; Exhaust: 0.016 inch. Tighten eccentric locknut.

5. Repeat Steps 2, 3 and 4 for each valve.

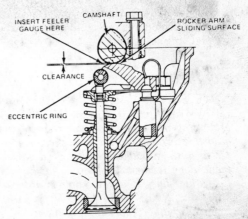

INSERT FEELER GAUGE HERE — CAMSHAFT — ROCKER ARM SLIDING SURFACE — CLEARANCE — ECCENTRIC RING

Valve train crossview—2.4L diesel engine

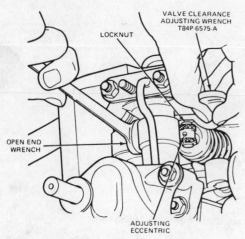

Eccentric adjustment—2.4L diesel engine

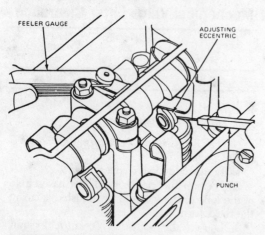

Valve clearance—2.4L diesel engine

6. Install the valve cover.
7. Start the engine and check for oil leaks.

Carburetor Adjustments

This section contains only carburetor adjustments as they normally apply to engine tuneup. Discriptions of the carburetor and complete adjustment procedures can be found in Chapter 4, under "Fuel System."

IDLE SPEED AND MIXTURE ADJUSTMENTS

NOTE: *Since the design of the 2700 VV and 7200 VV carburetor is different from all other Motorcraft carburetors in many respects, the adjusting procedures are necessarily different as well. Although the idle speed adjustment alone is identical, there is further information you will need to know in order to adjust the 2700 VV and 7200 VV properly. Refer to Chapter 4 for an explanation.*

NOTE: *In order to limit exhaust emissions,*

plastic caps have been installed on the idle fuel mixture screw(s), which prevent the carburetor from being adjusted to an overly rich idle fuel mixture. Under no circumstances should these limiters be modified or removed. A satisfactory idle should be obtained within the range of the limiter(s).

NOTE: *Refer to the procedure following this one for models equipped with fuel injection or for models equipped with an Automatic Overdrive Transmission (AOD).*

1. Start the engine and run it at idle until it reaches operating temperature (about 10–20 minutes, depending on outside temperatures). Stop the engine.

2. Check the ignition timing as outlined earlier in this chapter.

3. Remove the air cleaner, taking note of the hose locations, and check that the choke plate is in the open position (plate in vertical position). Check the accompanying illustrations to see where the carburetor adjustment locations are. If you cannot reach them with the air cleaner installed, leave it off temporarily. Otherwise, reinstall the air cleaner assembly including all the hose connections.

NOTE: *Leaving the air cleaner removed will affect the idle speed; therefore, adjust the curb idle speed to a setting 50–100 rpm higher than specified, if the air cleaner is off. When the air cleaner is reinstalled the idle speed should be to specifications.*

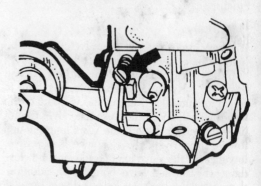

Location of idle speed adjustment—Carter RBS 1-V

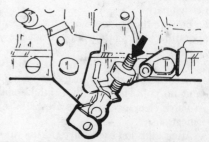

Location of idle speed adjustment—Motorcraft 4300 4-V

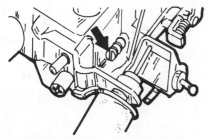

Location of idle speed adjustment—Rochester "Quadrajet" 4MV 4-V

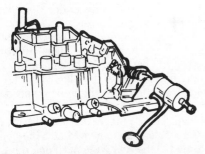

Location of idle speed adjustment—Carter "Thermoquad" 4-V

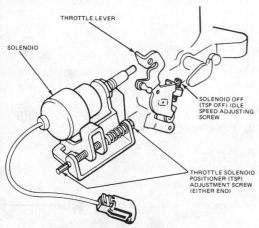

THROTTLE LEVER

SOLENOID

SOLENOID OFF (TSP OFF) IDLE SPEED ADJUSTING SCREW

THROTTLE SOLENOID POSITIONER (TSP) ADJUSTMENT SCREW (EITHER END)

Location of idle speed adjustment—Motorcraft 2100, 2150, 4300, 4350 (all with TSP)

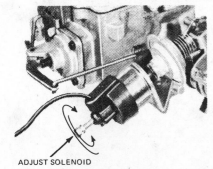

ADJUST SOLENOID

Location of idle speed adjustment—Motorcraft 2150 with solenoid dashpot TSP

4. Attach a tachometer to the engine, with the positive wire connected to the distributor side of the ignition coil, and the negative wire connected to a good ground, such as an engine bolt.

NOTE: *In order to attach an alligator clip to the distributor side (terminal) of the coil (primary connection), it will be necessary to lift off the connector and slide a female loop type connector (commercially available) down over the terminal threads. Then push down the rubber connector over the loop connector and connect the alligator clip of your tachometer. On late models a "tach" connector is provided.*

5. All idle speed adjustments are made with the headlights off (unless otherwise specified on the engine decal), with the air conditioning off (if so equipped), with all vacuum hoses connected, with the throttle solenoid positioner activated (connected, if so equipped), and with the air cleaner on. (See Note after Step 3.) Finally, all idle speed adjustments are made in Neutral on cars with manual transmission, and in Drive on cars equipped with automatic transmission.

CAUTION: *Whenever performing these adjustments, block all four wheels and set the parking brake.*

6a. On cars not equipped with a throttle solenoid positioner, the idle speed is adjusted with the curb idle speed adjusting screw. Start the engine. Turn the curb idle speed adjusting screw inward or outward until the correct idle speed (see "Tune-Up Specifications" chart) is reached, remembering to make the 50–100 rpm allowance if the air cleaner is removed.

6b. On cars equipped with a throttle solenoid positioner, the idle speed is adjusted with solenoid adjusting screw (nut), in two stages. Start the engine. The higher speed is adjusted with the solenoid connected. Turn the solenoid adjusting screw (nut) on 1 or 4 barrel carburetors, or the entire bracket on 2 barrel carburetors inward or outward until the correct higher idle speed (see "Turn-Up Specifications" chart) is reached, remembering to make the 50–100 rpm allowance if the air cleaner is removed. After making this adjustment on cars equipped with 2 barrel carburetors, tighten the solenoid adjusting locknut. The lower idle speed is adjusted with the solenoid lead wire disconnected near the harness (not at the carburetor). Place automatic transmission equipped cars in Neutral for this adjustment. Using the curb idle speed adjusting screw on the carburetor, turn the idle speed adjusting screw inward or outward until the correct lower idle speed (see "Tune-Up Specifications" chart) is reached, remembering again to make the 50–100 rpm allowance if the air cleaner is removed. Finally, reconnect the solenoid, slightly depress the throttle lever and allow the solenoid plunger to fully extend.

7. If removed, install the air cleaner. Recheck the idle speed. If it is not correct, Step 6 will have to be repeated and the approximate corrections made.

8. To adjust the idle mixture, turn the idle mixture screw(s) inward to obtain the smoothest idle possible within the range of the limiter(s).

9. Turn off the engine and disconnect the tachometer.

NOTE: *If any doubt exists as to the proper idle mixture setting for your car, have the exhaust emission level checked at a diagnostic center or garage with an exhaust (HC/CO) analyzer or an air/fuel ratio meter.*

Fuel Injection

GASOLINE ENGINES

NOTE: *Prior to adjusting the curb idle speed, set the parking brake and block all four wheels. Make all adjustments with the engine at normal operating temperature. Have all accessories turned off. If the underhood "Emissions Sticker" gives different specs and procedures than those following, always follow the sticker as it will reflect production changes and calibration differences.*

V6-Central Fuel Injection (CFI)

NOTE: *The EEC-IV system and an idle speed motor control the curb idle speed on models equipped with the V6 engine. The idle speed is not adjustable except for minimum and maximum throttle stop adjustment screw clearance. Too little clearance will prevent* *the throttle from closing as required thus causing a faster than normal idle speed. Any other problems with the system must be checked by EEC-IV system diagnosis.*

MINIMUM/MAXIMUM LIMIT ADJUSTMENT

NOTE: *Exact sequence must be followed when checking the adjustment.*

1. Adjustment is checked with the idle speed motor plunger fully retracted. Run the engine until normal operating temperature is reached, shut the engine off. Remove the air cleaner.

2. Locate the self test connector and self test input connector. Both are under the hood by the driver's side strut tower.

3. Connect a jumper wire between the single input connector and the signal return pin of the self test connector. The signal return pin is on the upper right of the plug when the plug is held straight on with the four prongs on the bottom facing you.

4. The motor plunger should retract when the jumper wire is connected and the ignition key turned to the Run position. If not, the EEC-IV system requires testing and service.

5. Wait about ten seconds until the plunger is fully retracted. Turn the key Off and remove the jumper.

6. If the idle speed was too high, remove the throttle stop adjusting screw and install a new one. With the throttle plates completely closed, turn the throttle stop adjusting screw in until a gap of .005 inch is present between the screw tip and the throttle lever contact surface. Turn the screw in an additional 1½ turns to complete the adjustment.

7. If the idle speed was too low, remove the dust cover from the motor tip. Push the tip back toward the motor to remove any play. Measure

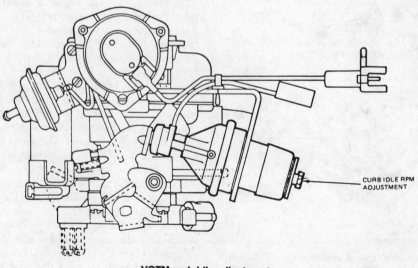

CURB IDLE RPM
ADJUSTMENT

VOTM curb idle adjustment

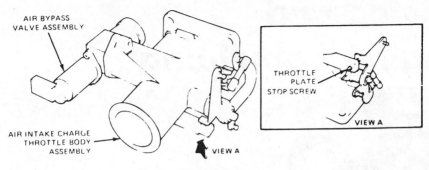

EFI adjustment

the clearance between the motor tip and throttle lever by passing a 9/32 inch drill bit in between, a slight drag is required.

8. If adjustment is required, turn the motor bracket adjusting screw until proper clearance is obtained. Tighten the lock and install the dust cover.

V8-Central Fuel Injection (CFI)

1. Connect a tachometer, start the engine and allow to reach normal operating temperature.

2. Shut the engine Off and restart. Run at about 2000 rpm for a minute. Allow the engine to return to idle and stabilize for about 30 seconds. Place the gear selector in Reverse. (Parking brake on and all four wheels blocked)

3. Adjust the curb idle as required using the saddle bracket adjusting screw.

4. If the rpms are too low, turn off the engine and turn the adjusting screw one full turn. If the speed is too high, turn off the engine and turn the screw counterclockwise.

5. Repeat Steps 2 and 4 until correct idle speed is obtained.

4 Cylinder EFI Turbo

NOTE: *Idle speed is controlled by the EEC-IV system and a air by-pass valve. If the fol-*

lowing procedure does not correct idle rpm, EEC-IV system diagnosis is required.

1. Run the engine until normal operating temperature is reached. Turn off all accessories.

2. Turn Off the engine. Disconnect the power lead to the idle speed by-pass control valve. Connect a tachometer to the engine.

3. Start the engine and run at 2000 rpm for two minutes. If the electric cooling fan comes on, disconnect the wiring harness connector.

4. Let the engine return to normal idling rpm and check speed on the tachometer.

5. Adjust rpm if necessary with the throttle plate stop screw.

6. Turn the engine Off and reconnect the by-pass valve lead and cooling fan harness.

7. Restart the engine and check idle speed.

2.4L DIESEL ENGINE

1. Connect a diesel engine tachometer to the engine. Start the engine and allow normal operating temperature to be reached. Check idle speed.

2. If adjustment is required, shut off the engine. Loosen the locknut on the throttle lever adjusting screw. Start engine and turn the adjusting screw until required rpm is reached.

3. Shut off the engine and tighten the locknut. Gap between the knurled nut and lever should be .020–.040 inches.

Engine and Engine Rebuilding

3

ENGINE ELECTRICAL

Distributor

REMOVAL AND INSTALLATION

1. Remove the air cleaner on V6 and V8 engines. On 4 and 6 cylinder in-line engines, removal of a thermactor (air) pump mounting bolt and drive belt will allow the pump to be moved to the side and permit access to the distributor. If necessary, disconnect the thermactor air filter and lines as well.

2. Remove the distributor cap and position the cap and ignition wires to the side.

3. Disconnect the wire harness plug from the distributor connector. Disconnect and plug the vacuum hoses from the vacuum diaphragm assembly. (DuraSpark III systems are not equipped with a vacuum diaphragm).

4. Rotate the engine (in normal direction of rotation) until No. 1 piston is on TDC (Top Dead Center) of the compression stroke. The TDC mark on the crankshaft pulley and the pointer should align. Rotor tip pointing at No. 1 position on distributor cap.

5. On DuraSpark I or II, turn the engine a slight bit more (if required) to align the stator (pick-up coil) assembly pole with an (the closest) armature pole. On DuraSpark III, the distributor sleeve groove (when looking down from the top) and the cap adaptor alignment slot should align. On models equipped with EECIV (1984 and later), remove the rotor (2 screws) and note the position of the "polarizing square" and shaft plate for reinstallation reference.

6. Scribe a mark on the distributor body and engine block to indicate the position of the rotor tip and position of the distributor in the engine. DuraSpark III and some EECIV system distributors are equipped with a notched base and will only locate at one position on the engine.

7. Remove the holddown bolt and clamp located at the base of the distributor. (Some DuraSpark III and EECIV system distributors are equipped with a special holddown bolt that requires a Torx head wrench for removal). Remove the distributor from the engine. Pay attention to the direction the rotor tip points when the drive gear disengages. For reinstallation purposes, the rotor should be at this position to insure proper gear mesh and timing.

8. Avoid turning the engine, if possible, while the distributor is removed. If the engine is turned from TDC position, TDC timing marks will have to be reset before the distributor is installed; Steps 4 and 5.

9. Position the distributor in the engine with the rotor aligned to the marks made on the distributor, or to the place the rotor pointed when the distributor was removed. The stator and armature or "polarizing square" and shaft plate should also be aligned. Engage the oil pump intermediate shaft and insert the distributor until fully seated on the engine, if the distributor does not fully seat, turn the engine slightly to fully engage the intermediate shaft.

10. Follow the above procedures on models equipped with an indexed distributor base. Make sure when positioning the distributor that

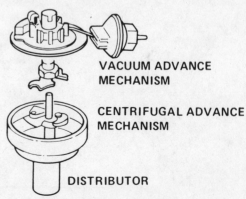

VACUUM ADVANCE MECHANISM

CENTRIFUGAL ADVANCE MECHANISM

DISTRIBUTOR

Dual advance distributor (typical)

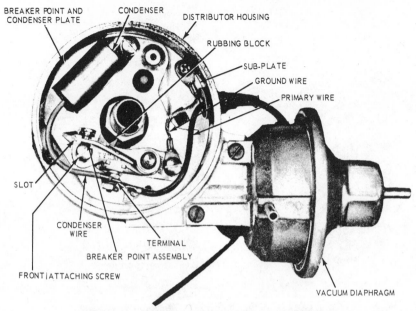

BREAKER POINT AND
CONDENSER PLATE

CONDENSER

DISTRIBUTOR HOUSING

RUBBING BLOCK

SUB-PLATE

GROUND WIRE

PRIMARY WIRE

SLOT

CONDENSER
WIRE

TERMINAL

BREAKER POINT ASSEMBLY

FRONT ATTACHING SCREW

VACUUM DIAPHRAGM

Conventional 6 cylinder distributor (cap and rotor removed)

the slot in the distributor base will engage the block tab and the sleeve/adaptor slots are aligned.

11. After the distributor has been fully seated on the block install the hold down bracket and bolt. On models equipped with an indexed base, tighten the mounting bolt. On other models, snug the mounting bolt so the distributor can be turned for ignition timing purposes.

12. The rest of the installation is in the reverse order of removal. Check and reset the ignition timing on applicable models.

NOTE: *A silicone compound is used on rotor tips, distributor cap contacts and on the inside of the connectors on the spark plugs cable and module couplers. Always apply*

Silicone Dielectric Compound after servicing any component of the ignition system. Various models use a multi-point rotor which do not require the application of dielectric compound.

Alternator

The alternator charging system consists of the alternator, voltage regulator, warning light, battery, and fuse link wire.

A failure of any component of the charging system can cause the entire system to stop functioning. Because of this, the charging system can be very difficult to troubleshoot when problems occur.

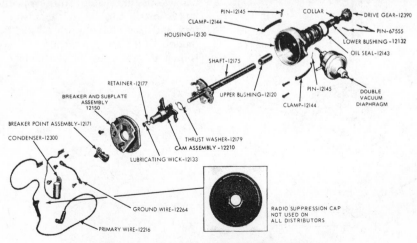

PIN-12145

CLAMP-12144

HOUSING-12130

COLLAR

DRIVE GEAR-12390

PIN-67555

LOWER BUSHING -12132

OIL SEAL-12143

SHAFT-12175

RETAINER-12177

BREAKER AND SUBPLATE
ASSEMBLY
12150

BREAKER POINT ASSEMBLY-12171

CONDENSER-12300

UPPER BUSHING-12120

PIN-12145

CLAMP-12144

DOUBLE
VACUUM
DIAPHRAGM

THRUST WASHER-12179

CAM ASSEMBLY -12210

LUBRICATING WICK-12133

GROUND WIRE-12264

PRIMARY WIRE-12216

RADIO SUPPRESSION CAP
NOT USED ON
ALL DISTRIBUTORS

Exploded view of conventional V8 distributor

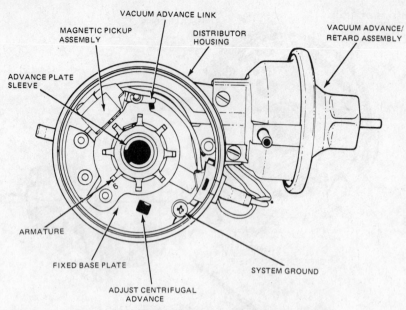

VACUUM ADVANCE LINK

MAGNETIC PICKUP ASSEMBLY

DISTRIBUTOR HOUSING

VACUUM ADVANCE/ RETARD ASSEMBLY

ADVANCE PLATE SLEEVE

ARMATURE

FIXED BASE PLATE

ADJUST CENTRIFUGAL ADVANCE

SYSTEM GROUND

Breakerless V8 distributor (cap and rotor removed)

When the ignition key is turned on, current flows from the battery, through the charging system indicator light on the instrument panel, to the voltage regulator, and to the alternator. Since the alternator is not producing any current, the alternator warning light comes on. When the engine is started, the alternator begins to produce current and turns the alternator light off. As the alternator turns and produces current, the current is divided in two ways: part to the battery to charge the battery and power the electrical components of the vehicle, and part is returned to the alternator to enable it to increase its output. In this situation, the alternator is receiving current from the battery and from itself. A voltage regulator is wired into the current supply to the alternator to prevent it from receiving too much current which would cause it to put out too much current. Conversely, if the voltage regulator does not allow the alternator to receive enough current, the battery will not be fully charged and will eventually go dead.

The battery is connected to the alternator at all times, whether the ignition key is turned on or not. If the battery were shorted to ground, the alternator would also be shorted. This would damage the alternator. To prevent this, a fuse link is installed in the wiring between the battery and the alternator on all 1970 and later models. If the battery is shorted, the fuse link is melted, protecting the alternator.

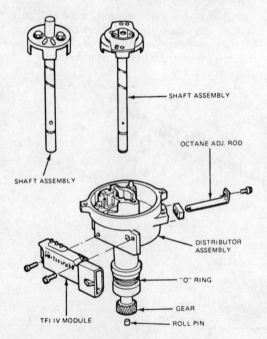

SHAFT ASSEMBLY

OCTANE ADJ. ROD

SHAFT ASSEMBLY

DISTRIBUTOR ASSEMBLY

"O" RING

TFI IV MODULE

GEAR

ROLL PIN

Universal TFI distributor

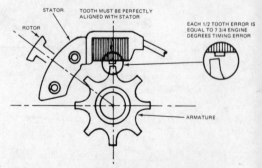

STATOR

TOOTH MUST BE PERFECTLY ALIGNED WITH STATOR

ROTOR

EACH 1/2 TOOTH ERROR IS EQUAL TO 7 3/4 ENGINE DEGREES TIMING ERROR

ARMATURE

Breakerless distributor static timing position

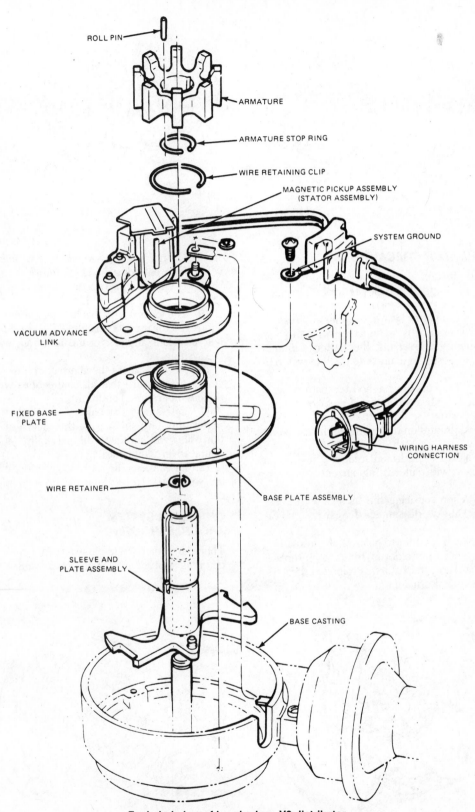

ROLL PIN

ARMATURE

ARMATURE STOP RING

WIRE RETAINING CLIP

MAGNETIC PICKUP ASSEMBLY
(STATOR ASSEMBLY)

SYSTEM GROUND

VACUUM ADVANCE
LINK

FIXED BASE
PLATE

WIRING HARNESS
CONNECTION

WIRE RETAINER

BASE PLATE ASSEMBLY

SLEEVE AND
PLATE ASSEMBLY

BASE CASTING

Exploded view of breakerless V8 distributor

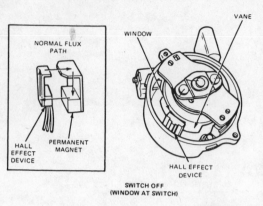

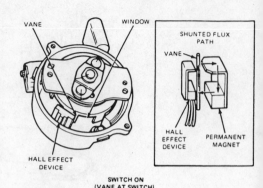

Hall Effect-On/Off switching

ALTERNATOR PRECAUTIONS

Several precautions must be observed with alternator equipped vehicles to avoid damaging the unit. They are as follows:

1. If the battery is removed for any reason, make sure that it is reconnected with the correct polarity. Reversing the battery connections may result in damage to the one-way rectifiers.

2. When utilizing a booster battery as a starting aid, always connect it as follows: positive to positive, and negative (booster battery) to a good ground on the engine of the car being started.

3. Never use a fast charger as a booster to start cars with alternating-current (AC) circuits.

4. When servicing the battery with a fast charger, always disconnect the car battery cables.

5. Never attempt to polarize an alternator.

6. Avoid long soldering times when replacing diodes or transistors. Prolonged heat is damaging to alternators.

7. Do not use test lamps of more than 12 volts (V) for checking diode continuity.

8. Do not short across or ground any of the terminals on the alternator.

9. The polarity of the battery, alternator, and regulator must be matched and considered before making any electrical connections within the system.

10. Never separate the alternator on an open circuit. Make sure that all connections within the circuit are clean and tight.

11. Disconnect the battery terminals when performing any service on the electrical system. This will eliminate the possibility of accidental reversal of polarity.

12. Disconnect the battery ground cable if arc welding is to be done on any part of the car.

CHARGING SYSTEM TROUBLESHOOTING

There are many possible ways in which the charging system can malfunction. Often the

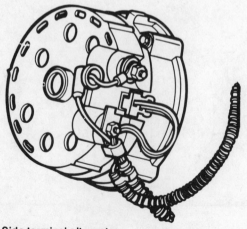

Side terminal alternator

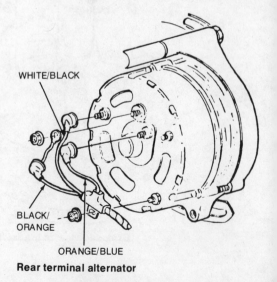

Rear terminal alternator

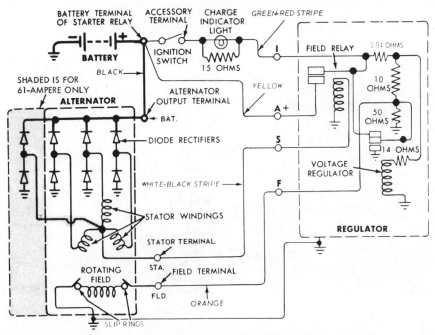

Alternator charging circuit w/indicator light—rear terminal type

source of a problem is difficult to diagnose, requiring special equipment and a good deal of experience. This is usually not the case, however, where the charging system fails completely and causes the dash board warning light to come on or the battery to become dead. To troubleshoot a complete system failure only two pieces of equipment are needed—a test light, to determine that current is reaching a certain point; and a current indicator (ammeter), to de-

termine the direction of the current flow and its measurement in amps.

This test works under three assumptions:

A. The battery is known to be good and fully charged;

B. The alternator belt is in good condition and adjusted to the proper tension;

C. All connections in the system are clean and tight.

NOTE: *In order for the current indicator to*

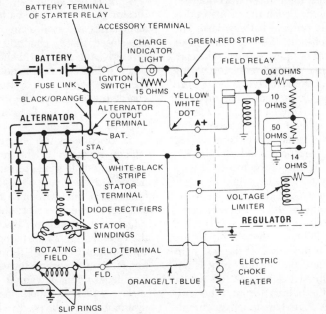

Alternator charging circuit w/indicator light—side terminal type

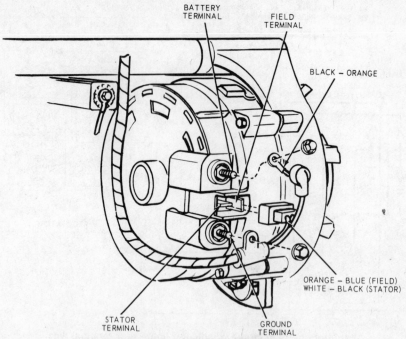

Alternator terminal locations—side terminal type

give a valid reading, the car must be equipped with battery cables which are of the same gauge size and quality as original equipment battery cables.

1. Turn off all electrical components on the car. Make sure the doors of the car are closed. If the car is equipped with a clock, disconnect the clock by removing the lead wire from the rear of the clock. Disconnect the positive battery cable from the battery and connect the ground wire on a test light to the disconnected positive battery cable. Touch the probe end of the test light to the positive battery post. The test light should not light. If the test light does light, there is a short or open circuit on the car.

2. Disconnect the voltage regulator wiring harness connector at the voltage regulator. Turn on the ignition key. Connect the wire on a test light to a good ground (engine bolt). Touch the probe end of a test light to the ignition wire connector into the voltage regulator wiring connector. This wire corresponds to the "I" terminal on the regulator. If the test light goes on, the charging system warning light circuit is complete. If the test light does not come on and the warning light on the instrument panel is on, either the resistor wire, which is parallel with the warning light, or the wiring to the voltage regulator, is defective. If the test light does not come on and the warning light is not on, either the bulb is defective or the power supply wire from the battery through the ignition switch to the bulb has an open circuit. Connect the wiring harness to the regulator.

3. Examine the fuse link wire in the wiring harness from the starter relay to the alternator. If the insulation on the wire is cracked or split, the fuse link may be melted. Connect a test light to the fuse link by attaching the ground wire on the test light to an engine bolt and touching the probe end of the light to the bottom of the fuse link wire where it splices into the alternator output wire. If the bulb in the test light does not light, the fuse link is melted.

4. Start the engine and place a current indicator on the positive battery cable. Turn off all electrical accessories and make sure the doors are closed. If the charging system is working properly, the gauge will show a draw of about 5 amps. If the system is not working properly, the gauge will show a draw of about 5 amps. A charge moves the needle toward the battery, a draw moves the needle away from the battery. Turn the engine off.

5. Disconnect the wiring harness from the voltage regulator at the regulator connector. Connect a male spade terminal (solderless connector) to each end of a jumper wire. Insert one end of the wire into the wiring harness connector which corresponds to the "A" terminal on the regulator. Insert the other end of the wire into the wiring harness connector which corresponds to the "F" terminal on the regulator. Position the connector with the jumper wire installed so that it cannot contact any metal surface under the hood. Position a current indicator gauge on the positive battery cable. Have an assistant start the engine. Observe the read-

ing on the current indicator. Have your assistant slowly raise the speed of the engine to about 2,000 rpm or until the current indicator needle stops moving, whichever comes first. Do not run the engine for more than a short period of time in this condition. If the wiring harness connector or jumper wire becomes excessively hot during this test, turn off the engine and check for a grounded wire in the regulator wiring harness. If the current indicator shows a charge of about three amps less than the output of the alternator, the alternator is working properly. If the previous tests showed a draw, the voltage regulator is defective. If the gauge does not show the proper charging rate, the alternator is defective.

REMOVAL AND INSTALLATION

1. Disconnect the negative battery cable from the battery.
2. Disconnect the wires from the alternator or generator.
3. Loosen the alternator mounting bolts and remove the drive belt.
   NOTE: *Some 1981 and later cars are equipped with a ribbed, K-section belt and automatic tensioner. A special tool must be made to remove the tension from the tensioner arm. Loosen the idler pulley pivot and adjuster bolts before using the tool. See the accompanying illustration for tool details.*
4. Remove the alternator mounting bolts and spacer (if equipped), and remove the alternator.
5. To install, position the alternator on its brackets and install the attaching bolts and spacer (if so equipped).
6. Connect the wires to the alternator.
7. Position the drive belt on the alternator pulley. Adjust the belt tension as outlined in Chapter 1.
8. Connect the negative battery cable.

Voltage Regulator

From 1971–73, all models were equipped with a nonadjustable electromechanical voltage regulator. In 1974, an adjustable transistorized unit was introduced, and all models through 1977

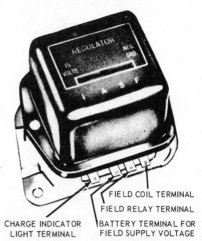

FIELD COIL TERMINAL
FIELD RELAY TERMINAL
BATTERY TERMINAL FOR FIELD SUPPLY VOLTAGE
CHARGE INDICATOR LIGHT TERMINAL

Electromechanical voltage regulator

were supplied with either type. A simple inspection will determine which regulator is on your vehicle. The cover of the electromechanical regulator is held in place by rivets, the transistorized unit uses screws. Beginning in 1978, a completely solid-state regulator is used.

REMOVAL AND INSTALLATION

1. Remove the battery ground cable. On models with the regulator mounted behind the battery, it is necessary to remove the battery hold-down, and to move the battery.
2. Remove the regulator mounting screws.
3. Disconnect the regulator from the wiring harness.
4. Connect the new regulator to the wiring harness.
5. Mount the regulator to the regulator mounting plate. The radio suppression condenser mounts under one mounting screw; the ground lead under the other mounting screw. Tighten the mounting screws.
6. If the battery was moved to gain access to the regulator, position the battery and install the hold-down. Connect the battery ground cable, and test the system for proper voltage regulation.

VOLTAGE LIMITER ADJUSTMENT
Transistorized Regulator Only

NOTE: *The only reason for making this adjustment is if the alternator field current voltage is too high or too low. The test to determine this information should be performed at a garage with professional testing equipment.*

1. Run the engine to normal operating temperature and then shut it off.
2. Remove the regulator cover.
3. Using a plastic strip as a screwdriver, turn

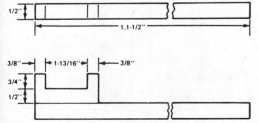

Fabricated absorber arm deflection tool

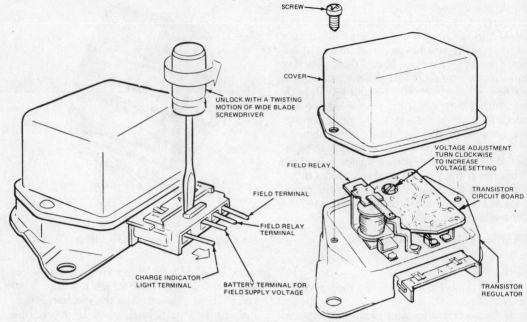

Voltage limiter adjustment—transistorized regulator only

the adjusting screw clockwise to increase the voltage setting, counterclockwise to decrease the setting.

4. Reinstall the regulator cover.

Starter

There are two different types of starter found on Ford and Mercury mid-size models; their use depends upon engine size. All 6 cylinder engines and most V8's are equipped with a positive engagement starter. A solenoid actuated starter is used on 429 and 460 V8 engines only. Since a greater amount of starting power is required by the 429 and 460 engines, the solenoid actuated starter is constructed with more coil and armature windings to deliver the necessary current. The presence of a solenoid mechanism is incidental and does not affect starting power.

The positive engagement starter system employs a starter relay, usually mounted inside the engine compartment on a fender wall, to transfer battery current to the starter. The relay is activated by the ignition switch and, when engaged, it creates a direct current from the battery to the starter windings. Simultaneously, the armature begins to turn and the starter drive is pushed out to engage the flywheel.

In the solenoid actuated starter system, battery current is first directed to a solenoid assembly which is mounted on the starter case. The current closes the splenoid contacts, which engages the drive pinion and directs current to the coil windings, causing the armature to rotate. While this system does not need a starter relay, some models were nevertheless equipped with one in order to simplify assembly procedures. These vehicles also have a connector link

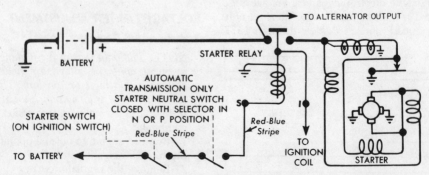

Positive engagement starter circuit

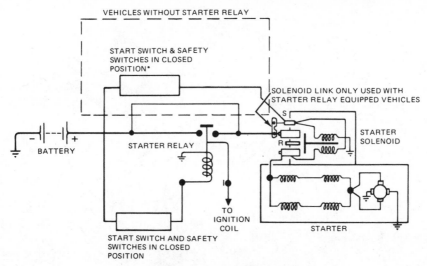

Solenoid actuated starter circuit

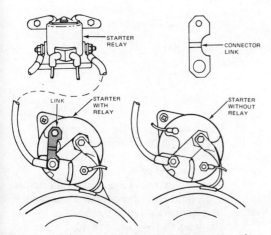

Solenoid connector link for use with starter relay

attached to the solenoid, which provides a hook up for the relay wire.

REMOVAL AND INSTALLATION

Except Diesel

1. Disconnect the negative battery cable.
2. Raise the front of the car and install jackstands beneath the frame. Firmly apply the parking brake and place blocks in back of the rear wheels.
3. Disconnect the heavy starter cable at the starter. On solenoid actuated starters (429 and 460 V8 only), label and disconnect the wires from the solenoid.
4. Turn the front wheels fully to the right. On some later models it will be necessary to remove the frame brace. On many models, it will be necessary to remove the two bolts re-

taining the steering idler arm to the frame to gain access to the starter.
5. Remove the starter mounting bolts and remove the starter.
6. Reverse the above procedure to install. Torque the mounting bolts to 12–15 ft. lbs. on starters with 3 mounting bolts and 15–20 ft. lbs. on starters with 2 mounting bolts. Torque the idler arm retaining bolts to 28–35 ft. lbs. (if removed). Make sure that the nut securing the heavy cable to the starter is snugged down tightly.

2.4L Diesel Engine

1. Disconnect the battery ground (negative) cable.
2. Remove the bolt holding the dipstick tube to the intake manifold.
3. Remove the wires from the starter solenoid. Remove the front starter support bracket.
4. Remove the two starter to torque converter housing mounting bolts.
5. Pull the dipstick tube outward slightly allowing clearance for starter motor removal. Remove the starter motor.
6. Position the starter to torque converter housing and install the two bolts. Tighten to 30–40 ft. lbs.
7. Install the starter support bracket and tighten the attaching bolts to 14–20 ft. lbs.
8. Connect the cables to the starter solenoid. Tighten the red wire to 80–120 inch lbs. Tighten the black wire to 25 inch lbs.
9. Reposition the dipstick to the intake manifold, install the bolt and tighten to 6–7 ft. lbs.
10. Install the battery ground cable.

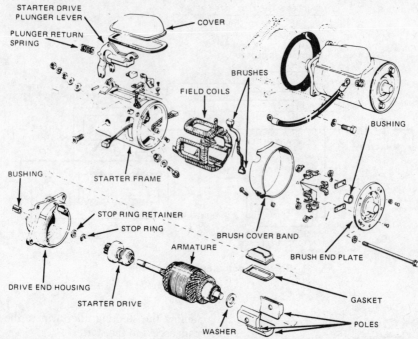

Exploded view of positive engagement starter

OVERHAUL—EXCEPT DIESEL

Brush Replacement

1. Remove starter from engine as previously outlined.

2. On positive engagement starters, remove the starter drive plunger lever cover and gasket.

3. On solenoid actuated starters, disconnect the copper strap from the starter terminal on the solenoid. Remove the retaining screws and detach the solenoid assembly from the starter housing.

4. Loosen and remove the brush cover band and remove the brushes from their holders.

5. Remove the two through bolts from the starter frame.

6. Separate the drive-end housing, starter frame and brush end plate assemblies.

7. On positive engagement starters, remove the starter drive plunger lever and pivot pin, and remove the armature.

8. On solenoid actuated starters:

 a. Remove the solenoid plunger and shift fork assembly. (If either the plunger or the fork is to be replaced, they can be separated by removing the roll pin.)

 b. Remove the armature and drive assembly from the frame.

9. Remove the ground brush retaining screws from the frame and remove the brushes.

10. Cut the insulated brush leads from the field coils, as close to the field connection point as possible.

11. Clean and inspect the starter motor.

12. Replace the brush end plate if the insulator between the field brush holder and the end plate is cracked or broken.

13. Position the new insulated field brushes lead on the field coil connection. Position and crimp the clip provided with the brushes to hold the brush lead to the connection. Solder the lead, clip, and connection together using resin core solder. Use a 300-watt soldering iron.

14. Install the ground brush leads to the frame with the retaining screws.

15. Reassemble in reverse order.

16. Torque the through bolts to 55–75 in. lbs.

17. If possible, connect the starter to a battery and check its operation before reinstalling it in the vehicle.

Drive Replacement

1. Remove the starter as outlined previously.

2. On positive engagement starters, remove the starter drive plunger lever and gasket and the brush cover band.

3. On solenoid actuated starters, disconnect the copper strap from the starter terminal on the solenoid. Remove the retaining screws and detach the solenoid assembly from the starter housing.

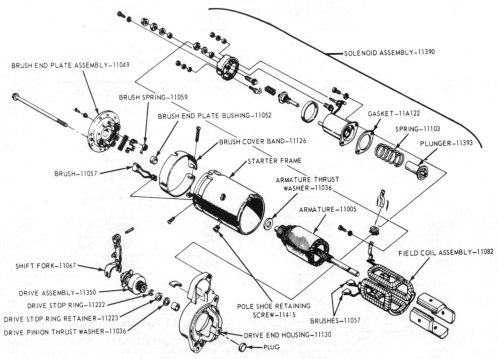

BRUSH END PLATE ASSEMBLY-11049

SOLENOID ASSEMBLY-11390

BRUSH SPRING-11059

BRUSH END PLATE BUSHING-11052

GASKET-11A122

SPRING-11103

PLUNGER-11393

BRUSH COVER BAND-11126

STARTER FRAME

BRUSH-11057

ARMATURE THRUST WASHER-11036

ARMATURE-11005

FIELD COIL ASSEMBLY-11082

SHIFT FORK-11067

DRIVE ASSEMBLY-11350

DRIVE STOP RING-11222

DRIVE STOP RING RETAINER-11223

DRIVE PINION THRUST WASHER-11036

POLE SHOE RETAINING SCREW-114:5

BRUSHES-11057

DRIVE END HOUSING-11130

PLUG

Exploded view of solenoid actuated starter

4. Remove the two through-bolts from the starter frame.

5. Separate the drive end housing from the starter frame.

NOTE: *On positive engagement starters, the starter drive plunger lever return spring may fall out after detaching the drive end housing. If not, remove it.*

6. On positive engagement starters, remove the pivot pin which attaches the starter drive plunger lever to the starter frame and remove the lever.

7. On solenoid actuated starters, remove the solenoid plunger and shift fork assembly. (If either the plunger or the fork is to be replaced, they can be separated by removing the roll pin.)

8. Remove the stop ring retainer and stop ring from the armature shaft.

9. Slide the starter drive off the armature shaft.

10. Examine the wear pattern on the starter drive teeth. There should be evidence of full contact between the starter drive teeth and the flywheel ring gear teeth. If there is evidence of irregular wear, examine the flywheel ring gear for damage and replace if necessary.

11. Reassemble in reverse order.

12. Apply a thin coat of white grease to the armature shaft before installing the drive gear. Place a small amount of grease in the drive end housing bearing.

13. Tighten the starter through bolts to 55–75 in. lbs.

14. If possible, connect the starter to a battery and check its operation before installing it in the vehicle.

ENGINE MECHANICAL

Engine Removal and Installation

NOTE: *Disconnect the negative battery cable before beginning any work. Always label all disconnected hoses, vacuum lines and wires, to prevent incorrect reassembly. Do not disconnect any air conditioning lines unless you are thoroughly familiar with A/C systems and the hazards involved; escaping refrigerant (freon) will freeze any surface it contacts, including skin and eyes. Have the system discharged professionally before required repairs are started.*

Gasoline Engine

1. Scribe the hood hinge outline on the under-hood, disconnect the hood and remove.

2. Drain the entire cooling system and crankcase.

3. Remove the air cleaner, disconnect the battery at the cylinder head. On automatic transmission equipped cars, disconnect the fluid

General Engine Specifications

Year	Engine No. Cyl Displacement (cu. in.)	Carb Type	■ Advertised Horsepower (@ rpm)	■ Advertised Torque @ rpm (ft. lbs.)	Bore and Stroke (in.)	Advertised Compression Ratio	Oil Pressure (psi) (@ 2000 rpm)
'71	6-250	1 bbl	145 @ 4000	232 @ 1600	3.682 x 3.910	9.0:1	35–60
	8-302	2 bbl	210 @ 4600	296 @ 2600	4.000 x 3.000	9.0:1	35–60
	8-351 C	2 bbl	240 @ 4600	355 @ 2600	4.000 x 3.500	9.5:1	35–60
	8-351 C	4 bbl	285 @ 5400	370 @ 3400	4.000 x 3.500	10.7:1	35–60
	8-429	4 bbl	360 @ 4600	480 @ 2800	4.362 x 3.590	10.5:1	35–75
	8-429 CJ	4 bbl	370 @ 5400	450 @ 3400	4.362 x 3.590	11.3:1	35–75
	8-429 SCJ	4 bbl	375 @ 5600	450 @ 3400	4.362 x 3.590	11.3:1	35–75
'72	6-250	1 bbl	99 @ 3600	184 @ 1600	3.680 x 3.910	8.0:1	35–60
	8-302	2 bbl	141 @ 4000	242 @ 2000	4.000 x 3.000	8.5:1	35–60
	8-351	2 bbl	164 @ 4000	276 @ 2000	4.000 x 3.500	8.6:1	35–85
	8-351 CJ	4 bbl	248 @ 5400	290 @ 3800	4.000 x 3.500	8.6:1	35–85
	8-400	2 bbl	168 @ 4200	297 @ 2200	4.000 x 4.000	8.4:1	35–85
	8-429	4 bbl	205 @ 4400	322 @ 2600	4.326 x 3.590	8.5:1	35–75
'73	6-250	1 bbl	92 @ 3200	197 @ 1600	3.680 x 3.910	8.0:1	35–60
	8-302	2 bbl	135, 137 @ 4200	228, 230 @ 2200	4.000 x 3.000	8.0:1	35–60
	8-351 W	2 bbl	156 @ 3800	260 @ 2400	4.000 x 3.500	8.0:1	50–70
	8-351 W	2 bbl	154, 159 @ 4000	246, 250 @ 2400	4.000 x 3.500	8.0:1	50–70
	8-351 CJ	4 bbl	246 @ 5400	312 @ 3600	4.000 x 3.500	8.0:1	50–70
	8-400	2 bbl	163, 168 @ 3800	300, 310 @ 2000	4.000 x 4.000	8.0:1	50–70
	8-429	4 bbl	197, 201 @ 4400	320, 322 @ 2600	4.362 x 3.590	8.0:1	35–75
	8-460 PI	4 bbl	274 @ 4600	392 @ 2800	4.362 x 3.850	8.8:1	50–75
'74	6-250	1 bbl	91 @ 3200	190 @ 1600	3.680 x 3.190	8.0:1	35–65
	8-302	2 bbl	140 @ 3800	230 @ 2600	4.000 x 3.000	8.0:1	35–55
	8-351 W	2 bbl	162 @ 4000	275 @ 2200	4.000 x 3.500	8.0:1	50–70
	8-351 C	2 bbl	163 @ 4200	278 @ 2000	4.000 x 3.500	8.0:1	50–70
	8-351 CJ	4 bbl	255 @ 5600	290 @ 3400	4.000 x 3.500	7.9:1	50–70
	8-400	2 bbl	170 @ 3400	330 @ 2000	4.000 x 4.000	8.0:1	50–70
	8-460	4 bbl	195 @ 3800	355 @ 2600	4.362 x 3.850	8.0:1	35–75
	8-460	4 bbl	200 @ 4000	355 @ 2600	4.362 x 3.850	8.0:1	35–75
	8-460 PI	4 bbl	260 @ 4400	380 @ 2700	4.362 x 3.850	8.8:1	50–75
'75–'76	8-351 W 49	2 bbl	154 @ 3800	268 @ 2200	4.000 x 3.500	8.2:1	40–65
	8-351 W Cal.	2 bbl	153 @ 3400	270 @ 2400	4.000 x 3.500	8.2:1	40–65
	8-351 M 49	2 bbl	148 @ 3800	243 @ 2400	4.000 x 3.500	8.0:1	50–75
	8-351 M Cal.	2 bbl	150 @ 3800	244 @ 2800	4.000 x 3.500	8.0:1	50–75
	8-400 49	2 bbl	158 @ 3800	276 @ 2000	4.000 x 4.000	8.0:1	50–75
	8-400 Cal.	2 bbl	144 @ 3600	255 @ 2200	4.000 x 4.000	8.0:1	50–75

General Engine Specifications (Cont.)

Year	Engine No. Cyl Displacement (cu. in.)	Carb Type	■ Advertised Horsepower (@ rpm)	■ Advertised Torque @ rpm (ft. lbs.)	Bore and Stroke (in.)	Advertised Compression Ratio	Oil Pressure (psi) (@ 2000 rpm)
'75–'76	8-460 49	4 bbl	216 @ 4000	366 @ 2600	4.362 x 3.850	8.0:1	40–65
	8-460 Cal.	4 bbl	217 @ 4000	365 @ 2600	4.362 x 3.850	8.0:1	40–65
	8-460 PI	4 bbl	266 @ 4000	374 @ 2600	4.263 x 3.850	8.0:1	40–65
'77–'78	8-302	2 bbl	130 @ 2400	243 @ 1800	3.000 x 3.000	8.4:1	40–60
	8-351 W	2 bbl	149 @ 3200	291 @ 1600	4.000 x 3.500	8.3:1	40–60
	8-351 M	2 bbl	161 @ 3600	285 @ 1800	4.000 x 3.500	8.0:1	50–75
	8-400	2 bbl	173 @ 3800	326 @ 1600	4.000 x 4.000	8.0:1	50–75
'79	8-302	2 bbl	140 @ 3600	250 @ 1800	4.000 x 3.000	8.4:1	40–65
	8-302 Cal.	vv	134 @ 3600	243 @ 2300	4.000 x 3.000	8.1:1	40–65
	8-351 M	2 bbl	152 @ 3600	270 @ 2200	4.000 x 3.500	8.0:1	51–75
	8-351 W	2 bbl	135 @ 3200	286 @ 1400	4.000 x 3.500	8.3:1	40–65
'80	8-255	2 bbl	119 @ 3800	194 @ 2200	3.680 x 3.000	8.8:1	40–60
	8-255 Cal.	vv	119 @ 3800	194 @ 2200	3.680 x 3.000	8.8:1	40–60
	8-302	2 bbl	134 @ 3600	232 @ 1600	4.000 x 3.000	8.4:1	40–60
	8-302	vv	131 @ 3600	231 @ 1400	4.000 x 3.000	8.4:1	40–60
'81–'82	4-140	2 bbl	88 @ 4600	118 @ 2600	3.781 x 3.126	9.0:1	40–60
	6-200	1 bbl	88 @ 3200	154 @ 1400	3.683 x 3.126	8.6:1	30–50
	6-232	2 bbl	112 @ 4000	175 @ 2600	3.814 x 3.388	8.8:1	40–60
	8-255	2 bbl	115 @ 3400	205 @ 2200	3.680 x 3.000	8.2:1	40–60
	8-255	vv	120 @ 3400	205 @ 2600	3.680 x 3.000	8.2:1	40–60
	8-302	2 bbl	160 @ 4200	247 @ 2400	4.000 x 3.000	8.4:1	40–60
	8-302	vv	130 @ 3400	235 @ 1800	4.000 x 3.000	8.4:1	40–50
'83	4-140	1bbl	86 @ 4600	117 @ 2600	3.781 x 3.126	9.0:1	40–60
	6-200	1 bbl	87 @ 3800	154 @ 1400	3.680 x 3.130	8.6:1	30–50
	6-232	2 bbl	112 @ 4000	175 @ 2600	3.810 x 3.390	8.7:1	40–60
	8-302	CFI	130 @ 3200	240 @ 2000	4.000 x 3.000	8.4:1	40–60
'84–'85	4-140	1 bbl	88 @ 4600	118 @ 2800	3.781 x 3.126	9.0:1	40–60
	4-140	EFI	145 @ 3800	180 @ 3600	3.781 x 3.126	8.0:1	40–60
	6-232	CFI	120 @ 3600	205 @ 1600	3.810 x 3.390	8.6:1	40–60
	6-232	2 bbl	112 @ 4000	175 @ 2600	3.810 x 3.390	8.6:1	40–60
	8-302	2 bbl	155 @ 3600	265 @ 2000	4.000 x 3.000	8.4:1	40–60
	8-302	CFI	140 @ 3200 ①	250 @ 1600 ①	4.000 x 3.000	8.4:1	40–60

■Beginning 1972 horsepower and torque are SAE net figures. They are measured at the rear of the transmission with all accessories installed and operating.
W: Windsor
C: Cleveland
M: Modified Cleveland
PI: Police interceptor
49: 49 states only
Cal: California only
VV: Variable Venturi
① H.O.: 165 @ 3800 245 @ 2000

Valve Specifications

Year	Engine No. Cyl. Displacement (cu. in.)	Seat Angle (deg)	Face Angle (deg)	Spring Test Pressure (lbs. @ in.)	Spring Intalled Height (in.)	Stem to Guide Clearance (in.)		Stem Diameter (in.)	
						Intake	Exhaust	Intake	Exhaust
'71	6-250	45	44	150 @ 1.22	1¹⁹⁄₃₂	.0008–.0025	.0010–.0027	.3104	.3102
	8-302	45	44	180 @ 1.23	1²¹⁄₃₂	.0010–.0027	.0015–.0032	.3420	.3415
	8-351 ①	45	44	215 @ 1.34	1²⁵⁄₃₂	.0010–.0027	.0015–.0032	.3420	.3415
	8-351 ②	45	44	210 @ 1.42	1¹³⁄₁₆	.0010–.0027	.0015–.0032	.3420	.3415
	8-351 ③	45	44	285 @ 1.31	1¹³⁄₁₆	.0010–.0027	.0015–.0032	.3420	.3415
	8-429	45	45	229 @ 1.33	1¹³⁄₁₆	.0010–.0027	.0010–.0027	.3420	.3420
'72–'76	6-250	45	44	150 @ 1.22	1¹⁹⁄₃₂	.0008–.0025	.0010–.0027	.3104	.3102
	8-302	45	44	200 @ 1.23	1¹¹⁄₁₆	.0010–.0027	.0015–.0032	.3420	.3415
	8-351 ①	45	44	200 @ 1.34	1²⁵⁄₃₂	.0010–.0027	.0015–.0032	.3420	.3415
	8-351 ②	45	44	210 @ 1.42	1¹³⁄₁₆	.0010–.0027	.0015–.0032	.3420	.3415
	8-351 ③	45	44	285 @ 1.23	1¹³⁄₁₆	.0010–.0027	.0015–.0032	.3420	.3415
	8-400	45	44	226 @ 1.39	1¹³⁄₁₆	.0010–.0027	.0015–.0032	.3420	.3515
	8-429	45	45	229 @ 1.33	1¹³⁄₁₆	.0010–.0027	.0010–.0027	.3420	.3420
'77–'78	6-250	45	44	150 @ 1.22	1¹⁹⁄₃₂	.0008–.0025	.0010–.0027	.3104	.3102
	8-302	45	44	200 @ 1.22	1⁹⁄₁₆	.0010–.0027	.0015–.0032	.3420	.3415
	8-351 ①	45	44	200 @ 1.34	1²⁵⁄₃₂	.0010–.0027	.0015–.0032	.3420	.3415
	8-351 ②	45	44	282 @ 1.32	1¹³⁄₁₆	.0010–.0027	.0015–.0032	.3420	.3415
	8-351 ③	45	44	285 @ 1.32	1¹³⁄₁₆	.0010–.0027	.0015–.0032	.3420	.3415
	8-400	45	44	226 @ 1.39	1¹³⁄₁₆	.0010–.0027	.0015–.0032	.3420	.3415
	8-460	45	44	253 @ 1.33	1¹³⁄₁₆	.0010–.0027	.0010–.0027	.3420	.3420
'79	8-302	45	44	④	⑤	.0010–.0027	.0015–.0032	.3420	.3415
	8-351 M	45	44	228 @ 1.39	1¹³⁄₁₆	.0010–.0027	.0015–.0032	.3420	.3415
	8-351 W	45	44	⑥	⑦	.0010–.0027	.0015–.0032	.3420	.3415
'80	8-255	45	44	⑦	⑧	.0010–.0027	.0015–.0032	.3420	.3415
	8-302	45	44	⑦	⑧	.0010–.0027	.0015–.0032	.3420	.3415
'81	4-140	45	44	⑨	1⁹⁄₁₆	.0010–.0027	.0015–.0032	.3420	.3415
	6-200	45	44	55 @ 1.59	1¹⁹⁄₃₂	.0008–.0025	.0010–.0027	.3104	.3102
	8-255	45	44	⑦	⑧	.0010–.0027	.0015–.0032	.3420	.3415
	8-302	45	44	⑦	⑧	.0010–.0027	.0015–.0032	.3420	.3415
'82–'85	4-140	45	44	75 @ 1.56	1⁹⁄₁₆	.0010–.0027	.0015–.0032	.3420	.3415
	6-200	45	44	55 @ 1.59	1¹⁹⁄₃₂	.0008–.0025	.0010–.0027	.3104	.3102
	6-232	⑨	⑩	202 @ 1.27	1¾	.0010–.0027	.0015–.0032	.3420	.3415
	8-255	⑨	⑩	⑪	⑧	.0010–.0027	.0015–.0032	.3420	.3415
	8-302	45	45	⑦	⑧	.0010–.0027	.0015–.0032	.3420	.3415

① Windsor heads
② Cleveland or modified Cleveland 2 bbl
③ Cleveland or modified Cleveland 4 bbl
④ Int.: 200 @ 1.31
  Exh.: 200 @ 1.20
⑤ Int.: 1¹¹⁄₁₆
  Exh.: 1⅝
⑥ Int.: 200 @ 1.34
  Exh.: 200 @ 1.20
⑦ Int.: 204 @ 1.36
  Exh.: 200 @ 1.20
⑧ Int.: 1¹¹⁄₁₆
  Exh.: 1¹⁹⁄₃₂
⑨ 44°30'–45°
⑩ 45°30'–45°45'
⑪ Int.: 192 @ 1.40
  Exh.: 191 @ 1.23

Crankshaft and Connecting Rod Specifications
All measurements are given in inches

Year	Engine No. Cyl. Displacement (cu. in.)	Crankshaft				Connecting Rod		
		Main Brg. Journal Dia	Main Brg. Oil Clearance	Shaft End-Play	Thrust on No.	Journal Diameter	Oil Clearance	Side Clearance
'81–'85	4-140	2.3982–2.3990	.0008–.0015 ⑧	.004–.008	3	2.0464–2.0472	.0008–.0015 ⑨	.0035–.0105
'81–'82	6-200	2.2482–2.2490	.0008–.0015 ⑧	.004–.008	5	2.1232–2.1240	.0008–.0015 ⑨	.0035–.0105
'82–'85	6-232	2.5185–2.5195	.0005–.0023 ⑩	.004–.008	3	2.1228–2.1236	.0008–.0026	.010–.020
'71–'77	6-250	2.3982–2.3990	.0005–.0022	.004–.008	5	2.1232–2.1240	.0008–.00024	.003–.010
'81–'82	8-255	2.2482–2.2490	.0005–.0015 ③⑪	.004–.008	3	2.1228–2.1236	.0008–.0015 ⑫	.010–.020
'71–'85	8-302	2.2482–2.2490	.0005–.0024 ⑤④	.004–.008	3	2.1228–2.1236	.0008–.0026	.010–.020
'73–'79	8-351W	2.9994–3.0002	.0013–.0030 ②	.004–.008	3	2.3103–2.3111	.0008–.0026 ⑦①	.010–.020
'71–'79	8-351C or M	2.7484–2.7492 ⑥	.0009–.0026 ⑦	.004–.008	3	2.3103–2.3111	.0008–.0026 ⑦①	.010–.020
'72–'78	8-400	2.9994–3.0002	.0011–.0028	.004–.008	3	2.3103–2.3111	.0011–.0026 ①	.010–.020
'71–'76	8-429, 460	2.9994–3.0002	.0010–.0020 ③	.004–.008	3	2.4992–2.5000	.0008–.0028	.010–.020

① .008–.0015 in. in 1974–77
② .008–.0025 in. in 1974–77
③ No. 1: .0010–.0015
④ .0005–.0015 in. in 1974–77
⑤ 302: .0001–.0005 No. 1 bearing only
⑥ 8-351C given; 8-351M: 2.9994–3.0002
⑦ 8-351C or M 4-bbl: .0011–.0015
⑧ .0008–.0026 allowed
⑨ .0008–.0024 allowed
⑩ Horiz.: .0009–.0027
⑪ 1982: .0005–.0024
⑫ 1982: .0007–.0020

Camshaft Specifications
(All measurements in inches)

Engine	Journal Diameter					Bearing Clearance	Lobe Lift		Endplay
	1	2	3	4	5		Intake	Exhaust	
4-140 (2.3L)	1.7713–1.7720	1.7713–1.7720	1.7713–1.7720	1.7713–1.7720	—	.001–.003	.2437①	.2437①	.001–.007
6-200 (3.3L)	1.8095–1.8105	1.8095–1.8105	1.8095–1.8105	1.8095–1.8105	—	.001–.003	.245	.245	.001–.007
6-232 (3.8L)	2.0505–2.0515	2.0505–2.0515	2.0505–2.0515	2.0505–2.0515	—	.001–.003	.240	.241	②
6-250 (4.1L)	1.8095–1.8105	1.8095–1.8105	1.8095–1.8105	1.8095–1.8105	—	.001–.003	.245	.245	.001–.007
8-255 (4.2L)	2.0805–2.0815	2.0655–2.0665	2.0505–2.0515	2.0355–2.0365	2.0205–2.0215	.001–.003	.2375	.2375	.001–.007
8-302 (5.0L)	2.0805–2.0815	2.0655–2.0665	2.0505–2.0515	2.0355–2.0365	2.0205–2.0215	.001–.003	.2375③	.2474③	.001–.003
8-351W (5.8L)	2.0805–2.0815	2.0655–2.0665	2.0505–2.0515	2.0355–2.0365	2.0205–2.0215	.001–.003	.260④	.260④	.001–.007
8-351M (5.8L) 8-400 (6.6L)	2.1238–2.1248	2.1238–2.1248	2.1238–2.1248	2.1238–2.1248	2.0205–2.0215	.001–.003	.235 .247	.235 .250	.001–.003
8-460 (7.5L)	2.1238–2.1248	2.1238–2.1248	2.1238–2.1248	2.1238–2.1248	2.1238–2.1248	.001–.003	.253④	.278④	.001–.006

① '84 and later: .2381
② Endplay controlled by button and spring on camshaft end.
③ HO engine: Intake—.2600; Exhaust—.2780
④ HO engine: Intake—.2780; Exhaust—.2830

Ring Gap (inches)

Year	Engine	Top Compression	Bottom Compression	Oil ① Control
1971–73	250	.010–.020	.010–.020	.015–.055
1974–82	200, 250	.008–.016	.008–.016	.015–.055
1971	302, 351	.010–.020	.010–.020	.015–.069
1971	429	.010–.020	.010–.020	.010–.035
1972–78	400	.010–.020	.010–.020	.015–.069
1972–85	Except 200, 250, 400	.010–.020	.010–.020	.015–.055 ②

① Steel Rails
② 1972–73 351 C is .015–.069

Ring Side Clearance (Inches)

Year	Engine	Top Compression	Bottom Compression	Oil Control
1971–85	All engines	.002–.004	.002–.004	Snug

Piston Clearance (Inches)

Year	Engine	Piston-to-Bore Clearance
1971–82	200, 250	0.0013–0.0021
1971–85	255, 302, 351W	0.0018–0.0026
1971–85	140, 351C, 351M, 400 429, 460	0.0014–0.0022 ①
1971	429 CJ and SCJ	0.0042–0.0050
1981–85	232	.0014–.0028

① 79–82 Turbo .0034–.0042
83–85 Turbo .0030–.0038

Torque Specifications
(All Readings in ft. lbs.)

Year	Engine No. Cyl Displacement (cu in.)	Cylinder Head Bolts *	Rod Bearing Bolts	Main Bearing Bolts	Crankshaft Pulley Bolt	Flywheel-to-Crankshaft Bolts	Manifold Intake	Exhaust
'71–'73	6-250	70–75	21–26	60–70	85–100	75–85	—	13–18
	8-302	65–72	19–24	60–70	70–90	75–85	23–25	12–16
	8-351	95–100	40–45	95–105 ②	70–90	75–85	23–25 (⁵⁄₁₆) 28–32 (³⁄₈) 6–9 (¼)	12–22
	8-400	95–105 ③	40–45	④	70–90	75–85	21–25 (⁵⁄₁₆) 27–33 (³⁄₈) 6–9 (¼)	12–16
	8-429, 460	130–140	40–45	95–105 ①	70–90	75–85	25–30	28–33
'74–'79	6-250	70–75	21–26	60–70	85–100	75–85	—	13–18
	8-302	65–72	19–24	60–70	35–50	75–85	19–27	12–16
	8-351W	105–112	40–45	95–105	35–50	75–85	19–27	18–24

Torque Specifications (Cont.)
(All Readings in ft. lbs.)

Year	Engine No. Cyl Displacement (cu in.)	Cylinder Head Bolts *	Rod Bearing Bolts	Main Bearing Bolts	Crankshaft Pulley Bolt	Flywheel-to-Crankshaft Bolts	Manifold	
							Intake	Exhaust
'74–'79	8-351C or M	95–105 ③	40–45	④	70–90	75–85	⑤	12–22
	8-400	95–105 ③	40–45	④	70–90	75–85	⑤	12–16
	8-460	130–140	40–45	95–105	35–50	75–85	22–32	28–33
'80–85	4-140	80–90 ⑨	30–36	80–90	100–120	54–64	14–21	16–23
	6-200	70–75	21–26	60–70	85–100	75–85	—	18–24
	6-232	65–81 ⑥	30–36 ⑥	62–81 ⑥	85–100	75–85	17–19	15–22
	8-255	65–75	19–24	60–70	70–90	75–85	18–20 ⑦	18–24
	8-302	65–75	19–24	60–70	70–90	75–85	23–25 ⑦	18–24

① 7/16 in. bolts—70–80 ft. lbs.
② 3/8 in. bolts—34–45 ft. lbs.
③ Three steps—55, 75, then maximum figure
④ 1/2 in.—13 bolts, 95–105, 3/8 in.—16 bolts, 35–45
⑤ 5/16 in. bolt, 21–25, 3/8 in. bolt, 22–32; 1/4 in. bolt, 6–9
⑥ Tighten to listed torque, loosen 2 complete turns, retighten to listed torque. Fasteners must be oil-coated
⑦ Torque cold, then retorque hot
⑧ Tighten in two steps: 50–60 then 80–90
* Tighten cylinder head bolts in three steps

Diesel 2.4L Specifications

ENGINE
Type .... 6-cylinder, in-line, 4-cycle, overhead valve, water-cooled
Bore .... 3.150 in. (80mm)
Stroke .... 3.189 in. (81mm)
Displacement .... 149 cu. in. (2442.9cc)
Compression ratio 23:1
Horsepower .... 114 at 4800 rpm
Minimum Torque .... 150 lb. ft. at 2400 rpm
Compression pressure .... 348 psi (2400 kPa)
Valve clearance (cold engine) .... Intake: 0.010 in. (0.3mm)
                                         Exhaust: 0.010 in. (0.3mm)
Cam Timing
   Intake valve opens .... 6° BTDC
   Intake valve closes .... 34° ABDC
   Exhaust valve opens .... 46° BBDC
   Exhaust valve closes .... 6° ATDC
   Intake valve lift .... 0.374 in. (9.5mm)
   Exhaust valve lift .... 0.376 in. (9.55mm)
Weight .... 433 lbs. (196.4 kg) dry
FUEL SYSTEM
Injection firing order 1 5 3 6 2 4
Idle speed .... 750 + 50 − 0 rpm
Fast idle (cold-start) speed .... 900–1050 rpm
Injection pump timing .... 2.5° BTDC at 750–800 rpm
LUBRICATION SYSTEM
Complete System w/o oil cooler .... 7.1 qts. (6.7L)
Complete System .... 7.9 qts. (7.5L)
Engine oil pressure .... 57–85 psi at 4000 rpm

NOTE: Due to the late introduction of this engine, normal specifications were unavailable at the time of publication.

Diesel 2.4L Torque Specifications

Description	Ft. lbs.	Description	Ft. lbs.
Main bearing caps	43–48	Sprocket to camshaft	40–47
Engine support straps	28–34	Bearing cap of camshaft	6–7
Valve cover	6–7		14–17
Oil trap to valve cover	11–14	Tensioning roller holder to crankcase	14–17
Cylinder head bolts		Clamping bolt in rocker arm	5–6.5
		Sprocket to auxiliary shaft	40–47
Step 1	36–43	Oil pressure switch	22–29
Step 2 (torque angle)	90 ± 5°	Oil pump to crankcase	16–17
Step 3 (torque angle)	90 ± 5°	Oil pump cover	6–7
Oil spray bar to cylinder head	14–17	Oil filter housing to crankcase	14–17
Oil drain plug	24–26	Oil filter cover	15–18
Oil pan to crankcase	6.5–7	Oil filter drain plug	7–9
Front/rear end covers to crankcase	6–7	Oil spray jet to crankcase	6–7
	14–17	Oil cooler oil lines to oil filter housing	22–29
Flywheel to crankshaft (installed with Loc-tite No. 270)	71–81	Oil lines to turbocharger	14–17
Vibration damper hub to crankshaft	282–311	Vacuum pump	6–7
Oil line from turbocharger to crankcase 22mm wide across flats hollow bolt	29–36	Pulse sensor to engine (holder)	6–7
		Glow plugs	14–22
Water pump to crankcase	14–17	Temperature switch to fuel filter housing	22
Fan coupling to water pump nut with left-hand threads	36	Wire to glow plug	3–4
Fan to fan coupling	6–7	Fuel filter housing to holder	31–35
Pulley to water pump	6–7	Injection pump to holder, rear (nuts and bolts)	14–17
Thermostat housing	6–7	Injection pump to holder, front	14–17
Bleeder screw	4–7	Electric shut-off to injection pump	11–18
Temperature sensor/temperature switch	12–14	Electric valve from cold start accelerator to injection pump	11–14
Intake manifold to cylinder head	14–17	Injection pump gear to injection pump	33–36
Exhaust manifold to cylinder head (upper row of staybolts installed with Loctite 270)	14–17	Tensioning torque for tensioning roller holder	33–36
Turbocharger to exhaust manifold	17–20	Tensioning roller holder to engine (M8 nut and bolt)	18
Exhaust to turbocharger	31–35	Combination fuel injector in cylinder head	29–33
Pulley/vibration damper to vibration damper hub	16–17	Injection line (coupling nut)	14–18
Connecting rod bolts		Nozzle holder to injection pump	33
Step 1	14	Spill valve to injection pump (hollow bolt)	14–22
Step 2 (torque angle)	70°		

cooler lines at the radiator. On the four cylinder, remove the exhuast manifold shroud.

4. Remove the upper and lower radiator hoses and remove the radiator. If equipped with air conditioning, unbolt the compressor and position compressor out of way with refrigerant lines intact. Unbolt and lay the refrigerant condenser forward without disconnecting refrigerant lines.

NOTE: *If there is not enough slack in the refrigerant lines to position the compressor out of the way, the refrigerant in the system must be evacuated (using proper safety precautions) before the lines can be disconnected from the compressor.*

5. Remove the fan, fan belt and upper pulley. On models equipped with an electric cooling fan, disconnect the power lead and remove the fan and shroud as an assembly.

6. Disconnect the heater hoses from the engine. On four cylinder engines, disconnect the heater hose from the water pump and choke fittings.

7. Disconnect the alternator wires at the alternator, the starter cable at the starter, the accelerator rod at the carburetor.

8. Disconnect and plug the fuel tank line at the fuel pump on models equipped with fuel injection, de-pressurize the fuel system.

9. Disconnect the coil primary wire at the coil. Disconnect wires at the oil pressure and water temperature sending units. Disconnect the brake booster vacuum line, if so equipped.

10. Remove the starter and dust seal.

11. With manual transmission, remove the clutch retracting spring. Disconnect the clutch equalizer shaft and arm bracket at the underbody rail and remove the arm bracket and equalizer shaft.

12. Raise the car and safely support on jackstands. Remove the flywheel or converter housing upper retaining bolts.

13. Disconnect the exhaust pipe or pipes at the exhaust manifold. Disconnect the right and left motor mount at the underbody bracket. Remove the flywheel or converter housing cover. On models equipped, disconnect the engine roll dampner on the left front of the engine to frame.

14. On manual shift, remove the lower wheel housing bolts.

15. On automatic transmission, disconnect throttle valve vacuum line at the intake manifold and disconnect the converter from the flywheel. Remove the converter housing lower retaining bolts. On power steering, disconnect power steering pump from cylinder head. Remove the drive belt and wire steering pump out of the way. Do not disconnect the hoses.

16. Lower the car. Support the transmission and flywheel or converter housing with a jack.

17. Attach an engine lifting hook. Lift the engine up and out of the compartment and onto workstand.

18. Place a new gasket on exhaust pipe flange.

19. Attach engine sling and lifting device. Lift engine from workstand.

20. Lower the engine into the engine compartment. Be sure the exhaust manifold(s) is in proper alignment with the muffler inlet pipe(s),

and the dowels in the block engage the holes in the flywheel housing.

On a car with automatic transmission, start the converter pilot into the crankshaft make sure converter studs align with flexplate holes.

On manual transmission, start the transmission main drive gear into the clutch disc. If the engine hangs up after the shaft enters, rotate the crankshaft slowly (with transmission in gear) until the shaft and clutch disc splines mesh. Rotate 4 cyl. engines clockwise only, when viewed from the front.

21. Install the flywheel or converter housing upper bolts.

22. Install the engine support insulator to bracket retaining nuts. Disconnect the engine lifting sling and remove lifting brackets.

23. Raise the front of car. Connect the exhaust line/s and tighten attachments.

24. Install the starter.

25. On manual transmission, install remaining flywheel housing-to-engine bolts. Connect clutch release rod. Position the clutch equalizer bar and bracket, and install retaining bolts. Install clutch pedal retracting spring.

26. On automatic transmission, remove the retainer holding the converter in the housing. Attach the converter to the flywheel. Install the converter housing inspection cover and the remaining converter housing retaining bolts.

27. Remove the support from the transmission and lower the car.

28. Connect the engine ground strap and coil primary wire.

29. Connect the water temperature gauge wire and the heater hose at coolant outlet housing. Connect the accelerator rod at the bellcrank.

30. On automatic transmission, connect the transmission filler tube bracket. Connect the throttle valve vacuum line.

31. On power steering, install the drive belt and power steering pump bracket. Install the bracket retaining bolts. Adust the drive belt to proper tension.

32. Remove the plug from the fuel tank line. Connect the flexible fuel line and the oil pressure sending unit wire.

33. Install the pulley, belt, spacer, and fan. Adjust belt tension.

34. Tighten the alternator adjusting bolts. Connect the wires and the battery ground cable. On the four cylinder, install the exhaust manifold shroud.

35. Install the radiator. Connect radiator hoses. On air conditioned cars, install the compressor and condensor.

36. On automatic transmission, connect fluid cooler lines. On cars with power brakes, connect the brake booster line.

37. Install oil filter. Connect heater hose at water pump and carburetor choke (4 cyl.).

38. Bring the crankcase to level with correct grade of oil. Run the engine at fast idle and check for leaks. Install the air cleaner and make final engine adjustments.

39. Install and adjust hood.

2.4L Diesel Engine

1. Disconnect the negative battery cable.

2. Disconnect the wiring assembly for the engine underhood light.

3. Scribe hinge mark locations and remove the hood.

4. Drain the cooling system. Drain the engine oil.

5. Remove the air cleaner assembly.

6. Remove the fan shroud attaching bolts and remove the fan shroud. Remove the engine cooling fan assembly.

7. Remove upper and lower radiator hoses.

8. Disconnect the transmission oil cooler tubes from the radiator fittings.

9. Remove the radiator assembly.

10. Disconnect the muffler inlet pipe.

11. Label and disconnect the vacuum hoses and wiring harnesses.

12. Disconnect the engine oil cooler hoses.

13. Disconnect the accelerator cable at the fuel injection pump.

14. Disconnect the fuel line from the tank to fuel injection pump.

15. Disconnect the transmission gear shift linkage.

16. Disconnect the battery ground cable at engine.

17. Remove the coolant expansion bottle and position it out of the way.

18. Disconnect the heater hoses at the dash panel (firewall).

19. Disconnect the wire to A/C compressor clutch.

20. Disconnect the power steering pump hose(s).

21. Disconnect the fuel line to the injectors.

22. Disconnect the wiring harness to instrument panel. Disconnect engine ground leads.

23. Install an engine support Tool D79F-6000-A or equivalent (bar and "J" hook or chain).

24. Raise the vehicle and safely support on jackstands.

25. Remove the muffler inlet pipe.

26. Remove the lower engine oil cooler bracket and brace.

27. Remove the stabilizer bar, bracket retaining bolts and position forward.

28. Remove the left hand front fender splash shield.

29. Disconnect the steering gear input shaft to steering column shaft coupling.

30. Remove the retainer nuts to the engine insulator supports.

31. Position a jack under the engine. Raise the engine assembly. Position the steering gear out of the way.

32. Lower the engine assembly.

33. Remove the converter housing access cover.

34. Remove the converter assembly retainer nuts.

35. Insert a pair of locking pliers in the converter housing to hold the converter in place during engine removal.

NOTE: *Make sure that the upper jaw of the locking pliers contacts the converter while clamped to the converter housing. This will apply adequate pressure on the converter to prevent separation during engine movements and removal.*

36. Remove No. 3 crossmember retainer nuts.

37. Remove the transmission gear shift lever bellcrank.

38. Raise the transmission.

39. Remove No. 3 crossmember retainer bolts. Lower the transmission.

40. Remove engine to transmission converter housing retainer bolts.

41. Install crossmember (No. 3) retainer bolts.

42. Lower the vehicle.

43. Install engine lifting equipment.

44. Remove the engine support Tool D79T-6000-A or equivalent.

45. Remove the engine assembly.

46. Position engine and install on engine work stand and service as necessary.

47. Install engine lifting equipment. Raise the engine and install in vehicle.

48. Install engine support Tool D79T-6000-A or equivalent.

49. Remove the engine lifting equipment. Raise vehicle and safely support on jackstands.

50. The remainder of the installation procedure is in reverse order of removal.

Valve Rocker Arm Cover

REMOVAL AND INSTALLATION

2.3L 4 Cylinder Engine
6 Cylinder In-Line Engines

1. Remove the air cleaner assembly and mounting brackets.

2. Label for identification and remove all wires and vacuum hoses interfering with valve cover removal. Remove the PCV valve with hose. Remove the accelerator control cable bracket if necessary.

NOTE: *4 Cylinder Turbocharged models require removal of the air intake tube and air throttle body. Refer to the "Fuel Injection" section of Chapter 4 for procedures.*

3. Remove the valve cover retaining bolts. On four cylinder models, the front bolts equipped with rubber sealing washers must be installed in the same location to prevent oil leakage.

4. Remove the valve cover. Clean all old gasket material from the valve cover and cylinder head gasket surfaces.

5 Install in reverse order of removal. Use oil resistant sealing compound and a new valve cover gasket. When installing the valve cover gasket, make sure all the gasket locating tangs are engaged into the cover notches provided.

V6 and V8 Engines

NOTE: *When disconnecting wires and vacuum lines, label them for reinstallation identification.*

1. Remove the air cleaner assembly.
2. On the right side;
   a. Disconnect the automatic choke heat chamber hose from the inlet tube near the right valve cover if equipped.
   b. Remove the automatic choke heat tube if equipped and remove the PCV valve and hose from the valve cover. Disconnect EGR valve hoses.
   c. Remove the thermactor bypass valve and air supply hoses as necessary to gain clearance.
   d. Disconnect the spark plug wires from the plugs with a twisting pulling motion; twist and pull on the boots only, never on the wire; position the wires and mounting bracket out of the way.
   e. Remove the valve cover mounting bolts; remove the valve cover.
3. On the left side;
   a. Remove the spark plug wires and bracket.
   b. Remove the wiring harness and any vacuum hoses from the bracket.
   c. Remove the valve cover mounting bolts and valve cover.
4. Clean all old gasket material from the valve cover and cylinder head mounting surfaces.
NOTE: *Some V6 engines do not use valve cover gaskets in product. Scrape away old RTV sealant and clean covers. Spread an even bead 3/16" wide of RTV sealant on the valve covers and reinstall, or install with gaskets.*
5. Installation is in reverse order of removal. Use oil resistant sealing compound and a new valve cover gasket. When installing the valve cover gasket, make sure all the gasket tangs are engaged into the cover notches provided.

2.4L Diesel Engine

1. Loosen the turbocharger crossover pipe boot clamps and remove the crossover pipe.
2. Disconnect the vacuum pump hose. Disconnect the breather hose.
3. Remove the oil trap. Remove the threaded sleeves that attach the rocker cover to the cylinder head. Remove the cover.
4. Inspect the cover gasket and vacuum pump mounting O-ring. Install a new gasket and O-ring if necessary. Clean all gasket mounting surfaces.
5. Install gasket and O-ring in position. Install cover after making sure the half-moon seal is fully seated in the cylinder head.
6. Tighten retainers to 10–12 ft. lbs.
7. Connect the oil trap, breather hose, vacuum hose and turbocharger crossover pipe.
8. Run the engine and check for oil and intake air leaks.

Rocker Arm (Cam Follower) and Hydraulic Lash Adjuster
REMOVAL AND INSTALLATION
Four Cylinder 140 Cu In. Engine

NOTE: *A special tool is required to compress the lash adjuster.*

1. Remove the valve cover and associated parts as required.
2. Rotate the camshaft so that the base circle of the cam is against the cam follower you intend to remove.
3. Remove the retaining spring from the cam follower, if so equipped.
4. Using special tool T74P-6565-B or a valve spring compressor tool, collapse the lash adjuster and/or depress the valve spring, as neces-

4-140 valve lash adjustment

sary, and slide the cam follower over the lash adjuster and out from under the camshaft.

5. Install the cam follower in the reverse order of removal. Make sure that the lash adjuster is collapsed and released before rotating the camshaft.

Rocker Arm Shaft/Rocker Arms
REMOVAL AND INSTALLATION
6 Cylinder In-Line Engines

1. Remove the rocker arm (valve) cover (see previous section).

2. Remove the rocker arm shaft mounting bolts, two turns at a time for each bolt. Start at the ends of the rocker shaft and work toward the middle.

3. Lift the rocker arm shaft assembly from the engine. Remove the pin and washer from each end of the shaft. Slide the rocker arms,

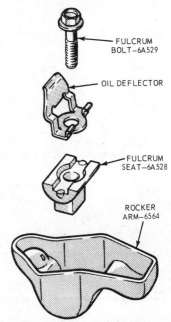

Rocker arm and related parts—351C, 351M, 400, 460 and 1972–73 429 V8

springs and supports off the shaft. Keep all parts in order or label them for position.

4. Clean and inspect all parts, replace as necessary.

5. Assemble the rocker shaft parts in reverse order of removal. Be sure the oil holes in the shaft are pointed downward. Reinstall the rocker shaft assembly on the engine.

NOTE: *Lubricate all parts with motor oil before installation.*

V6 and V8 Engines

1. Right side
   a. disconnect the automatic choke heat chamber air inlet hose.

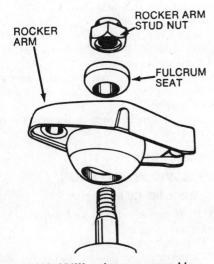

1971–78 302, 351W rocker arm assembly

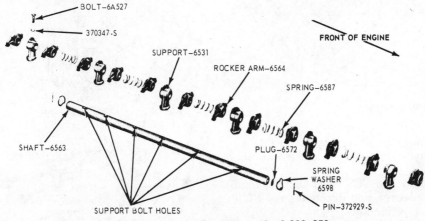

Rocker arm shaft assembly on the 6-200, 250

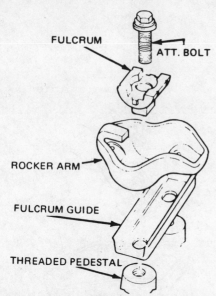

FULCRUM

ATT. BOLT

ROCKER ARM

FULCRUM GUIDE

THREADED PEDESTAL

1978–82 255, 302, 351W rocker arm assembly

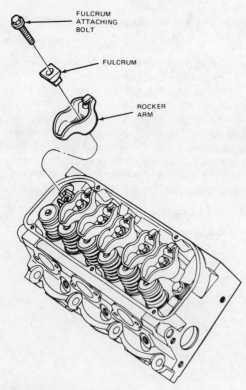

FULCRUM
ATTACHING
BOLT

FULCRUM

ROCKER
ARM

V6 rocker arm assembly

b. remove the air cleaner and duct.

c. remove the automatic choke heat tube (232, 302).

d. remove the PCV fresh air tube from the rocker cover, and disconnect the EGR vacuum amplifier hoses.

2. Remove the Thermactor by-pass valve and air supply hoses.

3. Disconnect the spark plug wires.

4. On the left side:

a. remove the wiring harness from the clips.

b. remove the rocker arm cover.

5. Remove the rocker arm stud nut or bolt, fulcrum seat and rocker arm.

6. Lubricate all parts with heavy SE oil before installation. When installing, rotate the crankshaft until the lifter is on the base of the cam circle (all the way down) and assemble the rocker arm. Torque the nut or bolt to 17–23 ft. lb.

NOTE: *Some later engines are using RTV sealant instead of valve cover gaskets.*

2.4L Diesel Engine

1. Disconnect the negative battery cable. Remove the valve cover and vacuum pump.

2. Rotate the engine until the base circle (heel) of the cam lobe for the rocker arm being removed is facing the rocker arm.

3. Remove the spring clip retaining the rocker arm. Compress the valve spring slightly using tool T84P6513C or the equivalent and remove the rocker arm.

CAUTION: *Be sure that the valve keys remain in position when slightly compressing the valve spring.*

4. Install the rocker arm in the reverse order of removal.

Intake Manifold

REMOVAL AND INSTALLATION

Four Cylinder 140 Cu In. Engine

NOTE: *If fuel-injected model, refer to the illustration provided.*

1. Drain the cooling system.

2. Remove the air cleaner and disconnect the throttle linkage from the carburetor.

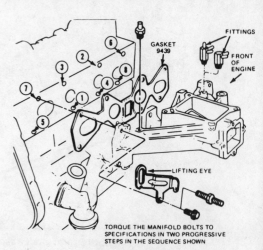

FITTINGS

GASKET
9439

FRONT
OF
ENGINE

LIFTING EYE

TORQUE THE MANIFOLD BOLTS TO
SPECIFICATIONS IN TWO PROGRESSIVE
STEPS IN THE SEQUENCE SHOWN

4-140 intake manifold installation

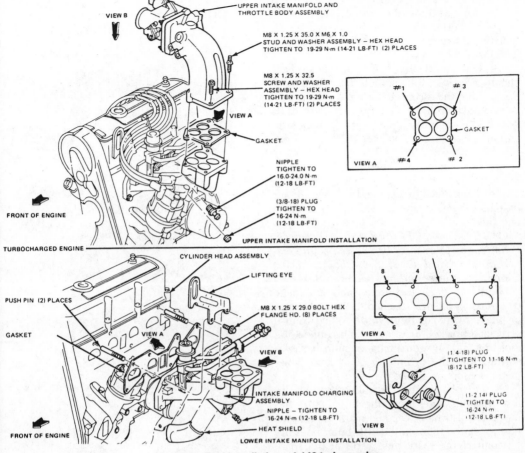

Intake manifold installation—4-140 turbo engine

3. Disconnect the fuel and vacuum lines from the carburetor.

4. Disconnect the carburetor solenoid wire at the quick-disconnect.

5. Remove the choke water housing and thermostatic spring from the carburetor.

6. Disconnect the water outlet and crankcase ventilation hoses from the intake manifold.

7. Disconnect the deceleration valve-to-carburetor hose (if equipped) at the carburetor.

8. Start from each end; work toward the middle; remove the intake manifold attaching bolts and remove the manifold.

9. Clean all old gasket material from the manifold and cylinder head.

10. Apply water-resistant sealer to the intake manifold gasket and position it on the cylinder head.

11. Install the intake manifold attaching nuts. Follow the sequence given in the illustrations.

12. Connect the water and crankcase ventilation hoses to the intake manifold.

13. Connect the deceleration valve-to-carburetor hose to the carburetor.

14. Position the choke water housing and thermostatic spring on the carburetor and engage the end of the spring coil in the slot and the choke adjusting lever. Align the tab on the spring housing. Tighten the choke water housing attaching screws.

15. Connect the carburetor solenoid wire.

16. Connect the fuel and vacuum lines to the carburetor.

17. Connect the throttle linkage to the carburetor.

18. Install the air cleaner and fill the cooling system.

Six Cylinder In-Line Engines

On six cylinder in-line engines, the intake manifold is integral with the cylinder head and cannot be removed.

V6 and V8 Engines

1. Drain the cooling system and disconnect the negative battery cable. Remove the air cleaner assembly.

2. Disconnect the upper radiator hose and water pump by-pass hose from the thermostat

housing and/or intake manifold. Disconnect the temperature sending unit wire connector. Remove the heater hose from the choke housing bracket and disconnect the hose from the intake manifold.

3. Disconnect the automatic choke heat chamber air inlet tube and electric wiring connector from the carburetor. Remove the crankcase ventilation hose, vacuum hoses and EGR hose and coolant lines (if equipped). Label the various hoses and wiring for reinstallation identification.

4. Disconnect the Thermactor air supply hose at the check valve. Loosen the hose clamp at the check valve bracket and remove the air by-pass valve from the bracket and position to one side.

CAUTION: *On CFI (fuel injected) engines. System pressure must be released before disconnecting fuel lines. See Chapter 4 for pressure release and fuel line procedures.*

5. Remove all carburetor and automatic transmission linkage attached to the carburetor or intake manifold. Remove the speed control servo and bracket, if equipped. Disconnect the fuel line and any remaining vacuum hoses or wiring from the carburetor, CFI unit, solenoids, sensors, or intake manifold.

6. On V8 engines, disconnect the distributor vacuum hoses from the distributor. Remove the distributor cap and mark the relative position of the rotor on the distributor housing. Disconnect the spark plug wires at the spark plugs and the wiring connector at the distributor. Remove the distributor hold-down bolt and remove the distributor. (See "Distributor Removal and Installation).

NOTE: *Distributor removal is not necessary on V6 engines.*

7. If your car is equipped with air conditioning and the compressor or mounting brackets interfere with manifold removal; remove the brackets and compressor and position out of the way. Do not disconnect any compressor lines.

8. Remove the intake manifold mounting bolts. Lift off the intake manifold and carburetor or CFI unit as an assembly.

NOTE: *The manifold on V6 engines is sealed at each end with an RTV type sealer. If prying at the front of the manifold is necessary to break the seal, take care not to damage the machined surfaces.*

9. Clean all gasket mounting surfaces. V6 engines have aluminum cylinder heads and intake manifold; exercise care when cleaning the old gasket material or RTV sealant from the machined surfaces.

10. Installation is in the reverse order of removal.

11. End seals are not used on V6 engines.

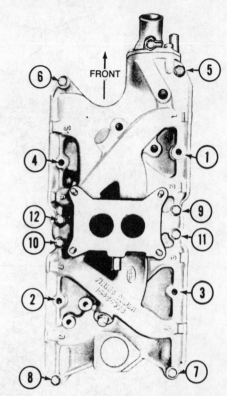

Intake manifold bolt torque sequence on the 8-255 and 302

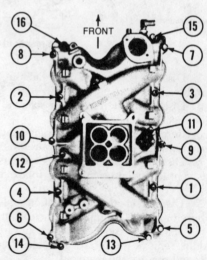

Intake manifold bolt tightening sequence—429 and 460 V8

Apply a ⅛ inch bead of RTV sealant at each end of the engine where the intake manifold seats. Install the intake gaskets and the manifold.

12. On V8 engines, make sure the intake gaskets interlock with the end seals. Use silicone rubber sealer (RTV) on the end seals.

13. After installing the intake manifold, run

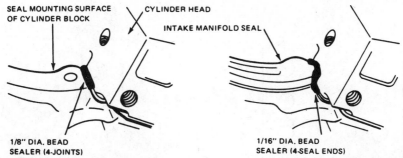

Sealer application area for intake manifold installation on all V8s except the 460

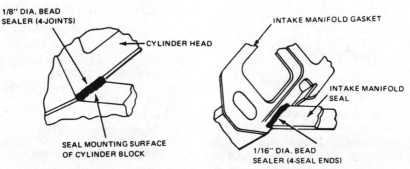

Sealer application area for intake manifold installation on the 8-460

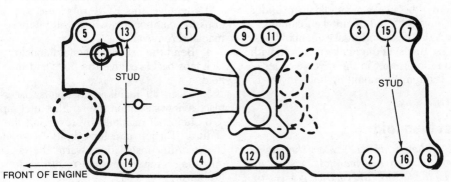

Intake manifold bolt tightening sequence—351W V8

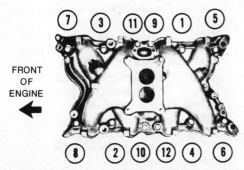

Intake manifold bolt tightening sequence—351C, 351M, 400 V8

a finger along the manifold ends to spread the RTV sealer and to make sure the end seals have not slipped out of place.

14. Torque the manifold mounting bolts to the required specifications in the proper sequence. Recheck the torque after the engine has reached normal operating temperature.

2.4L Diesel Engine

1. Disconnect the negative battery cable.
2. Remove the diagnostic plug bracket and position it out of the way. Disconnect the turbocharger boost pressure indicator connector.
3. Disconnect the engine oil dipstick tube

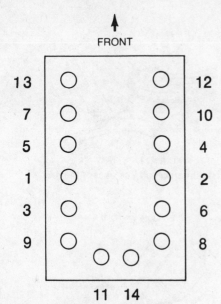

FRONT

V6 intake manifold torque sequence

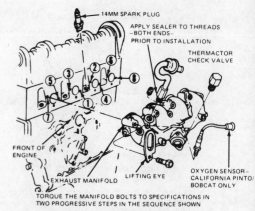

14MM SPARK PLUG
APPLY SEALER TO THREADS
–BOTH ENDS–
PRIOR TO INSTALLATION
THERMACTOR
CHECK VALVE
FRONT OF
ENGINE
EXHAUST MANIFOLD   LIFTING EYE
OXYGEN SENSOR–
CALIFORNIA PINTO/
BOBCAT ONLY
TORQUE THE MANIFOLD BOLTS TO SPECIFICATIONS IN
TWO PROGRESSIVE STEPS IN THE SEQUENCE SHOWN

4-140 exhaust manifold torque sequence

clamp from the intake manifold and position the dipstick out of the way. Disconnect and label hoses, lines and cables interfering with manifold removal. (See Chapter 4). Loosen the turbocharger air crossover pipe boot clamps and disconnect.

4. Remove the intake manifold to cylinder head attaching bolts and the intake manifold.

5. Clean the head and intake manifold gasket surfaces. Reinstall the intake manifold with a new mounting gasket in the reverse order of removal. Tighten the mounting bolts to 14–17 ft. lbs.

Exhaust Manifold

NOTE: *Although, in most cases, the engine does not have exhaust manifold gaskets installed by the factory, aftermarket gaskets are available from parts stores.*

REMOVAL AND INSTALLATION
Four Cylinder 140 Cu In. Engine

1. Remove the air cleaner.
2. Remove the heat shroud from the exhaust manifold. On turbocharged models, remove the turbocharger.
3. Place a block of wood under the exhaust pipe and disconnect the exhaust pipe from the exhaust manifold.
4. Remove the exhaust manifold attaching nuts and remove the manifold.
5. Install a light coat of graphite grease on the exhaust manifold mating surface and position the manifold on the cylinder head.
6. Install the exhaust manifold attaching nuts

and tighten them in the sequence shown in the illustration to 12–15 ft. lbs.

7. Connect the exhaust pipe to the exhaust manifold and remove the wood support from under the pipe.

8. Install the air cleaner.

Six Cylinder In-Line Engines

1. Remove the air cleaner and heat duct body.
2. Disconnect the muffler inlet pipe and remove the choke hot air tube from the manifold.
3. Remove the EGR tube and any other emission components which will interfere with manifold removal.
4. Bend the exhaust manifold attaching bolt lock tabs back, remove the bolts and the manifold.
5. Clean all manifold mating surfaces and place a new gasket on the muffler inlet pipe.
6. Reinstall manifold by reversing the procedure. Torque attaching bolts in sequence shown. After installation, warm the engine to operating temperature and re-torque to specifications.

V6, V8 Engines

1. If removing the right side exhaust manifold, remove the air cleaner and related parts and the heat stove, if so equipped.
2. On 351M and 400 engines: if the left exhaust manifold is being removed, first drain the engine oil and remove the oil filter. On some models (232, 255, 302 engines) dipstick and tube removal may be required. Remove and speed control brackets that interfere.
3. Disconnect the exhaust manifold(s) from the muffler (or converter) inlet pipe(s).

NOTE: *On certain vehicles with automatic transmission and column shift it may be necessary to disconnect the selector lever cross shaft for clearance.*

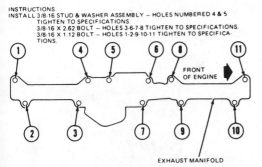

INSTRUCTIONS
INSTALL 3/8-16 STUD & WASHER ASSEMBLY — HOLES NUMBERED 4 & 5
TIGHTEN TO SPECIFICATIONS.
3/8-16 X 2.62 BOLT — HOLES 3-6-7-8 TIGHTEN TO SPECIFICATIONS.
3/8-16 X 1.12 BOLT — HOLES 1-2-9-10-11 TIGHTEN TO SPECIFICA-
TIONS.

FRONT
OF ENGINE

EXHAUST MANIFOLD

6-200, 250 exhaust manifold torque sequence

4. Disconnect the spark plug wires and re-move the spark plugs and heat shields. Disconnect the EGO sensor (models equipped), and heat control valve vacuum line (models equipped).

NOTE: *On some engines the spark plug wire heat shields are removed with the manifold. Transmission dipstick tube and thermactor air tube removal may be required on certain models. Air tube removal is possible by cutting the tube clamp at the converter.*

5. Remove the exhaust manifold attaching bolts and washers, and remove the manifold(s).

6. Inspect the manifold(s) for damaged gasket surfaces, cracks, or other defects.

7. Clean the mating surfaces of the manifold(s), cylinder head and muffler inlet pipe(s).

8. Install the manifold(s) in reverse order of removal. Torque the mounting bolts to the value listed in the "Torque Specifications" chart. Start with the centermost bolt and work outward in both directions.

NOTE: *Slight warpage may occur on V6 manifolds. Elongate the holes in the manifold as necessary. Do not, however, elongate the lower front No. 5 cylinder hole on the left side, nor the lower rear No. 2 cylinder hole on the right side. These holes are used as alignment pilots.*

2.4L Diesel Engine

1. Disconnect the battery ground cable.
2. Disconnect the muffler inlet pipe at the turbo outlet and cap turbo outlet.
3. Disconnect the EGR valve vacuum line.
4. Disconnect the inlet duct at turbo and cap turbo inlet.
5. Loosen the clamp at the turbo crossover pipe boot.
6. Remove the clamp attaching the turbo oil feed tube to the oil return tube.
7. Remove the bolts attaching the oil feed tube to the turbo.

CAUTION: *Cap the oil feed tube and oil feed inlet port on the turbo, to prevent contamination of the turbo oiling system.*

8. Disconnect the oil return line from the turbo oil drain port.

CAUTION: *Cap the oil return line and the oil return port on the turbo, to prevent contamination of the turbo oiling system.*

9. Remove the bolts attaching the exhaust manifold to the cylinder head and remove the exhaust manifold and turbo as an assembly. Cap turbo outlet to crossover pipe.

10. Clean the exhaust manifold and cylinder head gasket mating surfaces.

11. Install the exhaust manifold, with a new gasket, making sure the turbo outlet is installed in crossover pipe boot. Tighten bolts to 14–17 ft. lbs., and tighten the crossover pipe boot clamp.

12. Remove the caps and install the oil feed line, with a new gasket, on the turbo oil inlet port. Tighten bolts to 14–17 ft. lbs.

13. Remove the caps and connect the oil return line to the turbo oil return port. Tighten fitting 29–36 ft. lbs.

14. Install the oil feed tube to the exhaust manifold clamp and tighten to 6.5–7 ft. lbs.

15. Remove the cap and connect the inlet duct to the turbo inlet.

16. Remove the cap and connect the muffler inlet pipe to the turbo exhaust outlet. Tighten bolts to 31–35 ft. lbs.

17. Connect the EGR valve vacuum line.

18. Connect the battery ground cable.

19. Run the engine and check for intake, exhaust and oil leaks.

Turbocharger

NOTE: *The turbocharger is serviced by replacement only.*

REMOVAL AND INSTALLATION

NOTE: *Before starting removal/service procedures, clean the area around the turbocharger with a non-caustic solution. Cover the openings of component connections to prevent entry of dirt and foreign materials. Exercise care when handling the turbocharger not to nick, bend or in any way damage the compressor wheel blades.*

Except Diesel Engine

1. Disconnect the negative battery cable.
2. Drain the cooling system.
3. Loosen the upper clamp on the turbocharger inlet hose. Remove the two bolts mounting the throttle body discharge tube to the turbo.
4. Label for identification and location all vacuum hoses and tubes to the turbo and disconnect them.
5. Disconnect the PCV tube from the turbo

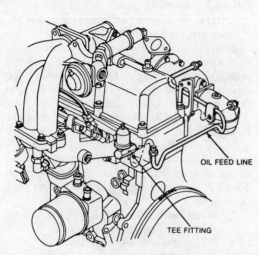

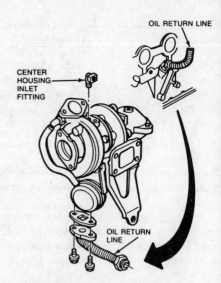

Turbo oil supply and return lines—4-140 engine

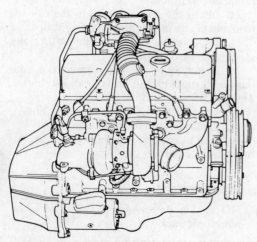

4-140 turbocharger installation

air inlet elbow. Remove the throttle body discharge tube and hose as an assembly.

6. Disconnect the ground wire from the air inlet elbow. Remove (disconnect) the water outlet connection (and fitting if a new turbo unit is to be installed) from the turbo center housing.

7. Remove the turbo oil supply feed line. Disconnect the oxygen sensor connector at the turbocharger.

8. Raise and support the front of the vehicle on jackstands. Disconnect the exhaust pipe from the turbocharger.

9. Disconnect the oil return line from the bottom of the turbocharger. Take care not to damage or kink the line.

10. Disconnect the water inlet tube at the turbo center housing.

11. Remove the lower turbo mounting

bracket to engine bolt. Lower the vehicle from the stands.

12. Remove the lower front mounting nut. Remove the three remaining mounting nuts evenly while sliding the turbocharger away from mounting.

13. Position a new turbocharger mounting gasket in position with the bead side facing outward. Install the turbocharger in position over the four mounting studs.

14. Position the lower mounting bracket over the two bottom studs. Using new nuts, start the two lower then the two upper mountings. Do not tighten completely at this time, allow for slight turbo movement.

15. Raise and support the front of the vehicle on jackstands.

16. Install and tighten the lower bracket to engine mounting bolt to 28–40 ft. lbs.

17. Position a new oil return line gasket and connect the return line. Tighten the mounting bolts to 14–21 ft. lbs.

18. Connect the water inlet tube assembly. Install the exhaust pipe to turbo. Tighten the mounting nuts to 25–35 ft. lbs.

19. Lower the vehicle. Tighten the turbo mounting nuts to 28–40 ft. lbs.

20. Connect the water outlet assembly to the turbocharger, tighten to 11–14 ft. lbs. Hold the fitting with a wrench when tightening the line.

21. Install the air inlet tube to the turbo inlet elbow (15–22 ft. lbs.). Tighten the clamp.

22. Connect the PCV tube and all vacuum lines.

23. Connect the oxygen sensor and other wiring and lines.

24. Connect the oil supply line. Connect the intake tube. Fill the cooling system.

25. Connect the negative battery cable. Start the engine and check for coolant leaks. Check vehicle operation.

NOTE: *When installing the turbocharger, or after an oil and filter change, disconnect the distributor feed harness and crank the engine with the starter motor until the oil pressure light on the dash goes out. Oil pressure must be up before starting the engine.*

2.4L Diesel Engine

CAUTION: *Do not accelerate the engine before engine oil pressure has been built up. Also do not switch off the engine while it is running at high speed (the turbocharger will continue to spin for a long time without oil pressure). These conditions can damage the engine and/or turbocharger.*

1. Remove the two bolts attaching the exhaust pipe to the turbocharger.
2. Remove the EGR tube and clamps.
3. Loosen the four hose clamps on the crossover tube and then remove tube.
4. Remove the air cleaner assembly and bellows. Cap turbocharger openings.
5. Remove the two oil supply line bolts on top of the turbocharger center housing.
6. Remove the clamp from oil lines.
7. Remove the oil return line.
8. Remove the bolt and sealing washers attaching the oil supply line to oil filter housing.
9. Disconnect and remove the EGR valve.
10. Remove the four bolts attaching the turbocharger to the exhaust manifold and remove the turbocharger.
11. Clean the mating surfaces of the turbocharger and exhaust manifold.
12. Position the turbocharger on the exhaust manifold and install the four mounting bolts. Tighten to 17–20 ft. lbs.
13. Install the EGR valve. Tighten to 18 ft. lbs.
14. Install the oil supply line using new seals. Tighten the bolt to 26–33 ft. lbs.
CAUTION: *Do not overtighten bolt. Oil leaks may occur if overtightened.*
15. Install the clamp retaining the oil lines.
16. Install the oil supply line bolts to the turbocharger housing and tighten to 15–18 ft. lbs.
17. Remove the protective caps from the turbocharger and install the air cleaner assembly and bellows.
18. Install the crossover tube. Tighten the hose clamps sung.
19. Install the EGR tube clamp.
20. Install the two bolts attaching the exhaust pipe to the turbocharger and tighten to 17–20 ft. lbs.

21. Run the engine and check for oil and air leaks.

Torque Specs

	Ft. Lbs. (in. lbs.)
EGR Valve	18
Hose Clamps	(15–22)
Oil Supply Line:	
To Turbo	15–18
To Engine Block	26–33
Oil Return Line—To Turbo	15–18
Turbocharger-to-Exhaust Manifold	17–20
Turbocharger-to-Exhaust Pipe	17–20

Cylinder Head
REMOVAL AND INSTALLATION

NOTE: *On cars with air conditioning, remove the mounting bolts and the drive belt, and position the compressor out of the way. Remove the compressor upper mounting bracket from the cylinder head.*
CAUTION: *If the compressor refrigerant lines do not have enough slack to permit repositioning of the compressor without first disconnecting the refrigerant lines, the air conditioning system will have to be evacuated by a trained air conditioning serviceman. Under no circumstances should an untrained person attempt to disconnect the air conditioning refrigerant lines.*

4 Cylinder 140 Engine

NOTE: *Set the engine to TDC position for No. 1 piston, if possible prior to head removal.*

1. Drain the cooling system.
2. Remove the air cleaner. Disconnect the negative battery cable.
3. Remove the valve cover. Note the location of the valve cover attaching screws that have rubber grommets.
4. Remove the intake and exhaust manifolds from the head. See the procedures for intake manifold, exhaust manifold, and turbocharger removal.
5. Remove the camshaft drive belt cover. Note the location of the belt cover attaching screws that have rubber grommets.
6. Loosen the drive belt tensioner and remove the belt.
7. Remove the water outlet elbow from the cylinder head with the hose attached.
8. Remove the cylinder head attaching bolts.
9. Remove the cylinder head from the engine.
10. Clean all gasket material and carbon from

ENGINE OVERHAUL

Most engine overhaul procedures are fairly standard. In addition to specific parts replacement procedures and complete specifications for your individual engine, this chapter also is a guide to accepted rebuilding procedures. Examples of standard rebuilding practice are shown and should be used along with specific details concerning your particular engine.

Competent and accurate machine shop services will ensure maximum performance, reliability and engine life. Procedures marked with the symbol shown above should be performed by a competent machine shop, and are provided so that you will be familiar with the procedures necessary to a successful overhaul.

In most instances it is more profitable for the do-it-yourself mechanic to remove, clean and inspect the component, buy the necessary parts and deliver these to a shop for actual machine work.

On the other hand, much of the rebuilding work (crankshaft, block, bearings, pistons, rods, and other components) is well within the scope of the do-it-yourself mechanic.

Tools

The tools required for an engine overhaul or parts replacement will depend on the depth of your involvement. With a few exceptions, they will be the tools found in a mechanic's tool kit (see Chapter 1). More in-depth work will require any or all of the following:
• a dial indicator (reading in thousandths) mounted on a universal base
• micrometers and telescope gauges
• jaw and screw-type pullers
• scraper
• valve spring compressor
• ring groove cleaner
• piston ring expander and compressor
• ridge reamer
• cylinder hone or glaze breaker

• Plastigage®
• engine stand

Use of most of these tools is illustrated in this chapter. Many can be rented for a one-time use from a local parts jobber or tool supply house specializing in automotive work.

Occasionally, the use of special tools is called for. See the information on Special Tools and the Safety Notice in the front of this book before substituting another tool.

Inspection Techniques

Procedures and specifications are given in this chapter for inspecting, cleaning and assessing the wear limits of most major components. Other procedures such as Magnaflux and Zyglo can be used to locate material flaws and stress cracks. Magnaflux is a magnetic process applicable only to ferrous materials. The Zyglo process coats the material with a flourescent dye penetrant and can be used on any material. Check for suspected surface cracks can be more readily made using spot check dye. The dye is sprayed onto the suspected area, wiped off and the area sprayed with a developer. Cracks will show up brightly.

Overhaul Tips

Aluminum has become extremely popular for use in engines, due to its low weight. Observe the following precautions when handling aluminum parts:
• Never hot tank aluminum parts (the caustic hot-tank solution will eat the aluminum)
• Remove all aluminum parts (identification tag, etc.) from engine parts prior to hot-tanking.
• Always coat threads lightly with engine oil or anti-seize compounds before installation, to prevent seizure.
• Never over-torque bolts or spark plugs, especially in aluminum threads.

Stripped threads in any component can be repaired using any of several commercial repair kits (Heli-Coil, Microdot, Keenserts, etc.)

When assembling the engine, any parts that will be in frictional contact must be pre-lubed to provide lubrication at initial start-up. Any product specifically formulated for this purpose can be used, but engine oil is not recommended as a pre-lube.

When semi-permanent (locked, but removable) installation of bolts or nuts is desired, threads should be cleaned and coated with Loctite® or other similar, commercial non-hardening sealant.

Repairing Damaged Threads

Several methods of repairing damaged threads are available. Heli-Coil® (shown here), Keenserts® and Microdot® are among the most widely used. All involve basically the same principle—drilling out stripped threads, tapping the hole and installing a pre-wound insert—making welding, plugging and oversize fasteners unnecessary.

Two types of thread repair inserts are usually supplied—a standard type for most Inch Coarse, Inch Fine, Metric Coarse and Metric Fine thread sizes and a spark plug type to fit most spark plug port sizes. Consult the individual manufacturer's catalog to determine exact applications. Typical thread repair kits will contain a selection of pre-wound threaded inserts, a tap (corresponding to the outside diameter threads of the insert) and an installation tool. Spark plug inserts usually differ because they require a tap equipped with pilot threads and a combined reamer/tap section. Most manufacturers also supply blister-packed thread repair inserts separately in addition to a master kit containing a variety of taps and inserts plus installation tools.

Before effecting a repair to a threaded hole, remove any snapped, broken or damaged bolts or studs. Penetrating oil can be used to free frozen threads; the offending item can be removed with locking pliers or with a screw or stud extractor. After the hole is clear, the thread can be repaired, as follows:

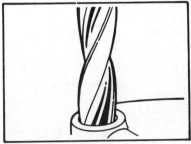

Drill out the damaged threads with specified drill. Drill completely through the hole or to the bottom of a blind hole

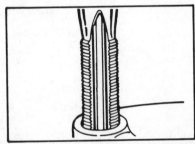

With the tap supplied, tap the hole to receive the thread insert. Keep the tap well oiled and back it out frequently to avoid clogging the threads

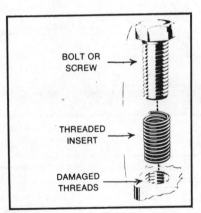

Damaged bolt holes can be repaired with thread repair inserts

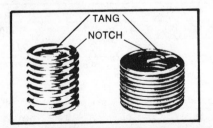

Standard thread repair insert (left) and spark plug thread insert (right)

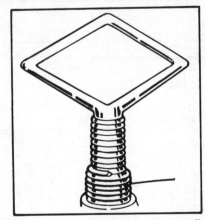

Screw the threaded insert onto the installation tool until the tang engages the slot. Screw the insert into the tapped hole until it is ¼–½ turn below the top surface. After installation break off the tang with a hammer and punch

Standard Torque Specifications and Fastener Markings

In the absence of specific torques, the following chart can be used as a guide to the maximum safe torque of a particular size/grade of fastener.

- There is no torque difference for fine or coarse threads.
- Torque values are based on clean, dry threads. Reduce the value by 10% if threads are oiled prior to assembly.
- The torque required for aluminum components or fasteners is considerably less.

U.S. Bolts

SAE Grade Number	1 or 2			5			6 or 7		
Number of lines always 2 less than the grade number.									
Bolt Size (Inches)—(Thread)	Maximum Torque			Maximum Torque			Maximum Torque		
	Ft./Lbs.	Kgm	Nm	Ft./Lbs.	Kgm	Nm	Ft./Lbs.	Kgm	Nm
¼—20	5	0.7	6.8	8	1.1	10.8	10	1.4	13.5
—28	6	0.8	8.1	10	1.4	13.6			
⁵⁄₁₆—18	11	1.5	14.9	17	2.3	23.0	19	2.6	25.8
—24	13	1.8	17.6	19	2.6	25.7			
⅜—16	18	2.5	24.4	31	4.3	42.0	34	4.7	46.0
—24	20	2.75	27.1	35	4.8	47.5			
⁷⁄₁₆—14	28	3.8	37.0	49	6.8	66.4	55	7.6	74.5
—20	30	4.2	40.7	55	7.6	74.5			
½—13	39	5.4	52.8	75	10.4	101.7	85	11.75	115.2
—20	41	5.7	55.6	85	11.7	115.2			
⁹⁄₁₆—12	51	7.0	69.2	110	15.2	149.1	120	16.6	162.7
—18	55	7.6	74.5	120	16.6	162.7			
⅝—11	83	11.5	112.5	150	20.7	203.3	167	23.0	226.5
—18	95	13.1	128.8	170	23.5	230.5			
¾—10	105	14.5	142.3	270	37.3	366.0	280	38.7	379.6
—16	115	15.9	155.9	295	40.8	400.0			
⅞—9	160	22.1	216.9	395	54.6	535.5	440	60.9	596.5
—14	175	24.2	237.2	435	60.1	589.7			
1—8	236	32.5	318.6	590	81.6	799.9	660	91.3	894.8
—14	250	34.6	338.9	660	91.3	849.8			

Metric Bolts

Relative Strength Marking	4.6, 4.8			8.8		
Bolt Markings						
Bolt Size Thread Size x Pitch (mm)	Maximum Torque			Maximum Torque		
	Ft./Lbs.	Kgm	Nm	Ft./Lbs.	Kgm	Nm
6 x 1.0	2–3	.2–.4	3–4	3–6	.4–.8	5–8
8 x 1.25	6–8	.8–1	8–12	9–14	1.2–1.9	13–19
10 x 1.25	12–17	1.5–2.3	16–23	20–29	2.7–4.0	27–39
12 x 1.25	21–32	2.9–4.4	29–43	35–53	4.8–7.3	47–72
14 x 1.5	35–52	4.8–7.1	48–70	57–85	7.8–11.7	77–110
16 x 1.5	51–77	7.0–10.6	67–100	90–120	12.4–16.5	130–160
18 x 1.5	74–110	10.2–15.1	100–150	130–170	17.9–23.4	180–230
20 x 1.5	110–140	15.1–19.3	150–190	190–240	26.2–46.9	160–320
22 x 1.5	150–190	22.0–26.2	200–260	250–320	34.5–44.1	340–430
24 x 1.5	190–240	26.2–46.9	260–320	310–410	42.7–56.5	420–550

CHECKING ENGINE COMPRESSION

A noticeable lack of engine power, excessive oil consumption and/or poor fuel mileage measured over an extended period are all indicators of internal engine wear. Worn piston rings, scored or worn cylinder bores, blown head gaskets, sticking or burnt valves and worn valve seats are all possible culprits here. A check of each cylinder's compression will help you locate the problems.

As mentioned in the "Tools and Equipment" section of Chapter 1, a screw-in type compression gauge is more accurate than the type you simply hold against the spark plug hole, although it takes slightly longer to use. It's worth it to obtain a more accurate reading. Follow the procedures below for gasoline and diesel-engined cars.

Gasoline Engines

1. Warm up the engine to normal operating temperature.
2. Remove all spark plugs.

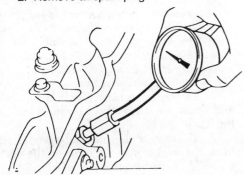

The screw-in type compression gauge is more accurate

3. Disconnect the high-tension lead from the ignition coil.
4. On carbureted cars, fully open the throttle either by operating the carburetor throttle linkage by hand or by having an assistant "floor" the accelerator pedal. On fuel-injected cars, disconnect the cold start valve and all injector connections.
5. Screw the compression gauge into the No. 1 spark plug hole until the fitting is snug.
NOTE: *Be careful not to crossthread the plug hole. On aluminum cylinder heads use extra care, as the threads in these heads are easily ruined.*
6. Ask an assistant to depress the accelerator pedal fully on both carbureted and fuel-injected cars. Then, while you read the compression gauge, ask the assistant to crank the engine two or three times in short bursts using the ignition switch.

7. Read the compression gauge at the end of each series of cranks, and record the highest of these readings. Repeat this procedure for each of the engine's cylinders. Compare the highest reading of each cylinder to the compression pressure specifications in the "Tune-Up Specifications" chart in Chapter 2. The specs in this chart are maximum values.

A cylinder's compression pressure is usually acceptable if it is not less than 80% of maximum. The difference between each cylinder should be no more than 12–14 pounds.

8. If a cylinder is unusually low, pour a tablespoon of clean engine oil into the cylinder through the spark plug hole and repeat the compression test. If the compression comes up after adding the oil, it appears that that cylinder's piston rings or bore are damaged or worn. If the pressure remains low, the valves may not be seating properly (a valve job is needed), or the head gasket may be blown near that cylinder. If compression in any two adjacent cylinders is low, and if the addition of oil doesn't help the compression, there is leakage past the head gasket. Oil and coolant water in the combustion chamber can result from this problem. There may be evidence of water droplets on the engine dipstick when a head gasket has blown.

Diesel Engines

Checking cylinder compression on diesel engines is basically the same procedure as on gasoline engines except for the following:

1. A special compression gauge adaptor suitable for diesel engines (because these engines have much greater compression pressures) must be used.
2. Remove the injector tubes and remove the injectors from each cylinder.
NOTE: *Don't forget to remove the washer underneath each injector; otherwise, it may get lost when the engine is cranked.*

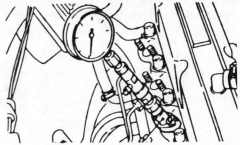

Diesel engines require a special compression gauge adaptor

3. When fitting the compression gauge adaptor to the cylinder head, make sure the bleeder of the gauge (if equipped) is closed.
4. When reinstalling the injector assemblies, install new washers underneath each injector.

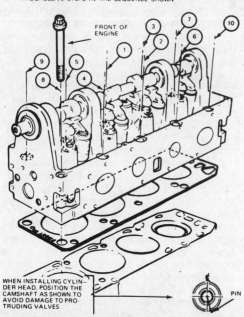

TORQUE THE CYLINDER HEAD BOLTS TO SPECIFICATIONS IN TWO PROGRESSIVE STEPS IN THE SEQUENCE SHOWN

FRONT OF ENGINE

WHEN INSTALLING CYLIN-DER HEAD, POSITION THE CAMSHAFT AS SHOWN TO AVOID DAMAGE TO PRO-TRUDING VALVES

PIN

4-140 cylinder head installation

the top of the cylinder block and pistons and from the bottom of the cylinder head.

11. Position a new cylinder head gasket on the engine. Rotate the camshaft so that the gear locating pin is at the five o'clock position to avoid damage to the valves and pistons.

NOTE: *If you encounter difficulty in positioning the cylinder head on the engine block, it may be necessary to install guide studs in the block to correctly align the head and the block. To fabricate guide studs, obtain two new cylinder head bolts and cut their heads off with a hack saw. Install the bolts in the holes in the engine block which correspond with cylinder head bolt holes Nos. 3 and 4, as identified in the cylinder head bolt tightening sequence illustration. Then, install the head gasket and head over the bolts. Install the cylinder head attaching bolts, replacing the studs with the original head bolts.*

12. Using a torque wrench, tighten the head bolts in the sequence shown in the illustration.

13. Install the camshaft drive belt. See "Camshaft Drive Belt Installation."

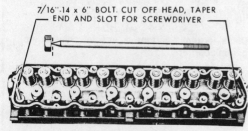

7/16"-14 x 6" BOLT. CUT OFF HEAD, TAPER END AND SLOT FOR SCREWDRIVER

Cylinder head guide stud fabrication

14. Install the camshaft drive belt cover and its attaching bolts. Make sure the rubber grommets are installed on the bolts. Tighten the bolts to 6–13 ft. lbs.

15. Install the water outlet elbow and a new gasket on the engine and tighten the attaching bolts to 12–15 ft. lbs.

16. Install the intake and exhaust manifolds. See the procedures for intake and exhaust manifold installation.

17. Install the air cleaner and the valve cover.

18. Fill the cooling system.

6 Cylinder In-Line Engines

1. Drain cooling system, remove the air cleaner and disconnect the negative battery cable.

NOTE: *On cars with air conditioning, remove the mounting bolts and the drive belt, and position the compressor out of the way of the left cylinder head. Remove the compressor upper mounting bracket from the cylinder head.*

CAUTION: *If the compressor refrigerant lines do not have enough slack to permit repositioning of the compressor without first disconnecting the refrigerant lines, the air conditioning system will have to be evacuated by a trained air conditioning serviceman. Under no circumstances should an untrained person attempt to disconnect the air conditioning refrigerant lines.*

2. Disconnect exhaust pipe at the manifold end, spring the exhaust pipe down and remove the flange gasket.

3. Disconnect the fuel and vacuum lines from the carburetor. Disconnect the intake manifold line at the intake manifold.

4. Disconnect the accelerator and retracting spring at the carburetor. Disconnect the transmission kick-down linkage, if equipped.

5. Disconnect the carburetor spacer outlet line at the spacer. Disconnect the radiator upper hose and the heater hose at the water outlet elbow. Disconnect the radiator lower hose and the heater hose at the water pump.

6. Disconnect the distributor vacuum control line at the distributor. Disconnect the gas filter line on the inlet side of the filter.

7. Disconnect and label the spark plug wires and remove the plugs. Disconnect the temperature sending unit wire.

8. Remove the rocker arm cover.

Cylinder head torque sequence for 6-200, 250

9. Remove the rocker arm shaft attaching bolts and the rocker arm and shaft assembly. Remove the valve pushrods, keep them in order for installation in their original positions.

10. Remove the remaining cylinder head bolts and lift off the cylinder head. Do not pry under the cylinder head as damage to the mating surfaces can easily occur.

To help in installation of cylinder head, two 6 in. x $\frac{7}{16}$–14 bolts with heads cut off and the head end slightly tapered and slotted, for installation and removal with a screwdriver, will reduce the possibility of damage during head replacement.

11. Clean the cylinder head and block surfaces. Be sure of flatness and no surface damage.

12. Apply cylinder head gasket sealer to both sides of the new gasket and slide the gasket down over the two guide studs in the cylinder block.

NOTE: *Apply gasket sealer only to steel shim head gaskets. Steel/asbestos composite head gaskets are to be installed without any sealer.*

13. Carefully lower the cylinder head over the guide studs. Place the exhaust pipe flange on the manifold studs (new gasket).

14. Coat the threads of the end bolts for the right side of the cylinder head with a small amount of water-resistant sealer. Install, but do not tighten, two head bolts at opposite ends to hold the head gasket in place. Remove the guide studs and install the remaining bolts.

15. Cylinder head torquing should proceed in three steps and in prescribed order. Tighten to 55 ft. lbs., then give them a second tightening to 65 ft. lbs. The final step is to 75 ft. lbs., at which they should remain undisturbed.

16. Lubricate both ends of the pushrods and install them in their original locations.

17. Apply lubricant to the rocker arm pads and the valve stem tips and position the rocker arm shaft assembly on the head. Be sure the oil holes in the shaft are in a down position.

18. Tighten all the rocker shaft retaining bolts to 30–35 ft. lbs. and do a preliminary valve adjustment (make sure there are no tight valve adjustments).

19. Hook up the exhaust pipe.

20. Reconnect the heater and radiator hoses.

21. Reposition the distributor vacuum line, the carburetor gas line and the intake manifold vacuum line on the engine. Hook them up to their respective connections and reconnect the battery cable to the cylinder head.

22. Connect the accelerator rod and retracting spring. Connect the choke control cable and adjust the choke. Connect the transmission kickdown linkage.

23. Reconnect the vacuum line at the dis-

tributor. Connect the fuel inlet line at the fuel filter and the intake manifold vacuum line at the vacuum pump.

24. Lightly lubricate the spark plug threads and install them. Connect spark plug wires and be sure the wires are all the way down in their sockets. Connect the temperature sending unit wire.

25. Fill the cooling system. Run the engine to stabilize all engine part temperatures.

26. Adjust engine idle speed and idle fuelair adjustment.

27. Coat one side of a new rocker cover gasket with oil-resistant sealer. Lay the treated side of the gasket on the cover and install the cover. Be sure the gasket seals evenly all around the cylinder head.

V6 Engine

1. Drain the cooling system.

2. Disconnect the cable from the battery negative terminal.

3. Remove the air cleaner assembly including air intake duct and heat tube.

4. Loosen the accessory drive belt idler. Remove the drive belt.

5. If the left cylinder head is being removed:

    a. If equipped with power steering, remove the pump mounting brackets' attaching bolts, leaving the hoses connected, place the pump/bracket assembly aside in a position to prevent the fluid from leaking out.

    b. If equipped with air conditioning, remove the mounting brackets' attaching bolts, leaving the hoses connected, position the compressor aside.

6. If the right cylinder head is being removed:

    a. Disconnect the thermactor diverter valve and hose assembly at the by-pass valve and downstream air tube.

    b. Remove the assembly.

    c. Remove the accessory drive idler.

    d. Remove the alternator.

    e. Remove the thermactor pump pulley. Remove the thermactor pump.

    f. Remove the alternator bracket.

    g. Remove the PCV valve.

7. Remove the intake manifold.

8. Remove the valve rocker arm cover attaching screws. Loosen the silicone rubber gasketing material by inserting a putty knife under the cover flange. Work the cover loose and remove. The plastic rocker arm covers will break if excessive prying is applied.

9. Remove the exhaust manifold(s).

10. Loose the rocker arm fulcrum attaching bolts enough to allow the rocker arm to be lifted off the pushroad and rotated to one side.

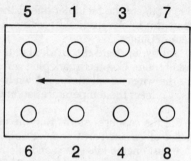

V6 cylinder head torque sequence

11. Remove the pushrods. Label the pushrods, they should be installed in the original position during assembly.

12. Remove the cylinder head attaching bolts. Remove the cylinder head(s).

13. Remove and discard the old cylinder head gasket(s). Discard the cylinder head bolts.

14. Lightly oil all bolt and stud bolt threads before installation except those specifying special sealant.

15. Clean the cylinder head, intake manifold, valve rocker arm cover and cylinder head gasket surfaces. If the cylinder head was removed for a cylinder head gasket replacement, check the flatness of the cylinder head and block gasket surfaces.

16. Position new head gasket(s) on the cylinder block using the dowels for alignment.

17. Position the cylinder heads to the block.

18. Apply a thin coating of pipe sealant or equivalent to the threads of the short cylinder head bolts (nearest to the exhaust manifold). Do not apply sealant to the long bolts. Lightly oil the cylinder head bolt flat washers. Install the flat washers and cylinder head bolts (Eight each side).

CAUTION: *Always use new cylinder head bolts to assure a leak tight assembly. Torque retention with used bolts can vary, which may result in coolant or compression leakage at the cylinder head mating surface area.*

19. Tighten the attaching bolts in sequence. Back-off the attaching bolts 2–3 turns. Repeat tightening sequence.

NOTE: *When the cylinder head attaching bolts have been tightened using the above sequential procedure, it is not necessary to retighten the bolts after extended engine operation. However, the bolts can be checked for tightness if desired.*

20. Dip each pushrod end in heavy engine oil. Install the push rods in their original position. For each valve rotate the crankshaft until the tappet rests on the heel (base circle) of the camshaft lobe.

21. Position the rocker arms over the push

rods, install the fulcrums, and tighten the fulcrum attaching bolts to 61–132 in. lbs.

CAUTION: *Fulcrums must be fully seated in cylinder head and pushrods must be seated in rocker arm sockets prior to final tightening.*

22. Lubricate all rocker arm assemblies with heavy engine oil. Finally tighten the fulcrum bolts to 19–25 ft. lbs. For final tightening, the camshaft may be in any position.

NOTE: *If the original valve train components are being installed, a valve clearance check is not required. If a component has been replaced, perform a valve clearance check.*

23. Install the exhaust manifold(s).

24. Apply a ⅛–³⁄₁₆ inch bead of RTV silicone sealant to the rocker arm cover flange. Make sure the sealer fills the channel in the cover flange. The rocker arm cover must be installed within 15 minutes after the silicone sealer application. After this time, the sealer may start to set-up, and its sealing effectiveness may be reduced.

25. Position the cover on the cylinder head and install the attaching bolts. Note the location of the wiring harness routing clips and spark plug wire routing clip stud bolts. Tighten the attaching bolts to 36–60 in. lbs. torque.

26. Install the intake manifold.

27. Install the spark plugs, if necessary.

28. Connect the secondary wires to the spark plugs.

29. Install the oil fill cap. If equipped with air conditioning, install the compressor mounting and support brackets.

30. On the right cylinder head:

   a. Install the PCV valve.

   b. Install the alternator bracket. Tighten attaching nuts to 30–40 ft. lbs.

   c. Install the thermactor pump and pump pulley.

   d. Install the alternator

   e. Install the accessory drive idler.

   f. Install the thermactor diverter valve and hose assembly. Tighten the clamps securely.

31. Install the accessory drive belt and tighten to the specified tension.

32. Connect the cable to the battery negative terminal.

33. Fill the cooling system with the specified coolant.

CAUTION: *This engine has an aluminum cylinder head and requires a special unique corrosion inhibited coolant formulation to avoid radiator damage.*

34. Start the engine and check for coolant, fuel, and oil leaks.

35. Check and, if necessary, adjust the curb idle speed.

36. Install the air cleaner assembly including the air intake duct and heat tube.

V8 Engines

1. Drain the cooling system.
2. Remove the intake manifold and the carburetor or CFI unit as an assembly.
3. Disconnect the spark plug wires, marking them as to placement. Position them out of the way of the cylinder head. Remove the spark plugs.
4. Disconnect the exhaust pipes at the manifolds.
5. Remove the rocker arm covers.
6. On cars with air conditioning, remove the mounting bolts and the drive belt, and position the compressor out of the way of the left cylinder head. Remove the compressor upper mounting bracket from the cylinder head.

NOTE: *If the compressor refrigerant lines do not have enough slack to permit repositioning of the compressor without first disconnecting the refrigerant lines, the air conditioning system will have to be evacuated by a trained air conditioning serviceman. Under no circumstances should an untrained person attempt to disconnect the air conditioning refrigerant lines.*

7. In order to remove the left cylinder head, on cars equipped with power steering, it may be necessary to remove the steering pump and bracket, remove the drive belt, and wire or tie the pump out of the way, but in such a way as to prevent the loss of its fluid.
8. In order to remove the right head it may be necessary to remove the alternator mounting bracket bolt and spacer, the ignition coil, and the air cleaner inlet duct from the right cylinder head.
9. In order to remove the left cylinder head on a car equipped with a Thermactor air pump system, disconnect the hose from the air manifold on the left cylinder head.
10. If the right cylinder head is to be removed on a car equipped with a Thermactor system, remove the Thermactor air pump and its mounting bracket. Disconnect the hose from the air manifold on the right cylinder head.
11. Loosen the rocker arm stud nuts enough to rotate the rocker arms to the side, in order to facilitate the removal of the pushrods. Remove the pushrods in sequence, so that they may be installed in their original positions. Remove the exhaust valve stem caps, if equipped.
12. Remove the cylinder head attaching bolts, noting their positions. Lift the cylinder head off the block. Remove and discard the old cylinder head gasket. Clean all mounting surfaces.
13. Installation is as follows: Position the new

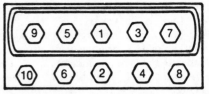

V8 cylinder head torque sequence

cylinder head gasket over the dowels on the block. Position new gaskets on the muffler inlet pipes at the exhaust manifold flange.

1. Position the cylinder head to the block, and install the head bolts, each in its original position. On engines on which the exhaust manifold has been removed from the head to facilitate removal, it is necessary to properly guide the exhaust manifold studs into the muffler inlet pipe flange when installing the head.
2. Step-torque the cylinder head retaining bolts first to 50 ft. lbs. then to 60 ft. lbs., and finally to the torque specification listed in the "Torque Specifications" chart. Tighten the exhaust manifold to cylinder head attaching bolts to specifications.
3. Tighten the nuts on the exhaust manifold studs at the muffler inlet flanges to 18 ft. lbs.
4. Clean and inspect the pushrods one at a time. Clean the oil passage within each pushrod with solvent and blow the passage out with compressed air. Check the ends of the pushrods for nicks, grooves, roughness, or excessive wear. Visually inspect the pushrods for straightness, and replace any bent ones. Do not attempt to straighten pushrods.
5. Install the pushrods in their original positions. Apply Lubriplate® or a similar product to the valve stem tips and to the pushrod guides in the cylinder head. Install the exhaust valve stem caps.
6. Apply Lubriplate® or a similar product to the fulcrum seats and sockets. Turn the rocker arms to their proper position and tighten the stud nuts enough to hold the rocker arms in position. Make sure that the lower ends of the pushrods have remained properly seated in the valve lifters. Tighten the stud nuts 17–23 ft. lbs. in the order given under the preliminary valve adjustment.
7. Install the valve covers.
8. Install the intake manifold and carburetor, following the procedure under "Intake Manifold Installation."
9. Reinstall all other items removed.

2.4L Diesel Engine

1. Disconnect the battery ground cable.
2. Drain the cooling system. Disconnect the heater hose(s).

3. Loosen and remove accessory drive belts.

4. Remove the valve cover.

5. Disconnect the diagnostic connectors.

6. Disconnect the coolant temperature switch and glow plug connector.

7. Disconnect the breather hose and bracket.

8. Remove the clamp attaching the oil dipstick tube to the intake manifold and position out of the way.

9. Disconnect the boost pressure switch connector.

10. Disconnect the radiator hose from the cylinder head.

11. Disconnect the temperature controlled idle boost coolant hose.

12. Remove the vacuum pump from cylinder head.

13. Disconnect No. 1 nozzle to the injection pump leak hose.

14. Disconnect the injection lines from the nozzles and injection pump.

CAUTION: *Cap nozzles and lines.*

15. Disconnect the turbocharger oil lines.

16. Rotate the crankshaft until No. 1 cylinder is at TDC of compression stroke (intake and exhaust valves on base circle). Install TDC Aligning Pin, T84P-6400-A or equivalent.

17. Loosen the camshaft drive sprocket retaining bolt.

18. Loosen the camshaft drive belt tensioning roller nut and bolt, and remove drive belt.

19. Loosen the cylinder head bolts in sequence, and remove cylinder head.

20. Clean gasket sealing surfaces on the cylinder head and crankcase. Check for warpage.

CAUTION: *Use care when cleaning gasket surfaces. Slight scoring of these surfaces can cause leakage due to high compression pressures.*

21. Clean the top of each piston.

22. Using a dial indicator D82L-4201-A and Piston Height Gauge D84P-6100-A or equivalent, measure the amount the piston top extends above crankcase gasket surface as follows:

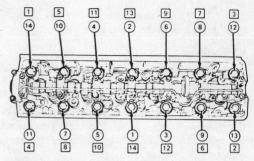

☐ REMOVAL ○ INSTALLATION

2.4L diesel engine—head bolt removal and installation sequence

a. Mount the dial indicator and bracket with dial indicator tip on piston.

b. Rotate the crankshaft to position piston at TDC, using dial indicator.

c. Zero the dial indicator with tip on crankcase.

d. Move the tip to the front of the piston. Record measurement.

e. Move the tip to the rear of the piston. Record measurement.

f. Repeat this procedure for each cylinder.

g. Average the two readings for each cylinder.

h. Using the measurement of highest piston, refer to the chart provided and select correct cylinder head gasket.

23. Clean carbon and oil deposits from the cylinder head bolts.

CAUTION: *Keep oil and/or antifreeze from entering cylinder head bolt holes. If either enters bolt holes, carefully blow out with compressed air. The presence of oil and/or antifreeze in bolt holes could result in insufficient cylinder head bolt tightening, or a cracked crankcase.*

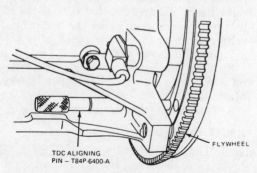

TDC alignment pin installation—2.4L diesel engine

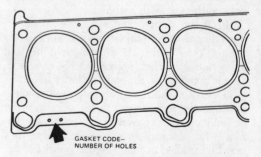

HIGHEST PISTON PROTRUSION OF ALL 6 PISTONS mm	CYL. HEAD GASKET CODE NO. OF HOLES	THICKNESS OF CYL. HEAD GASKET mm
0.60 – 0.70	1	1.4
0.70 – 0.85	2	1.5
0.85 – 1.00	3	1.6

2.4L diesel engine—cylinder head gasket identification

24. Position the correct cylinder head gasket on the crankcase.

25. Carefully lower the cylinder head onto the crankcase, using care not to damage gasket.

26. Install and tighten the cylinder head bolts, in sequence to 36–43 ft. lbs. Wait 15 minutes and tighten the bolts, in sequence an additional 90°.

27. Install and adjust the drive belt.

28. Connect the turbocharger oil lines and tighten to 14–17 ft. lbs.

29. Connect the nozzle high pressure lines to the nozzles and injection pump. Tighten to 14–18 ft. lbs., using fuel line wrench.

30. Connect No. 1 nozzle to the injection pump leak hose.

31. Install the vacuum pump on the cylinder head and tighten to 6–7 ft. lbs.

32. Connect the temperature controlled, idle boost coolant hose.

33. Connect the radiator hoses to the cylinder head.

34. Connect the oil pressure switch connector.

35. Install the oil dipstick tube.

36. Install the breather hose and bracket.

37. Connect the coolant temperature switch and glow plug connectors.

38. Connect the diagnostic connectors.

39. Install the valve cover loosely.

40. Install and adjust accessory drive belts.

41. Connect the heater hose(s).

42. Fill and bleed coolant system. Connect the battery ground cable.

43. Start and run engine for 15–20 minutes: shut off the engine, remove the valve cover and tighten the cylinder head bolts an additional 90°.

44. Install valve cover.

PRELIMINARY VALVE ADJUSTMENT

V6 and V8 Engines Only

This adjustment is actually part of the installation procedure for the individually mounted rocker arms found on the V-type engine, and is necessary to achieve an accurate torque value for each rocker arm nut.

By its nature, an hydraulic valve lifter will expand when it is not under load. Thus, when the rocker arms are removed and the pressure via the pushrod is taken off the lifter, the lifter expands to its maximum. If the lifter happens to be at the top of the camshaft lobe when the rocker arm is being reinstalled, a large amount of torque would be necessary when tightening the rocker arm nut just to overcome the pressure of the expanded lifter. This makes it very

difficult to get an accurate torque setting with individually mounted rocker arms. For this reason, the rocker arms are installed in a certain sequence which corresponds to the low points of the camshaft lobes.

1. Turn the engine until No. 1 cylinder is at TDC of the compression stroke and the timing pointer is aligned with the mark on the crankshaft damper.

2. Scribe a mark on the damper at this point.

3. Scribe two additional marks on the damper if V8, single line if V6. (see illustration).

4. With the timing pointer aligned with Mark 1 on the damper, tighten the following valves to the specified torque:

• *V6-232* No. 1 intake and exhaust; No. 3 intake and exhaust; No. 4 exhaust and No. 6 intake.

• *255, 302 (EXC. H.O), 429, and 460* No. 1, 7 and 8 Intake; No. 1, 5, and 4 Exhaust.

• *H.O. 302, 351 and 400* No. 1, 4 and 8 Intake; No. 1, 3 and 7 Exhaust.

5. Rotate the crankshaft 180° to point 2 and tighten the following valves:

• *V6-232* No. 2 intake; No. 3 exhaust; No. 4 intake; No. 5 intake and exhaust; No. 6 exhaust.

• *255, 302 (EXC. H.O) 429, and 460* No. 5 and 4 Intake; No. 2 and 6 Exhaust

• *H.O. 302, 351 and 400* No. 3 and 7 Intake; No. 2 and 6 Exhaust

6. Rotate the crankshaft 270° to point 3 and tighten the following valves:

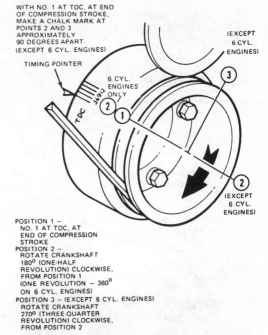

WITH NO. 1 AT TDC, AT END OF COMPRESSION STROKE, MAKE A CHALK MARK AT POINTS 2 AND 3 APPROXIMATELY 90 DEGREES APART. (EXCEPT 6 CYL. ENGINES)

TIMING POINTER

6 CYL. ENGINES ONLY

(EXCEPT 6 CYL. ENGINES)

(EXCEPT 6 CYL. ENGINES)

POSITION 1 – NO. 1 AT TDC, AT END OF COMPRESSION STROKE
POSITION 2 – ROTATE CRANKSHAFT 180° (ONE-HALF REVOLUTION) CLOCKWISE, FROM POSITION 1 (ONE REVOLUTION – 360° ON 6 CYL. ENGINES)
POSITION 3 – (EXCEPT 6 CYL. ENGINES) ROTATE CRANKSHAFT 270° (THREE-QUARTER REVOLUTION) CLOCKWISE, FROM POSITION 2

Crankshaft pulley marking for preliminary valve adjustment

• *302 (EXC. H.O), 429, and 460* No. 2, 3, and 6 Intake; No. 7, 3 and 8 Exhaust

• *H.O. 302, 351 and 400* No. 2, 5 and 6 Intake; No. 4, 5 and 8 Exhaust

7. Rocker arm tighten specifications are: 232, 255, 302 and 351W—tighten nut until it contacts the rocker shoulder, then torque to 18–20 ft. lbs.; 351C and 400—tighten bolt to 18–25 ft. lbs.; 429 and 460—tighten nut until it contacts rocker shoulder, then torque to 18–22 ft. lbs.

CYLINDER HEAD OVERHAUL

1. Remove the cylinder head(s) from the car engine (see Cylinder Head Removal and Installation). Place the head(s) on a workbench and remove any manifolds that are still connected. Remove all rocker arm retaining parts and the rocker arms, if still installed. On four cylinder engines, remove the camshaft (see Camshaft Removal).

2. Turn the cylinder head over so that the mounting surface is facing up and support evenly on wooden blocks.

CAUTION: *V6 engines use aluminum cylinder heads, exercise care when cleaning.*

3. Use a scraper and remove all of the gasket material stuck to the head mounting surface. Mount a wire carbon removal brush in an electric drill and clean away the carbon on the valves and head combustion chambers.

CAUTION: *When scraping or decarboniz-*

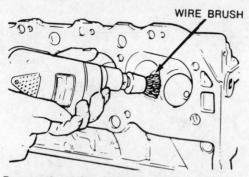

Remove the carbon from the cylinder head with a wire brush and electric drill

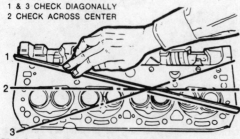

Check the cylinder head for warpage

ing the cylinder head take care not to damage or nick the gasket mounting surface.

4. Number the valve heads with a permanent felt-tip marker for cylinder location.

Resurfacing

If the cylinder head is warped resurfacing by a machine shop is required. Place a straightedge across the gasket surface of the head. Using feeler gauges, determine the clearance at the center and along the length between the head and straight-edge. Measure clearance at the center and along the lengths of both diagonals. If warpage exceeds .003 inches in a six inch span, or .006 inches over the total length the cylinder head must be resurfaced.

Valves and Springs
REMOVAL AND INSTALLATION

1. Block the head on its side, or install a pair of head-holding brackets made especially for valve removal.

2. Use a socket slightly larger than the valve stem and keepers, place the socket over the valve stem and gently hit the socket with a plastic hammer to break loose any varnish buildup.

3. Remove the valve keepers, retainer, spring shield and valve spring using a valve spring compressor (the locking C-clamp type is the easiest kind to use).

4. Put the parts in a separate container numbered for the cylinder being worked on; do not mix them with other parts removed.

5. Remove and discard the valve stem oil seal, a new seal will be used at assembly time.

6. Remove the valve from the cylinder head and place, in order, through numbered holes punched in a stiff piece of cardboard or wooden valve holding stick.

NOTE: *The exhaust valve stems, on some engines, are equipped with small metal caps. Take care not to lose the caps. Make sure to reinstall them at assembly time. Replace any caps that are worn.*

7. Use an electric drill and rotary wire brush to clean the intake and exhaust valve ports, combustion chamber and valve seats. In some cases, the carbon will need to be chipped away. Use a blunt pointed drift for carbon chipping, be careful around the valve seat areas.

8. Use a wire valve guide cleaning brush and safe solvent to clean the valve guides.

9. Clean the valves with a revolving wire brush. Heavy carbon deposits may be removed with the blunt drift.

NOTE: *When using a wire brush to clean carbon on the valve ports, valves etc., be sure that the deposits are actually removed, rather than burnished.*

10. Wash and clean all valve springs, keepers, retaining caps etc., in safe solvent.

11. Clean the head with a brush and some safe solvent and wipe dry.

12. Check the head for cracks. Cracks in the cylinder head usually start around an exhaust valve seat because it is the hottest part of the combustion chamber. If a crack is suspected but cannot be detected visually have the area checked with dye penetrant or other method by the machine shop.

13. After all cylinder head parts are reasonably clean check the valve stem-to-guide clearance. If a dial indicator is not on hand, a visual inspection can give you a fairly good idea if the guide, valve stem or both are worn.

14. Insert the valve into the guide until slightly away from the valve seat. Wiggle the valve sideways. A small amount of wobble is normal, excessive wobble means a worn guide or valve stem. If a dial indicator is on hand, mount the indicator so that the stem of the valve is at 90° to the valve stem, as close to the valve guide as possible. Move the valve off the seat, and measure the valve guide-to-stem clearance by rocking the stem back and forth to actuate the dial indicator. Measure the valve stem using a micrometer and compare to specifications to determine whether stem or guide wear is causing excessive clearance.

15. The valve guide, if worn, must be repaired before the valve seats can be resurfaced. Ford supplies valves with oversize stems to fit valve guides that are reamed to oversize for repair. The machine ship will be able to handle the guide reaming for you. In some cases, if the guide is not too badly worn, knurling may be all that is required.

16. Reface, or have the valves and valve seats refaced. The valve seats should be a true 45° angle. Remove only enough material to clean up any pits or grooves. Be sure the valve seat is not too wide or narrow. Use a 60° grinding wheel to remove material from the bottom of the seat for raising and a 30° grinding wheel to remove material from the top of the seat to narrow.

17. After the valves are refaced by machine, hand lap them to the valve seat. Clean the grinding compound off and check the position of face-to-seat contact. Contact should be close to the center of the valve face. If contact is close to the top edge of the valve narrow the seat; if too close to the bottom edge, raise the seat.

18. Valves should be refaced to a true angle of 44°. Remove only enough metal to clean up the valve face or to correct runout. If the edge of a valve head, after machining, is 1/32 inch or

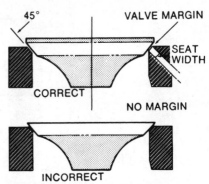

Valve seat width and centering

less replace the valve. The tip of the valve stem should also be dressed on the valve grinding machine, however, do not remove more than .010 inch.

19. After all valve and valve seats have been machined, check the remaining valve train parts (springs, retainers, keepers, etc.) for wear. Check the valve springs for straightness and tension.

20. Reassemble the head in the reverse order of disassembly using new valve guide seals and lubricating the valve stems. Check the valve spring installed height, shim or replace as necessary.

CHECKING VALVE SPRINGS

Place the valve spring on a flat surface next to a carpenters square. Measure the height of the spring, and rotate the spring against the edge of the square to measure distortion. If the spring height varies (by comparsion) by more than 1/16 inch or if the distortion exceeds 1/16 inch, replace the spring.

Have the valve springs tested for spring pressure at the installed and compressed (installed height minus valve lift) height using a valve spring tester. Springs should be within one pound, plus or minus each other. Replace springs as necessary.

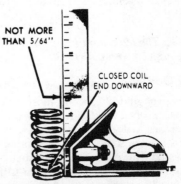

Check the valve spring free length and squareness

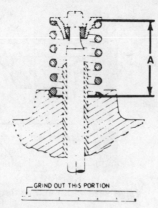

Measure the valve spring installed height (A) with a modified steel rule

VALVE SPRING INSTALLED HEIGHT

After installing the valve spring, measure the distance between the spring mounting pad and the lower edge of the spring retainer. Compare the measurement to specifications. If the installed height is incorrect, add shim washers between the spring mounting pad and the spring. Use only washers designed for valve springs; available at most parts houses.

VALVE STEM OIL SEALS

Umbrella type oil seals fitting on the valve stem over the top of the valve guide are used on the in-line six and eight cylinder engines. The four cylinder and V6 engine uses a positive valve stem seal using a Teflon insert. Teflon seals are available for other engines but usually require valve guide machining, consult your automotive machine shop for advice on having positive valve stem oil seals installed.

When installing valve stem oil seals, ensure that a small amount of oil is able to pass the seal to lubricate the valve stems and guide walls; otherwise, excessive wear will occur.

VALVE SEATS

If a valve seat is damaged or burnt and cannot be serviced by refacing, it may be possible to have the seat machined and an insert installed. Consult the automotive machine shop for their advice.

NOTE: *The aluminum heads on V6 engines are equipped with inserts.*

VALVE GUIDES

Worn valve guides can, in most cases, be reamed to accept a valve with an oversized stem. Valve guides that are not excessively worn or distorted may, in some cases, be knurled rather than reamed. However, if the valve stem is worn reaming for an oversized valve stem is the answer since a new valve would be required.

Knurling is a process in which metal is displaced and raised, thereby reducing clearance. Knurling also produces excellent oil control. The possibility of knurling instead of reaming the valve guides should be discussed with a machinist.

HYDRAULIC VALVE CLEARANCE

Hydraulic valve lifters operate with zero clearance in the valve train, and because of this the rocker arms are nonadjustable. The only means by which valve system clearances can be altered is by installing over or undersize pushrods; but, because of the hydraulic lifter's natural ability to compensate for slack in the valve train, all components of all the valve system should be checked for wear if there is excessive play in the system.

When a valve in the engine is in the closed position, the valve lifter is resting on the base circle of the camshaft lobe and the pushrod is in its lowest position. To remove this additional clearance from the valve train, the valve lifter expands to maintain zero clearance in the valve system. When a rocker arm is loosened or removed from the engine, the lifter expands to its fullest travel. When the rocker arm is reinstalled on the engine, the proper valve setting is obtained by tightening the rocker arm to a specified limit. But with the lifter fully expanded, if the camshaft lobe is on a high point it will require excessive torque to compress the lifter and obtain the proper setting. Because of this, when any component of the valve system has been removed, a preliminary valve adjustment procedure must be followed to ensure that when the rocker arm is reinstalled on the engine and tightened, the camshaft lobe for that cylinder is in the low position.

To determine whether a shorter or longer push rod is necessary, make the following check:

Mark the crankshaft pulley as described under "Preliminary Valve Adjustment" procedure. Follow each step in the procedure. As each valve is positioned, mount a suitable hydraulic lifter compressor tool on the rocker arm.

Slowly apply pressure to bleed down the lifter until the plunger is completely bottomed. Take care to avoid excessive pressure that might bend the pushrod. Hold the lifter in bottom position and check the available clearance between the rocker arm and the valve stem tip with a feeler gauge. If the clearance is less than specified, install an under-sized pushrod. If the clearance is greater than specified, install an over-sized pushrod. When compressing the valve spring to remove the pushrods, be sure the piston in the individual cylinder is below TDC to avoid contact between the valve and the piston. To replace a pushrod, it will be necessary to remove the valve rocker arm shaft assembly on in-line engines. Upon replacement of a valve pushrod, valve rocker arm shaft assembly or hydraulic valve lifter, the engine should not be cranked or rotated until the hydraulic lifters have had an opportunity to leak down to their normal operation position. The leak down rate can be accelerated by using the tool shown on the valve rocker arm and applying pressure in a direction to collapse the lifter.

Note: Collapsed tappet gap:

In-Line Engines
- Allowable—.085–.209
- Desired—.110–.184

V6 Engines
- Allowable—.088–.189

V8 Engines
- (255 cu in.)
  Allowable—.098–.198
  Desired—.123–.173
- (302 cu in. and 351)
  Allowable—.089–.193
  Desired—.096–.163

VALVE CLEARANCE—HYDRAULIC VALVE LASH ADJUSTERS

Four Cylinder 140 Cu In. Engine

Hydraulic valve lash adjusters are used in the valve train. These units are placed at the fulcrum point of the cam followers (or rocker arms). Their action is similar to the hydraulic tappets used in push rod engines.

1. Position the camshaft so that the base circle of the lobe is facing the cam follower of the valve to be checked.
2. Using the tool shown in the illustration, slowly apply pressure to the cam follower until the lash adjuster is completely collapsed. Hold the follower in this position and insert 0.045 in. feeler gauge between the base circle of the cam and the follower.

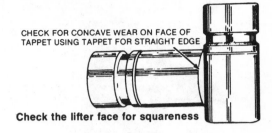

CHECK FOR CONCAVE WEAR ON FACE OF TAPPET USING TAPPET FOR STRAIGHT EDGE

Check the lifter face for squareness

NOTE: *The minimum gap is 0.035 in. and the maximum is 0.055 in. The desire gap is between 0.040 in. and 0.050 in.*

3. If the clearance is excessive, remove the cam follower and inspect it for damage.
4. If the cam follower seems OK measure the valve spring assembled height to be sure the valve is not sticking. See the Valve Specifications chart in this chapter.
5. If the valve spring assembled height is OK check the dimensions of the camshaft.
6. If the camshaft dimensions are OK the lash adjuster should be cleaned and tested.
7. Replace any worn parts as necessary.

NOTE: *For any repair that includes removal of the camshaft follower (rocker arm), each affected hydraulic lash adjuster must be collapsed after reinstallation of the camshaft follower, and then released. This step must be taken prior to any rotation of the camshaft.*

HYDRAULIC VALVE LIFTER INSPECTION

Remove the lifters from their bores and remove any gum and varnish with safe solvent. Check the lifters for concave wear. If the bottom of the lifter is worn concave or flat, replace the lifter. Lifters are built with a convex bottom, flatness indicates wear. If a worn lifter is detected, carefully check the camshaft for wear.

CAUTION: *Mark lifters for cylinder and position location: Lifter must be reinstalled in the same bore they were removed from.*

To test lifter leak down, submerge the lifter in a container of kerosene. Chuck a used pushrod or its equivalent into a drill press. Position the container of kerosene so the pushrod acts on the lifter plunger. Pump the lifter with the drill press until resistance increases. Pump several more times to bleed any air from the lifter. Apply very firm, constant pressure to the lifter and observe the rate which fluid bleeds out of the lifter. If the lifter bleeds down very quickly (less than 15 seconds), the lifter should be replaced. If the time exceeds 60 seconds, the lifter is sticking and should be cleaned or replaced. If the lifter is operating properly (leak down time 15–60 seconds) and not worn, lubricate and reinstall in engine.

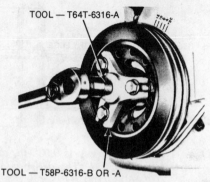

TOOL — T64T-6316-A

TOOL — T58P-6316-B OR -A

Using a puller to remove the damper on the 6-200, 250

Timing Cover and Chain

REMOVAL AND INSTALLATION

In-Line Six Cylinder Engines

1. Drain the cooling system and crankcase.
2. Disconnect the upper radiator hose from the intake manifold and the lower hose from the water pump. On cars with automatic transmission, disconnect the cooler lines from the radiator.
3. Remove the radiator, fan and pulley, and engine drive belts. On models with air conditioning, remove the condenser retaining bolts and position the condenser forward. *Do not disconnect the refrigerant lines.*
4. Remove the cylinder front cover retaining bolts and front oil pan bolts and gently pry the cover away from the block.

NOTE: *On 6-250 engine the oil pan must be removed prior to the front cover.*

5. Remove the crankshaft pulley bolt and use a puller to remove the vibration damper.
6. With a socket wrench of the proper size on the crankshaft pulley bolt, gently rotate the crankshaft in a clockwise direction until all slack is removed from the lift side of the timing chain. Scribe a mark on the engine block parallel to the present position on the left side of the chain. Next, turn the crankshaft in a counterclockwise direction to remove all the slack from the right

UNIVERSAL PULLER

Using a puller to remove the vibration damper on the V6 and V8

side of the chain. Force the left side of the chain outward with the fingers and measure the distance between the reference point and the present position of the chain. If the distance exceeds ½ inch, replace the chain and sprockets.

7. Crank the engine until the timing marks are aligned as shown in the illustration. Remove the bolt, slide sprocket and chain forward and remove as an assembly.
8. Position the sprockets and chain on the engine, making sure that the timing marks are aligned, dot to dot.
9. Reinstall the front cover, applying oil resistant sealer to the new gasket.

NOTE: *On 6-200 engines. Trim away the exposed portion of the old oil pan gasket flush with front of the engine block. Cut and position the required portion of a new gasket to the oil pan, applying sealer to both sides of it. Install oil pan on 6-250 engines.*

10. Install the fan, pulley and belts. Adjust belt tension.
11. Install the radiator, connect the radiator

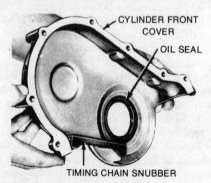

CYLINDER FRONT COVER

OIL SEAL

TIMING CHAIN SNUBBER

Timing gear cover on the 6-200, 250

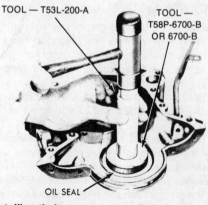

TOOL — T53L-200-A

TOOL — T58P-6700-B OR 6700-B

OIL SEAL

Installing timing gear cover oil seal

REFERENCE POINT

Measuring timing chain deflection—typical

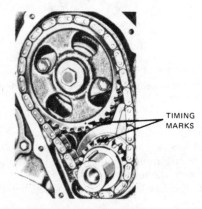

TIMING MARKS

6-200, 250 timing mark alignment

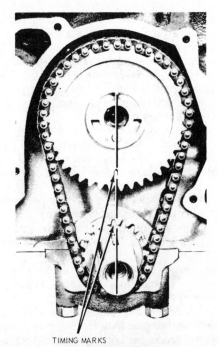

TIMING MARKS

V6 and V8 timing mark alignment

hoses and transmission cooling lines. If equipped with air conditioning, install the condenser.

12. Fill the crankcase and cooling system. Start the engine and check for leaks.

V6 Engine

1. Disconnect the negative battery cable from the battery. Drain the cooling system.

2. Remove the air cleaner and air duct assemblies.

3. Remove the radiator fan shroud and position back over the water pump. Remove the fan clutch assembly and shroud.

4. Remove all drive belts. If equipped with power steering, remove the pump with hoses attached and position out of the way. Be sure to keep the pump upright to prevent fluid leakage.

5. If your car is equipped with air conditioning, remove the front compressor mounting bracket. It is not necessary to remove the compressor.

6. Disconnect the coolant by-pass hose and the heater hose at the water pump.

7. Disconnect the upper radiator hose at the thermostat housing. Remove the distributor.

8. If your car is equipped with a trip-minder, remove the flow meter support bracket and allow the meter to be supported by the hoses.

9. Raise the front of the car and support on jackstands.

10. Remove the crankshaft pulley using a suitable puller. Remove the fuel pump shield.

11. Disconnect the fuel line from the carburetor at the fuel pump. Remove the mounting bolts and the fuel pump. Position pump out of the way with tank line still attached.

12. Drain the engine oil and remove the oil filter.

13. Disconnect the lower radiator hose at the water pump.

14. Remove the oil pan mounting bolts and lower the oil pan.
NOTE: *The front cover cannot be removed unless the oil pan is lowered.*

15. Lower the car from the jackstands.

16. Remove the front cover mounting bolts.
NOTE: *Water pump removal is not necessary.*
CAUTION: *A front cover mounting bolt is located behind the oil filter adapter. If the bolt is not removed and the cover is pried upon breakage will occur.*

17. Remove the timing indicator. Remove the front cover and water pump assembly.

18. Remove the camshaft thrust button and

spring from the end of the camshaft. Remove the camshaft sprocket attaching bolts.

19. Remove the camshaft sprocket, crankshaft sprocket and timing chain by pulling forward evenly on both sprockets. If the crankshaft sprocket is difficult to remove, position two small prybars, one on each side, behind the sprocket and pry forward.

20. Clean all gasket surfaces on the front cover, cylinder block, fuel pump and oil pan.

21. Install a new front cover oil seal. If a new front cover is to be installed: Install the oil pump, oil filter adapter and intermediate shaft from the old cover. Remove the water pump from the old cover, clean the mounting surface, install a new mounting gasket and the pump on the new front cover. Pump attaching bolt torque is 13–22 ft. lbs.

22. Rotate the crankshaft, if necessary, to bring No. 1 piston to TDC with the crankshaft keyway at the 12 o'clock position.

23. Lubricate the timing chain with motor oil. Install the chain over the two gears making sure the marks on both gears are positioned across from each other. Install the gears and chain on the cam and crankshaft. Install the camshaft mounting bolts. Tighten the bolts to 15–22 ft. lbs.

24. Install the camshaft thrust button and spring. Lubricate the thrust button with Polyethylene grease before installation.

NOTE: *The thrust button and spring must be bottomed in the camshaft seat and must not be allowed to fall out during front cover installation.*

25. Position a new cover gasket on the front of the engine and install the cover and water pump assemblies. Install the timing indicator. Torque the front cover bolts to 15–22 ft. lbs.

26. The remaining steps of installation are in the reverse order of removal.

CAUTION: *When installing the fuel pump, turn the crankshaft 180 degrees to position the fuel pump drive eccentric away from the fuel pump arm. Failure to turn the drive eccentric away from the pump arm can cause stress on the pump mounting threads and strip them out when installing the pump.*

V8 Engines

1. Drain cooling system, remove air cleaner and disconnect the battery.

2. Disconnect the transmission cooler lines and radiator hoses and remove the radiator.

3. Disconnect heater hose at water pump. Slide water pump by-pass hose clamp toward the pump.

4. Loosen alternator mounting bolts at the alternator. Remove the alternator support bolt at the water pump. Remove Thermactor pump

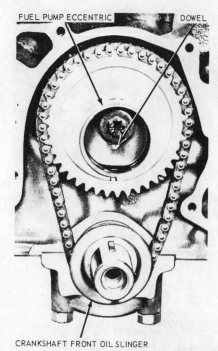

FUEL PUMP ECCENTRIC   DOWEL

CRANKSHAFT FRONT OIL SLINGER

Fuel pump eccentric and front oil slinger installed on the 8-255, 302, 351W

on all engines so equipped. If equipped with power steering or air conditioning, unbolt the component, remove the belt, and lay the pump aside with the lines attached.

5. Remove the fan, spacer, pulley, and drive belt.

6. Drain the crankcase.

7. Remove pulley from crankshaft pulley adapter. Remove cap screw and washer from front end of crankshaft. Remove crankshaft pulley adapter with a puller.

8. Disconnect fuel pump outlet line at the pump. Remove fuel pump retaining bolts and lay the pump to the side. Remove the engine oil dipstick.

9. Remove the front cover attaching bolts.

10. Remove the crankshaft oil slinger if so equipped.

11. Check timing chain deflection, using the procedure outlined in Step 6 of the in-line six cylinder cover and chain removal.

12. Rotate the engine until sprocket timing marks are aligned as shown in valve timing illustration.

13. Remove crankshaft sprocket cap screw, washers, and fuel pump eccentric. Slide both sprockets and chain forward and off as an assembly.

14. Position sprockets and chain on the camshaft and crankshaft with both timing marks dot to dot on a centerline. Install fuel pump eccentric, washers and sprocket attaching bolt.

Torque the sprocket attaching bolt to 40–45 ft. lbs.

15. Install crankshaft front oil slinger.

16. Clean front cover and mating surfaces of old gasket material. Install a new oil seal in the cover. Use a seal driver tool, if available.

17. Coat a new cover gasket with sealer and position it on the block.

NOTE: *Trim away the exposed portion of the oil pan gasket flush with the cylinder block. Cut and position the required portion of a new gasket to the oil pan, applying sealer to both sides of it.*

18. Install front cover, using a crank-shaft-to-cover alignment tool. Coat the threads of the attaching bolts with sealer. Torque attaching bolts to 12–15 ft. lbs.

19. Install fuel pump, connect fuel pump outlet tube.

20. Install crankshaft pulley adapter and torque attaching bolt. Install crankshaft pulley.

21. Install water pump pulley, drive belt, spacer and fan.

22. Install alternator support bolt at the water pump. Tighten alternator mounting bolts. Adjust drive belt tension. Install Thermactor pump if so equipped.

23. Install radiator and connect all coolant and heater hoses. Connect battery cables.

24. Refill cooling system and the crankcase. Install the dipstick.

25. Start engine and operate at fast idle.

26. Check for leaks, install air cleaner. Adjust ignition timing and make all final adjustments.

Front Cover Oil Seal

REMOVAL AND INSTALLATION

Except 4-140

It is recommended to replace the cover seal any time the front cover is removed.

NOTE: *On V6 engines, the seal may be removed, after the crank pulley is off without removing the cover.*

1. With the cover removed from the car, drive the old seal from the rear of cover with a pinpunch. Clean out the recess in the cover.

2. Coat the new seal with grease and drive it into the cover until it is fully seated. Check the seal after installation to be sure the spring is properly positioned in the seal.

Camshaft Drive Belt and Cover

Four Cylinder 140 cu in. Engine

The correct installation and adjustment of the camshaft drive belt is mandatory if the engine is to run properly. The camshaft controls the opening of the camshaft and the crankshaft.

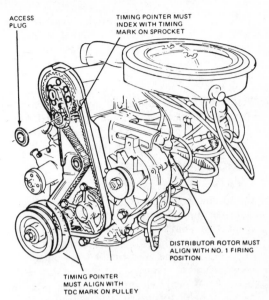

ACCESS PLUG

TIMING POINTER MUST INDEX WITH TIMING MARK ON SPROCKET

DISTRIBUTOR ROTOR MUST ALIGN WITH NO. 1 FIRING POSITION

TIMING POINTER MUST ALIGN WITH TDC MARK ON PULLEY

4-140 camshaft drive train installation

When any given piston is on the intake stroke the corresponding intake valve must be open to admit air/fuel mixture into the cylinder. When the same piston is on the compression and power strokes, both valves in that cylinder must be closed. When the piston is on the exhaust stroke, the exhaust valve for that cylinder must be open. If the opening and closing of the valves is not coordinated with the movements of the pistons, the engine will run very poorly, if at all.

The camshaft drive belt also turns the engine auxiliary shaft. The distributor is driven by the engine auxiliary shaft. Since the distributor controls ignition timing, the auxiliary shaft must be coordinated with the camshaft and the crankshaft, since both valves in any given cylinder must be closed and the piston in that cylinder near the top of the compression stroke when the spark plug fires.

Due to this complex interrelationship between the camshaft, the crankshaft and the auxiliary shaft, the cogged pulleys on each component must be aligned when the camshaft drive belt is installed.

TROUBLESHOOTING

Should the camshaft drive belt jump timing by a tooth or two, the engine could still run; but very poorly. To visually check for correct timing of the crankshaft, auxiliary shaft, and the camshaft follow this procedure:

NOTE: *There is an access plug provided in the cam drive belt cover so that the camshaft timing can be checked without moving the drive belt cover.*

1. Remove the access plug.

2. Turn the crankshaft until the timing marks on the crankshaft indicate TDC.

3. Make sure that the timing mark on the camshaft drive sprocket is aligned with the pointer on the inner belt cover. Also, the rotor of the distributor must align with the No. 1 cylinder firing position.

NOTE: *Never turn the crankshaft of any of the overhead cam engines in the opposite direction of normal rotation. Backward rotation of the crankshaft may cause the timing belt to slip and alter the timing.*

REMOVAL AND INSTALLATION

1. Set the engine to TDC as described in the troubleshooting section. The crankshaft and camshaft timing marks should align with their respective pointers and the distributor rotor should point to the No. 1 plug tower.

2. Loosen the adjustment bolts on the alternator and accessories and remove the drive belts. To provide clearance for removing the camshaft belt, remove the fan and pulley.

3. Remove the belt outer cover.

4. Remove the distributor cap from the distributor and position it out of the way.

5. Loosen the belt tensioner adjustment and pivot bolts. Lever the tensioner away from the belt and retighten the adjustment bolt to hold it away.

6. Remove the crankshaft bolt and pulley. Remove the belt guide behind the pulley.

7. Remove the camshaft drive belt.

8. Install the new belt over the crankshaft pulley first, then counter-clockwise over the auxiliary shaft sprocket and the camshaft sprocket. Adjust the belt fore and aft so that it is centered on the sprockets.

9. Loosen the tensioner adjustment bolt, allowing it to spring back against the belt.

10. Rotate the crankshaft two complete turns in the normal rotation direction to remove any belt slack. Turn the crankshaft until the timing check marks are lined up. If the timing has slipped, remove the belt and repeat the procedure.

11. Tighten the tensioner adjustment bolt to 14–21 ft. lbs., and the pivot bolt to 28–40 ft. lbs.

12. Replace the belt guide and crankshaft pulley, distributor cap, belt outer cover, fan and pulley, drive belts and accessories. Adjust the accessory drive belt tension. Start the engine and check the ignition timing.

Camshaft Drive Belt

REMOVAL AND INSTALLATION

2.4L Diesel Engine

1. Disconnect the negative battery cable. Drain the cooling system. Remove the upper radiator hose. Remove the fan shroud.

2. Remove all drive belts (alternator, air, etc.). Remove the fan and clutch and water pump pulley.

3. Remove the crankshaft damper and pulley.

4. Disconnect the heater hose from the thermostat housing.

5. Remove the four bolts attaching the camshaft drive belt cover to the crankcase and remove the cover.

6. Remove the valve cover. Turn the engine until No. 1 cylinder is at TDC on the compression stroke with the intake and exhaust valves on base circle (heel) of the cam. Install TDC Aligning Pin Tool T84P6400A or the equivalent between the lower engine block and the flywheel.

7. Install Cam Positioning Tool T84P6256A or the equivalent. Loosen the camshaft sprocket bolt.

8. Mark the belt, with a piece of chalk, in the direction of rotation if the belt is to be reused.

9. Loosen the bolts on the belt tensioner, relieve pressure and remove the belt.

10. If installing a new belt or one with less than 10,000 miles on it, insert a feeler gauge .098 inch between the Cam Positioning Tool T84P6256A (or equivalent) and the right front gasket mating surface of the cylinder head.

11. Install an Injection Pump Aligning Pin Tool T84P9000A (or equivalent) through the injection pump sprocket to hold it in position.

12. Rotate the cam sprocket clockwise against the pin. Install the camshaft drive belt.

13. Start the belt at the crankshaft, route the belt around the intermediate shaft sprocket, injection pump sprocket camshaft sprocket and finally the tension roller. Keep belt slack to a minimum during installation.

14. Hand tighten the belt tensioner until all slack is removed.

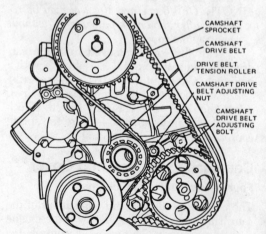

CAMSHAFT SPROCKET

CAMSHAFT DRIVE BELT

DRIVE BELT TENSION ROLLER

CAMSHAFT DRIVE BELT ADJUSTING NUT

CAMSHAFT DRIVE BELT ADJUSTING BOLT

2.4L diesel engine—camshaft drive belt installation

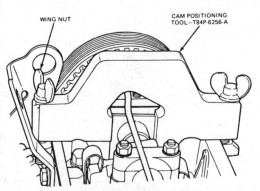

2.4L diesel engine—cam positioning tool installation

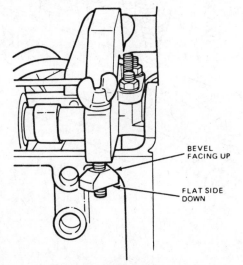

2.4L diesel engine—cam positioning tool nut position

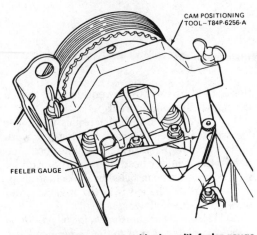

2.4L diesel engine—cam positioning with feeler gauge

15. Remove the Injection Pump Aligning Pin. Adjust the belt tension by applying 34–36 ft. lbs. using a dial type torque wrench. If the old drive belt (more than 10,000 miles) is rein-

2.4L diesel engine—injector pump alignment pin installation

stalled apply 23–25 ft. lbs. Tighten the two tensioner holding bolts to 15–18 ft. lbs.

16. Tighten the camshaft sprocket bolt to 41–47 ft. lbs. Check and adjust (if necessary) the injection pump timing.

17. Remove the Camshaft Positioning Tool and the TDC Alignment Tool.

18. Install the belt cover and tighten the mounting bolts to 6–7 ft. lbs.

19. Install the remaining components in the reverse order of removal.

Camshaft

REMOVAL AND INSTALLATION

Four Cylinder 140 cu in. Engine

NOTE: *The following procedure covers camshaft removal and installation with the cylinder head on or off the engine. If the cylinder head has been removed start at Step 9.*

1. Drain the cooling system. Remove the air cleaner assembly and disconnect the negative battery cable.

2. Remove the spark plug wires from the plugs, disconnect the retainer from the valve cover and position the wires out of the way. Disconnect rubber vacuum lines as necessary.

3. Remove all drive belts. Remove the alternator mounting bracket-to-cylinder head mounting bolts, position bracket and alternator out of the way.

4. Disconnect and remove the upper radiator hose. Disconnect the radiator shroud.

5. Remove the fan blades and water pump pulley and fan shroud. Remove cam belt and valve covers.

6. Align engine timing marks at TDC. Remove cam drive belt.

7. Jack up the front of the car and support on jackstands. Remove the front motor mount bolts. Disconnect the lower radiator hose from

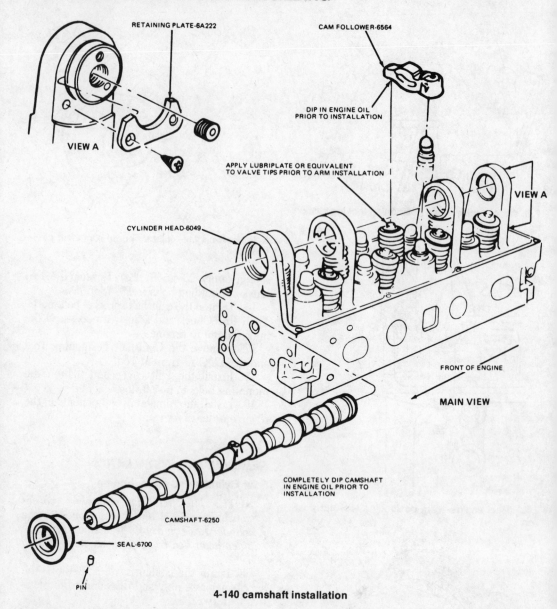

RETAINING PLATE-6A222

CAM FOLLOWER-6564

DIP IN ENGINE OIL
PRIOR TO INSTALLATION

VIEW A

APPLY LUBRIPLATE OR EQUIVALENT
TO VALVE TIPS PRIOR TO ARM INSTALLATION

CYLINDER HEAD-6049

VIEW A

FRONT OF ENGINE

MAIN VIEW

COMPLETELY DIP CAMSHAFT
IN ENGINE OIL PRIOR TO
INSTALLATION

CAMSHAFT-6250

SEAL-6700

PIN

4-140 camshaft installation

the radiator. Disconnect and plug the automatic transmission cooler lines.

8. Position a piece of wood on a floor jack and raise the engine carefully as far as it will go. Place blocks of wood between the engine mounts and crossmember pedestals.

9. Remove the rocker arms as described earlier in this chapter.

10. Remove the camshaft drive gear and belt guide using a suitable puller. Remove the front oil seal with a sheet metal screw and slide hammer.

11. Remove the camshaft retainer located on the rear mounting stand by unbolting the two bolts.

12. Remove the camshaft by carefully withdrawing toward the front of the engine. Cau-

tion should be used to prevent damage to cam bearings, lobes and journals.

13. Check the camshaft journals and lobes for wear. Inspect the cam bearings, if worn (unless the proper bearing installing tool is on hand), the cylinder head must be removed for new bearings to be installed by a machine shop.

14. Cam installation is in the reverse order of removal. See following notes.

NOTE: *Coat the camshaft with heavy SF oil before sliding it into the cylinder head. Install a new front seal. Apply a coat of sealer or teflon tape to the cam drive gear bolt before installation.*

NOTE: *After any procedure requiring removal of the rocker arms, each lash adjuster must be fully collapsed after assembly, then*

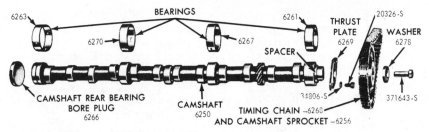

6-200, 250 camshaft and related parts

released. This must be done before the camshaft is turned. See Valve Clearance-Hydraulic Valve Lash Adjusters.

In-Line Six Cylinder Engines

1. Remove the cylinder head.
2. Remove the cylinder front cover, timing chain and sprockets as outlined in the preceding section.
3. Disconnect and remove the radiator, condenser and grille. Remove the gravel deflector.
4. Using a magnet, remove the valve lifters and keep them in order so that they can be installed in their original positions.
5. Remove the camshaft thrust plate and remove the camshaft by pulling it from the front of the engine. Use care not to damage the camshaft lobes or journals while removing the cam from the engine.
6. Before installing the camshaft, coat the lobes with engine assembly lubricant and the journals and all valve parts with heavy oil. Clean the oil passage at the rear of the cylinder block with compressed air.

V6 and V8 Engines

1. Remove or reposition the radiator, A/C condenser and grille components as necessary to provide clearance to remove the camshaft.

2. Remove the cylinder front cover and timing chain as previously described in this chapter.
3. Remove the intake manifold and related parts described earlier in this chapter.
4. Remove the crankcase ventilation valve and tubes from the valve rocker covers. Remove the EGR cooler, if so equipped.
5. Remove the rocker arm covers and loosen the valve rocker arm fulcrum bolts and rotate the rocker arms to the side.
6. Remove the valve push rods and identify them so that they can be installed in their original positions.
7. Remove the valve lifters and place them in a rack so that they can be installed in their original bores.
8. Remove the camshaft thrust plate or button and spring and carefully remove the camshaft by pulling toward the front of the engine. Be careful not to damage the camshaft bearings.
9. Before installing, oil the camshaft journals with heavy engine oil SF and apply Lubriplate® or equivalent to the lobes. Carefully slide the camshaft through the bearings.
10. Install the camshaft thrust plate with the groove towards the cylinder block.
11. Lubricate the lifters with heavy SF engine oil and install in their original bores.

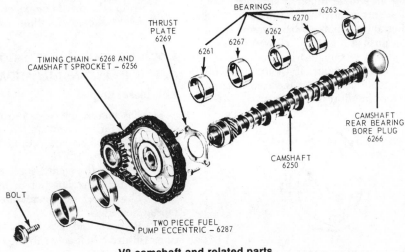

V8 camshaft and related parts

12. Apply Lubriplate® or equivalent to the valve stem tips and each end of the push rods. Install the push rods in their original position.

13. Lubricate the rocker arms and fulcrum seats with heave SF engine oil and position the rocker arms over the push rods.

14. Install all other parts previously removed.

15. Fill the crankcase and cooling system and adjust the timing.

2.4L Diesel Engine

1. Disconnect the negative battery cable.

2. Remove the valve cover and vacuum pump. Remove the fan and clutch assembly and all accessory drive belts.

3. Remove the camshaft drive belt cover. Remove all rocker arms.

4. Turn the engine until No. 1 piston is at TDC on the compression stroke. Install the TDC Alignment Pin (refer to cam belt section).

5. Loosen the camshaft sprocket bolt. Loosen the drive belt tensioner. Remove the drive belt and camshaft sprocket.

6. Mark the camshaft bearing caps for position and installation direction. Remove the bearing caps and the camshaft.

7. Install the camshaft in the reverse order of removal. Bearing caps are torqued to 6–7 ft. lbs. for the 6 mm nuts and 14–17 ft. lbs. for the 8mm nuts. Refer to the cam bolt removal and installation and various other procedures. Refer to Chapter 2 for Valve Adjustment.

CHECKING CAMSHAFT

Degrease the camshaft using safe solvent, clean all oil grooves. Visually inspect the cam lobes and bearing journals for excessive wear. If a lobe is questionable, check all lobes and journals with a micrometer.

Measure the lobes from nose to base and again at 90°. The lift is determined by subtracting the second measurement from the first. If all exhaust lobes and all intake lobes are not identical, the camshaft must be reground or replaced. Measure the bearing journals and compare to specifications. If a journal is worn there is a good chance that the cam bearings are worn too, requiring replacement.

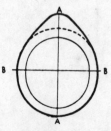

Camshaft lobe measurement

If the lobes and journals appear intact, place the front and rear cam journals in V-blocks and rest a dial indicator on the center journal. Rotate the camshaft to check for straightness, if deviation exceeds .001 inch, replace the camshaft.

Auxiliary Shaft
REMOVAL AND INSTALLATION
Four Cylinder 140 cu in. Engine

1. Remove the camshaft drive belt cover.

2. Remove the drive belt. Remove the auxiliary shaft sprocket. A puller may be necessary to remove the sprocket.

3. Remove the distributor and fuel pump.

4. Remove the auxiliary shaft cover and thrust plate.

5. Withdraw the auxiliary shaft from the block.

NOTE: *The distributor drive gear and the fuel pump eccentric on the auxiliary shaft must not be allowed to touch the auxiliary shaft bearings during removal and installation. Completely coat the shaft with oil before sliding it into place.*

6. Slide the auxiliary shaft into the housing and insert the thrust plate to hold the shaft.

7. Install a new gasket and auxiliary shaft cover.

NOTE: *The auxiliary shaft cover and cylinder front cover share a gasket. Cut off the old gasket around the cylinder cover and use half of the new gasket on the auxiliary shaft cover.*

8. Fit a new gasket into the fuel pump and install the pump.

9. Insert the distributor and install the auxiliary shaft sprocket.

10. Align the timing marks and install the drive belt.

11. Install the drive belt cover.

12. Check the ignition timing.

Engine Front Cover/Sprockets
REMOVAL AND INSTALLATION
2.4L Diesel Engine

1. Disconnect the battery ground cable.

2. Drain the cooling system.

3. Loosen and remove the accessory drive belts.

4. Remove the engine cooling fan.

5. Remove the vibration damper.

6. Disconnect the heater hose from thermostat housing.

7. Remove the four bolts attaching the camshaft drive belt cover to the crankcase and remove the cover.

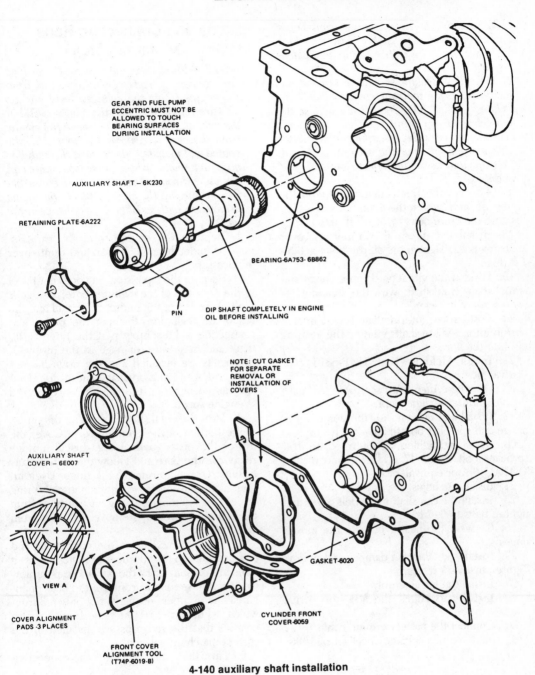

GEAR AND FUEL PUMP ECCENTRIC MUST NOT BE ALLOWED TO TOUCH BEARING SURFACES DURING INSTALLATION

AUXILIARY SHAFT – 6K230

RETAINING PLATE-6A222

BEARING-6A753- 6B862

PIN

DIP SHAFT COMPLETELY IN ENGINE OIL BEFORE INSTALLING

NOTE: CUT GASKET FOR SEPARATE REMOVAL OR INSTALLATION OF COVERS

AUXILIARY SHAFT COVER – 6E007

GASKET-6020

VIEW A

COVER ALIGNMENT PADS -3 PLACES

CYLINDER FRONT COVER-6059

FRONT COVER ALIGNMENT TOOL (T74P-6019-B)

4-140 auxiliary shaft installation

8. Remove the camshaft drive belt.

9. Remove the bolts attaching the intermediate shaft sprocket using Holding Tool T84P-6316-A or equivalent.

NOTE: *Be sure Allen head screws are aligned with holes in intermediate shaft sprocket.*

10. Remove the vibration damper flange and sprocket retaining bolt and remove the flange and sprocket using puller, T67L-3600-A or equivalent.

11. Remove the three oil pan-to-front cover attaching bolts. Loosen, but **DO NOT REMOVE,** the remaining oil pan bolts.

12. Remove the six bolts attaching the front cover to the crankcase, and remove cover.

13. Clean the front cover and crankcase gasket mating surfaces.

14. Inspect and replace the crankshaft and intermediate shaft oil seals, if necessary.

15. If the oil pan gasket is damaged, install a new pan gasket.

16. Install the new front cover gasket.

NOTE: *Coat the areas where front cover gasket meets oil pan gasket with a ¼ inch RTV Sealant, D6AZ-19562-A or equivalent sealer.*

NOTE: *RTV Sealant should be applied immediately prior to front cover installation. When applying RTV Sealant always use the bead size specified and join the components within 15 minutes of application. After this amount of time the sealant begins to "set-up" and its sealing effectiveness may be reduced.*

17. Position the front engine cover on the crankcase, and tighten the 6mm bolts to 6–7 ft. lbs. and the 8mm bolts to 14–17 ft. lbs.

18. Install the three oil pan-to-front cover attaching bolts. Tighten the oil pan bolts to 6.5–7 ft. lbs.

19. Position the vibration damper flange and sprocket on crankshaft, with the shoulder toward front of vehicle.

20. Position the intermediate shaft sprocket on the intermediate shaft, guiding the locating pin into the bore.

21. Install Holding Tool T84P-6316-A or equivalent.

NOTE: *Align Allen head screws in tool with holes in intermediate shaft.*

22. Install and tighten the vibration damper flange and sprocket bolt to 282–311 ft. lbs.

23. Install and tighten the intermediate shaft sprocket bolt to 40–47 ft. lbs. Remove Tool T84P-6316-A or equivalent.

24. Install and adjust the camshaft drive belt.

25. Install the camshaft drive belt cover and tighten bolts to 6–7 ft. lbs.

26. Connect the heater hose to thermostat housing.

27. Install the vibration damper and pulley. Tighten to 16–17 ft. lbs.

28. Install the fan assembly.

29. Install and adjust the accessory drive belts.

30. Connect the battery ground cable.

31. Start and idle engine. Check for oil leaks.

OIL SEAL, FRONT— CRANKSHAFT/INTERMEDIATE SHAFT

1. Remove the engine front cover.

2. Using an arbor press, press old seal(s) out of the front cover.

3. Position the new seals on the front cover and install, using T84P-6019-B for crankshaft seal, or T84P-6020-A or equivalent for intermediate shaft seal.

4. Lubricate the sealing lips with engine oil.

5. Install engine front cover.

Pistons and Connection Rods

REMOVAL AND INSTALLATION

NOTE: *Although, in most cases, the pistons and connecting rods can be removed from the engine (after the cylinder head and oil pan are removed) while the engine is still in the car; it is far easier to remove the engine from the car. If removing pistons with the engine still installed, disconnect the radiator hoses, automatic transmission cooler lines and radiator shroud. Unbolt front mounts before jacking up the engine. Block the engine in position with wooden blocks between the mounts.*

1. Remove the engine from the car. Remove cylinder head(s), oil pan and front cover (if necessary).

2. Because the top piston ring does not travel to the very top of the cylinder bore, a ridge is built up between the end of the travel and the top of the cylinder. Pushing the piston and connecting rod assembly past the ridge is difficult and may cause damage to the piston. If new rings are installed and the ridge has not been removed, ring breakage and piston damage can occur when the ridge is encountered at engine speed.

3. Turn the crankshaft to position the piston at the bottom of the cylinder bore. Cover the top of the piston with a rag. Install a ridge reamer in the bore and follow the manufacturer's instructions to remove the ridge. Use caution; avoid cutting too deeply or into the ring travel area. Remove the rag and cuttings from the top of the piston. Remove the ridge from all cylinders.

4. Check the edges of the connecting rod and bearing cap for numbers or matchmarks, if none are present mark the rod and cap numerically and in sequence from front to back of engine. The numbers or marks not only tell from which cylinder the piston came from but also ensures that the rod caps are installed in the correct matching position.

5. Turn the crankshaft until the connecting

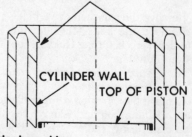

RIDGE CAUSED BY CYLINDER WEAR

CYLINDER WALL

TOP OF PISTON

Cylinder bore ridge

Match the connecting rod and cap with scribe marks

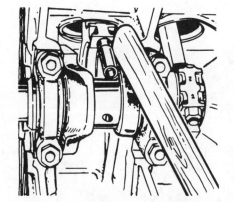

Push the piston out with a hammer handle

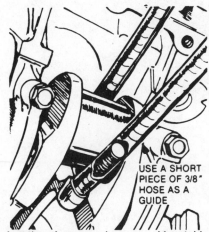

USE A SHORT PIECE OF 3/8″ HOSE AS A GUIDE

Use lengths of vacuum hose or rubber tubing to protect the crankshaft journals and cylinder walls during installation

rod is at the bottom of travel. Remove the two attaching nuts and the bearing cap. Take two pieces of rubber tubing and cover the rod bolts to prevent crank or cylinder scoring. Use a wooden hammer handle to help push the piston and rod up and out of the cylinder. Reinstall the rod cap in proper position. Remove all pistons and connecting rods. Inspect cylinder walls and deglaze or hone as necessary.

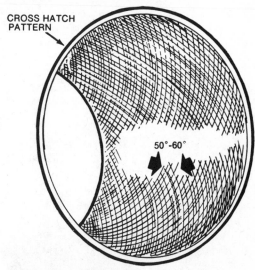

CROSS HATCH PATTERN

50°-60°

Cylinder bore after honing

6. Installation is in the reverse order of removal. Lubricate each piston, rod bearing and cylinder wall. Install a ring compressor over the piston, position piston with mark toward front of engine and carefully install. Position connecting rod with bearing insert installed over the crank journal. Install the rod cap with bearing in proper position. Secure with rod nuts and torque to proper specifications. Install all rod and piston assemblies.

CLEANING AND INSPECTION

1. Use a piston ring expander and remove the rings from the piston.
2. Clean the ring grooves using an appropriate cleaning tool, exercise care to avoid cutting too deeply.
3. Clean all varnish and carbon from the piston with a safe solvent. Do not use a wire brush or caustic solution on the pistons.
4. Inspect the pistons for scuffing, scoring, cracks, pitting or excessive ring groove wear. If wear is evident, the piston must be replaced.

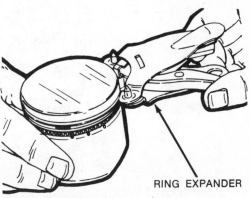

RING EXPANDER

Remove the piston rings

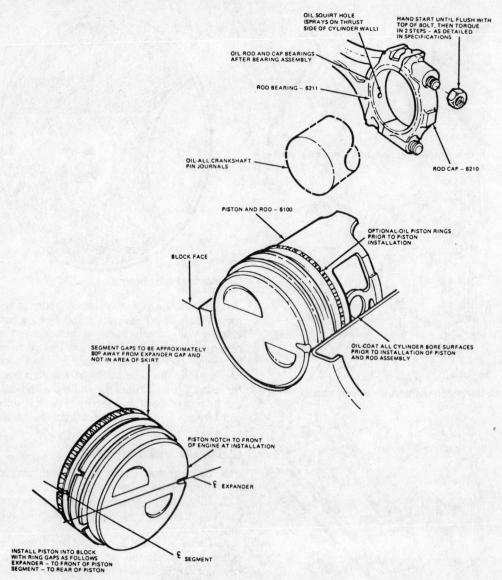

OIL SQUIRT HOLE
(SPRAYS ON THRUST
SIDE OF CYLINDER WALL)

HAND START UNTIL FLUSH WITH
TOP OF BOLT, THEN TORQUE
IN 2 STEPS – AS DETAILED
IN SPECIFICATIONS

OIL ROD AND CAP BEARINGS
AFTER BEARING ASSEMBLY

ROD BEARING – 6211

ROD CAP – 6210

OIL-ALL CRANKSHAFT
PIN JOURNALS

PISTON AND ROD – 6100

OPTIONAL-OIL PISTON RINGS
PRIOR TO PISTON
INSTALLATION

BLOCK FACE

OIL-COAT ALL CYLINDER BORE SURFACES
PRIOR TO INSTALLATION OF PISTON
AND ROD ASSEMBLY

SEGMENT GAPS TO BE APPROXIMATELY
80° AWAY FROM EXPANDER GAP AND
NOT IN AREA OF SKIRT

PISTON NOTCH TO FRONT
OF ENGINE AT INSTALLATION

ε EXPANDER

INSTALL PISTON INTO BLOCK
WITH RING GAPS AS FOLLOWS
EXPANDER – TO FRONT OF PISTON
SEGMENT – TO REAR OF PISTON

ε SEGMENT

4-140 piston rings and connecting rods

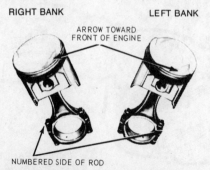

RIGHT BANK   LEFT BANK

ARROW TOWARD
FRONT OF ENGINE

NUMBERED SIDE OF ROD

Correct position of piston and rod—351C, 351M and 400 V8

5. Have the piston and connecting rod assembly checked by a machine shop for correct alignment, piston pin wear and piston diameter. If the piston has "collapsed" it will have to be replaced or knurled to restore original diameter. Connecting rod bushing replacement, piston pin fitting and piston changing can be handled by the machine shop.

CYLINDER BORE

1. Check the cylinder bore for wear using a telescope gauge and a micrometer, measure the cylinder bore diameter perpendicular to the piston pin at a point 2½ inches below the top

of the engine block. Measure the piston skirt perpendicular to the piston pin. The difference between the two measurements is the piston clearance. If the clearance is within specifications, finish honing or glaze breaking is all that is required. If clearance is excessive a slightly oversize piston may be required. If greatly oversize, the engine will have to be bored and .010 inch or larger oversized pistons installed.

FITTING AND POSITIONING PISTON RINGS

1. Take the new piston rings and compress them, one at a time into the cylinder that they will be used in. Press the ring about one inch below the top of the cylinder block using an inverted piston.

2. Use a feeler gauge and measure the distance between the ends of the ring; this is called measuring the ring end-gap. Compare the reading to the one called for in the specifications table. File the ends of the ring with a fine file to obtain necessary clearance.

NOTE: *If inadequate ring end-gap is utilized, ring breakage will result.*

3. Inspect the ring grooves on the piston for excessive wear or taper. If necessary have the grooves recut for use with a standard ring and spacer. The machine shop can handle the job for you.

Check the piston ring end gap

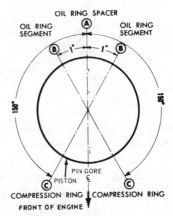

Piston ring spacing (all engines)

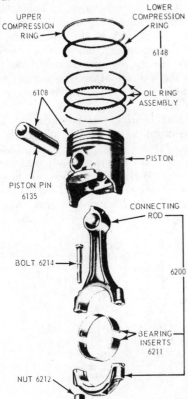

Typical piston and connecting rod assembly

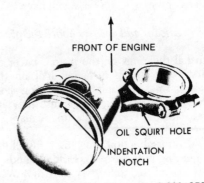

Piston and rod positioning on the 6-200, 250

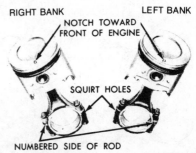

Piston and rod positioning on the V6-232, V8-255, 302, 351W, 429 and 460

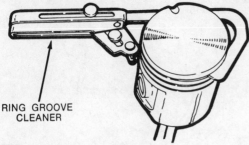

RING GROOVE
CLEANER

Clean the piston ring grooves

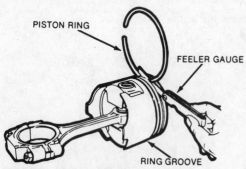

PISTON RING

FEELER GAUGE

RING GROOVE

Check the piston ring side clearance

4. Check the ring grooves by rolling the new piston ring around the groove to check for burrs or carbon deposits. If any are found, remove with a fine file. Hold the ring in the groove and measure side clearance with a feeler gauge. If clearance is excessive, spacer(s) will have to be added.

NOTE: *Always add spacers above the piston ring.*

5. Install the rings on the piston, lower oil ring first. Use a ring installing tool on the compression rings. Consult the instruction sheet that comes with the rings to be sure they are installed with the correct side up. A mark on the ring usually faces upward.

6. When installing oil rings; first, install the expanding ring in the groove. Hold the ends of the ring butted together (they must not overlap) and install the bottom rail (scraper) with the end about one inch away from the butted

end of the control ring. Install the top rail about an inch away from the butted end of the control but on the opposite side from the lower rail.

7. Install the two compression rings.

8. Consult the illustration for ring positioning, arrange the rings as shown, install a ring compressor and insert the piston and rod assembly into the engine.

Crankshaft and Bearings

1. Rod bearings can be installed when the pistons have been removed for servicing (rings etc.) or, in most cases, while the engine is still in the car. Bearing replacement, however, is far easier with the engine out of the car and disassembled.

2. For in car service, remove the oil pan, spark plugs and front cover if necessary. Turn the engine until the connecting rod to be serviced is at the bottom of travel. Remove the bearing cap, place two pieces of rubber hose over the rod cap bolts and push the piston and rod assembly up the cylinder bore until enough room is gained for bearing insert removal. Take care not to push the rod assembly up too far or the top ring will engage the cylinder ridge or come out of the cylinder and require head removal for reinstallation.

3. Clean the rod journal, the connecting rod end and the bearing cap after removing the old bearing inserts. Install the new inserts in the rod and bearing cap, lubricate them with oil. Position the rod over the crankshaft journal and install the rod cap. Make sure the cap and rod numbers match, torque the rod nuts to specifications.

4. Main bearings may be replaced while the engine is still in the car by "rolling" them out and in.

5. Special roll out pins are available from automotive parts houses or can be fabricated from a cotter pin. The roll out pin fits in the oil hole of the main bearing journal. When the crankshaft is rotated opposite the direction of

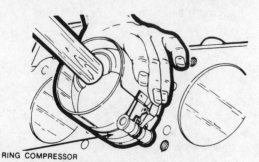

RING COMPRESSOR

Install the piston using a ring compressor

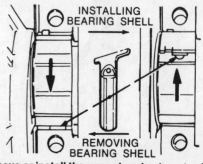

INSTALLING
BEARING SHELL

REMOVING
BEARING SHELL

Remove or install the upper bearing insert using a roll-out pin

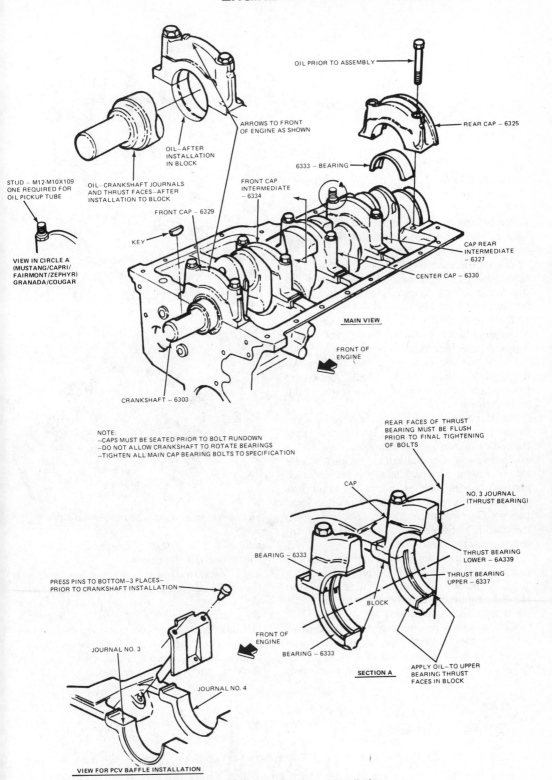

OIL PRIOR TO ASSEMBLY

REAR CAP – 6325

6333 – BEARING

ARROWS TO FRONT
OF ENGINE AS SHOWN

OIL–AFTER
INSTALLATION
IN BLOCK

OIL–CRANKSHAFT JOURNALS
AND THRUST FACES–AFTER
INSTALLATION TO BLOCK

STUD – M12-M10X109
ONE REQUIRED FOR
OIL PICKUP TUBE

FRONT CAP
INTERMEDIATE
– 6334

FRONT CAP – 6329

KEY

VIEW IN CIRCLE A
(MUSTANG/CAPRI/
FAIRMONT/ZEPHYR)
GRANADA/COUGAR

CAP REAR
INTERMEDIATE
– 6327

CENTER CAP – 6330

MAIN VIEW

FRONT OF
ENGINE

CRANKSHAFT – 6303

NOTE:
–CAPS MUST BE SEATED PRIOR TO BOLT RUNDOWN
–DO NOT ALLOW CRANKSHAFT TO ROTATE BEARINGS
–TIGHTEN ALL MAIN CAP BEARING BOLTS TO SPECIFICATION

REAR FACES OF THRUST
BEARING MUST BE FLUSH
PRIOR TO FINAL TIGHTENING
OF BOLTS

CAP

NO. 3 JOURNAL
(THRUST BEARING)

BEARING – 6333

THRUST BEARING
LOWER – 6A339

THRUST BEARING
UPPER – 6337

PRESS PINS TO BOTTOM–3 PLACES–
PRIOR TO CRANKSHAFT INSTALLATION

BLOCK

FRONT OF
ENGINE

JOURNAL NO. 3

BEARING – 6333

JOURNAL NO. 4

APPLY OIL–TO UPPER
BEARING THRUST
FACES IN BLOCK

SECTION A

VIEW FOR PCV BAFFLE INSTALLATION

4-140 crankshaft and main bearing installation

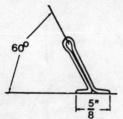

Home-made bearing roll-out pin

the bearing lock tab, the pin engages the end of the bearing and "rolls" out the insert.

6. Remove main bearing cap and roll out upper bearing insert. Remove insert from main bearing cap. Clean the inside of the bearing cap and crankshaft journal.

7. Lubricate and roll upper insert into position, make sure the lock tab is anchored and the insert is not "cocked". Install the lower bearing insert into the cap, lubricate and install on the engine. Make sure the main bearing cap is installed facing in the correct direction and torque to specifications.

8. With the engine out of the car. Remove the intake manifold, cylinder heads, front cover, timing gears and/or chain, oil pan, oil pump and flywheel.

9. Remove the piston and rod assemblies. Remove the main bearing caps after marking them for position and direction.

10. Remove the crankshaft, bearing inserts and rear main oil seal. Clean the engine block and cap bearing saddles. Clean the crankshaft and inspect for wear. Check the bearing journals with a micrometer for out-of-round condition and to determine what size rod and main bearing inserts to install.

11. Install the main bearing upper inserts and rear main oil seal half into the engine block.

12. Lubricate the bearing inserts and the crankshaft journals. Slowly and carefully lower the crankshaft into position.

13. Install the bearing inserts and rear main seal into the bearing caps, install the caps working from the middle out. Torque cap bolts to specifications in stages, rotate the crankshaft

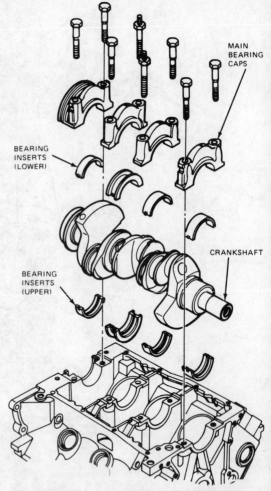

V6 crankshaft and main bearing installation

after each torque state. Note the illustration for thrust bearing alignment.

14. Remove bearing caps, one at a time and check the oil clearance with Plastigage®. Reinstall if clearance is within specifications. Check the crankshaft end-play, if within specifications install connecting rod and piston assemblies with new rod bearing inserts. Check connecting rod bearing oil clearance and side play, if correct assemble the rest of the engine.

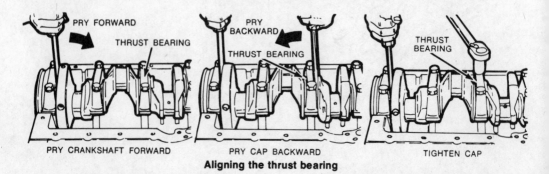

Aligning the thrust bearing

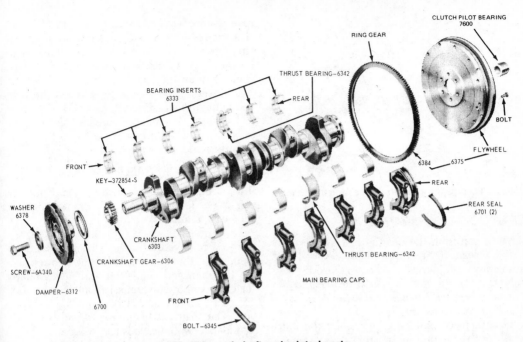

6-200, 250 crankshaft and related parts

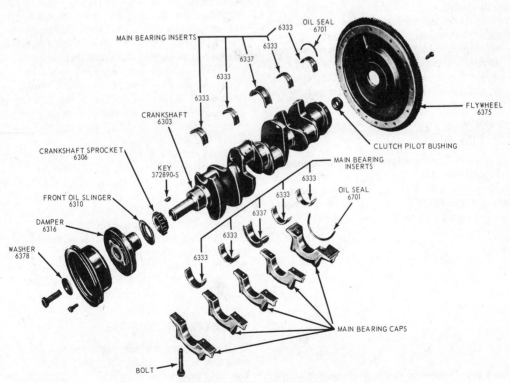

V8 crankshaft and related parts

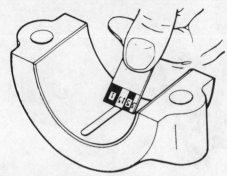

Measure Plastigage® to determine bearing clearance

BEARING OIL CLEARANCE

Remove cap from the bearing to be checked. Using a clean, dry rag, thoroughly clean all oil from crankshaft journal and bearing insert.

NOTE: *Plastigage® is soluble in oil; therefore, oil on the journal or bearing could result in erroneous readings.*

Place a piece of Plastigage® along the full width of the bearing insert, reinstall cap, and torque to specifications.

NOTE: *Specifications are given in the engine specifications earlier in this chapter.*

Remove bearing cap, and determine bearing clearance by comparing width of Plastigage® to the scale on Plastigage® envelope. Journal taper is determined by comparing width of the bearing insert, reinstall cap, and torque to specifications.

NOTE: *Do not rotate crankshaft with Plastigage® installed. If bearing insert and journal appear intact, and are within tolerances, no further main bearing service is required. If bearing or journal appear defective, cause of failure should be determined before replacement.*

CRANKSHAFT END-PLAY/CONNECTING ROD SIDE PLAY

Place a pry bar between a main bearing cap and crankshaft casting taking care not to damage any journals. Pry backward and forward, measure the distance between the thrust bearing and crankshaft with a feeler gauge. Com-

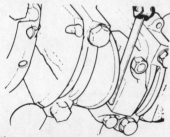

Check the connecting rod side clearance with a feeler gauge

pare reading with specifications. If too great a clearance is determined, a main bearing with a larger thrust surface or crank machining may be required. Check with an automotive machine shop for their advice.

Connecting rod clearance between the rod and crankthrow casting can be checked with a feeler gauge. Pry the rod carefully to one side as far as possible and measure the distance on the other side of the rod.

CRANKSHAFT REPAIRS

If a journal is damaged on the crankshaft, repair is possible by having the crankshaft machined to a standard undersize.

In most cases, however, since the engine must be removed from the car and disassembled, some thought should be given to replacing the damaged crankshaft with a reground shaft kit. A reground crankshaft kit contains the necessary main and rod bearings for installation. The shaft has been ground and polished to undersize specifications and will usually hold up well if installed correctly.

COMPLETING THE REBUILDING PRCOESS

Complete the rebuilding process as follows:

Fill the oil pump with oil, to prevent cavitating (sucking air) on initial engine start up. Install the oil pump and the pickup tube on the engine. Coat the oil pan gasket as necessary, and install the gasket and the oil pan. Mount the flywheel and the crankshaft vibration damper or pulley on the crankshaft.

NOTE: *Always use new bolts when installing the flywheel. Inspect the clutch shaft pilot bushing in the crankshaft. If the bushing is excessively worn, remove it with an expanding puller and a slide hammer, and tap a new bushing into place.*

Position the engine, cylinder head side up. Lubricate the lifters, and install them into their bores. Install the cylinder head, and torque it as specified. Insert the pushrods (where applicable), and install the rocker shaft(s) (if so equipped) or position the rocker.

Install the intake and exhaust manifolds, the carburetor(s), the distributor and spark plugs. Mount all accessories and install the engine in the car. Fill the radiator with coolant, and the crankcase with high quality engine oil.

BREAK-IN PROCEDURE

Start the engine, and allow it to run at low speed for a few minutes, while checking for leaks. Stop the engine, check the oil level, and fill as necessary. Restart the engine, and fill the cooling system to capacity. Check and adjust the ignition timing. Run the engine at low to medium speed (800–2500 rpm) for approximately ½ hour, and retorque the cylinder head bolts. Road test the car, and check again for leaks.

NOTE: *Some gasket manufacturers recommend not retorquing the cylinder head(s) due to the composition of the head gasket. Follow the directions in the gasket set.*

Oil Pan

REMOVAL AND INSTALLATION

NOTE: *Always raise and safely support the vehicle safely on jackstands. When raising the engine, place a piece of wood between the jack and jacking point, make sure the hood is opened and the fan blade does not touch*

the radiator or that radiator hoses or transmission lines are not stretched.

4-140 Engine

1. Disconnect negative battery cable.
2. Drain the crankcase and cooling system.
3. Remove the right and left engine support bolts and nuts or through bolts. Disconnect the hydraulic damper if equipped. Disconnect the upper and lower radiator hoses.
4. Using a jack, raise the engine as far as it will go. Place blocks of wood between the mounts and the chassis brackets. Remove the jack.
5. Remove the steering gear retaining nuts and bolts. Remove the bolt retaining the steering flex coupling to the steering gear. Position the steering gear forward and down.

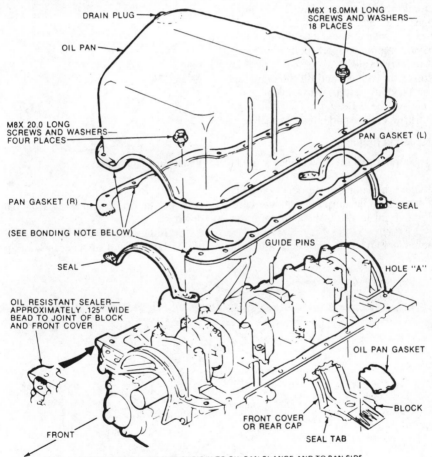

1. APPLY GASKET ADHESIVE EVENLY TO OIL PAN FLANGE AND TO PAN SIDE GASKETS. ALLOW ADHESIVE TO DRY PAST WET STAGE, THEN INSTALL GASKETS TO OIL PAN.
2. APPLY SEALER TO JOINT OF BLOCK AND FRONT COVER. INSTALL SEALS TO FRONT COVER AND REAR BEARING CAP AND PRESS SEAL TABS FIRMLY INTO BLOCK. BE SURE TO INSTALL THE REAR SEAL BEFORE THE REAR MAIN BEARING CAP SEALER HAS CURED.
3. POSITION 2 GUIDE PINS AND INSTALL THE OIL PAN. SECURE THE PAN WITH THE FOUR M8 BOLTS SHOWN ABOVE
4. REMOVE THE GUIDE PINS AND INSTALL AND TORQUE THE EIGHTEEN M6 BOLTS, BEGINNING AT HOLE "A" AND WORKING CLOCKWISE AROUND THE PAN.

4-140 oil pan bolt installation

6. Remove the shake brace and starter.

7. Remove the engine rear support to crossmember nuts.

8. Position a jack under the transmission and raise.

9. Remove oil pan retaining bolts. Remove the oil pan. It may be necessary to turn the crankshaft when removing the pan to avoid interference.

10. Position the new oil pan gasket and end seals to the cylinder block with cement.

11. Position the oil pan to the cylinder block and install its retaining bolts.

12. Lower the jack under the transmission and install the crossmember nuts.

13. Replace the oil filter.

14. Position the flex coupling to the steering gear and install the retaining bolt.

15. Install the steering gear.

16. Install the shake brace. Install the starter.

17. Raise the engine enough to remove the wood blocks. Lower the engine and remove the jack. Install engine support bolts and nuts. Connect radiator hoses.

18. Lower the vehicle and fill the crankcase with oil and cooling system with coolant.

19. Connect the battery.

20. Start the engine and check for leaks.

6 Cylinder Inline Engines

1. Disconnect two oil cooler lines at radiator.

2. Remove radiator top support two bolts. Remove or position fan shroud back over fan.

3. Remove oil level dipstick, drain crankcase.

4. Remove four bolts and nuts attaching

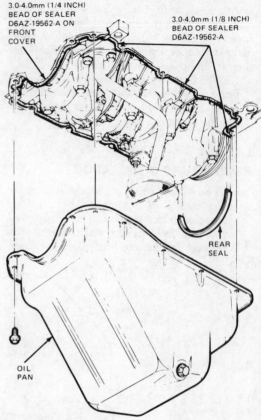

V6 oil pan installation

sway bar to chassis and allow sway bar to hang down.

5. Remove K brace.

6. Lower front steering rack and pinion, or

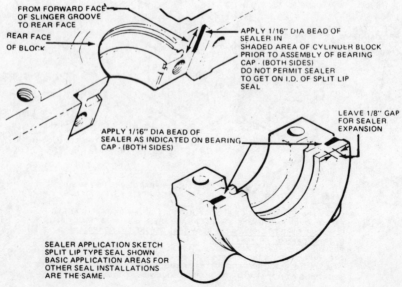

rear main oil seal installation on all except 4-140

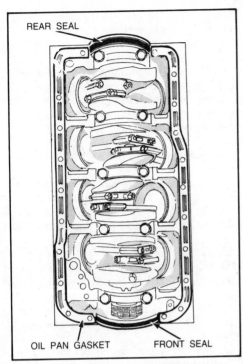

REAR SEAL

OIL PAN GASKET   FRONT SEAL

Typical oil pan gasket and seal installation

center link and linkage, if necessary for clearance.

7. Remove starter.

8. Remove two nuts attaching engine mounts to support brackets.

9. Loosen two rear insulator-to-crossmember attaching bolts.

10. Raise engine and place 1¼ in. spacer between engine support insulator and chassis brackets.

11. Position jack under transmission and raise slightly.

12. Remove oil pan attaching bolts and lower pan to crossmember. Position transmission cooler lines out of the way and remove oil pan (rotating crankshaft if required).

13. The oil pan has a two piece gasket. Coat the block surface and the oil pan gasket surfaces with oil resistant sealer, and position gaskets to cylinder block.

14. Position the oil pan seals in the cylinder front cover and rear bearing cap.

15. Insert gasket tabs under front and rear seals.

16. Position oil pan to cylinder block and install attaching bolts.

17. Position transmission cooler lines.

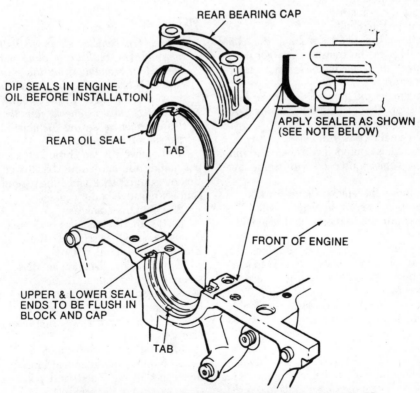

REAR BEARING CAP

DIP SEALS IN ENGINE
OIL BEFORE INSTALLATION

APPLY SEALER AS SHOWN
(SEE NOTE BELOW)

REAR OIL SEAL   TAB

FRONT OF ENGINE

UPPER & LOWER SEAL
ENDS TO BE FLUSH IN
BLOCK AND CAP

TAB

NOTE: CLEAN THE AREA WHERE SEALER IS TO BE APPLIED BEFORE INSTALLING THE SEALS. AFTER THE SEALS ARE IN PLACE, APPLY A 1/16 INCH BEAD OF SEALER AS SHOWN. *SEALER MUST NOT TOUCH SEALS*

4-140 rear main oil seal replacement

18. Lower jack under transmission.

19. Raise engine to remove spacers and lower engine to chassis.

20. Tighten two nuts attaching rear support insulator to crossmember.

21. Install two engine support to chassis through bolts and nuts.

22. Install starter motor and sway bar.

23. Install "K" brace, fill crankcase with oil.

24. Connect oil cooler lines to radiator and install upper radiator support.

25. Lower vehicle, start engine and check for leaks.

V6 (232) Engine

1. Remove the air cleaner assembly including the air intake duct. Drain the cooling system.

2. Remove the fan shroud attaching bolts and position the shroud back over the fan.

3. Remove the oil level dipstick.

4. Remove the screws attaching the vacuum solenoids to the dash panel. Lay the solenoids on the engine without disconnecting the vacuum hoses or electrical connectors.

5. Remove the exhaust manifold to exhaust pipe attaching nuts. Disconnect the radiator hoses from the radiator.

6. Drain the crankcase.

7. Remove the oil filter.

8. Remove the bolts attaching the shift linkage bracket to the transmission bell housing. Remove the starter motor for more clearance if necessary.

9. Disconnect the transmission cooler lines at the radiator. Remove power steering hose retaining clamp from frame.

10. Remove the converter cover.

11. On models equipped with rack and pinion steering vehicles proceed with the following steps.

   a. Remove the engine damper to No. 2 crossmember bracket attaching bolt. The damper must be disconnected from the crossmember.

   b. Disconnect steering flex coupling. Remove two bolts attaching steering gear to main crossmember and let steering gear rest on the frame away from oil pan.

12. Remove the nut and washer assembly attaching the front engine insulator to the chassis.

13. Raise the engine 2–3 in. or higher on some models and insert wood blocks between the engine mounts and the vehicle frame.

CAUTION: *Watch the clearance between the transmission dipstick tube and the thermactor downstream air tube. If the tubes contact before adequate pan-to-crossmember clearance is provided, lower the engine and*

remove the transmission dipstick tube and the downstream air tube.

14. Remove the oil pan attaching bolts. Work the oil pan loose and remove.

15. On models with limited clearance, lower the oil pan onto the crossmember. Remove the oil pickup tube attaching nut. Lower the pickup tube/screen assembly into the pan and remove the oil pan through the front of the vehicle.

16. Remove the oil pan seal from the main bearing cap.

17. Clean the gasket surfaces on the cylinder block, oil pan and oil pick-up tube.

18. Apply ⅛ in. bead of RTV sealer to all matching surfaces of oil pan and engine front cover.

19. Install the oil pan.

NOTE: *On models with limited clearance place the oil pick-up tube/screen assembly in the oil pan.*

20. Install all other components removed.

21. Fill the crankcase to the correct level with the oil.

22. Start the engine and check the fluid levels in the transmission.

23. Check for engine oil, and transmission fluid leaks.

V8 Engines

NOTE: *On vehicles equipped with a dual sump oil pan, both drain plugs must be removed to thoroughly drain the crankcase.*

NOTE: *When raising the engine for oil pan removal clearance; drain cooling system, disconnect hoses, check fan to radiator clearance when jacking. Remove radiator if clearance is inadequate.*

1. Remove the fan shroud attaching bolts, positioning the fan shroud back over the fan. Remove the dipstick and tube assembly. Disconnect negative battery cable.

2. Drain the crankcase.

3. Remove the stabilizer bar from the chassis (Versailles only). Disconnect the engine stabilizer on models equipped.

4. On rack and pinion models disconnect steering flex coupling. Remove two bolts attaching steering gear to main crossmember and let steering gear rest on frame away from oil pan. Disconnect power steering hose retaining clamp from frame.

5. Remove the starter motor.

6. Remove the idler arm bracket retaining bolts (models equipped) and pull the linkage down and out of the way.

7. Disconnect and plug the fuel line from the gas tank at the fuel pump. Disconnect and lower the exhaust pipe/converter assemblies if they will interfere with pan removal/

installation. Raise the engine and place two wood blocks between the engine mounts and the vehicle frame. Remove converter inspection cover.

NOTE: *On fuel injected models, depressurize system prior to line disconnection.*

8. Remove rear K braces (four bolts).

9. Remove the oil pan attaching bolts and lower oil pan to the frame.

10. Remove oil pump attaching bolts and the inset tube attaching nut from the No. 3 main bearing cap stud and lower the oil pump into the oil pan.

11. Remove the oil pan, rotating the crankshaft as necessary to clear the counterweights.

12. Clean the gasket mounting surfaces thoroughly. Coat the surfaces on the block and pan with sealer. Position the pan side gaskets on the engine block. Install the front cover oil seal on the cover, with the tabs over the pan side gaskets. Install the rear main cap seal with the tabs over the pan side gaskets.

13. Position oil pump and inlet tube into oil pan. Slide oil pan into position under the engine. With the oil pump intermediate shaft in position in the oil pump, position the oil pump to the cylinder block, and the inlet tube to the stud on No. 3 main bearing cap attaching bolt. Install the attaching bolts and nut and tighten to specification.

Position the oil pan on the engine and install the attaching bolts. Tighten the bolts (working from the center toward the ends) 9–11 ft. lbs. for ⁵⁄₁₆ in. bolts and 7–9 ft. lbs. for ¼ in. bolts.

14. Position the steering gear to the main crossmember. Install the two attaching bolts and tighten to specification. Connect steering flex coupling.

15. Position rear K braces and install the four attaching bolts.

16. Raise engine and remove wood blocks.

17. Install stabilizer bar (Versailles only).

18. Lower the engine and install engine mount attaching bolts. Tighten to specification. Install converter inspection cover.

19. Install oil dipstick and tube assembly, and fill crankcase with the specified engine oil. Install idler arm.

20. Connect transmission oil cooler lines. Connect battery cable.

21. Position the shroud to the radiator and install the two attaching bolts. Start the engine and check for leaks.

Oil Pump

REMOVAL AND INSTALLATION

Except V6 (232) Engines

1. Remove oil pan.

2. Remove oil pump inlet tube and screen assembly.

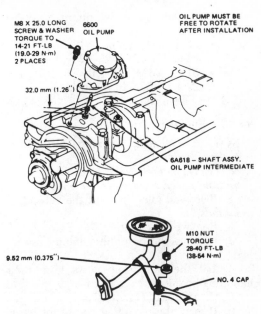

4-140 oil pump installation

3. Remove oil pump attaching bolts and remove oil pump gasket and intermediate shaft.

4. Prime oil pump by filling inlet and outlet port with engine oil and rotating shaft of pump to distribute it.

5. Position intermediate drive shaft into distributor socket.

6. Position new gasket on pump body and insert intermediate drive shaft into pump body.

7. Install pump and intermediate shaft as an assembly.

NOTE: *Do not force pump if it does not seat readily. The drive shaft may be misaligned with the distributor shaft. To align, rotate intermediate drive shaft into a new position.*

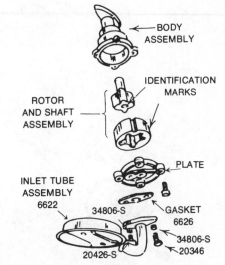

Oil pump used on 6 and 8 cylinder engines

8. Install and torque oil pump attaching screws to:

- 4 and 6-cyl. engines—12–15 ft. lbs.;
- 302 and 351 W—22–32 ft. lbs.;
- 351 C, 351M and 400—25–35 ft. lbs.;
- 429 and 460—20–25 ft. bls.

9. Install oil pan.

V6 (232) Engines

NOTE: *The oil pump is mounted in the front cover assembly.*

NOTE: *Oil pan removal is necessary for pick-up tube/screen replacement or service.*

1. Raise and safely support the vehicle on jackstands.

2. Remove the oil filter.

3. Remove the cover/filter mount assembly.

4. Lift the two pump gears from their mounting pocket in the front cover.

5. Clean all gasket mounting surfaces.

6. Inspect the mounting pocket for wear. If excessive wear is present, complete timing cover assembly replacement is necessary.

7. Inspect the cover/filter mount gasket to timing cover surface for flatness. Place a straight edge across the flat and check clearance with a feeler gauge. If the measured clearance exceeds .004 inch, replace the cover/filter mount.

8. Replace the pump gears if wear is excessive.

9. Remove the plug from the end of the pressure relief valve passage using a small drill and slide hammer. Use caution when drilling.

10. Remove the spring and valve from the bore. Clean all dirt, gum and metal chips from the bore and valve. Inspect all parts for wear. Replace as necessary.

11. Install the valve and spring after lubricating them with engine oil. Install a new plug flush with machined surface.

12. Install the pump gears and fill the pocket with petroleum jelly. Install cover/filter mount using a new mounting gasket. Tighten the mounting bolts to 18–22 ft. lbs. Install the oil filter, add necessary oil for correct level.

Rear Main Oil Seal

REMOVAL AND INSTALLATION

NOTE: *Refer to the "build" dates listed below to determine if the engine is equipped with a split-type or one piece rear main oil seal. Engines after the date indicated have a one-piece oil seal. 2.3 (140) OHC: after 9/28/81; 232 V6: after 4/1/83; 302 V8: after 12/1/82; 351W-V8: after 7/11/83. Engines prior to the date indicated are equipped with a split type seal.*

Split-Type Seal—Gas Engines

NOTE: *The rear oil seal installed in these engines is a rubber type (split-lip) seal.*

1. Remove the oil pan, and, if required, the oil pump.

2. Loosen all main bearing caps allowing the crankshaft to lower slightly.

NOTE: *The crankshaft should not be allowed to drop more than 1/32 in.*

3. Remove the rear main bearing cap and remove the seal from the cap and block. Be very careful not to scratch the sealing surface. Remove the old seal retaining pin from the cap, if equipped. It is not used with the replacement seal.

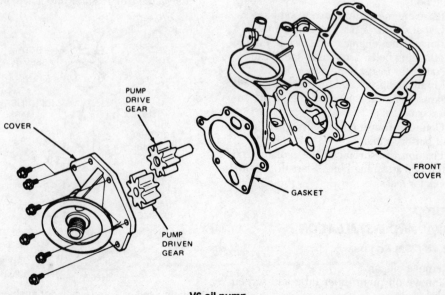

V6 oil pump

4. Carefully clean the seal grooves in the cap and block with solvent.

5. Soak the new seal halves in clean engine oil.

6. Install the upper half of the seal in the block with the undercut side of the seal toward the front of the engine. Slide the seal around the crankshaft journal until ⅜ in. protrudes beyond the base of the block.

7. Tighten all the main bearing caps (except the rear main bearing) to specifications.

8. Install the lower seal into the rear cap, with the undercut side facing the front of the engine. Allow ⅜ in. of the seal to protrude above the surface, at the opposite end from the block seal.

9. Squeeze a ¹⁄₁₆ in. bead of silicone sealant onto the areas shown.

10. Install the rear cap and torque to specifications.

11. Install the oil pump and pan. Fill the crankcase with oil, start the engine, and check for leaks.

One-Piece Seal—Gas Engines

1. Remove the transmission, clutch and flywheel or driveplate after refering to the appropriate section for instructions.

2. Punch two holes in the crankshaft rear oil seal on opposite sides of the crankshaft just above the bearing cap to cylinder block split line. Install a sheet metal screw in each of the holes or use a small slide hammer, and pry the crankshaft rear main oil seal from the block.

NOTE: *Use extreme caution not to scratch the crankshaft oil seal surface.*

3. Clean the oil seal recess in the cylinder block and main bearing cap.

4. Coat the seal and all of the seal mounting

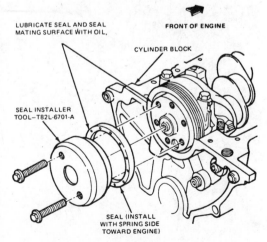

LUBRICATE SEAL AND SEAL MATING SURFACE WITH OIL,

FRONT OF ENGINE

CYLINDER BLOCK

SEAL INSTALLER TOOL—T82L-6701-A

SEAL (INSTALL WITH SPRING SIDE TOWARD ENGINE)

NOTE: REAR FACE OF SEAL MUST BE WITHIN 0.127mm (0.005-INCH) OF THE REAR FACE OF THE BLOCK

One piece rear main bearing oil seal installation

surfaces with oil and install the seal in the recess, driving it in place with an oil seat installation tool or a large socket.

5. Install the driveplate or flywheel and clutch and transmission in the reverse order of removal.

2.4L Diesel Engine

1. Raise the vehicle and safely support on jackstands.

2. Remove the transmission.

3. Remove the flywheel driveplate.

4. Remove the four oil pan to rear engine cover attaching bolts.

5. Loosen, but **DO NOT REMOVE** the remaining oil pan bolts.

6. Remove the six engine rear cover bolts and remove the cover.

7. Clean the crankcase and the engine rear cover gasket mating surfaces.

8. Replace the oil pan gasket, if damaged.

9. Using an arbor press, press the old seal out of the cover.

10. Position a new seal on the cover and press in using Crankshaft Rear Seal Replacer T84P-6701-A, or equivalent.

11. Lubricate the sealing lips on the seal with engine oil.

12. Position new rear cover gasket on the crankcase.

13. Apply gasket sealer at points where the rear cover gasket meets the oil pan gasket.

14. Position the rear cover on the crankshaft.

15. Install the rear cover bolts and tighten 6mm bolts to 6–7 ft. lbs. and 8mm bolts to 14–17 ft. lbs.

16. Install the four oil pan to rear cover attaching bolts. Tighten all oil pan bolts to 6.5–7 ft. lbs.

17. Install the flywheel.

18. Install the transmission.

19. Lower the vehicle.

20. Run the engine and check for oil leaks.

Radiator

REMOVAL AND INSTALLATION

1. Drain cooling system.

2. Disconnect upper, lower and overflow hoses at the radiator.

3. On automatic transmission-equipped cars, disconnect the fluid cooler lines at radiator.

4. Depending on model, remove the two top mounting bolts and remove radiator and shroud assembly, or remove the shroud mounting bolts and position the shroud out of the way, or remove the side mounting bolts. If the air conditioner condenser is attached to the

radiator, remove the retaining bolts and position the condenser out of the way. DO NOT disconnect the refrigerant lines.

5. Remove radiator attaching bolts or top brackets and lift out the radiator.

6. If a new radiator is to be installed, transfer the petcock from the old radiator to the new one. On cars equipped with automatic transmissions, transfer the fluid cooler line fittings from the old radiator.

7. Position the radiator and install, but do not tighten, the radiator support bolts. On cars equipped with automatic transmissions, connect the fluid cooler lines. Then tighten the radiator support bolts or shroud and mounting bolts.

8. Connect the radiator hoses. Close the radiator petcock. Fill and bleed the cooling system.

9. Start the engine and bring to operating temperature. Check for leaks.

10. On cars equipped with automatic transmissions, check the cooler lines for leaks and interference. Check transmission fluid level.

Water Pump

REMOVAL AND INSTALLATION

Gasoline Engines

1. Drain cooling system.

2. Disconnect the negative battery cable.

3. On cars with power steering, remove the drive belt.

4. If the vehicle is equipped with air conditioning, remove the idler pulley bracket and air conditioner drive belt.

5. On engines with Thermactor, remove the belt.

6. Disconnect the lower radiator hose and heater hose from the water pump.

7. On cars equipped with a fan shroud, remove the retaining screws and position the shroud rearward.

8. Remove the fan, fan clutch and spacer from the engine, and if the car is equipped with an electric motor driven fan, remove the fan as an assembly for working clearance.

9. On 4-cylinders, remove the cam belt outer cover.

10. On cars equipped with water pump mounted alternators, loosen alternator mounting bolts, remove the alternator belt and remove the alternator adjusting arm bracket from the water pump. If interference is encountered, remove the air pump pulley and pivot bolt. Remove the air pump adjusting bracket. Swing the upper bracket aside. Detach the air conditioner compressor and lay it aside. Do not disconnect any of the A/C lines. Remove any accessory mounting brackets from the water pump.

11. Loosen bypass hose at water pump, if equipped.

12. Remove water pump retaining screws and remove pump from engine.

13. Clean any gasket material from the pump mounting surface. On engines equipped with a water pump backing plate; remove the plate, clean gasket surfaces, install a new gasket and plate on the water pump.

NOTE: *The 250 6 cylinder engine originally uses a one-piece gasket for the cylinder front cover and water pump. Trim away the old gasket at the edge of the cylinder cover and replace with service gasket.*

14. Remove the heater hose fitting from the old pump and install it on the new pump.

15. Coat both sides of the new gasket with a water-resistant sealer, then install the pump reversing the procedure.

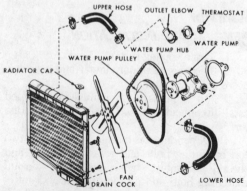

Typical cooling system and related parts—V8 with downflow radiator shown

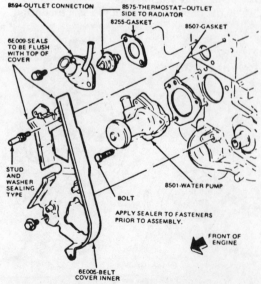

4-140 water pump, thermostat and inner timing bolt installation

2.4L Diesel Engine

1. Drain the cooling system.
2. Loosen and remove the accessory drive belts.
3. Remove the fan and motor assembly.
4. Remove the water pump pulley.
5. Disconnect the heater hose from the thermostat housing.
6. Remove the camshaft drive belt cover.
7. Remove the three bolts attaching the water pump to the crankcase and remove the water pump.

NOTE: *Do not loosen cam belt.*

8. Clean the gasket mating surfaces of the water pump and crankcase.
9. Install the water pump with a new gasket, on the crankcase and tighten bolts to 14–17 ft. lbs.
10. Install the camshaft drive belt cover and tighten bolts to 6–7 ft. lbs.
11. Connect the heater hose to the thermostat housing.
12. Install the water pump pulley and tighten bolts to 6–7 ft. lbs.
13. Install the fan and motor assembly.
14. Install and adjust the accessory drive belts.

Thermostat

REMOVAL AND INSTALLATION

1. Open the drain cock and drain the radiator so the coolant level is below the coolant outlet elbow which houses the thermostat.

NOTE: *On some models it will be necessary to remove the distributor cap, rotor and vacuum diaphragm in order to gain access to the thermostat housing mounting bolts.*

2. Remove the outlet elbow retaining bolts and position the elbow sufficiently clear of the intake manifold or cylinder head to provide access to the thermostat.
3. Remove the thermostat and the gasket.
4. Clean the mating surfaces of the outlet elbow and the engine to remove all old gasket material and sealer. Coat the new gasket with water-resistant sealer. Install the thermostat in

the block on 351W and 400 V8s (or in the intake manifold on 460 V8s), then install the gasket. On all other engines, position the gasket on the engine, and install the thermostat in the coolant elbow. The thermostat must be rotated clockwise to lock it in position on all 255, 302 and 351 W V8s. On 4-cylinders, be sure the full width of the heater outlet tube is visible within the thermostat port.

5. Install the outlet elbow and retaining bolts on the engine. Torque the bolts to 12–15 ft. lbs.
6. Refill the radiator. Run the engine at operating temperature and check for leaks. Recheck the coolant level.

Electro-Drive Cooling Fan

Gasoline Engines

Various models, are equipped with a bracket-mounted electric cooling fan that replaces the conventional water pump mounted fan.

Operation of the fan motor is dependent on engine coolant temperature and air conditioner compressor clutch engagement. The fan will run only when the coolant temperature is approximately 108°F or higher, or when the compressor clutch is engaged. The fan, motor and mount can be removed as an assembly after disconnecting the wiring harnesses and mounting bolts.

CAUTION: *The cooling fan is automatic and may come on at any time without warning even if the ignition is switched OFF. To avoid possible injury, always disconnect the negative battery cable when working near the electric cooling fan.*

2.4L Diesel Engine

1. Disconnect the battery ground cable.
2. Raise the vehicle and support on jackstands.

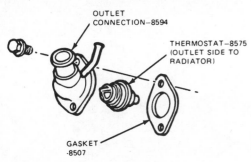

4-140 thermostat

OUTLET
CONNECTION–8594

THERMOSTAT–8575
(OUTLET SIDE TO
RADIATOR)

GASKET
-8507

Installing thermostat—typical

RECESS

BRIDGE

FLATS

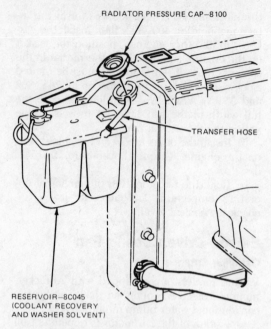

RADIATOR PRESSURE CAP—8100

TRANSFER HOSE

RESERVOIR—8C045
(COOLANT RECOVERY
AND WASHER SOLVENT)

Coolant Recovery System—Typical

3. Remove the bolts and nuts attaching the mounting brackets to the radiator support.

4. Disconnect the electrical connector to fan.

5. Remove the bolts securing the hood-latch to the radiator support and position the latch out of the way.

6. Remove the bolts and nuts attaching the mounting brackets to fan and motor assembly.

7. Remove the fan and motor assembly from the vehicle.

8. Position the fan and motor assembly in the vehicle.

9. Position the mounting brackets on the fan and motor assembly. Tighten the nuts to 4–5 ft. lbs.

10. Install the hood latch.

11. Connect the electrical connector to the fan and motor assembly.

12. Position the mounting brackets in the vehicle. Tighten the mounting bolts to 6–8 ft. lbs. Tighten mounting nuts to 4–5 ft. lbs.

13. Lower the vehicle.

14. Connect the battery ground cable.

Emission Controls and Fuel Systems

EMISSION CONTROLS

There are three basic sources of automotive pollution in the modern internal combustion engine. They are the crankcase with its accompanying blow-by vapors, the fuel system with its evaporation of unburned gasoline, and the combustion chambers with their resulting exhaust emissions. Pollution arising from the incomplete combustion of fuel generally falls into three categories; hydrocarbons (HC), carbon monoxide (CO), and oxides of nitrogen (NO$_x$).

Positive Crankcase Ventilation System

All models covered in this book are equipped with a positive crankcase ventilation (PCV) system to control crankcase blow-by vapors. The system consists of a PCV valve and oil separator mounted on top of the valve cover, a non-ventilated oil filler cap, and a pair of hoses supplying filtered intake air to the valve cover and delivering the crankcase vapors from the valve cover to the intake manifold (six-cylinder) or carburetor (V8).

The system functions as follows:

When the engine is running, a small portion of the gases which are formed in the combustion chamber leak by the piston rings and enter the crankcase. Since these gases are under pressure, they tend to escape from the crankcase and enter the atmosphere. If these gases are allowed to remain in the crankcase for any period of time, they contaminate the engine oil and cause sludge to build up in the crankcase. If the gases are allowed to escape into the atmosphere, they pollute the air, with unburned hydrocarbons. The job of the crankcase emission control equipment is to recycle these gases back into the engine combustion chamber where they are reburned.

Since the PCV valve works under severe load it is very important that it be replaced at the interval specified in the maintenance chart (see Chapter 1). Replacement involves removing the valve from the grommet in the rocker arm cover and installing a new valve. Do not attempt to clean a used valve.

Fuel Evaporative Control System

This system, which is found on all Ford and Mercury vehicles, is designed to prevent the evaporation of unburned gasoline. The system consists of a vacuum/pressure relief fuel filler cap, an expansion area at the top of the fuel tank, a foam-filled vapor separator mounted on top of the fuel tank, a carbon canister which stores fuel vapors and a number of hoses which connect the various components. The system functions as follows:

Changes in atmospheric temperature cause

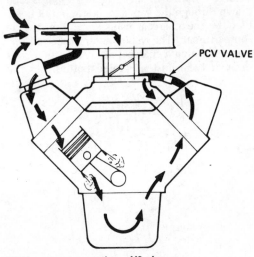

PCV system operation—V8 shown

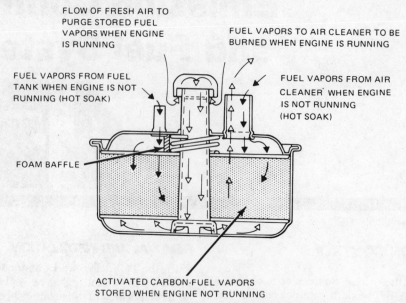

FLOW OF FRESH AIR TO PURGE STORED FUEL VAPORS WHEN ENGINE IS RUNNING

FUEL VAPORS TO AIR CLEANER TO BE BURNED WHEN ENGINE IS RUNNING

FUEL VAPORS FROM FUEL TANK WHEN ENGINE IS NOT RUNNING (HOT SOAK)

FUEL VAPORS FROM AIR CLEANER WHEN ENGINE IS NOT RUNNING (HOT SOAK)

FOAM BAFFLE

ACTIVATED CARBON-FUEL VAPORS STORED WHEN ENGINE NOT RUNNING

Evaporative emissions control canister

the gasoline in fuel tanks to expand or contract. If this expansion and consequent vaporization takes place in a conventional fuel tank, the fuel vapors escape through the filler cap or vent hose and pollute the atmosphere. The fuel evaporative emission control system prevents this by routing the gasoline vapors to the engine where they are burned.

As the gasoline in the fuel tank of a parked car begins to expand due to heat, the vapor that forms moves to the top of the fuel tank. The fuel tanks are enlarged so that there exists an area representing 10–20% of the total fuel tank volume above the level of the fuel tank filler tube where these gases may collect. The vapors then travel upward into the vapor separator which prevents liquid gasoline from escaping from the fuel tank. The fuel vapor is then drawn through the vapor separator outlet hose, then to the charcoal canister in the engine compartment. The vapor enters the canister, passes through a charcoal filter, and then exits through the canister's grated bottom. As the

vapor passes through the charcoal, it is cleansed of hydrocarbons, so that the air that passes out of the bottom of the canister is free of pollutants.

When the engine is started, vacuum from the carburetor draws fresh air into the canister. As the entering air passes through the charcoal in the canister, it picks up the hydrocarbons that were deposited there by the fuel vapors. This mixture of hydrocarbons and fresh air is then carried through a hose to the air cleaner. In the carburetor, it combines with the incoming air/fuel mixture and enters the combustion chambers of the engine where it is burned.

SERVICE

The only required service for the evaporative emissions control system is inspection of the various components at the interval specified in the maintenance chart (see Chapter 1). If the charcoal element in the canister is gummed up the entire canister should be repaced. Disconnect the canister purge hose from the air cleaner fitting, loosen the canister retaining bracket, lift out the canister. Installation is the reverse of removal.

Thermactor System

This system is found in the 1971 Cobra Jet and Super Cobra Jet engines, all 1974 models sold in California, and most 1975 and later models sold in the 50 states.

The Thermactor emission control system makes use of a belt-driven air pump to inject

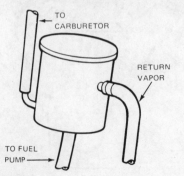

TO CARBURETOR

RETURN VAPOR

TO FUEL PUMP

Vapor separator

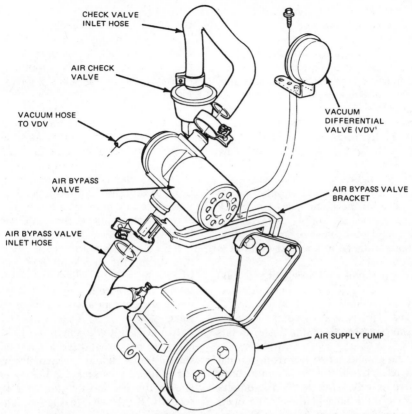

CHECK VALVE
INLET HOSE

AIR CHECK
VALVE

VACUUM HOSE
TO VDV

AIR BYPASS
VALVE

AIR BYPASS VALVE
INLET HOSE

VACUUM
DIFFERENTIAL
VALVE (VDV'

AIR BYPASS VALVE
BRACKET

AIR SUPPLY PUMP

Typical thermactor system components—catalytic equipped

fresh air into the hot exhaust stream through the engine exhaust ports. The result is the extended burning of those fumes which were not completely ignited in the combustion chamber, and the subsequent reduction of some of the hydrocarbon and carbon monoxide content of the exhaust emissions into harmless carbon dioxide and water.

The Thermactor system is composed of the following components:

1. Air supply pump (belt-driven)
2. Air by-pass valve
3. Check valves
4. Air manifolds (internal or external)
5. Air supply tubes (on external manifolds only).

Air for the Thermactor system is cleaned by means of a centrifugal filter fan mounted on the air pump driveshaft. The air filter does not require a replaceable element.

To prevent excessive pressure, the air pump is equipped with a pressure relief valve which uses a replaceable plastic plug to control the pressure setting.

The Thermactor air pump has sealed bearings which are lubricated for the life of the unit, and pre-set rotor vane and bearing clearances,

which do not require any periodic adjustments.

The air supply from the pump is controlled by the air by-pass valve, sometimes called a dump valve. During deceleration, the air by-pass valve opens, momentarily diverting the air supply through a silencer and into the atmosphere, thus preventing backfires within the exhaust system.

A check valve is incorporated in the air inlet side of the air manifolds. Its purpose is to prevent exhaust gases from backing up into the Thermactor system. This valve is especially important in the event of drive belt failure, and during deceleration, when the air by-pass valve is dumping the air supply.

The air manifolds and air supply tubes channel the air from the Thermactor air pump into the exhaust ports of each cylinder, thus completing the cycle of the Thermactor system.

SERVICE

The entire Thermactor system should be checked periodically according to the maintenance chart in Chapter 1. Use the following procedure to determine if the system is functioning properly.

NOTE: *See Chapter 1 for belt adjustment and replacement procedures.*

1. Remove air cleaner, if necessary.

2. Inspect all components of the thermactor system for any loose connections or other abnormal conditions—repair or replace as necessary.

3. Inspect the air pump drive belt for wear and tension—adjust or replace as necessary.

4. With the tramsmission in neutral or park and the parking brake on, start engine and bring to normal operating temperature.

5. Stop the engine. Connect a tachometer to the engine. Remove the air supply hose at the check valve. If the engine has two check valves, remove both air supply hoses at the check valves and plug off one hose. Position the open hose so that the air blast emitted is harmlessly dissipated.

6. Start the engine and accelerate to 1500 RPM. Place hand over the open hose. Air flow should be heard and felt. If no air flow is noted, the air bypass valve is defective and should be replaced. The procedure is outlined later in this section.

7. Let the engine speed return to normal idle. Pinch off and remove the vacuum hose from the bypass valve. Accelerate the engine to 1500 RPM. With hand held over the open end of the check valve hose (same as Step 6), virtually no air flow should be felt or heard.

If air flow is noted, the bypass valve is defective and is to be replaced.

8. Let the engine speed return to normal idle and reinstall the vacuum hose on the bypass valve vacuum hose nipple. Check hose routing to be sure it is not pinched or restricting normal vacuum signal flow.

9. With hand held over the open end of the check valve hose (same as Step 6), rapidly increase the engine speed to approximately 2500 RPM. Immediately release the throttle for the engine to return to normal idle. Air flow should be felt and/or heard to momentarily diminish or go to zero during the deceleration. If the air flow does not momentarily diminish or go to zero repeat the above using an engine speed of 3000–3200 RPM.

If air flow does not momentarily diminish or stop during the deceleration from 3000–3200 RPM, the vacuum differential control valve should be replaced. Omit this step if the system is not equipped with a differential vacuum valve.

10. Accelerate the engine to 1500 RPM and check for any exhaust gas leakage at the check valve. There should be virtually no pressure felt or heard when hand is held over the open end of the check valve for approximately 15 seconds. If excessive leakage is noted, replace the check valve(s).

CAUTION: *The check valve may be hot and*

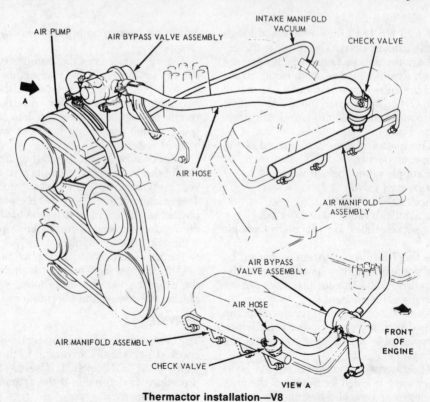

Thermactor installation—V8

capable of causing a burn if the hands are not protected.

11. If the engine is equipped with two check valves, repeat step 10 on the second valve.

12. Stop the engine and remove all the test equipment. Reconnect all the related components. Reinstall the air cleaner, if removed.

REMOVAL AND INSTALLATION

Thermactor Air Pump

1. Disconnect the air outlet hose at the air pump.

2. Loosen the pump belt tension adjuster.

3. Disengage the drive belt.

4. Remove the mounting bolt and air pump.

5. To install, position the air pump on the mounting bracket and install the mounting bolt.

6. Place drive belt in pulleys and attach the adjusting arm to the air pump.

7. Adjust the drive belt tension to specifications and tighten the adjusting arm and mounting bolts.

8. Connect the air outlet hose to the air pump.

Thermactor Air Pump Filter Fan

1. Loosen the air pump adjusting arm bolt and mounting bracket bolt to relieve drive belt tension.

2. Remove drive pulley attaching bolts and pull drive pulley off the air pump shaft.

3. Pry the outer disc loose; then, pull off the centrifugal filter fan with slip-joint pliers. CAUTION: *Do not attempt to remove the metal drive hub.*

4. Install a new filter fan by drawing it into position, using the pulley and bolts as an installer. Draw the fan evenly by alternately tightening the bolts, making certain that the outer edge of the fan slips into the housing. NOTE: *A slight interference with the housing bore is normal. After a new fan is installed, it may squeal upon initial operation, until its outer diameter sealing lip has worn*

in, which may require 20 to 30 miles of operation.

Thermactor Check Valve

1. Disconnect the air supply hose at the valve. (Use a 1¼ in. crowfoot wrench, the valve has a standard, right-hand pipe thread.)

2. Clean the threads on the air manifold adaptor (air supply tube on 302 V8 engine) with a wire brush. Do not blow compressed air through the check valve in either direction.

3. Install the check valve and tighten.

4. Connect the air supply hose.

Thermactor Air By-Pass Valve

1. Disconnect the air and vacuum hoses at the air by-pass valve body.

2. Position the air by-pass valve, and connect the respective hoses.

Vacuum Differential Control Valve

1. Remove the hose connections.

2. Unbolt the valve at its mounting bracket.

3. Install in reverse order.

Improved Combustion System (IMCO)

All models (except the 1971 429CJ and SCJ) are equipped with the Improved Combustion (IMCO) System. The IMCO system controls emissions arising from the incomplete combustion of the air/fuel mixture in the cylinders. The IMCO system incorporates a number of modifications to the distributor spark control system, the fuel system, and the internal design of the engine.

Internal engine modifications include the following: elimination of surface irregularities and crevices as well as a low surface area-to-volume ratio in the combustion chambers, a high-velocity intake manifold combined with short exhaust ports, selective valve timing and a higher temperature and capacity cooling system.

Modifications to the fuel system include the following: recalibrated carburetors to achieve a leaner air/fuel mixture, more precise calibration of the choke mechanism, the installation of idle mixture limiter caps and a heated air intake system.

Modifications to the distributor spark control system include the following: a modified centrifugal advance curve, the use of dual diaphragm distributors in most applications, a ported vacuum switch, a deceleration valve and a spark delay valve.

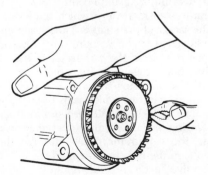

Thermactor air pump filter fan removal

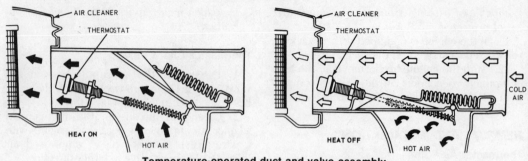

Temperature-operated duct and valve assembly

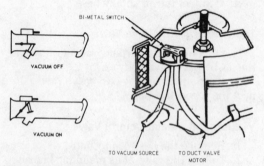

Vacuum-operated duct and valve assembly

SYSTEM DESCRIPTION

Heated Air Intake System

The heated air intake portion of the air cleaner consists of a thermostat (all 1971–72 models except the 351C and 400 V8), or bimetal switch and vacuum motor, and a spring-loaded temperature control door in the snorkel of the air cleaner. The temperature control door is located between the end of the air cleaner snorkel which draws in air from the engine compartment and the duct that carries heated air up from the exhaust manifold. When underhood temperature is below 90°F, the temperature control door blocks off underhood air from entering the air cleaner and allows only heated air from the exhaust manifold to be drawn into the air cleaner. When underhood temperature rises above 130°F, the temperature control door blocks off heated air from the exhaust manifold and allows only underhood air to be drawn into the air cleaner.

By controlling the temperature of the engine intake air this way, exhaust emissions are lowered and fuel economy is improved. In addition, throttle plate icing is reduced, and cold weather driveability is improved from the necessary leaner mixtures.

Dual Diaphragm Distributors

Dual diaphragm distributors are installed in most models and appear in many different engine/transmission/equipment combinations. The best way to tell if you have one is to take a look at your distributor vacuum capsule on the side of the distributor. One vacuum hose running from the vacuum capsule indicates a single diaphragm distributor. Two vacuum hoses means that you have a dual diaphragm unit.

The dual distributor diaphragm is a two-chambered housing which is mounted on the side of the distributor. The outer side of the housing is a distributor vacuum advance mechanism, connected to the carburetor by a vacuum hose. The purpose of the vacuum advance is to advance ignition timing according to the conditions under which the engine is operation. This device has been used on automobiles for many years now and its chief advantage is economical engine operation. The second side of the dual diaphragm is the side that has been added to help control engine exhaust emissions at idle and during deceleration.

The inner side of the dual diaphragm is connected by a vacuum hose to the intake manifold. When the engine is idling or decelerating, intake manifold vacuum is high and carburetor vacuum is low. Under these conditions, intake manifold vacuum, applied to the inner side of the dual diaphragm, retards ignition timing to promote more complete combustion of the air fuel mixture in the engine combustion chambers.

Ported Vacuum Switch (Distributor Vacuum Control Valve)

The distributor vacuum control valve is a temperature-sensitive valve which screws into the water jacket of the engine. Three vacuum lines are attached to the vacuum control valve: one which runs from the carburetor to the control valve, one which runs from the control valve to the distributor vacuum advance (outer) chamber, and one which runs from the intake manifold to the distributor vacuum control valve.

During normal engine operation, vacuum from the carburetor passes through the top nipple on the distributor control valve, through the valve to the second nipple on the valve, and out the second nipple on the valve to the

3-PORT PVS OPERATION

- **EGR/CSC** – switches EGR vacuum from EGR system to distributor advance with cold engine.
- **Cold Start Spark Advance (CSSA)** – supplies manifold vacuum to distributor below 125° F. coolant temperature.
- **Coolant Spark Control (CSC)** – cuts off distributor advance below hot engine temperature.
- **Cooling PVS** – switches advance vacuum from spark port to manifold vacuum if engine overheats.

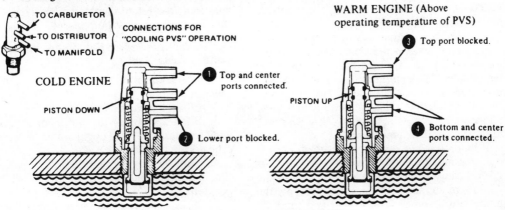

Ported vacuum switch (PVS) operation

distributor vacuum advance chamber. When the engine is idling however, carburetor vacuum is very low, so that there is little, if any, vacuum in the passageways described above.

If the engine should begin to overheat while idling, a check ball inside the distributor vacuum control which normally blocks off the third nipple of the valve (intake manifold vacuum) moves upward to block off the first nipple (carburetor vacuum). This applies intake manifold vacuum (third nipple) to the distributor vacuum advance chamber (second nipple). Since intake manifold vacuum is very high while the engine is idling, ignition timing is advanced by the application of intake manifold vacuum to the distributor vacuum advance chamber. This raises the engine idle speed and helps to cool the engine.

Deceleration Valve

Some IMCO-equipped 1971–72 engines are equipped with a distributor vacuum advance control valve (deceleration valve) which is used with dual-diaphragm distributors to further aid in controlling ignition timing. The deceleration valve is in the vacuum line which runs from the outer (advance) diaphragm to the carburetor—the normal vacuum supply for the distributor. During deceleration, the intake manifold vacuum rises causing the deceleration valve to close off the carburetor vacuum source and connect the intake manifold vacuum source to the distributor advance diaphragm. The increase in vacuum provides maximum ignition timing advance, thus providing more complete fuel combustion, and decreasing exhaust system backfiring.

Spark Delay Valve

The spark delay valve is a plastic, spring-loaded, color-coaded valve which is installed in the vacuum line to the distributor advance diaphragm on many models. Under heavy throttle applications, the valve will close, blocking normal carburetor vacuum to the distributor. After the designated period of closed time, the valve opens, restoring the carburetor vacuum to the distributor.

TESTING IMCO SYSTEM COMPONENTS

Heated Air Intake System

DUCT AND VALVE ASSEMBLY TEST

1. Either start with a cold engine or remove the air cleaner from the engine for at least half an hour. While cooling the air cleaner, leave the engine compartment hood open.

2. Tape a thermometer, of known accuracy, to the inside of the air cleaner so that it is near the temperature sensor unit. Install the air cleaner on the engine but do not fasten its securing nut.

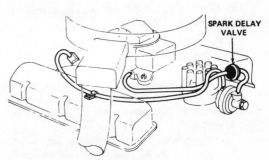

Spark delay valve installation

3. Start the engine. With the engine cold and the outside temperature less than 90°F, the door should be in the "heat on" position (closed to outside air).

4. Operate the throttle lever rapidly to one-half to three-quarters of its opening and release it. The air door should open to allow outside air to enter and then close again.

5. Allow the engine to warm up to normal temperature. Watch the door. When it opens to the outside air, remove the cover from the air cleaner. The temperature should be over 90°F and no more than 130°F; 105°F is about normal. If the door does not work within these temperature ranges, or fails to work at all, check for linkage or door binding.

If binding is not present and the air door is not working, proceed with the vacuum tests given below. If these indicate no faults in the vacuum motor and the door is not working, the temperature sensor is defective and must be replaced.

VACUUM MOTOR TEST

NOTE: *Be sure that the vacuum hose that runs between the temperature switch and the vacuum motor is not pinched by the retaining clip under the air cleaner. This could prevent the air door from closing*

1. Check all the vacuum lines and fittings for leaks. Correct any leaks. If none are found, proceed with the test.

2. Remove the hose which runs from the sensor to the vacuum motor. Run a hose directly from the manifold vacuum source to the vacuum motor.

3. If the motor closes the air door, it is functioning properly and the temperature sensor is defective.

4. If the motor does *not* close the door and no binding is present in its operation, the vacuum motor is defective and must be replaced.

NOTE: *If an alternate vacuum source is applied to the motor, insert a vacuum gauge in the line by using a T-fitting. Apply at least 9 in. Hg of vacuum in order to operate the motor.*

Dual Diaphragm Distributor Advance and Retard Mechanisms Test

1. Connect a timing light to the engine. Check the ignition timing.

NOTE: *Before proceeding with the tests, disconnect any spark control devices, distributor vacuum valves, etc. If these are left connected, inaccurate results may be obtained.*

2. Remove the retard hose from the distributor and plug it. Increase the engine speed. The timing should advance. If it fails to do so,

then the vacuum unit is faulty and must be replaced.

3. Check the timing with the engine at normal idle speed. Unplug the retard hose and connect it to the vacuum unit. The timing should instantly be retarded from 4°–10°. If this does not occur, the retard diaphragm has a leak and the vacuum unit must be replaced.

Ported Vacuum Switch (Distributor Vacuum Control Valve) Test

1. Check the routing and connection of all vacuum hoses.

2. Attach a tachometer to the engine.

3. Bring the engine up to the normal operating temperature. The engine must not be overheated.

4. Note the engine rpm, with the transmission in neutral, and the throttle in the curb idle position.

5. Disconnect the vacuum hose from the intake manifold at the temperature-sensing valve. Plug or clamp the hose.

6. Note the idle rpm with the hose disconnected. If there is no change in rpm, the valve is good. If there is a drop of 100 or more rpm, the valve should be replaced. Replace the vacuum line.

7. Check to make sure that the all-season cooling mixture meets specifications, and that the correct radiator cap is in place and functioning.

8. Block the radiator air flow to induce a higher-than-normal temperature condition.

9. Continue to operate until the engine temperature or heat indicator shows above normal.

If engine speed by time has increased 100 or more rpm, the temperature-sensing valve is satisfactory. If not, it should be replaced.

Spark Delay Valve Test

NOTE: *If the distributor vacuum line contains a cut-off solenoid, it must be open during this test.*

1. Detach the vacuum line from the distributor at the spark delay valve end. Connect a vacuum gauge to the valve, in its place.

2. Connect a tachometer to the engine. Start the engine and rapidly increase its speed to 2,000 rpm with the transmission in neutral.

3. As soon as the engine speed is increased, the vacuum gauge reading should drop to zero.

4. Hold the engine speed at a steady 2,000 rpm. It should take longer than two seconds for the gauge to register 6 in. Hg. If it takes less than two seconds, the valve is defective and must be replaced.

5. If it takes longer than the number of seconds specified in the application chart for the

gauge to reach 6 in. Hg, disconnect the vacuum gauge from the spark delay valve. Disconnect the hose which runs from the spark delay valve to the carburetor at the valve end. Connect the vacuum gauge to this hose.

6. Start the engine and increase its speed to 2,000 rpm. The gauge should indicate 10–16 in. Hg. If it does not, there is a blockage in the carburetor vacuum port or else the hose itself is plugged or broken. If the gauge reading is within specification, the valve is defective.

7. Reconnect all vacuum lines and remove the tachometer, once testing is completed.

REMOVAL AND INSTALLATION OF IMCO SYSTEM COMPONENTS

Temperature Operated Duct and Valve Assembly (Heated Air Intake System)

1. Remove the hex-head cap screws which secure the air intake duct and valve assembly to the air cleaner.

2. Remove the air intake duct and valve assembly from the engine.

3. If inspection reveals that the valve plate is sticking or the thermostat is malfunctioning, remove the thermostat and valve plates as follows:

a. Detach the valve plate tension spring from the valve plate using long-nose pliers. Loosen the thermostat locknut and unscrew the thermostat from the mounting bracket. Grasp the valve plate and withdraw it from the cut.

4. Install the air intake duct and valve assembly on the shroud tube.

5. Connect the air intake duct and valve assembly to the air cleaner and tighten the hex-head retaining cap screws.

6. If it was necessary to disassemble the thermostat and air duct and valve, assemble the unit as follows: Install the locknut on the thermostat, and screw the thermostat into the mounting bracket. Install the valve plate tension spring on the valve plate and duct.

7. Install the vacuum override motor (if applicable) and check for proper operation.

Vacuum Operated Duct and Valve Assembly (Heated Air Intake System)

1. Disconnect the vacuum hose at the vacuum motor.

2. Remove the hex cap screws which secure the air intake duct and valve assembly to the air cleaner.

3. Remove the duct and valve assembly from the engine.

4. Position the duct and valve assembly to the air cleaner and heat stove tube. Install the attaching cap screws.

5. Connect the vacuum line at the vacuum motor.

Ported Vacuum Switch (Distributor Vacuum Control Valve)

1. Drain about one gallon of coolant out of the radiator.

2. Tag the vacuum hoses that attach to the control valve and disconnect them.

3. Unscrew and remove the control valve.

4. Install the new control valve.

5. Connect the vacuum hoses.

6. Fill the cooling system.

Spark Delay Valve

1. Locate the spark delay valve in the distributor vacuum line and disconnect it from the line.

2. Install a new spark delay valve in the line, making sure that the black end of the valve is connected to the line from the carburetor and the color coded end is connected to the line from the spark delay valve to the distributor.

Distributor Modulator

DIST-O-VAC SYSTEM

NOTE: *This system is found on the following models only: 1971 vehicles equipped with automatic transmission and the 250 six cylinder engine or the 429 V8 engine with 4 bbl carburetor.*

The Three components of the Dist-O-Vac system are the speed sensor, the thermal switch, and the electronic control module. The electronic control module consists of two sub-assemblies: the electronic control amplifier and the three-way solenoid valve.

The speed sensor, a small unit mounted in the speedometer cable, contains a rotating magnet and a stationary winding which is insulated from ground. The magnet, which rotates with the speedometer cable, generates a small votage which increases directly with speed. This voltage is directed to the electronic control amplifier.

The thermal switch consists of a bimetallic-element switch which is mounted in the right door pillar and senses the temperature of the air. The switch is closed at 58°F or lower, and open at temperatures about 58°F. This switch is also connected to the electronic control amplifier.

Within the electronic control module case, there is a printed circuit board and an electronic amplifier. The speed sensor and thermal switch are connected to this assembly. The thermal switch is the dominant circuit. The thermal switch is the dominant circuit. When the temperature of the outside air is 58°F or

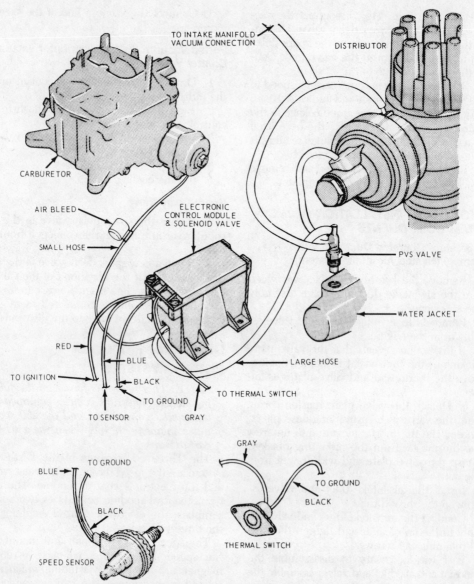

TO INTAKE MANIFOLD
VACUUM CONNECTION

DISTRIBUTOR

CARBURETOR

AIR BLEED

ELECTRONIC
CONTROL MODULE
& SOLENOID VALVE

SMALL HOSE

PVS VALVE

WATER JACKET

RED

BLUE

LARGE HOSE

TO IGNITION

BLACK

TO GROUND

TO THERMAL SWITCH

TO SENSOR

GRAY

GRAY

TO GROUND

BLUE

TO GROUND

BLACK

BLACK

THERMAL SWITCH

SPEED SENSOR

Distributor modulator (Dist-O-Vac) system schematic

lower, the circuit is closed, so that regardless of speed, the electronic control amplifier will not trigger the three-way solenoid valve. At temperatures above 58°F, however, the thermal switch circuit is open, allowing the circuit from the speed sensor to take over and control the action of the solenoid valve.

The three-way solenoid valve is located within the electronic control module and below the printed circuit board of the amplifier. It is vented to the atmosphere at the top, and connected at the bottom to the carburetor spark port (small hose) and the primary (advance) side of the dual-diaphragm distributor (large hose). The large hose is also channeled through the temperature-sensing valve. The small hose is equipped

with an air bleed to provide a positive airflow in the direction of the carburetor. The air bleed purges the hose of vacuum, thus assuring that raw gasoline will not be drawn through the hose and into the distributor diaphragm.

When the thermal switch is closed (air temperature 58°F or lower), or when it is open and the speed sensor is not sending out a strong enough voltage signal (speeds below approximately 35 mph), the amplifier will not activate the solenoid valve and the valve is in the closed position, blocking the passage of air from the small tube through the large tube. With the valve in this position, the larger hose is vented to the atmosphere through the top opening in the three-way valve assembly. Consequently, no vacuum is being supplied to the primary diaphragm on the distributor, and, therefore, no vacuum advance.

When the air temperature is above 85°F and/or the speed of the car is sufficient to generate the required voltage (35 mph or faster), the valve opens, blocking the vent to the atmosphere while opening the vacuum line from the carburetor spark port to the primary diaphragm of the distributor.

REMOVAL AND INSTALLATION OF SYSTEM COMPONENTS

Dist-O-Vac Temperature Sensor

1. Open the right door and remove the two screws which attach the temperature sensor to the right door pillar.
2. Disconnect the lead wires from the temperature sensor.
3. Connect the lead wires to the new sensor.
4. Position the sensor on the door pillar and install the attaching screws.

Dist-O-Vac Speed Sensor

1. Disconnect the lead wires from the sensor.
2. Disconnect the speed sensor from the speedometer cable.
3. Position the O-rings on both ends of the new speed sensor.
4. Connect both ends of the speedometer cable to the speed sensor.
5. Connect the lead wires to the speed sensor.

Three-way Solenoid Valve

1. Mark each of the vacuum hoses for identification and remove them from the valve.
2. Remove the valve from the engine by turning it counterclockwise, as you would a bolt.

3. Install in reverse order after lightly oiling the threads of the new valve. Be sure to connect the vacuum lines in correct order.

Electronic Control Module

1. Mark each of the vacuum hoses for identification and remove them from the module.
2. Label and remove the two wire harness connectors.
3. Unbolt the module from the fender wall.
4. Installation is the reverse of removal.

Electronic Spark Control

1972 models manufactured for sale in California equipped with a 250 Six, 351C 2 bbl, 351 CJ 4 bbl, or 400 V8 and automatic transmission, as well as all 429 Police Interceptor V8s, use the electronic spark control system.

Electronic Spark Control is a system which blocks off carburetor vacuum to the distributor vacuum advance mechanism under certain temperature and speed conditions. The Electronic Spark Control System consists of four components: a temperature sensor, a speed sensor, an amplifier, and a distributor modulator vacuum valve. The system serves to prevent ignition timing advance (by blocking off carburetor vacuum from the distributor vacuum advance mechanism) until the car reaches a speed of 35 mph when the ambient temperature is over 65°F.

The temperature sensor, which is mounted on the front face of the left door pillar, monitors the outside air temperature and relays this information to the amplifier. The amplifier, which is located under the instrument panel, controls the distributor modulator vacuum valve. The modulator valve, which is attached to the ignition coil mounting bracket, is connected into the carburetor vacuum line to the distributor, and is normally open. If the temperature of the

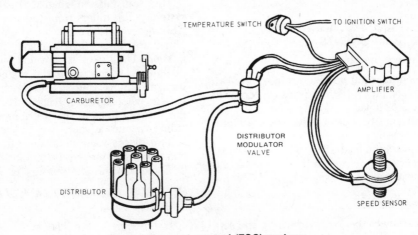

Electronic spark control (ESC) system

outside air is below 48°F, the contacts in the temperature sensor are open and no signal is sent to the amplifier. Since no signal is sent to the amplifier, the amplifier does not send a signal to the distributor modulator valve, and the vacuum passage from the carburetor to the distributor vacuum advance remains open. When the outside temperature rises to 65°F or above, the contacts in the temperature sensor close, and a signal is sent to the amplifier. The amplifier relays the message to the distributor modulator, which closes to block the vacuum passage to the distributor, preventing ignition timing advance.

When the ambient temperature is 65°F or above, ignition timing advance is prevented until the amplifier receives a signal from the speed sensor that the speed of the vehicle has reached 34 mph, and the distributor modulator vacuum valve can be opened to permit ignition timing advance.

The speed sensor is a miniature generator which is connected to the speedometer cable of the car. As the speedometer cable turns, the inside of the speed sensor turns with the speedometer cable. As the speed of the car increases, a rotating magnet in the speed sensor induces an electronic current in the stationary windings in the speed sensor. This current is sent to the amplifier. As the speed of the vehicle increases, the amount of current sent to the amplifier by the speed sensor increases proportionally. When the car reaches a speed of 35 mph, the amplifier signals the distributor modulator vacuum valve to open, allowing carburetor vacuum to be sent to the distributor vacuum advance chamber. This permits the ignition timing to advance.

It should be noted that this system operates only when the ambient temperature of 65°F or above, and then only when the speed of the car is below 35 mph.

REMOVAL AND INSTALLATION OF SYSTEM COMPONENTS

ESC Temperature Sensor

1. Open the right door and remove the two screws which attach the temperature sensor to the right door pillar.
2. Disconnect the lead wires from the temperature sensor.
3. Connect the lead wires to the newsensor.
4. Position the sensor on the door pillar and install the attaching screws.

ESC Speed Sensor

1. Disconnect the lead wires from the sensor.

2. Disconnect the speed sensor from the speedometer cable.
3. Position the O-rings on both ends of the new speed sensor.
4. Connect both ends of the speedometer cable to the speed sensor.
5. Connect the lead wires to the speed sensor.

ESC Amplifier

1. Locate the amplifier under the instrument panel, near the glove compartment.
2. Disconnect the wiring harness from the amplifier.
3. Remove the two amplifier attaching screws and remove the amplifier.
4. Position a new amplifier under the instrument panel and connect the wiring harness to it.
5. Install the two amplifier attaching screws.

ESC Distributor Vacuum Modulator Valve

1. Tag the hoses that attach to the modulator and disconnect them from the amplifier.
2. Disconnect the lead wires from the modulator.
3. Remove the No. 2 left front valve cover bolt (six-cylinder) or the inboard left front valve cover bolt and remove the modulator.
4. Position the new modulator on the valve cover and install the attaching bolt.
5. Connect the wires and hoses to the modulator.

Transmission Regulated Spark System

1972 models equipped with the 250 Six and manual transmission sold in the 49 states, and models equipped with the 351 CJ 4 bbl V8 sold in California use a transmission regulated spark control system.

The transmission regulated spark control system (TRS) differs from the Dist-O-Vac and ESC systems in that the speed sensor and amplifier are replaced by a switch on the transmission. The switch is activated by a mechanical linkage which opens the switch when the transmission is shifted into High gear. The switch, when opened, triggers the opening of the vacuum lines to the distributor, thus providing vacuum advance. So, in short, the TRS system blocks vacuum advance to the distributor only when the outside temperature is above 65°F and transmission is in First or Second gear.

REMOVAL AND INSTALLATION OF TRS SWITCH

1. Disconnect the TRS switch wire at the transmission.

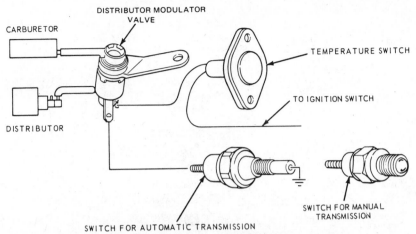

Transmission regulated spark (TRS) system schematic

2. Remove the TRS switch by turning it in a counterclockwise direction as you would a bolt.

3. Lightly oil the threads of the new switch and install in reverse order of removal. Torque to 15–20 ft. lbs. on manual transmissions; 4–8 ft. lbs. on automatic transmissions.

Exhaust Gas Recirculation System

All 1973 and later models are equipped with an exhaust gas recirculation (EGR) system to control oxides of nitrogen.

On V8 engines, exhaust gases travel through the exhaust gas crossover passage in the intake manifold. On 6 cylinder engines, an external tube carries exhaust manifold gases to a carburetor spacer. On spacer entry equipped engines, a portion of these gases are diverted into a spacer which is mounted under the carburetor. On floor entry models, a regulated portion of exhaust gases enters the intake manifold through a pair of small holes drilled in the floor of the intake manifold riser. The EGR control valve, which is attached to the rear of the spacer or intake manifold, consists of a vacuum diaphragm with an attached plunger which normally blocks exhaust gases from entering the intake manifold.

On all models, the EGR valve is controlled by a vacuum line from the carburetor which passes through a ported vacuum switch. The EGR ported vacuum switch provides vacuum to the EGR valve at coolant temperatures above 125°F. The vacuum diaphragm then opens the EGR valve permitting exhaust gases to flow through the carburetor spacer and enter the combustion chambers. The exhaust gases are relatively oxygen-free, and tend to dilute the combustion charge. This lowers peak combustion temperature thereby reducing oxides of nitrogen.

On some models equipped with a 351C, 400, 429 or 460 V8, an EGR subsystem, consisting of a speed sensor and control amplifier, prevents exhaust gases from entering the combustion mixture when the car is traveling 65 mph or faster.

The EGR systems on some 1976 and later models employ a backpressure transducer connected to an adapter between the EGR valve and the intake manifold. The transducer modulates EGR flow by varying the EGR valve vacuum signal according to exhaust backpressure. The variations in exhaust backpressure are sensed in the pressure cavity of the transducer spacer.

EGR SYSTEM TEST

1. Allow the engine to warm up, so that the coolant temperature has reached at least 125°F.

2. Disconnect the vacuum hose which runs from the temperature cut-in valve to the EGR valve at the EGR valve end. Connect a vacuum gauge to this hose with a T-fitting.

3. Increase engine speed. The gauge should indicate a vacuum. If no vacuum is present, check the following:

    a. The carburetor—look for a clogged vacuum port.

    b. The vacuum hoses—including the vacuum hoses to the transmission modulator.

    c. The temperature cut-in valve—if no vacuum is present at its outlet with the engine temperature above 125°F and vacuum available from the carburetor, the valve is defective.

4. If all the above tests are positive, check the EGR valve itself.

5. Connect an outside vacuum source and a vacuum gauge to the valve.

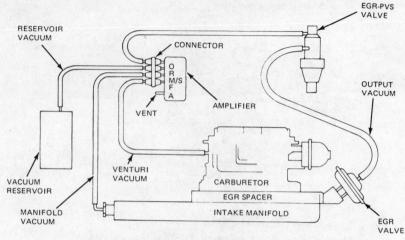

WITH SINGLE CONNECTOR VVA (1974 TYPE)

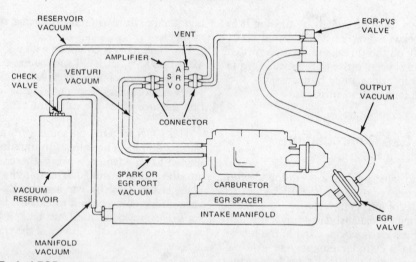

Typical EGR systems with vacuum amplifier—lower diagram is for 1975–78 models

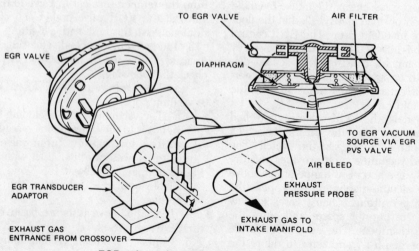

EGR valve exhaust backpressure tranducer

6. Apply vacuum to the EGR valve. The valve should open at 3–10 in. Hg, the engine idle speed should slow down and the idle quality should become more rough.

7. If this does not happen, i.e., the EGR valve remains closed, the EGR valve is defective and must be replaced.

8. If the valve stem moves but the idle remains the same, the valve orifice is clogged and must be cleaned.

> NOTE: *If an outside vacuum source is not available, disconnect the hose which runs between the EGR valve and the temperature cut-in valve and plug the hose connections on the cut-in valve. Connect the EGR valve hose to a source of intake manifold vacuum and watch the idle. The results should be the same as in steps 6–7, above.*

EGR SYSTEM SERVICE

Since the EGR system channels exhaust gases through quite narrow passages, deposits are likely to build up and eventually block the flow of gases. This necessitates servicing of the system at the interval specified in the maintenance chart (see Chapter 1). EGR system service consists of cleaning or replacing the EGR valve and cleaning all the exhaust gas channels.

EGR VALVE CLEANING

Remove the EGR valve for cleaning. Do not strike or pry on the valve diaphragm housing or supports, as this may damage the valve operating mechanism and/or change the valve calibration. Check orifice hole in the EGR valve body for deposits. A small hand drill of no more than 0.060 in. diameter may be used to clean the hole if plugged. Extreme care must be taken to avoid enlarging the hole or damaging the surface of the orifice plate.

> NOTE: *The remainder of this procedure refers only to EGR valves which can be disassembled. Valves which are riveted or otherwise permanently assembled cannot be cleaned and should be replaced if highly contaminated.*

Separate the diaphragm section from the main mounting body. Clean the valve plates, stem, and the mounting plate, using a small power-driven rotary type wire brush. Take care not to damage the parts. Remove deposits between stem and valve disc by using a steel blade or shim approximately 0.028 in. thick in a sawing motion around the stem shoulder at both sides of the disc.

The poppet must wobble and move axially before reassembly.

Clean the cavity and passages in the main body of the valve with a power-driven rotary wire brush. If the orifice plate has a hole less

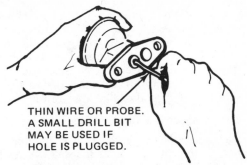

THIN WIRE OR PROBE. A SMALL DRILL BIT MAY BE USED IF HOLE IS PLUGGED.

Cleaning EGR valve orifice

than 0.050 in. it must be removed for cleaning. Remove all loosened debris using shop compressed air. Reassemble the diaphragm section on the main body using a new gasket between them. Torque the attaching screws to specification. Clean the orifice plate and the counterbore in the valve body. Reinstall the orifice plate using a small amount of contact cement to retain the plate in place during assembly of the valve to the carburetor spacer. Apply cement only to outer edges of the orifice plate to avoid restriction of the orifice.

EGR Supply Passages and Carburetor Space Cleaning

Remove the carburetor and carburetor spacer on engines so equipped. Clean the supply tube

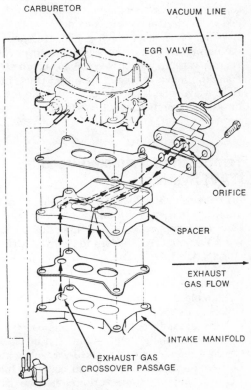

CARBURETOR
VACUUM LINE
EGR VALVE
ORIFICE
SPACER
EXHAUST GAS FLOW
INTAKE MANIFOLD
EXHAUST GAS CROSSOVER PASSAGE

EGR system spacer entry

with a small power-driven rotary type wire brush or blast cleaning equipment. Clean the exhaust gas passages in the spacer using a suitable wire brush and/or scraper. The machined holes in the spacer can be cleaned by using a suitable round wire brush. Hard encrusted material should be probed loose first, then brushed out.

EGR Exhaust Gas Channel Cleaning

Clean the exhaust gas channel, where applicable, in the intake manifold, using a suitable carbon scraper. Clean the exhaust gas entry port in the intake manifold by hand passing a suitable drill bit thru the holes to auger out the deposits. Do not use a wire brush. The manifold riser (bore(s)) should be suitably plugged during the above action to prevent any of the residue from entering the induction system.

Venturi Vacuum Amplifier System

Many 1974 and later models use a venturi vacuum amplifier in conjunction with the EGR system. The amplifier is used to boost a relatively weak venturi vacuum signal in the throat of the carburetor into a strong intake manifold vacuum signal to operate the EGR valve. This device improves driveability by more closely matching venturi airflow and EGR flow.

The amplifier features a vacuum reservoir and check valve to maintain an adequate vacuum supply regardless of variations in engine manifold vacuum. Also used in conjunction with the amplifier, is a relief valve, which will cancel the output EGR vacuum signal whenever the venturi vacuum signal is equal to, or greater than, the intake manifold vacuum. Thus, the EGR valve may close at or near wide-open throttle acceleration, when maximum power is needed.

Temperature Activated Vacuum (TAV) System

1973 cars using the 250 six-cylinder engine and automatic transmission built before March 15, 1973 are equipped with a Temperature Activated Vacuum (TAV) system to control distributor spark advance. The system contains a 3-way solenoid valve, an ambient temperature switch located in the front door hinge pillar, a vacuum bleed line to the carburetor airhorn and a spark delay valve.

When the ambient temperature is about 60°F, and contacts in the temperature sensor close and complete the circuit to the 3-way solenoid. This energizes the solenoid and connects the EGR vacuum port on the carburetor to the distributor vacuum advance. The EGR vacuum

signal is weaker than the normal spark port vacuum signal, thus supplying less vacuum advance once the outside temperature rises above 60°F. When the ambient temperature is below 49°F, the solenoid is deenergized and the distributor vacuum advance operates in the normal manner, thus aiding cold weather driveability.

Cold Temperature Activated Vacuum (CTAV) System

1973 cars using the 250 six-cylinder engine and automatic transmission built on or after March 15, 1973, as well as all 1974 models using the 250 six and automatic transmission are equipped with a Cold Temperature Activated Vacuum (CTAV) system to control distributor spark advance. This system is basically a refinement of the TAV system with the temperature switch relocated in the air cleaner and a latching relay added to maintain a strong vacuum signal at the distributor, whether it be EGR port or spark port carburetor vacuum, and to keep the system from intermittently switching vacuum signals when the intake air is between 49 and 60°F. When the temperature switch closes at 60°F, the latching relay (normally off) is energized and stays on until the ignition switch is turned off. The latching relay then overrides the temperature switch and forces the solenoid valve to keep the spark port vacuum system closed and open the EGR port vacuum system. This prevents full vacuum advance, once the engine is warmed-up, thereby lowering emissions.

Delay Vacuum By-Pass (DVB) System

All 1973 models equipped with the 351C or 400 V8 manufactured before March 15, 1973 are equipped with the Delay Vacuum By-pass spark control system. This system provides two paths by which carburetor vacuum can reach the distributor vacuum advance. The system consists of a spark delay valve, a check valve, a

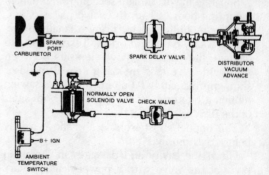

DELAY VACUUM BY-PASS SYSTEM SCHEMATIC

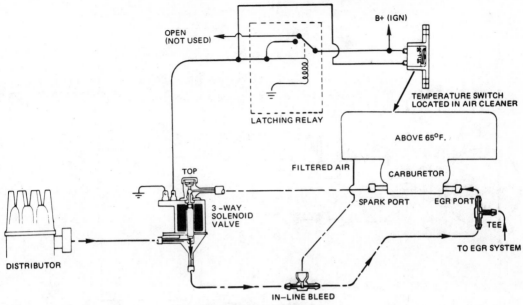

CTAV system schematic

solenoid vacuum valve, and an ambient temperature switch. When the ambient temperature is below 49°F, the temperature switch contacts are open and the vacuum solenoid is open (de-energized). Under these conditions, vacuum will flow from the carburetor, through the open solenoid, and to the distributor. Since the spark delay valve resists the flow of carburetor vacuum, the vacuum will always flow through the vacuum solenoid when it is open, since this is the path of least resistance. When the ambient temperature rises above 60°F, the contacts in the temperature switch (which is located in the door post) close. This passes ignition switch current to the solenoid, energizing the solenoid. This blocks one of the two vacuum paths. All distributor vacuum must now flow through the spark delay valve. When carburetor vacuum rises above a certain level on acceleration, a rubber valve in the spark delay valve blocks vacuum from passing through the valve for from 5 to 30 seconds. After this time delay has elasped, normal vacuum is supplied to the distributor. When the vacuum solenoid is closed, (temperature above 60°), the vacuum line from the solenoid to the distributor is vented to atmosphere. To prevent the vacuum that is passing through the spark delay valve from escaping through the solenoid into the atmosphere, a one-way check valve is installed in the vacuum line from the solenoid to the distributor.

EGR/Coolant Spark Control

The EGR/CSC system is used on most 1974 and later models. It regulates both distributor spark advance and the EGR valve operation according to coolant temperature by sequentially switching vacuum signals.

The major EGR/CSC system components are:
1. 95°F EGR-PVS valve;
2. Spark Delay Valve (SDV);
3. Vacuum check valve.

When the engine coolant temperature is below 82°F, the EGR-PVS valve admits carburetor EGR port vacuum (occurring at about 2,500 rpm) directly to the distributor advance diaphragm, through the one-way check valve.

At the same time, the EGR-PVS valve shuts off carburetor EGR vacuum to the EGR valve and transmission diaphragm.

When engine coolant temperature is 95°F and above, the EGR-PVS valve is actuated and directs carburetor EGR vacuum to the EGR valve and transmission instead of the distributor. At temperatures between 82–95°F, the EGR-PVS valve may be opened, closed, or in mid-position.

The SDV valve delays carburetor spark vacuum to the distributor advance diaphragm by restricting the vacuum signal through the SDV valve for a predetermined time. During normal acceleration, little or no vacuum is admitted to the distributor advance diaphragm until acceleration is completed, because of (1) the time delay of the SDV valve and (2) the rerouting of EGR port vacuum if the engine coolant temperature is 95°F or higher.

The check valve blocks off vacuum signal from the SDV to the EGR-PVS so that carburetor spark vacuum will not be dissipated when the EGR-PVS is actuated above 95°F.

The 235°F PVS is not part of the EGR/CSC

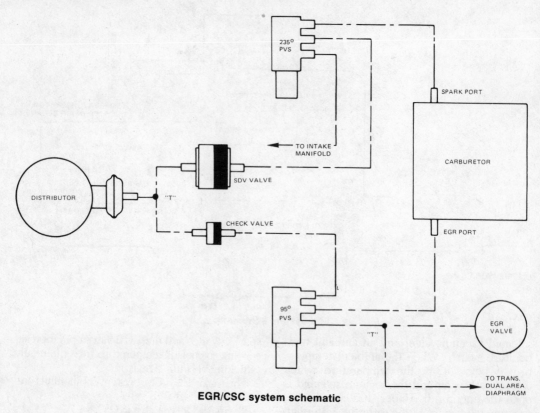

EGR/CSC system schematic

system, but is connected to the distributor vacuum advance to prevent engine overheating while idling (as on previous models). At idle speed, no vacuum is generated at either the carburetor spark port or EGR port and engine timing is fully retarded. When engine coolant temperature reaches 235°F, however, the valve is actuated to admit intake manifold vacuum to the distributor advance diaphragm. This advances the engine timing and speeds up the engine. The increase in coolant flow and fan speed lowers engine temperature.

Cold Start Spark Advance (CSSA)

All 1975 models using the 460 V8 and many 1976–78 models are equipped with the CSSA

System. It is a modification of the existing spark control system to aid in cold start driveability. The system uses a coolant temperature sensing vacuum switch located on the thermostat housing. When the engine is cold (below 125°F), it permits full manifold vacuum to the distributor advance diaphragm. After the engine warms up, normal spark control (retard) resumes.

Vacuum Operated Heat Control Valve (VOHV)

To further aid cold start driveability during engine warmup, most 1975 and later engines use a VOHV located between the exhaust manifold and the exhaust inlet (header) pipe.

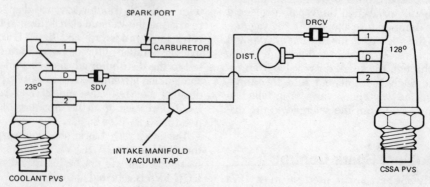

CSSA system schematic

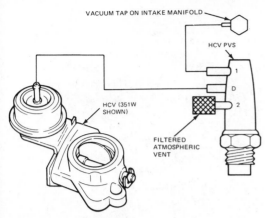

VOHV system schematic

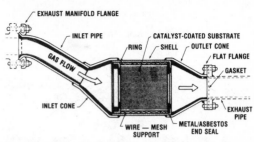

Sectional view of catalytic converter

When the engine is first started, the valve is closed, blocking exhaust gases from existing from one bank of cylinders. These gases are then diverted back through the intake manifold crossover passage under the carburetor. The result is quick heat to the carburetor and choke.

The VOHV is controlled by a ported vacuum switch which uses manifold vacuum to keep the vacuum motor on the valve closed until the coolant reaches a predetermined "warm-up" valve. When the engine is warmed-up, the PVS shuts off vacuum to the VOHV, and a strong return spring opens the VOHV butterfly.

Dual Signal Spark Advance (DSSA) System

The DSSA system is used on many 1975 and later model engines. It incorporates a spark delay valve (SDV) and a one-way check valve to provide improved spark and EGR function during mild acceleration.

The check valve prevents spark port vacuum from reaching the EGR valve and causing excessive EGR valve flow. It also prevents EGR port vacuum, which could result in improper

spark advance due to weakened signal. The SDV permits application of full EGR vacuum to the distributor vacuum advance diaphragm during mild acceleration. During steady speed or cruise conditions, EGR port vacuum is applied to the EGR valve and spark port vacuum is applied to the distributor vacuum advance diaphragm.

Catalytic Reactor (Converter) System

Starting in 1975, all models are equipped with a catalytic converter system to meet 1975 Federal and California emission control standards. California models are equipped with two converters, while models sold in the other 49 states have only one unit.

Catalytic converters convert noxious emissions of hydrocarbons (HC) and carbon monoxide (CO) into harmless carbon dioxide and water. The reaction takes place inside the reactor(s) at great heat using platinum or palladium metals as the catalyst. The 5 in. diameter units are installed in the exhaust system ahead of the mufflers. They are designed, if the engine is properly tuned, to last 50,000 miles before replacement.

NOTE: *Lead-free gasoline must be used on all converter equipped vehicles.*

Ford Electronic Engine Control System

EEC I

Ford's EEC I system was introduced in 1978, on the Lincoln Versailles. Designed to precisely control ignition timing, EGR and Thermactor (air pump) flow, the system consists of an Electrnoic Control Assembly (ECA), seven monitoring sensors, a Dura Spark II ignition module and coil, a special distributor assembly, and an EGR system designed to operate on air pressure.

The ECA is a solid state micro computer, consisting of a processor assembly and a calibration assembly. The processor continuously receives inputs from the seven sensors, which it converts to usable information for the calcu-

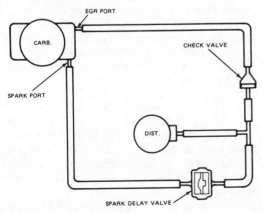

DSSA system schematic

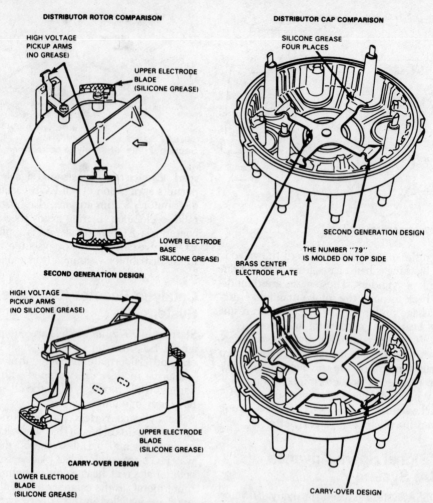

DISTRIBUTOR ROTOR COMPARISON

HIGH VOLTAGE
PICKUP ARMS
(NO GREASE)

UPPER ELECTRODE
BLADE
(SILICONE GREASE)

LOWER ELECTRODE
BASE
(SILICONE GREASE)

SECOND GENERATION DESIGN

HIGH VOLTAGE
PICKUP ARMS
(NO SILICONE GREASE)

UPPER ELECTRODE
BLADE
(SILICONE GREASE)

CARRY-OVER DESIGN

LOWER ELECTRODE
BLADE
(SILICONE GREASE)

DISTRIBUTOR CAP COMPARISON

SILICONE GREASE
FOUR PLACES

SECOND GENERATION DESIGN

THE NUMBER "79"
IS MOLDED ON TOP SIDE

BRASS CENTER
ELECTRODE PLATE

CARRY-OVER DESIGN

Comparison of early and later model EEC distributor caps

lating section of the computer. It also performs ignition timing, Thermactor and EGR flow calculations, processes the information and sends out signals to the ignition module and control solenoids to adjust the timing and flow of the systems accordingly. The calibration assembly contains the memory and programming for the processor.

Processor inputs come from sensors monitoring manifold pressure, barometric pressure, engine coolant temperature, inlet air temperature, crankshaft position, throttle position, and EGR valve position.

The manifold absolute pressure sensor determines changes in intake manifold pressure (barometric pressure minus manifold vacuum) which result from changes in engine load and speed, or in atmospheric pressure. Its signal is used by the ECA to set part throttle spark advance and EGR flow rate.

Barometric pressure is monitored by a sensor mounted on the firewall. Measurements

taken are converted into a useable electrical signal. The ECA uses this reference for altitude-dependent EGR flow requirements.

Engine coolant temperature is measured at the rear of the intake manifold by a sensor consisting of a brass housing containing a thermistor (resistance decreases as temperature rises). When reference voltage (about 9 volts, supplied by the processor to all sensors) is applied to the sensor, the resistance can be measured by the resulting voltage drop. Resistance is then interpreted as coolant temperature by the ECA. This sensor replaces both the PVS and EGR PVS in conventional systems. EGR flow is cut off by the ECA when a predetermined temperature value is reached. The ECA will also advance initial ignition timing to increase idle speed if the coolant overheats due to prolonged idle. A faster idle speed increases coolant and radiator air flow.

Inlet air temperature is measured by a sensor mounted in the air cleaner. It functions in

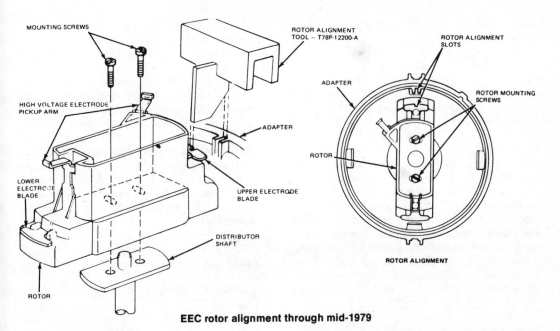

EEC rotor alignment through mid-1979

the same way as the coolant sensor. The ECA uses its signal for proper spark advance and Thermactor flow. At high inlet temperatures (above 90°F) the ECA modifies timing advance to prevent spark knock.

The crankshaft is fitted with a four-lobed powdered metal pulse ring, positioned 10° BTDC. Its position is constantly monitored by the crankshaft position sensor. Signals are sent to the ECA describing both the position of the crankshaft at any given moment, and the frequency of the pulses (engine rpm). These signals are used to determine optimum ignition timing advance. If either the sensor or wiring is broken, the ECA will not receive a signal, and thus be unable to send any signal to the ignition module. This will prevent the engine from starting.

The throttle position sensor is a rheostat connected to the throttle plate shaft. Changes in throttle plate angle change the resistance valve of the reference voltage supplied by the processor. Signals are interpreted in one of three ways by the ECA:
- Closed throttle (idle or deceleration)
- Part throttle (cruise)
- Full throttle (maximum acceleration)

A position sensor is built into the EGR valve. The ECA uses its signal to determine EGR valve position. The valve and position sensor are replaced as a unit, should either fail.

CAUTION: *Because of the complicated nature of this system, special diagnostic tools are necessary for troubleshooting. Any troubleshooting without these tools must be limited to mechanical checks of connectors and wiring.*

The distributor is locked in place during engine manufacture; no rotational adjustment is possible for initial ignition timing, since all timing is controlled by the ECA. There are no mechanical advance mechanisms or adjustments under the rotor, thus there is no need to remove it except for replacement.

EEC II

The second generation EEC II system was introduced in 1979 on full size Fords and Mercurys. It is based on the EEC I system used on the Versailles, but some changes have been made to reduce complexity and cost, increase the number of controlled functions, and improve reliability and performance.

In general, the EEC II system operates in the same manner as EEC I. An Electronic Control Assembly (ECA) monitors reports from six sensors, and adjusts the EGR flow, ignition timing, Thermactor (air pump) air flow, and carburetor air/fuel mixture in response to the incoming signals. Although there are only six sensors, seven conditions are monitored. The sensors are: (1) Engine Coolant Temperature, (2) Throttle Position, (3) Crankshaft Position, (4) Exhaust Gas Oxygen, (5) Barometric and Manifold Absolute Pressure, and (6) EGR Valve Position. These sensors function in the same manner as the EEC I sensors, and are described in the EEC I section. Note that inlet air temperature is not monitored in the EEC II system, and that the barometric and manifold pressure sensors have been combined into one unit. One more change from the previous system is in the location of the crankshaft sensor: it is mounted on the front of the engine, behind the vibration damper and crankshaft pulley.

The biggest difference between EEC I and EEC II is that the newer system is capable of continually monitoring and adjusting the carburetor air/fuel ratio. Monitoring is performed by the oxygen sensor installed in the right exhaust manifold; adjustment is made via an electric stepper motor installed on the model 7200 VV carburetor.

The stepper motor has four separate armature windings, which can be sequentially energized by the ECA. As the motor varies the position of the carburetor metering valve, the amount of control vacuum exposed to the fuel bowl is correspondingly altered. Increased vacuum reduces pressure in the fuel bowl, causing a leaner air/fuel mixture, and vice versa. During engine starting and immediately after, the ECA sets the motor at a point dependent on its initial position. Thereafter, the motor position is changed in response to the ECA calculations of the six input signals.

EEC II is also capable of controlling purging of vapors from the evaporative emission control storage canister. A canister purge solenoid, a combination solenoid and valve, is located in the line between the intake manifold purge fitting and the carbon canister. It controls the flow of vapors from the canister to the intake manifold, opening and closing in response to signals from the ECA.

CAUTION: *As is the case with EEC I, diagnosis and repair of the system requires special tools and equipment.*

The distributor is locked in place during engine manufacture; no rotational adjustment is possible for initial ignition timing, since all timing is controlled by the ECA. There are no mechanical advance mechanisms or adjustments under the ignition rotor, and thus there is no need to remove it except for replacement.

Air/fuel mixture is entirely controlled by the ECA; no adjustments are possible.

EEC III

EEC III was introduced in 1980. It is a third generation system developed entirely from EEC II. The only real differences between EEC II and III are contained within the Electronic Control Assembly (ECA) and the Dura-Spark ignition module. The EEC III system uses a separate program module which plugs into the main ECA module. This change allows various programming calibrations for specific applications to be made to the program module, while allowing the main ECA module to be standardized. Additionally, EEC III uses a Dura-Spark III ignition module, which contains fewer electronic functions than the Dura-Spark II module; the functions have been incorporated into the main ECA module. There is no interchangeability between the Dura-Spark II and III modules.

NOTE: *Since late 1979 emission controls and air/fuel mixtures have been controlled by various electronic methods. An electronically controlled feedback carburetor is used to precisely calibrate fuel metering, many vacuum check valves, solenoids and regulators have been added and the electronic control boxes (ECU and MCU) can be calibrated and programmed in order to be used by different engines and under different conditions.*

EEC IV

All 1984 and later engines use the EEC IV system.

The heart of the EEC-IV system is a microprocessor called an electronic control assembly (ECA). The ECA receives data from a number of sensors and other electronic components (switches, relays, etc.). Based on information received and information programmed in the ECA's memory, it generates output signals to control various relays, solenoids and other actuators. The ECA in the EEC-IV system has calibration modules located inside the assembly that contain calibration specifications for optimizing emissions, fuel economy and drive ability. The calibration module is called a PROM.

A potentiometer senses the position of the vane airflow meter in the engine's air induction system and generates a voltage signal that varies with the amount of air drawn into the engine. A sensor in the area of the vane airflow meter measures the temperature of the incoming air and transmits a corresponding electrical signal. Another temperature sensor inserted in the engine coolant tells if the engine is cold or warmed up. And a switch that senses throttle plate position produces electrical signals that tell the control unit when the throttle is closed or wide open.

A special probe (oxygen sensor) in the exhaust manifold measures the amount of oxygen in the exhaust gas, which is an indication of combustion efficiency, and sends a signal to the control unit. The sixth signal, Crankshaft position information, is transmitted by a sensor intergral with the new-design distributor.

The EEC IV microcomputer circuit processes the input signals and produces output control signals to the fuel injectors to regulate fuel discharged to the injectors. It also adjusts ignition spark timing to provide the best balance between driveability and economy.

NOTE: *Because of the complicated nature*

of the Ford system, special tools and procedures are necessary for testing and trouble-shooting.

The following emission control devices described can be tested and maintained, any not mentioned should be serviced by qualified mechanics using the required equipment.

GASOLINE ENGINE FUEL SYSTEM

Fuel Pump

A single-action, diaphragm-type, mechanical fuel pump, driven by the camshaft, is used on all models except the 1973–75 460 Police Interceptor V8 and models equipped with fuel injection. The mechanical fuel pump is located at the lower left-side of the engine block on in-line six-cylinder models, at the lower left-side of the cylinder front cover on V8 models and on the right side front on V6 models. The 1973–75 Police Interceptor engines use an electrical fuel pump located in the fuel tank beneath the vapor separator. The tank must be removed for electrical fuel pump service.

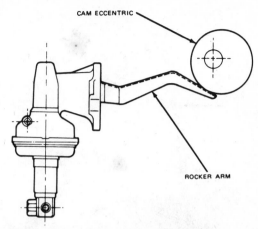

Typical mechanical fuel pump installation

MECHANICAL FUEL PUMP

Testing and Adjustment

No adjustments may be made to the fuel pump. Before removing and replacing the old fuel pump, the following test may be made while the pump is still installed on the engine.

1. If a fuel pressure gauge is available, connect the gauge to the engine and operate the engine until the pressure stops rising. Stop the engine and take the reading. If the reading is within the specifications given in the "Tune-Up Specifications" chart in Chapter 2, the malfunction is not in the fuel pump. Also check the pressure drop after the engine is stopped. A large pressure drop below the minimum specification indicates leaky valves. If the pump proves to be satisfactory, check the tank and inlet line.

2. If a fuel pressure gauge is not available, disconnect the fuel line at the pump outlet, place a vessel beneath the pump outlet, and crank the engine. A good pump will force the fuel out of the outlet in steady spurts. One pint in 25–30 seconds is a good flow. A worn diaphragm spring may not provide proper pumping action.

3. As a further test, disconnect and plug the fuel line from the tank at the pump, and hold your thumb over the pump inlet. If the pump is functioning properly, a suction indicates that

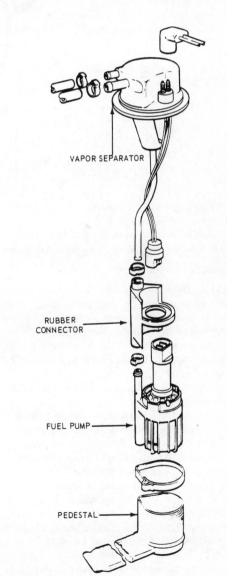

Electric fuel pump assembly—1973–75 460 PI V8

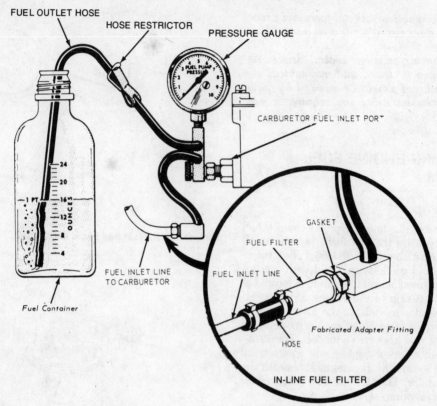

Fuel pump pressure and capacity test equipment

the pump diaphragm is leaking, or that the diaphragm linkage is worn.

4. Check the crankcase for gasoline. A ruptured diaphragm may leak fuel into the engine.

Removal and Installation

NOTE: *Before removing the pump, rotate the engine so that the low point of the cam lobe is against the pump arm. This can be determined by rotating the engine with the fuel pump mounting bolts loosened slightly; when tension (resistance) is removed from the arm, proceed.*

1. Disconnect the plug and inlet and outlet lines from the fuel pump.

2. Remove the fuel pump retaining bolts and carefully pull the pump and old gasket away from the block.

3. Discard the old gasket. Clean the mating surfaces on the block and position a new gasket on the block, using oil-resistant sealer.

4. Mount the fuel pump and gasket to the engine block, being careful to insert the pump lever (rocker arm) in the engine block, aligning it correctly above the camshaft lobe.

NOTE: *If resistance is felt while positioning the fuel pump on the block, the camshaft lobe is probably on the high position. To ease installation, connect a remote engine starter switch to the engine and "tap" the switch until resistance fades.*

5. While holding the pump securely against the block, install the retaining bolts. On six-cylinder engines, torque the bolts to 12–15 ft. lbs., and on V8, 20–24 ft. lbs.

6. Unplug and reconnect the fuel lines at the pump.

7. Start the engine and check for fuel leaks. Also check for oil leaks where the fuel pump attaches to the block.

ELECTRIC FUEL PUMP

Removal and Installation

NOTE: *A 1984 and later models equipped with a high output injected or turbocharged injected engine are equipped with two electric pumps. A low-pressure pump is mounted in the tank and a high pressure pump is externally mounted.*

CAUTION: *Before servicing any part of the fuel injection it is necessary to depressurize the system. A special tool is available for testing and bleeding the system.*

IN-TANK PUMP

1. Disconnect the negative battery cable.
2. Depressurize the system and drain as

much gas from the tank by pumping out through the filler neck.

3. Raise the back of the car and safely support on jackstands.

4. Disconnect the fuel supply, return and vent lines at the right and left side of the frame.

5. Disconnect the wiring to the fuel pump.

6. Support the gas tank, loosen and remove the mounting straps. Remove the gas tank.

7. Disconnect the lines and harness at the pump flange.

8. Clean the outside of the mounting flange and retaining ring. Turn the fuel pump lock ring counterclockwise and remove.

9. Remove the fuel pump.

10. Clean the mounting surfaces. Put a light coat of grease on the mounting surfaces and on the new sealing ring. Install the new fuel pump.

11. Installation is in the reverse order of removal. If single high pressure pump system, fill the tank with at least 10 gals. of gas. Turn the ignition key ON for three seconds. Repeat 6 or 7 times until the fuel system is pressurized. Check for any fitting leaks. Start the engine and check for leaks.

EXTERNAL PUMP

1. Disconnect the negative battery cable.

2. Depressurize the fuel system.

3. Raise and support the rear of the vehicle on jackstands.

4. Disconnect the inlet and outlet fuel lines.

5. Disconnect the electrical harness connection.

6. Bend down the retaining tab and remove the pump from the mounting bracket ring.

7. Install in reverse order, make sure the pump is indexed correctly in the mounting bracket insulator.

"Quick-Connect" Fuel Line Fittings

REMOVAL AND INSTALLATION

NOTE: *"Quick-Connect" (push) type fuel fittings are used on most models equipped with a pressurized fuel system. The fittings must be disconnected using proper procedures or the fitting may be damaged. Two types of retainers are used on the push connect fittings. Line sizes of ⅜ in. and 5/16 in. use a "hairpin" clip retainer, ¼ in. line connectors use a "duck bill" clip retainer.*

Hairpin Clip

1. Clean all dirt and/or grease from the fitting. Spread the two clip legs about an ⅛ inch each to disengage from the fitting and pull the clip outward from the fitting. Use finger pressure only, do not use any tools.

2. Grasp the fitting and hose assembly and pull away from the steel line. Twist the fitting and hose assembly slightly while pulling, if necessary, when a sticking condition exists.

3. Inspect the hairpin clip for damage, replace the clip if necessary. Reinstall the clip in position on the fitting.

4. Inspect the fitting and inside of the connector to insure freedom of dirt or obstruction. Install fitting into the connector and push together. A click will be heard when the hairpin clip snaps into proper connection. Pull on the line to insure full engagement.

Duck Bill Clip

1. A special tool is available from Ford for removing the retaining clips (Ford Tool No. T82L-9500-AH). If the tool is not on hand see Step 2. Align the slot on the push connector disconnect tool with either tab on the retaining clip. Insert the tool to disengage the clip. Pull the line from the connector.

2. If the special clip tool is not available, use a pair of narrow 6 in. channel lock pliers with a jaw width of 0.2 in. or less. Align the jaws of the pliers with the openings of the fitting case and compress the part of the retaining clip that engages the case. Compressing the retaining clip will release the fitting which may be pulled from the connector. Both sides of the clip must be compressed at the same time to disengage.

3. Inspect the retaining clip, fitting end and connector. Replace clip if any damage is apparent.

4. Push the line into the steel connector until a click is heard, indicating clip is in place. Pull on line to check engagement.

Electric Choke

Starting in 1973, all Fords use an electrically-assisted choke to reduce exhaust emissions of carbon monoxide during warmup. The system consists of a choke cap, a thermostatic spring, a bimetal sensing disc (switch) and a ceramic positive temperature coefficient (PTC) heater.

The choke is powered from the center tap of the alternator, so that current is constantly applied to the temperature sensing disc. The system is grounded through the carburetor body. At temperatures below approximately 60°F, the switch is open and no current is supplied to the ceramic heater, thereby resulting in normal unassisted thermostatic spring choke action. When the temperature rises above about 60°F, the temperature sensing disc closes and current is supplied to the heater, which in turn, acts on the thermostatic spring. Once the heater starts, it causes the thermostatic spring to pull

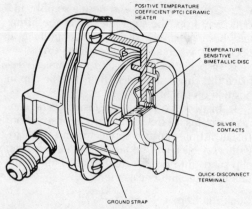

Electric choke components

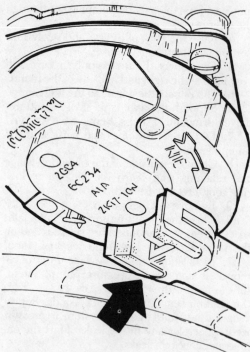

the choke plate(s) open within 1½ minutes, which is sooner than it would open if non-assisted.

OPERATIONAL TEST

1. Detach the electrical lead from the choke cap.

2. Use a jumper lead to connect the terminal on the choke cap and the wire terminal, so that the electrical circuit is still completed.

3. Start the engine.

4. Hook up a test light between the connector on the choke lead and ground.

5. The test light should glow. If it does not, current is not being supplied to the electrically-assisted choke.

Electric choke hookup

6. Connect the test light between the terminal on the alternator and the terminal on the choke cap. If the light now glows, replace the lead, since it is not passing current to the choke assist.

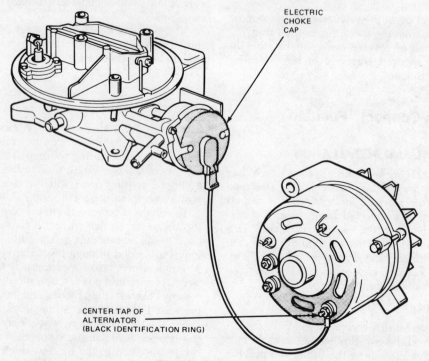

Electric choke wiring

CAUTION: *Do not ground the terminal on the alternator while performing Step 6.*

7. If the light still does not glow, the fault lies somewhere in the electrical system. Check the sytem out.

If the electrically-assisted choke receives power but still does not appear to be functioning properly, reconnect the choke lead and proceed with the rest of the test.

8. Tape the bulb end of the thermometer to the metallic portion of the choke housing.

9. If the electrically-assisted choke operates below 55°F, it is defective and must be replaced.

10. Allow the engine to warm up to between 80 and 100°F; at these temperatures the choke should operate for about 1½ minutes.

11. If it does not operate for this length of time, check the bimetallic spring to see if it is connected to the tang on the choke lever.

12. If the spring is connected and the choke is not operating properly, replace the cap assembly.

Carburetors

THROTTLE SOLENOID (ANTI-DIESELING SOLENOID) TEST

1. Turn the ignition key on and open the throttle. The solenoid plunger should extend (solenoid energize). 2. Turn the ignition off. The plunger should retract, allowing the throttle to close.

NOTE: *With the antidieseling de-energized, the carburetor idle speed adjusting screw must make contact with the throttle shaft to prevent the throttle plates from jamming in the throttle bore when the engine is turned off.*

3. If the solenoid is functioning properly and the engine is still dieseling, check for one of the following:

a. High idle or engine shut off speed;
b. Engine timing not set to specification;
c. Binding throttle linkage;
d. Too low an octane fuel being used.

Correct any of these problems as necessary.

4. If the solenoid fails to function as outlined in Steps 1–2, disconnect the solenoid leads; the solenoid should de-energize. If it does not, it is jammed and must be replaced.

5. Connect the solenoid to a 12 V power source and to ground. Open the throttle so that the plunger can extend. If it does not, the solenoid is defective.

6. If the solenoid is functioning correctly and no other source of trouble can be found, the fault probably lies in the wiring between the solenoid and the ignition switch or in the ignition switch itself. Remember to reconnect the solenoid when finished testing.

NOTE: *On some 1971 models, dieseling may occur when the engine is turned off because of feedback through the alternator warning light circuit. A diode kit is available from Ford to cure this problem*

CARBURETOR REMOVAL AND INSTALLATION

1. Remove the air cleaner.

2. Disconnect the throttle cable or rod at the throttle lever. Disconnect the distributor vacuum line, exhaust gas recirculation line (1973 and later models), inline fuel filter, choke heat tube and the positive crankcase ventilation hose at the carburetor.

3. Disconnect the throttle solenoid (if so equipped) and electric choke assist (1973 and later models) at their connectors.

4. Remove the carburetor retaining nuts. Lift off the carburetor carefully, taking care not to spill any fuel. Remove the carburetor mounting gasket and discard it. Remove the carburetor mounting spacer, if so equipped, from the intake manifold.

5. Prior to installation, clean the gasket mounting surfaces of the intake manifold, spacer (if so equipped), and carburetor. When using a spacer, use two new gaskets, sandwiching the spacer between the gaskets. If a spacer is not used, only one new carburetor mounting gasket is required.

6. Place the new gasket(s) and spacer (if so equipped) on the carburetor mounting studs. Position the carburetor on top of the gasket and hand tighten the retaining nuts. Then tighten the nuts in a crisscross pattern to 10–15 ft. lbs.

7. Connect the throttle linkage, the distributor vacuum line, exhaust gas recirculation line (1973 and later models), inline fuel filter, choke heat tube, positive crankcase ventilation hose, throttle solenoid (if so equipped) and electric-choke assist (1973 and later models).

8. Perform the preliminary adjustments of idle speed and mixture settings as outlined in Chapter 2.

OVERHAUL

All Types Except 2700 VV and 7200 VV

NOTE: *The 2700 VV and 7200 VV are part of the extremely sophisticated EEC system. Do not attempt to overhaul these units.*

Efficient carburetion depends greatly on careful cleaning and inspection during overhaul, since dirt, gum, water, or varnish in or on the carburetor parts are often responsible for poor performance.

Overhaul your carburetor in a clean, dust-free area. Carefully disassemble the carburetor, referring often to the exploded views. Keep all similar and look-alike parts segregated during the disassembly and cleaning to avoid accidental interchange during assembly. Make a note of all jet sizes.

When the carburetor is disassembled, wash all parts (except diaphragms, electric choke units, pump plunger, and any other plastic, leather, fiber, or rubber parts) in clean carburetor solvent. Do not leave parts in the solvent any longer than is necessary to sufficiently loosen the deposits. Excessive cleaning may remove the special finish from the float bowl and choke valve bodies, leaving these parts unfit for service. Rinse all parts in clean solvent and blow them dry with compressed air or allow them to air dry. Wipe clean all cork, plastic, leather, and fiber parts with a clean, lint-free cloth.

Blow out all passages and jets with compressed air and be sure that there are no restrictions or blockages. Never use wire or similar tools to clean jets, fuel passages, or air bleeds. Clean all jets and valves separately to avoid accidental interchange.

Check all parts for wear or damage. If wear or damage is found, replace the defective parts. Especially check the following:

1. Check the float needle and seat for wear. If wear is found, replace the complete assembly.

2. Check the float hinge pin for wear and the float(s) for dents or distortion. Replace the float if fuel has leaked into it.

3. Check the throttle and choke shaft bores for wear or an out-of-round condition. Damage or wear to the throttle arm, shaft, or shaft bore will often require replacement of the throttle body. These parts require a close tolerance of fit; wear may allow air leakage, which could affect starting and idling.

NOTE: *Throttle shafts and bushings are not included in overhaul kits. They can be purchased separately.*

4. Inspect the idle mixture adjusting needles for burrs or grooves. Any such condition requires replacement of the needle, since you will not be able to obtain a satisfactory idle.

5. Test the accelerator pump check valves. They should pass air one way but not the other. Test for proper seating by blowing and sucking on the valve. Replace the valve if necessary. If the valve is satisfactory, wash the valve again to remove breath moisture.

6. Check the bowl cover for warped surfaces with a straightedge.

7. Closely inspect the valves and seats for wear and damage, replacing as necessary.

8. After the carburetor is assembled, check the choke valve for freedom of operation.

Carburetor overhaul kits are recommended for each overhaul. These kits contain all gaskets and new parts to replace those which deteriorate most rapidly. Failure to replace all parts supplied with the kit (especially gaskets) can result in poor performance later.

Some carburetor manufacturers supply overhaul kits of three basic types: minor repair; major repair; and gasket kits. Basically, they contain the following:

Minor Repair Kits:
- All gaskets
- Float needle valve
- Volume control screw
- All diaphragms
- Spring for the pump diaphragm

Major Repair Kits:
- All jets and gaskets
- All diaphragms
- Float needle valve
- Volume control screw
- Pump ball valve
- Float
- Complete intermediate rod
- Intermediate pump lever
- Some cover hold-down screws and washers

Gasket Kits:
- All gaskets

After cleaning and checking all components, reassemble the carburetor, using new parts and referring to the exploded view. When reassembling, make sure that all screws and jets are tight in their seats, but do not overtighten as the tips will be distorted. Tighten all screws gradually, in rotation. Do not tighten needle valves into their seats; uneven jetting will result. Always use new gaskets. Be sure to adjust the float level when reassembling.

CARBURETOR ADJUSTMENTS

NOTE: *Adjustments for the 2700 VV, are covered following adjustments for all other carburetors.*

AUTOMATIC CHOKE HOUSING ADJUSTMENT

All Carburetors

By rotating the spring housing of the automatic choke, the reaction of the choke to engine temperature can be controlled. To adjust, remove the air cleaner assembly, loosen the thermostatic spring housing retaining screws and set the spring housing to the specified index mark. The marks are shown in the accompanying illustration. After adjusting the setting, tighten the retaining screws and replace the air cleaner assembly to the carburetor.

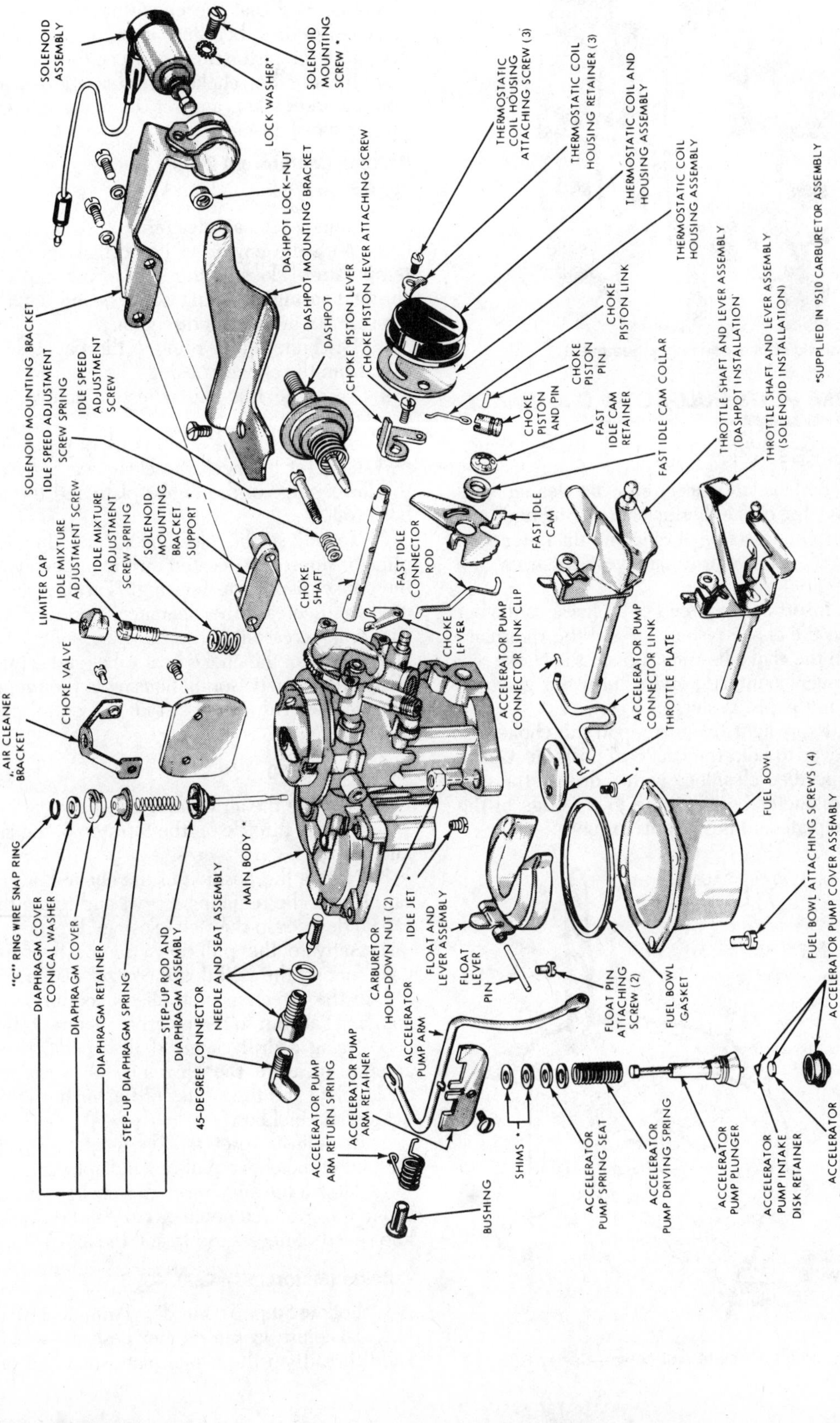

SOLENOID ASSEMBLY

LOCK WASHER*

SOLENOID MOUNTING SCREW *

THERMOSTATIC COIL HOUSING ATTACHING SCREW (3)

THERMOSTATIC COIL HOUSING RETAINER (3)

THERMOSTATIC COIL AND HOUSING ASSEMBLY

THERMOSTATIC COIL HOUSING ASSEMBLY

DASHPOT LOCK-NUT

DASHPOT MOUNTING BRACKET

DASHPOT

CHOKE PISTON LEVER

CHOKE PISTON LEVER ATTACHING SCREW

CHOKE PISTON LINK

CHOKE PISTON PIN

CHOKE PISTON AND PIN

FAST IDLE CAM RETAINER

FAST IDLE CAM COLLAR

THROTTLE SHAFT AND LEVER ASSEMBLY (DASHPOT INSTALLATION)

THROTTLE SHAFT AND LEVER ASSEMBLY (SOLENOID INSTALLATION)

SOLENOID MOUNTING BRACKET

IDLE SPEED ADJUSTMENT SCREW SPRING

IDLE SPEED ADJUSTMENT SCREW

LIMITER CAP

IDLE MIXTURE ADJUSTMENT SCREW

IDLE MIXTURE ADJUSTMENT SCREW SPRING

SOLENOID MOUNTING BRACKET SUPPORT *

CHOKE SHAFT

FAST IDLE CONNECTOR ROD

FAST IDLE CAM

ACCELERATOR PUMP CONNECTOR LINK CLIP

ACCELERATOR PUMP CONNECTOR LINK

THROTTLE PLATE

AIR CLEANER BRACKET

CHOKE VALVE

CHOKE LEVER

FUEL BOWL

"C" RING WIRE SNAP RING

CONICAL WASHER

DIAPHRAGM COVER

DIAPHRAGM RETAINER

STEP-UP DIAPHRAGM SPRING

STEP-UP ROD AND DIAPHRAGM ASSEMBLY

45-DEGREE CONNECTOR

DIAPHRAGM COVER

MAIN BODY *

NEEDLE AND SEAT ASSEMBLY

IDLE JET *

FLOAT AND LEVER ASSEMBLY

FLOAT LEVER

FUEL BOWL GASKET

FUEL BOWL ATTACHING SCREWS (4)

ACCELERATOR PUMP ARM RETURN SPRING

ACCELERATOR PUMP ARM RETAINER

ACCELERATOR PUMP ARM

CARBURETOR HOLD-DOWN NUT (2)

FLOAT PIN

FLOAT PIN ATTACHING SCREW (2)

SHIMS *

ACCELERATOR PUMP SPRING SEAT

ACCELERATOR PUMP DRIVING SPRING

ACCELERATOR PUMP PLUNGER

ACCELERATOR PUMP INTAKE DISK RETAINER

ACCELERATOR PUMP COVER ASSEMBLY

ACCELERATOR PUMP INTAKE DISK

BUSHING

Exploded view—Carter RBS-1V

*SUPPLIED IN 9510 CARBURETOR ASSEMBLY

THERMOSTATIC SPRING HOUSING INDEX MARK

CHOKE HOUSING INDEX MARK

Automatic choke housing adjustment

CHOKE PLATE PULL-DOWN CLEARANCE ADJUSTMENT

Carter RBS

1. Remove the carburetor air cleaner, and remove the choke thermostatic spring housing.

2. Bend a section of 0.026 in. diameter wire at a 90° angle approximately 1/8 in. from one end.

3. Insert the bent end of the wire gauge between the choke piston slot and the righthand slot in the choke housing. Rotate the choke piston lever counterclockwise until the gauge is snug in the piston slot.

4. Exert light pressure upon the choke piston lever to hold the gauge in position. Check the specified clearance with a drill of the correct diameter between the lower edge of the choke plate and the carburetor bore.

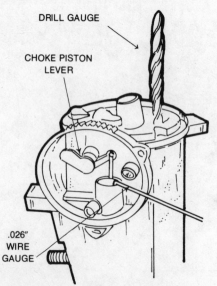

DRILL GAUGE

CHOKE PISTON LEVER

.026" WIRE GAUGE

Adjusting choke plate pull-down—Carter RBS

5. Choke plate pull-down clearance may be adjusted by bending the choke piston lever as required to obtain the desired clearance. It is recommended that the choke piston lever be removed prior to bending, in order to prevent distorting the piston link.

6. Install the choke thermostatic spring housing and gasket, and set the housing to the proper specification.

Autolite (Motorcraft) 2100

1970–74

1. Remove the air cleaner.

2. With the engine at its normal operating temperature, loosen the choke thermostatic spring housing retaining screws, and set the housing 90° in the rich direction.

3. Disconnect and remove the choke heat tube from the choke housing.

4. Turn the fast idle adjusting screw outward one full turn.

5. Start the engine. Use a drill of the specified diameter to check the clearance between the lower edge of the choke plate and the air horn wall.

6. To adjust the clearance, turn the diaphragm stopscrew (located on the underside of the choke diaphragm housing). Turning clockwise will decrease the clearance; counterclockwise will increase it.

7. Connect the choke heat tube, and set the choke thermostatic spring housing to the proper specification. Adjust the fast idle speed to specifications

Motorcraft 2150

1. Remove the air cleaner assembly.

2. Set the throttle on the top step of the fast idle cam.

3. Noting the position of the choke housing cap, loosen the retaining screws and rotate the cap 90 degrees in the rich (closing) direction.

4. Activate the pull-down motor by manually forcing the pull-down control diaphragm link in the direction of applied vacuum or by applying vacuum to the external vacuum tube.

5. Using a drill gauge of the specified diameter, measure the clearance between the choke plate and the center of the air horn wall nearest the fuel bowl.

6. To adjust, reset the diaphragm stop on the end of the choke pull-down diaphragm.

7. After adjusting, reset the choke housing cap to the specified notch. Check and reset fast idle speed, if necessary. Install the air cleaner.

Autolite (Motorcraft) 4300, 4350

1. Follow Steps 1–5 under "Autolite 1101."

2. To adjust, loosen the hex head screw (left-hand thread) on the choke plate shaft and pry

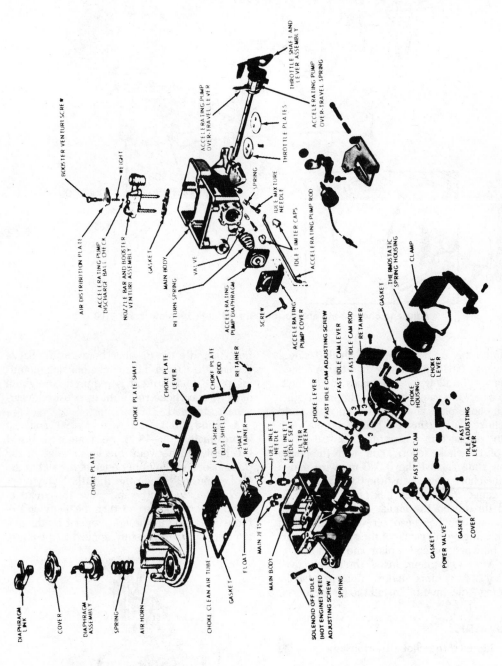

Exploded view—Autolite (Motorcraft) 2100-2V

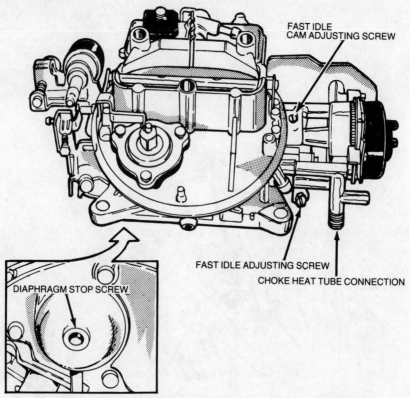

FAST IDLE
CAM ADJUSTING SCREW

DIAPHRAGM STOP SCREW

FAST IDLE ADJUSTING SCREW

CHOKE HEAT TUBE CONNECTION

Adjusting choke plate pull down—1971–74 Autolite (Motorcraft) 2100

the link away from the tapered shaft. Using a drill gauge 0.010 in. thinner than the specified clearance (to allow for tolerances in the linkage), insert the gauge between the lower edge of the choke plate and the air horn wall. Hold the choke plate against the gauge and maintain a light pressure in a counter-clockwise direction on the choke lever. Then, with the choke piston snug against the 0.036 in. wire gauge and the choke plate against the 0.010 in. smaller drill gauge, tighten the hex head screw (left-hand thread) on the choke plate shaft. After tightening the hex head screw, make a final check using a drill gauge of the specified clearance between the choke plate and air horn.

3. After adjustment, install the choke cover and adjust as outlined under "Automatic Choke Housing Adjustment." Install the air cleaner.

Holley 4150C

1. Remove the choke thermostatic housing cap.

2. Place the choke plate in the fully closed position by opening the throttle lever to about ⅓ throttle and pressing down on the front side of the choke plate. While holding the choke plate closed, release the throttle lever.

3. With the choke plate in the closed posi-

tion, measure the distance between the flat of the fast idle cam and the choke housing mounting post. If adjustment is required, straighten or bend the choke rod until the desired clearance is obtained.

4. Bend a 0.036 in. wire at a 90° angle at approximately ¹⁄₁₆–⅛ in. from one end. Insert the bent end between the lower edge of the piston slot and the upper edge of the slot in the choke housing. Open the throttle lever to approximately ⅓ throttle and rotate the choke lever counterclockwise so that the bent end of the wire is held in the housing slot by the piston slot with light pressure applied to the choke

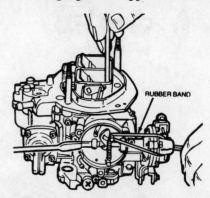

RUBBER BAND

Motorcraft 5200 choke plate pulldown adjustment

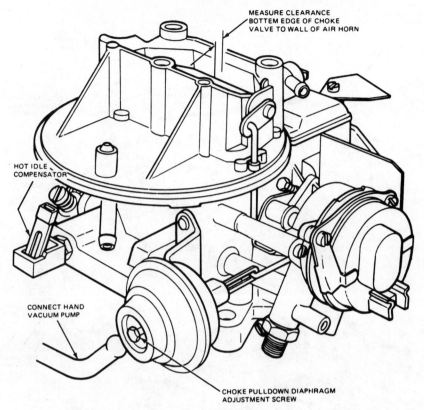

MEASURE CLEARANCE
BOTTOM EDGE OF CHOKE
VALVE TO WALL OF AIR HORN

HOT IDLE
COMPENSATOR

CONNECT HAND
VACUUM PUMP

CHOKE PULLDOWN DIAPHRAGM
ADJUSTMENT SCREW

Adjusting the choke plate pulldown on the Motorcraft 2150

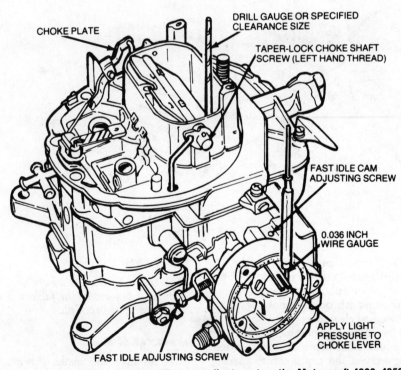

CHOKE PLATE

DRILL GAUGE OR SPECIFIED
CLEARANCE SIZE

TAPER-LOCK CHOKE SHAFT
SCREW (LEFT HAND THREAD)

FAST IDLE CAM
ADJUSTING SCREW

0.036 INCH
WIRE GAUGE

APPLY LIGHT
PRESSURE TO
CHOKE LEVER

FAST IDLE ADJUSTING SCREW

Choke plate pulldown and fast idle cam adjustment on the Motorcraft 4300, 4350

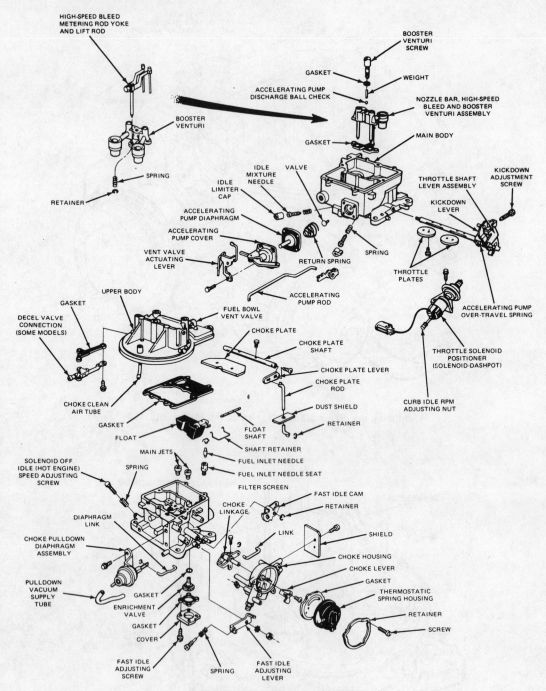

HIGH-SPEED BLEED METERING ROD YOKE AND LIFT ROD

BOOSTER VENTURI SCREW

GASKET

WEIGHT

ACCELERATING PUMP DISCHARGE BALL CHECK

NOZZLE BAR, HIGH-SPEED BLEED AND BOOSTER VENTURI ASSEMBLY

BOOSTER VENTURI

MAIN BODY

GASKET

SPRING

RETAINER

IDLE MIXTURE NEEDLE

VALVE

IDLE LIMITER CAP

THROTTLE SHAFT LEVER ASSEMBLY

KICKDOWN ADJUSTMENT SCREW

ACCELERATING PUMP DIAPHRAGM

KICKDOWN LEVER

ACCELERATING PUMP COVER

VENT VALVE ACTUATING LEVER

RETURN SPRING

SPRING

THROTTLE PLATES

UPPER BODY

ACCELERATING PUMP ROD

GASKET

FUEL BOWL VENT VALVE

ACCELERATING PUMP OVER-TRAVEL SPRING

DECEL VALVE CONNECTION (SOME MODELS)

CHOKE PLATE

CHOKE PLATE SHAFT

THROTTLE SOLENOID POSITIONER (SOLENOID-DASHPOT)

CHOKE PLATE LEVER

CHOKE PLATE ROD

CHOKE CLEAN AIR TUBE

DUST SHIELD

CURB IDLE RPM ADJUSTING NUT

GASKET

RETAINER

FLOAT

FLOAT SHAFT

MAIN JETS

SHAFT RETAINER

SOLENOID OFF IDLE (HOT ENGINE) SPEED ADJUSTING SCREW

SPRING

FUEL INLET NEEDLE

FUEL INLET NEEDLE SEAT

FILTER SCREEN

FAST IDLE CAM

DIAPHRAGM LINK

CHOKE LINKAGE

RETAINER

LINK

SHIELD

CHOKE PULLDOWN DIAPHRAGM ASSEMBLY

CHOKE HOUSING

CHOKE LEVER

GASKET

PULLDOWN VACUUM SUPPLY TUBE

GASKET

THERMOSTATIC SPRING HOUSING

ENRICHMENT VALVE

RETAINER

GASKET

SCREW

COVER

FAST IDLE ADJUSTING SCREW

SPRING

FAST IDLE ADJUSTING LEVER

Exploded view—Motorcraft 2150-2V

lever. Measure the distance between the air horn wall and the lower edge of the choke plate. If the clearance does not meet specifications, bend the adjusting tab on the choke lever to obtain the specified clearance.

5. Install the choke thermostatic housing. Be sure that the bimetallic loop is installed around the choke lever. Set the cap notch to specifications.

Holley 1946

NOTE: *On these carburetors, this adjustment is present at the factory and protected by a tamper-proof plug.*

Motorcraft 5200

1. Remove the choke thermostatic spring cover.

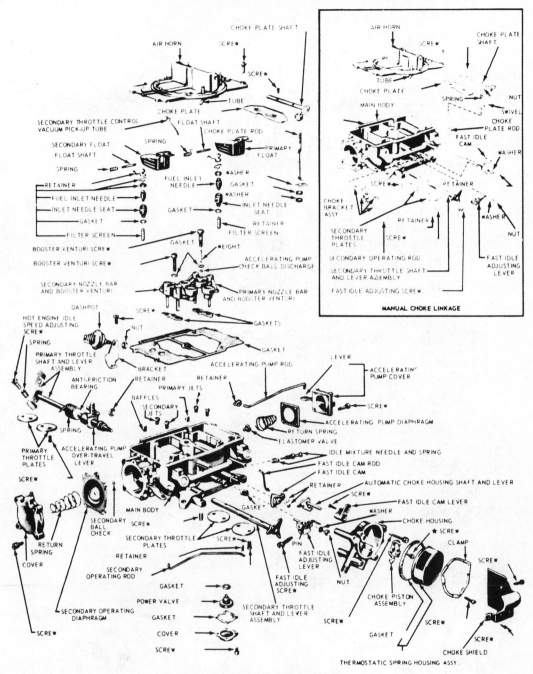

Exploded view—Autolite 4100-4V

2. Pull the coolant cover and the thermostatic spring cover assembly, or electric assist assembly out of the way.

3. Set the fast idle cam on the second step.

4. Push the diaphragm stem against its top and insert the specified gauge between the wall and the lower edge of the choke plate.

5. Apply sufficient pressure against the upper edge of the choke plate to take up any slack in the linkage.

6. Turn the adjusting screw in or out to get the proper clearance.

Carter YFA

PISTON TYPE CHOKE

NOTE: *This adjustment requires that the thermostatic spring housing and gasket (choke cap) are removed. Refer to the "Choke Cap" removal procedure below.*

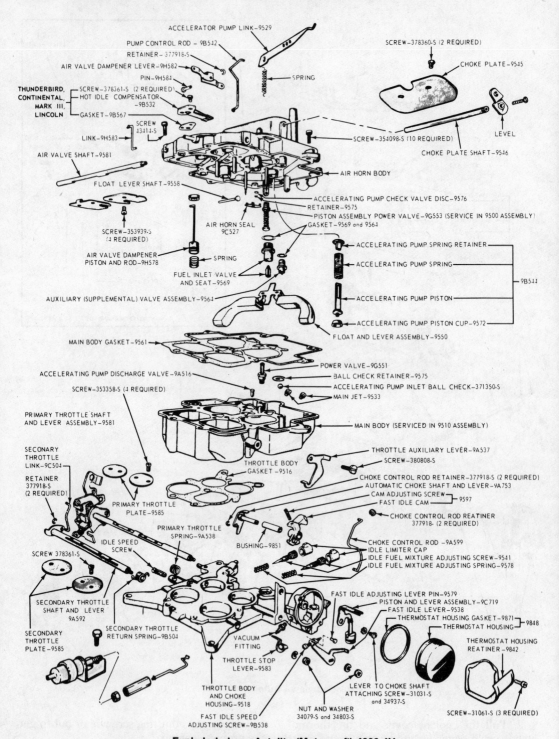

ACCELERATOR PUMP LINK-9529
PUMP CONTROL ROD-9B542
RETAINER-377918-S
AIR VALVE DAMPENER LEVER-9H582
PIN-9H584
THUNDERBIRD, SCREW-378361-S (2 REQUIRED)
CONTINENTAL, HOT IDLE COMPENSATOR-9B532
MARK III, GASKET-9B567
LINCOLN SCREW 43414-S
LINK-9H583
AIR VALVE SHAFT-9581
FLOAT LEVER SHAFT-9558
SCREW-353939-S (4 REQUIRED)
AIR VALVE DAMPENER PISTON AND ROD-9H578
SPRING
FUEL INLET VALVE AND SEAT-9569
AUXILIARY (SUPPLEMENTAL) VALVE ASSEMBLY-9564
AIR HORN SEAL 9C527

SCREW-378360-S (2 REQUIRED)
CHOKE PLATE-9545
LEVEL
SCREW-354098-S (10 REQUIRED)
CHOKE PLATE SHAFT-9546
SPRING
AIR HORN BODY
ACCELERATING PUMP CHECK VALVE DISC-9576
RETAINER-9575
PISTON ASSEMBLY POWER VALVE-9G553 (SERVICE IN 9500 ASSEMBLY)
GASKET-9569 and 9564
ACCELERATING PUMP SPRING RETAINER
ACCELERATING PUMP SPRING
9B544
ACCELERATING PUMP PISTON
ACCELERATING PUMP PISTON CUP-9572
FLOAT AND LEVER ASSEMBLY-9550

MAIN BODY GASKET-9561
ACCELERATING PUMP DISCHARGE VALVE-9A516
SCREW-353358-S (4 REQUIRED)
PRIMARY THROTTLE SHAFT AND LEVER ASSEMBLY-9581

POWER VALVE-9G551
BALL CHECK RETAINER-9575
ACCELERATING PUMP INLET BALL CHECK-371350-S
MAIN JET-9533
MAIN BODY (SERVICED IN 9510 ASSEMBLY)

SECONARY THROTTLE LINK-9C504
RETAINER 377918-S (2 REQUIRED)
PRIMARY THROTTLE PLATE-9585
IDLE SPEED SCREW
SCREW 378361-S
SECONDARY THROTTLE SHAFT AND LEVER 9A592
SECONDARY THROTTLE PLATE-9585
PRIMARY THROTTLE SPRING-9A538
BUSHING-9851
SECONDARY THROTTLE RETURN SPRING-9B504
VACUUM FITTING
THROTTLE STOP LEVER-9583
THROTTLE BODY AND CHOKE HOUSING-9518
FAST IDLE SPEED ADJUSTING SCREW-9B538
NUT AND WASHER 34079-S and 34803-S

THROTTLE BODY GASKET-9516
THROTTLE AUXILIARY LEVER-9A537
SCREW-380808-S
CHOKE CONTROL ROD RETAINER-377918-S (2 REQUIRED)
AUTOMATIC CHOKE SHAFT AND LEVER-9A753
CAM ADJUSTING SCREW
FAST IDLE CAM 9597
CHOKE CONTROL ROD REATINER 377918- (2 REQUIRED)
CHOKE CONTROL ROD-9A599
IDLE LIMITER CAP
IDLE FUEL MIXTURE ADJUSTING SCREW-9541
IDLE FUEL MIXTURE ADJUSTING SPRING-9578
FAST IDLE ADJUSTING LEVER PIN-9579
PISTON AND LEVER ASSEMBLY-9C719
FAST IDLE LEVER-9538
THERMOSTAT HOUSING GASKET-9871
THERMOSTAT HOUSING 9848
THERMOSTAT HOUSING REATINER-9842
LEVER TO CHOKE SHAFT ATTACHING SCREW-31031-S and 34937-S
SCREW-31061-S (3 REQUIRED)

Exploded view—Autolite (Motorcraft) 4300-4V

1. Remove the air cleaner assembly, then the choke cap.
2. Bend a 0.026 in. diameter wire gauge at a 90 degree angle approximately ⅛ in. from one end. Insert the bent end of the gauge between the choke piston slot and the right hand slot in the choke housing. Rotate the choke piston lever counterclockwise until the gauge is shut in the piston slot.

3. Apply light pressure on the choke piston

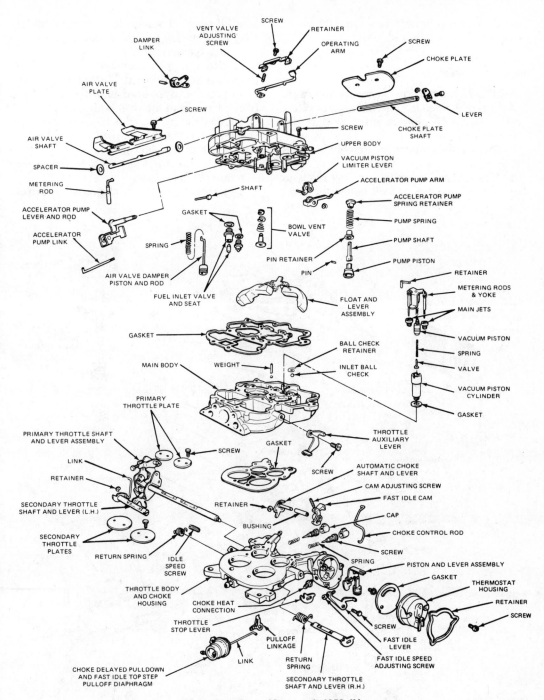

Exploded view—Motorcraft 4350-4V

lever to hold the gauge in place. Then measure the clearance between the lower edge of the choke plate and the carburetor bore using a drill with the diameter equal to the specified pulldown clearance.

4. Bend the choke piston lever to obtain the proper clearance.

5. Install the choke cap.

DIAPHRAGM TYPE CHOKE

1. Activate the pulldown motor by applying an external vacuum source.

2. Close the choke plate as far as possible without forcing it.

3. Using a drill of the specified size, measure the clearance between the lower edge of the choke plate and the air horn wall.

4. If adjustment is necessary, bend the choke diaphragm link as required.

CHOKE CAP REMOVAL

NOTE: *The automatic choke has two rivets and a screw, retaining the choke cap in place. There is a locking and indexing plate to prevent misadjustment.*

1. Remove the air cleaner assembly from the carburetor.

2. Check choke cap retaining ring rivets to determine if mandrel is well below the rivet head. If mandrel appears to be at or within the rivet head thickness, drive it down or out with a 1/16 inch diameter punch.

3. Use a 1/8 inch diameter of No. 32 drill. (.128 inch diameter) for drilling the rivet heads. Drill into the rivet head until the rivet head comes loose from the rivet body.

4. After the rivet head is removed, drive the remaining portion of the rivet out of the hole with a 1/8 inch diameter punch.

NOTE: *This procedure must be followed to retain the hole size.*

5. Repeat Steps 1–4 for the remaining rivet.

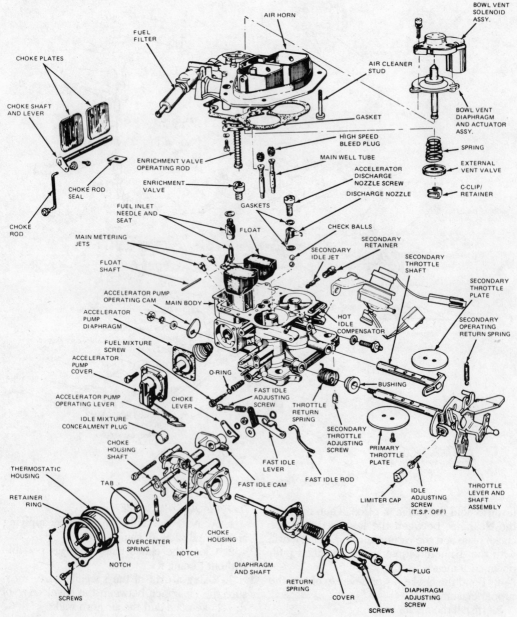

Motorcraft 5200 carburetor

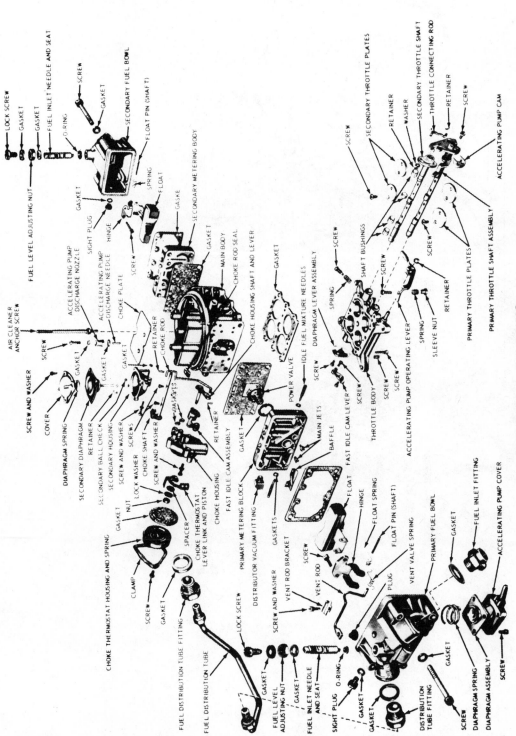

Exploded view—Holley 4150C

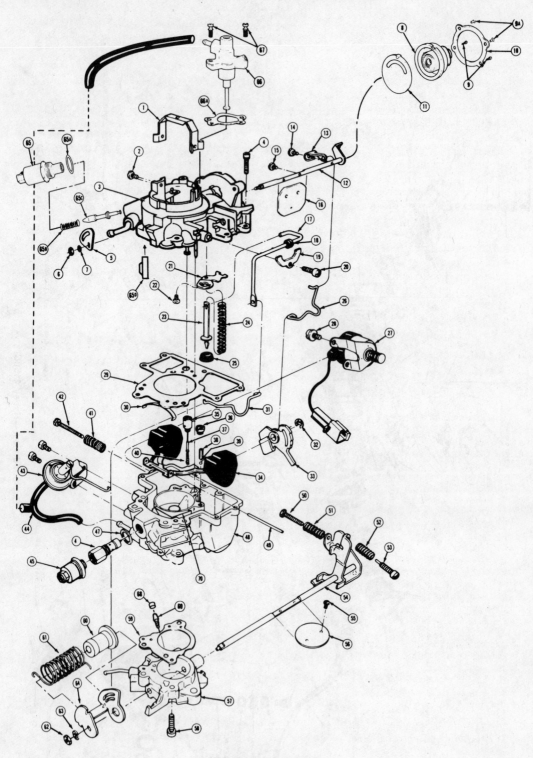

Holley 1946 carburetor

6. Remove the screw in the conventional manner.

INSTALLATION

1. Install choke cap gasket.
2. Install the locking and indexing plate.
3. Install the notched gasket.
4. Install choke cap, making certain that bi-metal loop is positioned around choke lever tang.
5. While holding cap in place, actuate choke plate to make certain bimetal loop is properly engaged with lever tang. Set retaining clamp over choke cap and orient clamp to match holes in casting (holes are not equally spaced). Make sure retaining clamp is not upside down.
6. Place rivet in rivet gun and trigger lightly to retain rivet (⅛ inch diameter × ½ inch long × ¼ inch diameter head).
7. Press rivet fully into casting after passing through retaining clamp and pop rivet (mandrel breaks off).
8. Repeat this step for the remaining rivet.

9. Install screw in conventional manner. Tighten to (17–20 in. lbs.)

FLOAT LEVEL ADJUSTMENT

Carter RBS

1. Remove the fuel bowl and its gasket.
2. Invert the main body of the carburetor, so that the float assembly is pressing against the inlet needle and seat. Measure the vertical distance from the main body casting surface for the fuel bowl to the raised tips formed on the outer ends of the float.
3. Measure for the specified setting at both ends of the float. If it is necessary to equalize the measurement, hold the float lever securely with needle-nose pliers at the narrow portion, and twist the float as required. While holding the float lever, adjust the float to the specified setting, while holding the tab of the float lever away from the inlet needle.

1. Air cleaner bracket (1)
2. Air cleaner bracket screw (2)
3. Air horn
4. Screw and washer (8)
5. Choke pulldown lever
6. Choke shaft nut
7. Lockwasher (1)
8. Choke bimetal assembly
9. Screw (2)
9A. Rivet (2)
10. Choke cover retainer
11. Choke thermostatic housing locating disc
12. Choke shaft and lever assembly
13. Choke control lever
14. Screw (1)
15. Screw (1)
16. Choke plate
17. Accelerator pump operating rod
18. Accelerator pump rod grommet
19. Rod retaining clamp
20. Screw (1)
21. Accelerator pump spring retaining plate
22. Screw (1)
23. Accelerator pump piston stem
24. Accelerator pump spring
25. Accelerator pump piston cup
26. Fast idle cam link
27. Anti-diesel solenoid
28. Screw (2)
29. Air horn gasket
30. Float-hinge retainer
31. Accelerator pump operating link
32. Retaining clip (fast idle cam)
33. Fast idle cam
34. Float assembly
35. Power valve body
36. Main metering jet
37. Power valve pin
38. Accelerator pump weight

39. Accelerator pump check ball
40. Power valve spring
41. Spring
42. Low idle (solenoid off) adjusting screw
43. Choke pulldown diaphragm assembly
44. Choke diaphragm vacuum hose
45. Fuel filter
46. Fuel inlet needle & seat assembly
47. Gasket
48. Main body assembly
49. Float hinge pin
50. Curb idle adjusting screw
51. Spring
52. Spring
53. Fast idle adjusting screw
54. Throttle shaft & Lever assembly
55. Screw (2)
56. Throttle plate
57. Throttle body assembly
58. Throttle body screw (3)
59. Throttle body gasket
60. Throttle return spring bushing
61. Throttle return spring
62. Nut
63. Lock washer
64. Throttle return spring bracket
65. Bowl vent solenoid
65A. Washer
65B. Spring
65C. Pintle
65D. Seal
66. Power valve piston assembly
66A. Gasket
67. Screw (2)
68. Idle mixture
69. Concealment plug
        idle mixture needle
70. Fuel bowl filler

Holley 1946 carburetor

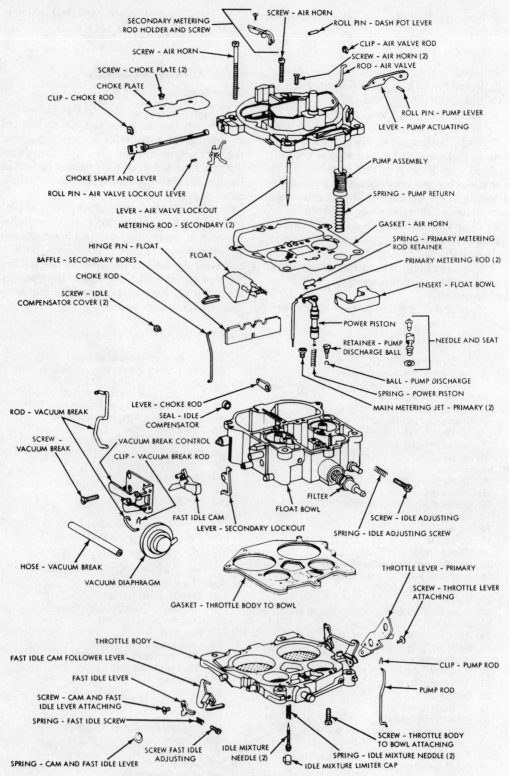

SECONDARY METERING ROD HOLDER AND SCREW

SCREW – AIR HORN

ROLL PIN – DASH POT LEVER

CLIP – AIR VALVE ROD

SCREW – AIR HORN (2)

ROD – AIR VALVE

SCREW – AIR HORN

SCREW – CHOKE PLATE (2)

CHOKE PLATE

CLIP – CHOKE ROD

ROLL PIN – PUMP LEVER

LEVER – PUMP ACTUATING

PUMP ASSEMBLY

SPRING – PUMP RETURN

CHOKE SHAFT AND LEVER

ROLL PIN – AIR VALVE LOCKOUT LEVER

LEVER – AIR VALVE LOCKOUT

METERING ROD – SECONDARY (2)

GASKET – AIR HORN

SPRING – PRIMARY METERING ROD RETAINER

HINGE PIN – FLOAT

BAFFLE – SECONDARY BORES

CHOKE ROD

FLOAT

PRIMARY METERING ROD (2)

INSERT – FLOAT BOWL

SCREW – IDLE COMPENSATOR COVER (2)

POWER PISTON

RETAINER – PUMP DISCHARGE BALL

NEEDLE AND SEAT

BALL – PUMP DISCHARGE

SPRING – POWER PISTON

MAIN METERING JET – PRIMARY (2)

LEVER – CHOKE ROD

SEAL – IDLE COMPENSATOR

ROD – VACUUM BREAK

VACUUM BREAK CONTROL

SCREW – VACUUM BREAK

CLIP – VACUUM BREAK ROD

FILTER

FLOAT BOWL

FAST IDLE CAM

LEVER – SECONDARY LOCKOUT

SCREW – IDLE ADJUSTING

SPRING – IDLE ADJUSTING SCREW

HOSE – VACUUM BREAK

VACUUM DIAPHRAGM

THROTTLE LEVER – PRIMARY

SCREW – THROTTLE LEVER ATTACHING

GASKET – THROTTLE BODY TO BOWL

THROTTLE BODY

FAST IDLE CAM FOLLOWER LEVER

FAST IDLE LEVER

SCREW – CAM AND FAST IDLE LEVER ATTACHING

SPRING – FAST IDLE SCREW

CLIP – PUMP ROD

PUMP ROD

SCREW – THROTTLE BODY TO BOWL ATTACHING

SPRING – CAM AND FAST IDLE LEVER

SCREW FAST IDLE ADJUSTING

IDLE MIXTURE NEEDLE (2)

SPRING – IDLE MIXTURE NEEDLE (2)

IDLE MIXTURE LIMITER CAP

Exploded view—Rochester Quadrajet 4MV-4V

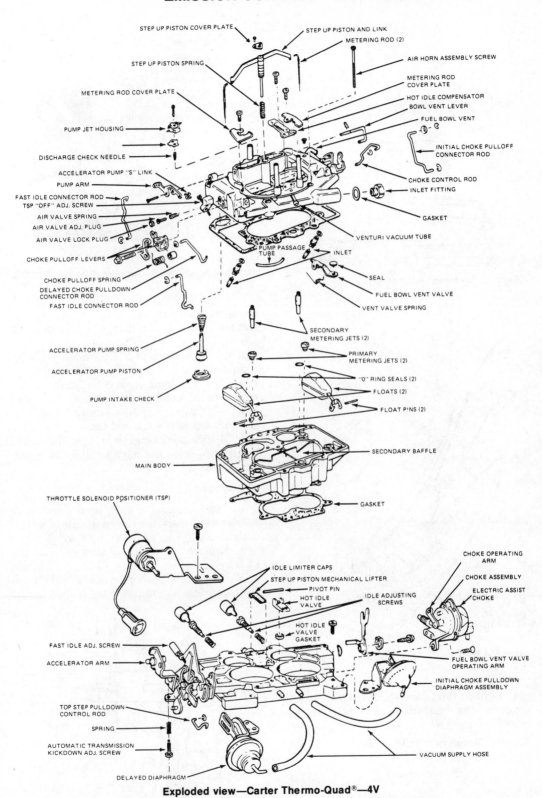

STEP UP PISTON COVER PLATE

STEP UP PISTON AND LINK

METERING ROD (2)

AIR HORN ASSEMBLY SCREW

STEP UP PISTON SPRING

METERING ROD COVER PLATE

METERING ROD COVER PLATE

HOT IDLE COMPENSATOR

BOWL VENT LEVER

FUEL BOWL VENT

PUMP JET HOUSING

DISCHARGE CHECK NEEDLE

INITIAL CHOKE PULLOFF CONNECTOR ROD

CHOKE CONTROL ROD

ACCELERATOR PUMP "S" LINK

PUMP ARM

INLET FITTING

FAST IDLE CONNECTOR ROD

TSP "OFF" ADJ. SCREW

AIR VALVE SPRING

AIR VALVE ADJ. PLUG

AIR VALVE LOCK PLUG

GASKET

VENTURI VACUUM TUBE

PUMP PASSAGE TUBE

INLET

CHOKE PULLOFF LEVERS

CHOKE PULLOFF SPRING

DELAYED CHOKE PULLDOWN CONNECTOR ROD

FAST IDLE CONNECTOR ROD

SEAL

FUEL BOWL VENT VALVE

VENT VALVE SPRING

SECONDARY METERING JETS (2)

PRIMARY METERING JETS (2)

ACCELERATOR PUMP SPRING

"O" RING SEALS (2)

ACCELERATOR PUMP PISTON

FLOATS (2)

FLOAT PINS (2)

PUMP INTAKE CHECK

SECONDARY BAFFLE

MAIN BODY

THROTTLE SOLENOID POSITIONER (TSP)

GASKET

CHOKE OPERATING ARM

IDLE LIMITER CAPS

STEP UP PISTON MECHANICAL LIFTER

CHOKE ASSEMBLY

PIVOT PIN

ELECTRIC ASSIST CHOKE

IDLE ADJUSTING SCREWS

HOT IDLE VALVE

HOT IDLE VALVE GASKET

FAST IDLE ADJ. SCREW

ACCELERATOR ARM

FUEL BOWL VENT VALVE OPERATING ARM

INITIAL CHOKE PULLDOWN DIAPHRAGM ASSEMBLY

TOP STEP PULLDOWN CONTROL ROD

SPRING

AUTOMATIC TRANSMISSION KICKDOWN ADJ. SCREW

VACUUM SUPPLY HOSE

DELAYED DIAPHRAGM

Exploded view—Carter Thermo-Quad®—4V

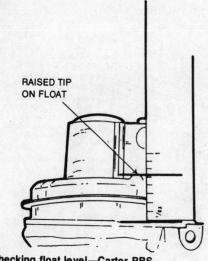

RAISED TIP
ON FLOAT

Checking float level—Carter RBS

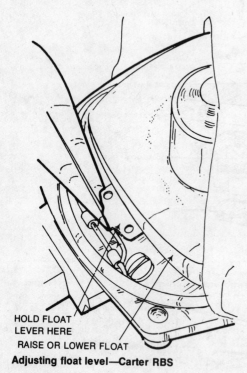

HOLD FLOAT
LEVER HERE

RAISE OR LOWER FLOAT

Adjusting float level—Carter RBS

4. Replace the gasket and fuel bowl. Install the carburetor if no further adjustments are required.

Autolite (Motorcraft) 2100, 2150

DRY ADJUSTMENT

This preliminary setting of the float level adjustment must be done with the carburetor removed from the engine.

1. Remove the air horn and see that the float is raised and the fuel inlet needle is seated. Check the distance between the top surface of

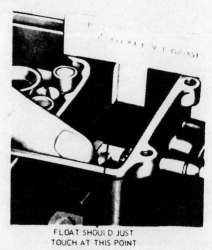

FLOAT SHOULD JUST
TOUCH AT THIS POINT

Dry float level check—Autolite (Motorcraft) 2100, 2150

the main body (with the gasket removed) and the top surface of the float. Depress the float tab to seat the fuel inlet needle. Take a measurement near the center of the float, at a point 1/8 in. from the free end. If you are using a prefabricated float gauge, place the gauge in the corner of the enlarged end section of the fuel bowl. The gauge should touch the float near the end, but not on the end radius.

2. If necessary, bend the tab on the end of the float to bring the setting within the specified limits.

WET ADJUSTMENT

1. Bring the engine to its normal operating temperature, park the car on as nearly level a surface as possible, and stop the engine.

2. Remove the air cleaner assembly from the carburetor.

3. Remove the air horn retaining screws and the carburetor identification tag. Leave the air

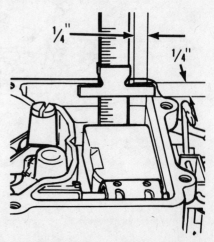

Motorcraft 2100, 2150 wet fuel level adjustment

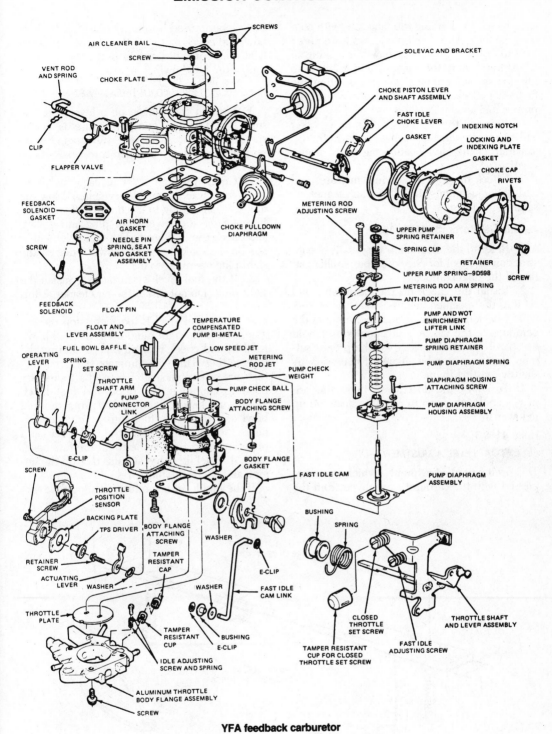

YFA feedback carburetor

horn and gasket in position on the carburetor main body. Start the engine, let it idle for several minutes, rotate the air horn out of the way, and remove the gasket to provide access to the float assembly.

4. With the engine idling, use a standard depth scale to measure the vertical distance from the top machined surface of the carburetor main body to the level of the fuel in the fuel bowl. This measurement must be made at least ¼ in. away from any vertical surface in order to assure an accurate reading.

5. Stop the engine before making any adjustment to the float level. Adjustment is ac-

complished by bending the float tab (with contacts the fuel inlet valve) up or down as required to raise or lower the fuel level. After making an adjustment, start the engine, and allow it to idle for several minutes before repeating the fuel level check. Repeat as necessary until the proper fuel level is attained.

6. Reinstall the air horn with a new gasket and secure it with the screws. Include the installation of the identification tag in its proper location.

7. Check the idle speed, fuel mixture, and dashpot adjustments. Install the air cleaner assembly.

Autolite (Motorcraft) 4300, 4350

1. Refer to the illustration for details of construction of a tool for checking the parallel setting of the dual pontoons.

2. Install the gauge on the carburetor and set it to the specified height.

3. Check the clearance and alignment of the pontoons to the gauge. Both pontoons should just barely touch the gauge for the proper setting. Pontoons may be aligned if necessary by slightly twisting them.

4. To adjust the float level, bend the primary needle tab down to raise the float and up to lower it.

Holly 4150C

FUEL FLOAT LEVEL ADJUSTMENT—DRY

This preliminary adjustment—which is accomplished with the carburetor removed from the car—is performed by simply inverting the fuel bowl and checking to see that the center of the float is an equal distance from the top and bottom of the fuel bowl.

FUEL FLOAT LEVEL ADJUSTMENT—WET

1. Position the vehicle on a level floor, be sure that the fuel pump pressure is within specifications, and operate the engine until normal operating temperature has been reached.

2. Check the fuel level in each fuel bowl separately. Place a suitable container below the fuel level sight plug to catch any fuel spillover. Remove the fuel level sight plug and gasket, and check the fuel level. The fuel level within the bowl should be at the lower edge of the sight plug opening $1/16$ in.

3. If the fuel level is satisfactory, install the sight plug. Do not install the air cleaner at this time.

4. If the fuel level is too high, stop the engine, install the sight plug, drain the fuel bowl, refill it, and check it again before altering the float setting. This will eliminate the possibility that dirt or foreign matter caused a temporary flooding condition. To drain the fuel bowl, loosen one lower retaining bolt from the fuel bowl and drain the fuel into a suitable container. Install the bolt and the fuel lever sight plug, and start the engine to fill the fuel bowl. After the fuel level has stabilized, stop the engine and check the fuel level.

If the fuel level is too high, it should be first

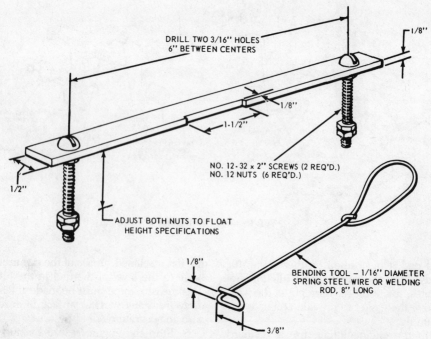

Float gauge and bending tool details—Autolite (Motorcraft) 4300, 4350

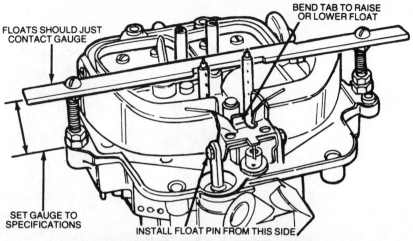

FLOATS SHOULD JUST CONTACT GAUGE

BEND TAB TO RAISE OR LOWER FLOAT

SET GAUGE TO SPECIFICATIONS

INSTALL FLOAT PIN FROM THIS SIDE

Motorcraft 4300, 4350 float level adjustment

lowered below specifications and then raised until it is just at the lower edge of the sight plug opening. If the level was too low it is necessary only to raise it to the specified level. If either is necessary, refer to the procedures for either adjustment.

TO LOWER FUEL LEVEL

1. With the engine stopped, loosen the lockscrew on top of the fuel bowl jusl enough to allow rotation of the adjusting nut underneath. Do not loosen the lockscrew or attempt to adjust the fuel level with the sight plug removed and the engine running because the pressure in the line will spray fuel out and present a fire hazard.

2. Turn the adjusting nut approximately ½ turn in to lower the fuel level below specifications (⅙ turn of the adjusting nut, depending on direction of rotation, will raise or lower the float assembly at the fuel level sight plug opening ³⁄₆₄ in.).

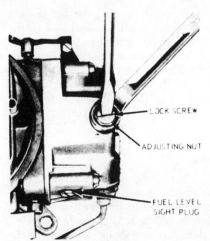

LOCK SCREW

ADJUSTING NUT

FUEL LEVEL SIGHT PLUG

Wet float level adjustment—Holley 4150C

3. Tighten the lockscrew and reinstall the fuel level sight plug. Start the engine. After the fuel level has stabilized, stop the engine and check the fuel level at the sight plug opening. The fuel level should be below specified limits. If it is not, repeat the previous steps, turning the adjusting nut an additional amount sufficient to lower the fuel below the specified level.

4. Loosen the lockscrew and turn the adjusting nut out in increments of ⅙ turn or less until the correct fuel level is achieved. After each adjustment, tighten the lockscrew, install the fuel level sight plug, and then start the engine and stabilize the fuel level. Check the fuel level at the sight plug opening. Install the sight plug and gasket.

5. Check the idle fuel mixture and idle speed adjustments. Adjust the carburetor as required.

TO RAISE FUEL LEVEL

Perform Steps 1, 4, and 5 under the procedure "To Lower Fuel Level."

Rochester Quadrajet 4MV

1. Remove the air horn assembly.

2. With an adjustable T-scale, measure the distance from the top of the float bowl surface (gasket removed) to the top of the float at the toe (locate gauging point ¹⁄₁₆ in. back from the toe on the float surface). Do not gauge on top of part number.

When checking the adjustment, make sure the float hinge pin is firmly seated and the float arm is held down against the float needle so that it is seated.

3. To adjust, bend the float pontoon up or down at the point shown in the illustration.

4. Install a new air horn gasket on the float bowl, then install the air horn.

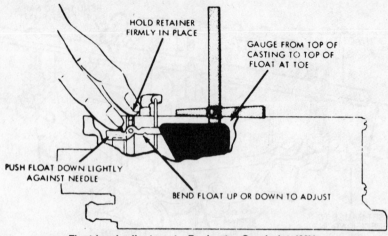

Float level adjustment—Rochester Quadrajet 4MV

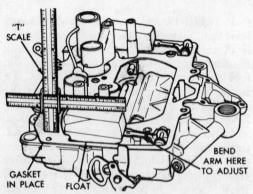

ThermoQuad float adjustment

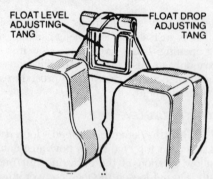

Motorcraft 5200 float adjustment

Carter Thermo-Quad®

1. Taking note of their placement, disconnect all linkages and rods which connect the bowl cover to the carburetor body.

2. Remove the 10 screws retaining the bowl cover to the body.

3. Using legs to protect the throttle valves, remove the bowl cover. Invert the bowl cover, taking care not to lose any of the small parts.

4. With the bowl cover inverted and the floats resting on the seated needle, measure the distance between the bowl cover (new gasket installed) to the bottom side of each float.

5. If not to specifications, bend the float lever to suit.

NOTE: *Never allow the lip of the float to be pressed against the needle when adjusting the float height.*

6. Reverse Steps 1–3 to install. Make sure that the float pin does not protrude past the edge of the bowl cover.

Motorcraft 5200

1. Remove the float bowl cover and hold it upside down.

2. With the float tang resting lightly on the spring loaded fuel inlet needle, measure the clearance between the edge of the float and the bowl cover.

3. To adjust the float, bend the float tang. Make sure that both floats are adjusted equally.

Holley 1946

1. Remove the air horn and place a finger over the hinge pin retainer and catch the accelerator pump ball when it falls out.

2. Lay a ruler across the housing under the floats. The lowest point of the floats should be just touching the ruler for all except California models. For California models, the ruler should just contact the heel (raised step) of the float.

3. Bend the tang of the float to adjust.

Carter YFA

1. Invert the air horn assembly and check the clearance from the top of the float to the surface of the air horn with a T-scale. The air horn should be held at eye level when gauging and the float arm should be resting on the needle pin.

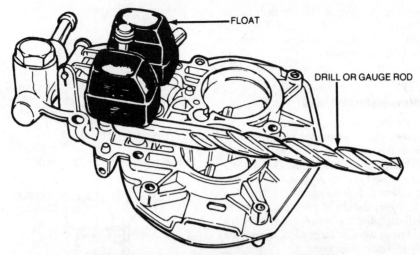

Measuring float clearance on the Motorcraft 5200

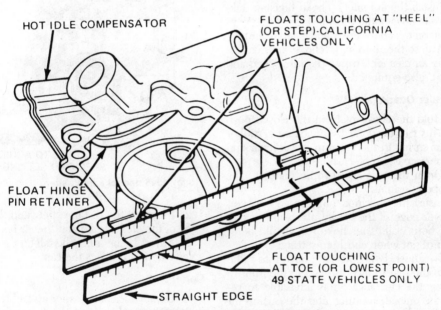

Holley 1946 float clearance adjustment

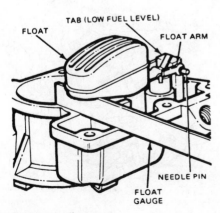

YFA float level adjustment

2. Do not exert pressure on the needle valve when measuring or adjusting the float. Bend the float arm as necessary to adjust the float level.

CAUTION: *Do not bend the tab at the end of the float arm as it prevents the float from striking the bottom of the fuel bowl when empty and keeps the needle in place.*

DECHOKE CLEARANCE ADJUSTMENT

Carter RBS

1. Remove the carburetor air cleaner.

2. Hold the throttle plate to the full open position while closing the choke plate as far as

possible without forcing it. Use a drill of the proper diameter (see "Carburetor Specifications" chart) to check the clearance between the choke plate and air horn.

3. Adjust as necessary by bending the tang on the throttle lever.

Autolite (Motorcraft) 4300, 4350

1. Remove the air cleaner assembly.

2. Remove the automatic choke spring housing from the carburetor.

3. With the throttle plate wide open and the choke plate closed as far as possible without forcing it, insert a drill gauge of the specified diameter between the choke plate and air horn.

4. To adjust, bend the arm on the choke trip lever. Bend downward to increase clearance and upward to decrease clearance. After adjusting, recheck the clearance.

5. Install the automatic choke housing, taking care to engage the thermostatic spring with the tang on the choke lever and shaft assembly.

6. Adjust the automatic choke setting. Install the air cleaner. Adjust the idle speed and dashpot, if so equipped.

Rochester Quadrajet 4MV

1. Hold the choke plate in the closed position. This can be done by attaching a rubber band or spring to the vacuum break lever and a stationary part of the carburetor.

2. Open the primary throttle plates to the wide open position.

3. Insert the specified plug gauge between the lower edge of the choke plates and inside the air horn wall. The choke rod should be in bottom of slot when checking setting.

4. To adjust, bend the tang on the fast idle lever to the rear to increase and to the front to decrease the clearance. It is advisable to recheck the unloader setting after the carburetor is installed on the engine by depressing the accelerator pedal.

Holley 1946

1. With the engine off, hold the throttle in the wide open position.

2. Insert the specified gauge between the upper edge of the choke plate and the air horn wall.

3. With a slight pressure against the choke shaft, a slight drag should be felt when the gauge is withdrawn.

4. To adjust, bend the unloader tab on the throttle lever.

Motorcraft 5200

1. Hold the throttle wide open. Remove all slack from the choke linkage by applying pressure to the upper edge of the choke plate.

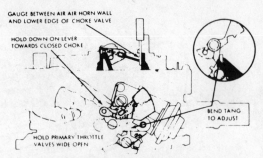

Dechoke adjustment—Rochester Quadrajet 4MV

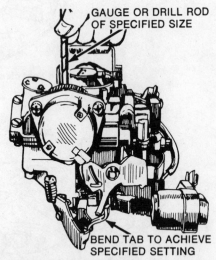

Holley 1946 dechoke adjustment

2. Measure the distance between the lower edge of the choke plate and the air horn wall.

3. Adjust by bending the tab on the fast idle lever where it touches the cam.

Carter YFA

1. Remove the air cleaner assembly.

2. Hold the throttle plate fully open and close

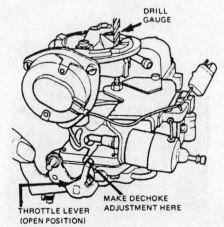

YFA dechoke adjustment

the choke plate as far as possible without forcing it. Use a drill of the proper diameter to check the clearance between the choke plate and air horn.

3. If the clearance is not within specification, adjust by bending the arm on the choke lever of the throttle lever. Bending the arm downward will decrease the clearance, and bending it upward will increase the clearance. Always recheck the clearance after making any adjustment.

ACCELERATOR PUMP STROKE ADJUSTMENT

Carter RBS

Unscrew the idle speed adjusting screw and open the choke plate so that the throttle plate is seated in its bore. Measure the distance between the flat surface of the main body casting and the top surface of the accelerating pump stem, as shown in the accompanying illustration. With the throttle in the wide-open position, measure the height again. The pump stroke is the difference between the first measurement and the second, and should be 0.400 in.

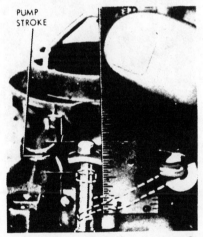

Accelerator pump stroke measurement—Carter RBS

Adjusting accelerator pump stroke—Carter RBS

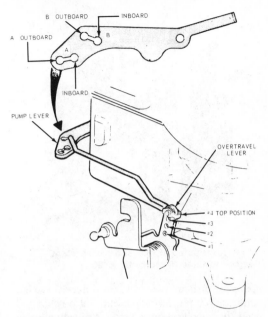

Accelerator pump stroke adjustment—Autolite (Motorcraft) 2100, 2150

The pump stroke may be adjusted by opening or closing the pump connector link at the offset portion as shown.

Autolite (Motorcraft) 2100, 2150

In order to keep the exhaust emission level of the engine within the specified limits, the accelerating pump stroke has been preset at the factory. The additional holes are provided for differing engine-transmission-body applications only. The primary throttle shaft lever (overtravel lever) has four holes and the accelerating pump link two holes to control the pump stroke. The accelerating pump operating rod should be in the overtravel lever hole number listed in the "Carburetor Specifications" chart, and in the inboard hole (hole closest to the pump plunger) in the accelerating pump link. If the pump stroke has been changed from the specified settings, use the following procedure to correct the stroke.

1. Release the operating rod from the retaining clip by pressing the tab end of the clip toward the rod while pressing the rod away from the clip until it disengages.

2. Position the clip over the specified hole (see "Carburetor Specifications" chart) in the overtravel lever. Press the ends of the clip together and insert the operating rod through the clip and the overtravel lever. Release the clip to engage the rod.

Autolite (Motorcraft) 4300

The pump stroke is preset at the factory to limit exhaust emissions. The additional holes in the

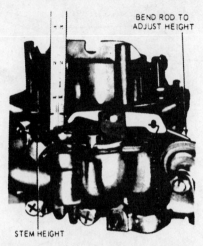

Accelerator pump stroke and piston stem height—Autolite (Motorcraft) 4300

operating arm are provided for different engine applications. The stroke should not be changed from the specified hole (see "Carburetor Specifications" chart).

The only adjustments possible are the pump stroke and pump stem height. To change the pump stroke, merely remove the pivot pin and reposition it in the specified hole. To adjust the pump stem height, bend the operating rod at the angles, taking care not to cause binds in the system.

Motorcraft 4350

The accelerator pump adjustment is preset at the factory for reduced exhaust emissions. Adjustment is provided only for different engine installations. The adjustment is internal, with three piston-to-shaft pin positions in the pump piston.

To check that the shaft pin is located in the specified piston hole, remove the carburetor air horn and invert it. Disconnect the accelerator pump from the operating arm by pressing downward on the spring and sliding the arm out of the pump shaft slot. Disassemble the spring and nylon keeper retaining the adjust-

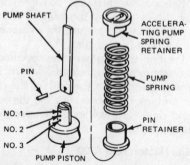

Accelerator pump stroke adjustment—Motorcraft 4350

ment pin. If the pin is not in its specified hole, remove it, reposition the shaft to the correct hole in the piston assembly and reinstall the pin. Then, slide the nylon retainer over the pin and position the spring on the shaft. Finally, compress the spring on the shaft and install the pump on the pump arm.

NOTE: *Under no circumstances should you adjust the stroke of the accelerator pump by turning the vacuum limiter lever adjusting nut. This adjustment is preset at the factory and modification could result in poor cold driveability.*

ANTI-STALL DASHPOT ADJUSTMENT

All Carburetors Except Rochester Quadrajet

Having made sure that the engine idle speed and mixture are correct and that the engine is at normal operating temperature, loosen the anti-stall dashpot locking nut (see accompanying illustration). With the throttle held closed,

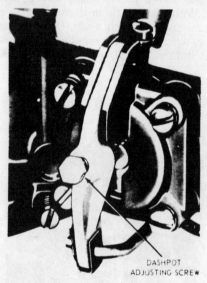

Anti-stall dashpot adjustment—Autolite 1100

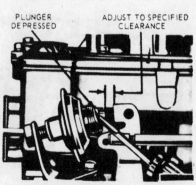

Typical anti-stall dashpot adjustment

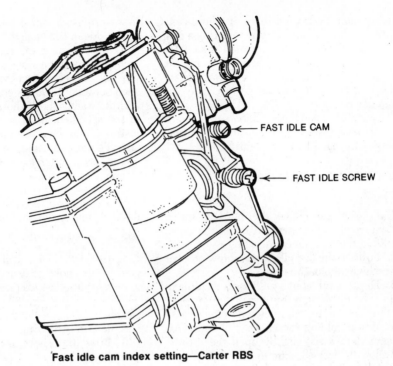

Fast idle cam index setting—Carter RBS

depress the plunger with a screwdriver blade and measure the clearance between the throttle lever and the plunger tip. If the clearance is not as specified in the "Carburetor Specifications" chart, turn the dashpot until the proper clearance is obtained between the throttle lever and the plunger tip. After tightening the locking nut, recheck the adjustment.

FAST IDLE CAM INDEX SETTING

Carter RBS

1. Position the fast idle screw on the kickdown step of the fast idle cam against the shoulder of the high step.

2. Adjust by bending the choke plate connecting rod to obtain the specified clearance between the lower edge of the choke plate and the carburetor bore.

Autolite 2100

1971–72

1. Loosen the choke thermostatic spring housing retaining screws and position the housing 90° in the rich direction.

2. Position the fast idle speed screw at the kick-down step of the fast idle cam. This kick-down step is identified by a small "V" stamped in the side of the casting.

3. Be sure that the fast idle cam is in the kick-down position while checking or adjusting the fast idle cam clearance. Check the clear-

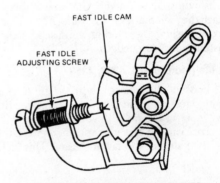

CONVENTIONAL ONE-PIECE FAST IDLE LEVER

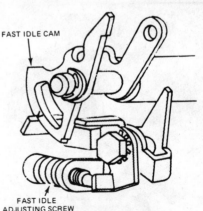

TWO-PIECE FAST IDLE LEVER
FOR 351-C AND 400 ENGINES

Fast idle cam index setting—Autolite (Motorcraft) 2100

ance between the lower edge of the choke plate and the wall of the air horn by inserting a drill of the specified diameter between them. Adjustment may be accomplished by turning the fast idle cam adjusting screw clockwise to increase or counterclockwise to decrease the clearance.

4. Set the choke thermostatic spring housing to specifications, and adjust the antistall dashpot, idle speed, and fuel mixture.

MOTORCRAFT 2100, 2150

1973–75

1. Loosen the choke thermostatic spring housing retaining screws and rotate the housing 90° in the rich direction.

2. Position the fast idle speed screw or lever on the high step of the cam.

3. Depress the choke pull-down diaphragm against the disphragm stop screw thereby placing the choke in the pull-down position.

4. While holding the choke pull-down diaphragm depressed, slightly open the throttle and allow the fast idle cam to fall.

5. Close the throttle and check the position of the fast idle cam or lever. When the fast idle cam is adjusted correctly, the screw should contact the "V" mark on the cam. Adjustment is accomplished by rotating the fast idle cam adjusting screw as needed.

Autolite (Motorcraft), 4300, 4350

1. Loosen the choke thermostatic spring housing retaining screws and position the housing 90° in the rich direction.

2. Position the fast idle speed screw at the kick-down step of the fast idle cam. This kick-down step is identified by a small "V" stamped in the side of the casting.

3. Be sure that the fast idle cam is in the kick-down position while checking or adjusting the fast idle cam clearance. Check the clearance between the lower edge of the choke plate and the wall of the air horn by inserting a drill of the specified diameter between them. Adjustment may be accomplished by turning the fast idle cam adjusting screw clockwise to increase or counterclockwise to decrease the clearance.

4. Set the choke thermostatic spring housing to specifications, and adjust the antistall dashpot, idle speed, and fuel mixture.

Motorcraft 5200

1. Insert a 5/32 in. drill between the lower edge of the choke plate and the air horn wall.

2. With the fast idle screw held on the second step of the fast idle cam, measure the clearance between the tang of the choke lever and the arm of the cam.

3. Bend the choke lever tang for adjustment.

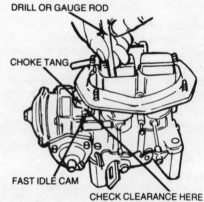

Motorcraft 5200 fast idle cam adjustment

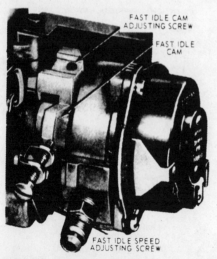

Fast idle cam index setting—Autolite (Motorcraft) 4300, 4350

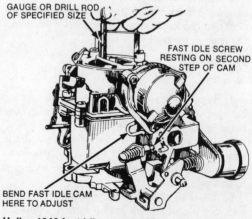

Holley 1946 fast idle cam position adjustment

Holley 1946

1. Position the fast idle adjusting screw on the second step of the fast idle cam.

2. Lightly move the choke plate towards the closed position.

3. Check the fast idle cam setting by placing the specified gauge between the upper edge of the choke plate and the air horn wall.

4. Bend the fast idle cam link to adjust.

Carter YFA

1. Put the fast idle screw on the second highest step of the fast idle cam against the shoulder of the high step.

2. Adjust by bending the choke plate connecting rod to obtain the specified clearance between the lower edge of the choke plate and the air horn wall.

AIR VALVE DASHPOT ADJUSTMENT

Rochester Quadrajet 4MV

1. Seat the vacuum break diaphragm, using an outside vacuum source.

2. With the air valve completely closed and the diaphragm seated, measure the clearance between the air valve dashpot rod and the air valve lever.

3. The dimension should be $\frac{1}{32}$ in. If not, bend the rod at the air valve end to adjust.

THROTTLE AND DOWNSHIFT LINKAGE ADJUSTMENT

Manual Transmission

Throttle linkage adjustments are not normally required, unless the carburetor or linkage have been removed from the car or otherwise disturbed. In all cases, the car is first brought to operating temperature, with the choke open and off the fast idle cam. The idle speed is then set to specifications (see Chapter 2).

Motorcraft 2700 VV and 7200 VV
DESIGN

Since the design of the 2700 VV (variable venturi) carburetor differs considerably from the other carburetors in the Ford lineup, an explanation in the theory and operation is presented here.

In exterior appearance, the variable venturi carburetor is similar to conventional carburetors and, like a conventional carburetor, it uses a normal float and fuel bowl system. However, the similarity ends there. In place of a normal choke plate and fixed area venturis, the 2700 VV carburetor has a pair of small oblong castings in the top of the upper carburetor body where you would normally expect to see the choke plate. These castings slide back and forth across the top of the carburetor in response to fuel-air demands. Their movement is controlled by a spring-loaded diaphragm valve regulated by a vacuum signal taken below the venturis in the throttle bores. As the throttle is opened, the strength of the vacuum signal increases, opening the venturis and allowing more air to enter the carburetor.

Fuel is admitted into the venturi area by means of tapered metering rods that fit into the main jets. These rods are attached to the venturis, and, as the venturis open or close in response to air demand, the fuel needed to maintain the proper mixture increases or decreases as the metering rods slide in the jets. In comparison to a conventional carburetor with fixed venturis and a variable air supply, this system provides much more precise control of the fuel-air supply during all modes of operation. Because of the variable venturi principle, there

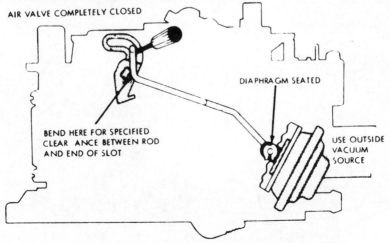

AIR VALVE COMPLETELY CLOSED

DIAPHRAGM SEATED

BEND HERE FOR SPECIFIED CLEARANCE BETWEEN ROD AND END OF SLOT

USE OUTSIDE VACUUM SOURCE

Air valve dashpot adjustment—Rochester Quadrajet 4MV

are fewer fuel metering systems and fuel passages. The only auxiliary fuel metering systems required are an idle trim, accelerator pump (similar to a conventional carburetor), starting enrichment, and cold running enrichment.

NOTE: *Adjustment, assembly and disassembly of this carburetor require special tools for some of the operations. These tools are available (see the Tools and Equipment Section). Do not attempt any operations on this carburetor without first checking to see if you need the special tools for that particular operation. The adjustment and repair procedures given here mention when and if you will need the special tools.*

The Motorcraft model 7200 variable venturi (VV) carburetor shares most of its design features with the model 2700 VV. The major difference between the two is that the 7200 is designed to work with Ford's EEC (electronic engine control) feedback system. The feedback system precisely controls the air/fuel ratio by varying signals to the feedback control monitor located on the carburetor, which opens or closes the metering valve in response. This expands or reduces the amount of control vacuum above the fuel bowl, leaning or richening the mixture accordingly.

FLOAT LEVEL ADJUSTMENT

1. Remove and invert the upper part of the carburetor, with the gasket in place.

2. Measure the vertical distance between the carburetor body, outside the gasket, and the bottom of the float.

3. To adjust, bend the float operating lever that contacts the needle valve. Make sure that the float remains parallel to the gasket surface.

FLOAT DROP ADJUSTMENT

1. Remove and hold upright the upper part of the carburetor.

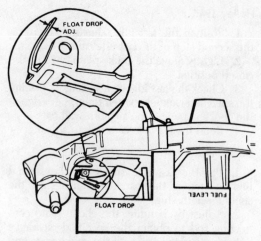

2700 VV float drop adjustment

2. Measure the vertical distance between the carburetor body, outside the gasket, and the bottom of the float.

3. Adjust by bending the stop tab on the float lever that contacts the hinge pin.

FAST IDLE SPEED ADJUSTMENT

1. With the engine warmed up and idling, place the fast idle lever on the step of the fast idle cam specified on the engine compartment sticker or in the specifications chart. Disconnect and plug the EGR vacuum line.

2. Make sure the high speed cam positioner lever is disengaged.

3. Turn the fast idle speed screw to adjust to the specified speed.

FAST IDLE CAM ADJUSTMENT

You will need a special tool for this job; Ford calls it a stator cap (#T77L-9848-A). It fits over the choke thermostatic lever when the choke cap is removed.

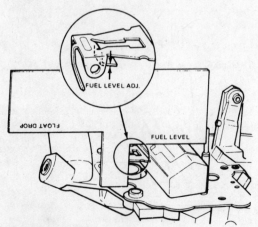

2700VV float adjustment

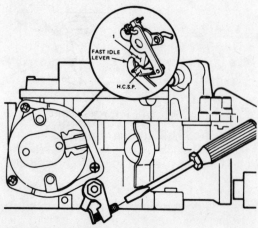

2700 VV fast idle speed adjustment

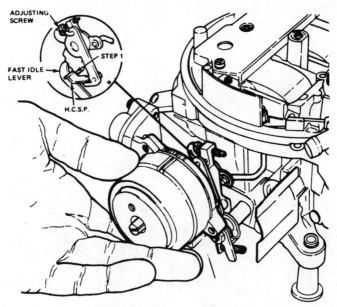

2700 VV fast idle cam adjustment

1. Remove the choke coil cap. On 1980 and later California models, the choke cap is riveted in place. The top rivets will have to be drilled out; the bottom rivet will have to be driven out from the rear. New rivets must be used upon installation.

2. Place the fast idle lever in the corner of the specified step of the fast idle cam (the highest step is first) with the high speed cam positioner retracted.

3. If the adjustment is being made with the carburetor removed, hold the throttle lightly closed with a rubber band.

4. Turn the stator cap clockwise until the lever contacts the fast idle cam adjusting screw.

5. Turn the fast idle cam adjusting screw until the index mark on the cap lines up with the specified mark on the casting.

6. Remove the stator cap. Install the choke coil cap and set to the specified housing mark.

COLD ENRICHMENT METERING ROD ADJUSTMENT

A dial indicator and the stator cap are required for this adjustment.

1. Remove the choke coil cap. See Step 1 of the "Fast Idle Cam Adjustment."

2. Attach a weight to the choke coil mechanism to seat the cold enrichment rod.

3. Install and zero a dial indicator with the tip on top of the enrichment rod. Raise and release the weight to verify zero on the dial indicator.

4. With the stator cap at the index position, the dial indicator should read the specified dimension. Turn the adjusting nut to correct.

5. Install the choke cap at the correct setting.

CONTROL VACUUM ADJUSTMENT

1977 Only

1. Make sure the idle speed is correct.

2. Using a 5/32 in. Allen wrench, turn the venturi valve diaphragm adjusting screw clockwise until the valve is firmly closed.

3. Connect a vacuum gauge to the vacuum tap on the venturi valve cover.

4. Idle the engine and use a 1/8 in. Allen wrench to turn the venturi by-pass adjusting screw to the specified vacuum setting. You may have to correct the idle speed.

5. Turn the venturi valve diaphragm adjusting screw counter-clockwise until the vacuum drops to the specified setting. You will have to work the throttle to get the vacuum to drop.

6. Reset the idle speed.

1980–82 Only

This adjustment is necessary only on non-feedback systems.

1. Remove the carburetor. Remove the venturi valve disphragm plug with a centerpunch.

2. If the carburetor has a venturi valve by-pass plug, remove it by removing the two cover retaining screws; invert and remove the by-pass screw plug from the cover with a drift. Install the cover.

3. Install the carburetor. Start the engine and allow it to reach normal operating temperature. Connect a vacuum gauge to the venturi

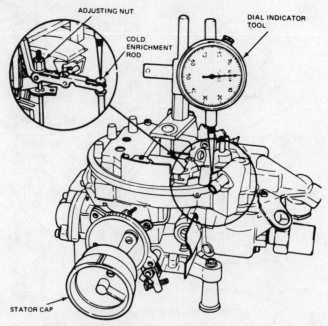

2700 VV cold enrichment metering rod adjustment

valve cover. Set the idle speed to 500 rpm with the transmission in Drive.

4. Push and hold the venturi valve closed. Adjust the bypass screw to obtain a reading of 8 in. H_2O on the vacuum gauge. Make sure the idle speed remains constant. Open and close the throttle and check the idle speed.

5. With the engine idling, adjust the venturi valve diaphragm screw to obtain a reading of 6 in. H_2O. Set the curb idle to specification.

Install new venturi valve bypass and diaphragm plugs.

INTERNAL VENT ADJUSTMENT
Through 1978 Only

This adjustment is required whenever the idle speed adjustment is changed.

1. Make sure the idle speed is correct.
2. Place a 0.010 in. feeler gauge between

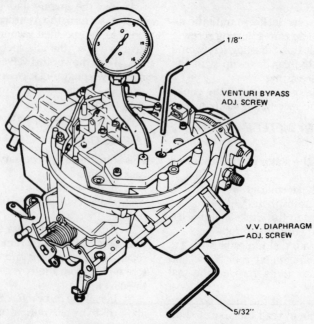

2700 VV control vacuum adjustment

the accelerator pump stem and the operating link.

3. Turn the nylon adjusting nut until there is a slight drag on the gauge.

VENTURI VALVE LIMITER ADJUSTMENT

1. Remove the carburetor. Take off the venturi valve cover and the two rollers.

2. Use a center punch to loosen the expansion plug at the rear of the carburetor main body on the throttle side. Remove it.

3. Use an Allen wrench to remove the venturi valve wide open stop screw.

4. Hold the throttle wide open.

5. Apply a light closing pressure on the venturi valve and check the gap between the valve and the air horn wall. To adjust, move the venturi valve to the wide open position and insert an Allen wrench into the stop screw hole. Turn clockwise to increase the gap. Remove the wrench and check the gap again.

6. Replace the wide open stop screw and turn it clockwise until it contacts the valve.

7. Push the venturi valve wide open and check the gap. Turn the stop screw to bring the gap to specifications.

8. Reassemble the carburetor with a new expansion plug.

CONTROL VACUUM REGULATOR ADJUSTMENT

There are two systems used. The earlier system's C.V.R. rod threads directly through the arm. The revised system, introduced in late 1977, has a ⅜ in. nylon hex adjusting nut on the C.V.R. rod and a flange on the rod.

Early System

1. Make sure that the cold enrichment metering rod adjustment is correct.

2. Rotate the choke coil cap half a turn

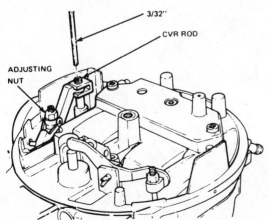

2700 VV control vacuum regulator adjustment

clockwise from the index mark. Work the throttle to set the fast idle cam.

3. Press down lightly on the regulator rod. If there is no down travel, turn the adjusting screw counter-clockwise until some travel is felt.

4. Turn the regulator rod clockwise with an Allen wrench until the adjusting nut just begins to rise.

5. Press lightly on the regulator rod. If there is any down travel, turn the adjusting screw clockwise in ¼ turn increments until it is eliminated.

6. Return the choke coil cap to the specified setting.

Revised System

The cold enrichment metering rod adjustment must be checked and set before making this adjustment.

1. After adjusting the cold enrichment metering rod, leave the dial indicator in place but remove the stator cap. Do not re-zero the dial indicator.

2. Press down on the C.V.R. rod until it bottoms on its seat. Measure this amount of travel with the dial indicator.

3. If the adjustment is incorrect, hold the ⅜ in. C.V.R. adjusting nut with a box wrench to prevent it from turning. Use a ³⁄₃₂ in. Allen wrench to turn the C.V.R. rod; turning counter-clockwise will increase the travel, and vice versa.

HIGH SPEED CAM POSITIONER ADJUSTMENT

Through 1979 Only

1. Place the high speed cam positioner in the corner of the specified cam step, counting the highest step as the first.

2. Place the fast idle lever in the corner of the positioner.

3. Hold the throttle firmly closed.

4. Remove the diaphragm cover. Adjust the diaphragm assembly clockwise until it lightly bottoms. Turn it counter-clockwise ½ to 1½ turns until the vacuum port and diaphragm hole line up.

5. Replace the cover.

IDLE MIXTURE ADJUSTMENT

Through 1977 Only

The results of this adjustment should be checked with an emissions tester, to make sure that emission limits are not exceeded. Idle mixture (idle trim) is not adjustable 1978 and later models.

1. Remove the air cleaner cover only.

2. Use a ³⁄₃₂ in. Allen wrench to adjust the

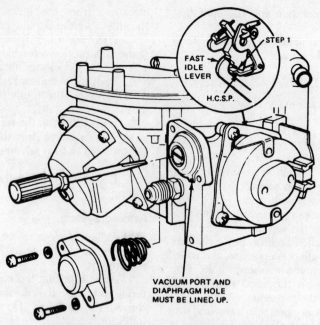

2700 VV high speed cam positioner adjustment

mixture for each barrel by turning the air adjusting screw. Turn clockwise to richen.

DISASSEMBLY

NOTE: *Special tools are required. If you have any doubts about your ability to successfully complete this procedure, leave it to a professional service person.*

Upper Body

1. Remove the fuel inlet fitting, fuel filter, gasket and spring.
2. Remove the screws retaining the upper body assembly and remove the upper body.
3. Remove the float hinge pin and float assembly.
4. Remove the fuel inlet valve, seat and gasket.

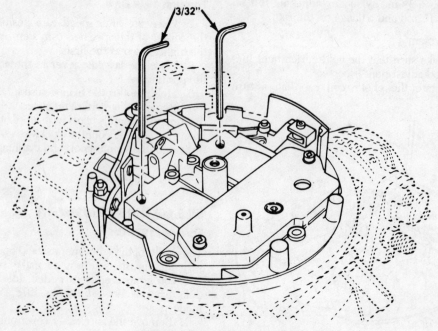

2700 VV idle mixture adjustment

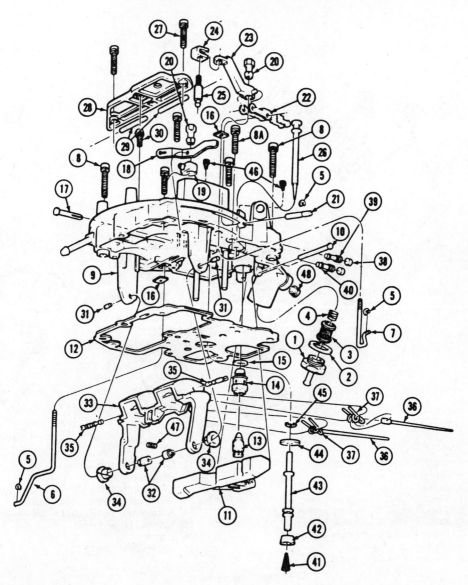

1. Fuel inlet fitting	17. Pin	33. Venturi valve
2. Fuel inlet fitting gasket	18. Accelerator pump link	34. Venturi valve pivot pin bushing
3. Fuel filter	19. Accelerator pump swivel	35. Metering rod pivot pin
4. Fuel filter spring	20. Nut	36. Metering rod
5. Retaining E-ring	21. Choke hinge pin	37. Metering rod spring
6. Accelerator pump rod	22. Cold enrichment rod lever	38. Cup plug
7. Choke control rod	23. Cold enrichment rod swivel	39. Main metering jet assembly
8. Screw	24. Control vacuum regulator	40. O-ring
8A. Screw	adjusting nut	41. Accelerator pump return spring
9. Upper body	25. Control vacuum regulator	42. Accelerator pump cup
10. Float hinge pin	26. Cold enrichment rod	43. Accelerator pump plunger
11. Float assembly	27. Screw	44. Internal vent valve
12. Float bowl gasket	28. Venturi valve cover plate	45. Retaining E-ring
13. Fuel inlet valve	29. Roller bearing	46. Idle trim screw
14. Fuel inlet seat	30. Venturi air bypass screw	47. Venturi valve limiter adjusting
15. Fuel inlet seat gasket	31. Venturi valve pivot plug	screw
16. Dust seal	32. Venturi valve pivot pin	48. Pipe plug

2700VV upper body

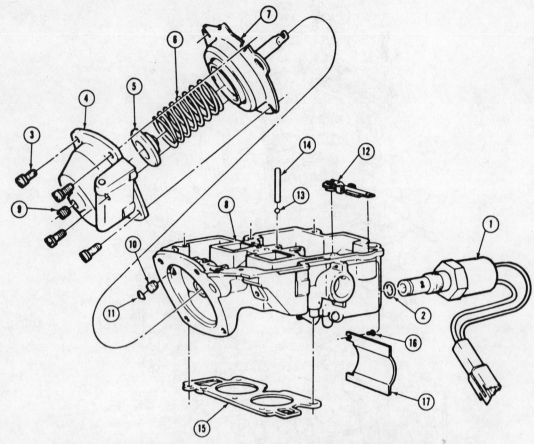

1. Cranking enrichment solenoid
2. O-ring seal
3. Screw
4. Venturi valve diaphragm cover
5. Venturi valve diaphragm spring guide
6. Venturi valve diaphragm spring
7. Venturi valve diaphragm assembly
8. Main body
9. Venturi valve adjusting screw
10. Wide open stop screw
11. Plug expansion
12. Cranking fuel control assembly
13. Accelerator pump check ball
14. Accelerator pump check ball weight
15. Throttle body gasket
16. Screw
17. Choke heat shield

2700VV main body

5. Remove the accelerator pump rod and the choke control rod.

6. Remove the accelerator pump link retaining pin and the link.

7. Remove the accelerator pump swivel and the retaining nut.

8. Remove the E-ring on the choke hinge pin and slide the pin out of the casting.

9. Remove the cold enrichment rod adjusting nut, lever and swivel; remove the control vacuum nut and regulator as an assembly.

10. Remove the cold enrichment rod.

11. Remove the venturi valve cover plate and roller bearings. Remove the venturi valve cover plate and roller bearings. Remove the venturi air bypass screw.

12. Using special tool T77P-9928-A, press the tapered plugs out of the venturi valve pivot pins.

13. Remove the venturi valve pivot pins, bushings and the venturi valve.

14. Remove the metering rod pivot pins, springs and metering rods. Be sure to mark the rods so that you know on which side they belong. Also, keep the venturi valve blocked open when working on the jets.

15. Using tool T77L-9533-B, remove the cup plugs.

16. Using tool T77L-9533-A, turn each main metering jet clockwise, counting the number of turns until they bottom in the casting. You will need to know the number of turns when you reassemble the carburetor. Remove the jets

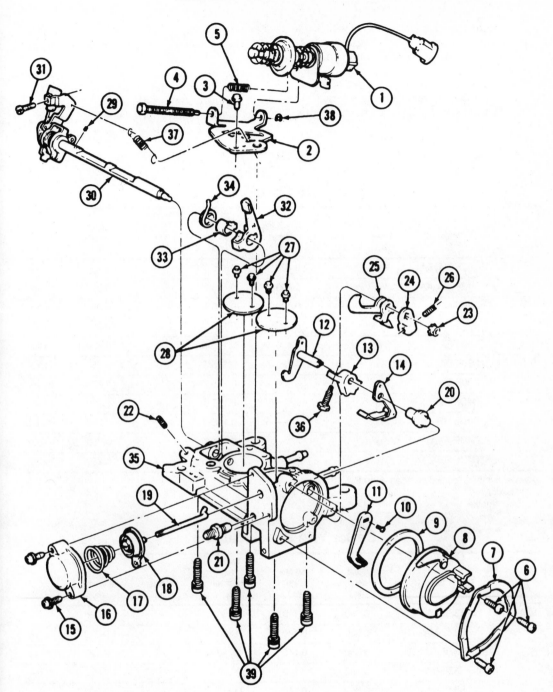

1. Throttle return control device
2. Throttle return control device bracket
3. Mounting screw
4. Adjusting screw
5. Adjusting screw spring
6. Screw
7. Choke thermostatic housing retainer
8. Choke thermostatic housing
9. Choke thermostatic housing gasket
10. Screw
11. Choke thermostatic lever
12. Choke lever and shaft assembly
13. Fast idle cam
14. High cam speed positioner assembly
15. Screw
16. High cam speed positioner diaphragm cover
17. High cam speed positioner diaphragm spring
18. High cam speed positioner diaphragm assembly
19. High cam speed positioner rod
20. Choke housing bushing

2700VV throttle body

and mark them so that you know on which side they belong. Don't lose the O-rings.

17. Remove the accelerator pump plunger assembly.

18. Remove the idle trim screws. Remove the venturi valve limiter adjusting screw.

19. To assemble the upper body, reverse the order.

Main Body

1. Remove the cranking enrichment solenoid and the O-ring seal.

2. Remove the venturi valve cover, spring guide, and spring. Remove the venturi valve.

3. Remove the throttle body.

4. Remove the choke heat shield.

5. Assembly is in reverse order.

Carter RBS Specifications

Year	Model ①	Float Level (in.)	Bowl Vent (in.)	Accelerator Pump (in.)	Fast Idle (rpm)	Fast Idle Throttle Plate (in.)	Choke Unloader (in.)	Choke
1971	D1ZF-HA, LA	9/16	—	0.400 ③	0.115 ②	—	0.250	Index
	D1ZF-NA, KA	9/16	—	0.400 ③	0.115 ②	—	0.250	1 Rich
1972	D20F-LA	9/16	—	0.400 ③	0.115 ②	—	0.250	Index
	D20F-MA	9/16	—	0.400 ③	0.115 ②	—	0.250	1 Rich
	D20F-SA	9/16	—	0.400 ③	0.115 ②	—	0.250	1 Rich
1973	D30F-BA	9/16	—	0.420 ③	0.115 ②	—	0.250	Index
	D30F-CA	9/16	—	0.400 ③	0.115 ②	—	0.250	Index
1974	D4DE-BB	9/16	—	—	0.115 ②	—	0.250	Index
	D4DE-SB	9/16	—	—	0.115 ②	—	0.250	Index
	D4DE-AAA	9/16	—	—	0.115 ②	—	0.250	1 Lean
	D4DE-AB	9/16	—	—	0.115 ②	—	0.250	Index

① Model numbers located on a tag or on the casting
② At kickdown
③ Closed throttle

Carter YFA Specifications

Year	Model ①	Float Level (in.)	Fast Idle Cam (in.)	Choke Plate Pulldown (in.)	Unloader (in.)	Dechoke (in.)	Choke
1983	E3ZE-LA	0.650	0.140	0.260	—	0.220	—
	E3ZE-MA	0.650	0.140	0.260	—	0.220	—
	E3ZE-TB	0.650	0.140	0.240	—	0.220	—
	E3ZE-UA	0.650	0.140	0.240	—	0.220	—
	E3ZE-VA	0.650	0.140	0.260	—	0.220	—
	E3ZE-YA	0.650	0.140	0.260	—	0.220	—
	E3ZE-NB	0.650	0.160	0.260	—	0.220	—
	E3ZE-PB	0.650	0.160	0.260	—	0.220	—
	E3ZE-ASA	0.650	0.160	0.260	—	0.220	—
	E3ZE-APA	0.650	0.140	0.240	—	0.220	—
	E3ZE-ARA	0.650	0.140	0.240	—	0.220	—
	E3ZE-ADA	0.650	0.140	0.260	—	0.220	—
	E3ZE-AEA	0.650	0.140	0.260	—	0.220	—

Carter YFA Specifications (Cont.)

Year	Model ①	Float Level (in.)	Fast Idle Cam (in.)	Choke Plate Pulldown (in.)	Unloader (in.)	Dechoke (in.)	Choke
1983	E3ZE-ACA	0.650	0.140	0.260	—	0.220	—
	E3ZE-ATA	0.650	0.160	0.260	—	0.220	—
	E3ZE-ABA	0.650	0.140	0.260	—	0.220	—
	E3ZE-UB	0.650	0.140	0.240	—	0.220	—
	E3ZE-TC	0.650	0.140	0.240	—	0.220	—
1984–85	E4ZE-HC, DB	0.650	0.140	0.260	—	0.270	—
	E4ZE-MA, NA	0.650	0.140	0.240	—	0.270	—
	E4ZE-PA, RA	0.650	0.140	0.260	—	0.270	—
	E5ZE-CA	0.650	0.140	0.260	—	0.270	—
	E4ZE-PB, RB	0.650	0.140	0.240	—	0.270	—

① Model number located on the tag or casting

Autolite (Motorcraft) 2100, 2150 Specifications

Year	(9510) * Carburetor Identification	Dry Float Level (in.)	Wet Float Level (in.)	Pump Setting Hole # ①	Choke Plate Pulldown (in.)	Fast Idle Cam Linkage Clearance (in.)	Fast Idle (rpm)	Dechoke (in.)	Choke Setting
1971	D1YF-DA	7/16	13/16	3	0.200	0.160	1500	0.060	Index
	D1MF-JA	7/16	13/16	3	0.190	0.160	1500	0.060	1 Rich
	D1MF-FA	7/16	13/16	3	0.200	0.160	1500	0.060	1 Rich
1972	D2AF-FB	7/16	13/16	3	0.140	0.130	1500	0.030	Index
	D2AF-GB	7/16	13/16	3	0.140	0.130	1500	0.030	Index
	D2AF-HA	7/16	13/16	2	0.150	0.130	1400	0.060	1 Rich
	D2GF-AA	7/16	13/16	2	0.150	0.130	1400	0.060	1 Rich
	D2GF-BA	7/16	13/16	2	0.150	0.130	1400	0.060	1 Rich
	D2MF-FB	7/16	13/16	4	0.180	0.150	1500	0.060	1 Rich
	D2OF-KA	7/16	13/16	2	0.150	0.130	1400	0.060	1 Rich
	D2OF-VB	7/16	13/16	3	0.190	0.160	1400	0.030	2 Rich
	D2WF-CA	7/16	13/16	3	0.190	0.160	1400	0.030	2 Rich
	D2ZF-FA	7/16	13/16	2	0.150	0.130	1400	0.060	1 Rich
	D2ZF-LA	7/16	13/16	3	0.240	0.210	1500	0.030	1 Rich
1973	D3AF-CE	7/16	13/16	3	②	②	1500	②	1 Rich
	D3AF-DC	7/16	13/16	3	②	②	1500	②	3 Rich
	D3GF-AF	7/16	13/16	2	②	②	1400	②	3 Rich
	D3GF-BB	7/16	13/16	2	②	②	1250	②	3 Rich
	D3ZF-EA	7/16	13/16	2	②	②	1400	②	1 Rich
	D3AF-KA	7/16	13/16	3	②	②	1500	②	3 Rich
	D3MF-AE	7/16	13/16	3	②	②	1500	②	3 Rich
	D3MF-BA	7/16	13/16	3	②	②	1500	②	3 Rich

Autolite (Motorcraft) 2100, 2150 Specifications (Cont.)

Year	(9510) * Carburetor Identification	Dry Float Level (in.)	Wet Float Level (in.)	Pump Setting Hole # ①	Choke Plate Pulldown (in.)	Fast Idle Cam Linkage Clearance (in.)	Fast Idle (rpm)	Dechoke (in.)	Choke Setting
1974	D4AE-DA	7/16	13/16	2	②	②	1500	②	1 Rich
	D4AE-EA	7/16	13/16	2	②	②	1500	②	3 Rich
	D4AE-FA	7/16	13/16	3	②	②	1500	②	3 Rich
	D4AE-GA	7/16	13/16	3	②	②	1500	②	3 Rich
	D4DE-LA	7/16	13/16	2	②	②	1500	②	3 Rich
	D4DE-RB	7/16	13/16	2	②	②	1500	②	3 Rich
	D4OE-FA	7/16	13/16	2	②	②	1500	②	3 Rich
	D4AE-HB	7/16	13/16	3	②	②	1500	②	3 Rich
	D4DE-NB	7/16	13/16	2	②	②	1500	②	3 Rich
	D4DE-PA	7/16	13/16	2	②	②	1500	②	3 Rich
	D4OE-CA	7/16	13/16	2	②	②	1500	②	3 Rich
	D4ME-BA	7/16	13/16	3	②	②	1500	②	3 Rich
	D4ME-CA	7/16	13/16	3	②	②	1500	②	3 Rich
1975	D5ZE-AC	3/8	3/4	2	0.145	②	1500	②	2 Rich
	D5ZE-BC	3/8	3/4	2	0.145	②	1500	②	2 Rich
	D5ZE-CC	3/8	3/4	3	0.145	②	1500	②	2 Rich
	D5ZE-DC	3/8	3/4	2	0.145	②	1500	②	2 Rich
	D5DE-AA	7/16	13/16	2	0.140	②	1500	②	3 Rich
	D5DE-BA	7/16	13/16	2	0.140	②	1500	②	3 Rich
	D5DE-JA	7/16	13/16	2	0.140	②	1500	②	3 Rich
	D5ZE-JA	7/16	13/16	2	0.140	②	1500	②	3 Rich
	D5OE-AA	7/16	13/16	2	0.140	2	1500	②	3 Rich
	D5OE-DA	7/16	13/16	2	0.140	②	1500	②	3 Rich
	D5DE-HA	7/16	13/16	3	0.140	②	1500	②	3 Rich
	D5DE-UA	7/16	13/16	2	0.140	②	1500	②	3 Rich
	D5OE-BA	7/16	13/16	3	0.125	②	1500	②	3 Rich
	D5OE-CA	7/16	13/16	3	0.125	②	1500	②	3 Rich
	D5OE-GA	7/16	13/16	2	0.125	②	1500	②	3 Rich
	D5AE-AA	7/16	13/16	3	0.125	②	1500	②	3 Rich
	D5AE-EA	7/16	13/16	3	0.125	②	1500	②	3 Rich
	D5ME-BA	7/16	13/16	2	0.125	②	1500	②	3 Rich
	D5ME-FA	7/16	13/16	2	0.125	②	1500	②	3 Rich
1976–77	D5ZE-BE	3/8	3/4	2	0.105	②	1600 ③	②	3 Rich
	D6ZE-AA	3/8	3/4	2	0.100	②	1600 ③	②	3 Rich
	D6ZE-BA	3/8	3/4	2	0.100	②	1600 ③	②	3 Rich
	D6ZE-CA	13/32	3/4	2	0.110	②	1600 ③	②	3 Rich
	D6ZE-DA	3/8	3/4	3	0.110	②	1600 ③	②	3 Rich
	D5DE-AEA	7/16	13/16	2	0.160	②	2000 ④	②	3 Rich
	D5DE-AFA	7/16	13/16	2	0.160	②	2000 ④	②	3 Rich

Autolite (Motorcraft) 2100, 2150 Specifications (Cont.)

Year	(9510) * Carburetor Identification	Dry Float Level (in.)	Wet Float Level (in.)	Pump Setting Hole # ①	Choke Plate Pulldown (in.)	Fast Idle Cam Linkage Clearance (in.)	Fast Idle (rpm)	Dechoke (in.)	Choke Setting
	D5WE-FA	7/16	13/16	2	0.160	②	2000 ④	②	3 Rich
	D6ZE-JA	7/16	13/16	2	0.160	②	2000 ④	②	3 Rich
	D6OE-AA	7/16	13/16	3	0.160	②	2000 ④	②	3 Rich
	D6OE-BA	7/16	13/16	3	0.160	②	2000 ④	②	3 Rich
	D6OE-CA	7/16	13/16	3	0.160	②	2000 ④	②	3 Rich
	D6WE-AA	7/16	13/16	2	0.160	②	1350 ⑤	②	3 Rich
	D6WE-BA	7/16	13/16	2	0.160	②	1350 ⑤	②	3 Rich
	D6AE-HA	7/16	13/16	2	0.160	②	1350 ⑤	②	3 Rich
	D6ME-AA	7/16	13/16	2	0.160	②	1350 ⑤	②	3 Rich
1978	D84E-EA	7/16	13/16	2	0.110	⑥	⑦	—	3 Rich
	D8AE-JA	3/8	3/4	3	0.167	⑥	⑦	—	3 Rich
	D8BE-ACA	7/16	3/4	4	0.155	⑥	⑦	—	2 Rich
	D8BE-ADA	7/16	13/16	2	0.110	⑥	⑦	—	3 Rich
	D8BE-AEA	7/16	13/16	2	0.110	⑥	⑦	—	4 Rich
	D8BE-AFA	7/16	13/16	2	0.110	⑥	⑦	—	4 Rich
	D8BE-MB	3/8	13/16	3	0.122	⑥	⑦	—	Index
	D8DE-HA	19/32	13/16	3	0.157	⑥	⑦	—	Index
	D8KE-EA	19/32	13/16	2	0.135	⑥	⑦	—	3 Rich
	D8OE-BA	3/8	3/4	3	0.167	⑥	⑦	—	3 Rich
	D8OE-EA	19/32	13/16	2	0.136	⑥	⑦	—	Index
	D8OE-HA	7/16	13/16	3	0.180	⑥	⑦	—	2 Rich
	D8SE-CA	19/32	13/16	3	0.150	⑥	⑦	—	2 Rich
	D8ZE-TA	3/8	3/4	4	0.135	⑥	⑦	—	Index
	D8ZE-UA	3/8	3/4	4	0.135	⑥	⑦	—	Index
	D8WE-DA	7/16	13/16	4	0.143	⑥	⑦	—	1 Rich
	D8YE-AB	3/8	13/16	3	0.122	⑥	⑦	—	Index
	D8SE-DA, EA	7/16	13/16	3	0.147	⑥	⑦	—	3 Rich
	D8SE-FA, GA	3/8	13/16	3	0.147	⑥	⑦	—	3 Rich
1979	D9AE-AHA	7/16	13/16	3	0.147	⑥	⑦	0.250	3 Rich
	D9AE-AJA	7/16	13/16	3	0.147	⑥	⑦	0.250	3 Rich
	D9AE-ANB	7/16	13/16	3	0.129	⑥	⑦	—	1 Rich
	D9AE-APB	7/16	13/16	3	0.129	⑥	⑦	—	1 Rich
	D9AE-AVB	7/16	13/16	3	0.129	⑥	⑦	—	1 Rich
	D9AE-AYA	7/16	13/16	3	0.129	⑥	⑦	—	1 Rich
	D9AE-AYB	7/16	13/16	3	0.129	⑥	⑦	—	1 Rich
	D9AE-TB	7/16	13/16	3	0.129	⑥	⑦	—	2 Rich
	D9AE-UB	7/16	13/16	3	0.129	⑥	⑦	—	2 Rich
	D9BE-VB	7/16	13/16	3	0.153	⑥	⑦	0.250	2 Rich
	D9BE-YB	7/16	13/16	3	0.153	⑥	⑦	—	2 Rich

Autolite (Motorcraft) 2100, 2150 Specifications (Cont.)

Year	(9510) * Carburetor Identification	Dry Float Level (in.)	Wet Float Level (in.)	Pump Setting Hole # ①	Choke Plate Pulldown (in.)	Fast Idle Cam Linkage Clearance (in.)	Fast Idle (rpm)	Dechoke (in.)	Choke Setting
1979	D9DE-NB	$7/16$	$13/16$	3	0.153	⑥	⑦	0.250	2 Rich
	D9DE-RA	$7/16$	$13/16$	2	0.125	⑥	⑦	0.115	3 Rich
	D9DE-RB	$7/16$	$13/16$	2	0.125	⑥	⑦	0.115	3 Rich
	D9DE-RD	$7/16$	$13/16$	2	0.125	⑥	⑦	—	3 Rich
	D9DE-SA	$7/16$	$13/16$	2	0.125	⑥	⑦	0.250	3 Rich
	D9DE-SC	$7/16$	$13/16$	2	0.125	⑥	⑦	—	3 Rich
	D9ME-BA	$7/16$	$13/16$	2	0.136	⑥	⑦	0.115	Index
	D9ME-CA	$7/16$	$13/16$	2	0.136	⑥	⑦	0.115	Index
	D9OE-CB	$7/16$	$13/16$	3	0.132	⑥	⑦	0.115	3 Rich
	D9OE-DB	$7/16$	$13/16$	3	0.132	⑥	⑦	—	3 Rich
	D9OE-EA	$7/16$	$13/16$	3	0.132	⑥	⑦	0.115	2 Rich
	D9OE-FA	$7/16$	$13/16$	3	0.132	⑥	⑦	0.115	2 Rich
	D9SE-GA	$7/16$	$13/16$	3	0.150	⑥	⑦	0.250	2 Rich
	D9VE-LC	$7/16$	$13/16$	3	0.145	⑥	⑦	0.250	3 Rich
	D9VE-SA	$7/16$	$13/16$	3	0.147	⑥	⑦	—	3 Rich
	D9VE-UB	$7/16$	$13/16$	3	0.155	⑥	⑦	0.250	3 Rich
	D9VE-VA	$3/8$	$3/4$	3	0.145	⑥	⑦	—	3 Rich
	D9VE-YB	$3/8$	$3/4$	2	0.145	⑥	⑦	0.250	3 Rich
	D9WE-CB	$7/16$	$13/16$	3	0.132	⑥	⑦	—	3 Rich
	D9WE-DB	$7/16$	$13/16$	3	0.132	⑥	⑦	—	3 Rich
	D9WE-EB	$7/16$	$13/16$	3	0.132	⑥	⑦	—	2 Rich
	D9WE-FB	$7/16$	$13/16$	3	0.132	⑥	⑦	—	2 Rich
	D9WE-JA	$7/16$	$13/16$	3	0.150	⑥	⑦	0.250	2 Rich
	D9WE-MB	$7/16$	$13/16$	3	0.132	⑥	⑦	—	1 Rich
	D9WE-NB	$7/16$	$13/16$	3	0.132	⑥	⑦	—	1 Rich
	D9YE-EA	$7/16$	$13/16$	3	0.118	⑥	⑦	0.115	1 Rich
	D9YE-FA	$7/16$	$13/16$	3	0.118	⑥	⑦	0.115	1 Rich
	D9YE-AB	$7/16$	$13/16$	3	0.118	⑥	⑦	0.115	Index
	D9YE-BB	$7/16$	$13/16$	3	0.118	⑥	⑦	0.115	Index
	D9YE-CA	$7/16$	$13/16$	2	0.118	⑥	⑦	0.115	Index
	D9YE-DA	$7/16$	$13/16$	2	0.118	⑥	⑦	0.115	Index
	D9ZE-AYA	$7/16$	$13/16$	3	0.138	⑥	⑦	0.115	Index
	D9ZE-BFB	$7/16$	$13/16$	2	0.125	⑥	⑦	—	3 Rich
	D9ZE-BGB	$7/16$	$13/16$	2	0.125	⑥	⑦	—	3 Rich
	D9ZE-BHB	$7/16$	$13/16$	2	0.125	⑥	⑦	0.250	3 Rich
	D9ZE-BJB	$7/16$	$13/16$	2	0.125	⑥	⑦	—	3 Rich
1980	EO4E-PA, RA	—	$13/16$	2	0.104	⑥	⑦	$1/4$	⑦
	EOBE-AUA	—	$13/16$	3	0.116	⑥	⑦	$1/4$	⑦
	EODE-SA, TA	—	$13/16$	2	0.104	⑥	⑦	$1/4$	⑦

Autolite (Motorcraft) 2100, 2150 Specifications (Cont.)

Year	(9510) * Carburetor Identification	Dry Float Level (in.)	Wet Float Level (in.)	Pump Setting Hole # ①	Choke Plate Pulldown (in.)	Fast Idle Cam Linkage Clearance (in.)	Fast Idle (rpm)	Dechoke (in.)	Choke Setting
	EOKE-CA, DA	—	13/16	3	0.116	⑥	⑦	1/4	⑦
	EOKE-GA, HA	—	13/16	3	0.116	⑥	⑦	1/4	⑦
	EOKE-JA, KA	—	13/16	3	0.116	⑥	⑦	1/4	⑦
	D84E-TA, UA	—	13/16	2	0.125	⑥	⑦	1/4	⑦
	EO4E-ADA, AEA	—	13/16	2	0.104	⑥	⑦	1/4	⑦
	EO4E-CA	—	13/16	2	0.104	⑥	⑦	1/4	⑦
	EO4E-EA, FA	—	13/16	2	0.104	⑥	⑦	1/4	⑦
	EO4E-JA, KA	—	13/16	2	0.137	⑥	⑦	1/4	⑦
	EO4E-SA, TA	—	13/16	2	0.104	⑥	⑦	1/4	⑦
	EO4E-VA, YA	—	13/16	2	0.104	⑥	⑦	1/4	⑦
	EODE-TA, VA	—	13/16	2	0.104	⑥	⑦	1/4	⑦
	EOSE-GA, HA	—	13/16	2	0.104	⑥	⑦	1/4	⑦
	EOSE-LA, MA	—	13/16	2	0.104	⑥	⑦	1/4	⑦
	EOSE-NA	—	13/16	2	0.104	⑥	⑦	1/4	⑦
	EOSE-PA	—	13/16	2	0.137	⑥	⑦	1/4	⑦
	EOVE-FA	—	13/16	2	0.104	⑥	⑦	1/4	⑦
	EOWE-BA, CA	—	13/16	2	0.137	⑥	⑦	1/4	⑦
	D9AE-ANA, APA	—	13/16	3	0.129	⑥	⑦	1/4	⑦
	D9AE-AVA, AYA	—	13/16	3	0.129	⑥	⑦	1/4	⑦
	EOAE-AGA	—	13/16	3	0.159	⑥	⑦	1/4	⑦
1981	EIKE-CA	7/16	0.810	3	0.124	⑥	⑦	0.250	⑦
	EIKE-EA	7/16	0.810	3	0.124	⑥	⑦	0.250	⑦
	EIKE-DA	7/16	0.810	3	0.124	⑥	⑦	0.250	⑦
	EIKE-FA	7/16	0.810	3	0.124	⑥	⑦	0.250	⑦
	EIWE-FA	7/16	0.810	2	0.120	⑥	⑦	0.250	⑦
	EIWE-EA	7/16	0.810	2	0.120	⑥	⑦	0.250	⑦
	EIWE-CA	7/16	0.810	2	0.120	⑥	⑦	0.250	⑦
	EIWE-DA	7/16	0.810	2	0.120	⑥	⑦	0.250	⑦
	EIAE-YA	7/16	0.810	3	0.124	⑥	⑦	0.250	⑦
	EIAE-ZA	7/16	0.810	3	0.124	⑥	⑦	0.250	⑦
	EIAE-ADA	7/16	0.810	3	0.124	⑥	⑦	0.250	⑦
	EIAE-AEA	7/16	0.810	3	0.124	⑥	⑦	0.250	⑦
	EIAE-TA	—	0.810	2	0.104	⑥	⑦	0.250	⑦
	EIAE-UA	—	0.810	2	0.104	⑥	⑦	0.250	⑦
1982	E2ZE-BAA	13/32	0.780	2	0.172	⑥	1400	0.250	⑧
	E2ZE-BBA	13/32	0.780	2	0.172	⑥	1400	0.250	⑧
	E3CE-LA	7/16	0.810	3	0.103	⑥	2200	0.250	⑧
	E3CE-MA	7/16	0.810	3	0.103	⑥	2200	0.250	⑧
	E3CE-JA	7/16	0.810	3	0.103	⑥	2200	0.250	⑧

Autolite (Motorcraft) 2100, 2150 Specifications (Cont.)

Year	(9510) * Carburetor Identification	Dry Float Level (in.)	Wet Float Level (in.)	Pump Setting Hole # ①	Choke Plate Pulldown (in.)	Fast Idle Cam Linkage Clearance (in.)	Fast Idle (rpm)	Dechoke (in.)	Choke Setting
1982	E3CE-KA	7/16	0.810	3	0.103	⑥	2200	0.250	⑧
	E3CE-NA	7/16	0.810	3	0.120	⑥	2100	0.250	⑧
	E3CE-PA	7/16	0.810	3	0.120	⑥	2100	0.250	⑧
1983	E3CE-AA	7/16	0.810	3	0.103	⑥	2200	0.250	⑧
	E3CE-BA	7/16	0.810	3	0.103	⑥	2200	0.250	⑧
	E3CE-GA	7/16	0.810	3	0.103	⑥	2200	0.250	⑧
	E3CE-HA	7/16	0.810	3	0.103	⑥	2200	0.250	⑧
	E3CE-EA	7/16	0.810	3	0.113	⑥	2100	0.250	⑧
	E3CE-FA	7/16	0.810	3	0.113	⑥	2100	0.250	⑧
	E3SE-ATA	7/16	0.810	3	0.113	⑥	2200	0.250	⑧
	E3SE-AUA	13/16	0.810	3	0.113	⑥	2200	0.250	⑧
	E3SE-ALA	7/16	0.810	3	0.107	⑥	2200	0.250	⑧
	E3SE-AMA	7/16	0.810	3	0.107	⑥	2200	0.250	⑧
	E3SE-BDA	7/16	0.810	3	0.107	⑥	2200	0.250	⑧
	E3SE-BEA	7/16	0.810	3	0.107	⑥	2200	0.250	⑧
	E3SE-ANA	7/16	0.810	3	0.101	⑥	2200	0.250	⑧
	E3SE-APA	7/16	0.810	3	0.101	⑥	2200	0.250	⑧
	E3SE-AJA	7/16	0.810	3	0.107	⑥	2200	0.250	⑧
	E3SE-BFA	7/16	0.810	3	0.107	⑥	2200	0.250	⑧
	E3SE-BGA	7/16	0.810	3	0.107	⑥	2200	0.250	⑧
	E3SE-EA	7/16	0.810	3	0.113	⑥	2200	0.250	⑧
	E3SE-FA	7/16	0.810	3	0.113	⑥	2200	0.250	⑧
	E3SE-LA	7/16	0.810	3	0.107	⑥	2200	0.250	⑧
	E3SE-MA	7/16	0.810	3	0.107	⑥	2200	0.250	⑧
	E3SE-JA	7/16	0.810	3	0.101	⑥	2200	0.250	⑧
	E3SE-KA	7/16	0.810	3	0.101	⑥	2200	0.250	⑧
	E3SE-NA	7/16	0.810	3	0.107	⑥	2200	0.250	⑧
	E3SE-PA	7/16	0.810	3	0.107	⑥	2200	0.250	⑧
	E3SE-GA	7/16	0.810	3	0.120	⑥	2100	0.250	⑧
	E3SE-HA	7/16	0.810	3	0.120	⑥	2100	0.250	⑧
	E3AE-TA	7/16	0.810	3	0.103	⑥	2200	0.250	⑧
	E3AE-ADA	7/16	0.810	3	0.103	⑥	2200	0.250	⑧
	E3AE-UA	7/16	0.810	3	0.103	⑥	2200	0.250	⑧
	E3AE-AEA	7/16	0.810	3	0.103	⑥	2200	0.250	⑧
	E3AE-TA	7/16	0.810	3	0.103	⑥	2200	0.250	⑧
	E3AE-UA	7/16	0.810	3	0.103	⑥	2200	0.250	⑧
	E3AE-RA	7/16	0.810	3	0.103	⑥	2200	0.250	⑧
	E3AE-SA	7/16	0.810	3	0.103	⑥	2200	0.250	⑧
	E3AE-EA	7/16	0.810	2	—	⑥	1550	0.250	⑧

Autolite (Motorcraft) 2100, 2150 Specifications (Cont.)

Year	(9510) * Carburetor Identification	Dry Float Level (in.)	Wet Float Level (in.)	Pump Setting Hole # ①	Choke Plate Pulldown (in.)	Fast Idle Cam Linkage Clearance (in.)	Fast Idle (rpm)	Dechoke (in.)	Choke Setting
1984–85	E3EA-EA	7/16	0.810	2	—	⑥	1550	0.250	⑧
	E4CE-AA	7/16	0.810	3	0.103	⑥	2200	0.250	2NR
	E4CE-BA	7/16	0.810	3	0.103	⑥	2200	0.250	2NR
	E4SE-CA	7/16	0.810	3	0.103	⑥	2200	0.250	⑧
	E4SE-DA	7/16	0.810	3	0.103	⑥	2200	0.250	⑧
	E5AE-CA	7/16	0.810	2	—	⑥	1550	0.250	⑧

* Basic carburetor number for Ford products
① With link in inboard hole of pump lever
② Electric choke; see procedure in text
③ Figure given is for manual transmission; for automatics add 100 RPM.
④ Figure given is for 49 states Granada and Monarch; for Calif. Granada and Monarch and all Torino, Montego and Cougar models, figure is 1400 RPM.
⑤ Figure given is for 49 states model; Calif. specification is 1150 RPM.
⑥ Opposite V- notch
⑦ See underhood sticker
⑧ V-notch

Carter Thermo-Quad Specifications

Year	Model ①	Float Setting (in.)	Secondary Throttle Linkage (in.)	Secondary Air Valve Opening (in.)	Secondary Air Valve Spring (turns)	Accelerator Pump (in.)	Choke Control Lever (in.)	Choke Unloader (in.)	Vacuum Kick (in.)	Fast Idle Speed (rpm)
1974	6488S	1	②	1/2	1 1/4	31/64	3 1/8	.310	21	1800
	6452S	1	②	1/2	1 1/4	35/64	3 3/8	.310	4	1900
	6453S	1	②	1/2	1 1/4	31/64	3 3/8	.310	21	1900
	6454S	1	②	1/2	1 1/4	31/64	3 3/8	.310	4	1900
	6455S	1	②	1/2	1 1/4	31/64	3 3/8	.310	21	1900
	6489S	1	②	1/2	1 1/4	31/64	3 3/8	.310	21	2000
	6496S	1	②	1/2	1 1/4	31/64	3 3/8	.310	21	2000
	6456S	1	②	1/2	1 1/4	31/64	3 3/8	.310	4	1700
	6457S	1	②	1/2	1 1/4	31/64	3 3/8	.310	21	1800
	6459	1	②	1/2	1 1/4	31/64	3 3/8	.310	21	1800
	6460S	1	②	1/2	1 1/4	31/64	3 3/8	.310	21	1700
	6461S	1	②	1/2	1 1/4	31/64	3 3/8	.310	21	1700
	6462S	1	②	1/2	1 1/4	31/64	3 3/8	.310	21	1700
	6463S	1	②	1/2	1 1/4	31/64	3 3/8	.310	21	1700

① Model numbers located on the tag or on the casting
② Adjust link so primary and secondary stops both contact at same time
NOTE: All choke settings are fixed

Autolite (Motorcraft) 4300, 4350 Specifications

Year	(9510)* Carburetor Identification ①	Dry Float Level (in.)	Pump Hole Setting	Choke Plate Pulldown (in.)	Fast Idle Cam Linkage (in.)	Fast Idle (rpm)	Dechoke (in.)	Choke Setting	Dashpot
1971	D1AF-MA	$^{49}/_{64}$	2	0.220	—	1350	—	Index	$^1/_{16}$
	D1OF-EA	$^{13}/_{16}$	2	0.180	0.160	1250	—	Index	—
	D1OF-AAA	$^{13}/_{16}$	2	0.200	0.180	1400	—	Index	—
	D1SF-AA	$^{49}/_{64}$	2	0.220	—	1350	—	Index	$^1/_{16}$
	D1VF-AA	$^{49}/_{64}$	2	0.220	0.170	1250	—	1 Rich	0.100
1972	D2AF-AA	$^{49}/_{64}$	1	0.220	0.200	1350	—	2 Rich	—
	D2AF-LA	$^{49}/_{64}$	1	0.215	0.190	1900	—	2 Rich	—
	D2SF-AA	$^{49}/_{64}$	1	0.220	0.200	1350	—	2 Rich	—
	D2SF-BA	$^{49}/_{64}$	1	0.220	0.200	1350	—	2 Rich	—
	D2VF-AA	$^{49}/_{64}$	1	0.230	0.200	1250	—	Index	—
	D2VF-BA	$^{49}/_{64}$	1	0.230	0.200	1250	—	Index	—
	D2ZF-AA	$^{13}/_{16}$	1	0.200	0.180	1200	—	Index	—
	D2ZF-BB	$^{13}/_{16}$	1	0.200	0.200	1200	—	Index	—
	D2ZF-DA	$^{13}/_{16}$	1	0.200	0.200	1200	—	Index	—
	D2ZF-GA	$^{13}/_{16}$	1	0.200	0.180	1200	—	Index	—
1973	D3VF-DA	0.76	1	0.210	0.190	1350	—	Index	—
	D3ZF-AC	0.82	1	0.180	0.180	1300	—	Index	—
	D3ZF-BC	0.82	1	0.170	0.170	1300	—	INR	—
	D3ZF-CD	0.82	1	0.180	0.180	1300	—	Index	—
	D3AF-HA	0.76	1	0.210	0.200	1350	—	Index	—
	D3AF-EB	0.88	1	0.200	0.200	1900	—	Index	—
1974	D4AE-AA	$^3/_4$	1	0.230	0.200	1900	—	Index	—
	D4AE-NA, D4VE-AB	$^3/_4$	1	0.220	0.200	1250	—	Index	—
	D4TE-ATA	$^{13}/_{16}$	1	0.220	0.180	1250	—	Index	—
	D4OE-AA	$^{13}/_{16}$	1	0.180	0.180	1800	—	Index	—
1975	D5VE-AD	$^{15}/_{16}$	1	②	0.160	1600	0.300	2 Rich	—
	D5VE-BA	$^{15}/_{16}$	1	②	0.160	1600	0.300	2 Rich	—
	D5AE-CA	$^{31}/_{32}$	1	②	0.160	1600	0.300	2 Rich	—
	D5AE-DA	$^{31}/_{32}$	1	②	0.160	1600	0.300	2 Rich	—
1976–77	D6AE-CA	1.00	2	0.140 ③	0.140	1350	0.30	2 Rich	—
	D6AE-FA	1.00	2	0.140 ③	0.140	1350	0.30	2 Rich	—
	D6AE-DA	1.00	2	0.160 ④	0.160	1350	0.30	2 Rich	—

* Basic carburetor number for Ford products.
① The identification tag is on the bowl cover.
② Initial—0.160 in.
   Delayed—0.190 in.
③ Initial Figure given; delayed—0.190
④ Initial Figure given; delayed—0.210

Motorcraft Model 2700 VV Specifications

Year	Model	Float Level (in.)	Float Drop (in.)	Fast Idle Cam Setting (notches)	Cold Enrichment Metering Rod (in.)	Control Vacuum (in. H₂O)	Venturi Valve Limiter (in.)	Choke Cap Setting (notches)	Control Vacuum Regulator Setting (in.)
1977–78	All	1³⁄₆₄	1¹⁵⁄₃₂	1 Rich/3rd step	.125	5.0	⁶¹⁄₆₄	Index	—
1979	D9ZE-LB	1³⁄₆₄	1¹⁵⁄₃₂	1 Rich/2nd step	.125	①	②	Index	.230
	D84E-KA	1³⁄₆₄	1¹⁵⁄₃₂	1 Rich/3rd step	.125	5.5	⁶¹⁄₆₄	Index	—
1980	All	1³⁄₆₄	1¹⁵⁄₃₂	1 Rich/4th step	.125	③	④	⑤	.075
1981	EIAE-AAA	1.015–1.065	1.435–1.485	—	—	③	④	⑤	—

① Venturi Air Bypass 6.8–7.3
  Venturi Valve Diaphragm 4.6–5.1
② Limiter Setting .38–.42
  Limiter Stop Setting .73–.77
③ See text
④ Opening gap: 0.99–1.01
  Closing gap: 0.94–0.98
⑤ See underhood decal

Rochester Quadrajet Specifications

Year	Carburetor Identification ①	Float Level (in.)	Air Valve Spring	Pump Rod (in.)	Vacuum Break (in.)	Secondary Opening (in.)	Choke Rod (in.)	Choke Unloader (in.)	Fast Idle Speed (rpm)
1971	DOOF-A	1¹⁄₃₂	0.030	⁵⁄₁₆	0.140	—	0.130	0.300	1800 ②
	DOOF-E	1¹⁄₃₂	0.030	⁵⁄₁₆	0.190	—	0.166	0.300	2000 ②

① The carburetor identification tag is located at the rear of the carburetor on one of the air horn screws.
② Second step of cam.

Motocraft (Holley) Model 5200 Specifications

Year	(9510)* Carburetor Identification ①	Dry Float Level (in.)	Pump Hole Setting	Choke Plate Pulldown (in.)	Fast Idle Cam Linkage (in.)	Fast Idle (rpm)	Dechoke (in.)	Choke Setting
1981	EIZE-YA	.41–.51	2	0.200	.080	②	0.200	②
	EOEE-RB	.41–.51	2	0.200	.080	②	0.200	②
	EIZE-VA	.41–.51	2	0.200	.080	②	0.200	②
	D9EE-ANA	.41–.51	2	0.240	0.720	②	0.200	②
	D9EE-APA	.41–.51	2	0.240	0.120	②	0.200	②

*Basic carburetor number
① Figure given is for all manual transmissions; for automatic trans. the figures are: (49 states) 2000 RPM; (Calif.) 1800 RPM.
② See underhood decal

Holly 4150C Specifications

Year	Carb. Part No. ①	Float Level (Dry) (in.)	Accelerator Pump Lever Adjustment (in.)	Choke Setting (in.)	Choke Unloader Clearance (in.)	Fast Idle On Car (rpm)	Choke Vacuum Break (in.)
1971	R4800-A	②	0.015	1.320 ③	0.350	2200	0.350
	R4801-A	②	0.015	1.320 ③	0.350	2200	0.350
	R4802-A	②	0.015	1.320 ③	0.350	2200	0.350
	R4803-A	②	0.015	1.320 ③	0.350	2200	0.350

① Located on tag attached to carburetor, or on the casting or choke plate
② The fuel level is adjusted to the lower edge of the sight plug hole on the Holley 4150C carburetor.
③ Bottom of throttle body to center of hole in operating lever

Motorcraft Model 7200 VV Specifications

Year	Model	Float Level (in.)	Float Drop (in.)	Fast Idle Cam Setting (notches)	Cold Enrichment Metering Rod (in.)	Control Vacuum (in. H₂O)	Venturi Valve Limiter (in.)	Choke Cap Setting (notches)
1979	D9AE-ACA	1³⁄₆₄	1¹⁵⁄₃₂	1 Rich/3rd step	.125	7.5	.73–.77 ①	Index
	D9ME-AA	1³⁄₆₄	1¹⁵⁄₃₂	1 Rich/3rd step	.125	7.5	.73–.77 ①	Index
1980	All	1³⁄₆₄	1¹⁵⁄₃₂	1 Rich/3rd step	.125	②	③	④
1981	D9AE-AZA	1.015–1.065	1.435–1.485	1 Rich/3rd step	.125	②	⑤	Index
	EIAE-LA	1.015–1.065	1.435–1.485	0.360/2nd step	⑦	②	⑥	INR
	EIAE-SA	1.015–1.065	1.435–1.485	0.360/2nd step	⑦	②	⑥	INR
	EIVE-AA	1.015–1.065	1.435–1.485	0.360/2nd step	⑦	②	③	Index
1982	E2AE-LB	1.010–1.070	1.430–1.490	0.360/2nd step	⑧	②	⑨	Index
	E2DE-NA	1.010–1.070	1.430–1.490	0.360/2nd step	⑧	②	⑨	Index
	E2AE-LC	1.010–1.070	1.430–1.490	0.360/2nd step	⑧	②	⑨	Index
	E25E-FA	1.010–1.070	1.430–1.490	0.360/2nd step	⑧	②	⑨	Index
	E25E-GB	1.010–1.070	1.430–1.490	0.360/2nd step	⑧	②	⑨	Index
	E2SE-GA	1.010–1.070	1.430–1.490	0.360/2nd step	⑧	②	⑨	Index
	E2AE-RA	1.010–1.070	1.430–1.490	0.360/2nd step	⑩	②	⑨	Index
	E1AE-ACA	1.010–1.070	1.430–1.490	0.360/2nd step	⑩	②	⑨	Index
	E2SE-DB	1.010–1.070	1.430–1.490	0.360/2nd step	⑪	②	⑨	Index
	E2SE-DA	1.010–1.070	1.430–1.490	0.360/2nd step	⑪	②	⑨	Index
	E1AE-SA	1.010–1.070	1.430–1.490	0.360/2nd step	⑫	②	⑬	1 Rich
	E2AE-MA	1.010–1.070	1.430–1.490	0.360/2nd step	⑫	②	⑬	1 Rich
	E2AE-MB	1.010–1.070	1.430–1.490	0.360/2nd step	⑫	②	⑬	1 Rich
	E2AE-TA	1.010–1.070	1.430–1.490	0.360/2nd step	⑫	②	⑬	Index
	E2AE-TB	1.010–1.070	1.430–1.490	0.360/2nd step	⑫	②	⑬	Index
	E25E-AC	1.010–1.070	1.430–1.490	0.360/2nd step	⑪	②	⑨	Index
	E1AE-AGA	1.010–1.070	1.430–1.490	0.360/2nd step	⑫	②	⑨	Index
	E2AE-NA	1.010–1.070	1.430–1.490	0.360/2nd step	⑫	②	⑨	Index
1983–84	E2AE-NA	1.010–1.070	1.430–1.490	0.360/2nd step	⑫	②	⑨	Index
	E2AE-AJA	1.010–1.070	1.430–1.490	0.360/2nd step	⑫	②	⑨	Index
	E2AE-APA	1.010–1.070	1.430–1.490	0.360/2nd step	⑫	②	⑨	Index
	E2AE-AJA	1.010–1.070	1.430–1.490	0.360/2nd step	⑫	②	⑨	Index
	E2AE-APA	1.010–1.070	1.430–1.490	0.360/2nd step	⑫	②	⑨	Index

① Limiter Stop Setting: .99–1.01
② See text
③ Opening gap: 0.99–1.01
   Closing gap: 0.39–0.41
④ See underhood decal
⑤ Maximum opening: 99/1.01
   Wide open on throttle: .94/.98
⑥ Maximum opening: .99/1.01
   Wide open on throttle: .74/.76
⑦ 0°F—0.490 @ starting position
   75°F—0.475 @ starting position
⑧ 0°F—0.525 @ starting position
   75°F—0.445 @ starting position
⑨ Maximum opening: .99/1.01
   Wide open on throttle: .39/.41
⑩ 0°F—0.490 @ starting position
   75°F—0.445 @ starting position
⑪ 0°F—0.525 @ starting position
   75°F—0.475 @ starting position
⑫ 0°F—0.490 @ starting position
   75°F—0.460 @ starting position
⑬ Maximum opening: .99/1.01
   Wide open on throttle: .74/.76

Model 1946

Year	Part Number	Float Level (in.)	Choke Pulldown (in.)	Dechoke (in.)	Fast Idle Cam (in.)	Accelerator Pump Stroke Slot
1981	EIBE-AFA	.69	.113	.150	.082	#2
	EIBE-AKA	.69	.113	.150	.082	#2
	EOBE-CA	.69	.100	.150	.070	#2
	EOBE-AA	.69	.100	.150	.070	#2
1982	EIBE-AGA	.69	.120	.150	.086	#2
	E2BE-CA	.69	.110	.150	.078	#2
	E2BE-BA	.69	.110	.150	.078	#2
	E2BE-JA	.69	.110	.150	.078	#2
	E2BE-HA	.69	.110	.150	.078	#2
	E2BE-TA	.69	.110	.150	.078	#2
	E2BE-SA	.69	.110	.150	.078	#2
1983	E2BE-CA	.69	.110	.150	.078	#2
	E2BE-BA	.69	.110	.150	.078	#2
	E2BE-TA	.69	.110	.150	.078	#2
	E2BE-SA	.69	.110	.150	.078	#2
	E3SE-CA	.69	.105	.150	.078	#2
	E3SE-DA	.69	.105	.150	.078	#2
	E3SE-AA	.69	.095	.150	.078	#2
	E3SE-BA	.69	.095	.150	.078	#2

FUEL INJECTION

Central Fuel Injection

DESCRIPTION

Central Fuel Injection (CFI) is a throttle body injection system in which two fuel injectors are mounted in a common throttle body, spraying fuel down through the throttle valves at the bottom of the body and into the intake manifold.

OPERATION

Fuel is supplied from the fuel tank by a high pressure, in-tank fuel pump. The fuel passes through a filter and is sent to the throttle body where a regulator keeps the fuel delivery pressure at a constant 39 psi. The two fuel injectors are mounted vertically above the throttle plates and are connected in line with the fuel pressure regulator. Excess fuel supplied by the pump, but not needed by the engine, is returned to the fuel tank by a steel fuel return line.

The fuel injection system is linked with and controlled by the Electronic Engine Control (EEC) system.

Air and Fuel Control

The throttle body assembly is comprised of six individual components which perform the job of mixing the air and fuel to the ideal ratio for controlling exhaust emissions and providing performance and economy. The six components are: air control, fuel injector nozzles, fuel pressure regulator, fuel pressure diagnostic valve, cold engine speed control, and throttle position sensor.

Air Control

Air flow to the engine is controlled by two butterfly valves mounted in a two piece, die-cast aluminum housing called the throttle body. The butterfly valves, or throttle valves, are identical in design to the throttle plates of a conventional carburetor and are actuated by a similar linkage and pedal cable arrangement.

Fuel Injector Nozzles

The fuel injector nozzles are mounted in the throttle body and are electro-mechanical devices which meter and atomize the fuel delivered to the engine. The injector valve bodies consist of a solenoid actuated pintle and needle valve assembly. An electrical control signal from the EED electronic processor activates the solenoid causing the pintle to move inward off its seat and allowing fuel to flow. The fuel flow through the injector is controlled by the amount of time the injector solenoid holds the pintle off its seat.

Fuel Pressure Regulator

The fuel pressure regulator is mounted on the throttle body. The regulator smooths out fuel pressure drops from the fuel pump. It is not sensitive to back pressure in the return line to the tank.

A second function of the pressure regulator is to maintain fuel supply pressure upon engine and fuel pump shut down. The regulator acts as a check valve and traps fuel between itself and the fuel pump. This promotes rapid start ups and helps prevent fuel vapor formation in the lines, or vapor lock. The regulator makes sure that the pressure of the fuel at the injector nozzles stays at a constant 39 psi.

Fuel Pressure Diagnostic Valve

A Schrader-type diagnostic pressure valve is located at the top of the throttle body. This valve can be used by service personnel to monitor fuel pressure, bleed down the system pressure prior to maintenance and to bleed out air which may have been introduced during assembly or filter servicing. A special Ford tool (T80L-9974-A) is used to accomplish these procedures.

CAUTION: *Under no circumstances should compressed air be forced into the fuel system using the diagnostic valve.*

Cold Engine Speed Control

The cold engine speed control serves the same purpose as the fast idle speed device on a carbureted engine, which is to raise engine speed during cold engine idle. A throttle stop cam positioner is used. The cam is positioned by a bimetal spring and an electric heating element. The cold engine speed control is attached to the throttle body. As the engine heats up, the fast idle cam on the cold engine speed control is gradually repositioned by the bimetal spring, heating element and EEC computer until normal idle speed is reached. The EEC computer automatically kicks down the fast idle cam to a lower step (lower engine speed) by supplying vacuum to the automatic kickdown motor which

physically moves the high speed cam a predetermined time after the engine starts.

Throttle Position Sensor

This sensor is attached to the throttle body and is used to monitor changes in throttle plate position. The throttle position sensor sends this information to the computer, which uses it to select proper air/fuel mixture, spark timing and EGR control under different engine operating conditions.

Fuel System Inertia Switch

In the event of a collision, the electrical contacts in the inertia switch open and the fuel pump automatically shuts off. The fuel pump will shut off even if the engine does not stop running. The engine, however, will stop a few seconds after the fuel pump stops. It is not possible to restart the engine until the inertia switch is manually reset. The switch is located in the luggage compartment on the left hinge support on all models. To reset, depress both buttons on the switch at the same time.

CAUTION: *Do not reset the inertia switch until the complete fuel system has been inspected for leaks.*

FUEL CHARGING ASSEMBLY REMOVAL AND INSTALLATION

1. Remove the air cleaner.
2. Release the pressure from the fuel system at the diagnostic valve using Tool T80L-9974-A or its equivalent.
3. Disconnect the throttle cable and transmission throttle valve lever.
4. Disconnect the fuel, vacuum and electrical connections. Use care to prevent combustion of spilled fuel.
5. Remove the fuel charging assembly retaining nuts then remove the fuel charging assembly.
6. Remove the mounting gasket from the intake manifold.
7. Installation is the reverse of removal. Tighten the fuel charging assembly nuts to 120 inch lb.

THROTTLE BODY DISASSEMBLY AND ASSEMBLY

1. Remove the air cleaner mounting stud in order to separate the upper body from the throttle body.
2. Turn the fuel charging assembly (Throttle Body) over and remove the four screws from the bottom of the throttle body.
3. Separate the throttle body (lower half) from the main body (upper half).
4. Remove the old gasket. If stuck and

scraping is necessary, use only a plastic or dull scraper. Take care not to damage gasket surfaces.

5. Remove the three pressure regulator mounting screws. Remove the pressure regulator.

6. Disconnect the electrical connectors at each injector by pulling outward on the connector and not on the wire. Loosen but do not remove the wiring harness retaining screw. Push in on the harness tabs to remove from the upper body.

7. Remove the fuel injector retaining screw. Remove the injection retainer.

8. Pull the injectors, one at a time, from the upper body. Mark the injectors for identification, they must be reinstalled in the same position (choke or throttle side). Each injector is equipped with a small O-ring. If the O-ring does not come out with the injector, carefully pick out of body.

9. Remove the fuel diagnostic valve assembly.

10. Remove the choke cover by drilling the retaining rivets. A ⅛ in. or No. 30 drill is required. A choke mounting kit for reinstallation is available from Ford.

11. Remove the choke cap retaining ring, choke cap and gasket. Remove the thermostat lever screw and lever. Remove the fast idle cam assembly and control rod positioner.

12. Hold the control diaphragm cover in position and remove the two mounting screws. Carefully remove the cover, spring and pull down diaphragm.

13. Remove the fast idle retaining nut, fast idle cam adjuster lever, fast idle lever and E-clip.

14. Remove the potentiometer (sensor) connector bracket retaining screw. Mark the throttle body and throttle position sensor for correct reinstallation position. Remove the throttle sensor retaining screws and slide the sensor off of the throttle shaft. Remove the throttle positioner retaining screw and remove the throttle positioner.

15. Perform any necessary cleaning or repair.

16. Assemble the upper body by first installing the fuel diagnostic fuel pressure valve assembly.

17. Lubricate the new injector O-rings with a light grade oil. Install the O-rings on each injector. Install the injectors in their appropriate choke or throttle side position. Use a light, twisting, pushing motion to install the injectors.

18. Install the injector retainer and tighten the retaining screw to 30–60 inch lbs.

19. Install the injector wiring harness and snap into position. Tighten the harness retaining screw to 8–10 inch lbs.

20. Snap the electrical connectors into position on the injectors. Lubricate the fuel pressure regulator O-ring with light oil. Install the O-ring and new gasket on the regulator, install the regulator and tighten retaining screws to 27–40 inch lbs.

21. Install the throttle positioner onto the throttle body. Tighten the retaining screw to 32–44 inch lbs.

22. Hold the throttle sensor (potentiometer) with the location identification mark (see step 14) in the 12 o'clock position. The two rotary tangs should be at 3 o'clock and 9 o'clock positions.

23. Slide the sensor onto the throttle shaft with the identification mark still in the 12 o'clock position. Hold the sensor firmly against the throttle body.

24. Rotate the sensor until the identification marks on the sensor and body are aligned. Install the retaining screws and tighten to 13–18 inch lbs.

25. Install the sensor wiring harness bracket retaining screw, tighten to 18–22 inch lbs. Install the E-clip, fast idle lever, fast idle adjustment lever and fast idle retaining nut. Tighten the retaining nut to 16–20 inch lbs.

26. Install the pull down diaphragm, spring and cover. Hold the cover in position and tighten the retaining screws to 13–19 inch lbs.

27. Install the fast idle control rod positioner, fast idle cam and the thermostat lever. Tighten the retaining screw to 13–19 inch lbs.

28. Install the choke cap gasket, bi-metal spring, cap and retaining ring. Install new rivets and snug them with the rivet gun. Do not break rivets, loosely install so choke cover can rotate. Index choke and break rivets to tighten.

29. Install the gasket between the main body and the throttle body. Place the throttle body in position. Install the four retaining screws loosely. Install the air cleaner stud and tighten to 70–95 inch lbs. Tighten the four retaining screws.

30. The rest of the assembly is in the reverse order of disassembly.

ELECTRONIC CONTROL SYSTEM

Electronic Control Assembly (ECA)

The Electronic Control Assembly (ECA) is a solid-state micro-computer consisting of a processor assembly and a calibration assembly. It is located under the instrument panel or passenger's seat and is usually covered by a kick panel. 1981–82 models use an EEC III engine control system, while 1983 and later models use

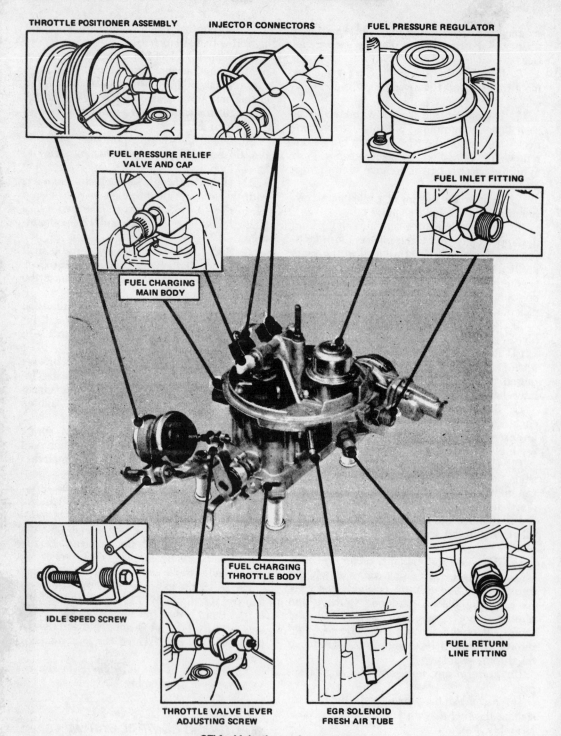

THROTTLE POSITIONER ASSEMBLY

INJECTOR CONNECTORS

FUEL PRESSURE REGULATOR

FUEL PRESSURE RELIEF
VALVE AND CAP

FUEL INLET FITTING

FUEL CHARGING
MAIN BODY

IDLE SPEED SCREW

FUEL CHARGING
THROTTLE BODY

THROTTLE VALVE LEVER
ADJUSTING SCREW

EGR SOLENOID
FRESH AIR TUBE

FUEL RETURN
LINE FITTING

CFI fuel injection and components

the EEC IV. Although the two systems are similar in appearance and operation, the ECA units are not interchangeable. A multipin connector links the ECA with all system components. The processor assembly is housed in an aluminum case. It contains circuits designed to continuously sample input signals from the engine sensors. It then calculates and sends out proper control signals to adjust air/fuel ratio, spark timing and emission system operation. The processor also provides a continuous reference voltage to the B/MAP, EVP and TPS sensors.

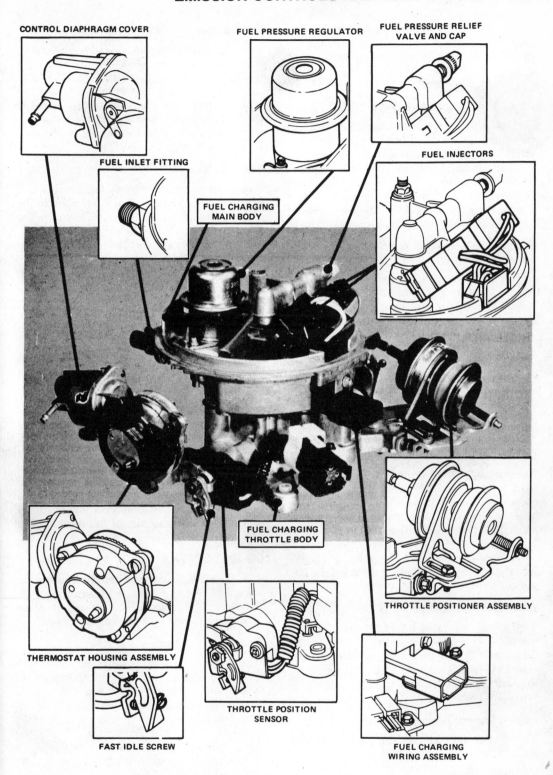

CONTROL DIAPHRAGM COVER

FUEL PRESSURE REGULATOR

FUEL PRESSURE RELIEF VALVE AND CAP

FUEL INLET FITTING

FUEL CHARGING MAIN BODY

FUEL INJECTORS

FUEL CHARGING THROTTLE BODY

THROTTLE POSITIONER ASSEMBLY

THERMOSTAT HOUSING ASSEMBLY

THROTTLE POSITION SENSOR

FUEL CHARGING WIRING ASSEMBLY

FAST IDLE SCREW

EEC III reference voltage is 8–10 volts, while EEC IV systems use a 5 volt reference signal. The calibration assembly is contained in a black plastic housing which plugs into the top of the processor assembly. It contains the memory and programming information used by the processor to determine optimum operating conditions. Different calibration information is used in different vehicle applications, such as California or Federal models. For this reason, careful identification of the engine, year, model and type of electronic control system is essential to insure correct component replacement.

ENGINE SENSORS

Air Charge Temperature Sensor (ACT)

The ACT is threaded into the intake manifold air runner. It is located behind the distributor on V6 engines and directly below the accelerator linkage on V8 engines. The ACT monitors air/fuel charge temperature and sends an appropriate signal to the ECA. This information is used to correct fuel enrichment for variations in intake air density due to temperature changes.

Barometric & Manifold Absolute Pressure Sensors (B/MAP)

The B/MAP sensor on V8 engines is located on the right fender panel in the engine compartment. The MAP sensor used on V6 engines is separate from the barometric sensor and is located on the left fender panel in the engine compartment. The barometric sensor signals the ECA of changes in atmospheric pressure and density to regulate calculated air flow into the engine. The MAP sensor monitors and signals the ECA of changes in intake manifold pressure which result from engine load, speed and atmospheric pressure changes.

Crankshaft Position (CP) Sensor

The purpose of the CP sensor is to provide the ECA with an accurate ignition timing reference (when the piston reaches 10° BTDC) and injector operation information (twice each crankshaft revolution). The crankshaft vibration damper is fitted with a 4 lobe "pulse ring." As the crankshaft rotates, the pulse ring lobes interrupt the magnetic field at the tip of the CP sensor.

EGR Valve Position Sensor (EVP)

This sensor, mounted on EGR valve, signals the computer of EGR opening so that it may subtract EGR flow from total air flow into the manifold. In this way, EGR flow is excluded from air flow information used to determine mixture requirements.

Engine Coolant Temperature Sensor (ECT)

The ECT is threaded into the intake manifold water jacket directly above the water pump bypass hose. The ECT monitors coolant temperature and signals the ECA, which then uses these signals for mixture enrichment (during cool operation), ignition timing and EGR operation. The resistance value of the ECT increases with temperature, causing a voltage signal drop as the engine warms up.

Exhaust Gas Oxygen Sensor (EGO)

The EGO is mounted in the right side exhaust manifold on V8 engines, in the left and right side exhaust manifolds on V6 models. The EGO monitors oxygen content of exhaust gases and sends a constantly changing voltage signal to the ECA. The ECA analyzes this signal and adjusts the air/fuel mixture to obtain the optimum (stoichiometric) ratio.

Knock Sensor (KS)

This sensor is used on various models equipped with the 3.8L V6 engine. It is attached to the intake manifold in front of the ACT sensor. The KS detects engine vibrations caused by preignition or detonation and provides information to the ECA, which then retards the timing to eliminate detonation.

Thick Film Integrated Module Sensor (TFI)

The TFI module sensor plugs into the distributor just below the distributor cap and replaces the CP sensor on some engines. Its function is to provide the ECA with ignition timing information, similar to what the CP sensor provides.

Throttle Position Sensor (TPS)

The TPS is mounted on the right side of the throttle body, directly connected to the throttle shaft. The TPS senses throttle movement and position and transmits an appropriate electrical signal to the ECA. These signals are used by the ECA to adjust the air/fuel mixture, spark timing and EGR operation according to engine load at idle, part throttle, or full throttle. The TPS is nonadjustable.

ON-CAR SERVICE

NOTE: *Diagnostic and test procedures on the EEC III and EEC IV electronic control systems require special test equipment. Have the testing done by a professional.*

Fuel Pressure Tests

The diagnostic pressure valve (Schrader type) is located at the top of the Fuel charging main body. This valve provides a convenient point for service personnel to monitor fuel pressure, bleed down the system pressure prior to maintenance, and to bleed out air which may become trapped in the system during filter replacement. A pressure gauge with an adapter is required to perform pressure tests.

CAUTION: *Under no circumstances should compressed air be forced into the fuel system using the diagnostic valve. Depressing the pin in the diagnostic valve will relieve system pressure by expelling fuel into the throttle body.*

System Pressure Test

Testing fuel pressure requires the use of a special pressure gauge (T80L-9974-A or equivalent) that attaches to the diagnostic pressure tap on the fuel charging assembly. Depressurize the fuel system before disconnecting any lines.

1. Disconnect fuel return line at throttle body (in-tank high pressure pump) or at fuel rail (in-line high pressure and in-tank low pressure pumps) and connect the hose to a one-quart calibrated container. Connect pressure gauge.

2. Disconnect the electrical connector to the fuel pump. The connector is located ahead of fuel tank (in-tank high pressure pump) or just forward of pump outlet (in-line high pressure pump). Connect auxiliary wiring harness to connector of fuel pump. Energize the pump for 10 seconds by applying 12 volts to the auxiliary harness connector, allowing the fuel to drain into the calibrated container. Note the fuel volume and pressure gauge reading.

3. Correct fuel pressure should be 35–45 psi (241–310 kPa). Fuel volume should be 10 ozs. in 10 seconds (minimum) and fuel pressure should maintain minimum 30 psi (206 kPa) immediately after pump cut-off.

If pressure condition is met, but fuel flow is not, check for blocked filter(s) and fuel supply lines. After correcting problem, repeat test procedure. If fuel flow is still inadequate, replace high pressure pump. If flow specification is met but pressure is not, check for worn or damaged pressure regulator valve on throttle body. If both pressure and fuel flow specifications are met, but pressure drops excessively after de-energization, check for leaking injector valve(s) and/or pressure regulator valve. If injector valves and pressure regulator valve are okay, replace high pressure pump. If no pressure or flow is seen in fuel system, check for blocked filters and fuel lines. If no trouble is found, replace in-line fuel pump, in-tank fuel pump and the fuel filter inside the tank.

Fuel Injector Pressure Test

1. Connect pressure gauge T80L-9974-A, or equivalent, to fuel pressure test fitting. Disconnect coil connector from coil. Disconnect electrical lead from one injector and pressurize fuel system. Disable fuel pump by disconnecting inertia switch or fuel pump relay and observe pressure gauge reading.

2. Crank engine for 2 seconds. Turn ignition OFF and wait 5 seconds, then observe pressure drop. If pressure drop is 2–16 psi (14–110 kPa), the injector is operating properly. Reconnect injector, activate fuel pump, then repeat the procedure for other injector.

3. If pressure drop is less than 2 psi (14 kPa)

or more than 16 psi (110 kPa), switch electrical connectors on injectors and repeat test. If pressure drop is still incorrect, replace disconnected injector with one of the same color code, then reconnect both injectors properly and repeat test.

4. Disconnect and plug vacuum hose to EGR valve. It may be necessary to disconnect the idle speed control (3.8L V6) or throttle kicker solenoid (5.0L V8) and use the throttle body stop screw to set engine speed. Start and run the engine at 1800 RPM (2000 rpm on 1984 and later models). Disconnect left injector electrical connector. Note rpm after engine stabilizes (around 1200 rpm). Reconnect injector and allow engine to return to high idle.

5. Perform same procedure for right injector. Note difference between rpm readings of left and right injectors. If difference is 100 rpm or less, check the oxygen sensor. If difference is more than 100 rpm, replace both injectors.

CFI COMPONENT TESTS

NOTE: *Complete CFI system diagnosis requires the use of special test equipment. Have the system tested professionally.*

Before beginning any component testing, always check the following:

• Check ignition and fuel systems to ensure there is fuel and spark.

• Remove air cleaner assembly and inspect all vacuum and pressure hoses for proper connection to fittings. Check for damaged or pinched hoses.

• Inspect all sub-system wiring harnesses for proper connections to the EGR solenoid valves, injectors, sensors, etc.

• Check for loose or detached connectors and broken or detached wires. Check that all terminals are sealed firmly and are not corroded. Look for partially broken or frayed wires or any shorting between wires.

• Inspect sensors for physical damage. Inspect vehicle electrical system. Check battery for full charge and cable connections for tightness.

• Inspect the relay connector and make sure the ECA power relay is securely attached and making a good ground connection.

High Pressure In-Tank Pump

Disconnect electrical connector just forward of the fuel tank. Connect voltmeter to body wiring harness connector. Turn key ON while watching voltmeter. Voltage should rise to battery voltage, then return to zero after about 1 second. Momentarily turn key to START position. Voltage should rise to about 8 volts while cranking. If voltage is not as specified, check electrical system.

High Pressure In-Line & Low Pressure In-Tank Pumps

Disconnect electrical connector at fuel pumps. Connect voltmeter to body wiring harness connector. Turn key ON while watching voltmeter. Voltage should rise to battery voltage, then return to zero after about 1 second. If voltage is not as specified, check inertia switch and electrical system. Connect ohmmeter to in-line pump wiring harness connector. If no continuity is present, check continuity directly at in-line pump terminals. If no continuity at in-line pump terminals, replace in-line pump. If continuity is present, service or replace wiring harness.

Connect ohmmeter across body wiring harness connector. If continuity is present (about 5 ohms), low pressure pump circuit is OK. If no continuity is present, remove fuel tank and check for continuity at in-tank pump flange terminals on top of tank. If continuity is absent at in-tank pump flange terminals, replace assembly. If continuity is present at in-tank pump but not in harness connector, service or replace wiring harness to in-tank pump.

Solenoid and Sensor Resistance Tests

All CFI components must be disconnected from the circuit before testing resistance with a suitable ohmmeter. Replace any component whose measured resistance does not agree with the specifications chart. Shorting the wiring harness across a solenoid valve can burn out the

CFI Resistance Specifications

Component	Resistance (Ohms)
Air Charge Temp (ACT)	
1981–83	1700–60,000
1984	1100–58,000
Coolant (ECT) Sensor	
1981–83	1100–8000
1984—Engine Off	1300–7700
1984—Engine On	1500–4500
Crank Position Sensor	100–640
FGB	30–70
EGR Vent Solenoid	30–70
Fuel Pump Relay	50–100
Throttle Kicker Solenoid	50–100
Throttle Position Sensor	
1981–83 Closed Throttle	3000–5000
1984 Closed Throttle	550–1100
Wide Open Throttle	More than 2100
TAB Solenoid	50–100
TAD Solenoid	50–100

circuitry in the ECA that controls the solenoid valve actuator. Exercise caution when testing solenoid valves to avoid accidental damage to ECA.

Electronic Multi-Point Injection (EFI)

DESCRIPTION

The Electronic Fuel Injector System (EFI) is classified as a multi-point, pulse time, mass air flow fuel injection system. Fuel is metered into the intake air stream in accordance with engine demand through four injectors mounted on a tuned intake manifold. A blow-through turbocharger system is utilized to reduce fuel delivery time and increase power.

An on board vehicle electronic engine control (EEC) computer accepts inputs from various engine sensors to compute the required fuel flow rate necessary to maintain a prescribed air/fuel ration throughout the entire engine operational range. The computer then outputs a command to the fuel injectors to meter the approximate quantity of fuel.

OPERATION

The fuel delivery sub-system consists of a high pressure, chassis mounted, electric fuel pump delivering fuel from the fuel tank through a 20 micron fuel filter to a fuel charging manifold assembly.

The fuel charging manifold assembly incorporates electrically actuated fuel injectors directly above each of the engine's four intake ports. The injectors, when energized, spray a metered quantity of fuel into the intake air stream.

A constant fuel pressure drop is maintained across the injector nozzles by a pressure regulator. The regulator is connected in series with the fuel injectors and positioned down stream from them. Excess fuel supplied by the pump, but not required by the engine, passes through the regulator and returns to the fuel tank through a fuel return line.

All injectors are energized simultaneously, once every crankshaft revolution. The period of time that the injectors are energized (injector "on time" or the pulse width) is controlled by the vehicles' Engine Electronic Control (EEC) computer. Air entering the engine is measured by a vane air flow meter located between the air cleaner and the fuel charging manifold assembly. This air flow information and input from various other engine sensors is used to compute the required fuel flow rate necessary to maintain a prescribed air/fuel ratio for the given engine operation. The computer de-

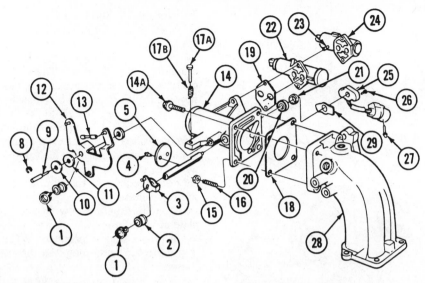

1. Spring—carburetor throttle return
2. Bushing—accelerator pump overtravel spring (2)
3. Lever—engine throttle
4. Screw—M4 × .7 × 8
5. Plate—air intake charge throttle
6. Shaft—air intake charge throttle
7. Spring—secondary throttle return
8. E-ring
9. Hub—throttle control
10. Spacer
11. Washer—nylon (2)
12. Lever—throttle control
13. Rod—engine secondary throttle control
14. Body—air intake charge throttle
14A. Bolt M8 × 1.25 × 30 hex flange head (2 req'd)
15. Nut—M8 (2 req'd)
16. Stud—M8 × 42.5 (2 req'd)
17A. Screw throttle stop
17B. Spring—throttle return control
18. Gasket—air charge control to intake manifold
19. Gasket—air bypass valve
20. Seal—throttle control shaft
21. Bushing—carburetor throttle shaft
22. Valve assembly—throttle air bypass
23. Bolt—M6 × 1.0 × 20 hex head flange
24. Valve assembly—throttle air bypass (alt.)
25. Potentiometer throttle position
26. Screw and washer assembly M4 × 22
27. Screw—M4 × 0.7 × 14.0 hex. washer tap
28. Manifold—intake upper
29. Gasket T.P.S.

4-140 engine—EFI components

termines the needed injector pulse width and outputs a command to the injector to meter the exact quantity of fuel.

COMPONENT DESCRIPTION

Fuel Injectors

The four fuel injector nozzles are electro-mechanical devices which both meter and atomize fuel delivered to the engine. The injectors are mounted in the lower intake manifold and are positioned so that their tips are directing fuel just ahead of the engine intake valves. The injector bodies consist of a solenoid actuated pintle and needle valve assembly. An electrical control signal from the Electronic Engine Control unit activates the injector solenoid causing the pintle to move inward off the seat, allowing fuel to flow. Since the injector flow orifice is fixed and the fuel pressure drop across the injector tip is constant, fuel flow to the engine is regulated by how long the solenoid is energized. Atomization is obtained by countouring

the pintle at the point where the fuel separates.

Fuel Pressure Regulator

The fuel pressure regulator is attached to the fuel supply manifold assembly downstream of the fuel injectors. It regulates the fuel pressure supplied to the injectors. The regulator is a diaphragm operated relief valve in which one side of the diaphragm senses fuel pressure and the other side is subjected to intake manifold pressure. The nominal fuel pressure is established by a spring preload applied to the diaphragm. Balancing one side of the diaphragm with manifold pressure maintains a constant fuel pressure drop across the injectors. Fuel, in excess of that used by the engine, is bypassed through the regulator and returns to the fuel tank.

Air Vane Meter Assembly

The air vane meter assembly is located between the air cleaner and the throttle body and is mounted on a bracket near the LH shock

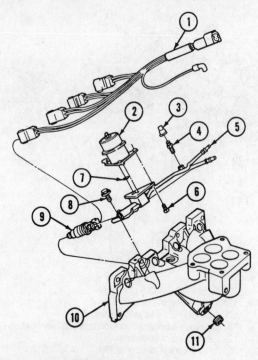

1. Wiring harness—fuel charging
2. Regulator assembly—fuel pressure
3. Cap—fuel pressure relief
4. Valve assembly—fuel pressure relief
5. Manifold assembly—fuel injection fuel supply
6. Screw—M5 × 0.8 × 10 socket head (3 req'd)
7. Seal—$\frac{5}{16}$ × .070 O-ring
8. Bolt (2 req'd)
9. Injector assembly—fuel (4 req'd)
10. Manifold—intake lower
11. Plug

4-140 engine—EFI components

tower. The vane air meter contains two sensors which furnish input to the Electronic Control Assembly—a vane airflow sensor and a vane air temperature. The air vane meter measures the mass of air flow to the engine. Air flow through the body moves a vane mounted on a pivot pin. This vane is connected to a variable resistor (potentiometer) which in turn is connected to a 5 volt reference voltage. The output of this potentiometer varies depending on the volume of air flowing through the sensor. The temperature sensor in the air vane meter measures the incoming air temperature. These two inputs, air volume and temperature, are used by the Electronic Control Assembly to compute the mass air flow. This valve is then used to compute the fuel flow necessary for the optimum air/fuel ratio which is fed to the injectors.

Air Throttle Body Assembly

The throttle body assembly controls air flow to the engine through a single butterfly-type valve.

The throttle position is controlled by conventional cable/cam throttle linkage. The body is a single piece die casting made of aluminum. It has a single bore with an air bypass channel around the throttle plate. This bypass channel controls both cold and warm engine idle airflow control as regulated by an air bypass valve assembly mounted directly to the throttle body. The valve assembly is an electromechanical device controlled by the EEC computer. It incorporates a linear actuator which positions a variable area metering valve.

Other features of the air throttle body assembly include:

• An adjustment screw to set the throttle plate at a minimum idle airflow position.
• A preset stop to locate the WOT position.
• A throttle body mounted throttle position sensor.
• A PCV fresh air source located up-stream of the throttle plate.
• Individual ported vacuum taps (as required) for PCV and EVAP control signals.

Fuel Supply Manifold Assembly

The fuel supply manifold assembly is the component that delivers high pressure fuel from the vehicle fuel supply line to the four fuel injectors. The assembly consists of a single preformed tube or stamping with four injector connectors, a mounting flange for the fuel pressure regulator, a pressure relief valve for diagnostic testing or field service fuel system pressure bleed down and mounting attachments which locate the fuel manifold assembly and provide fuel injector retention.

Air Intake Manifold

The air intake manifold is a two piece (upper and lower intake manifold) aluminum casting. Runner lengths are tuned to optimize engine torque and power output. The manifold provides mounting flanges for the air throttle body assembly, fuel supply manifold and accelerator control bracketry and the EGR valve and supply tube. Vacuum taps are provided to support various engine accessories. Pockets for the fuel injectors are machined to prevent both air and fuel leakage. The pockets, in which the injectors are mounted, are placed to direct the injector fuel spray immediately in front of each engine intake valve.

COMPONENT REMOVAL AND INSTALLATION

Fuel Charging Assembly

NOTE: *If any of the sub-assemblies are to be serviced and/or removed, with the fuel charging assembly mounted to the engine, the following steps must be taken.*

1. Make sure the ignition key is in the off position.
2. Drain the coolant from the radiator.
3. Disconnect the negative battery cable.
4. Remove the fuel cap to relieve fuel tank pressure.
5. Relieve the pressure from the fuel system at the pressure relief valve. Special tool T80L-9974-A or its equal is needed for this procedure.
6. Disconnect the fuel supply line.
7. Identify and disconnect the fuel return lines and vacuum connections.
8. Disconnect the injector wiring harness by disconnecting the ECT sensor in the heater supply tube, under the lower intake manifold.
9. Disconnect the air by-pass connector from EEC harness.

NOTE: *Not all assemblies may be serviceable while on the engine. In some cases, removal of the fuel charging assembly may facilitate service of the various sub-assemblies. To remove the entire fuel charging assembly, the following should be observed.*

10. Remove the engine air cleaner outlet tube between the vane air meter and air throttle body by loosening two clamps.
11. Disconnect and remove the accelerator and speed control cables (if so equipped) from the accelerator mounting bracket and throttle lever.
12. Disconnect the top manifold vacuum fitting connections by disconnecting:
    a. Rear vacuum line to the dash panel vacuum tree.
    b. Front vacuum line to the air cleaner and fuel pressure regulator.
13. Disconnect the PCV system by removing the following:
    a. Two large forward facing connectors on the throttle body and intake manifold.
    b. Throttle body port hose at the straight plastic connector.
    c. Canister purge line at the straight plastic connector.
    d. PCV hose at the valve cover.
    e. Unbolt the PCV separator support bracket from cylinder head and remove PCV system.
14. Disconnect the EGR vacuum line at the EGR valve.
15. Disconnect the EGR tube from the upper intake manifold by removing the two flange nuts.
16. Remove the dipstick and its tube.
17. Remove the fuel return line.
18. Remove six manifold mounting nuts.

19. Remove the manifold with wiring harness and gasket.
20. Installation is the reverse of removal. Tighten the manifold bolts 12–15 ft. lbs.

Fuel Pressure Regulator

NOTE: *Before attempting this procedure depressurize the fuel system.*

1. Remove the vacuum line at the pressure regulator.
2. Remove the three Allen retaining screws from the regulator housing.
3. Remove the pressure regulator, gasket and O-ring. Discard gasket and inspect O-ring for deterioration.

NOTE: *If scraping is necessary be careful not to damage the gasket surface.*

4. Installation is the reverse of removal. Lubricate the O-ring with light oil prior to installation. Tighten the three screws 27–40 inch lbs.

Fuel Injector Manifold Assembly

1. Remove the fuel tank cap. Release the pressure from the fuel system.
2. Disconnect the fuel supply and return lines.
3. Disconnect the wiring harness from the injectors.
4. Disconnect the vacuum line from the fuel pressure regulator valve.
5. Remove the two fuel injector manifold retaining bolts.
6. Carefully disengage the manifold from the fuel injectors. Remove the manifold.
7. Installation is the reverse of removal. Torque the fuel manifold bolts 15–22 ft. lbs.

Pressure Relief Valve

1. If the fuel charging assembly is mounted to engine, the fuel system must be depressurized.
2. Using an open end wrench or suitable deep well socket, remove the pressure relief valve from the injection manifold.
3. Installation is the reverse of removal. Torque the valve 48–84 inch lbs.

Throttle Position Sensor

1. Disconnect the throttle position sensor from the wiring harness.
2. Remove the two retaining screws.
3. Remove the throttle position sensor.
4. Installation is the reverse of removal. Torque the sensor screws 11–16 inch lbs.

NOTE: *This throttle position sensor is not adjustable.*

Ford Electronic Fuel Injection Troubleshooting

Symptom	Possible Problem Areas
Surging, backfire, misfire, runs rough	1. EEC distributor rotor registry ① 2. EGR solenoid(s) defective 3. Distributor, cap, body, rotor, ignition wires, plugs, coil defective 4. Pulse ring behind vibration damper misaligned or damaged 5. Spark plug fouling
Stalls on deceleration	1. EGR solenoid(s) or valve defective 2. EEC distributor rotor registry ①
Stalls at idle	1. Idle speed wrong 2. Throttle kicker not working
Hesitates on acceleration	1. Acceleration enrichment system defective 2. Fuel pump ballast bypass relay not working
Fuel pump noisy	1. Fuel pump ballast bypass relay not working
Engine won't start	1. Fuel pump power relay defective, no spark, EGR system defective, no or low fuel pressure 2. Crankshaft position sensor not seated, clearance wrong, defective 3. Pulse ring behind vibration damper misaligned, sensor tabs damaged 4. Power and ground wires open or shorted, poor electrical connections 5. Inertia switch tripped
Engine starts and stalls or runs rough	1. Fuel pump ballast wire defective 2. Manifold absolute pressure (MAP) sensor circuit not working 3. Low fuel pressure 4. EGR system problem 5. Microprocessor and calibration assembly faulty
Starts hard when cold	1. Cranking signal circuit faulty

Air Bypass Valve Assembly

1. Disconnect the air bypass valve assembly connector from the wiring harness.

2. Remove the two air bypass valve retaining screws.

3. Remove the air bypass valve and gasket.

NOTE: *If necessary to remove the gasket by scraping, be careful not to damage the gasket surface.*

4. Installation is the reverse of removal. Torque the air bypass valve assembly 71–102 inch lbs.

Air Intake Throttle Body

1. Remove four throttle body nuts. Make sure that the throttle position sensor connector and air by-pass valve connector have been disconnected from the harness. Disconnect air cleaner outlet tube.

2. Identify and disconnect vacuum hoses.

3. Remove throttle bracket.

4. Carefully separate the throttle body from the upper intake manifold.

5. Remove and discard the gasket between the throttle body and the upper intake manifold.

NOTE: *If scraping is necessary be careful not to damage gasket surfaces, or allow any material to drop into the manifold.*

6. Installation is the reverse of removal. Tighten the throttle body to upper intake manifold nuts 12–15 ft. lbs.

Upper Intake Manifold

1. Disconnect the air cleaner outlet tube from the air intake throttle body.

2. Unplug the throttle position sensor from the wiring harness.

3. Unplug the air by-pass valve connector.

4. Remove three upper manifold retaining bolts.

5. Remove upper manifold assembly.

6. Remove and discard the gasket from the lower manifold assembly.

NOTE: *If scraping is necessary be careful not to damage gasket surfaces, or allow any material to drop into the lower manifold.*

7. Installation is the reverse of removal. Tighten the upper intake manifold bolts 15–22 ft. lbs. Use a new gasket between the manifolds.

Fuel Injector

NOTE: *The fuel system must be depressurized prior to starting this procedure.*

1. Disconnect the fuel supply and return lines.

2. Remove the vacuum line from the fuel pressure regulator.

3. Disconnect the wiring harness.

4. Remove the fuel injector manifold assembly.

5. Carefully remove the connectors from the individual injectors.

6. Grasping the injectors body, pull up while gently rocking the injector from side to side.

7. Inspect the injector O-rings (two per injector) for signs of deterioration. Replace as needed.

8. Inspect the injector "plastic hat" (covering the injector pintle) and washer for signs of deterioration. Replace as needed. If a hat is missing, look for it in the intake manifold.

9. Installation is the reverse of removal. Lubricate all O-rings with a light oil. Carefully seat the fuel injector manifold assembly on the four injectors and secure the manifold with the attaching bolts. Torque the bolts 15–22 ft. lbs.

Vane Air Meter

1. Loosen the hose clamp which secures engine air cleaner outlet hose to the vane meter assembly.

2. Remove air intake and outlet tube from the air cleaner.

3. Disengage four spring clamps and remove air cleaner front cover and air cleaner filter panel.

4. Remove the two screw and washer assemblies which secure the air meter to its bracket. Remove the vane air meter assembly.

5. Installation is the reverse of removal.

DIESEL ENGINE FUEL SYSTEM

Injection Pump

REMOVAL AND INSTALLATION

1. Disconnect the battery ground cable. Drain the cooling system.

2. Remove the accessory drive belts.

3. Remove the fan and clutch assembly or electric motor and fan assembly.

4. Remove the camshaft drive belt.

5. Install Injection Pump Sprocket Aligning Pin T84P-9000-A or equivalent and remove nut and washer attaching sprocket to the injection pump.

6. Install puller T67L-3600-A or equivalent and remove the sprocket. Remove the woodruff key from pump shaft.

7. Disconnect the clamp attaching the oil dipstick tube to the intake manifold, and position out of the way.

8. Disconnect the turbo pressure indicator switch connector. Remove the diagnostic plug bracket and position out of the way.

9. Loosen the clamp attaching the turbo crossover pipe boot to the intake manifold.

10. Remove the nuts attaching the intake manifold to cylinder head, and remove the intake manifold.

NOTE: *To prevent fuel system contamination, cap all fuel lines and fittings.*

11. Disconnect and cap the nozzle fuel lines at nozzles.

12. Remove the injection nozzle lines from injection pump using Fuel Line Nut Wrench T84P-9396-A or equivalent. Install caps on each end of each fuel line and pump fitting as it is removed and identify each fuel line accordingly.

13. Disconnect the coolant hoses from the idle speed boost housing.

14. Disconnect the electrical connectors to the fuel shut-off and cold start accelerator valves, micro-switch and fuel pressure switch.

15. Disconnect the nozzle return line at the injectpon pump.

16. Disconnect the fuel return hose from the fuel return line on the left fender apron.

17. Disconnect the fuel inlet hose from the fuel inlet line on the left fender apron.

18. Disconnect the vacuum hoses at the altitude compensation valve. Note position of hoses, so they may be returned to the original position.

19. Disconnect the throttle cable and speed control cable, if equipped, from the injection pump.

20. Remove the three nuts attaching the injection pump to mounting bracket.

21. Remove the two nuts attaching the injection pump to the engine front cover, and remove the injection pump.

22. Install the injection pump in position. Line up the mark on the front cover with the mark on the injection pump mounting boss. Install attaching nuts and bolts. Tighten to 14–17 ft. lbs.

23. Connect the throttle cable, and speed control cable, if so equipped.

24. Remove the protective caps and install the fuel inlet hose to the fuel inlet line on left fender apron. Connect the fuel return hose to the fuel return line on the left fender apron.

25. Connect the vacuum hoses to the altitude compensation valve. Refer to the VECI decal. (underhood sticker).

26. Connect the nozzle return line to the injection pump.

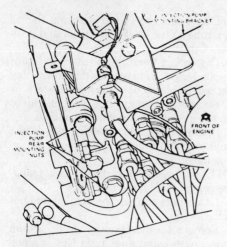

Injection pump rear mounting bolts—2.4L diesel engine

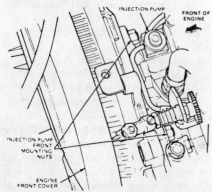

Injection pump front mounting bolts—2.4L diesel engine

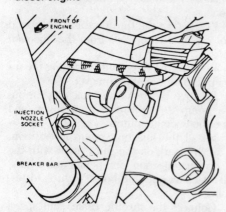

Injector nozzle removal and installation

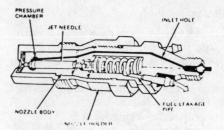

Injector nozzle

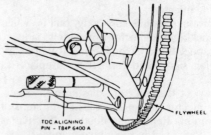

TDC aligning tool installation—2.4L diesel engine

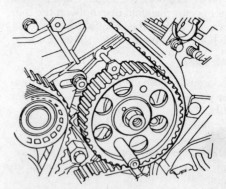

Injector pump aligning tool—2.4L diesel engine

27. Connect the electrical connectors to the fuel pressure sensor, micro-switch, cold start accelerator valve and fuel shut-off valve.

28. Connect the coolant hoses to the idle speed boost housing.

29. Install the fuel lines on injection pump, using Tool T84P-9396-A or equivalent, and tighten to 14–17 ft. lbs.

30. Connect the fuel lines to the nozzles and tighten to 14–17 ft. lbs.

31. Clean the intake manifold and cylinder head gasket mating surfaces. Position a new intake manifold gasket on the cylinder head, and install the intake manifold. Be sure the intake manifold inlet port is inserted into the turbo crossover pipe boot. Tighten attaching bolts to 14–17 ft. lbs. Tighten the clamp at the crossover pipe boot.

32. Install the diagnostic plug bracket on the cylinder head, and tighten to 14–17 ft. lbs.

33. Connect the turbo pressure indicator switch connector.

34. Position the oil dipstick tube to the intake manifold and install clamp.

35. Install the woodruff key in injection pump shaft.

36. Install the sprocket on injection pump. Install injection Pump Aligning Pin T84P-9000-

A or equivalent, in sprocket. Install the sprocket attaching washer and nut and tighten to 33–36 ft. lbs.

37. Install and adjust camshaft drive belt.

38. Install the camshaft drive belt cover and tighten to 6–7 ft. lbs.

39. Install fan and clutch assembly or electric motor and fan assembly.

40. Install and adjust the accessory drive belts.

41. Fill and bleed the cooling system.

42. Air bleed the fuel system.

43. Adjust the injection pump timing.

44. Connect the battery ground cable.

45. Start the engine and check for fuel, coolant and oil leaks.

46. Adjust the curb idle, fast idle and injection pump timing.

Fuel Shut-Off Valve
REMOVAL AND INSTALLATION

1. Disconnect the battery ground cable.

2. Remove the nut attaching the electrical connector to the shut-off valve and remove the connector.

3. Remove the shut-off valve.

CAUTION: *Piston and spring may fall out when removing valve.*

4. Replace the O-ring and valve, and install the valve on the injection pump. Tighten to 11–18 ft. lbs.

CAUTION: *Piston and spring may fall out when installing valve.*

5. Install the connector on the shut-off valve. Tighten nut to 3–3.5 ft. lbs.

6. Connect the battery ground cable. Run the engine and check for fuel leaks.

Injection Nozzles
REMOVAL AND INSTALLATION

1. Pull off the leak oil lines from the injector nozzles.

NOTE: *Make sure area around injector is clean.*

2. Remove the fuel lines at the injectors and at the fuel injection pump with Fuel Line Wrench T84P-9395-A or equivalent. Cap all fuel lines and openings as the fuel lines are removed.

3. Unscrew the fuel injectors with Injector Nozzle Socket T84P-9527-A or equivalent. Note injector order for installation.

NOTE: *On injectors with sensors, disconnect the sensor plug wires and guide sensor wires through Injector Nozzle Socket T84P-9527-A or equivalent, while installing tool on the injector.*

4. Plug the cylinder block injector nozzle opening.

5. Clean the injector nozzle opening in the cylinder block.

6. Install new heat shields into the injection nozzle openings.

7. Apply a copper based, anti-sieze compound to the injector nozzle threads. Remove the protective plug in the cylinder block and install injector nozzles in original positions with Injector Nozzle Socket T84P-9527-A or equivalent. Tighten to 30–33 ft. lbs.

NOTE: *On injectors with sensors, guide the sensor plug wire through socket before installing the injector nozzle. Reconnect the sensor wire after nozzle installation.*

8. Remove the protective caps from the fuel lines, injector pump and injector nozzles and install fuel lines using Fuel Line Wrench T84P-9396-A or equivalent. Tighten to 15–18 ft. lbs.

Injection Nozzle Fuel Lines
REMOVAL AND INSTALLATION

1. If all the fuel lines are being removed, remove the intake manifold, and then remove all the fuel lines as an assembly.

NOTE: *Do not remove the two clamps holding the fuel lines together.*

2. Remove fuel line(s) at the injector nozzles and at the fuel injection pump with Fuel Line Wrench T84P-9395-A or equivalent. Cap all fuel lines and openings as fuel lines are removed.

3. If only one fuel line is being removed, remove the clamps holding fuel lines together and remove the fuel line.

4. If the fuel lines are being installed as an assembly, remove the protective caps and install fuel lines (with clamps installed) to the injector nozzles and injection pump using Fuel Line Wrench T84P-9395-A or equivalent.

5. If only one fuel line is being installed, remove protective caps and position fuel line to the injector nozzle, and injection line using Fuel Line Wrench T84P-9395-A or equivalent. Install clamps holding the fuel lines together.

6. Install the intake manifold if it was previously removed.

Glow Plugs
REMOVAL AND INSTALLATION

1. Disconnect the battery ground cable.

2. Unscrew the glow plug electrical connection and remove the wire.

3. Remove the glow plug using a 12mm deepwell socket.

4. Coat the glow plug threads with a copper based, anti-seize compound.

5. Install the glow plug into the engine block using a 12mm deepwell socket.

6. Tighten the glow plug to 15–22 ft. lbs.

7. Connect the electrical wire to the glow plug with the nut and tighten to 3–4 ft. lbs.

8. Connect the battery ground cable.

Fuel Filter

REMOVAL AND INSTALLATION

1. Drain the fuel from the fuel filter by opening the vent screw on the top of the filter and then depressing the drain valve on the bottom of the filter.

2. Disconnect the Water-in-Fuel sensor connector.

3. Remove the filter cartridge using a standard oil filter wrench, if necessary.

4. Remove the protective cover.

5. Remove the drain valve from the old filter and install on the new filter.

6. Install the protective cover.

7. Coat the surface of the sealing gasket with engine oil and install the filter on the adapter. Turn the filter until the gasket contacts the sealing surface of the filter adapter.

8. Turn the filter an additional one-half turn.

9. Close the vent screw.

10. Start the engine and check for fuel leaks, tightening the filter further, if necessary.

Fuel Heater

REMOVAL AND INSTALLATION

1. Disconnect the water-in-fuel sensor connector, fuel temperature sensor and fuel heater connector.

2. Drain the fuel from the fuel filter by opening the vent screw on the top of the filter and depressing the drain valve on the bottom of the filter.

3. Remove the filter cartridge using a standard oil filter wrench, if necessary.

4. Remove the fuel lines from the fuel filter adapter.

5. Remove the two bolts retaining the fuel heater/filter adapter to the bracket, and remove from vehicle.

6. Unscrew the fuel heater assembly from the fuel filter adapter.

7. Coat the seal with engine oil and install the fuel heater on the fuel filter adapter.

8. Position the fuel filter adapter (with fuel heater attached) to the bracket and install with two bolts. Tighten to 29–40 ft. lbs.

9. Coat the surface of the sealing gasket with engine oil and install the filter on the adapter. Turn the filter until the gasket contacts the sealing surface of the filter adapter. Turn the filter an additional half turn.

10. Connect the Fuel-in-Water sensor, temperature sensor and fuel heater connectors.

11. Reconnect the fuel lines to the fuel filter and tighten the vent screw.

12. Start the engine and check for fuel leaks, tightening the filter further, if necessary.

Electric Fuel Pump

REMOVAL AND INSTALLATION

1. Disconnect the electric fuel pump electrical connector.

2. Remove the hose clamp on the inlet and outlet lines and remove the hoses from the fuel pump.

3. Remove the two fuel pump retaining screws and remove the fuel pump.

4. To install, reverse the removal steps. Tighten attaching screws to 9–11 ft. lbs.

HEATER

Non-Air Conditioned Cars

HEATER CORE REMOVAL AND INSTALLATION

Torino, Montego, Elite, LTD II, Cougar and Thunderbird Through 1979

1. Drain coolant.
2. Disconnect both heater hoses at the firewall.
3. Remove the nuts retaining the heater assembly to the firewall.
4. Disconnect temperature and defroster cables at heater.
5. Disconnect wires from resistor, and disconnect blower motor wires and clip retaining heater assembly to defroster nozzle.
6. Remove glove box.
7. Remove bolt and nut connecting the right air duct control to instrument panel. Remove nuts retaining right air duct and remove duct assembly.
8. Remove heater assembly to bench.

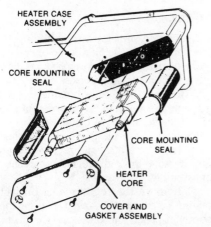

HEATER CASE ASSEMBLY

CORE MOUNTING SEAL

CORE MOUNTING SEAL

HEATER CORE

COVER AND GASKET ASSEMBLY

Typical heater core removal on all non-air conditioned cars, except 1981–82 Cougar

9. Open the case and remove the core.
10. Installation is the reverse of removal.

1981–82 Cougar

It is not necessary to remove the heater case for access to the heater core.

1. Drain enough coolant from the radiator to drain the heater core.
2. Loosen the heater hose clamps on the engine side of the firewall and disconnect the heater hoses. Cap the heater core tubes.
3. Remove the glove box liner.
4. Remove the instrument panel-to-cowl brace retaining screws and remove the brace.
5. Move the temperature lever to warm.
6. Remove the heater core cover screws. Remove the cover through the glove box.
7. Loosen the heater case mounting nuts on the engine side of the firewall.
8. Push the heater core tubes and seal toward the interior of the car to loosen the core.
9. Remove the heater core through the glove box opening.
10. Service as necessary, install in the reverse order of removal.

Thunderbird, XR7, LTD and Marquis—1980 and Later

1. Disconnect the negative battery cable.
2. Drain the cooling system.
3. Remove the instrument panel (see instrument panel removal and installation).
4. Disconnect the heater hoses from the heater core tubes. Plug the heater hoses and core tubes to prevent coolant spillage during removal.
5. Working under the hood at the firewall, remove the two nuts retaining the evaporator (heater) case to the dash.
6. From under the dash, remove the screws attaching the heater assembly support bracket and air inlet duct support bracket to the top cowl panel.

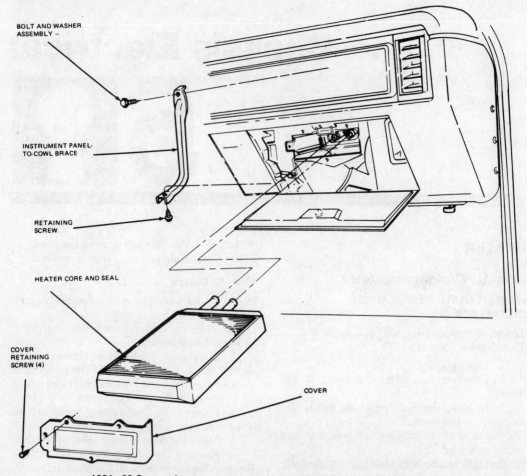

BOLT AND WASHER
ASSEMBLY —

INSTRUMENT PANEL-
TO-COWL BRACE

RETAINING
SCREW

HEATER CORE AND SEAL

COVER
RETAINING
SCREW (4)

COVER

1981–82 Cougar heater core removal on cars without air conditioning

7. Remove the nut retaining the bracket at the left end of the heater assembly to the dash panel, and the nut retaining the bracket below the case to the dash panel.

8. Carefully pull the heater assembly away from the dash panel to gain access to the screws that retain the heater core access cover to the evaporator (heater) case.

9. Remove the cover retaining screws and the cover.

10. Lift the heater core and seals from the case. Remove the seals from the core tubes.

11. Install the heater core in the reverse order of removal. Fill the system with the correct coolant mix.

BLOWER MOTOR REMOVAL AND INSTALLATION

The blower motor on all models except the 1980–82 Cougar XR-7, Thunderbird and 1982 Lincoln Continental is located inside the heater assembly. To replace the blower motor on all models except the 1980 and later Cougar XR-7 and Thunderbird, and 1981–82 Cougar, re-

move the heater assembly from the car. Once the heater assembly is removed, it is a simple operation to remove the motor attaching bolts and remove the motor. On all models except as noted, the motor and cage are removed as an assembly.

1981–82 Cougar

The right side ventilator assembly must be removed for access to the blower motor and wheel.

1. Remove the retaining screw for the right register duct mounting bracket.

2. Remove the screws holding the control cable lever assembly to the instrument panel.

3. Remove the glove box liner.

4. Remove the plastic rivets securing the grille to the floor outlet, and remove the grille.

5. Remove the right register duct and register assembly:

   a. Remove the register duct bracket retaining screw on the lower edge of the instrument panel, and disengage the duct from the opening and remove through the glove box opening.

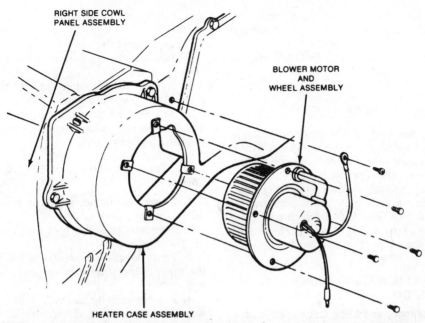

RIGHT SIDE COWL
PANEL ASSEMBLY

BLOWER MOTOR
AND
WHEEL ASSEMBLY

HEATER CASE ASSEMBLY

Typical blower motor removal on non-air conditioned cars, except 1981–82 Cougar

b. Insert a thin blade under the retaining tab and pry the tab toward the louvers until retaining tab pivot clears the hole in the register opening. Pull the register assembly end out from the housing only enough to prevent the pivot from going back into the pivot hole. Pry the other retaining tab loose and remove the register assembly from the opening.

6. Remove the retaining screws securing the ventilator assembly to the blower housing. The upper right screw can be reached with a long extension through the register opening; the upper left screw can be reached through the

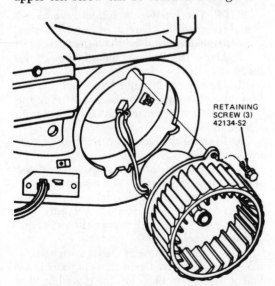

RETAINING
SCREW (3)
42134-S2

Blower motor removal on 1981–82 Cougar without air conditioning

glove box opening. The other two screws are on the bottom of the assembly.

7. Slide the assembly to the right, then down and out from under the instrument panel.

8. Remove the motor lead wire connector from the register and push it back through the hole in the case. Remove the right side cowl trim panel for access, and remove the ground terminal lug retaining screw.

9. Remove the hub clamp spring from the motor shaft and remove the blower wheel.

10. Remove the blower motor bolts from the housing and remove the motor.

Thunderbird, XR7, LTD and Marquis—1980 and Later

1. Disconnect the negative battery cable.

2. Remove the glove compartment and disconnect the hose from the outside-recirc door vacuum motor.

3. Remove the lower instrument panel right side to cowl attaching bolt.

4. Remove the screw attaching the support brace to the top of the air inlet duct.

5. Disconnect the blower motor power lead at the wire connector.

6. Remove the nut retaining the blower housing lower support bracket to the evaporator (heater) case.

7. Remove the screw attaching the top of the air inlet duct to the heater assembly.

8. Move the air duct and blower housing assembly down and away from the heater case.

9. Remove the air inlet duct and blower housing assembly from the vehicle.

10. Remove the blower motor mounting plate screws and remove the blower motor and wheel assembly from the housing.

11. Service as necessary. Install in the reverse order of removal.

Air-Conditioned Models

NOTE: *Removal of the heater-air conditioner (evaporator) housing, if necessary, requires evacuation of the air conditioner refrigerant. This operation requires special tools and training. Failure to follow proper safety precautions may cause personal injury. It is recommended that discharging and charging of the A/C system be performed by an experienced professional mechanic.*

HEATER CORE REMOVAL AND INSTALLATION

Torino, Montego, and Elite; Cougar through 1976

1. Drain the cooling system and disconnect the heater hoses at the core.

2. Remove the glove box.

3. Remove the two snap clips and the heater air outlet register from the plenum.

4. Remove the temperature control cable assembly mounting screw, and disconnect the end of the cable from the blend door crank arm.

5. Remove the blue and red vacuum hoses from the high-low door vacuum motor; the yellow hose from the panel-defrost door motor,

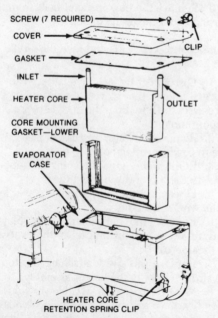

Typical heater core removal on air conditioned cars

and the brown hose from the inline tee connector.

6. Disconnect the wires at the resistor block.

7. Remove the ten screws and the rear half of the plenum.

8. Remove the mounting nut from the heater core tube support bracket.

9. Reverse the procedure to install, taking care to apply body sealer around the case flanges to insure a positive seal.

LTD II, Thunderbird through 1979, 1977–79 Cougar

1. Drain the engine coolant and disconnect the hoses from the core.

2. Remove the heater core cover plate, under the hood.

3. Press down on the core and tilt it toward the front of the vehicle to release it from the seal.

4. Pull the core up and out.

5. To install, press downward on the core and tilt it toward the rear to engage the notch on the seal with the flange on the housing. Replace any deformed sealer. Install all other parts.

1980–82 XR-7 and Thunderbird, 1982 Continental

Heater core removal and installation for air conditioned models is the same as the procedure given earlier for non-air conditioned models. It is not necessary to discharge the A/C system; simply pull the evaporator case far enough away from the firewall to reach the heater core cover screws.

Versailles

NOTE: *The refrigerant system components and charge do not have to be disturbed when removing and installing the heater core.*

1. Drain the coolant and disconnect the battery.

2. Disconnect 2 heater hose clamps at the firewall in the engine compartment. Plug the core tubes to prevent coolant leakage during removal.

3. Remove the heat distribution duct from the instrument panel.

4. On models through 1978, remove the seat belt interlock module and bracket.

5. Remove the glovebox liner.

6. Loosen the right door sill scuff plate, right A pillar trim cover, and remove the right cowl side trim panel.

7. Loosen instrument panel-to-right cowl side bolt and remove the instrument panel brace bolt at the lower rail, below the glove box.

8. On models with ATC, remove the instrument panel crash pad.

9. On models with ATC, remove the radio speaker or panel cowl brace.

10. Remove the 4 nozzle-to-cowl bracket mounting screws.

11. Lift the defroster nozzle upward through the crash pad opening.

12. Disconnect the vacuum hoses from the A/C-Defrost and Heat-Defrost door motors. Remove the screw from the clip holding the vacuum harness to the plenum.

13. Remove 2 Heat/Defrost door mounting nuts and swing the motor rearward on the door crankarm.

14. Remove 2 screws attaching the plenum to the left mounting bracket. Then remove the screws and clips securing the plenum to the evaporator case.

15. Swing the bottom of the plenum away from the evaporator case to disengage the S-clip on the forward flange of the Plenum. Raise the plenum to clear the tabs on the top of the evaporator case.

16. Move the plenum to the left as far as possible (about 4 inches), pulling rearward on the instrument panel to gain clearance. Take care when pulling back on the instrument panel to avoid cracking the plastic panel.

NOTE: *There is very little clearance between the plenum and the wiper motor assembly.*

17. Pull the heater core to the left using the tab molded into the rear heater core seal. As the rear surface of the heater core clears the evaporator case, pull the core rearward and downward to clear the instrument panel.

18. Reverse the procedure to install.

NOTE: *Before installing the core, make sure that the heater core tube to firewall seal is in place between the evaporator case and the firewall.*

1981–82 Cougar

The instrument panel must be removed for access to the heater core.

1. Disconnect the battery ground cable.

2. Remove the instrument panel pad:

a. Remove the screws attaching the instrument cluster trim panel to the pad.

b. Remove the screw attaching the pad to the panel at each defroster opening.

c. Remove the screws attaching the edge of the pad to the panel.

3. Remove the steering column opening cover.

4. Remove the nuts and bracket retaining the steering column to the instrument panel and lay the column against the seat.

5. Remove the instrument panel to brake pedal support screw at the column opening.

6. Remove the screws attaching the lower brace to the panel below the radio, and below the glove box.

7. Disconnect the temperature cable from the door and case bracket.

8. Unplug the 7-port vacuum hose connectors at the evaporator case.

9. Disconnect the resistor wire connector and the blower feed wire.

10. Remove the screws attaching the top of the panel to the cowl. Support the panel while doing this.

11. Remove the one screw at each end attaching the panel to the cowl side panels.

12. Move the panel rearward and disconnect the speedometer cable and any wires preventing the panel from lying flat on the seat.

13. Drain the coolant and disconnect the heater hoses from the heater core. Plug the core tubes.

14. Remove the nuts retaining the evaporator case to the firewall in the engine compartment.

15. Remove the case support bracket screws and air inlet duct support bracket.

16. Remove the nut retaining the bracket to the dash panel at the left side of the evaporator case, and the nut retaining the bracket below the case to the dash panel.

17. Pull the case assembly away from the panel to get to the screws retaining the heater core cover to the case.

18. Remove the cover screws and the cover.

19. Lift the heater core and seals from the evaporator case.

20. Service as required. Reinstall in the reverse order of removal.

Thunderbird, XR7, LTD and Marquis-1983 and later-Manual Air Conditioning

CAUTION: *This procedure requires the evacuation of the air conditioning system. This operation should not be attempted by anyone lacking the skill and experience to do so safely, as the freon gas can cause serious injury on contact. Have the system discharged, evacuated and recharged by a professional if in doubt.*

NOTE: *Heater core removal requires instrument panel and heater/evaporator case assembly removal.*

1. Disconnect the negative battery cable.

2. Remove the instrument panel (see instrument panel removal and installation).

3. Discharge the air conditioning system at the service access gauge port located on the suction line. See the CAUTION NOTICE at the beginning of this procedure.

4. Once the air conditioning system has been discharged, remove the high and low pressure hoses. Use a second wrench to hold

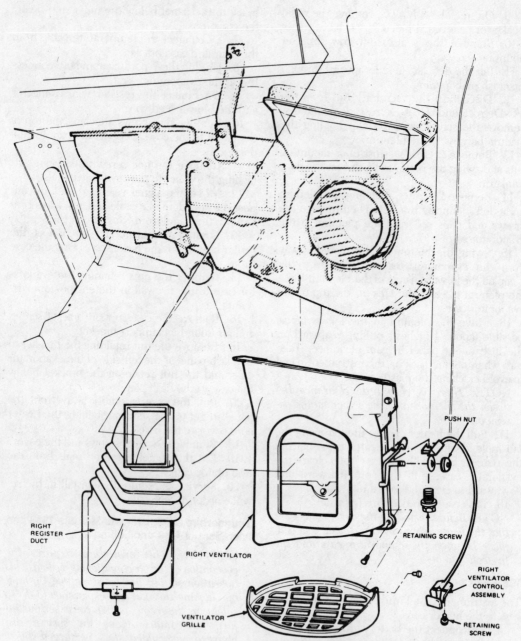

RIGHT
REGISTER
DUCT

RIGHT VENTILATOR

VENTILATOR
GRILLE

PUSH NUT

RETAINING SCREW

RIGHT
VENTILATOR
CONTROL
ASSEMBLY

RETAINING
SCREW

Right ventilator and register duct removal on non-air conditioned 1981–82 Cougar

the fittings when loosening the lines. Plug the hose openings to prevent dirt and moisture from entering.

5. Drain the cooling system and remove the heater hoses from the heater core tubes. Plug the hoses and the heater core tubes.

6. Remove the screw that attaches the air inlet duct and blower housing support brace to the cowl top panel under the dash.

7. Disconnect the vacuum supply hose from the in-line vacuum check valve in the engine compartment.

8. Disconnect the blower motor wiring connector.

9. From under the hood, remove the two nuts retaining the evaporator case to the fire-wall.

10. From under the dash, remove the screw attaching the evaporator case support bracket to the cowl top panel.

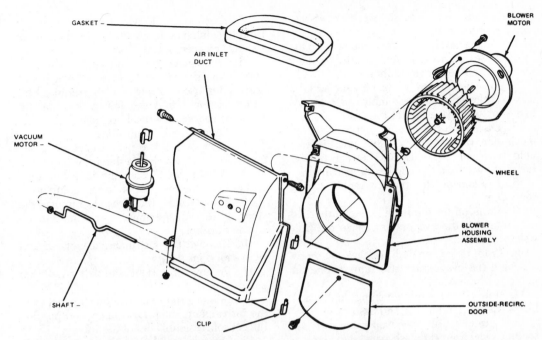

Air inlet duct and blower housing on air conditioned 1981–82 Cougar

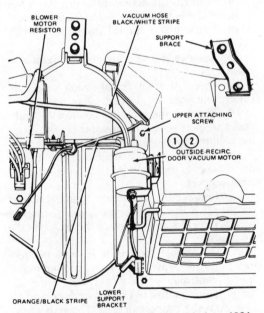

Air inlet and blower system assembled on 1981–82 Cougar

11. Remove the nut that retains the bracket below the evaporator case to the dash panel.

12. Carefully pull the evaporator case away from the dash panel and remove the case from the vehicle.

13. Remove the heater core access cover from the evaporator case.

14. Remove the heater core and seals from the case. Remove the seals from the core fitting tubes.

15. Service as required. Install in the reverse order of removal. Fill the cooling system with the correct coolant mix. Have the air-conditioning system charged. See the CAUTION NOTICE at the beginning of this procedure.

Continental (1983), Thunderbird, XR7, LTD and Marquis-1983 and later-Automatic Air Conditioning

CAUTION: *This procedure requires the evacuation of the air conditioning system. This operation should not be attempted by anyone lacking the skill and experience to do so safely, as the freon gas can cause serious injury on contact. Have the system discharged, evacuated, and recharged by a professional if in doubt.*

NOTE: *Core removal requires instrument panel and evaporator case assembly removal.*

1. Disconnect the negative battery cable.

2. Remove the instrument panel. (see instrument panel removal and installation).

3. Discharge the air conditioning system at the service access gauge port located on the suction line. See the CAUTION NOTICE at the beginning of this procedure.

4. Once the air conditioning system has been discharged, remove the high and low pressure hoses. Use a second wrench to hold the receiver fittings when loosening the lines.

Plug the hose openings to prevent dirt and moisture from entering.

5. Drain the cooling system and remove the heater hoses from the heater core tubes. Plug the hoses and heater core tubes.

6. Remove the screw attaching the air inlet duct and blower housing assembly support brace to the top cowl panel under the dash.

7. Disconnect the vacuum supply hose from the in-line vacuum check valve and the vacuum hose from the TBL (Thermal Blower Lockout Switch) in the engine compartment.

8. Disconnect the blower motor wiring connector.

9. From under the hood, remove the two nuts retaining the evaporator case to the firewall.

10. From under the dash, remove the screw attaching the evaporator case support bracket to the cowl top panel.

11. Remove the screw retaining the bracket below the evaporator case and dash panel.

12. Carefully pull the evaporator case assembly away from the dash panel and remove the assembly from the vehicle.

13. Remove the heater core access cover screws and the cover.

14. Lift the heater core and seals from the case assembly.

15. Remove the seals from the core.

16. Service as required. Install in the reverse order of removal. Fill the cooling system with the correct mixture of coolant. Have the air conditioning system recharged. See CAUTION NOTICE at the beginning of this procedure.

Mark VII-1984 and later-Automatic Air Conditioning

CAUTION: *This procedure requires discharge of the air conditioning system. This operation should not be attempted by anyone lacking the skill and experience to do so safely, as the freon gas can cause serious injury on contact. Have the system discharged, evacuated and recharged by a professional if in doubt.*

NOTE: *Heater core removal requires instrument panel and heater/evaporator case assembly removal.*

1. Disconnect the negative battery cable and drain the cooling system.

2. Discharge the refrigerant from the air conditioning system. See the CAUTION NOTICE at the beginning of this procedure.

3. Remove the air cleaner assembly from the engine.

4. Disconnect the heater hoses from the heater core tubes at the firewall. Plug the heater hoses and core tubes.

5. Disconnect the wire harness connector from the clutch cycling switch located on top of the suction accumulator/drier.

6. Disconnect the liquid line and the accumulator/drier inlet tube from the evaporator core tubes. New O-rings will be required for re-installation. Hold the line connection fittings with a second wrench to prevent damage. Plug all lines after disconnecting.

7. Remove the two nuts retaining the accumulator/drier bracket to the firewall.

8. Position the drier and the liquid line aside and remove the two evaporator retaining nuts.

9. From inside the vehicle, remove the steering column opening cover from the instrument panel.

10. Remove the instrument panel left and right sound insulators.

11. Remove the right and left cowl trim panels.

12. Remove the right side finish panel from the instrument panel. Disconnect and position the console assembly out of the way.

13. Carefully pry the defroster opening grille from the instrument panel.

14. Remove the screw attaching the lower center of the instrument panel to the floor brace.

15. Remove the shroud from the steering column.

16. Remove the steering column reinforcement.

17. Disconnect the transmission gear indicator cable from the steering column.

18. Remove the steering column to brake pedal support retaining nuts and lay the steering column down against the front seat.

19. Remove the nut attaching the instrument panel to the brake pedal and steering column support.

20. Remove the instrument panel attaching screws. Pull the panel forward and disconnect wire connectors etc. and place the panel on the front seat.

21. Disconnect the wiring harness connectors from the blower motor and blower motor speed controller. Disconnect the automatic temperature control (ATC) sensor hose and elbow from the evaporator case. Disconnect the ATC harness at the control assembly.

22. Disconnect the antenna cable from the radio and the strap retaining the cable to the evaporator case.

23. Disconnect the rear seat duct adaptor from the floor duct.

24. Remove the bolts attaching the evaporator case to the panel and remove the evaporator assembly from the vehicle.

25. Remove the screws attaching the heater core access cover from the evaporator case. Remove the cover. Lift the heater core and seals

from the evaporator case. Remove the seals from the core tubes. Service as required.

26. Position the evaporator assembly in position and install the three mounting bolts but do not tighten at this time. Be sure that the evaporator drain tube is through the dash opening and is not pinched or kinked.

27. Install the two evaporator case mounting nuts at the firewall under the hood. Tighten the three mounting bolts inside the vehicle that were previously installed.

28. Position the instrument panel near the dash panel (firewall) and connect the radio antenna, ATC harness, blower motor and controller harnesses, and the ATC sensor hose and elbow and all other instrument harness connectors that were removed.

29. Position the instrument panel and secure, be sure that the A/C plenum, attached to the instrument panel, is aligned and sealed at the evaporator case opening.

30. Install the nut retaining the instrument panel to the brake pedal and steering column support. Position the steering column to the brake pedal and column support bracket and install the retaining nuts.

31. Connect the transmission gear selector indicator cable and adjust if necessary.

32. Install the steering column opening reinforcement. Install the steering column shroud. Install the screw that attaches the lower center of the instrument panel to the floor brace.

33. Install the defroster grille. Install the right and left side cowl trim panels. Install the right and left side instrument panel sound insulators.

34. Install the rear seat heater duct assembly. Install the console assembly. Install the instrument panel right side finish panel and the steering column opening cover.

35. Install the remaining components in the reverse order of removal. Have the A/C system recharged (see the CAUTION NOTICE at the beginning of this procedure) and check system operation.

Continental-1984 and later-Automatic Air Conditioning

CAUTION: *This procedure requires the evacuation of the air conditioning system. This operation should not be attempted by anyone lacking the skill and experience to do so safely, as the freon gas can cause serious injury on contact. Have the system discharged, evacuated and recharged by a professional if in doubt.*

NOTE: *Heater core removal requires instrument panel and heater/evaporator case assembly removal.*

1. Disconnect the negative battery cable and drain the cooling system.

2. Discharge the refrigerant from the air conditioning system. See the CAUTION NOTICE at the beginning of this procedure.

3. Remove the air cleaner assembly from the engine.

4. Disconnect the heater hoses at the heater core tubes. Plug the hoses and core tubes.

5. Disconnect the wiring harness connector from the clutch cycling pressure switch located on top of the suction accumulator/drier.

6. Disconnect the liquid line and the accumulator/drier inlet tube from the evaporator core tubes. New O-rings will be required for re-installation. Hold the connector fitting with a second wrench to prevent damage while disconnecting the lines. Cap the lines.

7. Remove the two nuts retaining the drier bracket to the firewall. Position the drier and lines out of the way. Remove the two nuts that mount the evaporator to the firewall.

8. From inside the vehicle, remove the steering column opening cover from the instrument panel.

9. Remove the instrument panel right and left sound insulators.

10. Remove the right and left side cowl trim panels.

11. Remove the ash tray receptacle from the instrument panel. Remove the two screws attaching the lower center of the instrument panel to the floor brace.

12. Remove the shroud from the steering column and disconnect the transmission gear indicator cable from the steering column.

13. Remove the instrument panel pad. Remove the steering column to brake pedal support retaining nuts and lower the steering column to the front seat.

14. Remove the nut attaching the instrument panel to the brake pedal and steering column support.

15. Remove the instrument panel attaching screws and lay the panel on the front seat after disconnecting the necessary wire harness connectors.

16. Disconnect the wiring harness connectors from the blower motor wires and the blower motor speed controller.

17. Disconnect the automatic temperature control (ATC) sensor hose and elbow from the evaporator case.

18. Disconnect the ATC harness at the control assembly.

19. Disconnect the radio antenna cable from the radio and from the retaining strap.

20. Use a sharp knife and carefully slit the

carpet on the top of the transmission tunnel. Fold back the carpet to expose the rear seat heater duct.

21. Use a saw or hot knife to cut the top and side of the duct. Remove the top of the duct.

22. Remove the three evaporator case mounting bolts and remove the evaporator assembly.

23. Remove the screws that retain the heater core access cover. Remove the cover. Lift the heater core and tube seals from the evaporator case. Service the assembly as required.

24. Position the evaporator assembly to the dash (firewall) panel and install the three mounting bolts but do not tighten them at this time.

25. Make sure that the evaporator drain tube is through the opening in the dash and is not pinched or kinked. Install and tighten the two evaporator case mounting nuts on the firewall in the engine compartment.

26. Tighten the three case mounting bolts inside the vehicle.

27. Place the top piece that was cut from the rear seat heat duct into position and secure with duct tape. Be sure to cover all seams to prevent air leakage. Position the carpet back over the duct.

28. Position the instrument panel near the dash (firewall) and connect the radio antenna, ATC harness, blower motor and controller harnesses, ATC sensor hose and elbow and all other harness connectors removed from the instrument panel.

29. Position the instrument panel and secure with the mounting screws. Be sure that the A/C plenum, attached to the instrument panel, is properly aligned and sealed at the evaporator outlet opening.

30. Install the nut that attaches the instrument panel to the brake pedal and steering column support.

31. Position the steering column to the brake pedal and column support and install the retaining nuts.

32. Connect the transmission gear selector indicator cable and adjust if necessary.

33. Install the steering column opening reinforcement. Install the steering column shroud.

34. Install the two screws to attach the lower center of the instrument panel to the floor brace. Install the right and left side cowl trim panels.

35. Install the right and left side instrument panel sound insulators. Install the instrument panel pad. Install the steering column opening cover.

36. Install the remaining components in the reverse order of removal. Have the A/C system recharged (see the CAUTION NOTICE at the beginning of this procedure) and check system operation.

BLOWER MOTOR REMOVAL AND INSTALLATION

Torino, Montego, Elite; Cougar Through 1976

1. Disconnect the battery and take out the glove box.

2. Remove the recirculating air duct. On 1975 and later models, remove the instrument panel pad and side cowl trim.

3. Remove the screws which attach the blower lower housing to the firewall and bracket.

4. Disconnect the vacuum line from the actuator and move it out of the way.

5. Disconnect the plug from the resistor block and lift out the resistor block.

6. Remove all blower housing flange screws, separate blower housing halves, and unscrew and remove blower assembly.

7. Remove the blower wheel.

8. Install the blower wheel on the motor.

9. Install the motor and shell and ground wire in the case.

10. Install blower assembly into lower housing, and reassemble housing.

11. Connect the wires.

12. Fasten the resistor block to the plenum.

13. Install the recirculating air duct.

14. Install the screws which attach the blower lower housing to the firewall and bracket.

15. Install the glove box and connect the battery. Install the pad and trim.

1977–79 Cougar, LTD II and Thunderbird

1. Remove the two screws from around the instrument cluster opening, the screw above the steering column and the two screws from above the glove box door.

2. Remove the screw from the top right surface of the upper finish panel.

3. Pull the panel pad rearward then up to disengage the clips.

4. Remove the glove box.

5. Remove the side cowl trim panel.

6. Remove the instrument panel attachment on the right side.

7. Remove the blower housing-to-dash attaching nut in the engine compartment and the one in the passenger compartment.

8. Disconnect the outside air recirculating door vacuum hose and the blower motor wiring.

9. Remove the blower assembly and remove the motor and the wheel as an assembly.

10. Reverse to install.

Versailles

1. Disconnect the negative battery cable.

2. Loosen the passenger side door sill scuff plate and the right A pillar trim cover. Remove the right cowl side trim panel.

3. Remove the bolt retaining the lower side

of the instrument panel to the cowl. Remove the right cowl side brace bolt.

4. Disconnect the wiring harness connectors at the blower motor.

5. If so equipped, remove the cooling tube from the blower motor.

6. Remove the 4 screws retaining the blower motor and wheel assembly to the scroll. To remove the motor, pull rearward on the lower edge of the instrument panel to provide clearance. Do not remove the mounting plate from the blower motor.

7. Installation is the reverse of removal. If necessary, cement the cooling tube to the blower motor.

1980–82 Cougar XR-7 and Thunderbird 1981–82 Cougar, 1982 Continental

The air inlet duct and blower housing assembly must be removed for access to the blower motor.

1. Remove the glove box liner and disconnect the hose from the vacuum motor.

2. Remove the instrument panel lower right side to cowl attaching bolt.

3. Remove the screw attaching the brace to the top of the air inlet duct.

4. Disconnect the motor wire.

5. Remove the housing lower support bracket to case nut.

6. Remove the side cowl trim panel and remove the ground wire screw.

7. Remove the attaching screw at the top of the air inlet duct.

8. Remove the air inlet duct and housing assembly down and away from the evaporator case.

9. Remove the four blower motor mounting plate screws and remove the blower motor and wheel as an assembly from the housing. Do not remove the mounting plate from the motor.

Thunderbird, XR7, LTD and Marquis-1983 and later-Manual Air Conditioning

NOTE: *Follow the previous procedure for 1980–82 models.*

Continental, Thunderbird, XR7, LTD and Marquis-1983 and later-Automatic Air Conditioning

1. Remove the glove compartment (and shield on Continental models) and disconnect the hose from the outside recir door vacuum motor.

2. Remove the instrument panel lower right side to side cowl attaching bolt.

3. Remove the screw attaching the support brace to the top of the air duct.

4. Disconnect the power lead for the blower motor at the wire connector.

5. Remove the nut retaining the blower

motor housing lower support bracket to the evaporator case.

6. Remove the side cowl trim panel. On Continental models; open the ash tray and remove the receptacle and remove the two screws attaching the instrument panel to the transmission tunnel at the ashtray opening.

7. Remove the screw attaching the top of the air inlet duct to the evaporator case.

8. Move the air inlet duct and blower housing assembly down and away from the evaporator case. Remove the assembly.

9. Remove the blower plate mounting screws and remove the blower motor and wheel assembly.

10. Service as required. Install in the reverse order of removal.

Instrument Cluster
REMOVAL AND INSTALLATION

CAUTION: *Extreme care must be exercised during the removal and installation of the instrument cluster and dash components to avoid damage or breakage. Wooden paddles should be used to separate dash components, if required. Tape or cover dash areas that may be damaged by the removal and installation of the dash components.*

NOTE: *During the removal and installation procedures, slight variations may be required from the general outline, to facilitate the removal and installation of the instrument panel and cluster components, due to slight changes from model year to model year.*

1971

1. Disconnect the battery.

2. Remove one retaining screw from the lower edge of the dash pad at the left of the instrument cluster.

3. Remove the five pad-to-instrument panel screws across the bottom edge of the pad to the right of the cluster.

4. Pull the pad and retainer assembly free from the clips on the instrument panel.

5. Disconnect the speaker and remove the pad.

6. Remove the four screws that retain the cluster to the panel and move the cluster part way out of the panel.

7. Disconnect the speedometer cable, the multiple plug which goes to the printed circuit and the feed plug which services the tachometer or clock, if so equipped.

8. Disengage the three light bulb and socket assemblies from their receptacles.

9. Disconnect the cable and the five vacuum hoses from the heater control, and feed plug to the heater control switch and the connector to the heater control light.

10. Remove the cluster. Reverse the procedure to install.

1972

1. Disconnect the battery ground cable.
2. Remove the three upper and four lower retaining screws from the instrument cluster trim cover and remove the trim cover.
3. Remove the two upper and two lower screws retaining the instrument cluster to the instrument panel.
4. Pull the cluster away from the instrument panel; disconnect the speedometer cable connector.
5. Disconnect the cluster feed plug from its receptacle in the printed circuit.
6. Remove the belts and park light sockets from the receptacles (if so equipped).
7. On vehicles equipped with the performance cluster, disconnect the clock and tachometer wire loom at the connector.
8. Remove the cluster from the vehicle.
9. Install the "belts" and "park" light sockets into their proper receptacles, if so equipped. On vehicles equipped with the performance cluster, connect the clock and tachometer wire loom at the connector.
10. Connect the instrument cluster multiple connector to the printed circuit.
11. Align the speedometer cable connector with the speedometer adaptor and push the speedometer cable on the speedometer with a twisting motion until the catch is engaged.
12. Position the cluster to the instrument panel.
13. Install the four cluster retaining screws.
14. Position the cluster front trim cover and install the seven retaining screws.
15. Connect the battery ground cable.

1973–77

1. Disconnect the negative battery cable.
2. Remove the steering column cover.
3. Disconnect the speedometer cable and the wire plugs to the printed circuit.
4. Remove the cluster trim cover.
5. Remove the screw attaching the transmission selector lever indicator cable to the column.
6. Remove the instrument cluster retaining screws and lift the cluster from the instrument panel.
7. Reverse the above procedure to install, taking care to ensure that the selector pointer is aligned.

1978–80 Lincoln Continental, 1980 and Later Mark VI

1. Disconnect the battery ground cable.
2. Remove the lower steering column cover.

3. Remove the instrument cluster trim cover. 1979 and later, remove the bottom half of the steering column shroud.
4. Reach behind the cluster and disconnect the cluster electrical feed plug and the speedometer cable.
5. Unsnap and remove the steering column shroud cover, if not previously done. Disconnect the transmission indicator cable from the tab in the shroud retainer.
6. Remove the attaching screw for the transmission indicator cable bracket to steering column. Disconnect the cable loop from the pin on the steering column.
7. Remove the cluster retaining screws and remove the cluster assembly.
8. The installation is the reverse of the removal procedure.

AUXILIARY INSTRUMENT CLUSTER

1. Remove the main instrument cluster as previously outlined.
2. Remove the auxiliary cluster housing trim from the instrument panel.
3. Disconnect the electrical connection from the rear of the cluster.
4. Remove the auxiliary instrument cluster from the rear, through the opening of the removed main instrument cluster.
5. The installation is the reverse of the removal procedure.

1978–79 Mark V

1. Disconnect the negative battery cable.
2. Remove the three screws retaining the upper access cover to the instrument panel pad.
3. Remove one screw retaining the lower cluster applique cover below the instrument panel.
4. Remove the steering column shroud.
5. Remove the heated rear window control knob.
6. From under the instrument panel, depress the headlamp switch knob and shaft release button and pull the knob and shaft from the light switch.
7. Remove the headlamp switch bezel, the wiper/washer control knob and bezel.
8. Remove the cigar lighter from its socket and remove the four screws retaining the cluster front cover.
9. Using a standard right angle screwdriver, gradually withdraw the studs in sequence along the edges of the finish panel.
10. Remove the cluster front cover.
11. Remove one screw attaching the shift quadrant control cable bracket to the steering column and disconnect the cable while the transmission selector is in the "PARK" position.

12. Reach under the instrument panel and disconnect the speedometer cable.

13. Remove the cluster to instrument panel retaining screws and pull the cluster away from the instrument panel.

14. Disconnect the electrical connectors and tilt the cluster out, bottom first, and move the cluster towards the center of the vehicle and remove.

15. The installation of the cluster is the reverse of the removal procedure.

1978–79 Thunderbird, LTD II and Cougar

STANDARD CLUSTER

1. Disconnect the negative battery cable.

2. Remove the instrument cluster trim cover and attaching screws.

3. Remove the clock or cover attaching screws. Remove the clock or cover.

4. Remove the retaining screws from the instrument cluster to instrument panel.

5. Pull the cluster away from the instrument panel and disconnect the speedometer cable and the cluster electrical connector.

6. Remove the cluster from the instrument panel.

7. The installation is the reverse of the removal procedure.

PERFORMANCE CLUSTER

1. Disconnect the negative battery cable.

2. Remove the instrument cluster trim cover and attaching screws.

3. Remove the instrument cluster retaining screws, pull the cluster away from the panel and disconnect both the speedometer cable and the cluster electrical connector.

4. Disconnect the overlay harness connector and remove the cluster from the dash.

5. The installation is the reverse of the removal procedure.

1980 and Later Thunderbird, Cougar XR-7 and Continental

1. Disconnect the negative battery cable.

2. Disconnect the speedometer cable (Standard cluster).

3. Remove the instrument panel trim cover and steering column lower shroud.

4. Remove the cluster retaining screws (Electronic cluster).

5. Remove the attaching screw from the transmission indicator quadrant cable bracket to the steering column. Disconnect the cable loop from the pin on the steering column.

6. Remove the cluster retaining screws (Standard cluster).

7. Pull the cluster away from the instrument panel and disconnect the speedometer cable (Electronic cluster).

8. Disconnect the electrical connections from the cluster. Disconnect the ground wire (Electronic cluster).

9. Remove the cluster from the instrument panel.

10. Reverse the removal procedure to install.

1981 and Later Cougar

NOTE: *Certain special ordered cluster assemblies have two printed circuits.*

1. Disconnect the battery negative cable.

2. Remove the steering column shroud and the cluster trim cover.

3. Remove one screw from the shift quadrant control cable bracket to steering column and disconnect the cable loop from the pin on the shift cane lever. Remove the plastic clamp from around the steering column.

4. Remove the retaining screws holding the cluster to the instrument panel.

5. Pull the cluster away from the instrument panel and disconnect the speedometer cable. Disconnect the electrical connectors and remove the cluster from the dash.

6. To install the cluster, reverse the removal procedure.

Versailles

1. Disconnect the negative battery cable.

2. Remove the retaining screws from the lower cluster applique cover, below the steering column.

3. Remove the steering column shroud.

4. From under the instrument panel, release the headlamp switch control knob and shaft assembly.

5. Remove the threaded headlight switch bezel.

6. Remove the retaining screws from the cluster front cover.

7. Insert a right angle standard tip screwdriver along the edges of the finish panel, withdrawing the studs in sequence gradually around the outer edge of the panel.

8. Remove the cluster front cover.

9. If the vehicle is equipped with automatic transmission, remove one screw attaching the shift quadrant control cable bracket to the steering column. Disconnect the cable loop from the pin on the steering column.

10. From under the instrument panel, disconnect the speedometer cable.

11. Remove the retaining screws and pull the cluster away from the instrument panel.

12. Disconnect the electrical connectors from the rear of the cluster.

13. Remove the cluster from the instrument panel.

14. To install the cluster, reverse the removal procedure.

1983 and Later LTD, Marquis

STANDARD CLUSTER

1. Disconnect the negative battery cable.
2. Disconnect the speedometer cable. Remove the screws retaining the cluster trim panel and remove the panel.
3. Remove the steering wheel shroud. Remove the screw retaining the shift indicator control cable to the steering column. Disconnect the indicator cable loop from the shift lever pin. Remove the plastic clamp from the steering column.
4. Remove the cluster retaining screws. Disconnect the cluster feed plug from the printed circuit. Disconnect the engine warning lamp.
5. Remove the instrument cluster.
6. Install the cluster in the reverse order of removal.

ELECTRONIC CLUSTER

1. Disconnect the negative battery cable.
2. Remove the screws retaining the lower instrument cluster trim panel. Remove the steering column cover.
3. Remove the screws retaining the instrument cluster to the instrument panel.
4. Remove the screw attaching the transmission indicator cable bracket to the steering column. Disconnect the cable loop from the pin on the steering column.
5. Carefully pull the instrument cluster away from the panel and disconnect the speedometer cable. Disconnect the cluster feed plug and ground receptacle from the cluster back plate.
6. Remove the cluster assembly.
7. Install the cluster in the reverse order of removal.

Instrument Panel

NOTE: *For Continental and Mark VII models, refer to the instructions under Automatic Air Conditioning Heater Core Removal.*

REMOVAL AND INSTALLATION

1983 and Later—Thunderbird/Cougar (Manual A/C)

1. Disconnect the ground cable from battery.
2. Remove the three screws attaching steering column opening cover to instrument panel. Then, pull the panel rearward to disengage the clips and remove the cover.
3. Remove the three screws attaching the reinforcement to the instrument panel below the steering column opening and remove the reinforcement.
4. Remove the two nuts retaining the hood latch release handle mounting bracket to the brake pedal support below the steering column.
5. Remove the sound insulator from under left side of the instrument panel.
6. Remove the two nuts retaining the steering column clamp to the brake pedal support and allow the steering column to rest on the seat.
7. Remove the instrument panel pad.
8. Disconnect the speedometer cable from the speedometer head.
9. Remove the two screws attaching the console tray (automatic transmission) or console cover around the gear shift lever (manual transmission) to the console. Then, remove the tray or cover from the console.
10. Remove the four console switch panel cover attachment screws. Disconnect the switch wires and remove the switch panel.
11. Open the console box cover and remove the two screws from the bottom of the console box and the two screws from the top front of the box.
12. Remove the two screws attaching front end of the console to the lower edge of the instrument panel.
13. Remove the two screws attaching the bracket at the front end of console and lower the edge of the instrument panel to the floor pan. Then, lift the rear end of the console and pull the console rearward to disengage it from the instrument panel. Position the console out of the way.
14. Remove the two plastic push pins attaching the glove box door straps to the glove box. Allow the glove box and door to hang by the hinge.
15. Remove the one bolt attaching instrument panel brace to the instrument panel at the glove box opening.
16. Remove the one nut attaching the lower edge of the instrument panel to the brake pedal support.
17. Remove the one bolt attaching a second instrument panel brace to the lower edge of instrument panel just to the left of the console extension.
18. Remove the one bolt attaching each end of the instrument panel to the cowl side panel.
19. Support the instrument panel and remove the three screws attaching top edge of instrument panel to cowl top panel.
20. Cover the steering column and seats. Then, carefully position the instrument panel toward seat disconnecting wires and vacuum

harness as necessary. Allow instrument panel to rest on front seat.

21. Place the instrument panel in position and connect any wires and vacuum harness that were disconnected during instrument panel removal. Then, install the three screws to attach top edge of instrument panel to cowl top panel.

22. Install one bolt to attach each end of instrument panel to cowl side panel.

23. Install one bolt each to attach the instrument panel left and right braces to the lower edge of instrument panel near the console extension.

24. Install a nut to attach lower edge of instrument panel to the brake pedal support.

25. Position the console to vehicle and install two screws to attach the front bracket to the floor.

26. Install two screws to attach the console box to the floor and two screws to attach the top front of box to the support bracket.

27. Position the console switch panel to the console and connect wires. Then, install four panel cover attaching screws.

28. Position the console tray or cover around gear shift lever to console and install the two attaching screws.

29. Connect the speedometer cable to the speedometer.

30. Install the instrument panel pad.

31. Position the steering column to brake pedal support and install retaining clamp (two nuts).

32. Position the reinforcement across the steering column opening of instrument panel and install the three attaching screws.

33. Position the steering column opening cover to the instrument panel and install three attaching screws.

34. Install the sound insulator under left side of instrument panel.

35. Connect the support straps to the glove box.

36. Connect the ground cable to the battery.

37. Check for proper operation of all instruments and controls.

1983 and Later—LTD/Marquis (Manual A/C)

1. Remove the instrument panel upper finish panel and pad assemblies.

2. Loosen the steering column and carefully lower only enough for access to transmission gear shaft selector lever and cable assembly.

NOTE: *Care must be used to assure that the column is not lowered too far to prevent damage to the selector lever and/or cable.*

3. Reach between the steering column and the instrument panel and gently lift the selector lever cable off the shift selector lever. Then, remove the cable clamp from the steering column tube.

4. Lay the steering column to rest on the front seat.

5. Remove one screw attaching the instrument panel to the brake pedal support at the steering column opening.

6. Disconnect the temperature control cable from the temperature blend door and the evaporator case bracket.

7. Disconnect the vacuum hose connectors at the evaporator case.

8. Disconnect the blower resistor wire connector from the resistor on the evaporator housing, and the blower motor feed wire at the in-line connector near the blower resistor wire connector.

9. Support the instrument panel and remove three screws attaching the top of the instrument panel to the cowl.

10. Remove one screw attaching each end of the instrument panel to the cowl side panels.

11. Remove two screws holding instrument panel to floor.

12. Move the instrument panel rearward and disconnect the speedometer cable from the speedometer and any wires that will not allow the instrument panel to lay on the front seat. Use care not to scratch the instrument panel or the steering column.

13. Place the instrument panel near the installed position and connect any wires or connectors that were disconnected during removal.

14. Connect the speedometer cable to the speedometer.

15. Place the instrument panel in position and install one screw at each end of the instrument panel.

16. Install three screws along the top front edge of the instrument panel.

17. Install two screws retaining instrument panel to floor.

18. Connect the temperature control cable to the temperature blend door crank arm and the bracket.

1983 and Later—Thunderbird/Cougar (Automatic A/C)

1. Disconnect the ground cable from the battery.

2. Remove three screws attaching the steering column opening cover to the instrument panel. Then, pull the panel rearward to disengage the clips and remove the cover.

3. Remove three screws attaching the reinforcement to the instrument panel below the

steering column opening and remove the reinforcement.

4. Remove two nuts retaining the hood latch release handle mounting bracket to the brake pedal support below the steering column.

5. Remove the sound insulator from under the left side of the instrument panel.

6. Remove two nuts retaining steering column clamp to the brake pedal support and allow the steering column to rest on the seat.

7. Remove the instrument panel pad.

8. Disconnect the speedometer cable from the speedometer head.

9. Remove two screws attaching the console tray (automatic transmission) or the console cover around the gear shift lever (standard transmission) to the console. Then, remove the tray or cover from the console.

10. Remove four console switch panel cover attaching screws. Disconnect the switch wires and remove the switch panel.

11. Open the console box cover and remove two screws from the bottom of the console box and two screws from the top front of the box.

12. Remove two screws attaching the front end of the console to the lower edge of the instrument panel.

13. Remove two screws attaching the bracket at the front end of the console and lower edge of the instrument panel to the floor pan. Then, lift the rear end of the console and pull the console rearward to disengage it from the instrument panel. Position the console out of the way.

14. Remove two plastic push pins attaching the glove box door straps to the glove box. Allow the glove box and door to hang by the hinge.

15. Remove one bolt attaching the instrument panel brace to the instrument panel at the glove box opening.

16. Remove one nut attaching the lower edge of the instrument panel to the brake pedal support.

17. Remove one bolt attaching a second instrument panel brace to the lower edge of the instrument panel just to the left of the console extension.

18. Remove one bolt attaching each end of the instrument panel to the cowl side panel.

19. Support the instrument panel and remove three screws attaching the top edge of the instrument panel to the cowl top panel.

20. Cover the steering column and seats. Then, carefully position the instrument panel toward the seat disconnecting wires and vacuum harness as necessary. Allow the instrument panel to rest on the front seat.

21. Place the instrument panel in position and connect any wires and vacuum harness that were disconnected during instrument panel removal. Then, install the three screws to attach the top edge of the instrument panel to the cowl top panel.

22. Install one bolt to attach each end of the instrument panel to the cowl side panel.

23. Install one bolt each to attach the instrument panel left and right braces to the lower edge of the instrument panel near the console extension.

24. Install the nut to attach the lower edge of the instrument panel to the brake pedal support.

25. Position the console to the vehicle and install two screws to attach the front bracket to the floor.

26. Install two screws to attach the console box to the floor and two screws to attach the top front of the box to the support bracket.

27. Position the console switch panel to the console and connect the wires. Then install the four panel cover attaching screws.

28. Position the console tray or the cover around the gear shift lever to the console and install the two attaching screws.

29. Connect the speedometer cable to the speedometer.

30. Install the instrument panel pad.

31. Position the steering column to the brake pedal support and install the retaining clamp (two nuts).

32. Position the reinforcement across the steering column opening of the instrument panel and install the three attaching screws.

33. Position the steering column opening cover to the instrument panel and install the three attaching screws.

34. Install the sound insulator under the left side of the instrument panel.

35. Connect the support straps to the glove box.

36. Connect the ground cable to the battery.

37. Check for proper operation of all instruments and controls.

1983 and Later—LTD/Marquis (Automatic A/C)

1. Remove the instrument panel upper finish panel and pad assemblies.

2. Loosen the steering column and carefully lower only enough for access to transmission gear shift selector lever and cable assembly.

NOTE: *Care must be used to assure that the column is not lowered too far to prevent damage to the selector lever and/or cable.*

3. Reach between the steering column and the instrument panel and gently lift the selector lever cable off the shift selector lever. Then, remove the cable clamp from the steering column tube.

4. Lay the steering column to rest on the front seat.

5. Remove one screw attaching the instrument panel to the brake pedal support at the steering column opening.

6. Disconnect the servo motor from the temperature blend door.

7. Disconnect the vacuum hose connectors at the evaporator case.

8. Disconnect the blower resistor wire connector from the resistor on the evaporator housing, and the blower motor feed wire at the in-line connector near the blower resistor wire connector.

9. Support the instrument panel and remove three screws attaching the top of the instrument panel to the cowl.

10. Remove one screw attaching each end of the instrument panel to the cowl side panels.

11. Remove two screws holding instrument panel to floor.

12. Move the instrument panel rearward and disconnect the speedometer cable from the speedometer and any wires that will not allow the instrument panel to lay on the front seat. Use care not to scratch the instrument panel or the steering column.

13. Place the instrument panel near the installed position and connect any wires or connectors that were disconnected during removal.

14. Connect the servo motor to the temperature blend door crank arm and the bracket.

15. Connect the vacuum hoses at the 7-port connectors and the blower motor wires at the resistor and in-line connector near the resistor.

16. Connect the speedometer cable to the speedometer.

17. Place the instrument panel in position and install one screw at each end of the instrument panel.

18. Install three screws along the top front edge of the instrument panel.

19. Install two screws retaining instrument panel to floor.

20. Install the screw attaching the instrument panel to the brake pedal support.

21. Position the steering column near the brake pedal support.

22. Connect the transmission gear shift selector lever cable to the shift selector lever. Then, connect the cable clamp to the steering column tube.

23. Position the steering column against the brake pedal support and install the four attaching nuts.

24. Adjust the transmission selector indicator as necessary.

25. Install the steering column shroud.

26. Position the steering column opening cover to the instrument panel and install the two attaching screws.

27. Install the instrument panel pad and connect the ground cable to the battery.

Speedometer Cable
REMOVAL AND INSTALLATION

NOTE: *Depending on year and model, some dash panels or the instrument cluster may require removal to gain access to the rear of the speedometer.*

1. Reach up behind the speedometer and depress the flat, quick-disconnect tab, while pulling back on the cable.

2. If the inner cable is broken, raise and support the car and remove the cable-to-transmission clamp and pull the cable from the transmission.

3. Pull the core from the cable.

4. Installation is the reverse of removal. Lubricate the core with speedometer cable lubricant prior to installation.

Radio
REMOVAL AND INSTALLATION
1971–79

1. Disconnect the negative cable from the battery.

2. Pull off the radio control knobs and remove the nuts and washers that retain the radio to the instrument panel.

3. Disconnect the antenna lead. On AM models, the jack is on the right (passenger) side of the radio and, on AM/FM models, it is at the rear.

4. Disconnect the speaker, power, and dial light leads at their respective quick-disconnects.

5. Remove the radio support bracket(s).

6. Lower the radio from the instrument panel and remove it.

7. To install, position the radio on the floor below its mounting location and attach the antenna, speaker, power, and dial light leads if they will reach. Then place the radio in the instrument panel and install the retaining nuts and washers. Connect all leads not previously connected.

8. Install the radio support bracket(s).

9. Push the radio control knobs onto their shafts.

10. Connect the negative cable to the battery.

11. Adjust the antenna trimmer, if necessary, and check radio operation.

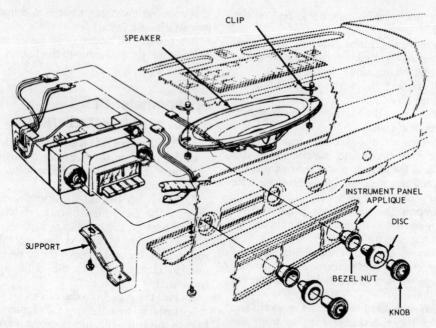

Typical radio installation

Versailles

1. Disconnect the negative battery cable.
2. Remove the headlight switch from the instrument panel. Remove the heater, air conditioner, windshield wiper/washer knobs, and radio knobs and discs.
3. Remove the six screws which attach the applique to the instrument panel and remove the applique. Disconnect the antenna lead-in cable from the radio.
4. Remove the four screws which attach the radio bezel to the instrument panel. Slide the radio and bezel out of the lower rear support bracket and instrument panel opening toward the interior far enough to disconnect the electrical connections, and remove the radio.
5. Remove the nut attaching the rear support bracket to the radio and remove the bracket. Remove the nuts and washer from the radio control shafts and remove the bezel.
6. To install, attach the rear support bracket to the radio. Install the bezel, washers and nuts.
7. Insert the radio with rear support bracket and bezel through the instrument panel opening far enough to connect the electrical leads and antenna lead-in cable. Install the radio upper rear support bracket into the lower rear support bracket.
8. Center the radio and bezel in the opening and install the four bezel attaching screws.
9. Install the instrument panel applique with its six attaching screws. Install all knobs removed from the instrument panel and radio. Install the headlight switch.
10. Connect the negative battery cable.

1981–82 Cougar

1. Disconnect the negative battery cable.
2. Disconnect the electrical, speaker, and antenna leads from the radio.
3. Remove the knobs, discs, and control shaft nuts and washers from the radio shafts.
4. Remove the ash tray receptacle and bracket.
5. Remove the rear support nut from the radio.
6. Remove the instrument panel lower reinforcement and the heater or air conditioning floor ducts.
7. Remove the radio from the rear support, and drop the radio down and out from behind the instrument panel.
8. To install, reverse the removal procedure.

1980 and Later Thunderbird and Cougar XR-7, 1982 Continental, 1983 and Later LTD, Marquis and Cougar

1. Disconnect the negative battery cable.
2. Remove the radio knobs (pull off). Remove the center trim panel.
3. Remove the radio mounting plate screws. Pull the radio towards the front seat to disengage it from the lower bracket.
4. Disconnect the radio and antenna connections.
5. Remove the radio. Remove the nuts and washers (conventional radios) or mounting plate screws (electronic radios) as necessary.
6. On electronic radios, install the mounting plates before installing the retaining nuts

and washers or screws. The rest of installation is the reverse of removal.

Windshield Wipers

MOTOR REMOVAL AND INSTALLATION

Torino, Montego, LTD II With Non-Hidden Wipers

1. Disconnect battery and wiper motor connector.
2. Remove cowl top left vent screen by removing four retaining drive pins.
3. Remove wiper link retaining clip from wiper motor arm.
4. Remove three wiper motor retaining bolts, and remove wiper motor and mounting bracket.
5. To install motor, place wiper motor and mounting bracket against firewall and install three retaining bolts.
6. Position wiper link on motor drive arm, and install connecting clip. Be sure to force clip locking flange into locked position.
7. Install cowl top vent screen and secure with four drive pins.
8. Check motor operation and connect wiring plugs.

1977 Versailles

1. Remove instrument cluster.
2. If air conditioned, remove center connector and duct assembly. Remove mounting bracket screw behind center duct, disconnect assembly from plenum chamber and left duct, and pull center connector and duct assembly out through cluster opening.
3. Working through cluster opening, disconnect two pivot shaft links from motor drive arm by removing retaining clip.
4. Disconnect wiring plug at motor, remove three retaining bolts, and remove motor through cluster opening.
5. To install motor, bolt motor to mounting plate with three retaining bolts.
6. Connect right pivot shaft link to motor and then connect left pivot shaft link. Lock clip.
7. On air conditioned vehicles, insert end of center connector and duct assembly near mounting bracket into left duct and opposite end into plenum chamber.
8. Secure assembly with mounting bracket screw.
9. Install instrument cluster, and check operation of wiper motor.

1978–80 Versailles

1. Disconnect the battery ground cable.
2. Remove the instrument panel pad, retained by eight screws.
3. Remove the speaker mounting bracket, disconnect and remove the speaker.

4. Remove the interlock module from the bracket and disconnect the multiple connector.
5. Remove the motor bracket bolts and the drive arm clip. Remove the motor.
6. Install in reverse order.

Torino, Elite, LTD II, Montego; Cougar and Thunderbird Through 1979 (Hidden Wipers)

1. Disconnect the battery ground cable.
2. Remove the wiper arm and blade assemblies from the pivot shafts.
3. Remove the left cowl screen for access through the cowl opening. Disconnect the linkage drive arm from the motor output arm crankpin by removing the retaining clip. From the engine side of the firewall, disconnect the two push-on wire connectors from the motor.
4. Remove the three bolts which retain the motor to the firewall and remove the motor. If the output arm catches on the firewall during removal, hand turn the arm clockwise, so that it will clear the opening in the firewall.
5. Before installing the motor, be sure that the output arm is in the Park position.

1980–83 Thunderbird and Cougar XR-7 1981–82 Cougar, 1982–83 Continental, 1983 and LTD/Marquis

1. Disconnect the ground cable.
2. Remove the right hand wiper arm (on LTD and Marquis models remove the left side assembly also) from the pivot shaft and lay it on the top grille.
3. Remove the cowl top grille screws.
4. Reach under the left front corner of the grille to disconnect the linkage drive arm from the motor crank by removing the retaining clip.
5. Disconnect the electrical connector. Remove the motor mounting bolts and remove the motor.
6. Install in reverse order.

1984 and Later Mark VII, Thunderbird and Cougar

1. Turn the ignition switch to the On position. Turn the wiper switch on, when the blades are straight up on the windshield, turn the key switch Off.
2. Disconnect the negative battery cable. Remove the arm and blade assemblies.
3. Remove the left side leaf guard screen. Disconnect the linkage drive arm from the wiper motor after removing the retaining clip.
4. Disconnect the electrical wiring harness connector from the wiper motor. Remove the wiper motor mounting bolts and the motor.
5. Install in the reverse order of removal. Before installing the arm and blade assemblies, turn on the key and allow the motor to cycle. Turn the wiper control switch Off so that the

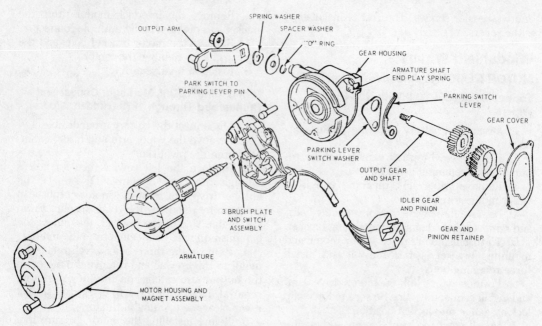

Typical single or two-speed wiper motor disassembled

drives and motor will stop in the park position. Install the arm and blade assemblies.

Ignition Lock Cylinder
REPLACEMENT

1. Disconnect the negative battery cable.
2. On cars with a fixed steering column, re-

move the steering wheel trim pad and the steering wheel. Insert a stiff wire into the hole located in the lock cylinder housing. On some models with a tilt steering wheel, this hole is located on the outside of the column near the 4-way flasher button making it unnecessary to remove the wheel. On most late models, re-move the four column shroud screws and re-

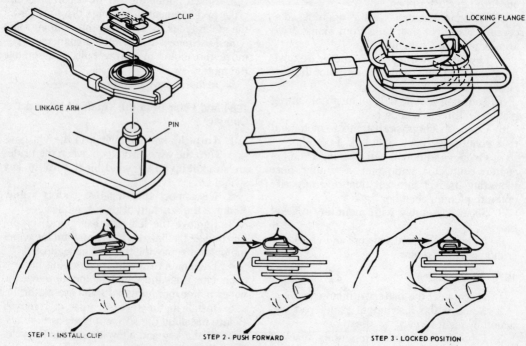

Removing or installing wiper arms connecting clips

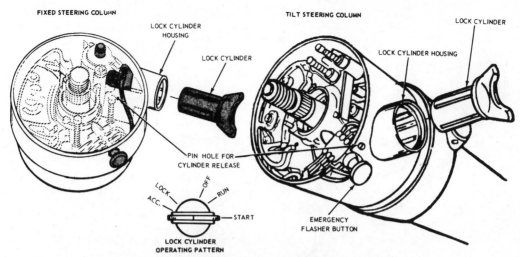

Lock cylinder replacement on locking type column

move the shroud halves. The hole in the casting is angled down toward the seat. Insert a ⅛ in. diameter wire.

3. Place the gear shift lever in Reverse on standard shift cars and in park on cars with automatic transmissions and turn the ignition key to the "on" position.

4. Depress the wire and remove the lock cylinder and wire.

5. Insert a new cylinder into the housing and turn to the "off" position. This will lock the cylinder into position.

6. Reinstall the steering wheel and pad.

7. Connect the negative battery cable.

Ignition Switch

REPLACEMENT

1. Disconnect the negative battery cable.

2. Remove shrouding from the steering column. Detach and lower the steering column from the brake support bracket if necessary for clearance.

3. Disconnect the switch wiring at the multiple plug. On most 1982 and later models place the ignition key in the On (run) position. Refer to the instruction sheet packed with the switch.

4. Remove the two nuts that retain the switch to steering column. On the models specified in Step 2, the break-off head bolts that attach the switch to the lock cylinder housing must be drilled out with a ⅛ in. drill. Remove the bolts with an Easy-Out extractor. Disengage the ignition switch from the pin.

5. On models with a steering column-mounted gearshift lever, disconnect the ignition switch plunger from the ignition switch actuator rod and remove the ignition switch. On

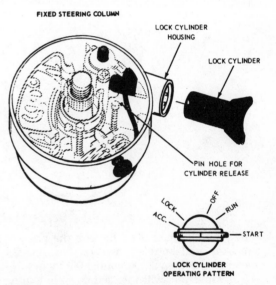

Lock cylinder replacement

models with a floor mounted gearshift lever, remove the pin that connects the switch plunger to the switch actuator and remove the switch.

6. To re-install the switch, place both locking mechanism at top of column and switch itself in Lock or Run position, depending on year and model. Check the key switch to insure approximate correct position. The Run position is about 90° from Lock. New switches are held in lock by plastic shipping pins. To pin existing switches, pull the switch plunger out as far as it will go and push back in to first detent. Insert ³⁄₃₂ in. diameter wire into locking hole in the top of the switch.

7. Connect the switch plunger to the switch actuator rod.

8. Position the switch on the column and

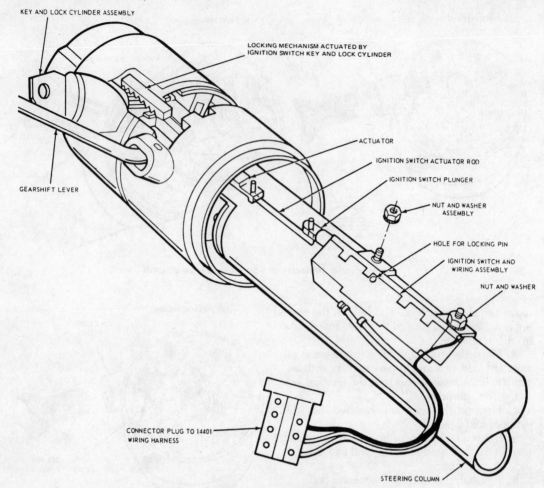

KEY AND LOCK CYLINDER ASSEMBLY

LOCKING MECHANISM ACTUATED BY
IGNITION SWITCH KEY AND LOCK CYLINDER

GEARSHIFT LEVER

ACTUATOR

IGNITION SWITCH ACTUATOR ROD

IGNITION SWITCH PLUNGER

NUT AND WASHER
ASSEMBLY

HOLE FOR LOCKING PIN

IGNITION SWITCH AND
WIRING ASSEMBLY

NUT AND WASHER

CONNECTOR PLUG TO 14401
WIRING HARNESS

STEERING COLUMN

Ignition switch assembly

install the attaching nuts. Be sure the proper break-off head bolts are used on the models mentioned in Step 2. Do not tighten them.

9. Move the switch up and down to locate the mid-position of rod lash, and then tighten the nuts. On the models specified in Step 2, tighten the bolts until the heads break off.

10. Remove the locking pin or wire. Connect the electrical connector. Reconnect the battery cable and check for proper switch operation.

11. Attach the steering column to the brake support bracket and install the shrouding.

Seat-Belt/Starter Interlock

1974–75 Models

All 1974 and some 1975 Ford and Mercury vehicles are equipped with the Federally-required starter interlock system. The purpose of this system is to force the wearing of seat belts.

The system includes a warning light and buzzer (as in late 1972 and 1973), weight sen-

sors in the front seats, switches in the out-board front seat belt retractors, and an electronic control module. The center front seat is tied into the warning light and buzzer system, but not into the starter interlock.

The electronic control module requires that the driver and right front paasenger first sit down, then pull out their seat belts. If this is not done, the starter will not operate, but the light and buzzer will. The sequence must be followed each time the engine is started unless the driver and passenger have remained seated and buckled. If the seat belts have been pulled out and left buckled, the engine will not start. The switches in the retractors must be cycled for each start. If the belts are released after the start, the light and buzzer will operate.

Turn Signal Flasher Locations

1971	On fuse board to left of column
1972 and later	On fuse panel

STARTER INTERLOCK DELETION — ALL VEHICLES SO EQUIPPED — 1974–75

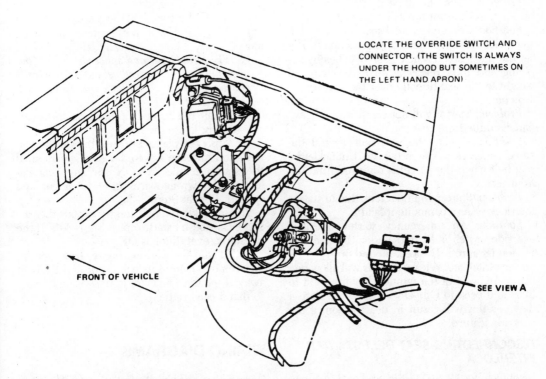

LOCATE THE OVERRIDE SWITCH AND CONNECTOR. (THE SWITCH IS ALWAYS UNDER THE HOOD BUT SOMETIMES ON THE LEFT HAND APRON)

FRONT OF VEHICLE

SEE VIEW A

CAUTION: SET THE PARKING BRAKE AND REMOVE THE IGNITION KEY BEFORE ANY REWORK IS PERFORMED.
(IF THE NO. 640 CIRCUIT IS ACCIDENTALLY SPLICED INTO THE NO. 32 OR NO. 33 CIRCUITS, THE CAR WILL START IN GEAR)

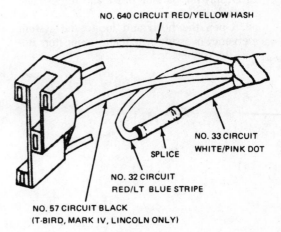

NO. 640 CIRCUIT RED/YELLOW HASH

NO. 33 CIRCUIT WHITE/PINK DOT

SPLICE

NO. 32 CIRCUIT RED/LT BLUE STRIPE

NO. 57 CIRCUIT BLACK (T-BIRD, MARK IV, LINCOLN ONLY)

VIEW A

Seat belt/starter interlock system deletion—all models

If the system should fail, preventing starting, the interlock by-pass switch under the hood can be used. This switch permits one start without interference from the interlock system. This by-pass switch can also be used for servicing purposes.

TROUBLESHOOTING

If the starter will not crank or the warning buzzer will not shut off, perform the following checks:
checks:

Problem: Front seat occupant sits on a pre-buckled seat belt.

Solution: Unbuckle the prebuckled belt, fully retract, extract, and then rebuckle the belt.

Problem: The front seat occupants are buckled, but the starter will not crank.

Solution: The unoccupied seat sensor switch stuck closed before the seat was occupied. Reset the unoccupied seat sensor switches by applying and then releasing 50 lbs or more of weight to the seat directly over the seat sensor switches.

Problem: Starter will not crank with a heavy parcel on the front seat.

Solution: Buckle the seat belt around the parcel somewhere else in the car. Unbuckle the seat belt when the parcel is removed from the front seat.

Problem: Starter will not crank due to starter interlock system component failure.

Solution: An emergency starter interlock override switch is located under the hood on the fender apron. Depress the red push button on the switch and release it. This will allow one complete cycle of the ignition key from Off to Start and back to Off. Do not tape the button down as this will result in deactivation of the override feature.

DISCONNECTING SEAT BELT/STARTER INTERLOCK

As of October 29, 1974, it is legal to disconnect the seat belt/starter interlock system. However, the warning light portion of the system must be left operational.

1. Apply the parking brake and remove the ignition key.

2. Open the hood and locate the system emergency override switch and connector. Remove the connector.

3. Cut the white wire(s) with the pink dots (#33 circuit) and the red wire(s) with the light blue stripe (#32 circuit).

4. Splice the two (four) wires together and tape the splice. Use a "butt" connector if available.

NOTE: *Do not cut and splice the other connector wires. If the red/yellow hash wire is spliced to any of the other wires the car will start in gear.*

5. Install the connector back on the override switch. Close the hood.

6. Apply the parking brakes, buckle the seat belt, and turn the key to the "ON" position. If the starter cranks in "ON" or any gear selected, the wrong wires have been cut and spliced. Repeat Steps 3–5.

7. Unbuckle the belt and try to start the car. If the car doesn't start, repeat Steps 3–5. If the car starts, everything is OK.

8. To stop the warning buzzer from operating, remove it from its connector and throw it away. Tape the connector to the wiring harness so that it can't rattle.

WIRING DIAGRAMS

Wiring diagrams have been left out of this book. As cars have become more complex, and available with longer and longer option lists, wiring diagrams have grown in size and complexity also. It has become virtually impossible to provide a readable reproduction in a reasonable number of pages. Information on ordering wiring diagrams from the vehicle manufacturer can be found in the owners manual.

6

MANUAL TRANSMISSION

NOTE: *A manual transmission was not available in Mid-Size Models, from 1974 through 1980.*

REMOVAL AND INSTALLATION

1971–73

1. On floor-shift models, remove the boot retainer and shift lever. Raise the car, taking proper safety precautions.

2. Disconnect the driveshaft at the rear universal joint and remove the driveshaft.

3. Disconnect the speedometer cable at the transmission extension. On transmission regulated spark equipped cars, disconnect the lead wire at the connector.

4. Disconnect the gearshift rods from the transmission shift levers. If the car is equipped with a four-speed, remove the bolts that secure the shift control bracket to the extension housing.

5. Remove the bolt holding the extension housing to the rear support, and remove the muffler inlet pipe bracket-to-housing bolt.

6. Remove the two rear support bracket insulator nuts from the underside of the cross-member. Remove the cross-member.

NOTE: *On 1972 and later models the no. 3 crossmember's mounting bolts have a plastic locking compound on the threads. To remove the insulator nuts, heat them with a torch.*

7. Place a jack (equipped with a protective piece of wood) under the rear of the engine oil pan. Raise the engine, slightly.

8. Remove the transmission-to-fly-wheel housing bolts. On clutch removal only, install two guide studs into the bottom attaching bolt holes.

NOTE: *On 429 cu in. engines, the upper left-hand transmission attaching bolt is a seal bolt.*

Carefully note its position so that it may be reinstalled in its original position.

9. Slide the transmission back and out of the car.

10. Start the transmission extension housing up and over the rear support. After moving the transmission back just far enough for the pilot shaft to clear the clutch housing, move it upward into position onto the transmission guide studs.

11. Slide the transmission forward and into place against the flywheel housing.

12. Remove the guide studs and torque the transmission to flywheel bolts to 37–42 ft. lbs.

13. Position the crossmember to the frame and install the attaching bolts. Slowly lower the engine onto the crossmember.

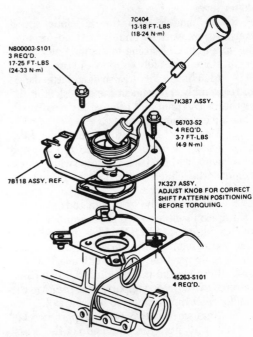

Shift lever installation on model 82ET 4-speed

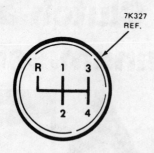

7K327
REF.

WITH LEVER IN NEUTRAL POSITION, INSTALL LOCKING
NUT 7C404 UNTIL HAND TIGHT. THEN INSTALL KNOB
7K327 UNTIL HAND TIGHT. BACK KNOB OFF UNTIL
SHIFT PATTERN ALIGNS WITH THE   OF DRIVE LINE.
TIGHTEN LOCKING NUT 13-18 FT-LBS (18-24 N·m) NO THREADS
SHALL BE VISIBLE AFTER NUT HAS BEEN TIGHTENED.
SHIFT PATTERN ALIGNMENT MUST BE WITHIN ±15⁰
OF ℄ OF DRIVE LINE.

Shift knob installation on model 82ET 4-speed

14. Install the insulator-to-cross-member nuts. Torque the nuts to 30–50 ft. lbs.

15. Connect the gear shift rods and the speedometer cable. On cars with transmission-regulated spark, connect the lead wire at the plug connector. On floor-shift models, install the shift lever and boot.

16. Connect the driveshaft.

17. Refill the transmission to the proper level.

1981 and Later

NOTE: *Procedure includes clutch removal and installation.*

1. Disconnect and remove starter and dust ring, if the clutch is to be removed. On floor-shift models, remove the boot retainer and shifter lever.

2. On models with the ET four speed transmission: working under the hood, remove the upper clutch housing-to-engine bolts.

3. Raise and safely support the car.

4. Matchmark the driveshaft and axle flange for reassembly. Disconnect the driveshaft at the rear universal joint and remove the driveshaft. Plug the extension housing.

5. Disconnect the speedometer cable at the transmission extension. Disconnect the seat belt sensor wires and the back-up lamp switch wires. Remove the clutch lever boot and cable on models so equipped.

6. Disconnect the gear shift rods from the transmission shift levers. If car is equipped with four speed, except SROD models, remove bolts that secure shift control bracket to extension housing. Support the engine with a jack.

7. Remove the bolt holding the extension housing to the rear support, and remove the muffler inlet pipe bracket to housing bolt.

8. Remove the two rear support bracket insulator nuts from the underside of the cross-member. Remove crossmember.

9. Place a jack (equipped with a protective piece of wood) under the rear of the engine oil pan. Raise or lower the engine slightly as necessary to provide access to the bolts.

NOTE: *Depending on year and model, the flywheel housing may be removed with the transmission (internal bolts fastened from inside housing) if this is the case, unbolt the housing from engine and remove as an assembly with the transmission.*

10. Remove transmission-to-flywheel housing bolts.

11. Slide the transmission back and out of the car. It may be necessary to slide the catalytic converter bracket forward to provide clearance on some models.

12. To remove the clutch, remove release lever retracting spring. Disconnect pedal at the equalizer bar, or the clutch cable from the housing, as applicable.

13. Remove bolts that secure engine rear plate to front lower part of bellhousing.

14. Remove bolts that attach bell housing to cylinder block and remove housing and release lever as a unit. Remove the clutch release lever by pulling it through the window in the housing until the retainer spring disengages from the pivot.

15. Loosen six pressure plate cover attaching bolts evenly to release spring pressure. Mark cover and flywheel to facilitate reassembly in same position.

16. Remove six attaching bolts while holding pressure plate cover. Remove pressure plate and clutch disc.

CAUTION: *Do not depress the clutch pedal while the transmission is removed.*

17. Before installing the clutch, clean the flywheel surface. Inspect the flywheel and pressure plate for wear, scoring, or burn marks (blue color). Light scoring and wear may be cleaned up with emery paper; heavy wear may require refacing of the flywheel or replacement of the damaged parts.

18. Attach the clutch disc and pressure plate assembly to the flywheel. The three dowel pins on the flywheel, if so equipped, must be properly aligned. Damaged pins must be replaced. Avoid touching the clutch plate surface. Tighten the bolts finger tight.

19. Align the clutch disc with the pilot bushing. Torque cover bolts to 12–14 ft. lbs. with the four cylinder, 12–20 ft. lbs. for all others.

20. Lightly lubricate the release lever fulcrum ends. Install the release lever in the flywheel housing and install the dust shield.

21. Apply very little lubricant on the release bearing retainer journal. Fill the groove in the release bearing hub with grease. Clean all ex-

cess grease from the inside bore of the hub to prevent clutch disc contamination. Attach the release bearing and hub on the release lever.

22. Make sure the flywheel housing and engine block are clean. Any missing or damaged mounting dowels must be replaced. Install the flywheel housing and torque the attaching bolts to 38–61 ft. lbs. on all V8s and 250 sixes, 38–55 ft. lbs. on 200 sixes, and 28–38 ft. lbs. on fours and 170-V6s. Install the dust cover and torque the bolts to 17–20 ft. lbs.

23. Connect the release rod or cable and the retracting spring. Connect the pedal-to-equalizer-rod at the equalizer bar.

24. Install starter and dust ring.

25. After moving the transmission back just far enough for the pilot shaft to clear the clutch housing, move it upward and into position on the flywheel housing. It may be necessary to put the transmission in gear and rotate the output shaft to align the input shaft and clutch splines.

26. Move the transmission forward and into place against the flywheel housing, and install the transmission attaching bolts finger-tight.

27. Tighten the transmission bolts to 37–42 ft. lbs. on all cars.

28. Install the crossmember and torque the mounting bolts to 20–30 ft. lbs. Slowly lower the engine onto the crossmember.

29. Torque the rear mount to 30–50 ft. lbs.

30. Connect gear shift rods and the speedometer cable.

31. Remove the plug from the extension housing and install the driveshaft, aligning the marks made previously.

32. Refill transmission to proper level. On floorshift models, install the boot retainer and shift lever.

LINKAGE ADJUSTMENT

3-Speed Column Shift

If the transmission shifts hard or a gear will not engage, the gear shift rods may need adjustment. Move the selector lever through all shift positions to be certain that the crossover operation is smooth. If not, adjust the gear shift rods.

1. Place the lever in Neutral.

2. Loosen the two gear shift rod adjustment nuts.

3. Insert 3/16 in. diameter alignment pin through First and Reverse gear shift lever and Second and Third gear shift lever. Align the levers to insert the pin.

4. Tighten the gear shift rod adjustment nuts and remove the pin.

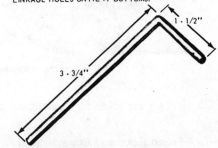

AN ALIGNMENT TOOL CAN BE MADE FROM 1/4" DIAMETER DRILL ROD BENT TO AN "L" SHAPE. THE EXTENSIONS SHOULD BE 1 - 1/2" AND 3 - 3/4" FROM THE ELBOW. SHORT END OF ALIGNMENT TOOL SHOULD BE INSERTED INTO CONTROL BRACKET AND LINKAGE HOLES UNTIL IT BOTTOMS.

¼ in. alignment rod

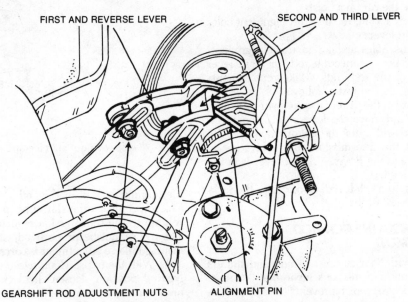

Column shift linkage adjustment

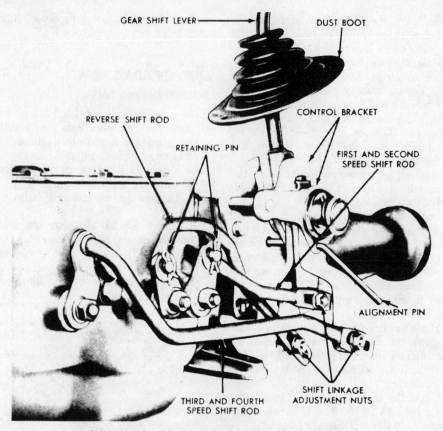

GEAR SHIFT LEVER

DUST BOOT

REVERSE SHIFT ROD

CONTROL BRACKET

RETAINING PIN

FIRST AND SECOND
SPEED SHIFT ROD

ALIGNMENT PIN

THIRD AND FOURTH
SPEED SHIFT ROD

SHIFT LINKAGE
ADJUSTMENT NUTS

Adjusting the floor shift linkage on 1971–73 models

5. Check the gear lever for smooth cross-over.

1971–73 4-Speed Floor and Console Shift

1. Place the hand shifter lever in Neutral, then raise the car on a hoist.

2. Insert a ¼ in. rod into the alignment holes of the shift levers.

3. If the holes are not in exact alignment, check for bent connecting rods or loose lever locknuts at the rod ends. Make replacements or repairs, then adjust as follows.

4. Loosen the three rod-to-lever retaining locknuts and move the levers until the ¼ in. gauge rod will enter the alignment holes. Be sure that the transmission shift levers are in Neutral, and the Reverse shifter lever is in the Neutral detent.

5. Install the shift rods and torque the locknuts to 18–23 ft. lbs.

TRANSMISSION LOCK ROD ADJUSTMENT

Models with floor or console-mounted shifters and manual transmissions incorporate a transmission lock rod which prevents the shifter from being moved from the Reverse position when

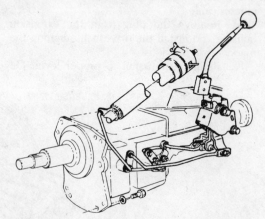

1972–73 4-speed floor shift linkage and lock rod

the ignition lock is in the "off" position. The lock rod connects the shift tube in the steering column to the transmission reverse lever. The lock rod cannot be properly adjusted until the manual linkage adjustment is correct.

1. With the transmission selector lever in the Neutral position, loosen the lock rod adjustment nut on the transmission Reverse lever.

2. Insert a 0.180 in. diameter rod (no. 15

drill bit) in the gauge pin hole located at the six o'clock position on the steering column socket casting, directly below the ignition lock.

3. Manipulate the pin until the casting will not move with the pin inserted.

CLUTCH

REMOVAL AND INSTALLATION

1971–73

1. Disconnect and remove the starter and dust ring. On floor-shift models, remove the boot retainer and shift lever.

2. Raise the car, taking proper safety precautions.

3. Remove the transmission as outlined in the manual transmission removal section.

4. Remove the release lever retracting spring and disconnect the pedal at the equalizer bar.

5. Remove the bolts that secure the engine rear plate to the front lower part of the bellhousing.

6. Remove the bolts that attach the bellhousing to the cylinder block and remove the housing and release lever as a unit.

7. Loosen the six pressure plate cover attaching bolts evenly to release spring pressure. Mark the cover and flywheel to facilitate reassembly in the same position.

8. Remove the six attaching bolts while holding the pressure plate cover.

9. Remove the pressure plate and clutch disc.

10. Wash the flywheel surface with alcohol.

11. Attach the clutch disc and pressure plate assembly to the flywheel with the bolts fingertight.

12. Using a clutch centering arbor, or an input shaft out of an old transmission, align the clutch disc with the pilot bearing (bushing). While holding the centering shaft firmly against the pilot bearing, torque the pressure plate retaining bolts, diagonally in rotation, to a final figure of 12–20 ft. lbs.

13. Apply a small amount of lubricant to the release lever fulcrum ends. Install the release lever in the flywheel housing and install the dust shield.

14. Lightly lubricate the release bearing retainer journal. Attach the release bearing and hub on the release lever.

15. Install the flywheel housing. Torque the attaching bolts to 40–50 ft. lbs. Install the dust cover and torque the bolts to 17–20 ft. lbs.

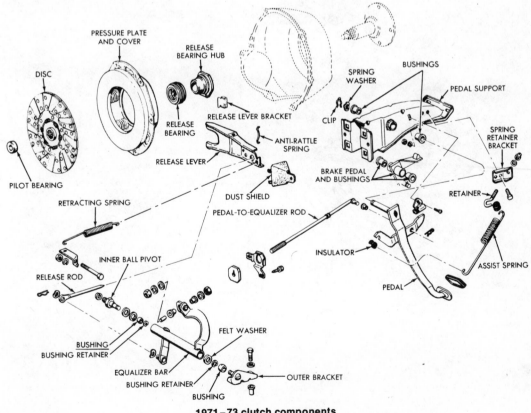

1971–73 clutch components

16. Connect the release rod and the retracting spring. Connect the pedal to equalizer rod at the equalizer bar.

17. Install the starter and dust ring.

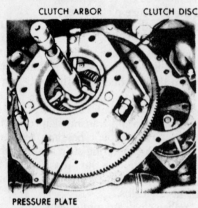

CLUTCH ARBOR   CLUTCH DISC

PRESSURE PLATE

Installing clutch disc

18. Install the transmission as outlined in the manual transmission installation section.

1981 and Later

NOTE: *Clutch removal and installation procedures are included in the previous transmission removal section.*

CLUTCH PEDAL ADJUSTMENT

The free travel of the clutch pedal should be checked every six months or 6,000 miles and adjusted whenever the clutch does not engage properly or when new clutch parts are installed. Improper adjustment of clutch pedal free travel is one of the most frequent causes of clutch failure and can be a contributing factor in transmission failures.

1981–82 models require no free-play adjustment. A clutch pedal height adjustment is required instead.

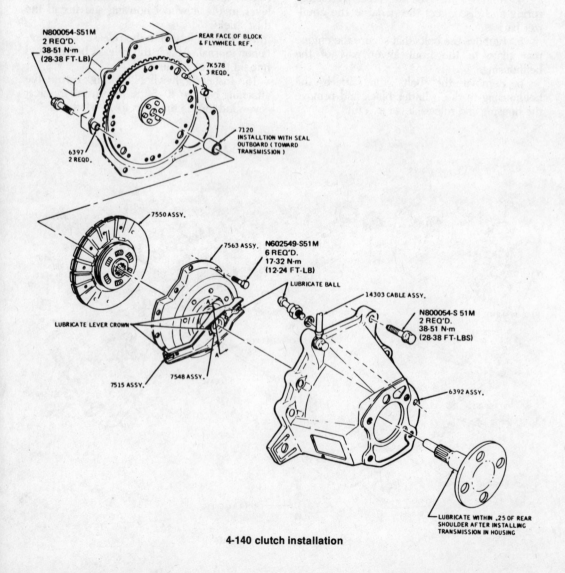

N800054-S51M
2 REQ'D.
38-51 N·m
(28-38 FT-LB)

REAR FACE OF BLOCK
& FLYWHEEL REF.

7K578
3 REQD.

7120
INSTALLTION WITH SEAL
OUTBOARD (TOWARD
TRANSMISSION)

6397
2 REQD.

7550 ASSY.

7563 ASSY.

N602549-S51M
6 REQ'D.
17-32 N·m
(12-24 FT-LB)

LUBRICATE BALL

14303 CABLE ASSY.

N800054-S 51M
2 REQ'D.
38-51 N·m
(28-38 FT-LBS)

LUBRICATE LEVER CROWN

7515 ASSY.

7548 ASSY.

6392 ASSY.

LUBRICATE WITHIN .25 OF REAR
SHOULDER AFTER INSTALLING
TRANSMISSION IN HOUSING

4-140 clutch installation

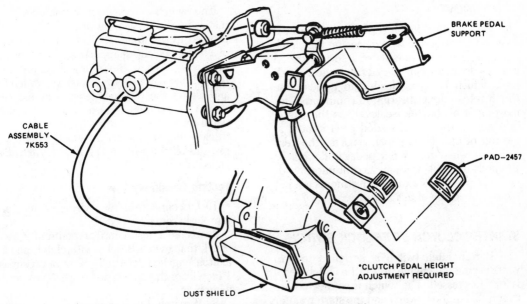

1981–82 clutch pedal and cable assembly

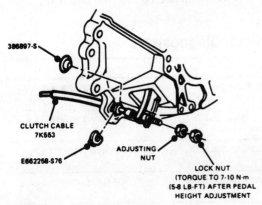

4-140 clutch pedal adjustment

1971–1973

1. Disconnect the clutch return spring from the release lever.

2. Loosen the release lever rod locknut and adjusting nut.

3. Move the clutch release lever rearward until the release bearing lightly contacts the pressure plate release fingers.

4. Adjust the length of the rod adaptor until the adaptor seats in the release lever pocket.

5. Insert the specified feeler gauge against the back face of the rod adaptor. Tighten the adjusting nut finger-tight against the gauge. The proper feeler gauge sizes (in in.) and their respective years of application are as follows.

6. Tighten the locknut against the adjusting nut, being careful not to disturb the adjustment. Torque the locknut to 10–15 ft. lbs. and remove the feeler gauge.

7. Install the clutch return spring.

8. Depress and release the clutch pedal a minimum of five times and recheck the free-play setting with a feeler gauge. Readjust if necessary.

9. With the engine running at 3,000 rpm and the transmission in Neutral, check the pedal free travel. The free travel at this speed must be at least ½ in. Free travel must be exactly to specification. Otherwise, the release fingers may contact the release bearing continuously, resulting in premature bearing and clutch failure.

1981 and Later

NOTE: *All 1981 and later models have self-adjusting clutches. No adjustments are necessary.*

Self-Adjusting Clutch

The free play in the clutch is adjusted by a built in mechanism that allows the clutch controls to be self-adjusted during normal operation.

The self-adjusting feature should be checked every 5000 miles. This is accomplished by insuring that the clutch pedal travels to the top of its upward position. Grasp the clutch pedal with your hand or put your foot under the clutch pedal, pull up on the pedal until it stops. Very little effort is required (about 10 lbs.) During the application of upward pressure, a click may be heard which means an adjustment was necessary and has been accomplished.

COMPONENTS

The self-adjusting clutch control mechanism is automatically adjusted by a device on the clutch pedal. The system consists of a spring loaded gear quadrant, a spring loaded pawl, and a clutch cable which is spring loaded to preload the clutch release lever bearing to compensate for movement of the release lever, as the clutch disc wears. The spring loaded pawl located at the top of the clutch pedal, engages the gear quadrant when the clutch pedal is depressed and pulls the cable through its continuously adjusted stroke. Clutch cable adjustments are not required because of this feature.

STARTER/CLUTCH INTERLOCK SWITCH

The starter/clutch switch is designed to prevent starting the engine unless the clutch pedal is fully depressed. The switch is connected between the ignition switch and the starter motor relay coil and maintains an open circuit with the clutch pedal up (clutch engaged).

The switch is designed to self-adjust automatically the first time the clutch pedal is pressed to the floor. The self-adjuster consists of a two-piece clip snapped together over a serrated rod. When the plunger or rod is extended, the clip bottoms out on the switch body and allows the rod to ratchet over the serrations to a position determined by the clutch pedal travel limit. In this way, the switch is set to close the starter circuit when the clutch is pressed all the way to the floor (clutch disengaged).

Testing Continuity

1. Disconnect in-line wiring connector at jumper harness.
2. Using a test lamp or continuity tester, check that switch is open with clutch pedal up (clutch engaged), and closed at approximately 1 inch from the clutch pedal full down position (clutch disengaged).
3. If switch does not operate, check to see if the self-adjusting clip is out of position on the rod. It should be near the end of the rod.

Self-Adjusting Clutch Diagnosis

Condition	Possible Source	Action
Clutch does not disengage.	Pawl binding due to entrapped sound absorber	Remove contamination and free up pawl.
Clutch gears clash while shifting.	Pawl does not fully engage due to missing or weak pawl spring	Install new spring (pawl).
Pedal makes racheting noise while traveling to floor.	Teeth stripped on pawl or quadrant	Replace worn components.
Pedal travels to floor with no effort or noise.	Pawl does not engage quadrant due to missing spring	Install new spring (pawl).
Excessive pedal effort over 20 kg (45 lbs).*	Damaged or worn cable	Inspect cable. Replace if kinked or crushed.
	Clutch cable excessive wear	Disconnect cable from release lever. Check for smooth operation or binding. Replace if operation is erratic.
	Clutch pedal binding	Disconnect cable from release lever. Check for free pedal movement. Free up as required.
	Clutch release lever binding	Inspect and service as required.
	Clutch disc worn or pressure plate damaged	Service as required
Vehicle will not start with clutch pedal fully depressed.	Clutch interlock switch improperly adjusted.	Reposition self-adjusting clip or rod on press and release clutch pedal.
	Clutch interlock switch damaged.	Perform continuity test. Replace switch if necessary.
	Starter, wiring or battery damaged.	Refer to Section 28-02 and/or Section 31-02.

*NOTE: In the event of a sheared teeth condition on the pawl or quadrant, the pedal efforts are to be evaluated after installation of new components. If the pedal efforts are in excess of 45 lbs., the clutch disc, pressure plate or clutch cable may require replacement.

4. If the self-adjusting clip is out of position, remove and reposition the clip to about 1 inch from the end of the rod.

5. Reset the switch by pressing the clutch pedal to the floor.

6. Repeat Step 2. If switch is damaged, replace it.

REMOVAL AND INSTALLATION

Starter/Clutch Interlock Switch

1. Disconnect the wiring connector.

2. Remove the retaining pin from the clutch pedal.

3. Remove the switch bracket attaching screw.

4. Lift the switch and bracket assembly upward to disengage tab from pedal support.

5. Move the switch outward to disengage actuating rod eyelet from clutch pedal pin and remove switch from vehicle.

NOTE: *Always install the switch with the self-adjusting clip about 1 inch from the end of the rod. The clutch pedal must be fully up (clutch engaged). Otherwise, the switch may be misadjusted.*

6. Place the eyelet end of the rod onto the pivot pin.

7. Swing the switch assembly around to line up hole in the mounting boss with the hole in the bracket.

8. Install the attaching screw.

9. Replace the retaining pin in the pivot pin.

10. Connect the wiring connector.

Clutch Pedal Assembly

1. Remove the starter/clutch interlock switch.

2. Remove the clutch pedal attaching nut.

3. Pull the clutch pedal off the clutch pedal shaft.

4. Align the square hole of the clutch pedal with the clutch pedal shaft and push the clutch pedal on.

5. Install the clutch pedal attaching nut and tighten to 32–50 ft. lbs.

6. Install the starter/clutch interlock switch.

Self-Adjusting Assembly

1. Disconnect the battery cable from the negative terminal of the battery.

2. Remove the steering wheel using a steering wheel puller Tool T67L-3600-A or equivalent.

3. Remove the lower dash panel section to the left of the steering column.

4. Remove the shrouds from the steering column.

5. Disconnect the brake lamp switch and the master cylinder pushrod from the brake pedal.

6. Rotate the clutch quadrant forward and unhook the clutch cable from the quadrant. Allow the quadrant to slowly swing rearward.

7. Remove the bolt holding the brake pedal support bracket lateral brace to the left side of the vehicle.

8. Disconnect all electrical connectors to the steering column.

9. Remove the four nuts that hold the steering column to the brake pedal support bracket and lower the steering column to the floor.

10. Remove the four booster nuts that hold the brake pedal support bracket to the dash panel.

11. Remove the bolt that holds the brake pedal support bracket to the underside of the instrument panel, and remove the brake pedal support bracket assembly from the vehicle.

12. Remove the clutch pedal shaft nut and the clutch pedal as outlined.

13. Slide the self-adjusting mechanism out of the brake pedal support bracket.

14. Remove the self-adjusting mechanism shaft bushings from either side of the brake pedal support bracket and replace if worn.

15. Lubricate the self-adjusting mechanism shaft with motor oil and install the mechanism into the brake pedal support bracket.

16. Position the quadrant towards the top of the vehicle. Align the flats on the shaft with the flats in the clutch pedal assembly, and install the retaining nut. Tighten to 32–50 ft. lbs.

17. Position the brake pedal support bracket assembly beneath the instrument panel aligning the four holes with the studs in the dash panel. Install the four nuts loosely. Install the bolt through the support bracket into the instrument panel and tighten to 13–25 ft. lbs.

18. Tighten the four booster nuts that hold the brake pedal support bracket to the dash panel to 13–25 ft. lbs.

19. Connect the brake lamp switch and the master cylinder pushrod to the brake pedal.

20. Attach the clutch cable to the quadrant.

21. Position the steering column onto the four studs in the support bracket and start the four nuts.

22. Connect the steering column electrical connectors.

23. Install the steering column shrouds.

24. Install the brake pedal support lateral brace.

25. Tighten the steering column attaching nuts to 20–37 ft. lbs.

26. Install the lower dash panel section.

27. Install the steering wheel.

28. Connect the battery cable to the negative terminal on the battery.

29. Check the steering column for proper operation.

30. Depress the clutch pedal several times to adjust cable.

Quadrant Pawl, Self-Adjusting

1. Remove the self-adjusting mechanism.

2. Remove the two hairpin clips that hold the pawl and quadrant on the shaft assembly.

3. Remove the quadrant and quadrant spring.

4. Remove the pawl spring.

5. Remove the pawl.

6. Lubricate the pawl and quadrant pivot shafts with M1C75B or equivalent grease.

7. Install pawl. Position the teeth of the pawl toward the longer shaft, and the spring hole at the end of the arm. Do not position the spring hole beneath the arm.

8. Insert the straight portion of the spring into the hole, with the coil up.

9. Keeping the straight portion in the hole rotate the spring 180 degrees to the left and slide the coiled portion of the spring over the boss.

10. Hook the bent portion of the spring under the arm.

11. Install the retainer clip on opposite side of spring.

12. Place the quadrant spring on the shaft with the bent portion of the spring in the hole in the arm.

13. Place the lubricated quadrant on the shaft aligning the projection at the bottom of the quadrant to a position beneath the arm of the shaft assembly. Push the pawl up so the bottom tooth of the pawl meshes with bottom tooth of quadrant.

14. Install the quadrant retainer pin.

15. Grasp the straight end of the quadrant spring with pliers and position behind the ear on the quadrant.

16. Install the self-adjusting mechanism.

17. Install the clutch pedal assembly.

Clutch Cable Assembly

1. Lift the clutch pedal to its upward most position to disengage the pawl and quadrant. Push the quadrant forward, unhook the cable from the quadrant and allow to slowly swing rearward.

2. Open the hood and remove the screw that holds the cable assembly isolater to the dash panel.

3. Pull the cable through the dash panel and into the engine compartment. On 2.3L EFI turbocharged and 5.0L engines, remove cable bracket screw from fender apron.

4. Raise the vehicle and safely support on jackstands.

5. Remove the dust cover from the bell housing.

6. Remove the clip retainer holding the cable assembly to the bell housing.

7. Slide the ball on the end of the cable assembly through the hole in the clutch release lever and remove the cable.

8. Remove the dash panel isolater from the cable.

9. Install the dash panel isolater on the cable assembly.

10. Insert the cable through the hole in the bell housing and through the hole in the clutch release lever. Slide the ball on the end of the cable assembly away from the hole in the clutch release lever.

11. Install the clip retainer that holds the cable assembly to the bell housing.

12. Install the dust shield on the bell housing.

13. Push the cable assembly into the engine compartment and lower the vehicle. On 2.3L EFI turbocharged and 5.0L engines, install cable bracket screw in fender apron.

14. Push the cable assembly into the hole in the dash panel and secure the isolater with a screw.

15. Install the cable assembly by lifting the clutch pedal to disengage the pawl and quadrant, then, pushing the quadrant forward, hook the end of the cable over the rear of the quadrant.

16. Depress clutch pedal several times to adjust cable.

AUTOMATIC TRANSMISSION

NEUTRAL START SWITCH ADJUSTMENT

NOTE: *The neutral safety switch on AOD and ZF transmission is non-adjustable.*

Console Shift

1. With the manual linkage properly adjusted and the brakes on, try to engage the starter at each position on the quadrant. The starter should engage only in Neutral and Park positions.

2. Remove the shift handle from the shift lever and the console from the vehicle.

3. Loosen the switch attaching screws and move the shift lever back and forward until the gauge pin .091 in. (no. 43 drill) can be inserted fully.

4. Place the shift lever firmly against the neutral detent stop and slide the switch backward and forward until the switch lever contacts the shift lever.

5. Tighten the switch attaching screws and check starter engagement as in Step 1.

6. Reinstall the console and shift linkage.

Column Shift

1. With the manual linkage properly adjusted and the brakes on, try to engage the starter in each position on the quadrant. The starter should engage only in Neutral or Park.

2. Place the shift lever in the Neutral detent.

3. Disconnect the start switch wires at the plug connector. Disconnect the vacuum hoses, if any. Remove the screws securing the neutral start switch to the steering column and remove the switch. Remove the actuator lever along with the Type III switches.

4. With the switch wires facing up, move the actuator lever fully to the left and insert the gauge pin (no. 43 drill) into gauge pin hole at point A. See the accompanying figure. On a Type III switch, be sure the gauge pin is inserted a full ½ in.

5. 5. With the pin in place, move the actuator lever to the right until the positive stop is engaged.

6. On Type I and Type II switches, remove the gauge pin and insert it at point B. On Type III switches, remove the gauge pin, align two holes in the switch at point A, and reinstall the gauge pin.

7. Reinstall the switch on the steering column. Be sure that the shift lever is engaged in the Neutral detent.

8. Connect the switch wires and vacuum hoses, and remove the gauge pin.

9. Check starter engagement as in Step 1.

NOTE: *1972 and later models with column-mounted selector do not incorporate a Neutral start switch. The driver of the vehicle is prevented from starting the car in any other gear except Park or Neutral by the transmission locking device in the ignition switch on the steering column.*

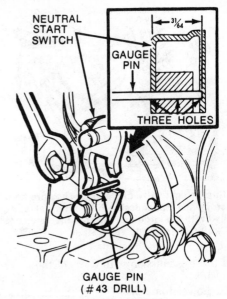

GAUGE PIN
(#43 DRILL)

C4 neutral start switch adjustment

CHANGING TRANSMISSION FLUID AND PAN REMOVAL

NOTE: *Refer to Chapter 1 for current fluid requirements.*

C3, C4, C5

1. Raise the vehicle, so that the transmission oil pan is readily accessible. Safely support on jackstands.

2. Disconnect the fluid filler tube from the pan and allow the fluid to drain into an appropriate container.

3. Remove the transmission oil pan attaching bolts, pan and gasket.

To install the transmission oil pan:

4. Clean the transmission oil pan and transmission mating surfaces.

5. Install the transmission oil pan in the reverse order of removal, torquing the attaching bolts to 16–16 ft. lbs. and using a new gasket.

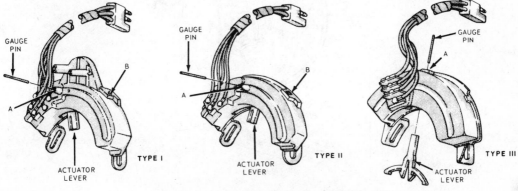

Neutral start switch adjustment—1971 column shift

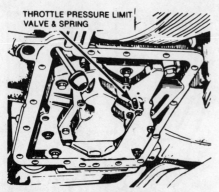

C4 throttle limit valve and spring. They are held in place by the transmission filter. The valve is installed with the large end towards the valve body, the spring fits over the valve stem.

Fill the transmission with 3 qts of the correct type fluid.

6. Lower the vehicle. Start the engine and move the gear selector through shift pattern. Allow the engine to reach normal operating temperature.

7. Check the transmission fluid. Add fluid, if necessary, to maintain correct level.

C6, CW, FMX, and AOD

1. Raise the car and support on jackstands.
2. Place a drain pan under the transmission.
3. Loosen the pan attaching bolts and drain the fluid from the transmission.
4. When the fluid has drained to the level of the pan flange, remove the remaining pan bolts working from the rear and both sides of the pan to allow it to drop and drain slowly.

5. When all of the fluid has drained, remove the pan and clean it thoroughly. Discard the pan gasket.

6. Place a new gasket on the pan, and install the pan on the transmission. Tighten the attaching bolts to 12–16 ft. lbs.

7. Add three quarts of fluid to the transmission through the filler tube.

8. Lower the vehicle. Start the engine and move the gear selector through shift pattern. Allow the engine to reach normal operating temperature.

9. Check the transmission fluid. Add fluid, if necessary, to maintain correct level.

ZF Transmission

NOTE: *Fluid change is required every 30,000 miles. Required fluid is Dexron® II or equivalent.*

1. Raise and support the vehicle safely.
2. Place a drain pan underneath the transmission oil pan.
3. Remove the drain plug and allow the fluid to drain.
4. After all of the fluid has drained, clean the drain plug and reinstall. Tighten the drain plug to 11 ft. lbs.
5. Lower the vehicle. Add three quarts of fluid through the transmission filler tube.
6. Start the engine and check the fluid level after moving the selector through all positions. Add fluid, if necessary, to correct level.

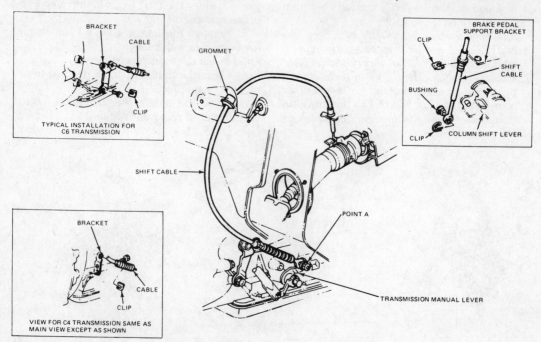

Manual linkage adjustment—column shift

SHIFT LINKAGE ADJUSTMENT

Column Shift

1. With the engine off, place the gear selector in the D (Drive) position, or D (overdrive) position (AOD). Either hang a weight on the shifter or have an assistant sit in the car and hold the selector against the stop.

2. Loosen the adjusting nut or clamp at the shift lever so that the shift rod is free to slide. On models with a shift cable, remove the nut from the transmission lever and disconnect the cable from the transmission.

3. Place the manual shift lever on the transmission in the D (Drive) or D (Overdrive) position. This is the second detent position from the full counterclockwise position.

4. Tighten the adjusting bolt. On cars with a cable, position the cable end on the transmission lever stud, aligning the flats. Tighten the adjusting nut.

5. Check the pointer alignment and transmission operation for all selector positions. If not correct, adjust linkage.

Floor or Console Shift

1. Place the transmission shift lever in D.

2. Raise the vehicle and loosen the manual lever shift rod retaining nut. Move the transmission lever to D_1 or D position. D is the fourth detent from the rear.

3. With the transmission shift lever and transmission manual lever in position, tighten the nut at point A to 10–20 ft. lbs.

4. Check transmission operation for all selector lever detent positions.

NOTE: *All 1971 models with a floor or console-mounted selector lever have incorpo-* rated a transmission lockout rod to prevent the transmission selector from being moved out of the Park position when the ignition lock is in the "off" position. The lock rod connects the shift tube in the steering column to the transmission manual lever. The lock rod cannot be properly adjusted until the manual linkage adjustment is correct.

DOWNSHIFT (THROTTLE) LINKAGE ADJUSTMENT

All Models Except (AOD) Automatic Overdrive and ZF Transmission

1. With the engine off, disconnect the throttle and downshift return springs, if equipped.

2. Hold the carburetor throttle lever in the wide open position against the stop.

3. Hold the transmission downshift linkage in the full downshift position against the internal stop.

4. Turn the adjustment screw on the carburetor downshift lever to obtain 0.010–0.080 in. clearance between the screw tip and the throttle shaft lever tab.

5. Release the transmission and carburetor to their normal free positions. Install the throttle and downshift return springs, if removed.

AOD

1. With the engine off, remove the air cleaner and make sure the fast idle cam is released— the throttle lever must be at the idle stop.

2. Turn the linkage lever adjusting screw counterclockwise until the end of the screw is flush with the face of the lever.

3. Turn the linkage adjustment screw in until there is a maximum clearance of .005 in. be-

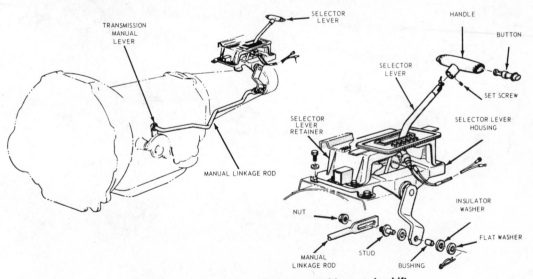

Early type manual linkage adjustment with console shift

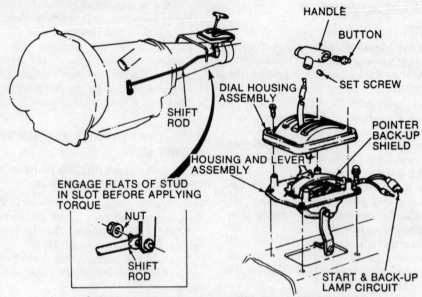

Later type automatic transmission floor shift linkage

tween the throttle lever and the end of the adjustment screw.

4. Turn the linkage lever adjusting screw clockwise three full turns. A minimum of one turn is permissible if the screw travel is limited.

5. If it is not possible to turn the adjusting screw at least one full turn or if the initial gap of .005 in. could not be obtained, perform the linkage adjustment at the transmission.

AOD Alternate Method

If unable to adjust the throttle valve control linkage at the carburetor, as described above, proceed as follows.

1. At the transmission, loosen the 8 mm bolt

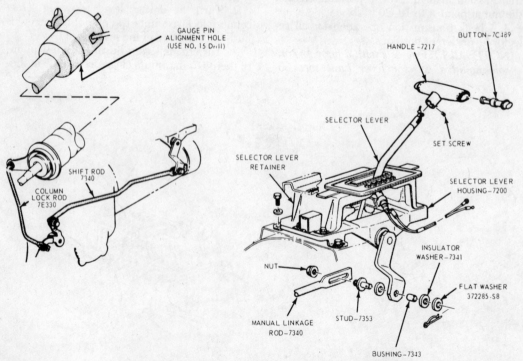

Manual linkage adjustment—1971 console shift with lockrod

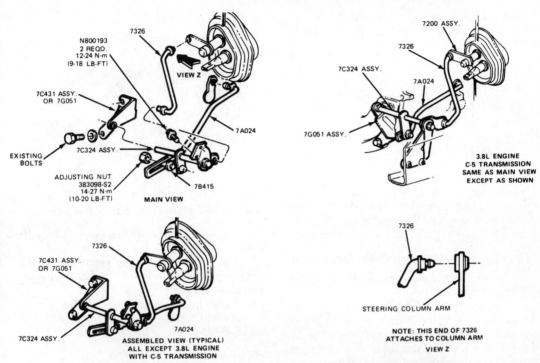

Manual linkage on column shift automatic transmission, 1981–82 Cougar

on the throttle valve (TV) control rod sliding trunnion block. Make sure the trunnion block slides freely on the control rod.

2. Push up on the lower end of the TV control rod to insure that the carburetor linkage lever is held against the throttle lever. When the pressure is released, the control rod must stay in position.

3. Force the TV control lever on the transmission against its internal stop. While maintaining pressure tighten the trunnion block bolt. Make sure the throttle lever is at the idle stop.

AOD IDLE SPEED ADJUSTMENT

Whenever it is necessary to adjust the idle speed by more than 50 rpm either above or below the

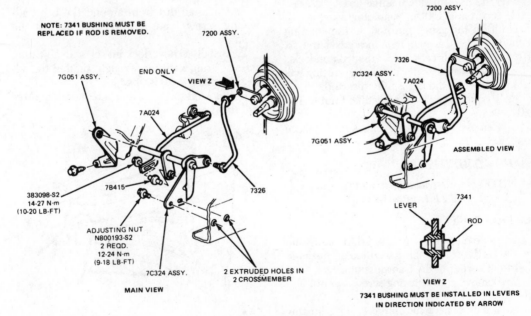

Rod-type column shift linkage on Thunderbird, XR-7, and Continental

factory specifications, the adjustment screw on the linkage lever at the carburetor should also be adjusted to the following specifications:

Idle Speed Change (rpm)	Adjustment Screw Turns
• 50–100 increase	1½ turns out
• 50–100 decrease	1½ turns in
• 100–150 increase	2½ turns out
• 100–150 decrease	2½ turns in

After making any idle speed adjustments, make sure the linkage lever and throttlelever are in contact with the throttle lever at its idle stop and verify that the shift lever is in N (neutral).

ZF Transmission-Kickdown Cable Adjustment

1. Set the injection pump top lever to the full throttle position.
2. Tighten the rear adjusting nut on the threaded barrel of the adjusting cable until a gap of 1.5 inches exists between the edge of the crimped bead on the cable closest to the barrel and the end of the threaded barrel.
3. Tighten the forward adjusting nut to 80–106 inch lbs. to lock the cable assembly to the bracket maintaining the correct position.
4. Recheck the gap, readjust if necessary.

LOCK ROD ADJUSTMENT

1971 Console Shift

1. With the transmission selector lever in the Drive position, loosen the lock rod adjustment nut on the transmission manual lever.
2. Insert a 0.180 in. diameter rod (no. 15 drill bit) in the gauge pin hole in the steering column socket casting. It is located at the six o'clock position directly below the ignition lock.
3. Manipulate the pin so that the casting will not move when the pin is fully inserted.
4. Torque the lock rod adjustment nut to 10–20 ft. lbs.
5. Remove the pin and check the linkage operation.

BAND ADJUSTMENTS

NOTE: *No external adjustments are possible on AOD and ZF transmissions.*

C3 Front Band

1. Wipe clean the area around the adjusting screw on the side of the transmission, near the left front corner of the transmission.
2. Remove the adjusting screw locknut and discard it.
3. Install a new locknut on the adjusting screw but do not tighten it.

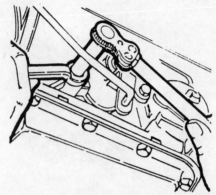

C4, C5 and C6 intermediate band adjustment

4. Tighten the adjusting screw to *exactly 10 ft. lbs.*
5. Back off the adjusting screw *exactly 1½ turns* on models through 1979, and 2 turns on 1980 and later models.
6. Hold the adjusting screw so that it *does not turn* and tighten the adjusting screw locknut to 35–45 ft. lbs.

C4 and C5 Intermediate Band

1. Clean all the dirt from the adjusting screw and remove and discard the locknut.
2. Install a new locknut on the adjusting screw using a torque wrench, tighten the adjusting screw to 10 ft. lbs.
3. Back off the adjusting screw *exactly 1¾ turns* for the C4 and 4¼ turns for the C5.
4. Hold the adjusting screw steady and tighten the locknut to 35 ft. lbs.

C4, and C5 Low-Reverse Band

1. Clean all dirt from around the band adjusting screw, and remove and discard the locknut.
2. Install a new locknut of the adjusting screw. Using a torque wrench, tighten the adjusting screw to 10 ft. lbs.
3. Back off the adjusting screw *exactly three full turns.*

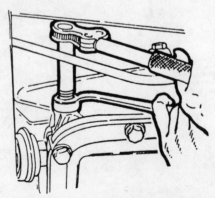

C4, and C5 low-reverse band adjustment

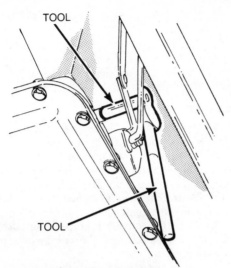

C6 intermediate band adjustment

4. Hold the adjusting screw steady and tighten the locknut to 35 ft. lbs.

C6 Intermediate Band Adjustment

1. Raise the car on a hoist or place it on jack stands.

2. Clean the threads of the intermediate band adjusting screw.

3. Loosen the adjustment screw locknut.

4. Tighten the adjusting screw to 10 ft. lbs. and back the screw off *exactly 1½ turns*. Tighten the adjusting screw locknut to 35 ft. lbs.

FMX, CW Front Band Adjustment

1. Drain the transmission fluid and remove the oil pan, fluid filter screen, and clip.

2. Clean the pan and filter screen and remove the old gasket.

3. Loosen the front servo adjusting screw locknut.

4. Pull back the actuating rod and insert a ¼ in. spacer bar between the adjusting screw and the servo piston stem. Tighten the adjusting screw to 10 in. lbs. torque. Remove the spacer bar and tighten the adjusting screw *an additional ¾ turn*. Hold the adjusting screw fast and tighten the locknut securely (20–25 ft. lbs.).

5. Install the transmission fluid filter screen and clip. Install pan with a new pan gasket.

6. Refill the transmission to the mark on the dipstick. Start the engine, run for a few minutes, shift the selector lever through all positions, and place it in Park. Recheck the fluid level and add fluid if necessary.

FMX, CW Rear Band Adjustments

On certain cars with a console floor shift, the entire console shift lever and linkage will have

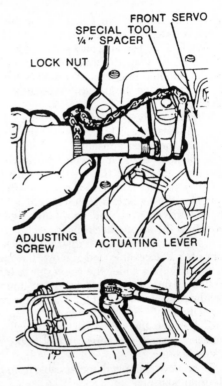

FMX and CW front band (top) and rear band (bottom) adjustments

to be removed to gain access to the rear band external adjusting screw.

1. Locate the external rear band adjusting screw on the transmission case, clean all dirt from the threads, and coat the threads with light oil.

NOTE: *The adjusting screw is located on the upper right-side of the transmission case. Access is often through a hole in the front floor to the right of center under the carpet.*

2. Loosen the locknut on the rear band external adjusting screw.

3. Using torque wrench tighten the adjusting screw to 10 ft. lbs. torque. If the adjusting screw is tighter than 10 ft. lbs. torque, loosen the adjusting screw and retighten to the proper torque.

4. Back off the adjusting screw *exactly 1½ turns*. Hold the adjusting screw steady while tightening the locknut to the proper torque (35–40 ft. lbs.).

Transmission Removal and Installation

C3

Removal

1. Raise and safely support the vehicle.

2. Place a drain pan under the transmission fluid pan. Starting at the rear of the pan

and working toward the front, loosen the attaching bolts and allow the fluid to drain. Then remove all of the pan attaching bolts except two at the front, to allow the fluid to further drain. After all the fluid has drained, install two bolts on the rear side of the pan to temporarily hold it in place.

3. Remove the converter drain plug access cover and adapter plate bolts from the lower end of the converter housing.

4. Remove the four flywheel to converter attaching nuts. Crank the engine to turn the converter to gain access to the nuts, using a wrench on the crankshaft pulley attaching bolt. **On belt driven overhead camshaft engines, never turn the engine backwards.**

5. Crank the engine until the converter drain plug is accessible and remove the plug. Place a drain pan under the converter to catch the fluid. After all the fluid has been drained from the converter, reinstall the plug and tighten to specification.

6. Remove the driveshaft and install the extension housing seal replacer tool in the extension housing.

7. Remove the speedometer cable from the extension housing.

8. Disconnect the shift rod at the transmission manual lever. Disconnect the downshift rod at the transmission downshift lever.

9. Remove the starter-to-converter housing attaching bolts and position the starter out of the way.

10. Disconnect the neutral start switch wires from the switch.

11. Remove the vacuum line from the transmission vacuum unit.

12. Position a transmission jack under the transmission and raise it slightly.

13. Remove the engine rear support-to-crossmember nut.

14. Remove the crossmember-to-frame side support attaching bolts and remove the crossmember.

15. Remove the inlet pipe steady rest from the inlet pipe and rear engine support; then disconnect the muffler inlet pipe at the exhaust manifold and secure it.

16. Lower the jack under the transmission and allow the transmission to hang.

17. Position a jack to the front of the engine and raise the engine to gain access to the two upper converter housing-to-engine attaching bolts.

18. Disconnect the oil cooler lines at the transmission. Plug all openings to keep out dirt.

19. Remove the lower converter housing-to-engine attaching bolts.

20. Remove the transmission filler tube.

21. Secure the transmission to the jack with a safety chain.

22. Remove the two upper converter housing-to-engine attaching bolts. Move the transmission to the rear and down to remove it from under the vehicle.

Installation

1. Tighten the converter drain plug to 20-30 ft. lb. if not previously done.

2. Position the converter to the transmission making sure the converter hub is fully engaged in the pump gear. The dimension given in the illustration is for guidance only. It does not indicate engagement.

3. With the converter properly installed, place the transmission on the jack and secure with safety chain.

4. Rotate the converter so the drive studs and drain plug are in alignment with their holes in the flywheel.

5. With the transmission mounted on a transmission jack, move the converter and transmission assembly forward into position being careful not to damage the flywheel and the converter pilot.

During this move, to avoid damage, do not allow the transmission to get into a nosed down position as this will cause the converter to move forward and disengage from the pump gear. The converter must rest squarely against the flywheel. This indicates that the converter pilot is not binding in the engine crankshaft.

6. Install the two upper converter housing-to-engine attaching bolts and tighten to 28-38 ft. lb.

7. Remove the safety chain from the transmission.

8. Insert the filler tube in the stub tube and secure it to the cylinder block with the attaching bolt. Tighten the bolt to 28-38 ft. lb. If the stub tube is loosened or dislodged, it should be replaced.

9. Install the oil cooler lines in the retaining clip at the cylinder block. Connect the lines to the transmission case.

10. Remove the jack supporting the front of the engine.

11. Position the muffler inlet pipe support bracket to the converter housing and install the four lower converter housing-to-engine attaching bolts. Tighten the bolts to 28-38 ft. lb.

12. Raise the transmission. Position the crossmember to the frame side supports and install the attaching bolts. Tighten the bolts to 30-40 ft. lb.

13. Lower the transmission and install the rear engine support-to-crossmember nut. Tighten the nut to 30-40 ft. lb.

14. Remove the transmission jack.

15. Install the vacuum hose on the transmission vacuum unit. Install the vacuum line into the retaining clip.

16. Connect the neutral start switch plug to the switch.

17. Install the starter and tighten the attaching bolts.

18. Install the four flywheel-to-converter attaching nuts.

When assembling the flywheel to the converter, first install the attaching nuts and tighten to 20–34 lb. ft.

19. Install the converter drain plug access cover and adaptor plate bolts. Tighten the bolts to 15–20 ft. lb.

20. Connect the muffler inlet pipe to the exhaust manifold.

21. Connect the transmission shift rod to the manual lever.

22. Connect the downshift rod to the downshift lever.

23. Connect the speedometer cable to the extension housing.

24. Install the driveshaft. Tighten the companion flange U-bolt attaching nuts to 30 ft. lb.

25. Adjust the manual and downshift linkage as required.

26. Lower the vehicle. Fill the transmission to the proper level with Dexron® II.

Pour in five quarts of fluid; then run the engine and add fluid as required.

27. Check the transmission, converter assembly and oil cooler lines for leaks.

C4

Removal

1. Raise and safely support the vehicle.

2. Place the drain pan under the transmission fluid pan. Remove the fluid filler tube from the pan and drain the transmission fluid. On some models it may be necessary to loosen the pan attaching bolts and allow the fluid to drain. Start loosening the bolts at the rear of the pan and work toward the front. Finally remove all of the pan attaching bolts except two at the front, to allow the fluid to further drain. After the fluid has drained, install two bolts on the rear side of the pan to temporarily hold it in place.

3. Remove the converter drain plug access cover from the lower end of the converter housing.

4. Remove the converter-to-flywheel attaching nuts. Place a wrench on the crankshaft pulley attaching bolt to turn the converter to gain access to the nuts.

5. With the wrench on the crankshaft pulley attaching bolt, turn the converter to gain access to the converter drain plug. Then, remove the plug. Place a drain pan under the converter to catch the fluid. After the fluid has been drained from the converter, reinstall the plug.

6. Remove the drive shaft and install the extension housing seal replacer tool in the extension housing.

7. Remove the vacuum line hose from the transmission vacuum unit. Disconnect the vacuum line from the retaining clip. Disconnect the transmission regulated spark (T.R.S.) switch wire at the transmission, if so equipped.

8. Remove the engine support to crossmember bolts or nuts.

9. Remove the speedometer cable from the extension housing.

10. Disconnect the oil cooler lines from the transmission case.

11. Disconnect the selector rod or cable at the transmission manual lever. Disconnect the downshift rod at the transmission downshift lever.

12. On console and floor shift vehicles, disconnect the column lock rod at the transmission, if so equipped.

13. Disconnect the starter cable. Remove the starter attaching bolts and remove the starter from the converter housing.

14. Remove the bolt that secures the transmission fluid filler tube to the cylinder head and lift the fluid filler tube from the case.

15. Position the transmission jack to support the transmission and secure the transmission to the jack with a safety chain.

16. Remove the crossmember attaching bolts and lower the crossmember.

17. Remove the five converter housing-to-engine attaching bolts. Lower the transmission and remove it from under the vehicle.

Installation

1. Torque the converter drain plug to 20–30 ft. lb.

2. Position the converter to the transmission making sure the converter drive flats are fully engaged in the pump gear.

3. With the converter properly installed, place the transmission on the jack. Secure the transmission to the jack with the safety chain.

4. Rotate the converter so that the studs and drain plug are in alignment with their holes in the flywheel.

5. With the transmission mounted on a transmission jack, move the converter and transmission assembly forward into position, using care not to damage the flywheel and the converter pilot. The converter must rest squarely against the flywheel. This indicates that

the converter pilot is not binding in the engine crankshaft.

6. Install the five converter housing-to-engine attaching bolts. Torque the bolts to 23–28 ft. lb. Remove the safety chain from the transmission.

7. Position the crossmember and install the attaching bolts. Torque the bolts to 40–50 ft. lb.

8. Lower the transmission and install the engine support to crossmember bolts or nuts. Torque the bolts or nuts to 30–40 ft. lb.

9. Install the flywheel to the converter attaching nuts. Torque the nuts to 23–28 ft. lb.

11. Remove the transmission jack. Install the fluid filler tube in the transmission case or pan. Secure the tube to the cylinder head with the attaching bolt. Install the vacuum hose on the transmission vacuum unit. Install the vacuum line retaining clip. Connect the transmission regulated spark (T.R.S.) switch wire to the switch, if so equipped.

12. Connect the fluid cooling lines to the transmission case.

13. Connect the downshift rod to the downshift lever.

14. Connect the selector rod or cable to the transmission manual lever. Connect the column lock rod on console and floor shift vehicles, if so equipped.

15. Connect the speedometer cable to the extension housing.

16. Install the converter housing cover and torque the attaching bolts to 12–16 ft. lb.

18. Install the starter and torque the attaching bolts to 25–30 ft. lb. Connect the starter cable.

19. Install the drive shaft. Torque the companion flange U-bolts attaching nuts to 25–30 ft. lb.

20. Lower the vehicle. Fill the transmission to the proper level with fluid. Adjust the manual and downshift linkage as required.

C5

Removal

1. Open the hood and install protective covers on the fenders.

2. Disconnect the battery negative cable.

3. On Cougar models equipped with a 3.8L engine, remove the air cleaner assembly.

4. Remove the fan shroud attaching bolts and position the shroud back over the fan.

5. On Cougar models equipped with a 3.8L engine, loosen the clamp and disconnect the thermactor air injection hose at the catalytic converter check valve. The check valve is located on the right side of the engine compartment near the dash panel.

6. On Cougar models equipped with a 3.8 L engine, remove the two transmission-to-engine attaching bolts located at the top of the transmission bell housing. These bolts are accessible from the engine compartment.

7. Raise and safely support the vehicle.

8. Remove the driveshaft.

9. Disconnect the muffler inlet pipe from the catalytic converter outlet pipe. Support the muffler/pipe assembly by wiring it to a convenient underbody bracket.

10. Remove the nuts attaching the exhaust pipe(s) to the exhaust manifold(s).

11. Pull back on the catalytic converters to release the converter hangers from the mounting bracket.

12. Remove the speedometer clamps bolt and pull the speedometer out of the extension housing.

13. Separate the neutral start switch harness connector.

14. Disconnect the kick down rod at the transmission lever.

15. Disconnect the shift linkage at the linkage bellcrank. On vehicles equipped with floor mounted shift, remove the shift cable routing bracket attaching bolts and disconnect the cable at the transmission lever.

16. Remove the converter dust shield.

17. Remove the torque converter to drive plate attaching nuts. To gain access to the converter nuts, turn the crankshaft and drive plate using a ratchet handle and socket on the crankshaft pulley attaching bolt.

18. Remove the starter attaching bolts.

19. Loosen the nuts attaching the rear support to the No. 3 crossmember.

20. Position a transmission jack under transmission oil pan. Secure the transmission to the jack with a safety chain.

21. Remove the through bolts attaching the No. 3 crossmember to the body brackets.

22. Lower the transmission enough to allow access to the cooler line fittings. Disconnect the cooler lines.

23. On Cougar models, remove the (4) remaining transmission-to-engine attaching bolts (2 each side). On all other models, remove the (6) transmission-to-engine attaching bolts.

24. Pull the transmission back to disengage the converter studs from the drive plate. Lower the transmission out of the vehicle.

Installation

1. Raise the transmission into the vehicle. As the transmission is being slowly raised into position, rotate the torque converter until the studs and drain plug are aligned with the holes in the drive plate.

2. Move the converter/transmission as-

sembly forward against the back of the engine. Make sure the converter studs engage the drive plate and that the transmission dowels on the back of the engine engage the bolt holes in the bell-housing.

3. On Cougar models equipped with a 3.8L engine, install four transmission-to-engine attaching bolts (2 each side). On all other models, install the (6) transmission-to-engine attaching bolts. Tighten the attaching bolts to 40–50 ft. lb.

4. Connect the cooler lines.

5. Raise the transmission and install the No. 3 crossmember through bolts. Tighten the attaching nuts to 20–30 ft. lb.

6. Remove the safety chain and transmission jack.

7. Tighten the rear support attaching nuts to 30–50 ft. lb.

8. Position the starter and install the attaching bolts.

9. Install the torque converter to drive plate attaching nuts. Tighten the attaching nuts to 20–30 ft. lb.

10. Position the dust shield and on vehicles with column mounted shift, position the linkage bellcrank bracket. Install the attaching bolts and tighten to 12–16 ft. lb.

11. Connect the shift linkage to the linkage bellcrank. On vehicles equipped with floor mounted shift, connect the cable to the shift lever and install the routing bracket attaching bolt.

12. Connect the kick down rod to the transmission lever.

13. Connect the neutral start switch harness.

14. Install the speedometer and the clamp bolt. Tighten the clamp bolt to 36–54 in. lb.

15. Install the catalytic converters using new seal(s) at the pipe(s) to exhaust manifold connection(s).

16. Install the pipe(s) to exhaust manifold attaching nuts. Do not tighten the attaching nuts.

17. Remove the wire supporting the muffler/pipe assembly and connect the pipe to the converter outlet. Do not tighten the attaching nuts.

18. Align the exhaust system and tighten the manifold and converter outlet attaching nuts.

19. Install the driveshaft.

20. Check and if necessary, adjust the shift linkage.

21. Lower the vehicle.

22. On Cougar models equipped with a 3.8L engine, install the two transmission-to-engine attaching bolts located at the top of the transmission bell housing.

23. On Cougar models equipped with a 3.8L

engine, connect the thermactor air injection hose to the converter check valve.

24. Position the fan shroud and install the attaching bolts.

25. On Cougar models equipped with a 3.8L engine, install the air cleaner assembly.

26. Connect the battery negative cable.

27. Start the engine. Make sure the engine cranks only when the selector lever is positioned in the neutral (N) or Park (P) detent.

28. Fill the transmission with type H fluid.

29. Raise the vehicle and inspect for fluid leaks.

C6

Removal

1. Working from the engine compartment, remove the two bolts retaining the fan shroud to the radiator.

2. Connect a remote control starter button on Torino and Motego vehicles equipped with a 400 CID engine.

3. Raise and safely support the vehicle.

4. Place the drain pan under the transmission fluid pan. Starting at the rear of the pan and working toward the front, loosen the attaching bolts and allow the fluid to drain. Finally remove all of the pan attaching bolts except two at the front, to allow the fluid to further drain. After the fluid has drained, install two bolts on the rear side of the pan to temporarily hold it in place.

5. Remove the converter drain plug access cover and adapter plate bolts from the lower end of the converter housing.

6. Remove the converter-to-flywheel attaching nuts. On Torino and Montego vehicles equipped with a 400 CID engine, crank the engine until the nuts are accessible.

7. Crank the engine on Torino and Montego vehicles with a 400 CID engine to turn the converter to gain access to the converter drain plug. Then, remove the plug. Place a drain pan under the converter to catch the fluid. After the fluid has been drained from the converter, reinstall the plug.

8. Disconnect the drive shaft from the rear axle and slide the shaft rearward from the transmission. Install a seal installation tool in the extension housing to prevent fluid leakage.

9. Disconnect the speedometer cable from the extension housing.

10. Disconnect the downshift rod from the transmission downshift lever.

11. Disconnect the shift cable from the manual lever at the transmission.

12. Remove the two bolts that secure the shift cable bracket to the converter housing and position the cable and bracket out of the way.

13. Remove the starter motor attaching bolts and position the starter out of the way.

14. Disconnect the rubber hose from the vacuum diaphragm at the rear of the transmission. Remove the vacuum tube from the retaining clip at the transmission. Disconnect the transmission regulated spark (T.R.S.) switch wire at the transmission, if so equipped.

15. Disconnect the muffler inlet pipe at the exhaust manifolds and allow the pipe to hang.

16. Remove the crossmember to frame side support bolts and nuts. Remove the nuts securing the rear engine supports to the crossmember. Position a jack under the transmission and raise it slightly. Remove the bolts securing the rear engine supports to the extension housing and remove the crossmember and rear supports from the vehicle.

17. Loosen the parking brake adjusting nut at the equalizer and remove the cable from the idler hook attached to the floor pan.

18. Lower the transmission, then disconnect the oil cooler lines from the transmission case.

19. Secure the transmission to the jack with a chain.

20. Remove the six bolts that attach the converter housing to the cylinder block.

21. Remove the bolt that secures the transmission filler tube to the cylinder block. Lift the filler tube and dipstick from the transmission.

22. Move the transmission away from the cylinder block.

23. Carefully lower the transmission and remove it from under the vehicle.

24. Remove the converter and mount the transmission in a holding fixture.

Installation

1. Torque the converter drain plug to 14–28 ft. lb.

2. Position the converter to the transmission making sure the converter drive flats are fully engaged in the pump gear.

3. With the converter properly installed, place the transmission on the jack. Secure the transmission to the jack with the safety chain.

4. Rotate the converter so that the studs and drain plug are in alignment with their holes in the flywheel.

5. With the transmission mounted on a transmission jack, move the converter and transmission assembly forward into position using care not to damage the flywheel and converter pilot. The converter must rest squarely against the flywheel. This indicates that the converter pilot is not binding in the engine crankshaft.

6. Install a new O-ring on the lower end of the transmission filler tube. Insert the tube in the transmission case and secure the tube to the engine with the attaching bolt.

7. Install the converter housing-to-engine attaching bolts. Torque the bolts to 40–50 ft. lb. Remove the safety chain from the transmission.

8. Connect the oil cooler lines to the transmission case.

9. Raise the transmission.

10. Position the parking brake cable in the idler hook and tighten the adjusting nut at the equalizer.

11. Place the rear engine supports on the crossmember and position the crossmember on the frame side supports.

12. Secure the engine rear supports to the extension housing with the attaching bolts. Torque the bolts to 35–40 ft. lb.

13. Remove the transmission jack from under the vehicle and install the crossmember-to-frame side support bolts and nuts. Torque the bolts and nuts to 35–40 ft. lb.

14. Install and torque the engine rear support-to-crossmember attaching nuts.

15. Connect the muffler inlet pipe to the exhaust manifolds.

16. Connect the vacuum line to the vacuum diaphragm making sure that the metal tube is secured in the retaining clip. Connect the transmission regulated spark (T.R.S.) switch wire to the switch, if so equipped.

17. Position the starter motor to the converter housing and secure it with the attaching bolts.

18. Install the torque converter-to-flywheel attaching nuts and torque them to 20–30 ft. lb.

19. Position the shift cable bracket to the converter housing and install the two attaching bolts.

20. Connect the shift cable to the manual lever at the transmission.

21. Connect the downshift rod to the lever on the transmission.

22. Connect the speedometer cable to the extension housing.

23. Install the drive shaft.

24. Install the converter drain plug access cover and adapter plate bolts. Torque the bolts to 12–16 ft. lb.

25. Adjust the manual and downshift linkage as required.

26. Lower the vehicle.

27. Working from the engine compartment, position the fan shroud to the radiator and secure with the two attaching bolts.

28. Remove the remote starter button on Torino and Montego vehicles equipped with the 400 CID engine.

29. Fill the transmission to the proper level

with Type F for 1971–76 models and Dexron® II for 1977 and later.

30. Check the transmission, converter assembly and oil cooler lines for leaks.

CW and FMX

Removal

1. Position the vehicle in the work area, but do not raise at this time.

2. Remove the two upper bolts and lockwashers which attach the converter housing to the engine.

3. Raise and safely support the vehicle.

4. Place the drain pan under the transmission fluid pan. Starting at the rear of the pan and working toward the front, loosen the attaching bolts and allow the fluid to drain. Finally remove all of the pan attaching bolts except two at the front, to allow the fluid to further drain. With fluid drained, install two bolts on the rear side of the pan to temperarily hold it in place.

5. Remove the converter drain plug access cover from the lower end of the converter housing.

6. Remove the converter-to-flywheel attaching nuts. Place a wrench on the crankshaft pulley attaching bolt to turn the converter to gain access to the nuts.

7. With the wrench on the crankshaft pulley attaching bolt, turn the converter to gain access to the converter drain plug, and remove the plug. Place a drain pan under the converter to catch the fluid. After the fluid has been drained, reinstall the plug.

8. Disconnect the driveshaft from the rear companion flange (marking it to assure correct assembly). Slide the shaft rearward from the transmission. Position a seal installation tool in the extension housing to prevent fluid leakage.

9. Disconnect the vacuum hoses from the vacuum diaphragm unit and the tube from the extension housing clip.

10. Install the converter housing front plate to hold the converter in place when the transmission is removed. Under no conditions should the converter be left attached to the engine when the transmission is removed. This could damage the input shaft, converter and pump.

11. Disconnect the starter cables from the starter and remove the starter.

12. Disconnect the oil cooler lines from the transmission.

13. Disconnect the downshift linkage from the transmission.

14. Disconnect the selector rod or cable from the transmission manual lever.

15. Disconnect the speedometer cable from the extension housing. Disconnect the exhaust inlet pipes at the exhaust manifolds (LTD II, Thunderbird and Cougar).

16. Support the transmission on a transmission jack. Secure the transmission to the jack with safety chain. Remove the two engine rear support to transmission bolts. Remove the two crossmember to frame side rail attaching bolts and nuts. Raise the transmission slightly to take the weight off the crossmember. Remove the rear support to crossmember bolt and nut and remove the crossmember.

17. Lower the transmission slightly and disconnect the fluid filler tube.

18. Remove the remaining converter housing to engine attaching bolts. Move the transmission and converter assembly to the rear and down to remove it.

Installation

1. Torque the converter drain plug to 15–28 ft. lb.

2. If the converter has been removed from the converter housing, carefully position the converter to the transmission making sure the converter drive flats are fully engaged in the pump gear.

3. With the converter properly installed, place the transmission on the jack. Secure the transmission to the jack with safety chain.

4. Rotate the converter until the studs and drain plug are in alignment with their holes in the flywheel.

5. With the transmission mounted on a transmission jack, move the converter and transmission assembly forward into position, using care not to damage the flywheel and converter pilot. The converter must rest squarely against the flywheel. This indicates that the converter pilot is not binding in the engine crankshaft.

6. Install the lower converter housing-to-engine bolts. Torque bolts to 40–50 ft. lb. Remove the safety chain from the transmission.

7. Connect the fluid filler tube.

8. Install the crossmember.

9. Lower the transmission until the extension housing rests on the crossmember, and then install the rear support-to-crossmember bolts. Connect the exhaust inlet pipes at the exhaust manifolds (LTD II, Thunderbird and Cougar).

10. Install the converter attaching nuts. Install the access plates.

11. Connect the oil cooler inlet and outlet lines to the transmission case.

12. Coat the front universal joint yoke seal and spline with C1AZ-19590B lubricant (or equivalent), and install the drive shaft. Be sure that the drive shaft markings match those of the companion flange for correct balance.

13. Connect the speedometer cable at the transmission.

14. Connect the manual selector rod or cable to the transmission manual lever.

15. Connect the downshift linkage at the transmission downshift lever.

16. Install the starter motor and connect the starter cables.

17. Connect the vacuum hoses to the vacuum diaphragm unit and the tube to its clip.

18. Lower the transmission and install the upper two converter housing-to-engine bolts. Torque bolts to 40–50 ft. lb.

19. Lower the vehicle and fill the transmission with type F fluid.

20. Check the transmission, converter assembly, and fluid cooler lines for fluid leaks. Adjust the manual and downshift linkages.

AUTOMATIC OVERDRIVE (AOD)

Removal

1. Raise and safely support the vehicle.

2. Place the drain pan under the transmission fluid pan. Starting at the rear of the pan and working toward the front, loosen the attaching bolts and allow the fluid to drain. Finally remove all of the pan attaching bolts except two at the front, to allow the fluid to further drain. With fluid drained, install two bolts on the rear side of the pan to temporarily hold it in place.

3. Remove the converter drain plug access cover from the lower end of the converter housing.

4. Remove the converter-to-flywheel attaching nuts. Place a wrench on the crankshaft pulley attaching bolt to turn the converter to gain access to the nuts.

5. Place a drain pan under the converter to catch the fluid. With the wrench on the crankshaft pulley attaching bolt, turn the converter to gain access to the converter drain plug and remove the plug. After the fluid has been drained, reinstall the plug.

6. Disconnect the driveshaft from the rear axle and slide shaft rearward from the transmission. Install a seal installation tool in the extension housing to prevent fluid leakage.

7. Disconnect the cable from the terminal on the starter motor. Remove the three attaching bolts and remove the starter motor. Disconnect the neutral start switch wires at the plug connector.

8. Remove the rear mount-to-crossmember attaching bolts and the two crossmember-to-frame attaching bolts.

9. Remove the two engine rear support-to-extension housing attaching bolts.

10. Disconnect the TV linkage rod from the transmission TV lever. Disconnect the manual rod from the transmission manual lever at the transmission.

11. Remove the two bolts securing the bellcrank bracket to the converter housing.

12. Raise the transmission with a transmission jack to provide clearance to remove the crossmember. Remove the rear mount from the crossmember and remove the crossmember from the side supports.

13. Lower the transmission to gain access to the oil cooler lines.

14. Disconnect each oil line from the fittings on the transmission.

15. Disconnect the speedometer cable from the extension housing.

16. Remove the bolt that secures the transmission fluid filler tube to the cylinder block. Lif the filler tube and the dipstick from the transmission.

17. Secure the transmission to the jack with the chain.

18. Remove the converter housing-to-cylinder block attaching bolts.

19. Carefully move the transmission and converter assembly away from the engine and, at the same time, lower the jack to clear the underside of the vehicle.

20. Remove the converter and mount transmission in a holding fixture.

Installation

1. Tighten the converter drain plug to 20–28 ft. lb.

2. Position the converter on the transmission, making sure the converter drive flats are fully engaged in the pump gear by rotating the converter.

3. With the converter properly installed, place the transmission on the jack. Secure the transmission to the jack with a chain.

4. Rotate the converter until the studs and drain plug are in alignment with the holes in the flywheel.

IMPORTANT: Lube pilot.

5. Align the yellow balancing marks on converter and flywheel for Continental.

6. Move the converter and transmission assembly forward into position, using care not to damage the flywheel and the converter pilot. The converter must rest squarely against the flywheel. This indicates that the converter pilot is not binding in the engine crankshaft.

7. Install and tighten the converter housing-to-engine attaching bolts to 40–50 ft. lb. Make sure that the vacuum tube retaining clips are properly positioned.

8. Remove the safety chain from around the transmission.

9. Install a new O-ring on the lower end of

the transmission filler tube. Insert the tube in the transmission case and secure the tube to the engine with the attaching bolt.

10. Connect the speedometer cable to the extension housing.

11. Connect the oil cooler lines to the right side of transmission case.

12. Position the crossmember on the side supports. Positon the rear mount on the crossmember and install the attaching bolt and nut.

13. Secure the engine rear support to the extension housing and tighten the bolts to 35–40 ft. lb.

14. Lower the transmission and remove the jack.

15. Secure the crossmember to the side supports with the attaching bolts and tighten them to 35–40 ft. lb.

16. Position the bellcrank to the converter housing and install the two attaching bolts.

17. Connect the TV linkage rod to the transmission TV lever. Connect the manual linkage rod to the manual lever at the transmission.

18. Secure the converter-to-flywheel attaching nuts and tighten them to 20–30 ft. lb.

19. Install the converter housing access cover and secure it with the attaching bolts.

20. Secure the starter motor in place with the attaching bolts. Connect the cable to the terminal on the starter. Connect the neutral start switch wires at the plug connector.

21. Connect the driveshaft to the rear axle.

22. Adjust the shift linkage as required.

23. Adjust throttle linkage.

24. Lower the vehicle.

25. Fill the transmission to the correct level with Dexron® II. Start the engine and shift the transmission to all ranges, then recheck the fluid level.

ZF TRANSMISSION

Removal and Installation

1. Remove the kickdown cable and insert from the injection pump side lever and cable bracket located in the engine compartment.

2. Place the transmission gear selector in the Neutral position.

3. Raise and safely support the vehicle.

4. Remove the outer manual lever and nut from the transmission manual shift lever shaft.

5. Remove the position sensor from the converter housing.

6. Remove the engine to transmission brace from the lower end of the converter housing and engine block. On models with columnshift, remove the two bolts that secure the bellcrank bracket to the brace.

7. Place a suitable wrench on the crankshaft pulley center bolt and turn the engine to gain access to the converter to drive plate mounting bolts. Remove the fastening nuts, turning the engine as necessary.

8. Drain the fluid from the transmission. Remove the driveshaft after marking the rear driveshaft yoke and companion flange for reinstallation reference.

9. Disconnect the neutral safety switch electrical connector. Remove the vibration damper from the transmission extension housing.

10. Position a suitable transmission type floor jack under the transmission for support.

11. Remove the rear transmission support to crossmember attaching nuts and the two crossmember to side support attaching bolts.

12. Remove the transmission to exhaust system support brackets.

NOTE: *Exhaust system hardware may have to be removed in order gain enough clearance for crossmember removal.*

13. Disconnect the transmission cooler lines from the transmission fittings. See "Quick Disconnect Fitting" instructions in the Fuel Section Chapter.

14. Disconnect the speedometer wiring harness from the transmission extension housing.

15. Remove the starter motor mounting bolts and the starter motor.

16. Secure the transmission to the floor jack, and lower the jack slightly.

17. Remove the four converter housing to engine attaching bolts.

18. Remove the transmission filler tube and dipstick.

19. Carefully move the transmission back and away from the engine. Be sure the converter is mounted fully on the transmission. Lower the transmission and remove from the car.

20. Remove the transmission from the jack and service as required.

21. Secure the transmission on the jack. Insure that the converter is positioned fully back on the transmission shaft and that the mounting studs are in approximate alignment with the crankshaft mounted flexplate hole positions.

22. Move the transmission assembly into position and raise. Align the mounting studs to flexplate and position the transmission. The converter face must fit squarely against the flexplate indicating that the converter pilot is not binding on the engine crankshaft.

23. Install the transmission fluid filler tube and install the four converter housing to engine mounting bolts. Tighten the mounting bolts to 38–48 ft. lbs.

24. Connect the transmission cooler lines to the transmission. Connect the speedometer wiring harness to its connector. Install the ex-

tension housing vibration damper. Tighten the mounting bolts to 18–25 ft. lbs.

25. Install the rear exhaust system support.

26. Install the crossmember on the side supports and secure the mounting bolts and nuts. Secure the rear engine support to the extension housing and crossmember. Install any removed exhaust system hardware.

27. Install and tighten the converter to flexplate mounting nuts to 20–34 ft. lbs.

28. Install the engine to transmission brace on the lower end of the converter housing. Tighten the bolts to 15–18 ft. lbs.

29. On models equipped with a column mounted shift, install the bellcrank bracket on the transmission brace. Tighten the bolts to 10–20 ft. lbs.

30. Remove the transmission jack.

31. Guide the kickdown cable up into the engine compartment.

32. Install the manual control outer lever onto the transmission lever shaft. Tighten the mounting nut to 10–20 ft. lbs.

33. Connect the neutral safety switch harness. Install the position sensor to the converter housing.

34. Install the driveshaft after aligning the flange reference marks.

35. Lower the vehicle and adjust the shift linkage and kickdown cable as required.

36. Add an initial amount of transmission fluid, start the engine and move the transmission control lever through all positions. Recheck the fluid level and add if necessary.

DRIVELINE

Driveshaft and U-Joints

The driveshaft is the means by which the power from the engine and transmission (in the front of the car) is transferred to the differential and rear axles, and finally to the rear wheels.

The driveshaft assembly incorporates two universal joints—one at each end—and a slip yoke at the front end of the assembly, which fits into the back of the transmission.

All driveshafts are balanced when installed in a car. It is therefore imperative that before applying undercoating to the chassis, the driveshaft and universal joint assembly be completely covered to prevent the accidental application of undercoating to the surfaces, and the subsequent loss of balance.

DRIVESHAFT REMOVAL

The procedure for removing the driveshaft assembly—complete with universal joint and slip yoke—is as follows:

1. Mark the relationship of the rear driveshaft yoke and the drive pinion flange of the axle. If the original yellow alignment marks are visible, there is no need for new marks. The purpose of this marking is to facilitate installation of the assembly in its exact original position, thereby maintaining proper balance.

2. Remove the four bolts or "U" clamps which hold the rear universal joint to the pinion flange. Wrap tape around the loose bearing caps in order to prevent them from falling off the spider.

3. Pull the driveshaft toward the rear of the vehicle until the slip yoke clears the transmission housing and the seal. Plug the hole at the rear of the transmission housing or place a container under the opening to catch any fluid which might leak.

UNIVERSAL JOINT OVERHAUL

1. Position the driveshaft assembly in a sturdy vise.

2. Remove the snap-rings which retain the bearings in the slip yoke (front only) and in the driveshaft (front and rear).

3. Using a large punch or an arbor press, drive one of the bearings in toward the center of the universal joint, which will force the opposite bearing out.

4. As each bearing is pressed or punched far enough out of the universal joint assembly that it is accessible, grip it with a pair of pliers, and pull it from the driveshaft yoke. Drive or press the spider in the opposite direction in order to make the opposite bearing accessible, and pull it free with a pair of pliers. Use this procedure to remove all bearings from both universal joints.

5. After removing the bearings, lift the spider from the yoke.

6. Thoroughly clean all dirt and foreign

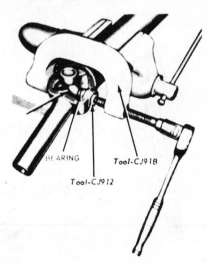

BEARING   Tool-CJ91B

Tool-CJ912

Removing universal joint bearing

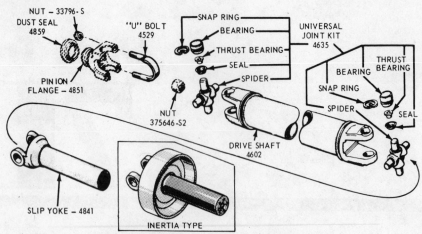

Driveshaft and universal joints disassembled

matter from the yokes on both ends of the driveshaft.

NOTE: *When installing new bearings in the yokes, it is advisable to use an arbor press. However, if this tool is not available, the bearings should be driven into position with extreme care, as a heavy jolt on the needle bearings can easily damage or misalign them, greatly shortening their life and hampering their efficiency.*

7. Start a new bearing into the yoke at the rear of the driveshaft.

8. Position a new spider in the rear yoke and press (or drive) the new bearing ¼ in. below the outer surface of the yoke.

9. With the bearing in position, install a new snap-ring.

10. Start a new bearing into the opposite side of the yoke.

11. Press (or drive) the bearing until the opposite bearing—which you have just in-stalled—contacts the inner surface of the snap-ring.

12. Install a new snap-ring on the second bearing. It may be necessary to grind the surface of this second snap-ring.

13. Reposition the driveshaft in the vise, so that the front universal joint is accessible.

14. Install the new bearings, new spider, and new snap-rings in the same manner as you did for the rear universal joint.

15. Position the slip yoke on the spider. Install new bearings, nylon thrust bearings, and snap-rings.

16. Check both reassembled joints for freedom of movement. If misalignment of any part is causing a bind, a sharp rap on the side of the yoke with a brass hammer should seat the bearing needle and provide the desired freedom of movement. Care should be exercised to firmly support the shaft end during this operation, as well as to prevent blows to the bear-

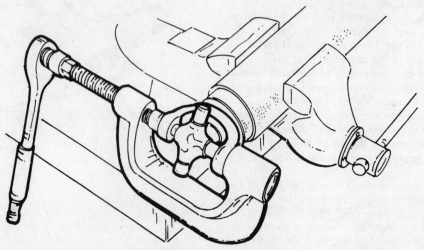

Installing universal joint bearing

ings themselves. Under no circumstances should a driveshaft be installed in a car if there is any binding in the universal joints.

DOUBLE CARDAN JOINT REPLACEMENT (REAR)

1. Working at the rear axle end of the shaft, mark the position of the spiders, the center yoke, and the centering socket yoke as related to the companion flange. The spiders must be assembled with the bosses in their original position to provide proper clearances.

2. Position tool CJ91B or equivalent as shown in the illustration. Thread the tool clockwise until the bearing protrudes approximately ⅜ inch out of the yoke.

3. Remove the driveshaft from the vise.

4. Tighten the bearing in the vise and tap on the yoke to free the bearing from the center yoke. Do not tap on the drive shaft tube.

5. Reposition tool CJ91B or equivalent on the yoke and force the opposite bearing outward and remove it.

6. Position the tool on one of the remaining bearings and force it outward approximately ⅜ inch.

7. Grip the bearing in the vise and tap on the weld yoke to free the bearing from the center yoke. **Do not tap on the driveshaft tube.**

8. Reposition the tool on the yoke to press out the remaining bearing.

9. Remove the spider from the center yoke.

10. Remove the bearings from the driveshaft yoke as outlined above and remove the spider from the yoke.

11. Insert a suitable tool into the centering ball socket located in the companion flange and pry out the rubber seal. Remove the retainer, three piece ball seat, washer and spring from the ball socket.

12. Inspect the centering ball socket assembly for worn or damaged parts. If any damage is evident replace the entire assembly.

13. Insert the spring, washer, three piece ball seat and retainer into the ball socket.

14. Using a suitable tool, install the centering ball socket seal.

15. Position the spider in the driveshaft yoke. Make sure the spider bosses are in the same position as originally installed. Press in the bearing cups with tool CJ91B or equivalent. Install the internal snap rings provided in the repair kit.

16. Position the center yoke over the spider ends and press in the bearing cups. Install the snap rings.

17. Install the spider in the companion flange yoke. Make sure the spider bosses are in the position as originally installed. Press on the bearing cups and install the snap rings.

18. Position the center yoke over the spider ends and press on the bearing cups. Install the snap rings.

DRIVESHAFT INSTALLATION

1. Carefully inspect the rubber seal on the output shaft and the seal in end of the transmission extension housing. Replace them if they are damaged.

2. Examine the lugs on the axle pinion flange and replace the flange if the lugs are shaved or distorted.

3. Coat the yoke spline with special-purpose lubricant. The Ford art number for this lubricant is B8A-19589-A.

4. Remove the plug from the rear of the transmission housing.

5. Insert the yoke into the transmission housing and onto the transmission output shaft. Make sure that the yoke assembly does not bottom on the output shaft with excessive force.

6. Locate the marks which you made on the rear driveshaft yoke and the pinion flange prior to removal of the driveshaft assembly. Install the driveshaft assembly with the marks properly aligned.

7. Install the U-bolts and nuts or bolts which attach the universal joint to the pinion flange. Torque the U-bolt nuts to 8–15 ft. lbs. Flange bolts are tighten to 70–95 ft. lbs.

REAR AXLE ASSEMBLY

Both integral and removable carrier type axles are used.

The axle type and ratio are stamped on a plate attached to a rear housing cover bolt. Axle types also indicate whether the axle shafts are retained by C-locks. To properly identify a C-lock axle, drain the lubricant, remove the rear cover and look for the C-lock on the end of the axle shaft in the differential side gear bore. If the axle has no cover (solid housing) it is not a "C"-lock. If the second letter of the axle model code is F, it is a Traction-Lok axle. Always refer to the axle tag code and ratio when ordering parts.

Axle and Bearing

REMOVAL AND INSTALLATION

Except C-Lock Type

NOTE: *Bearings must be pressed on and off the shaft with an arbor press. Unless you have access to one, it is inadvisable to attempt any repair work on the axle shaft bearing assemblies.*

1. Remove the wheel, tire, and brake drum. With disc brakes, remove the caliper, retainer

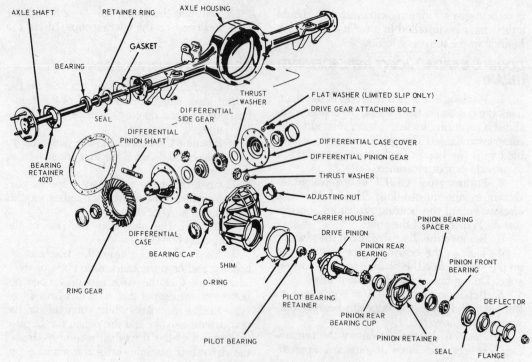

AXLE SHAFT

RETAINER RING

AXLE HOUSING

GASKET

BEARING

THRUST WASHER

FLAT WASHER (LIMITED SLIP ONLY)

DRIVE GEAR ATTACHING BOLT

SEAL

DIFFERENTIAL SIDE GEAR

DIFFERENTIAL PINION SHAFT

DIFFERENTIAL CASE COVER

DIFFERENTIAL PINION GEAR

BEARING RETAINER 4020

THRUST WASHER

ADJUSTING NUT

CARRIER HOUSING

PINION BEARING SPACER

DRIVE PINION

PINION REAR BEARING

PINION FRONT BEARING

DIFFERENTIAL CASE

BEARING CAP

SHIM

O-RING

PILOT BEARING RETAINER

PINION REAR BEARING CUP

DEFLECTOR

RING GEAR

PINION RETAINER

SEAL

FLANGE

PILOT BEARING

Removable carrier axle assembly

nuts, and rotor. New anchor plate bolts will be needed for reassembly.

2. Remove the nuts holding the retainer plate to the backing plate, or axle shaft retainer bolts from the housing. Disconnect the brake line with drum brakes.

3. Remove the retainer and install nuts, finger-tight, to prevent the brake backing plate from being dislodged.

4. Pull out the axle shaft and bearing assembly, using a slide hammer.

On models with a tapered roller bearing, the tapered cup will normally remain in the axle housing when the shaft is removed. The cup must be removed from the housing to prevent seal damage when the shaft is reinstalled. The cup can be removed with a slide hammer and an expanding puller.

NOTE: *If end-play is found to be excessive, the bearing should be replaced. Shimming the bearing is not recommended as this ignores end-play of the bearing itself and could result in improper bearing seating.*

5. Using a chisel, nick the bearing retainer in 3 or 4 places. The retainer does not have to be cut, but merely collapsed sufficiently to allow the bearing retainer to be slid from the shaft.

6. Press off the bearing and install the new one by pressing it into position. With tapered bearings, place the lubricated seal and bearing on the axle shaft (cup rib ring facing the flange). Make sure that the seal is the correct length. Disc brake seal rims are black, drum brake seal rims are grey. Press the bearing and seal onto the shaft.

7. Press on the new retainer.

NOTE: *Do not attempt to press the bearing and the retainer on at the same time.*

8. On ball bearing models, to replace the seal: remove the seal from the housing with an expanding cone type puller and a slide hammer. The seal must be replaced whenever the shaft is removed. Wipe a small amount of sealer onto the outer edge of the new seal before installation; do not put sealer on the sealing lip. Press the seal into the housing with a seal installation tool.

9. Assemble the shaft and bearing in the housing, being sure that the bearing is seated properly in the housing. On ball bearing models, be careful not to damage the seal with the shaft. With tapered bearings, first install the tapered cup on the bearing, and lubricate the outer diameter of the cup and the seal with axle lube. Then install the shaft and bearing assembly into the housing.

10. Install the retainer, drum or rotor and caliper, wheel and tire. Bleed the brakes.

C-Lock Type

1. Jack up and support the rear of the car.

2. Remove the wheels and tires from the brake drums.

3. Place a drain pan under the housing and drain the lubricant by loosening the housing cover.

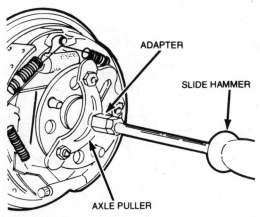

Typical axle shaft removal

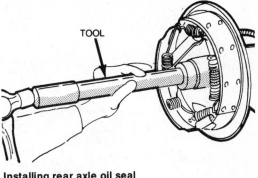

Installing rear axle oil seal

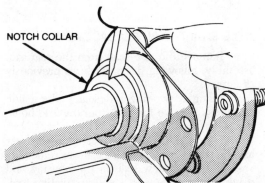

Loosening the bearing retaining ring on the 6¾ inch rear axle

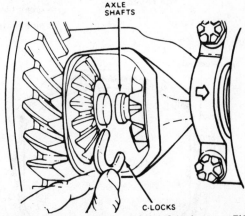

Removal and installation of the C-locks on a 7½ inch rear axle

4. Remove the locks securing the brake drums to the axle shaft flanges and remove the drums.

5. Remove the housing cover and gasket, if used.

6. Position jackstands under the rear frame member and lower the axle housing. This is done to give easy access to the inside of the differential.

7. Working through the opening in the differential case, remove the side gear pinion shaft lockbolt and the side gear pinion shaft.

8. Push the axle shafts inward and remove the C-locks from the inner end of the axle shafts. Temporarily replace the shaft and lockbolt to retain the differential gears in position.

9. Remove the axle shafts with a slide hammer. Be sure the seal is not damaged by the splines on the axle shaft.

10. Remove the bearing and oil seal from the housing. Both the seal and bearing can be removed with a slide hammer. Two types of bearings are used on some axles, one requiring a press fit and the other a loose fit. A loose fitting bearing does not necessarily indicate excessive wear.

11. Inspect the axle shaft housing and axle shafts for burrs or other irregularities. Replace

any work or damaged parts. A light yellow color on the bearing journal of the axle shaft is normal, and does not require replacement of the axle shaft. Slight pitting and wear is also normal.

12. Lightly coat the wheel bearing rollers with axle lubricant. Install the bearings in the axle housing until the bearing seats firmly against the shoulder.

13. Wipe all lubricant from the oil seal bore, before installing the seal.

14. Inspect the original seals for wear. If necessary, these may be replaced with new seals, which are prepacked with lubricant and do not require soaking.

15. Install the oil seal.

CAUTION: *Installation of the seal without the proper tool can cause distortion and seal leakage. Seals may be colored coded for side identification. Do not interchange seals from side to side, if they are coded.*

16. Remove the lockbolt and pinion shaft. Carefully slide the axle shafts into place. Be careful that you do not damage the seal with the splined end of the axle shaft. Engage the splined end of the shaft with the differential side gears.

17. Install the axle shaft C-locks on the in-

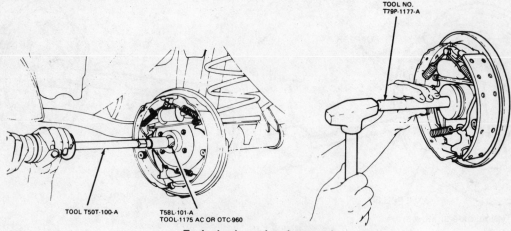

TOOL NO.
T79P-1177-A

TOOL T50T-100-A

T58L-101-A
TOOL-1175 AC OR OTC-960

Typical axle seal replacement

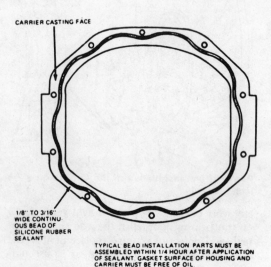

CARRIER CASTING FACE

1/8" TO 3/16"
WIDE CONTINU-
OUS BEAD OF
SILICONE RUBBER
SEALANT

TYPICAL BEAD INSTALLATION PARTS MUST BE
ASSEMBLED WITHIN 1/4 HOUR AFTER APPLICATION
OF SEALANT. GASKET SURFACE OF HOUSING AND
CARRIER MUST BE FREE OF OIL.

Installing sealer on rear axle housing cover

ner end of the axle shafts and seat the C-locks in the counterbore of the differential side gears.

18. Rotate the differential pinion gears until the differential pinion shaft can be installed. Install the differential pinion shaft lockbolt. Tighten to 15–22 ft. lbs.

19. Install the brake drum on the axle shaft flange.

20. Install the wheel and tire on the brake drum and tighten the attaching nuts.

21. Clean the gasket surface of the rear housing and install a new cover gasket and the housing cover. Some models do not use a "paper" gasket. On these models, apply a bead of silicone sealer on the gasket surface. The bead should run inside of the bolt holes.

22. Raise the rear axle so that it is in the running position. Add the amount of specified lubricant to bring the lubricant level to ½ in. below the filler hole.

AXLE SHAFT SEAL REPLACEMENT

1. Remove the axle shaft from the rear axle assembly, following the procedures previously discussed.

2. Using a two-fingered seal puller (slide hammer), remove the seal from the axle housing.

3. Thoroughly clean the recess in the rear axle housing from which the seal was removed.

4. Position a new seal on the housing and drive it into place with a seal installation tool. If this tool is not available, a wood block may be substituted.

NOTE: *Although the right and left-hand seals are identical, there are many different types of seals which have been used on rear axle assemblies. It is advisable to have one of the old seals with you when you are purchasing new ones.*

5. When the seal is properly installed, install the axle shaft.

Differential Overhaul

A differential overhaul is a complex, highly technical, and time-consuming operation—one which requires a great many tools, extensive knowledge of the unit and the way it works, and a high degree of mechanical experience and ability. It is highly advisable that the amateur mechanic not attempt any work on the differential unit.

Improved Traction Differentials

Ford calls their improved traction differential "Traction-Lok". In this assembly, a multiple-disc clutch is employed to control differential action. Repair procedures are the same as for conventional axles (within the scope of this book).

Suspension and Steering

FRONT SUSPENSION

Coil Spring On Upper Arm Suspension

On these models, the front coil springs are mounted on top of the upper control arm to a tower in the sheet metal of the body. This type of mounting provides good stability. The lower arm and stabilizing strut substitute for the conventional A frame and serve to guide the lower part of the spindle through its cycle of up-and-down movement. The rod-type stabilizing strut is mounted between two rubber buffer pads and the front end to cushion fore and aft thrust of the suspension. The effective length of this rod is variable and must be considered in maintenance. Ball joints are of the usual steel construction.

NOTE: *Extreme caution should be exercised when removing or installing coil springs.*

COIL SPRING REMOVAL AND INSTALLATION

1. Raise the hood and remove the shock absorber upper mounting bracket bolts.
2. Raise the front of the vehicle and place safety stands under the end of the lower control arms.
3. Remove the shock absorber lower attaching nuts, washer, and insulators.
4. Remove the wheel cover hub cap.
5. Remove the wheel cover or hub cap.
6. Remove the grease cap, cotter pin, nut lock, adjusting nut, and outer bearing.
7. Pull the wheel, tire and hub and drum off the spindle as an assembly.
8. Install a spring compressor.
9. Compress the spring until all tension is removed from the control arms.
10. Remove the two upper control arm attaching nuts and swing the control arm outboard.

11. Release the spring compressor cautiously and remove it.
12. Remove the spring.
13. Place the upper spring insulator on the spring and secure it in place with tape.
14. Position the spring in the spring tower and compress it with the spring compressor.
15. Swing the upper control arm and install the attaching nuts. Torque the nuts to 75–100 ft. lbs.
16. Release the spring pressure and guide spring into the upper arm spring seat. The end of the spring must be not more than ½ in. from the tab on the spring seat.
17. Remove the spring compressor and position the wheel, tire, and hub and drum on spindle.
18. Install bearing, washer, and adjusting nut.
19. On cars with disc brakes, loosen adjusting nut three turns and rock wheel hub and rotor assembly in and out to push disc brake pads away from rotor.
20. While rotating wheel, hub and drum assembly, torque the adjusting nut to 17–25 ft. lbs. to seat the bearing.
21. With 1⅛ in. box wrench back off the adjusting nut ½ turn, and tighten nut to 10–15 in. lbs. or finger-tight.
22. Position the lock on adjusting nut and install new cotter pin. Bend the ends of the pin around the castellated flange of the nut lock.
23. Check the front wheel rotation and install the grease cap and hub cap.
24. Install shock absorber and upper bracket assembly, making sure shock absorber lower studs have insulators and are in pivot plate holes.
25. Install nuts and wahsers on the lower studs and torque to 8–21 ft. lbs.
26. Install the nuts on the shock absorber upper bracket and torque to 20–28 ft. lbs.
27. Remove safety stands and lower the vehicle.

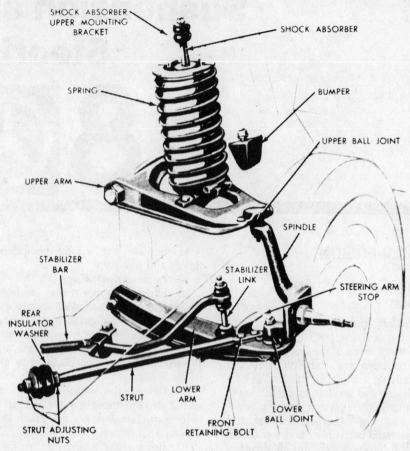

SHOCK ABSORBER
UPPER MOUNTING
BRACKET

SHOCK ABSORBER

SPRING

BUMPER

UPPER BALL JOINT

UPPER ARM

SPINDLE

STABILIZER
BAR

STABILIZER
LINK

STEERING ARM
STOP

REAR
INSULATOR
WASHER

STRUT

LOWER
ARM

LOWER
BALL JOINT

STRUT ADJUSTING
NUTS

FRONT
RETAINING BOLT

1971 front suspension assembly—coil spring on upper arm type

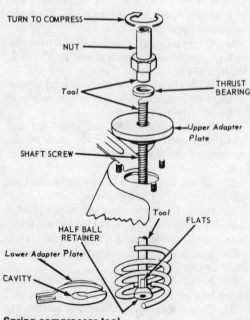

TURN TO COMPRESS

NUT

Tool

THRUST
BEARING

Upper Adapter
Plate

SHAFT SCREW

Tool

FLATS

HALF BALL
RETAINER

Lower Adapter Plate

CAVITY

Spring compressor tool

SHOCK ABSORBER REMOVAL AND INSTALLATION

1. Raise the hood and remove the three shock absorber-to-spring tower attaching bolts.

2. Raise the front of the vehicle and place jackstands under the lower control arms.

3. Remove the shock absorber lower attaching nuts, washers, and insulators.

4. Lift the shock absorber and upper bracket from the spring tower and remove the bracket from the shock absorber. Remove the insulators from the lower attaching studs.

5. Install the upper mounting bracket on the shock absorber and torque to 20–30 ft. lbs. Install the insulators on the lower attaching studs.

6. Place the shock absorber and upper bracket assembly in the spring tower, making sure that the shock absorber lower studs are in the pivot plate holes.

7. Install the two washers and attaching nuts on the lower studs of the shock absorbers and torque to 8–12 ft. lbs.

8. Install the three shock absorber upper

mounting bracket attaching nuts and torque them to 15–25 ft. lbs. Remove the jackstands and lower the vehicle.

Upper Control Arm

When upper control arm bushings become low on lubrication, they become very noisy. This can often be corrected by lubrication and it is not necessary to replace the bushings. On early models that do not contain grease plugs it is necessary to drill and tap the bushing to accept a grease fitting. On later models with grease plugs it is difficult to remove the plug and grease the bushing with conventional tools. Ford has available an upper A-arm lubrication kit which greatly eases the performance of this operation.

REMOVAL AND INSTALLATION

1. Remove the shock absorber and upper mounting bracket from the car as an assembly.
2. Raise the vehicle and remove the wheel and tire as an assembly.
3. Install the spring compressor tool.
4. Place a safety stand under the lower arm.
5. Remove the cotter pin from the upper ball joint stud and loosen the nut.
6. Using a suitable tool, loosen the ball joint in the spindle then, remove the nut and lift the stud from the spindle.
7. Remove the upper arm attaching nuts from the engine compartment and remove the upper arm.
8. To install the arm, position it on the mounting bracket and install the attaching nuts on the inner shaft attaching bolts.
NOTE: *The original equipment keystone-type lockwashers must be used with the inner shaft attaching nuts and bolts.*

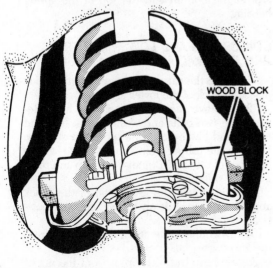

WOOD BLOCK

Upper arm support block installed

9. Install the upper ball joint stud in the spindle and tighten the nut to 60–80 ft. lbs. Install a new cotter pin.
10. Remove the spring compressor and position spring on upper arm. Install wheel and check front end alignment.

Lower Ball Joint/Control Arm
INSPECTION

The lower ball joint is an integral part of the lower control arm. If the lower ball joint is defective the entire lower control arm must be replaced.

1. Raise the vehicle on a hoist or floor jack so that the front wheel falls to the full down position.
2. Have an assistant grasp the bottom of the tire and move the wheel in and out.
3. As the wheel is being moved, observe the lower control arm where the spindle attaches to it.
4. Any movement between the lower part of the spindle and the lower control arm indicates a bad control arm which must be replaced.
NOTE: *During this check, the upper ball joint will be unloaded and may move; this is normal and not an indication of a bad ball joint. Also, do not mistake a loose wheel bearing for a worn ball joint.*

Lower Ball Joint/Control Arm
REMOVAL AND INSTALLATION

1. Position an upper control arm support between the upper arm and side rail.
2. Raise the vehicle, position jackstands, and remove the wheel and tire.
3. Remove the stabilizer bar-to-link attaching nut and disconnect the bar from the link.
4. Remove the link bolt from the lower arm.
5. Remove the strut bar-to-lower attaching nuts and bolts.
6. Remove the lower ball joint cotter pin and back off the nut. Using a suitable tool, loosen the ball joint stud in the spindle.
7. Remove the nut from the arm and lower the arm.
8. Remove the lower arm-to-under-body cam attaching parts and remove the arm.
9. To install, position the lower arm in the underbody and install the ball joint and cam attaching parts loosely.
10. Install the stabilizer and strut and torque the attaching parts to specifications.
11. Torque the lower arm pivot and ball joint stud to specifications.
12. Lower the car and remove the upper arm support.
13. Front end alignment must be rechecked.

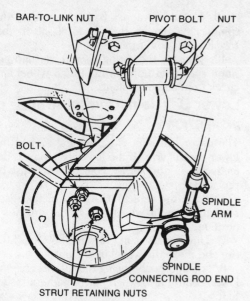

Lower control arm installed

Upper Ball Joint

INSPECTION

1. Raise the vehicle on a hoist or floor jack so that the front wheels hang in the full down position.

2. Have an assistant grasp the wheel top and bottom and apply alternate in and out pressure to the top and bottom of the wheel.

3. Radial play of ¼ in. is acceptable measured at the inside of the wheel adjacent to the upper arm.

NOTE: *This radial play measurement is multiplied at the outer circumference of the tire and should not be measured here. Measure only at the inside of the wheel.*

REMOVAL AND INSTALLATION

1. Position a support between the upper arm and frame rail.

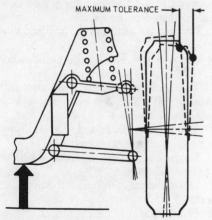

Measuring upper ball joint radial play

2. Raise and safely support the vehicle. Remove the tire and wheel.

3. Remove the upper ball joint cotter pin and loosen the nut.

4. Using a suitable tool, loosen the ball joint in the spindle.

5. Remove the three ball joint retaining rivets using a large chisel.

6. Remove the nut from the ball joint stud and remove the ball joint.

7. Clean and remove all burrs from the ball joint mounting area of the control arm before installing the new ball joint.

8. Install the ball joint in the upper arm using the service part nuts and bolts. Do not attempt to rivet a new ball joint to the arm.

9. Install and torque the ball joint stud nut and install the cotter pin.

10. Lubricate the new joint with a hand grease gun only, using an air pressure gun may loosen the ball joint seal.

11. Install the wheel, lower the vehicle, and remove the upper arm support.

12. Check the front end alignment.

Coil Spring on Lower Arm Suspension

Each front wheel rotates on a spindle. The spindle's upper and lower ends attach to the upper and lower ball joints which mount to an upper and lower arm respectively. The upper arm pivots on a bushing and shaft assembly bolted to the frame. The lower arm pivots on the No. 2 crossmember bolt. The coil spring is seated between the lower arm and the top of the spring housing on the underside of the upper arm. A shock absorber is bolted to the lower arm at the bottom and the top of the spring housing.

COIL SPRING AND LOWER CONTROL ARM REMOVAL AND INSTALLATION

1. Raise the car and support it with stands placed in back of the lower arms.

2. Remove the wheel from the hub. Remove the two bolts and washers that hold the caliper and brake hose bracket to the spindle. Remove the caliper from the rotor and wire it back out of the way. Remove the hub and rotor from the spindle.

3. Disconnect the lower end of the shock absorber and push it up to the retracted position.

4. Disconnect the stabilizer bar link from the lower arm.

5. Remove the cotter pins from the upper and lower ball joint stud nuts.

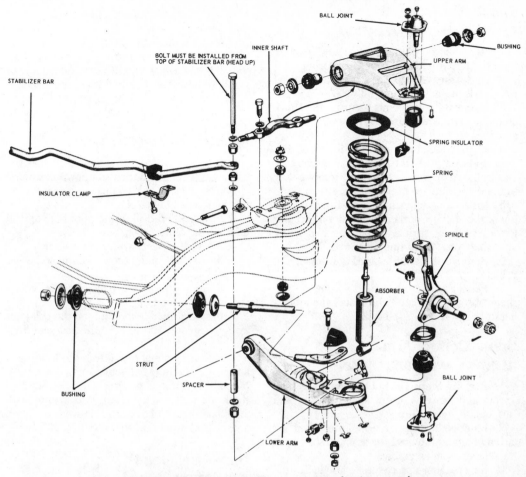

1972 and later coil spring on lower arm type front suspension

6. Remove the two bolts and nuts holding the strut to the lower arm.

7. Loosen the lower ball joint stud nut two turns. Do not remove this nut.

8. Install spreader tool T57P-3006-A between the upper and lower ball joint studs.

9. Expand the tool until the tool exerts considerable pressure on the studs. Tap the spindle near the lower stud with a hammer to loosen the stud with tool pressure only.

10. Position the floor jack under the lower arm and remove the lower ball joint stud nut.

11. Lower the floor jack and remove the spring and insulator.

12. Remove the A-arm-to-crossmember attaching parts and remove the arm from the car.

13. Reverse the above procedure to install. If the lower control arm was replaced because of damage, check front end alignment. Torque lower arm-to-no. 2 crossmember nut to 60–90 ft. lbs. Torque the strut-to-lower arm bolts to 80–115 ft. lbs. The caliper-to-spindle bolts are torqued to 90–120 ft. lbs. Torque the ball joint-to-spindle attaching nut to 60–90 ft. lbs.

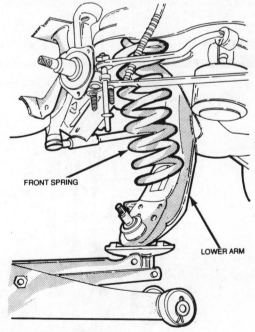

Removing front spring

Shock Absorber
REMOVAL AND INSTALLATION

1. Remove the nut, washer, and bushing from the upper end of the shock absorber.
2. Raise the vehicle on a hoist and install jackstands under the frame rails.
3. Remove the two bolts securing the shock absorber to the lower arm and remove the shock absorber.
4. Inspect the shock absorber for leaks. Extend and compress the unit several times to check the damping action and remove any trapped air. Replace in pairs if necessary.
5. Install a new bushing and washer on the top of the shock absorber and position the unit inside the front spring. Install the two lower attaching bolts and torque them to 8–15 ft. lbs.
6. Remove the safety stands and lower the vehicle.
7. Place a new bushing and washer on the shock absorber top stud and install the attaching nut. Torque to 22–30 ft. lbs.

Upper Control Arm
REMOVAL AND INSTALLATION

1. Perform Steps 1–11 of the previous "Coil Spring and Lower Control Arm Removal and Installation" procedure.
2. Remove the upper arm inner shaft attaching bolts and remove the arm and shaft from the chassis as an assembly.
3. Reverse above procedure to install. Torque the ball joint-to-spindle attaching nut to 60–90 ft. lbs.
4. Adjust front end alignment.

Lower Ball Joint
INSPECTION

1. Raise the vehicle by placing a floor jack under the lower arm or, raise the vehicle on a

hoist and place a jackstand under the lower arm and lower the vehicle onto it to remove the preload from the lower ball joint.
2. Have an assistant grasp the top and bottom of the wheel and apply alternate in and out pressure to the top and bottom of the wheel.
3. Radial play of ¼ in. is acceptable measured at the inside of the wheel adjacent to the lower arm.

REMOVAL AND INSTALLATION

1. Raise the vehicle on a hoist and allow the front wheels to fall to their full down position.
2. Drill a ⅛ in. hole completely through each ball joint attaching rivet.
3. Use a ⅜ in. drill in the pilot hole to drill off the head of the rivet.
4. Drive the rivets from the lower arm.
5. Place a jack under the lower arm and lower the vehicle about 6 in.
6. Remove the lower ball joint stud cotter pin and attaching nut.
7. Using a suitable tool, loosen the ball joint from the spindle and remove the ball joint from the lower arm.
8. Clean all metal burrs from the lower arm and install the new ball joint, using the service part nuts and bolts to attach the ball joint to the lower arm. Do not attempt to rivet the ball joint again once it has been removed.
9. Check front end alignment.

Upper Ball Joint
INSPECTION

1. Raise the vehicle by placing a floor jack under the lower arm. Do not allow the lower arm to hang freely with the vehicle on a hoist or bumper jack.
2. Have an assistant grasp the top and bottom of the tire and move the wheel in and out.
3. As the wheel is being moved, observe the upper control arm where the spindle attaches to it. Any movement between the upper part of the spindle and the upper ball joint indicates a bad ball joint which must be replaced.
  NOTE: *During this check, the lower ball joint will be unloaded and may move; this is normal and not an indication of a bad ball joint. Also, do not mistake a loose wheel bearing for a defective ball joint.*

REMOVAL AND INSTALLATION

1. Raise the vehicle and support on jackstands allowing the front wheels to fall to their full down position.
2. Drill a ⅛ in. ho.e completely through each ball joint attaching rivet.
3. Using a large chisel, cut off the head of each rivet and drive them from the upper arm.

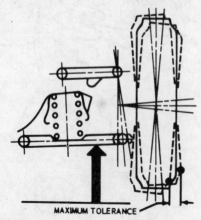

MAXIMUM TOLERANCE

Measuring lower ball joint radial play

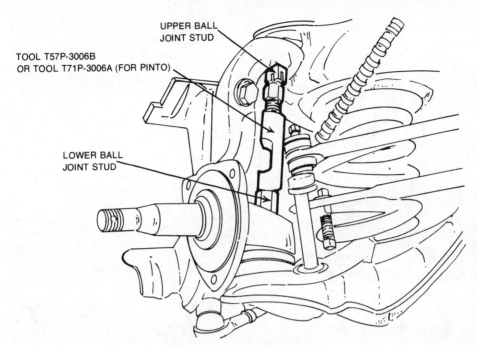

TOOL T57P-3006B
OR TOOL T71P-3006A (FOR PINTO)

UPPER BALL
JOINT STUD

LOWER BALL
JOINT STUD

Loosening lower ball joint stud

4. Place a jack under the lower arm and lower the vehicle about 6 in.

5. Remove the cotter pin and attaching nut from the ball joint stud.

6. Using a suitable tool, loosen the ball joint stud from the spindle and remove the ball joint from the upper arm.

7. Clean all metal burrs from the upper arm and install the new ball joint, using the service part nuts and bolts to attach the ball joint to the upper arm. Do not attempt to rivet the ball joint again once it has been removed.

8. Check front end alignment.

MacPherson Strut Suspension

The design utilizes shock struts with coil springs mounted between the lower arm and a spring pocket in the No. 2 crossmember. The shock struts are non-repairable, and must be replaced as a unit. The ball joints lower suspension arm bushings are not separately serviced, and they also must be replaced by replacing the suspension arm assembly. The ball joint seal can be replaced separately.

SPRINGS

NOTE: *Always use extreme caution when working with coil springs. Make sure the vehicle is supported sufficiently.*

Removal

1. Raise the front of the vehicle and place safety stands under both sides of the jack pads just back of the lower arms.

2. Remove the wheel and tire assembly.

3. Disconnect the stabilizer bar link from the lower arm.

4. Remove the steering gear bolts, and move the steering gear out of the way.

5. Disconnect the tie rod from the steering spindle.

6. Using a spring compressor, install one plate with the pivot ball seat down into the coils of the spring. Rotate the plate, so that it is fully seated into the lower suspension arm spring seat.

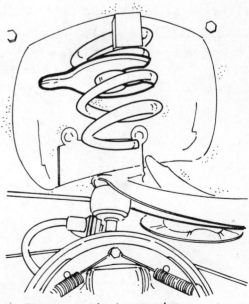

MacPherson strut front suspension

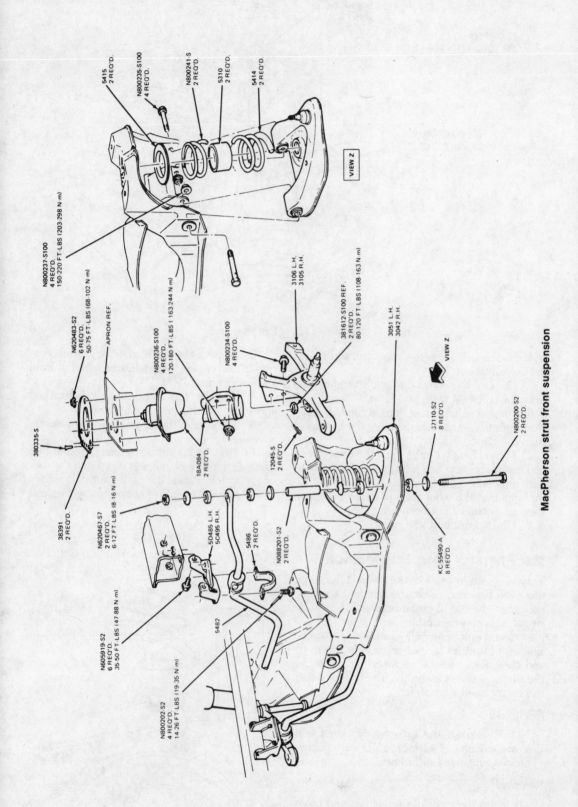

MacPherson strut front suspension

VIEW Z

5415
2 REQ'D.

N800235-S100
4 REQ'D.

N800241-S
2 REQ'D.

5310
2 REQ'D.

5414
2 REQ'D.

N800237-S100
4 REQ'D.
150-220 FT-LBS (203-298 N·m)

N620483-S2
6 REQ'D.
50-75 FT-LBS (68-102 N·m)

APRON REF.

N800226-S100
4 REQ'D.
120-180 FT-LBS (163-244 N·m)

N800234-S100
4 REQ'D.

3106 L.H.
3105 R.H.

381612-S100 REF.
2 REQ'D.
80-120 FT-LBS (108-163 N·m)

3051 L.H.
3042 R.H.

380335-S

38391
2 REQ'D.

N620467-S7
2 REQ'D.
6-12 FT-LBS (8-16 N·m)

18A084
2 REQ'D.

12045-S
2 REQ'D.

VIEW Z

37110-S2
8 REQ'D.

N800200-S2
2 REQ'D.

N605919-S2
6 REQ'D.
35-50 FT-LBS (47-88 N·m)

50D485 L.H.
5C495 R.H.

5486
2 REQ'D.

N088201-S2
2 REQ'D.

KC 55490-A
8 REQ'D.

N800202-S2
4 REQ'D.
14-26 FT-LBS (19-35 N·m)

5482

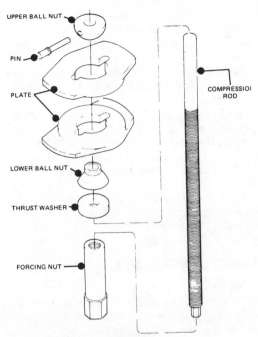

Exploded view of a MacPherson strut

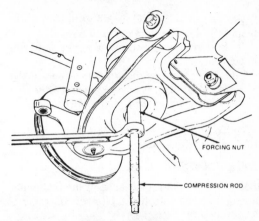

Spring compressed for removal

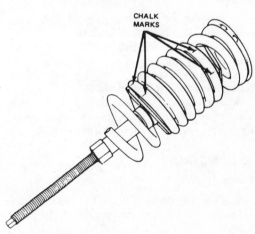

Spring removed from car

7. Install the other plate with the pivot ball seat up into the coils of the spring. Insert the ball nut through the coils of the spring, so it rests in the upper plate.

8. Insert the compression rod into the opening in the lower arm through the lower and upper plate. Install the upper ball nut on the rod, and return the securing pin.

NOTE: *This pin can only be inserted one way into the upper ball nut because of a stepped hole design.*

9. With the upper ball nut secured turn the upper plate, so it walks up the coil until it contacts the upper spring seat.

10. Install the lower ball nut, thrust bearing and forcing nut on the compression rod.

11. Rotate the nut until the spring is compressed enough so that it is free in its seat.

12. Remove the two lower control arm pivot bolts and nuts, and disengage the lower arm from the frame crossmember and remove the spring assembly.

13. If a new spring is to be installed, mark the position of the upper and lower plates on the spring with chalk. Measure the compressed length of the spring as well as the amount of the spring curvature to assist in the compressing and installation of a new spring.

14. Loosen the nut to relieve spring tension, and remove the tools from the spring.

Installation

1. Assemble the spring compressor tool, and locate it in the same position as indicated in Step 13 of the removal procedure.

NOTE: *Before compressing the coil spring, be sure the upper ball nut securing pin is inserted properly.*

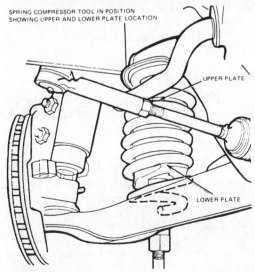

Spring compressor in position

2. Compress the coil spring until the spring height reaches the dimension in Step 13.

3. Position the coil spring assembly into the lower arm.

NOTE: *Make sure that the lower end of the spring is properly positioned between the two holes in the lower arm spring pocket depression.*

4. To finish installing the coil spring reverse the removal procedure.

BALL JOINTS

Ball joints are not replaceable. If the ball joints are found to be defective the lower control arm assembly must be replaced.

Inspection

1. Support the vehicle in normal driving position with both ball joints loaded.

2. Wipe the grease fitting and checking surface, so they are free of dirt and grease. The checking surface is the round boss into which the grease fitting is threaded.

3. The checking surface should project outside the cover. If the checking surface is inside the cover, replace the lower arm assembly.

SHOCK STRUT

Removal

1. Place the ignition key in the unlocked position to permit free movement of the front wheels.

2. Working from the engine compartment remove the nut that attaches the strut to the upper mount. A screwdriver in the slot will hold the rod stationary while removing the nut.

NOTE: *The vehicle should not be driven while the nut is removed so make sure the car is in position for hoisting purposes.*

3. Raise the front of the vehicle by the lower control arms, and place safety stands under the frame jacking pads, rearward of the wheels.

4. Remove the tire and wheel assembly.

5. Remove the brake caliper, rotor assembly, and dust shield.

6. Remove the two lower nuts and bolts attaching the strut to the spindle.

7. Lift the strut up from the spindle to compress the rod, then pull down and remove the strut.

Installation

1. With the rod half extended, place the rod through the upper mount and hand start the mount as soon as possible.

2. Extend the strut and position into the spindle.

3. Install the two lower mounting bolts and hand start the nuts.

4. Tighten the nut that attaches the strut to the upper body mount to 60–75 ft. lbs. This can be done from inside the engine compartment.

NOTE: *Position a suitable tool in the slot to hold the rod stationary while the nut is being tightened.*

5. Remove the suspension load from the lower control arms by lowering the hoist and tighten the lower mounting nuts to 150 ft. lbs.

6. Raise the suspension control arms and install the brake caliper, rotor assembly and dust shield.

7. Install the tire and wheel assembly.

8. Remove the safety stands and lower the vehicle.

LOWER CONTROL ARM

Removal

1. Raise the front of the vehicle and position safety stands under both sides of the jack pads, just to the rear of the lower arms.

2. Remove the wheel and tire assembly.

3. Disconnect the stabilizer bar link from the lower arm.

4. Remove the disc brake caliper, rotor and dust shield.

5. Remove the steering gear bolts and position out of the way.

6. Remove the cotter pin from the ball joint stud nut, and loosen the ball joint nut one or two turns.

7. Tap the spindle sharply to relieve the stud pressure.

8. Remove the tie-rod end from the spindle. Place a floor jack under the lower arm, supporting the arm at both bushings. Remove both lower arm bolts, lower the jack and remove the coil spring as outlined earlier in the chapter.

9. Remove the ball nut and remove the arm assembly.

Installation

1. Place the new arm assembly into the spindle and tighten the ball joint nut to 100 ft. lbs. Install the cotter pin.

2. Position the coil spring in the upper spring pocket. Make sure the insulator is on top of the spring and the lower end is properly positioned between the two holes in the depression of the lower arm.

3. Carefully raise the lower arm with the floor jack until the bushings are properly positioned in the crossmember.

4. Install the lower arm bolts and nuts, finger tight only.

5. Install and tighten the steering gear bolts.

6. Connect the tie-rod end and tighten the nut to 35–47 ft. lbs.

7. Connect the stabilizer link bolt and nut and tighten to 10 ft. lbs.

8. Install the brake dust shield, rotor and caliper.

9. Install the wheel and tire assembly.

10. Remove the safety stands and lower the vehicle. After the vehicle has been lowered to the floor and at curb height, tighten the lower arm nuts to 210 ft. lbs.

Air Suspension

WARNING: *Do not remove an air spring under any circumstances when there is pressure in the air spring. Do not remove any components supporting an air spring without either exhausting the air or providing support for the air spring.*

COMPONENTS

Suspension Fasteners

Suspension fasteners are important attaching parts in that they could affect performance of vital components and systems and/or could result in major service expense. They must be replaced with fasteners of the same part number, or with an equivalent part, if replacement becomes necessary. **Do not** use a replacement part of lesser quality or substitute design. Torque values must be used, as specified, during assembly to assure proper retention of parts. New fasteners must be used whenever old fasteners are loosened or removed and when new component parts are installed.

Air Spring Suspension

• Air compressor (less dryer), regenerative dryer, O-ring, mounting bracket and the isolator mounts are all serviced as separate components.

• Height sensors and modules are replaceable.

• Air springs are replaceable as assemblies (including the solenoid valve).

• Air spring solenoid valves and external O-rings are replaceable.

• Air lines are replaceable, however quick connect unions and bulk tubing are available to mend a damaged air line.

• Collet and O-rings of the quick connect type fittings are replaceable.

Front Suspension

• Gas filled shock absorber struts must be replaced as assemblies. They are not serviceable. Replace only the damaged shock absorber strut. It is not necessary to replace in matched pairs.

• Strut upper mounts may be replaced individually.

• Air springs are replaced as assemblies. It is not necessary to replace in pairs.

• The lower control arm is replaceable as an assembly with the ball joint and bushings included.

• The spindle is replaceable.

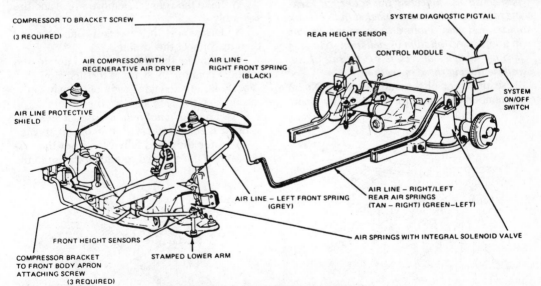

THE SYSTEM CONSISTS OF AN ELECTRIC AIR COMPRESSOR WITH REGENERATIVE AIR DRYER, THREE ELECTRONIC HEIGHT SENSORS, EIGHT QUICK CONNECT AIR FITTINGS, FOUR AIR SPRINGS WITH INTEGRAL SOLENOIDS, FOUR ONE-PIECE AIR LINES CONNECTING EACH SPRING TO THE COMPRESSOR AND A CONTROL MODULE WITH A SINGLE CHIP MICROCOMPUTER.

Air suspension system

• The stabilizer bar is replaceable with stabilizer bar-to-body insulators included.

• The stabilizer bar-to-body bushing is replaceable.

Rear Suspension

The following rear suspension components may be replaced individually:

• Gas filled shock absorbers must be replaced as assemblies. They are not serviceable. Replace only the damaged shock absorber. It is not necessary to replace in matched pairs.

• Air springs are replaced as assemblies. It is not necessary to replace in pairs.

Lower control arms, including both end bushings, are replaceable as assemblies. (Must be replaced in pairs).

• Upper control arms, including body end bushing, are replaceable as assemblies. (Must be replaced in pairs).

• Upper control arm axle and bushings are replaceable individually. (Must be replaced in pairs).

• Stabilizer bar is replaceable with stabilizer bar-to-axle insulator included.

• Stabilizer bar-to-body bushings are replaceable.

JACKING AND SUPPORTING

CAUTION: *The electrical power supply to the air suspension system must be shut off prior to hoisting, jacking or towing an air suspension vehicle. This can be accomplished by disconnecting the battery or turning off the power switch located in the trunk on the LH side. Failure to do so may result in unexpected inflation or deflation of the air springs which may result in shifting of the vehicle during these operations.*

Raise the front of the vehicle at the No. 2 crossmember until the tires are above the floor.

Support the vehicle body with jackstands at each front corner and then lower the floor jack so that the front suspension is in full rebound. Repeat this procedure for the rear suspension, except raise the body at the rear jacking location.

AIR SPRING SYSTEM

CAUTION: *Power to the air system must be shut-off by turning the air suspension switch (in luggage compartment) Off or by disconnecting the battery when servicing any air suspension components.*

• Do not attempt to install or inflate any air spring that has become unfolded.

• Any spring which has unfolded must be refolded, prior to being installed in a vehicle.

• Do not attempt to inflate any air spring which has been collapsed while uninflated from the rebound hanging position to the jounce stop.

• After inflating an air spring in hanging position, it must be inspected for proper shape.

• Failure to follow the above procedures may result in a sudden failure of the air spring or suspension system.

Air Spring Solenoid

The air spring solenoid valve has a two stage solenoid pressure relief fitting similar to a radiator cap. A clip is first removed, and rotation of the solenoid out of the spring will release air from the assembly before the solenoid can be removed.

1. Turn the air suspension switch Off.

2. Raise the vehicle. Remove wheel and tire assembly.

3. Disconnect the electrical connector and then disconnect the air line.

4. Remove the solenoid clip. Rotate the solenoid counterclockwise to the first stop.

5. Pull the solenoid straight out slowly to the second stop to bleed air from the system.

CAUTION: *Do not fully release solenoid until air is completely bled from the air spring.*

6. After the air is fully bled from the system, rotate the solenoid counterclockwise to the

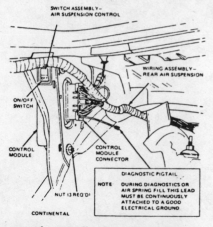

Air suspension cut-off switch—Continental

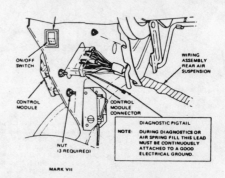

Air suspension cut-off switch—Mark VII

third stop, and remove the solenoid from the air spring assembly.

7. Check the solenoid O-ring for abrasion or cuts. Replace O-ring as required. Lightly grease the O-ring area of solenoid with silicone dielectric compound WA-10, D7AZ-19A331-A or equivalent.

8. Insert the solenoid into the air spring end cap and rotate clockwise to the third stop, push into the second stop, then rotate clockwise to the first stop.

9. Install solenoid clip. Connect the air line and the electrical connector.

10. Refill the air spring(s). Install the wheel and tire assembly.

Air Spring Fill

1. Turn On the air suspension switch. Diagnostic pigtail is to be ungrounded.

2. Connect a battery charger to reduce battery drain.

3. Cycle the ignition from the Off to Run position, hold in the Run position for a minimum of five seconds, then return to the Off position. Driver's door is open with all other doors shut.

4. Change the diagnostic pigtail from an ungrounded state to a grounded state by attaching a lead from the diagnostic pigtail to vehicle ground. The pigtail must remain grounded during the spring fill sequence.

5. While applying the brakes, turn the ignition switch to the Run position. (The door must be open. Do not start the vehicle). The warning lamp will blink continuously once every two seconds to indicate the spring pump sequence has been entered.

6. To fill a rear spring(s), close and open the door once. After a 6 second delay, the rear spring will be filled for 60 seconds.

7. To fill a front spring(s), close and open the door twice. After a 6 second delay, the front spring will be filled for 60 seconds.

8. To fill rear and front springs, fill the rear springs first (Step 6). When the rear fill has finished, close and open the door once to initiate the front spring fill.

9. Terminate the air spring fill by turning the ignition switch to Off, actuating the brake, or ungrounding the diagnostic pigtail. The diagnostic pigtail must be ungrounded at the end of spring fill.

10. Lower vehicle and start engine. Allow the vehicle to level with doors closed.

Air Spring—Front or Rear

1. Turn the air suspension switch Off.

2. Raise and support the vehicle. Suspension must be at full rebound.

3. Remove tire and wheel assembly.

4. Remove the air spring solenoid.

5. Remove the spring to lower arm fasteners. Remove the clip for front spring and/or remove bolts for rear spring.

6. Push down on the spring clip on the collar of the air spring and rotate collar counterclockwise to release the spring from the body spring seat. Remove the air spring.

7. Install the air spring solenoid. Correctly position the solenoid. For LH installation (front or rear spring), the notch on the collar is to be in line with the centerline of the solenoid. For RH installation (front or rear), the flat on the collar is to be in line with the centerline of the solenoid.

8. Install the air spring into the body spring seat, taking care to keep the solenoid air and electrical connections clean and free of damage. Rotate the air spring collar until the spring clip snaps into place. Be sure that the air spring collar is retained by the three rolled tabs on the body spring seat.

9. Attach and secure the lower arm to spring attachment with suspension at full rebound and supported by the shock absorbers.

CAUTION: *The air springs may be damaged if suspension is allowed to compress before spring is inflated.*

11. Replace the tire and wheel assembly.

12. Lower the vehicle until the tire and wheel assembly are 1–3 inches above floor. Refill the air spring(s).

Air Compressor and Dryer Assembly

1. Turn the air suspension switch Off.

2. Disconnect the electrical connector located on the compressor.

3. Remove the air line protector cap from the dryer by releasing the two latching pins located on the bottom of the cap 180 degrees apart.

4. Disconnect the four air lines from dryer.

5. Remove the three screws retaining the air compressor to mounting bracket.

6. Position the air compressor and dryer assembly to the mounting bracket and install the three mounting screws.

7. Connect the four air lines into the dryer.

8. Connect the electrical connection. Install the air line protector cap onto the dryer.

9. Turn the air suspension switch On.

Dryer, Air Compressor

1. Turn the air suspension switch Off.

2. Remove the air line protector cap from the dryer by releasing the two latching pins located on the bottom of the cap 180 degrees apart.

3. Disconnect the four air lines from the dryer.

4. Remove the dryer retainer clip and screw.

5. Remove from the head assembly.

6. Check to ensure the old O-ring is not in the head assembly.

7. Check the dryer end to ensure new O-ring is in proper position.

8. Insert the dryer into the head assembly and install the retainer clip and screw.

9. Connect the four air lines into the dryer.

10. Install the air line protector cap onto the dryer.

11. Turn the air suspension switch On.

Mounting Bracket, Air Compressor

1. Turn the air suspension switch Off.

2. Remove the air compressor and dryer assembly.

3. Raise and support the vehicle on jackstands.

4. Remove the left front tire and wheel assembly.

5. Remove the left front inner fender liner.

6. Remove the three bolts attaching the mounting bracket to body side apron.

7. Position the mounting bracket to the body side apron with the two locating tabs.

8. Secure the three bolts attaching the bracket to the body side apron.

9. Install the left front inner fender liner.

10. Install the tire and wheel assembly.

11. Lower the vehicle.

12. Install compressor and dryer assembly. Turn the air suspension switch On.

Height Sensors—Front

1. Turn the air suspension switch Off.

2. Disconnect the sensor electrical connector. The front sensor connectors are located in the engine compartment behind the shock towers.

3. Push the front sensor connector through the access hole in the rear of the shock tower.

4. Raise and support the vehicle on jackstands. Suspension must be at full rebound.

5. Disconnect the bottom and then the top end of the sensor from the attaching studs.

6. Disconnect the sensor wire harness from the plastic clips on the shock tower and remove sensor.

7. Connect the top and then the bottom end of the sensor to the attaching studs. Route the sensor electrical connector as required to connect to the vehicle wire harness.

8. Lower the vehicle. Connect the sensor connector. Turn the air suspension switch On.

Height Sensor—Rear

1. Turn the air suspension switch Off.

2. Disconnect the sensor electrical connec-

tor located in the luggage compartment in front of the forward trim panel. Also pull the luggage compartment carpet back for access to the sensor sealing grommet located on the floor pan.

3. Raise and support the vehicle on jackstands. Suspension must be at full rebound.

4. Disconnect the bottom and then the top end of the sensor from the attaching studs.

5. Push upwards on the sealing grommet to unseat and then push sensor through the floor pan hole into the luggage compartment.

6. Lower the vehicle.

7. Connect the sensor connector and then push sensor through the floor pan hole being sure to seat the sealing grommet. Replace the luggage compartment carpet.

8. Raise and support the vehicle on jackstands.

9. Connect the top and then the bottom end of the sensor. Lower the vehicle.

10. Turn the air suspension switch On.

Control Module

1. Turn the air suspension switch Off. Ignition switch is also to be Off.

2. Remove the LH luggage compartment trim panel.

3. Disconnect the wire harness from the module.

4. Remove the three attaching nuts.

5. Remove the module.

6. Position the module and secure it with the three attaching nuts.

7. Connect the wire harness to the module.

8. Attach the LH luggage compartment trim panel. Turn the air suspension switch On.

Nylon Air Line

If a leak is detected in an air line, it can be serviced by carefully cutting the line with a sharp knife to ensure a good, clean, straight cut. Then, install a service fitting. If more tube is required, it can be obtained in bulk. The four air lines are color coded to show which spring they are connecting, but do not require orientation at the air compressor dryer. A protective plastic cap and convoluted tube protect the air lines from the dryer rearward over the left shock tower in the engine compartment. Routing of the lines after exiting the protective tube follows:

• **Left Front/Grey:** Down and through the rear wall of the left shock tower to the air spring solenoid.

• **Right Front/Back:** To cowl and along cowl on the right side of the vehicle, forward and down through the rear wall of the right shock tower to the air spring solenoid.

• **Left Rear/Green, Right Rear/Tan:** Through the left side apron into the fender well, through the left upper dash panel (sealing grommet) into the passenger compartment, down the dash panel to the left rocker, along the rocker to the left rear fender well, over the fender well into the luggage compartment. The left air line goes down through the floor pan (sealing grommet) in front of the left rear shock tower. The right air line goes across the rear seat support and then down through the floor pan (sealing grommet) in front of the right rear shock tower.

Quick Connect Fittings

If a leak is detected in any of the eight quick connect fittings, it can be serviced using a repair kit containing a new O-ring, collet, release ring, and O-ring removal tool. The outer housing of the fitting cannot be serviced.

To remove the collet and O-ring, insert a scrap piece of air line, grasp the air line firmly (do not use pliers) and pull straight out (DO NOT use the release button). A force of 30–50 lbs. is required to remove the collet. After the retainer is removed, use the repair tool to remove the old O-ring.

To service, insert the new O-ring and seat it in the bottom of the fitting housing. Then, insert the new collet, being sure the end with four prongs is inserted. Press the collet into position with finger pressure. Install the new release button.

O-ring Seals

The areas that have O-ring seals that can be serviced are:
• Air compressor head to dryer: One O-ring.
• Air spring solenoid to end cap: Two O-rings each solenoid.
• Quick connect fitting: Four O-rings at dryer, one O-ring at each spring.
If air leaks are detected in these areas, the components can be removed, following the procedures outlines in this Section, and new O-rings can be installed.

Air Suspension Switch

1. Disconnect the electrical connector.
2. Depress the retaining clips that retain the switch to the brace, and remove switch.
• 3. Push the switch into position in the brace, making sure retaining clips are fully seated.
4. Connect electrical connector.

Compressor Relay

1. Disconnect the electrical connector.
2. Remove the screw retaining the relay to the left front shock tower and remove the relay.

3. Position the relay on the shock tower and install the retaining screw.
4. Connect the electrical connector.

FRONT SUSPENSION COMPONENTS

CAUTION: *Power to the air system must be shut-off by turning the air suspension switch (in luggage compartment) Off or by disconnecting the battery when servicing any suspension components.*

Stabilizer Bar Link Insulators

To replace the link insulators on each stabilizer link, use the following procedure:
1. Turn the air suspension switch Off.
2. Raise the vehicle and support on jackstands.
3. Remove the nut, washer, and insulator from the end of the stabilizer bar link attaching bolt.
4. Remove the bolt and the remaining washers, insulators and spacer.
5. Install the stabilizer bar link insulators by reversing the removal procedure.
6. Tighten the attaching nut.
7. Lower the vehicle. Turn air suspension system On.

Stabilizer Bar and/or Bushing

1. Turn the air suspension switch Off.
2. Raise the vehicle and support on jackstands.
3. Disconnect the stabilizer bar from each link and bushing U-clamps. Remove the stabilizer bar assembly.
4. Remove the adapter brackets and U-clamps.
5. Cut the worn bushings from the stabilizer bar.
6. Coat the necessary parts of the stabilizer bar with Ford Rubber Suspension Insulator Lubricant. E25Y-19553-A or equivalent, and slide bushings onto the stabilizer bar. Reinstall the U-clamps.
7. Reinstall the adapter brackets on the U-clamps.
8. Using a new nut and bolt, secure each end of the stabilizer bar to the lower suspension arm.
9. Using new bolts, clamp the stabilizer bar to the attaching brackets on the side rail.
10. Lower the vehicle. Turn air suspension switch On.

Shock Strut Replacement

1. Turn the air suspension switch Off.
2. Turn the ignition key to the unlocked position to allow free movement of the front wheels.
3. From the engine compartment, loosen

but do not remove the one 16mm strut-to-upper mount attaching nut. A suitable tapered tool inserted in the slot will hold the rod stationary while loosening the nut. The vehicle should be in place to be raised and must not be driven with the nut loosened or removed.

4. Raise and support the vehicle. Position safety stands under the lower control arms as far outboard as possible being sure that the lower sensor mounting bracket is clear. Lower until vehicle weight is supported by the lower arms.

5. Remove tire and wheel assembly.

6. Remove the brake caliper and wire out of the way.

7. Remove the strut-to-upper mount attaching nut and then the two lower nuts and bolts attaching the strut to the spindle.

NOTE: *The strut should be held firmly during the removal of the last bolt since the gas pressure will cause the strut to fully extend when removed.*

8. Lift the strut up from the spindle to compress the rod and then remove the strut.

9. Prime the new strut by extending and compressing the strut rod five times.

10. Place the strut rod through the upper mount, hand start and secure a new 16mm nut.

11. Compress the strut, and position onto the spindle.

12. Install two new lower mounting bolts, and hand start the nuts.

13. Raise the vehicle to remove load from the lower control arms, and tighten the lower mounting nuts.

14. Install the brake caliper, install the tire and wheel assembly.

15. Remove safety stands and lower the vehicle to the ground.

16. Turn air suspension switch On.

NOTE: *Front wheel alignment should be checked and adjusted, if out of specification.*

Upper Mount Assembly

NOTE: *Upper mounts are one piece units and cannot be disassembled.*

1. Turn the air suspension system Off.

2. Turn the ignition key to the unlocked position to allow free movement of the front wheels.

3. From the engine compartment, loosen but do not remove the three 12mm upper mount retaining nuts. Vehicle should be in place over a hoist and must not be driven with these nuts removed. Do not remove the pop rivet holding the camber plate in position.

4. Loosen 16 mm strut rod nut at this time.

5. Raise the vehicle and position safety stands under the lower control arms as far outboard as possible being sure that the lower sensor mounting bracket is clear. Lower until

the vehicle weight is supported by the lower arms.

6. Remove the tire and wheel assembly.

7. Remove brake caliper and rotate out of position and wire securely out of the way.

8. Remove the upper mount retaining nuts and the two lower nuts and bolts that attach the strut to the spindle.

NOTE: *The strut should be held firmly during the removal of the last bolt since the gas pressure will cause the strut to fully extend when removed.*

9. Lift the strut up from the spindle to compress the rod, and then remove the strut.

10. Remove the upper mount from the strut.

11. Install a new upper mount on the strut and hand start a new 16mm nut.

12. Position the upper mount studs into the body and start and secure three new nuts. Secure the strut rod 16mm nut.

13. Compress the strut and position onto the spindle.

14. Install two new lower mounting bolts, and hand start nuts.

15. Raise the vehicle to remove load from the lower control arms and tighten the lower mounting nuts to 126–179 ft. lbs.

16. Install the brake caliper. Install the tire and wheel assembly.

17. Remove safety stands and lower vehicle to the ground.

18. Turn air suspension switch On.

19. Front wheel alignment should be checked and adjusted if out of specification.

Spindle Assembly

1. Turn the air suspension switch Off.

2. Raise and support the vehicle on jackstands.

3. Remove the wheel and tire assembly.

4. Remove the brake caliper, rotor and dust shield.

5. Remove the stabilizer link from the lower arm assembly.

6. Remove the tie rod end from the spindle.

7. Remove the cotter pin from the ball joint stud nut, and loosen the nut one or two turns.

CAUTION: *DO NOT remove the nut from the ball joint stud at this time.*

8. Tap the spindle boss smartly to relieve stud pressure.

9. Place a floor jack under the lower arm, compress the air spring and remove the stud nut.

10. Remove the two bolts and nuts attaching the spindle to the shock strut. Compress the shock strut until working clearance is obtained.

11. Remove the spindle assembly.

12. Place the spindle on the ball joint stud, and install the new stud nut. DO NOT tighten at this time.

13. Lower the shock strut until the attaching holes are in line with the holes in the spindle. Install two new bolts and nuts.

14. Tighten ball joint stud nut and install cotter pin.

15. Lower the floor jack from under the suspension arm, and remove jack.

16. Tighten the shock strut to spindle attaching nuts.

17. Install stabilizer bar link and tighten attaching nut.

18. Attach the tie rod end, and tighten the retaining nut.

19. Install the disc brake dust shield, rotor, and caliper.

20. Install the wheel and tire assembly.

21. Remove the safety stands, and lower the vehicle.

22. Turn air suspension switch On.

23. Front wheel alignment should be checked and adjusted if out of specification.

Suspension Control Arm

1. Turn the air suspension switch Off.

2. Raise the vehicle and support on jackstands, so the control arms hang free (full rebound).

3. Remove the wheel and tire assembly.

4. Disconnect the tie rod assembly from the steering spindle.

5. Remove the steering gear bolts, if necessary, and position the gear so that the suspension arm bolt may be removed.

6. Disconnect the stabilizer bar link from the lower arm.

7. Disconnect the lower end of the height sensor from the lower control arm sensor mounting stud. Remove the sensor mounting stud and unscrew from lower arm, noting the position of stud on the lower arm bracket.

8. Remove the cotter pin from the ball joint stud nut, and loosen the ball joint nut one or two turns. DO NOT remove the nut at this time. Tap spindle boss smartly to relieve stud pressure.

9. Vent the air spring(s) to atmospheric pressure. Then, reinstall the solenoid.

10. Remove the air spring to lower arm fastener clip.

11. Remove the ball joint nut, and raise the entire strut and spindle assembly (strut, rotor, caliper and spindle). Wire it out of the way to obtain working room.

12. Remove the suspension arm to crossmember nuts and bolts, and remove the arm from the spindle.

13. Position the arm into the crossmember and install new arm to crossmember bolts and nuts. DO NOT tighten at this time.

14. Remove the wire from the strut and spindle assembly and attach to the ball joint stud. Install a new ball joint stud nut. DO NOT tighten at this time.

15. Position the air spring in the arm and install a new fastener.

16. Attach the sensor mounting stud and screw to lower arm in the same position as original arm location. Connect the lower end of sensor to the lower arm mounting stud.

17. With a suitable jack, raise the suspension arm to curbheight.

18. With the jack still in place, tighten the lower arm to crossmember attaching nut to 150–180 ft. lbs.

19. Tighten ball joint stud nut to 100–120 ft. lbs., and install a new cotter pin. Remove jack.

20. Install the steering gear to crossmember bolts and nuts (if removed). Hold the bolts, and tighten nuts to 90–100 ft. lbs.

21. Position the tie rod assembly into the steering spindle, and install the retaining nut. Tighten the nut to 35 ft. lbs., and continue tightening the nut to align the next castellation with cotter pin hole in the stud. Install a new cotter pin.

22. Connect the stabilizer bar link to the lower suspension arm, and tighten the attaching nut to 9–12 ft. lbs.

23. Install the wheel and tire assembly, and lower the vehicle but DO NOT allow tires to touch the ground.

24. Turn the air suspension switch On.

25. Refill the air spring(s).

26. Front wheel alignment should be checked and adjusted if out of specification.

REAR SUSPENSION

Shock Absorber

CAUTION: *Power to the air system must be shut-off by turning the air suspension switch (in luggage compartment) Off or by disconnecting the battery when servicing any suspension components.*

1. Turn the air suspension switch Off.

2. Open the luggage compartment and remove inside trim panels to gain access to the upper shock stud.

3. Loosen but do not remove the shock rod attaching nut.

4. Raise the vehicle and position two safety stands under the rear axle. Lower the vehicle until weight is supported by the rear axle.

5. Remove the upper attaching nut, washer and insulator and then remove the lower shock protective cover (right shock only) and lower

shock absorber cross bolt and nut from the lower shock brackets.

6. From under the vehicle, compress the shock absorber to clear it from the hold in the upper shock tower.

CAUTION: *Shock absorbers will extend unassisted. Do not apply heat or flame to the shock absorber tube during removal.*

7. Remove the shock absorber.

8. Prime the new shock absorber by extending and compressing shock absorber five times.

9. Place the inner washer and insulator on the upper attaching stud. Position stud through shock tower mounting hole and position an insulator, washer on stud from the luggage compartment. Hand start the attaching nut and then secure.

10. Place the shock absorber's lower mounting eye between the ears of the lower shock mounting bracket, compressing shock as required. Insert the bolt, (bolt head must seat on the inboard side of the shock bracket), through the shock bracket and the shock absorber mounting eye. Hand start and then secure the original attaching nut.

11. Install the protective cover, to the RH shock absorber. This is done by inserting the bolt point and nut into the cover's open end, sliding the cover over the shock bracket, and snapping the closed end of the cover over the bolt head. Properly installed, the cover will completely conceal the bolt point, nut, and bolt head. The rounded or closed end of the cover should be pointing inboard.

12. Raise the vehicle and remove safety stands from under axle, then lower the vehicle.

13. Reinstall the inside trim panels.

14. Turn air suspension switch On.

Lower Control Arm

NOTE: *If one arm requires replacement, replace the other arm also.*

1. Turn the air suspension switch Off.

2. Raise and support the vehicle so that the suspension will be at full rebound.

3. Remove tire and wheel assembly.

4. Vent air spring(s) to atmospheric pressure. Then, reinstall the solenoid.

5. Remove the two air spring-to-lower arm bolts and remove the air spring from the lower arm.

6. Remove the frame-to-arm and the axle-to-arm bolts and remove the arm from the vehicle.

7. Position the lower arm assembly into the front arm brackets, and insert a new, arm-to-frame pivot bolt and nut with nut facing outwards. DO NOT tighten at this time.

8. Position the rear bushing in the axle bracket and install a new arm-to-axle pivot bolt and nut with nut facing outwards. DO NOT tighten at this time.

9. Install two new air spring-to-arm bolts. DO NOT tighten at this time.

10. Using a suitable jack, raise the axle to curb height. Tighten the lower arm front bolt, the rear pivot bolt, and the air spring to arm bolt being sure that the air spring piston is flat on the lower arm. Remove the jack.

11. Replace tire and wheel assembly.

12. Lower the vehicle.

13. Turn the air suspension switch On.

14. Refill the air spring(s).

Upper Control Arm and Axle Bushing

NOTE: *If one arm requires replacement, replace the other arm also.*

1. Turn the air suspension switch Off.

2. Raise and support the vehicle so that the suspension will be at full rebound.

3. On the RH side detach rear height sensor from side arm. Note position of the sensor adjustment bracket on the upper arm.

4. Remove the upper arm-to-axle pivot bolt and nut.

5. Remove the upper arm-to-frame pivot bolt and nut. Remove upper arm from vehicle.

If upper arm axle bushing is to be replaced, use Tool T78P-5638-A or equivalent and the following procedure:

6. Place the upper arm axle bushing remover tool in position and remove the bushing assembly.

7. Using the installer tool, install the bushing assembly into the bushing ear of the rear axle.

8. Place the upper arm into the bracket of body side rail. Insert a new upper arm-to-frame pivot bolt and nut (nut facing outboard). DO NOT tighten at this time.

9. Align the upper arm-to-axle pivot hole with the hole in the axle bushing. If required, raise the axle using a suitable jack to align. Install a new pivot bolt and nut (nut inboard). DO NOT tighten at this time.

10. On the RH side, reattach rear height sensor to the arm. Set the adjustment bracket to the same position as on the replaced arm and tighten nut.

11. Using a suitable jack, raise the axle to curb height, and tighten the front upper arm bolt, and the rear upper arm bolt.

12. Remove the jackstands supporting the axle.

13. Lower the vehicle.

14. Turn the air suspension switch On.

Stabilizer Bar Link Insulators

1. Turn the air suspension switch Off.

2. Raise and support the vehicle on jackstands.

3. Remove the nut, washer and insulator from the end of the stabilizer bar link attaching bolt.

4. Remove the bolt and the remaining spacer, washer and insulators.

5. Install the stabilizer bar link insulators by reversing the removal procedure. A new bolt and nut must be used.

6. Tighten the attaching nut.

7. Lower the vehicle.

8. Turn the air suspension switch On.

Stabilizer Bar Bushings

1. Turn the air suspension switch Off.

2. Raise and support the vehicle on jackstands.

3. Disconnect the stabilizer bar from each link and bushing U-clamp. Remove the stabilizer bar assembly.

4. Remove the U-clamps.

5. Cut the worn bushings from the stabilizer bar.

6. Coat the necessary parts of the stabilizer bar with Ford Rubber Suspension Insulator Lubricant E25Y-19553-A or equivalent and slide new bushings onto the stabilizer bar. Reinstall U-clamps.

7. Using new bolts and nuts, attach stabilizer bar to the axle. Do not tighten bolts at this time.

8. Using new bolts and nuts, attach the link end of the stabilizer bar to the body. Tighten the link attaching nut and then the axle attaching bolts.

9. Lower the vehicle.

10. Turn the air suspension switch On.

Wheel Alignment
EXCEPT MACPHERSON STRUT

NOTE: *The procedure for checking and adjusting front wheel alignment requires specialized equipment and professional skills. The following descriptions and adjustment procedures are for general reference only.*

Front wheel alignment is the position of the front wheels relative to each other and to the vehicle. It is determined, and must be maintained to provide safe, accurate steering with minimum tire wear. Many factors are involved in wheel alignment and adjustments are provided to return those that might change due to normal wear to their original value. The factors which determine wheel alignment are dependent on one another; therefore, when one of the factors is adjusted, the others must be adjusted to compensate.

Descriptions of these factors and their affects on the car are provided below.

NOTE: *Do not attempt to check and adjust the front wheel alignment without first making a thorough inspection of the front suspension components.*

CAMBER

Camber angle is the number of degrees that the centerline of the wheel in inclined from the vertical. Camber reduces loading of the outer wheel bearing and improves the tire contact patch while cornering.

CASTER

Caster angle is the number of degrees that a line drawn through the steering knuckle pivots is inclined from the vertical, toward the front or rear of the car (when viewed from the side of the car). Caster improves the directional stability and decreases susceptibility to crosswinds or road surface deviations.

TOE-IN

Toe-in is the difference of the distance between the centers of the front and rear of the front wheels. It is most commonly measured in inches, but is occasionally referred to as an angle between the wheels. Toe-in is necessary to compensate for the tendency of the wheels to deflect rearward while in motion. Due to this

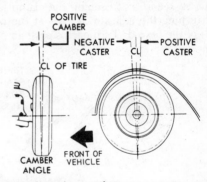

Caster and camber angles

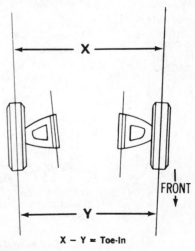

$$X - Y = \text{Toe-In}$$

Toe-in

tendency, the wheels of a vehicle, with properly adjusted toe-in, are traveling straight forward when the vehicle itself is traveling straight forward, resulting in directional stability and minimum tire wear.

Steering wheel spoke misalignment is often an indication of incorrect front end alignment. Care should be exercised when aligning the front end to maintain steering wheel spoke position. When adjusting the tie rod ends, adjust each an equal amount (in the opposite direction) to increase or decrease toe-in. If, following toe-in adjustment, further adjustments are necessary to center the steering wheel spokes, adjust the tie-rod ends an equal amount in the same direction.

ADJUSTMENT PROCEDURES

1971

Caster is adjusted by lengthening or shortening the struts at the frame crossmember. To adjust, turn both nuts an equal number of turns in the same direction. Caster adjustments should be within 1/4° of the opposing side of the car.

To adjust camber, loosen the lower control arm pivot bolt and rotate the eccentrics.

Adjust toe-in by loosening the clamp bolts, and turning the adjuster sleeves at the outer ends of the tie-rod. Turn each sleeve an equal

amount in the opposite direction, in order to maintain steering wheel spoke alignment.

1972 and Later

Install Ford tool T65P-3000D, or its equivalent, on the frame rail, position the hooks around the upper control arm pivot shaft, and tighten the adjusting nuts slightly. Loosen the pivot shaft retaining bolts to permit adjustment.

To adjust caster, loosen or tighten either the front or rear adjusting nut. After adjusting caster, adjust the camber by loosening or tightening both nuts an equal amount. Tighten the shaft retaining bolts to specifications, remove the tool, and recheck the adjustments.

Adjust toe-in by loosening the clamp bolts, and turning the adjuster sleeves at the outer

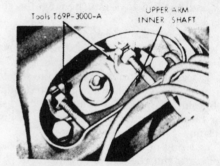

Caster and camber adjustments—1972 and later

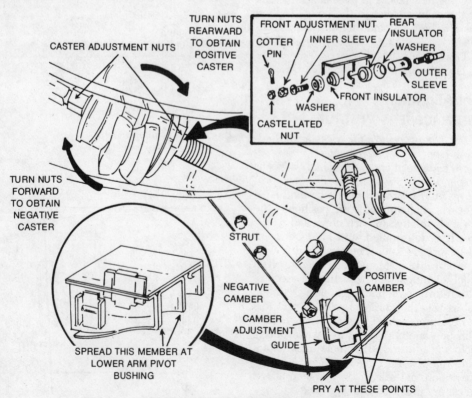

Caster and camber adjustments—1971

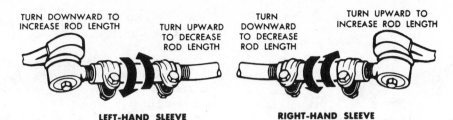

Tie-rod (toe-in) adjustments

ends of the tie-rod. Turn the sleeves an equal amount in the opposite direction, to maintain steering wheel spoke alignment.

MACPHERSON STRUT

The caster and camber are set at the factory and cannot be changed. Only the toe is adjustable.

Toe Adjustment

Toe is the difference in width (distance), between the front and rear inside edges of the front tires.

1. Turn the steering wheel, from left to right, several times and center.

NOTE: *If car has power steering, start the engine before centering the steering wheel.*

2. Secure the centered steering wheel with a steering wheel holder, or any device that will keep it centered.

3. Release the tie-rod end bellows clamps so the bellows will not twist while adjustment is made. Loosen the jam nuts on the tie-rod ends. Adjust the left and right connector sleeves until each wheel has one-half of the desired toe setting.

4. After the adjustment has been made, tighten the jam nuts and secure the bellows clamps. Release the steering wheel lock and check for steering wheel center. Readjust, if necessary until steering wheel is centered and toe is within specs.

Wheel Alignment Specifications

Year	Model	Caster Range (deg)	Caster Pref Setting	Camber Range (deg)	Camber Pref Setting	Toe-in (in.)	Steering Axis Inclination (deg)	Wheel Pivot Ratio (deg) Inner	Wheel Pivot Ratio (deg) Outer
'71	All	1¼N to ¼N	¾N	½N to 1P	¼P	⅛ to ⅜	7⅔	20	①
'72–'73	All	1¼N to 2¾P	¾P	¼N to 1¾P	¾P	1/16 to 7/16	7⅔	20	17¾
'74	All	½P to 3½P	2P	Left ⅜N to 1⅝P Right ⅞N to 1⅛P	½P ⅛P	0 to ⅜	9	20	18⁷/64
'75–'79	All	3¼P to 4¾P	4P	Left ¼N to 1¼P Right ½N to 1P	½P ¼P	0 to ⅜	9	20	18¹/10
'78–'80	Versailles	1¼N to ¼P	½N	½N to 1P	¼P	0 to ¼	6¾	20	②
'80–'82	Thunderbird, XR-7	⅛P to 1⅞P	1P	½N to 1¼P	⅜P	1/16 to 5/16	15⅓	20	19.77
'80–'82	Cougar	⅛P to 1⅞P	1P	5/16N to 1 3/16P	7/16P	1/16 to 5/16	15¼	20	19.84
'82	Continental	1¾N to 2¼P	1¼P	½N to 1¼P	⅜P	0 to ¼	15¼	20	19.84
'83–'85	Thunderbird Cougar XR-7	½P to 2P	1¼P	½N to 1P	¼P	1/16 to 5/16	—	20	19.73
'83–'85	LTD, Marquis (Sedan)	1⅛P to 2⅛P	1⅛P	5/16N to 1 3/16P	7/16	1/16 to 5/16	—	20	19.84
'83–'85	LTD, Marquis (Station Wagon)	⅛N to 1⅞P	⅞P	¼N to 1¼P	½P	1/16 to 5/16	—	20	19.84
'82–'83	Continental	⅜P to 2⅛P	1¼P	½N to 1¼P	⅜P	0 to ¼	—	20	19.13

① Manual steering—17° 19'; power steering—17° 49'
N Negative
P Positive

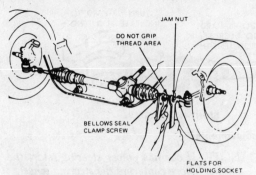

JAM NUT

DO NOT GRIP
THREAD AREA

BELLOWS SEAL
CLAMP SCREW

FLATS FOR
HOLDING SOCKET

Toe adjustment on MacPherson strut front ends

REAR SUSPENSION

NOTE: *Refer to previous Air Suspension section for procedures on models so equipped.*

1971 Fairlanes, Torinos and Montegos utilize a semi-elliptic leaf spring suspension. The axle housing is supported by a pair of leaf springs mounted on spring pads on the axle housing. The housing is secured to the center of the springs by two U-bolts, retaining plates and nuts. Each spring is suspended from the underbody side rail by a hanger at the front and a shackle at the rear. The shock absorbers are mounted between the leaf spring retaining plates and brackets bolted to the crossmember. Some high-performance 1971 models were equipped with staggered rear shock absorbers.

1972 and later models use a four-link coil spring suspension. The axle housing is suspended from the frame by an upper and lower trailing arm and a shock absorber at each side of the vehicle. These arms pivot in the frame members and the rear axle housing brackets. Each coil spring is mounted between a lower seat which is welded to the axle housing or lower arm and an upper seat which is integral with the frame. The shock absorbers are bolted to the spring upper seats at the top and brackets mounted on the axle housing at the bottom. The upper trailing arms are attached to the frame crossmember brackets at the front and brackets located near the outer ends of the axle housing at the rear. Both lower arms attach similarly to the frame side members and the axle housing brackets. A rear stabilizer bar attached to the frame side rail brackets and the two axlehousing brackets is available as optional equipment.

Leaf Spring Suspension

LEAF SPRING REMOVAL AND INSTALLATION

1. Raise the vehicle and place supports beneath the underbody and under the axle.

2. Disconnect the lower end of the shock absorber from the spring clip plate and position it out of the way. Remove the supports from under the axle.

3. Remove the spring plate nuts from the U-bolts and remove the clip plate. Raise the rear axle just enough to remove the weight of the housing from the spring.

4. Remove the two rear shackle attaching nuts, the shackle bar, and the two inner bushings.

5. Remove the rear shackle assembly and two outer bushings.

6. Remove the nut from the spring mounting bolt and tap the bolt out of the bushing at the front hanger. Lift out the spring assembly.

7. If the front hanger bushing is to be replaced, it may be necessary to take the spring assembly to a machine shop and have the old bushing pressed out and a new one pressed in.

8. Inspect the rear shackle and hanger assembly, bushings, and studs for wear, damage, cracks, or distortion. Check for broken spring leaves. Inspect the anti-squeak inserts between the leaves. Inspect the spring clips for worn or damaged threads. Check the spring clip plate and insulator retainers for distortion. If the spring center tie bolt requires replacement, clamp the spring in a vise to keep the spring compressed during bolt removal and replacement. Replace all parts found to be defective.

NOTE: *All used attaching components (nuts, bolts, etc.) must be discarded and replaced with new ones prior to reassembly. This is due to the extreme stresses and weather conditions imposed on the attaching hardware. If a used component is reinstalled, it may break.*

9. Position the leaf spring under the axle housing and insert the shackle assembly into the rear hanger bracket and the rear eye of the spring.

10. Install the shackle inner bushings, the shackle plate, and the locknuts. Hand tighten the locknuts.

11. Position the spring front eye in the front hanger, slip the washer on the front hanger bolt, and, from the inboard side, insert the bolt through the hanger and eye. Install the locknut on the hanger bolt and tighten finger-tight.

12. Lower the rear axle housing so that it rests on the spring. Place the spring plate on the U-bolts. Install the U-bolt nuts and torque to 35–50 ft. lbs.

13. Attach the lower end of the shock absorber to the spring plate using a new nut.

14. Place safety stands under the axle housing, lower the vehicle until the spring is in the approximate curb load position, and then torque the front hanger stud locknut to 90–110 ft. lbs.

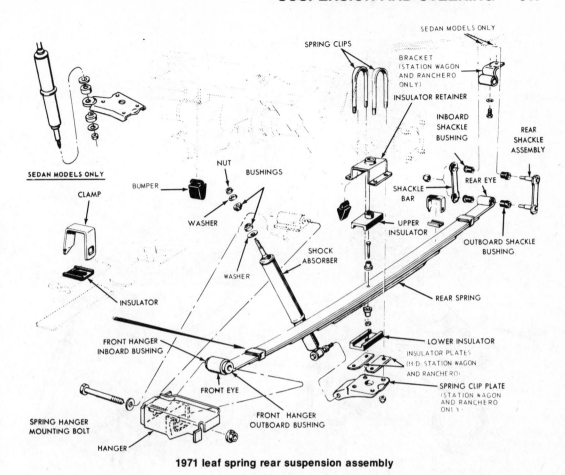

1971 leaf spring rear suspension assembly

15. Torque the locknuts on the rear shackle to 18–29 ft. lbs. Close the hole in the inner rail with a body plug.

16. Remove the safety stands and lower the vehicle.

SHOCK ABSORBER REMOVAL AND INSTALLATION

1. Remove the spare from the trunk. On the Ranchero, remove the attaching screws and lift the forward half of the floor panel from the body; remove the access cover from the opening in the floor pan over the shock absorber. On station wagon models, remove the access cover from the opening in the seat riser over the shock absorber.

2. On all other models, fold back the floor mat in the trunk and remove the shock absorber access cover from the floor pan. Remove the nut, outer washer, and rubber bushing from the top of the shock absorber.

3. Raise the vehicle and remove the attaching nut, outer washer and bushing from the shock absorber at the spring plate. Compress the shock absorber and remove it from the vehicle.

4. If the shock absorber is not in need of replacement but requires new bushings, remove the inner bushings and washers from the shock absorber studs.

NOTE: *All standard equipment shock absorbers are not refillable and cannot be repaired. Wipe off the shock absorber then extend and compress it several times. Severe leakage or weak action requires replacement. As a general rule, shock absorbers should be replaced in pairs (front and rear sets).*

5. Position the inner washer and bushing on each shock absorber stud.

6. Expand the shock absorber and place it between the spring plate and the mounting in the floor pan.

7. Connect the lower stud to the spring plate and install the bushing, outer washer, and a new nut on the stud. Make sure that the spring plate is free of burrs. On the Ranchero, torque the stud nut to 15–25 ft. lbs. and install the forward half of the floor panel.

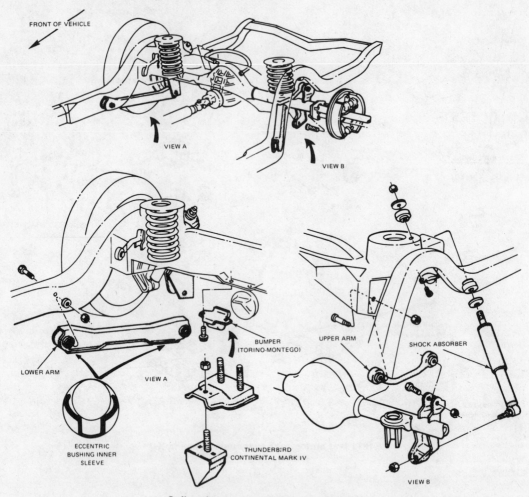

FRONT OF VEHICLE

VIEW A

VIEW B

LOWER ARM

VIEW A

ECCENTRIC
BUSHING INNER
SLEEVE

BUMPER
(TORINO-MONTEGO)

THUNDERBIRD
CONTINENTAL MARK IV

UPPER ARM

SHOCK ABSORBER

VIEW B

Coil spring rear suspension assembly

8. From inside the trunk, install the bushing, outer washer, and new attaching nut to the upper mounting stud, and torque to 15–25 ft. lbs. On station wagon models, replace the floor bed panel.

9. Replace and secure the spare in the trunk.

Coil Spring Suspension

COIL SPRING

Spring Between Axle Housing and Frame

1. Place a jack under the rear axle housing. Raise the vehicle and place jackstands under the frame side rails.

2. Disconnect the lower studs of the shock absorbers from the mounting brackets on the axle housing.

3. Lower the axle housing until the springs are fully released.

4. Remove the springs and insulators from the vehicle.

5. Place the insulators in each upper seat and position the springs between the upper and lower seats.

6. With the springs in position, raise the axle housing until the lower studs of the rear shock absorbers reach the mounting brackets on the axle housing. Connect the lower studs and install the attaching nuts.

7. Remove the jackstands and lower the vehicle.

Spring Between Lower Control Arm and Frame

NOTE: *If one spring must be replaced, the other should be replaced also. If the car has a stabilizer bar, the bar must be removed first.*

1. Raise and support the car at the rear crossmember, while supporting the axle with a jack.

2. Lower the axle until the shocks are fully extended.

3. Place a jack under the lower arm pivot bolt. Remove the pivot bolt and nut. Carefully

and slowly lower the arm until the spring load is relieved.

4. Remove the spring and insulators.

5. To install, tape the insulator in place in the frame, and place the lower insulator in place on the arm. Install the internal damper in the spring.

6. Position the spring in place and slowly raise the jack under the lower arm. Install the pivot bolt and nut, with the nut facing outwards. Do not tighten the nut.

7. Raise the axle to curb height, and tighten the lower pivot bolt to 70–100 ft. lbs.

8. Install the stabilizer bar, if removed. The proper torque is 20–27 ft. lbs. Remove the crossmember stands and lower the car.

SHOCK ABSORBER

NOTE: *Purge a new shock of air by repeatedly extending it in its normal position and compressing it while inverted.*

Spring Between Axle Housing and Frame

1. Raise the vehicle and install jackstands.

2. Remove the shock absorber outer attaching nut, washer and insulator from the stud at the top side of the spring upper seat. Compress the shock sufficiently to clear the spring seat hole, and remove the inner insulator and washer from the upper attaching stud.

3. Remove the locknut and disconnect the shock absorber lower stud at the mounting bracket on the axle housing. Remove the shock absorber.

4. Position a new inner washer and insulator on the upper attaching stud. Place the upper stud in the hole in the upper spring seat. While maintaining the shock in this position, install a new outer insulator, washer, and nut on the stud from the top side of the spring upper seat.

5. Extend the shock absorber. Locate the lower stud in the mounting bracket hole on the axle housing and install the locknut.

Spring Between Lower Control Arm and Frame

1. Remove the upper attaching nut, washer, and insulator. Access is through the trunk on sedans or side panel trim covers on station wagons and hatchbacks. Sedan studs have rubber caps.

2. Raise the car. Compress the shock to clear the upper tower. Remove the lower nut and washer; remove the shock.

3. Purge the shock of air and compress. Place the lower mounting eye over the lower stud and install the washer and a new locking nut. Do not tighten the nut yet.

4. Place the insulator and washer on the up-

per stud. Extend the shock, installing the stud through the upper mounting hole.

5. Torque the lower mounting nut to 40–55 ft. lbs.

6. Lower the car. Install the outer insulator and washer on the upper stud, and install a new nut. Tighten to 14–26 ft. lbs. **Install the trim** panel on station wagons and hatchbacks or the rubber cap on sedans.

STEERING

Steering Wheel

REMOVAL AND INSTALLATION

1971–74

1. Open the hood and disconnect the negative cable from the battery.

2. On models equipped with safety crash pads, remove the crash pad attaching screws from the underside of the steering wheel spoke and remove the pad. Remove the horn button or ring by pressing down evenly and turning it counterclockwise approximately 20 degrees and then lifting it from the steering wheel. Disconnect the shorn wires.

3. Remove the nut at the end of the shaft. Mark the steering shaft and hub prior to removal. Install a steering wheel puller on the end of the shaft and remove the wheel.

CAUTION: *The use of a knock-off type steering wheel puller or the use of a hammer on the steering shaft will damage the column bearing and, on collapsible columns, the column itself may be damaged.*

4. Lubricate the horn switch brush plate and the upper surface of the steering shaft upper bushing with Lubriplate or a similar product. Transfer all serviceable parts to the new steering wheel.

5. Position the steering wheel on the shaft so that the alignment marks made prior to removal line up. Install a new locknut and torque it to 20–30 ft. lbs. Connect the horn wires.

6. Install the horn button or ring by turning it clockwise and install the crash pad.

1975 and Later

1. Open the hood and disconnect the negative cable from the battery.

2. On models with safety crash pads, remove the crash pad attaching screws from the underside of the steering wheel spoke and remove the pad. On all models equipped with a horn button, remove the horn button or ring by pressing down evenly and turning it counterclockwise approximately 20° and then lifting

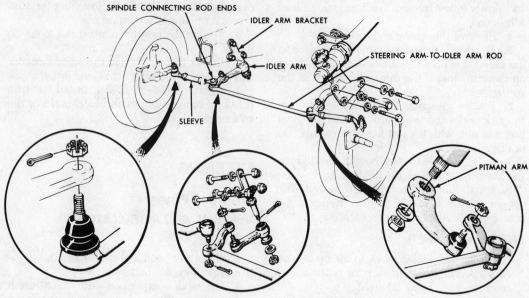

SPINDLE CONNECTING ROD ENDS

IDLER ARM BRACKET

STEERING ARM-TO-IDLER ARM ROD

IDLER ARM

SLEEVE

PITMAN ARM

Typical manual steering linkage

it from the steering wheel. On 1981 and later models, pull straight out on the hub cover. Disconnect the horn wires from the crash pad on models so equipped.

3. Remove and discard the nut from the end of the shaft. Install a steering wheel puller on the end of the shaft and remove the wheel.

CAUTION: *The use of a knock-off type steering wheel puller or the use of a hammer on the steering shaft will damage the collapsible column.*

4. Lubricate the upper surface of the steering shaft upper bushing with white grease. Transfer all serviceable parts to the new steering wheel.

5. Position the steering wheel on the shaft so that the alignment marks line up. Install a locknut and torque it to 30–40 ft. lbs. Connect the horn wires.

6. Install the horn button or ring by turning it clockwise or install the crash pad.

TURN SIGNAL SWITCH REPLACEMENT

1971–74

1. Open the hood and disconnect the negative battery cable.

2. Remove the retaining screw from the underside of each steering wheel spoke and remove the crash pad and horn switch cover as an assembly.

3. Remove the steering wheel retaining nut. Remove the steering wheel as outlined in the steering wheel "Removal and Installation" section.

4. Remove the turn signal handle from the side of the column. Remove the emergency flasher retainer and knob, if so equipped.

5. Remove the wire assembly cover and disconnect the wire connector plugs. Record the location and color code of each wire and tape the wires together. Make sure that the horn wires are disconnected. Remove the plastic cover from the wiring harness. Attach a piece of heavy cord to the switch wires to pull them through the column during installation.

6. Remove the retaining clips and attaching screws from the turn signal switch and lift the switch and wire assembly from the top of the column.

7. Tape the ends of the new switch wires together and transfer the pull cord to these wires.

8. Pull the wires down through the column with the cord and attach the new switch to the column hub.

9. Connect the wiring plugs to their mating plugs at the lower end of the column and install the plastic cover at the harness.

10. Install all retaining clips and wire assembly covers that were removed and install the turn signal handle. Install the emergency flasher retainer and knob, if so equipped.

11. Install the steering wheel and retaining nut as outlined in the "Steering Wheel Removal and Installation" section.

12. Install the horn ring or button. Install the crash pad with the retaining screws at the underside of each steering wheel spoke.

13. Connect the negative battery cable and test the operation of the turn signals, horn, and emergency flashers, if so equipped.

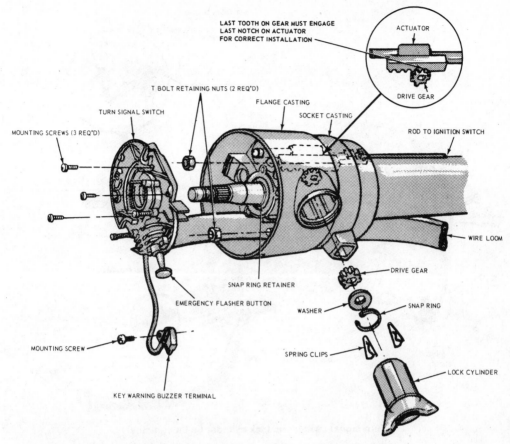

LAST TOOTH ON GEAR MUST ENGAGE
LAST NOTCH ON ACTUATOR
FOR CORRECT INSTALLATION

ACTUATOR

DRIVE GEAR

T BOLT RETAINING NUTS (2 REQ'D)

FLANGE CASTING

SOCKET CASTING

TURN SIGNAL SWITCH

ROD TO IGNITION SWITCH

MOUNTING SCREWS (3 REQ'D)

WIRE LOOM

DRIVE GEAR

SNAP RING RETAINER

EMERGENCY FLASHER BUTTON

WASHER

SNAP RING

MOUNTING SCREW

SPRING CLIPS

LOCK CYLINDER

KEY WARNING BUZZER TERMINAL

Turn signal switch and lock cylinder on fixed columns

LTD II, Montego, Torino, Versailles, 1975–79 Cougar, 1977–79 Thunderbird

1. Open the hood and disconnect the negative battery cable.

2. Remove the steering wheel.

3. Unscrew the turn signal handle from the side of the column. Remove the emergency flasher retainer and knob, if so equipped.

4. Remove the wire assembly cover and disconnect the wire connector plugs. Record the location and color code of each wire and tape the wires together. Make sure that the horn wires are disconnected. Remove the plastic cover from the wiring harness. Attach a piece of heavy cord to the switch wires to pull them through the column during installation.

5. Remove the retaining clips and attaching screws from the turn signal switch and pull the switch and wire assembly from the top of the column.

6. Tape the ends of the new switch wires together and transfer the pull cord to these wires.

7. Pull the wires down through the column with the cord and attach the new switch to the column hub.

8. Connect the wiring plugs to their mating plugs at the lower end of the column and install the plastic cover at the harness.

9. Install all retaining clips and wire assembly covers that were removed and install the turn signal handle. Install the emergency flasher retainer and knob, if so equipped.

10. Install the steering wheel and retaining nut.

11. Connect the negative battery cable.

1980 and Later Thunderbird and Cougar XR-7, 1981 and Later Cougar, 1982 and Later Continental and Mark VII, 1983 and Later LTD and Marquis

1. Remove the four screws retaining the steering column shroud.

2. Remove the turn signal lever by pulling and twisting straight out.

3. Peel back the foam shield. Disconnect the two electrical connectors.

4. Remove the two attaching screws and disengage the switch from the housing.

5. To install, position the switch to the housing and install the screws. Stick the foam to the switch.

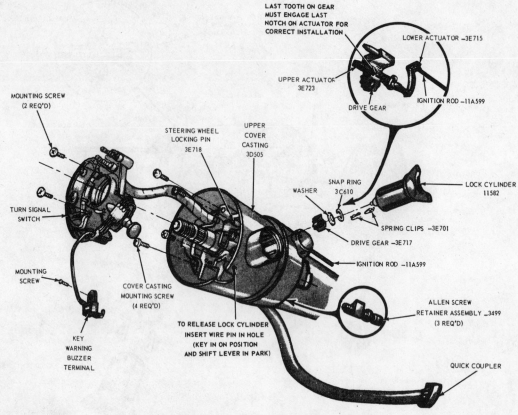

LAST TOOTH ON GEAR
MUST ENGAGE LAST
NOTCH ON ACTUATOR FOR
CORRECT INSTALLATION

LOWER ACTUATOR –3E715

UPPER ACTUATOR
3E723

IGNITION ROD –11A599

DRIVE GEAR

MOUNTING SCREW
(2 REQ'D)

STEERING WHEEL
LOCKING PIN
3E718

UPPER
COVER
CASTING
3D505

SNAP RING
3C610

WASHER

LOCK CYLINDER
11582

TURN SIGNAL
SWITCH

SPRING CLIPS –3E701

DRIVE GEAR –3E717

IGNITION ROD –11A599

MOUNTING
SCREW

COVER CASTING
MOUNTING SCREW
(4 REQ'D)

ALLEN SCREW
RETAINER ASSEMBLY –3499
(3 REQ'D)

KEY
WARNING
BUZZER
TERMINAL

TO RELEASE LOCK CYLINDER
INSERT WIRE PIN IN HOLE
(KEY IN ON POSITION
AND SHIFT LEVER IN PARK)

QUICK COUPLER

Turn signal switch and lock cylinder on tilt columns

6. Install the lever by aligning the key and pushing the lever fully home.

7. Install the two electrical connectors, test the switch, and install the shroud.

Manual Steering, Except Rack and Pinion

STEERING GEAR INSPECTION

Before any steering gear adjustments are made, it is recommended that the front end of the car be raised and a thorough inspection be made for stiffness or lost motion in the steering gear, steering linkage, and front suspension. Worn or damaged parts should be replaced, since a satisfactory adjustment of the steering gear cannot be obtained if bent or badly worn parts exist.

It is also very important that the steering gear be properly aligned in the car. Misalignment of the gear places a stress on the steering worm shaft, therefore a proper adjustment is impossible. To align the steering gear, loosen the mounting bolts to permit the gear to align itself. Check the steering gear mounting seat and if there is a gap at any of the mounting bolts, proper alignment may be obtained by placing

shims where excessive gap appears. Tighten the steering gear bolts. Alignment of the gear in the car is very important and should be done carefully so that a satisfactory, trouble-free gear adjustment may be obtained.

STEERING WORM AND SECTOR GEAR ADJUSTMENT

The ball nut assembly and the sector gear must be adjusted properly to maintain a minimum amount of steering shaft end-play and a minimum amount of back-lash between the sector gear and the ball nut. There are only two adjustments that may be done on this steering gear and they should be done as given below:

1. Disconnect the pitman arm from the steering pitman-to-idler arm rod.

2. Loosen the locknut on the sector shaft adjustment screw and turn the adjusting screw counterclockwise.

3. Measure the worm bearing preload by attaching an in. lbs. torque wrench to the steering wheel nut. With the steering wheel off center, note the reading required to rotate the input shaft about 1½ turns to either side of center. If the torque reading is not about 4–5 in. lbs., adjust the gear as given in the next step.

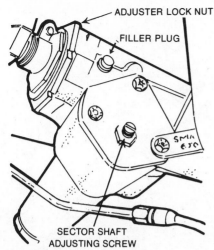

ADJUSTER LOCK NUT

FILLER PLUG

SECTOR SHAFT
ADJUSTING SCREW

Manual steering gear adjustment

4. Loosen the steering shaft bearing adjuster locknut and tighten or back off the bearing adjusting screw until the preload is within the specified limits.

5. Tighten the steering shaft bearing adjuster locknut and recheck the preload torque.

6. Turn the steering wheel slowly to either stop. Turn *gently* against the stop to avoid possible damage to the ball return guides. Then rotate the wheel 2¾ turns to center the ball nut.

7. Turn the sector adjusting screw clockwise until the proper torque (9–10 in. lbs.) is obtained that is necessary to rotate the worm gear past its center (high spot).

8. While holding the sector adjusting screw, tighten the sector screw adjusting locknut to 32–40 ft. lbs. and recheck the backlash adjustment.

9. Connect the pitman arm to the steering arm-to-idler arm rod.

STEERING GEAR REMOVAL AND INSTALLATION

1. Remove the bolt(s) that retains the flex coupling to the steering shaft.

2. Remove the nut and lock washer that secures the Pitman arm to the sector shaft. Using a puller, remove the Pitman arm from the sector shaft. Do not hammer on the end of the puller as this can damage the steering gear.

3. On vehicles with standard transmissions it may be necessary to disconnect the clutch linkage to obtain clearance. On 8-cylinder models, it may be necessary to lower the exhaust system.

4. Remove the bolts that attach the steering gear to the side rail. Remove the gear.

5. Position the steering gear and flex coupling on the steering shaft. Install steering gear-to-side rail bolts and torque to 50 to 65 ft. lb.

6. Install the clutch linkage if disconnected. Reposition the exhaust system if it was lowered.

7. Place the Pitman arm on the sector shaft and install the attaching nut and lock washer. Torque the nut to 150 to 225 ft. lb.

8. Install the flex coupling attaching nut(s) and torque to 18–23 ft. lb.

Manual Steering, Rack and Pinion Type

ADJUSTMENTS

The rack and pinion gear provides two means of service adjustment. The gear must be removed from the vehicle to perform both adjustments.

Support Yoke to Rack

1. Clean the exterior of the steering gear thoroughly and mount the gear by installing two long bolts and washers through the mounting boss bushings and attaching to Bench Mounted Holding Fixture, Tool T57L-500-B or equivalent.

2. Remove the yoke cover, gasket, shims, and yoke spring.

3. Clean the cover and housing flange areas thoroughly.

4. Reinstall the yoke and cover, omitting the gasket, shims, and the spring.

5. Tighten the cover bolts lightly until the cover just touches the yoke.

6. Measure the gap between the cover and the housing flange. With the gasket, add selected shims to give a combined pack thickness 0.13–0.15mm (.005–.006 inch) greater than the measured gap.

7. Remove the cover.

8. Assemble the gasket next to the housing flange, then the selected shims, spring, and cover.

9. Install cover bolts, sealing the threads with ESW-M46-132A or equivalent, and tighten.

10. Check to see that the gear operates smoothly without binding or slackness.

Pinion Bearing Preload

1. Clean the exterior of the steering gear thoroughly and place the gear in the bench mounted holding fixture as outlined under Support Yoke to Back Adjustment.

2. Loosen the bolts of the yoke cover to relieve spring pressure on the rack.

3. Remove the pinion cover and gasket. Clean the cover flange area thoroughly.

4. Remove the spacer and shims.

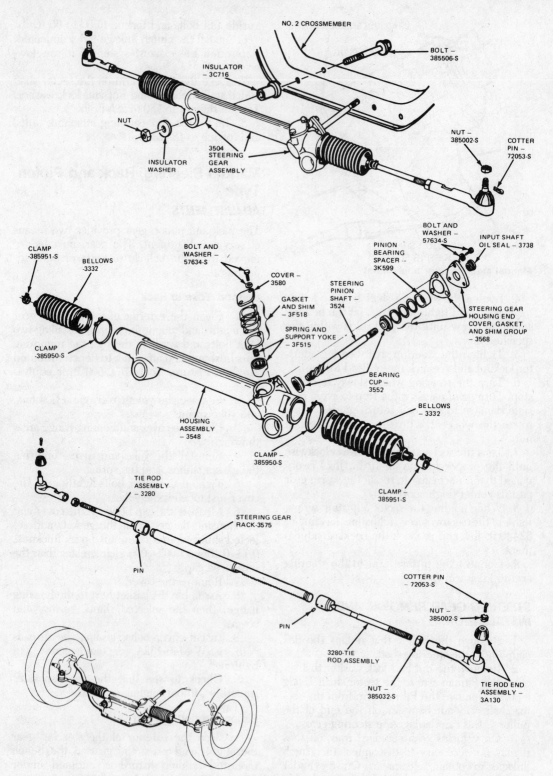

Typical rack and pinion steering gear linkage

5. Install a new gasket, and fit shims between the upper bearing and the spacer until the top of the spacer is flush with the gasket. Check with a straightedge, using light pressure.

6. Add one shim (.0025–.005) to the pack in order to preload the bearings. The spacer must be assembled next to the pinion cover.

7. Install the cover and bolts.

Tie Rod Articulation Effort

1. Install hook end of pull scale through the hole in the tie rod end stud. Effort to move the tire rod should be 1–5 pounds. Do not damage tie rod neck.

2. Replace ball joint/tie rod assembly if effort falls outside this range. Save the tie rod end for use on the new tie rod assembly.

REMOVAL AND INSTALLATION

1. Disconnect the negative battery cable from the battery.

2. Remove the one bolt retaining the flexible coupling to the input shaft.

3. Leave the ignition key in the ON position, and raise the vehicle on a hoist.

4. Remove the two tie rod end retaining cotter pins and nuts. Separate the studs from the spindle arms, using the ball joint separator tool. Do not use a hammer or similar tool as this may damage spindle arms or rod studs.

5. Support the steering gear, and remove the two nuts, insulator washers, and bolts retaining the steering gear to the No. 2 crossmember.

6. Remove the steering gear assembly from the vehicle.

7. Insert the input shaft into the flexible coupling aligning the flats and position the steering gear to the No. 2 crossmember. Install the two bolts.

8. Connect the tie rod ends to the spindle arms, and install the two retaining nuts. Tighten the nuts to specifications, and install the two cotter pins.

9. Lower the vehicle, and install the one bolt retaining the flexible coupling to the input shaft. Tighten the bolt to specifications.

10. Turn the ignition key to the OFF position.

11. Connect the negative battery cable to the battery.

12. Check the toe, and reset if necessary.

Power Steering

Four Different power steering systems have been used:

Bendix Non-Integral System
• 1971 All
• All Versailles

Ford Integral System
• 1972–79 All except Versailles, 1974 Torino and Montego with the 8-302 engine, and 1975–76 models with the 8-351 engine and without air conditioning

Saginaw Integral System
• 1974 Torino and Montego with the 8-302 engine
• 1975–76 models with the 8-351 engine and without air conditioning

Ford Integral Rack and Pinion System
• From 1980 All

ADJUSTMENTS

Bendix Non-Integral System

WORM AND SECTOR

The ball nut assembly and sector gear must be properly adjusted to steering shaft end play (a factor of preload adjustment) and backlash between the sector gear and ball nut. Only two adjustments can be made. Perform these operations in the following order to avoid damage to the gear.

1. Disconnect the linkage from the gear by removing the Pitman arm from the sector shaft.

2. Loosen the nut that locks the sector adjusting screw and turn the screw counterclockwise. Remove the horn pad from the steering wheel.

3. Measure worm bearing preload by attaching an in. lb. torque wrench to the steering wheel nut. With the steering wheel off center, measure the pull required to rotate the input shaft approximately one and one-half turns to either side of center.

4. If preload is 3–8 in. lb., loosen the worm shaft bearing adjuster lock nut and tighten or loosen the bearing adjuster (as required) to bering the preload within the specified limits.

5. Tighten the worm shaft bearing adjuster lock nut to 60–80 ft. lb. and recheck preload.

6. Turn the steering wheel slowly to one stop. Turn gently against the stop to avoid damage to the ball return guides. Rotate the wheel to center the ball nut. 6½ turns should be needed to rotate the steering wheel lock-to-lock. Divide by two to determine the center position. The blind tooth on the gear input shaft should be at the 12 o'clock position when centered.

7. Torque the sector adjusting screw clockwise until resistance is felt. Using an in. lb.

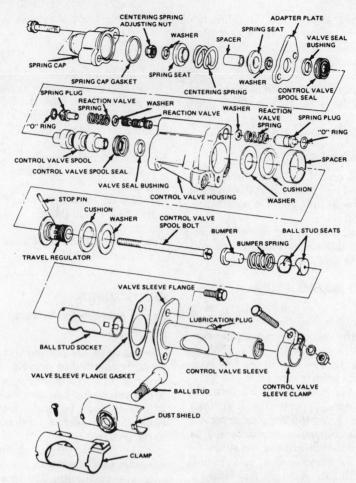

Exploded view of the Bendix linkage system control valve

torque wrench, recheck the center mesh load by rotating the steering shaft approximately 90 degrees either way across center. If the mesh-load is not within 10–16 in. lb., turn sector shaft adjusting screw until meshload is within specification. Hold the sector shaft adjusting screw and torque the locknut to 32–40 ft. lb.

8. Re-check preload adjustment by turning the steering wheel one and one-half turns from center.

9. Connect the Pitman arm to the sector shaft.

CONTROL VALVE CENTERING

1. Raise the vehicle and remove two spring cap attaching screws and lock washer assemblies. Remove the spring cap and discard the spring cap gasket. Never start the engine with the spring cap removed.

2. Torque the centering spring adjusting nut to 90–100 in. lb. Do not tighten beyond specification. Loosen the same spring adjusting nut ¼ turn.

NOTE: *Because the control valve spool bolt and nut may turn together slightly, be sure that only the nut-relative-to-bolt movement is counted.*

3. Lubricate spring cap and gasket and position on valve housing. Lubricate and install the two screw and washer assemblies. Torque to 72–100 in. lb.

4. Lower the vehicle.

Ford Integral System

MESH LOAD

During the vehicle breaking-in period, some factory adjustments may change. These changes will not necessarily affect operation of the steering gear assembly, and need not be adjusted unless there is excessive lash or other malfunctioning. Adjust the total-overcenter position load to eliminate excessive lash between the sector and rack teeth as follows:

1. Disconnect the Pitman arm from the sector shaft.

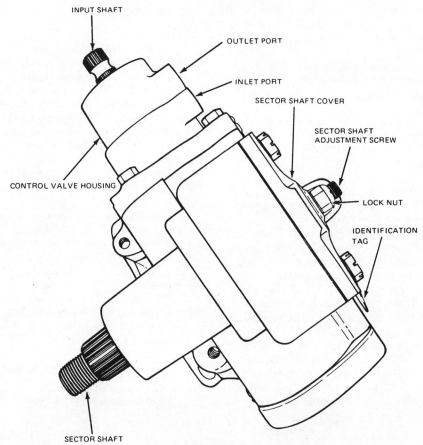

INPUT SHAFT

OUTLET PORT

INLET PORT

SECTOR SHAFT COVER

SECTOR SHAFT
ADJUSTMENT SCREW

CONTROL VALVE HOUSING

LOCK NUT

IDENTIFICATION
TAG

SECTOR SHAFT

Ford integral power steering gear

2. Disconnect the fluid return line at the reservoir and cap the reservoir return line pipe.

3. Place the end of the return line in a clean container and turn the steering wheel from left to right to discharge the fluid from the gear.

4. Turn the steering wheel to 45 degrees from the left stop.

5. Using an in. lb. torque wrench on the steering wheel nut, determine the torque required to rotate the shaft slowly approximately ⅛ turn from the 45 degree position.

6. Turn the steering wheel back to center, and determine the torque required to rotate the shaft back and forth across the center position. Loosen the nut, and turn the adjuster screw until the reading is 11 to 12 in. lb. greater than the torque measured at 45 degrees from the stop. Tighten the nut while holding the screw in place.

7. Recheck the readings and replace the Pitman arm and steering wheel hub cover.

8. Connect the fluid return line to the reservoir and fill the reservoir. Do not pry against the reservoir to obtain proper belt load. Pressure may deform the reservoir causing it to leak.

9. Recheck belt tension and adjust, if necessary. Torque the bolts and nut to 30 to 40 ft. lb.

VALVE SPOOL CENTERING CHECK

1. Install a 0–2000 psi pressure gauge in the pressure line between the power steering pump outlet port and the integral steering gear inlet port. Be sure the valve on the gauge is fully open.

2. Check the fluid level and add fluid, if necessary.

3. Start the engine and turn the steering wheel from stop-to-stop to bring the steering lubricant to normal operating temperature. Turn off the engine and recheck fluid level. Add fluid, if necessary.

4. With the engine running at approximately 1000 rpm and the steering wheel centered, attach an in. lb. torque wrench to the steering wheel nut. Apply sufficient torque in each direction to get a gauge reading of 250 psi.

5. The reading should be the same in both directions at 250 psi. If the difference between

the readings exceeds 4 in. lb., remove the steering gear and install a thicker or thinner valve centering shim in the housing. Use as many shims as necessary, but do not allow thickness of the shim pack to exceed .030 inch. The piston must be able to bottom on the valve housing face. No clearance is allowed in this area.

6. Test for clearance between the piston end and valve housing face as follows:

a. Hold the valve assembly so the piston is up and try to turn the input shaft to the right.

b. If there is no clearance, the input shaft will not turn. If there is clearance, the piston and worm will rotate together.

c. If two or more shims must be used to center the spool valve, and a restriction or interference condition is experienced when turning the piston to its stop on the valve housing, replace the shaft and control assembly. If steering effort is heavy to the left, increase shim thickness. If steering effort is light to the left, decrease shim thickness.

7. When performing the valve spool centering check outside the vehicle, use the procedures described above except take torque and pressure readings at the right and left stops instead of at either side of center.

Saginaw Integral System

MESH LOAD

1. Disconnect the Pitman arm from the sector shaft. Remove the steering wheel hub.

2. Disconnect the fluid return line at the reservoir, and cap the reservoir return line pipe.

3. Place the end of the return line in a clean container and turn the steering wheel from left to right to discharge the fluid from the gear.

4. Turn the gear one-half turn off center in either direction. Using a 24 in. lb torque wrench on the steering wheel nut, determine the torque required to rotate the shaft slowly through a 20 degree arc.

5. Turn the gear back to center and repeat Step 4. Loosen the adjuster lock nut and turn the screw inward using a 7/32-inch Allen wrench, until the reading is 6 in. lb. greater than the reading taken in Step 4. Retighten the lock nut while holding the screw in place.

6. Recheck the readings and replace the Pitman arm and steering wheel hub.

7. Connect the fluid return line to the reservoir and fill the reservoir.

Ford Integral Rack and Pinion System

The power rack and pinion steering gear provides for only one service adjustment. The gear

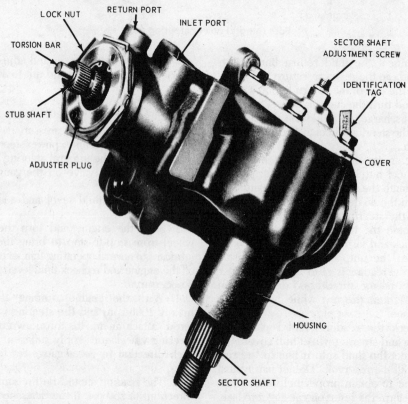

Saginaw integral steering gear

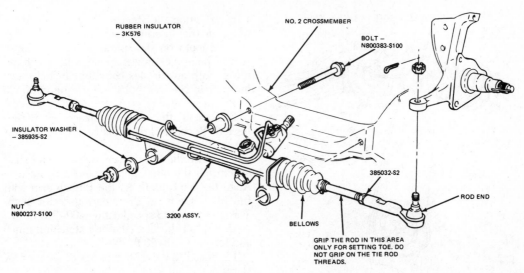

RUBBER INSULATOR – 3K576

NO. 2 CROSSMEMBER

BOLT – N800383-S100

INSULATOR WASHER – 385935-S2

385032-S2

ROD END

NUT N800237-S100

3200 ASSY.

BELLOWS

GRIP THE ROD IN THIS AREA ONLY FOR SETTING TOE. DO NOT GRIP ON THE TIE ROD THREADS.

Ford power rack and pinion steering gear

must be removed from the vehicle to perform this adjustment.

RACK YOKE PLUG PRELOAD

1. Clean the exterior of the steering gear thoroughly.

2. Install two long bolts and washers through the bushings, and attach to the bench mounted holding fixture, Tool T57L-500-B or equivalent.

3. Do not remove the external pressure lines, unless they are leaking or damaged. If these lines are removed, they must be replaced with new lines.

4. Drain the power steering fluid by rotating the input shaft lock-to-lock twice using Tool T74P-3504-R or equivalent. Cover ports on valve housing with shop cloth while draining gear.

5. Insert an lb-in torque wrench with maximum capacity of 30–60 in. lb. into the input shaft torque adapter, Tool T74P-3504-R or equivalent. Position the adapter and wrench on the input shaft splines.

6. Loosen the yoke plug locknut with wrench, Tool T78P-3504-H or equivalent.

7. Loosen yoke plug with a ¾ inch socket wrench.

8. With the rack at the center of travel, tighten the yoke plug to 45–50 in. lb. Clean the threads of the yoke plug prior to tightening to prevent a false reading.

9. Back off the yoke plug approximately ⅛ turn (44 degrees min. to 54 degrees max.) until the torque required to initiate and sustain rotation of the input shaft is 7–18 in. lb.

10. Place Tool T78P-3504-H or equivalent on the yoke plug locknut. While holding the yoke plug, tighten the locknut to 44–66 ft. lb. Do not allow the yoke plug to move while

tightening or the preload will be affected. Recheck input shaft torque after tightening locknut.

11. If the external pressure lines were removed, they must be replaced with new service line. Remove the copper seals from the housing ports prior to installation of new lines.

STEERING GEAR REMOVAL AND INSTALLATION

Bendix Non-Integral System

1. Remove the bolt(s) that retains the flex coupling to the steering shaft.

2. Remove the nut and lock washer that secures the Pitman arm to the sector shaft.

3. Raise the vehicle and disconnect the two fluid lines from the power cylinder and drain the lines.

4. Remove the pal nut, attaching nut, washer, and the insulator from the end of the power cylinder rod.

5. Remove the cotter pin and castellated nut that secures the power cylinder stud to the centerlink.

6. Disconnect the power cylinder stud from the centerlink. It is necessary to use the steering arm remover tool, No. T64P-3590-F. Use of any other tool will result in damage to the power cylinder.

7. Remove the insulator sleeve and washer from the end of the power cylinder rod. Remove the cylinder rod. Remove the cylinder rod boot and discard the clamp.

8. Inspect the tube fittings and seats in the power cylinder for damage. Replace the seats in the cylinder or the tubes as required. If any tube seat is removed, a new seat must be used.

9. Using Tool T64P-3590-F remove the

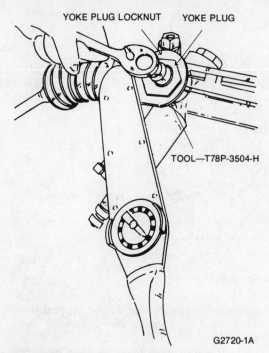

YOKE PLUG LOCKNUT   YOKE PLUG

TOOL—T78P-3504-H

G2720-1A

Tightening yoke plug locknut

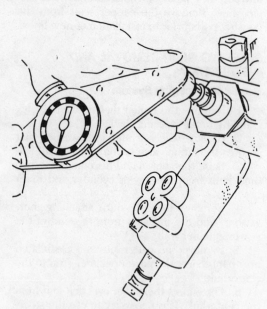

Adjusting yoke bearing preload

Pitman arm from the sector shaft. Do not hammer on the end of the puller as this can damage the steering gear.

10. On vehicles with standard transmissions it may be necessary to disconnect the clutch linkage to obtain clearance. On 8 cylinder models, it may be necessary to lower the exhaust system.

11. Remove the bolts that attach the steering gear to the side rail. Remove the gear.

12. Position the steering gear and flex coupling on the steering shaft. Be sure that the missing tooth on the spline of the gear input shaft is pointing straight up and aligns with the blind tooth on the flex coupling. Install steering gear-to-side rail bolts and torque to 50–60 ft. lb.

13. Install the clutch linkage if disconnected. Reposition the exhaust system if it was lowered.

14. Place the Pitman arm on the sector shaft and install the attaching nut and lock washer. Align the blind tooth on the Pitman arm with the blind tooth on the steering sector shaft. Torque the nut to specification 200–225 ft. lb.

15. Install the flex coupling attaching nut(s) and torque to 18–23 ft. lb.

16. Install the cylinder rod boot with a new clamp.

17. Install the washer, sleeve, and the insulator on the end of the power cylinder rod.

18. Extend the rod as far as possible. Insert the rod in the bracket on the frame and compress the rod, if necessary, to insert the stud in the centerlink. Secure the stud with a castellated nut and a cotter pin. Torque the nut to 35–47 ft. lb.

19. Secure the power cylinder rod with an insulator, washer, nut, and pal nut. Torque the hex nut to 18–34 ft. lb. and the pal nut to 36–60 ft. lb.

20. Connect the two fluid lines into the correct power cylinder ports. Position the lines so that they are parallel to each other, and tighten. Torque the tube nuts to 21–30 ft. lb.

21. Lower the vehicle and fill the fluid reservoir with fluid to the cross-hatched area on the dip stick.

22. Start the engine and run it at idle speed for about two minutes to warm the fluid, then turn the steering wheel all the way to the left and right several times and check the system for leaks.

23. Increase the engine speed to about 1,000 RPM and turn the steering wheel all the way to the left and right several times.

24. Stop the engine and check the control valve and hose connections; repair any leaks.

25. Check the fluid level and refill, if necessary.

Ford Integral System

1. Tag the pressure and return lines for future identification.

2. Disconnect the pressure and return lines from the steering gear. Plug the lines and ports in the gear to prevent entry of dirt.

3. Remove the bolts that secure the flexible coupling to the steering gear and column.

4. Raise the vehicle and remove the sector shaft attaching nut.

5. Remove the Pitman arm from the sector shaft with Tool T64P-3590-F. Remove the tool from the Pitman arm. Do not damage the seals.

6. On vehicles with standard transmissions, remove the clutch release lever retracting spring to provide clearance for removing the steering gear.

7. Support the steering gear. Remove the steering gear attaching bolts.

8. Remove the clamp bolt that holds the flexible coupling to the steering gear. Work the gear free of the flex coupling and remove.

9. If the flex coupling did not come off with the gear, lift it off the shaft.

10. Slide the flex coupling into place on the steering shaft assembly. Turn the steering wheel so the spokes are in the normal position.

11. Center the steering gear input shaft.

12. Slide the steering gear input shaft into the flex coupling and into place on the frame side rail. Install the attaching bolts and torque to 35–40 ft. lb.

13. Be sure the wheels are in the straight ahead position. Then install the Pitman arm on the sector shaft. Install and tighten the sector shaft and attaching bolts. Torque the bolts to 55–70 ft. lb.

14. Move the flex coupling into place on the input and steering column shaft. Install the attaching bolts and torque to 18–22 ft. lb.

15. Connect the pressure and the return lines to the steering gear. Tighten the lines.

16. Disconnect the coil wire.

17. Fill the reservoir. Turn on the ignition and turn the steering wheel from stop-to-stop to distribute the fluid.

18. Recheck the fluid level and add fluid, if necessary.

19. Install the coil wire. Start the engine and turn the steering wheel from left to right. Inspect for fluid leaks.

Saginaw Integral System

1. Disconnect the pressure and return lines from the steering gear. Plug the lines and ports in the gear to prevent entry of dirt.

2. Remove the bolts that secure the flex coupling to the steering gear and column.

3. Raise the vehicle and remove the Pitman arm attaching nut and lock washer.

4. Using Tool T64P-3590-F, remove the Pitman arm from the sector shaft. Do not hammer on the end of the tool when pulling the Pitman arm from the shaft. Damage to the gear or cover could result. Remove the tool from the Pitman arm.

5. On vehicles with standard transmissions, remove the clutch release lever retract-

ing spring to provide clearance for removing the steering gear.

6. Support the steering gear. Remove the steering gear attaching bolts.

7. Work the steering gear free of the flex coupling and remove.

8. Lift the flex coupling off the shaft if it did not come off with the gear.

9. Slide the flex coupling into place on the steering shaft. Turn the steering wheel so that the spokes are in their normal position.

10. Center the steering gear input shaft.

11. Slide the steering gear input shaft into the flex coupling and into place on the frame side rail. Install the attaching bolts and torque to 45–50 ft. lb.

12. Be sure that the wheels are in the straight-ahead position. Then install the Pitman arm on the sector shaft. Install the sector shaft attaching nut and torque to 200 ft. lb.

13. Move the flex couplihng into place on the input shaft and steering column shaft. Install the attaching bolts and torque to 18–23 ft. lb.

14. Connect the pressure and the return lines to the steering gear. Tighten the lines.

15. Disconnect the coil wire. Fill the pump reservoir. Crank the engine with the starter and continue adding fluid until the level remains constant. Turn the steering wheel from side to side without hitting the stops. Turn off ignition and recheck the fluid level. Add fluid, if necessary.

16. Reconnect the coil wire. Start the engine and allow it to run for several minutes. Turn the steering wheel from stop to stop.

17. Turn off the engine and recheck the fluid level. Add fluid, if necessary.

Ford Integral Rack and Pinion System

1. Disconnect the negative battery cable from the battery.

2. Remove the one bolt retaining the flexible coupling to the input shaft.

3. Leave the ignition key in the On position, and raise the vehicle on a hoist.

4. Remove the two tie rod end retaining cotter pins and nuts. Separate the studs from the spindle arms, using the ball joint separator tool.

5. Support the steering gear, and remove the two nuts, insulator, washers, and bolts retaining the steering gear to the No. 2 crossmember. Lower the gear slightly to permit access to the pressure and return line fittings.

6. Disconnect the pressure and return lines from the steering gear valve housing. Plug the lines and parts in the valve housing to prevent entry of dirt.

7. Remove the steering gear assembly from the vehicle.

8. Support and position the steering gear, so that the pressure and return line fittings can be connected to the valve housing. Tighten the fittings to 15–20 ft. lb. The design allows the hoses to swivel when tightened properly. Do not attempt to eliminate looseness by over-tightening, since this can cause damage to the fittings.

NOTE: *The rubber insulators must be pushed completely inside the gear housing before the installation of the gear housing on the No. 2 crossmember.*

9. No gap is allowed between the insulator and the face of the gear boss. A rubber lubricant should be used to facilitate proper installation of the insulators in the gear housing. Insert the input shaft into the flexible coupling, and position the steering gear to the No. 2 crossmember. Install the two bolts, insulator washers, and nuts. Tighten the two nuts to 80–100 ft. lb.

10. Connect the tie rod ends to the spindle arms, and install the two retaining nuts. Tighten the nuts to 35–45 ft. lb., then, after tightening to specification, tighten the nuts to their nearest cotter pin castellation, and install two new cotter pins.

11. Lower the vehicle, and install the one bolt retaining the flexible coupling to the input shaft. Tighten the bolt to 18–23 ft. lb.

12. Turn the ignition key to the Off position.

13. Connect the negative battery cable to the battery.

14. Remove the coil wire.

15. Fill the power steering pump reservoir.

16. Engage the starter, and cycle the steering wheel to distribute the fluid. Check the fluid level and add as required.

17. Install the coil wire, start the engine, and cycle the steering wheel. Check for fluid leaks.

18. If the tie rod ends were loosened, check the wheel alignment.

Power Steering Pump
REMOVAL AND INSTALLATION

1. Drain the fluid from the pump reservoir by disconnecting the fluid return hose at the pump. Disconnect the pressure hose from the pump.

2. Remove the mounting bolts from the front of the pump. On eight cylinder engines through 1977, there is a nut on the rear of the pump that must be removed. After removal, move the pump inward to loosen the belt tension and remove the belt from the pulley. Remove the pump from the car.

3. To install the pump, position on mount-ing bracket and loosely install the mounting bolts and nuts. Put the drive belt over the pulley and move the pump outward against the belt until the proper belt tension is obtained. Do not pry against the pump body. Measure the belt tension with a belt tension gauge for the proper adjustment. Only in cases where a belt tension gauge is not available should the belt deflection method be used.

4. Tighten the mounting bolts and nuts.

Tie Rod End
REPLACEMENT
Torino, Montego, Elite, LTD II, 1975–79 Cougar, 1977–79 Thunderbird

1. Raise and support the front end.

2. Remove the cotter pin and nut from the rod end ball stud.

3. Loosen the sleeve and clamp bolts and remove the rod end from the spindle arm center link using a ball joint separator.

4. Remove the rod end from the sleeve, counting the exact number of turns required.

5. Install the new end using the exact number of turns it took to remove the old one.

6. Install all parts. Torque the stud to 40–43 ft. lbs. and the clamp to 20–22 ft. lbs.

7. Check the toe-in.

Versailles

1. Raise and support the front end.

2. Remove and discard the cotter pin and nut from the rod end ball stud.

3. Disconnect the rod end from the spindle arm or center link.

4. Loosen the rod sleeve clamp bolts and turn the rod to remove. Count the exact number of turns required.

5. Install a new rod end using the exact number of turns it took to remove the old one.

6. Install all parts in reverse of removal. Torque stud to 40–43 ft. lbs. and clamp to 20–22 ft. lbs.

7. Check the toe-in.

Rack and Pinion Models

1. Remove the cotter pin and nut at the spindle. Separate the tie rod end stud from the spindle with a puller.

2. Matchmark the position of the locknut with paint on the tie rod. Unscrew the locknut. Unscrew the tie rod end, counting the number of turns required to remove.

3. Install the new end the same number of turns. Attach the tie rod end stud to the spindle. Install the nut and torque to 35 ft. lbs., then continue to tighten until the cotter pin holes align. Install a new cotter pin. Check the toe and adjust if necessary, then torque the tie rod end locknut to 35 ft. lbs.

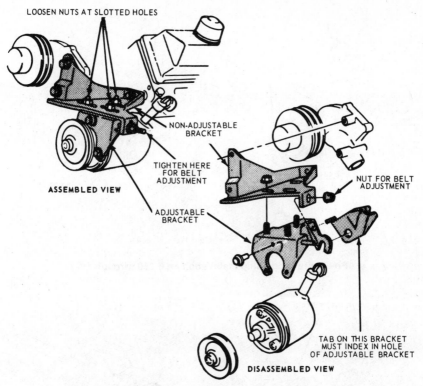

LOOSEN NUTS AT SLOTTED HOLES

NON-ADJUSTABLE BRACKET

TIGHTEN HERE FOR BELT ADJUSTMENT

ASSEMBLED VIEW

ADJUSTABLE BRACKET

NUT FOR BELT ADJUSTMENT

TAB ON THIS BRACKET MUST INDEX IN HOLE OF ADJUSTABLE BRACKET

DISASSEMBLED VIEW

Power steering pump installation on 429 and 460 engines

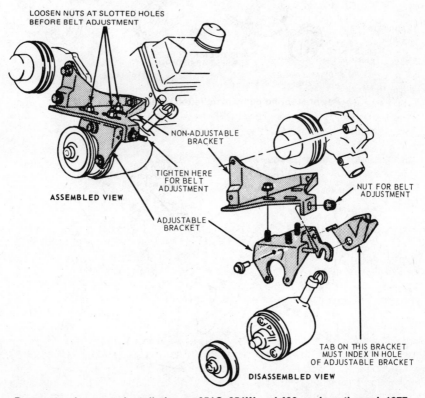

LOOSEN NUTS AT SLOTTED HOLES BEFORE BELT ADJUSTMENT

NON-ADJUSTABLE BRACKET

TIGHTEN HERE FOR BELT ADJUSTMENT

ASSEMBLED VIEW

ADJUSTABLE BRACKET

NUT FOR BELT ADJUSTMENT

TAB ON THIS BRACKET MUST INDEX IN HOLE OF ADJUSTABLE BRACKET

DISASSEMBLED VIEW

Power steering pump installation on 351C, 351W and 400 engines through 1977

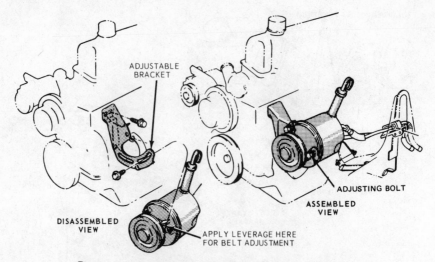

Power steering pump installation on 6-250 through 1977

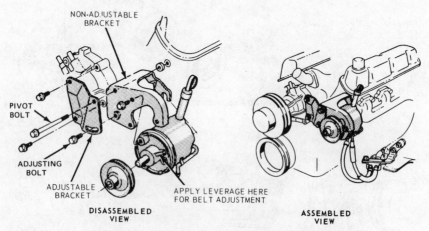

Power steering pump installation on 302 through 1977

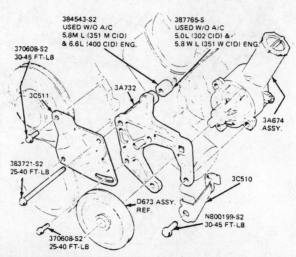

Power steering pump installation on all 1978–79 models except Versailles

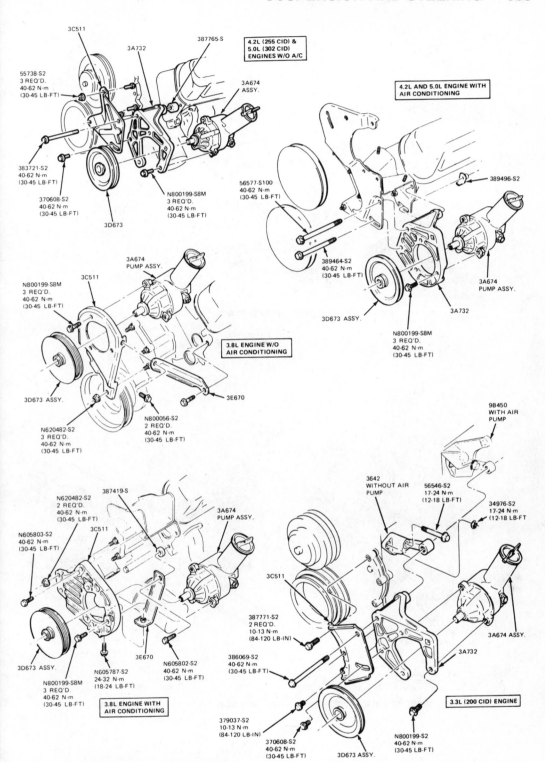

**4.2L (255 CID) &
5.0L (302 CID)
ENGINES W/O A/C**

3C511

3A732

387765-S

55738-S2
3 REQ'D.
40-62 N·m
(30-45 LB-FT)

3A674
ASSY.

383721-S2
40-62 N·m
(30-45 LB-FT)

370608-S2
40-62 N·m
(30-45 LB-FT)

3D673

N800199-S8M
3 REQ'D.
40-62 N·m
(30-45 LB-FT)

**4.2L AND 5.0L ENGINE WITH
AIR CONDITIONING**

389496-S2

56577-S100
40-62 N·m
(30-45 LB-FT)

389464-S2
40-62 N·m
(30-45 LB-FT)

3D673 ASSY.

3A674
PUMP ASSY.

3A732

N800199-S8M
3 REQ'D.
40-62 N·m
(30-45 LB-FT)

3A674
PUMP ASSY.

3C511

N800199-S8M
3 REQ'D.
40-62 N·m
(30-45 LB-FT)

3D673 ASSY.

N620482-S2
3 REQ'D.
40-62 N·m
(30-45 LB-FT)

N800056-S2
2 REQ'D.
40-62 N·m
(30-45 LB-FT)

3E670

**3.8L ENGINE W/O
AIR CONDITIONING**

9B450
WITH AIR
PUMP

3642
WITHOUT AIR
PUMP

56546-S2
17-24 N·m
(12-18 LB-FT)

34976-S2
17-24 N·m
(12-18 LB-FT)

N620482-S2
2 REQ'D.
40-62 N·m
(30-45 LB-FT)

387419-S

3A674
PUMP ASSY.

N605803-S2
40-62 N·m
(30-45 LB-FT)

3C511

3C511

387771-S2
2 REQ'D.
10-13 N·m
(84-120 LB-IN)

3A674 ASSY.

3A732

3E670

N605802-S2
40-62 N·m
(30-45 LB-FT)

386069-S2
40-62 N·m
(30-45 LB-FT)

3D673 ASSY.

N605787-S2
24-32 N·m
(18-24 LB-FT)

N800199-S8M
3 REQ'D.
40-62 N·m
(30-45 LB-FT)

**3.8L ENGINE WITH
AIR CONDITIONING**

379037-S2
10-13 N·m
(84-120 LB-IN)

370608-S2
40-62 N·m
(30-45 LB-FT)

3D673 ASSY.

N800199-S2
40-62 N·m
(30-45 LB-FT)

3.3L (200 CID) ENGINE

Power steering pump installation on 1982 Thunderbird, XR-7 and Continental

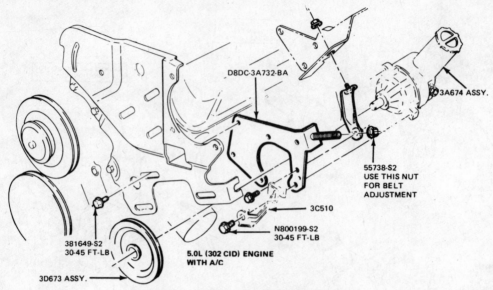

D8DC-3A732-BA

3A674 ASSY.

55738-S2
USE THIS NUT
FOR BELT
ADJUSTMENT

3C510

N800199-S2
30-45 FT-LB

381649-S2
30-45 FT-LB

5.0L (302 CID) ENGINE
WITH A/C

3D673 ASSY.

Power steering pump installation on Versailles

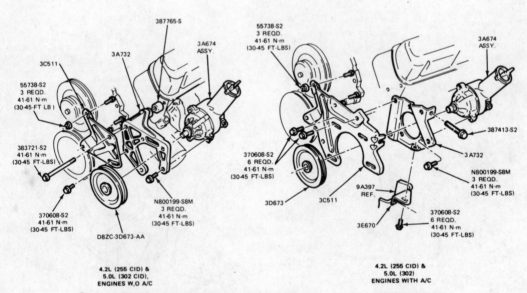

387765-S

3A732

3A674
ASSY.

3C511

55738-S2
3 REQD.
41-61 N·m
(30-45-FT LB)

383721-S2
41-61 N·m
(30-45 FT-LBS)

370608-S2
41-61 N·m
(30-45 FT-LBS)

D8ZC-3D673-AA

N800199-S8M
3 REQD.
41-61 N·m
(30-45 FT-LBS)

55738-S2
3 REQD.
41-61 N·m
(30-45 FT-LBS)

3A674
ASSY.

387413-S2

3A732

N800199-S8M
3 REQD.
41-61 N·m
(30-45 FT-LBS)

370608-S2
6 REQD.
41-61 N·m
(30-45 FT-LBS)

9A397
REF.

3D673

3C511

3E670

370608-S2
6 REQD.
41-61 N·m
(30-45 FT-LBS)

4.2L (255 CID) &
5.0L (302 CID),
ENGINES W,O A/C

4.2L (255 CID) &
5.0L (302)
ENGINES WITH A/C

Power steering pump installation on all 1980–81 models except Versailles

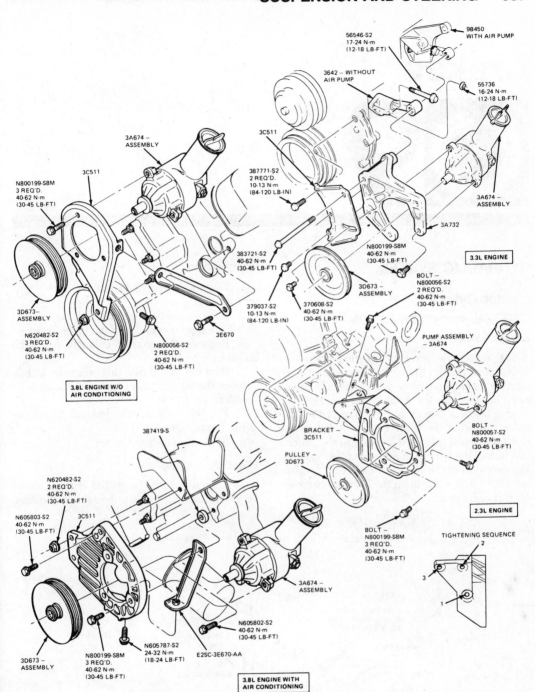

56546-S2
17-24 N·m
(12-18 LB-FT)

9B450
WITH AIR PUMP

3642 — WITHOUT
AIR PUMP

55736
16-24 N·m
(12-18 LB-FT)

3A674 —
ASSEMBLY

3C511

3C511

387771-S2
2 REQ'D.
10-13 N·m
(84-120 LB-IN)

3A674 —
ASSEMBLY

N800199-S8M
3 REQ'D.
40-62 N·m
(30-45 LB-FT)

3A732

3C511

383721-S2
40-62 N·m
(30-45 LB-FT)

N800199-S8M
40-62 N·m
(30-45 LB-FT)

3.3L ENGINE

BOLT —
N800056-S2
2 REQ'D.
40-62 N·m
(30-45 LB-FT)

3D673 —
ASSEMBLY

3D673 —
ASSEMBLY

379037-S2
10-13 N·m
(84-120 LB-IN)

370608-S2
40-62 N·m
(30-45 LB-FT)

N620482-S2
3 REQ'D.
40-62 N·m
(30-45 LB-FT)

3E670

N800056-S2
2 REQ'D.
40-62 N·m
(30-45 LB-FT)

PUMP ASSEMBLY
— 3A674

**3.8L ENGINE W/O
AIR CONDITIONING**

387419-S

BRACKET —
3C511

PULLEY —
3D673

BOLT —
N800057-S2
40-62 N·m
(30-45 LB-FT)

2.3L ENGINE

N620482-S2
2 REQ'D.
40-62 N·m
(30-45 LB-FT)

N605803-S2
40-62 N·m
(30-45 LB-FT)

3C511

BOLT —
N800199-S8M
3 REQ'D.
40-62 N·m
(30-45 LB-FT)

TIGHTENING SEQUENCE

2

3

1

3A674 —
ASSEMBLY

N605802-S2
40-62 N·m
(30-45 LB-FT)

3D673 —
ASSEMBLY

N800199-S8M
3 REQ'D.
40-62 N·m
(30-45 LB-FT)

N605787-S2
24-32 N·m
(18-24 LB-FT)

E2SC-3E670-AA

**3.8L ENGINE WITH
AIR CONDITIONING**

Power steering pump installation on 1982 Cougar

Brakes

HYDRAULIC SYSTEM

Master Cylinder
REMOVAL AND INSTALLATION
Except 4 Wheel Anti-Lock

A dual or tandem-type master cylinder is used. This system divides the brake hydraulic system into two, independent and hydraulically separated halves, with the front of the cylinder operating the rear brakes and the rear of the cylinder operating the front brakes. A failure in one system will still allow braking in the other. Whenever the hydraulic pressure is unequal in the two systems, a pressure differential valve activates a warning light on the instrument panel to warn the driver.

POWER BRAKES

1. Disconnect the brake lines from the master cylinder.
2. Remove the two nuts and lockwashers that attach the master cylinder to the brake booster.
3. Remove the master cylinder from the booster.
4. Reverse the above procedure to install. Torque the master cylinder attaching nuts to 13–25 ft. lb.
5. Fill the master cylinder and bleed the entire brake system.
6. Refill the master cylinder.

STANDARD BRAKES

1. Disconnect the negative battery cable. Working under the dash, disconnect the mas-

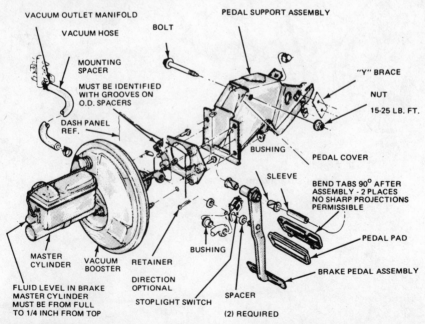

Master cylinder installation on 1972–79 models with power assist, except Versailles

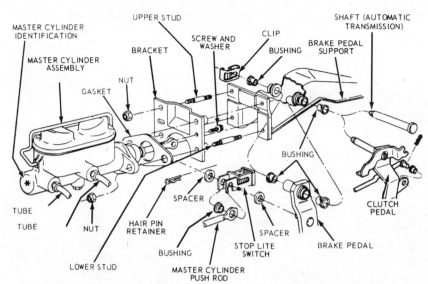

Master cylinder installation—1971 models with non-power brakes

ter cylinder pushrod from the brake pedal. The pushrod cannot be removed from the master cylinder.

2. Disconnect the stoplight switch wires and remove the switch from the brake pedal, using care not to damage the switch.

3. Disconnect the brake lines from the master cylinder.

4. Remove the attaching screws from the firewall and remove the master cylinder from the car.

5. Reinstall in reverse of the above order,

leaving the brake line fittings loose at the master cylinder. Torque the master cylinder nuts to 13–25 ft. lb.

6. Fill the master cylinder and, with brake lines loose, slowly bleed the air from the master cylinder using the foot pedal.

OVERHAUL

Except 4 Wheel Anti-Lock

1. Remove the cylinder from the car and drain the brake fluid.

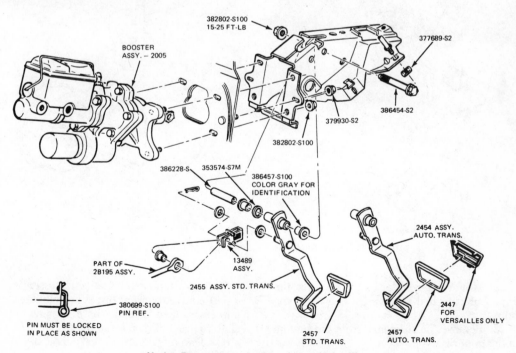

Hydro-Boost power brake system, Versailles

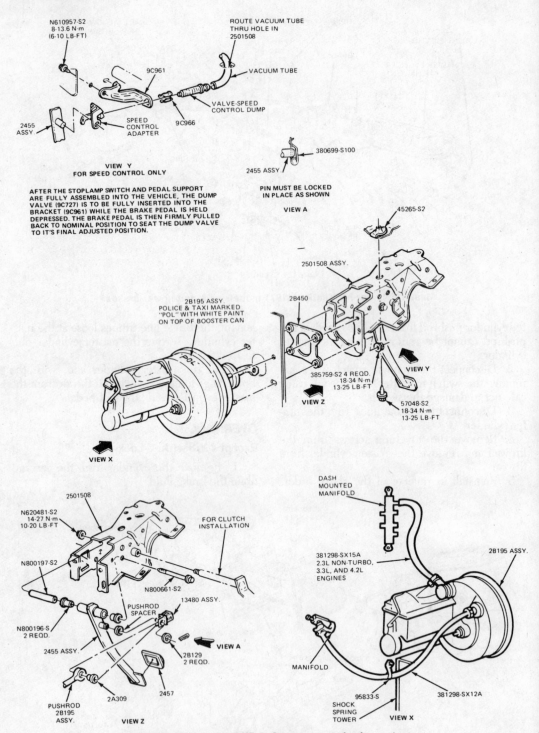

N610957-S2
8-13.6 N·m
(6-10 LB-FT)

ROUTE VACUUM TUBE
THRU HOLE IN
2501508

9C961

VACUUM TUBE

VALVE-SPEED
CONTROL DUMP

2455
ASSY.

SPEED
CONTROL
ADAPTER

9C966

380699-S100

2455 ASSY.

VIEW Y
FOR SPEED CONTROL ONLY

AFTER THE STOPLAMP SWITCH AND PEDAL SUPPORT
ARE FULLY ASSEMBLED INTO THE VEHICLE, THE DUMP
VALVE (9C727) IS TO BE FULLY INSERTED INTO THE
BRACKET (9C961) WHILE THE BRAKE PEDAL IS HELD
DEPRESSED. THE BRAKE PEDAL IS THEN FIRMLY PULLED
BACK TO NOMINAL POSITION TO SEAT THE DUMP VALVE
TO IT'S FINAL ADJUSTED POSITION.

PIN MUST BE LOCKED
IN PLACE AS SHOWN

VIEW A

45265-S2

2501508 ASSY.

2B450

2B195 ASSY.
POLICE & TAXI MARKED
"POL" WITH WHITE PAINT
ON TOP OF BOOSTER CAN

VIEW Y

385759-S2 4 REQD.
18-34 N·m
13-25 LB-FT

VIEW Z

57048-S2
18-34 N·m
13-25 LB-FT

VIEW X

2501508

N620481-S2
14-27 N·m
10-20 LB-FT

FOR CLUTCH
INSTALLATION

N800197-S2

N800661-S2

13480 ASSY.

PUSHROD
SPACER

N800196-S
2 REQD.

2455 ASSY.

VIEW A

2B129
2 REQD.

PUSHROD
2B195
ASSY.

2A309

2457

VIEW Z

DASH
MOUNTED
MANIFOLD

381298-SX15A
2.3L NON-TURBO,
3.3L, AND 4.2L
ENGINES

2B195 ASSY.

MANIFOLD

95833-S

SHOCK
SPRING
TOWER

VIEW X

381298-SX12A

1980–82 Thunderbird, XR-7, Cougar power brake system

2. Mount the cylinder in a vise so that the outlets are up then remove the seal from the hub.

3. Remove the stopscrew from the bottom of the front reservoir.

4. Remove the snap-ring from the front of

the bore and remove the rear piston assembly.

5. Remove the front piston assembly using compressed air. Cover the bore opening with a cloth to prevent damage to the piston.

6. Clean metal parts in brake fluid and discard the rubber parts.

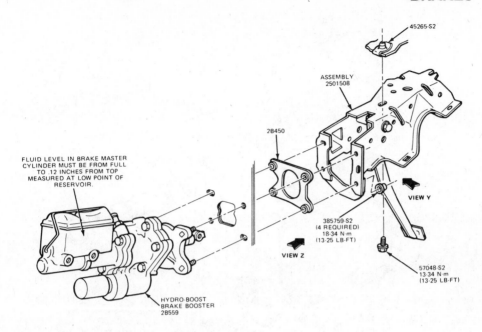

FLUID LEVEL IN BRAKE MASTER CYLINDER MUST BE FROM FULL TO .12 INCHES FROM TOP MEASURED AT LOW POINT OF RESERVOIR.

HYDRO-BOOST BRAKE BOOSTER 2B559

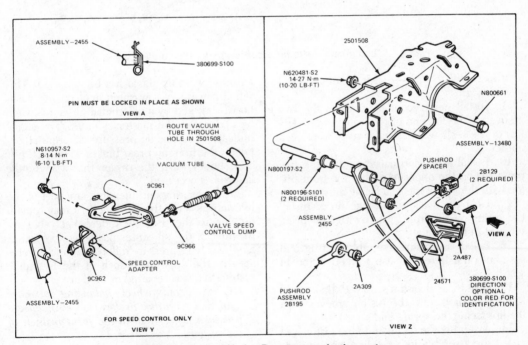

1982 Continental Hydro-Boost power brake system

7. Inspect the bore for damage or wear, and check the pistons for damage and proper clearance in the bore.

CAUTION: *Late models are equipped with aluminum master cylinders. DO NOT HONE. If the bore is pitted or scored deeply, the master cylinder assembly must be replaced.*

8. If the bore is only slightly scored or pitted it may be honed. Always use hones that are in good condition and completely clean the cylinder with brake fluid when the honing is completed. If any evidence of contamination exists in the master cylinder, the entire hydraulic system should be flushed and refilled with clean brake fluid. Blow out the passages with compressed air.

NOTE: *Rebuilding Kit may contain secondary and primary piston assemblies instead*

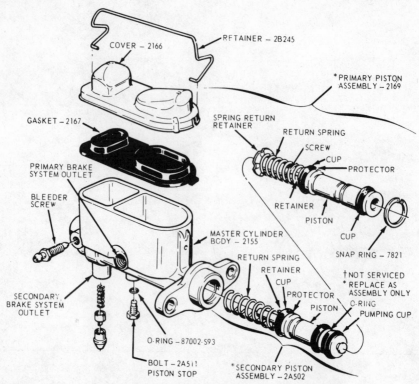

COVER — 2166

RETAINER — 2B245

*PRIMARY PISTON
ASSEMBLY — 2169

GASKET — 2167

SPRING RETURN
RETAINER

RETURN SPRING

SCREW

CUP

PROTECTOR

PRIMARY BRAKE
SYSTEM OUTLET

RETAINER

PISTON

CUP

BLEEDER
SCREW

SNAP RING — 7821

MASTER CYLINDER
BODY — 2155

RETURN SPRING

RETAINER

CUP

†NOT SERVICED
*REPLACE AS
ASSEMBLY ONLY

PROTECTOR

O-RING

SECONDARY
BRAKE SYSTEM
OUTLET

PISTON

PUMPING CUP

O-RING — 87002-S93

BOLT — 2A511
PISTON STOP

*SECONDARY PISTON
ASSEMBLY — 2A502

Dual master cylinder disassembled—disc brakes

*of just rubber seals—seal installation is not
required.*

9. Install new secondary seals in the two
grooves in the flat end of the front piston. The
lips of the seals will be facing away from each
nother.

10. Install a new primary seal and the seal
protector on the opposite end of the front piston with the lips of the seal facing outward.

11. Coat the seals with brake fluid. Install
the spring on the front piston with the spring
retainer in the primary seal.

12. Insert the piston assembly, spring end
first, into the bore and use a wooden rod to
seat it.

13. Coat the rear piston seals with brake fluid
and install them into the piston grooves with
the lips facing the spring end.

14. Assemble the spring onto the piston and
install the assembly into the bore spring first.
Install the snap-ring.

15. Hold the piston train at the bottom of
the bore and install the stopscrew. Install a new
seal on the hub. Bench-bleed the cylinder or
install and bleed the cylinder on the car.

Pressure Differential Warning Valve

Since the introduction of dual master cylinders
to the hydraulic brake system, a pressure differential warning signal has been added. This
signal consists of a warning light on the dash-
board activated by a differential pressure switch
located below the master cylinder. The signal
indicates a hydraulic pressure differential between the front and rear brakes of 80–150 psi,
and should warn the driver that a hydraulic
failure has occurred.

After repairing and bleeding any part of the
hydraulic system the warning light may remain
on due to the pressure differential valve remaining in the off-center position. To centralize the valve a pressure difference must be created in the opposite branch of the hydraulic
system that was repaired or bled last.

NOTE: *Front wheel balancing of cars
equipped with disc brakes may also cause a
pressure differential in the front branch of
the system.*

VALVE CENTERING PROCEDURE

To centralize the valve:

1. Turn the ignition to either the "acc" or
"on" position.

2. Check the fluid level in the master cylinder reservoirs. Fill to within ¼ in. of the top
if necessary.

3. Depress the brake pedal firmly. The valve
will centralize itself causing the brake warning
light to go out.

4. Turn the ignition off.

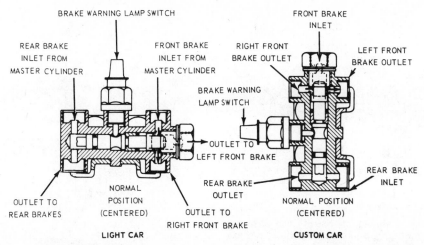

Pressure differential valve and brake light warning switch on models with front drum brakes

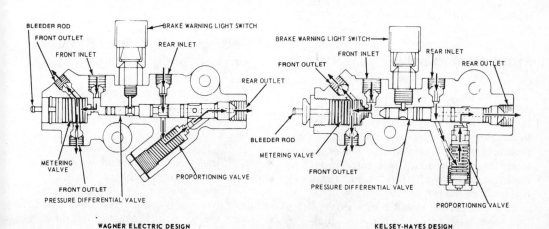

Control valve assembly on front disc brake models through 1979

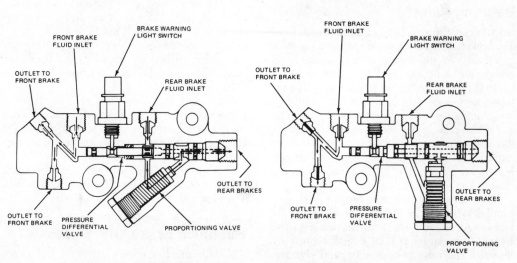

Control valve assembly on models with 4-wheel disc brakes

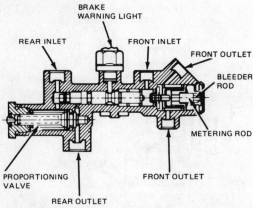

1980–82 3-way aluminum control valve assembly (contains metering, pressure differential and proportioning valves)

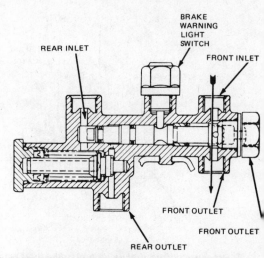

1980–82 2-way aluminum control valve assembly (contains pressure differential and proportioning valves)

5. Prior to driving the vehicle, check the operation of the brakes and obtain a firm pedal.

Proportioning Valve

On vehicles equipped with front disc and rear drum brakes, a proportioning valve is an important part of the system. It is installed in the hydraulic line to the rear brakes. Its function is to maintain the correct proportion between line pressures to the front and rear brakes. *No attempt at adjustment of this valve should be made, as adjustment is preset and tampering will result in uneven braking action.*

To assure correct installation when replacing the valve, the outlet to the rear brakes is stamped with the letter "R."

Metering Valve

On vehicles through 1980 equipped with front disc brakes, a metering valve is used. This valve is installed in the hydraulic line to the front brakes, and functions to delay pressure build-up to the front brakes on application. Its purpose is to reduce front brake pressure until rear brake pressure builds up adequately to overcome the rear brake shoe return springs. In this way disc brake pad life is extended because it prevents the front disc brakes from carrying all or most of the braking load at low operating line pressures.

The metering valve can be checked very simply. With the car stopped, gently apply the brakes. At about 1 in. of travel, a very small change in pedal effort (like a small bump) will be felt if the valve is operating properly. Metering valves are not serviceable and must be replaced if defective.

Bleeding the Hydraulic System

NOTE: *See 4 Wheel Anti-Lock section if vehicle is equipped with system.*

NOTE: *Since the front and rear hydraulic systems are independent, if it is known that only one system has air in it, only that system has to be bled.*

1. Fill the master cylinder with brake fluid.

2. Install a 3/8 in. box-end wrench to the bleeder screw on the right rear wheel.

3. Push a piece of small-diameter rubber tubing over the bleeder screw until it is flush against the wrench. Submerge the other end of the rubber tubing in a glass jar partially filled with clean brake fluid. Make sure the rubber tube fits on the bleeder screw snugly.

4. Have a friend apply pressure to the brake pedal. Open the bleeder screw and observe the bottle of brake fluid. If bubbles appear in the glass jar; there is air in the system. When your friend has pushed the pedal to the floor, immediately close the bleeder screw before he releases the pedal.

5. Repeat this procedure until no bubbles appear in the jar. Refill the master cylinder right front and left front wheels, in that order. Periodically refill the master cylinder so it does not run dry.

6. Center the pressure differential warning valve as outlined in the "Pressure Differential Warning Valve" section.

Hydraulic Brake Line Check

The hydraulic brake lines and brake linings are to be inspected at the recommended intervals in the maintenance schedule. Follow the steel tubing from the master cylinder to the flexible hose fitting at each wheel. If a section of the tubing is found to be damaged, replace the entire section with tubing of the same type (steel, not copper), size, shape, and length. When installing a new section of brake tubing, flush clean brake fluid or denatured alcohol through to remove any dirt or foreign material from the line. Be sure to flare both ends to provide sound, leak-proof connections. When bending the tubing to fit the underbody contours, be careful not to kink or crack the line. Torque all hydraulic connections to 10–15 lbs.

Check the flexible brake hoses that connect the steel tubing to each wheel cylinder. Replace the hose if it shows any signs of softening, cracking, or other damage. When installing a new front brake hose, position the hose to avoid contact with other chassis parts. Place a new copper gasket over the hose fitting and thread the hose assembly into the front wheel cylinder. A new rear brake hose must be positioned clear of the exhaust pipe or shock absorber. Thread the hose into the rear brake tube connector. When installing either a new front or rear brake hose, engage the opposite end of the hose to the bracket on the frame. Install the horseshoe-type retaining clip and connect the tube to the hose with the tube fitting nut.

Always bleed the system after hose or line replacement. Before bleeding, make sure that the master cylinder is topped up with high-temperature, extra-heavy-duty fluid of at least SAE 70R3 quality.

Power Assist

VACUUM BOOSTER REMOVAL AND INSTALLATION

1. Working inside the car below the instrument panel, disconnect the booster valve operating rod from the brake pedal assembly.

2. Open the hood and disconnect the wires from the stop light switch at the brake master cylinder.

3. Disconnect the brake line at the master cylinder outlet fitting.

4. Disconnect the manifold vacuum hose from the booster unit.

5. Remove the four bracket-to-dash panel attaching bolts.

6. Remove the booster and bracket assembly from the dash panel, sliding the valve operating rod out from the engine side of the dash panel.

7. Mount the booster and bracket assembly to the dash panel by sliding the valve operating rod in through the hole in the dash panel, and installing the attaching bolts.

8. Connect the manifold vacuum hose to the booster.

9. Connect the brake line to the master cylinder outlet fitting.

10. Connect the stop light switch wires.

11. Working inside the car below the instrument panel, install the rubber boot on the valve operating rod at the passenger side of the dash panel.

12. Connect the valve operating rod to the brake pedal with the bushings, eccentric shoulder bolt, and nut.

HYDRO-BOOST HYDRAULIC BOOSTER REMOVAL AND INSTALLATION

A hydraulically powered brake booster was used on these models. The power steering pump provides the fluid pressure to operate both the brake booster and the power steering gear.

The hydro-boost assembly contains a valve which controls pump pressure while braking, a lever to control the position of the valve and a boost piston to provide the force to operate a conventional master cylinder attached to the front of the booster. The hydro-boost also has a reserve system, designed to store sufficient pressurized fluid to provide at least 2 brake applications in the event of insufficient fluid flow from the power steering pump. The brakes can also be applied unassisted if the reserve system is depleted.

Before removing the hydro-boost, discharge the accumulator by making several brake applications until a hard pedal is felt.

1. Working from inside the vehicle, below the instrument panel, disconnect the pushrod from the brake pedal. Disconnect the stoplight switch wires at the connector. Remove the hairpin retainer. Slide the stoplight switch off the brake pedal far enough for the switch outer hole to clear the pin. Remove the switch from the pin. Slide the pushrod, nylon washers and bushing off the brake pedal pin.

2. Open the hood and remove the nuts attaching the master cylinder to the hydro-boost. Remove the master cylinder. Secure it to one side without disturbing the hydraulic lines.

3. Disconnect the pressure, steering gear and return lines from the booster. Plug the lines to prevent the entry of dirt.

4. Remove the nuts attaching the hydroboost. Remove the booster from the firewall, sliding the pushrod link out of the engine side of the firewall.

5. Install the hydro-boost on the firewall and install the attaching nuts.

6. Install the master cylinder on the booster.

7. Connect the pressure, steering gear and return lines to the booster.

8. Working below the instrument panel,

install the nylon washer, booster pushrod and bushing on the brake pedal pin. Install the switch so that it straddles the pushrod with the switch slot on the pedal pin and the switch outer hole just clearing the pin. Slide the switch completely onto the pin and install the nylon washer. Attach these parts with the hairpin retainer. Connect the stoplight switch wires and install the wires in the retaining clip.

9. Remove the coil wire so that the engine will not start. Fill the power steering pump and engage the starter. Apply the brakes with a pumping action. Do not turn the steering wheel until air has been bled from the booster.

10. Check the fluid level and add as required. Start the engine and apply the brakes, checking for leaks. Cycle the steering wheel.

11. If a whine type noise is heard, suspect fluid aeration.

4 WHEEL ANTI-LOCK BRAKE SYSTEM

The 4 Wheel Anti-Lock brake system is a compact integral power brake system that uses brake fluid for both brake function and hydraulic boost. Individual front wheel brake circuits and a combined rear wheel brake circuit are used. Major components of the system are:

MASTER CYLINDER AND HYDRAULIC BOOSTER

The master cylinder and brake booster are mounted in the conventional manner. The booster control valve is located in a parallel bore above the master cylinder centerline and is operated by a lever mechanism connected to the brake pedal pushrod.

ELECTRIC PUMP AND ACCUMULATOR

A high pressure electric pump runs for short periods at frequent intervals to charge the hydraulic accumulator. The accumulator is a gas filled pressure chamber that is part of the pump and motor assembly. The pump, motor and accumulator are mounted to the master cylinder/booster assembly.

VALVE BODY ASSEMBLY

The valve body contains three pairs of solenoid valves, one pair for each front wheel and the third pair for both the rear wheels combined. The paired solenoid valves are inlet/outlet valves with the inlet valve normally open and the outlet valve normally closed. The valve body is bolted to the inboard side of the master cylinder/booster assembly.

RESERVOIR AND FLUID LEVEL WARNING SWITCHES

A translucent plastic reservoir having two main chambers is connected to the pump assembly and master cylinder by two low pressure hoses. Integral fluid level switches are part of the reservoir cap assembly. The reservoir is mounted to the hydraulic unit with a screw and bracket and a push-in tube outlet that seats in a grommet mounted in the brake booster housing.

WHEEL SENSORS

Four variable relutance electronic sensor assemblies are used, each is provided with a 104 tooth ring. Each sensor is connected to an electronic controller through a wiring harness. The front sensors are bolted to front spindle mounted brackets. The front toothed sensor rings are pressed into the inside of the front disc rotors. The rear sensors are bolted to the rear brake axle adapters. The toothed rear sensor rings are pressed on the axle shafts, inboard of the axle shaft flange.

ELECTRONIC CONTROLLER

The electronic controller is a non-repairable unit consisting of two microprocessors and the necessary circuitry for operation. The controller monitors system operation during normal driving as well as during anti-lock (panic) braking. Under wheel locking conditions signals are triggered from the controller that open and close solenoid valves resulting in moderate pulsations in the brake pedal and equal anti-locking control to all four wheels.

System Operation

The hydraulic pmp maintains between 2030 to 2610 psi pressure in the accumulator which is connected by a high pressure hose to the booster chamber and control valve. When the brakes are applied, a scissor-lever mechanism activates the control valve and pressure, proportional to brake pedal travel, enters the booster chamber. The pressure is transmitted through the normally open solenoid valve through the proportioning valve to the rear brakes. The same pressure moves the booster piston against the master cylinder piston, shutting off the central valves in the master cylinder. This applies pressure to the front wheels through the two normally open solenoid valves. The electronic controller monitors the electromechanical components of the system. Malfunction of the anti-lock system will cause the electronic controller to shut off or inhibit the anti-lock system. Normal power assisted braking remains if the anti-lock system shuts off. Malfunctions are

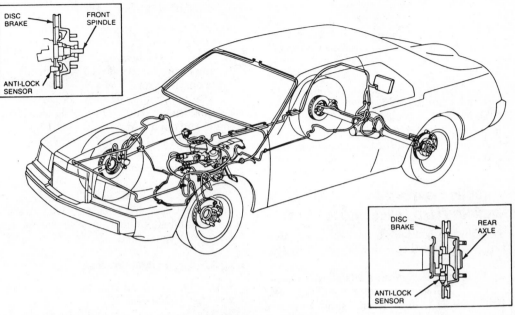

Anti-skid brake system

indicated by one or two warning lamps inside the vehicle.

The four wheel anti-lock system is selfmonitoring. When the ignition switch is placed in the Run position, the electronic controller will perform a preliminary selfcheck on the anti-lock electrical system as indicated by a three to four second illumination of the amber "Check Anti-Lock Brakes" lamp in the overhead console.

During vehicle operation, including normal and anti-lock braking operation is continually monitored. Should a problem occur, either the "Check Anti-Lock Brakes" or the "Brake" warning lamp(s) will be illuminated. Inspection of the system and any necessary repairs should be done before any further vehicle operation.

Brake System Bleeding

NOTE: *The 4 Wheel Anti-Lock brake system is under high accumulator hydraulic pressure most of the time.*
CAUTION: *Before servicing any component which contains high pressure, it is mandatory that the high pressure in the system be discharged.*

SYSTEM DISCHARGING (DEPRESSURIZING)

Turn the ignition to the Off position. Pump the brake pedal a minimum of twenty times until an increase in pedal force is clearly felt.

FRONT BRAKE BLEEDING

The front brakes can be bled in the conventional manner, with or without the accumulator being charged. Refer to the previous brake bleeding section at the beginning of this Chapter for instructions.

REAR BRAKE BLEEDING

A fully charged accumulator is required for successful rear brake system bleeding. Once accumulator pressure is applied to the system,

Anti-skid hydraulic cylinder/booster unit

the rear brakes can be bled by opening the rear caliper bleeder screw while holding the brake pedal in the applied position with the ignition switch in the Run position. Repeat the procedure until an air free flow of brake fluid comes from the bleeder screw. Close the bleeder screw. Add fluid to the master cylinder reservoir until required level is reached.

CAUTION: *Care must be used when opening the bleeder screws. The fluid is under high pressure and could cause injury if splashed into eyes etc.*

Hydraulic Reservoir

CHECKING FLUID LEVEL AND REFILLING

1. With the ignition switch On, pump the brake pedal until the hydraulic pump motor starts.

2. Wait until the pump shuts off and check the brake fluid level in the reservoir. If the level is below the MAX fill line, add fluid until the line is reached.

NOTE: *Do not overfill, the level maybe over the MAX line depending upon the accumulator charge. Perform above procedure before adding or removing brake fluid.*

Component Removal and Installation

HYDRAULIC CYLINER/BOOSTER UNIT ASSEMBLY

CAUTION: *Depressurize the system before working on the system.*

1. Disconnect the negative battery cable.

2. Disconnect the electrical connectors from the fluid reservoir cap, main valve, solenoid valve body, pressure warning switch, hydraulic pump motor and the ground connector from the master cylinder. Label for reinstallation identification.

3. Disconnect the brake lines from the solenoid valve body and plug them to prevent fluid loss.

4. Disconnect the booster pushrod from the brake pedal by first disconnecting the stoplight switch wires at the connecter on the brake pedal. Then, remove the hairpin connector at the stoplight switch and slide the switch off the pedal pin until the large end of the switch (outer hole) is off of the pin. Remove the switch using a twisting motion. Remove the unit's four retaining nuts at the firewall.

5. Remove the booster from the engine compartment.

6. Install in the reverse order. Bleed the brake system.

HYDRAULIC ACCUMULATOR

CAUTION: *Depressurize the system before working on the system.*

1. Disconnect the negative battery cable. Disconnect the electrical connecter at the hydraulic pump motor.

2. Use a 8mm hex wrench, loosen and unscrew the accumulator. Do not allow any dirt to enter the open port.

3. Loosen and remove the accumulator mounting block, if necessary.

4. Install in the reverse order using new O-ring seals.

5. Turn the ignition switch to the On position. Check that the "Check Anti-Lock Brakes" lamp goes out after a maximum of one minute. Fill the reservoir as necessary.

HYDRAULIC PUMP MOTOR

CAUTION: *Depressurize the system before working on the system.*

1. Disconnect the negative battery cable.

2. Disconnect the electrical connections at the hydraulic pump motor and pressure warning switch.

3. Use an 8mm hex wrench and remove the accumulator, make sure no dirt falls into the open port.

4. Remove the suction line between the reservoir and the pump at the reservoir by twisting the hose and pulling. Plug the hose to prevent fluid loss. Install a plugged piece of large vacuum hose on the reservoir nipple to prevent fluid loss.

5. Remove the banjo bolt (hollow hex headed bolt) connecting the high pressure hose to the booster housing, at the housing. Be sure to catch and save the sealing O-rings, one on each side of the banjo bolt head.

6. Remove the allen headed bolt attaching the pump and motor assembly to the extension housing which is located directly under the accumulator. A long extension and universal swivel socket will help reach the bolt.

7. Move the pump assembly toward the engine and remove the retainer pin on the inboard side of the extension housing. Remove the pump and motor assembly.

8. Installation is in the reverse order of removal. Tighten the allen head bolt to 5–7 ft. lbs. Tighten the banjo bolt to 12–15 ft. lbs. after installing new O-rings (if necessary). Install a new O-ring on the accumulator and tighten to 30–40 ft. lbs.

9. Turn the ignition switch to On. Check that the "Check Anti-Lock Brakes" lamp goes out after a maximum of one minute. Check the brake fluid level in the reservoir, add fluid if necessary.

RESERVOIR ASSEMBLY

CAUTION: *Depressurize the system before working on the system.*

1. Disconnect the negative battery cable.
2. Remove the electrical connectors from the reservoir cap. Unlock and remove the cap.
3. Empty the reservoir of as much fluid as possible using a large rubber syringe or suction gun.
4. Remove the line between the pump and reservoir, from the reservoir by twisting and pulling the hose from the reservoir fitting.
5. Remove the return line between the reservoir and master cylinder at the reservoir in the same manner as Step 4.
6. Remove the allen head reservoir mounting screw.
7. Pry the reservoir from the booster housing carefully. Be sure the short sleeve and O-ring are removed from the booster housing.
8. Install the reservoir mounting bracket in its guide on the bottom of the reservoir. Check to be sure that the short sleeve and O-ring are in position at the bottom of the reservoir. Wet the mounting grommet with brake fluid.
9. Insert the reservoir into the grommet as far as it will go on the booster housing, make sure the short sleeve and O-ring are in place. The reservoir should be held vertical to the booster during installation.
10. The rest of the installation is in the reverse order of removal.
11. Fill the reservoir to the correct level with a charged accumulator.

ELECTRONIC CONTROLLER

The controller is located in the luggage compartment in front of the forward trim panel.

1. Disconnect the 35 pin connector from the controller.
2. Remove the three retaining screws holding the controller to the seat back brace and remove the controller.
3. Install in the reverse order.

PRESSURE SWITCH

CAUTION: *Depressurize the system before working on the system.*

1. Disconnect the negative battery cable.
2. Disconnect the valve body seven pin connector. Failure to disconnect the connector can result in damage to the connector if struck by removal tool.
3. Remove the pressure switch with special socket T85P20215B or equivalent.
4. Inspect the mounting O-ring, replace if necessary. Install the switch in the reverse order of removal. Tighten to 15–25 ft. lbs.

FRONT WHEEL SENSOR

1. Disconnect the harness connector on the inside of the engine compartment for either the right or left sensor.
2. Raise and support the front side of the vehicle to be worked on. Remove wheel, caliper and disc rotor assemblies.
3. Disengage the wire grommet at the shock tower and draw the sensor cable carefully through the grommet mounting hole. Remove the harness from the mounting brackets.
4. Loosen the 5mm set screw that hold the sensor to the mounting bracket. Remove the sensor through the hole in the disc brake splash shield.
5. Clean the sensor face, if reusing the original sensor. Install in the reverse order of removal. Install a new paper spacer on the sensor mounting flange before installation.

REAR WHEEL SENSOR

1. Disconnect the sensor connector for the side requiring service. The connector is located on the inside of the luggage compartment behind the forward trim panel.
2. Lift the carpet and push the sensor wire mounting grommet through the mounting hole.
3. Raise and support the rear of the vehicle. Remove the wire harness from the retaining brackets and C-clip. Pull rearward on the clip to disengage.
4. Remove the wheel, caliper and rotor assemblies.
5. Remove the sensor mounting bolt. Slip the grommet out of the splash shield and pull the sensor wire through the hole.
6. Install in the reverse order. If the original sensor is to be used clean the sensor face. Install a new paper spacer on the sensor mounting flange before installation.

SENSOR RING-FRONT WHEEL

NOTE: *Toothed sensor ring replacement requires the use of an arbor press, an automotive machine shop or well equipped garage should be able to handle the job.*

1. Remove the rotor assembly.
2. Position the rotor face up on the arbor press bed.
3. Using the proper adapters, press each stud down until they contact the sensor ring.
4. Position an approximate adapter on the top of all five studs and press the studs and sensor ring from the rotor.
5. Install the studs into the rotor using the press. Install the sensor ring with the press until the ring bottoms in position.
6. Install the rotor in the reverse order of removal.

SENSOR RING-REAR WHEEL

1. Remove the rear axle shaft. Install the necessary adapter between the axle shaft flange and sensor ring.

2. Position the axle in an arbor press and remove the sensor ring.

3. Press the sensor ring into position until a gap of 47mm (1.8 inch) between the sensor ring and face of the axle flange is obtained.

4. Reinstall the axle shaft and removed components.

DRUM BRAKES

1971 was the last year that drum brakes were standard equipment on the front of the Ford mid-size cars. Starting in 1972, sliding caliper disc brakes are standard equipment on the front, with drum brakes on the rear. Front discs were an option in 1971.

Duo-Servo Self-Adjusting Drum Brakes

Drum brakes on all Ford Mid-Size cars employ single-anchor, internal-expanding, and self-adjusting brake assemblies. The automatic adjuster continuously maintains correct operating clearance between the linings and the drums by adjusting the brake in small increments in direct proportion to lining wear. When applying the brakes while backing up, the linings tend to follow the rotating drum counterclock-

wise, thus forcing the upper end of the primary shoe against the anchor pin. Simultaneously, the wheel cylinder pushes the upper end of the secondary shoe and cable guide outward, away from the anchor pin. This movement of the secondary shoe causes the cable to pull the adjusting lever upward and against the end of the tooth on the adjusting screw star wheel. As lining wear increases, the upward travel of the adjusting lever also increases. When the linings have worn sufficiently to allow the lever to move upward far enough, it passes over the end of the tooth and engages it. Upon release of the brakes, the adjusting spring pulls the adjuster level downward, turning the star wheel and expanding the brakes.

INSPECTION

1. Raise the front or rear of the car and support the car with safety stands. Make sure the parking brake is not on.

2. If you are going to check the rear brakes, remove the lug nuts that attach the wheels to the axle shaft and remove the tires and wheels from the car. Using a pair of pliers, remove the tinnerman nuts from the wheel studs. Pull the brake drum off the axle shaft. If the brakes are adjusted too tightly to remove the drum, see Step 4. If you can remove the drum, see Step 5.

3. If you are going to check the front brakes, then the front tire, wheel and brake drum can be removed as an assembly. Remove the hub cap, then either pry the dust cover off the spin-

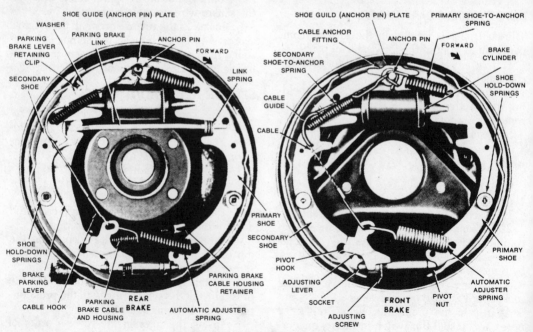

Self-adjusting drum brake assemblies

dle with a screwdriver or pull it off with a pair of channel-lock pliers. Remove the cotter pin from the spindle. Slide the nut lock off the adjusting nut, then loosen the adjusting nut until it reaches the end of the spindle. Do not remove the adjusting nut yet. Grab the tire and pull it out toward yourself, then push it back into position. This will free the outer wheel bearing from the drum hub. If the brakes are adjusted up too tightly to allow the drum to be pulled off them, go to step four and loosen up the brakes, then return here. Remove the adjusting nut, washer and outer bearing from the spindle. Pull the tire, wheel, and brake drum off the spindle.

4. If the brakes are too tight to remove the drum, get under the car (make sure you have safety stands under the car to support it) and remove the rubber plug from the bottom of the brake backing plate. Shine a flashlight into the slot in the plate. You will see the top of the adjusting screw star wheel and the adjusting lever for the automatic brake adjusting mechanism. To back off on the adjusting screw, you must first insert a small, thin screwdriver or a piece of firm wire (coat-hanger wire) into the adjusting slot and push the adjusting lever away from the adjusting screw. Then, insert a brake adjusting spoon into the slot and engage the top of the star wheel. Lift up on the bottom of the adjusting spoon to force the adjusting screw star wheel downward. Repeat this operation until the brake drum is free of the brake shoes and can be pulled off.

5. Clean the brake shoes and the inside of the brake drum. There must be at least 1/16 in. of brake lining above the heads of the brake shoe attaching rivets. The lining should not be cracked or contaminated with grease or brake fluid. If there is grease or brake fluid on the lining it must be replaced and the source of the

leak must be found and corrected. Brake fluid on the lining means leaking wheel cylinders. Grease on the brake lining means a leaking grease retainer (front wheels) or axle seal (rear brakes). If the lining is slightly glazed but otherwise in good condition, it can be cleaned up with medium sandpaper. Lift up the bottom of the wheel cylinder boots and inspect the ends of the wheel cylinders. A small amount of fluid in the end of the cylinders should be considered normal. If fluid runs out of the cylinder when the boots are lifted, however, the wheel cylinder must be rebuilt or replaced. Examine the inside of the brake drum; it should have a smooth, dull finish. If excessive brake shoe wear caused grooves to wear in the drum it must be machined or replaced. If the inside of the drum is slightly glazed, but otherwise good, it can be cleaned up with medium sandpaper.

6. If no repairs are required, install the drum and wheel. If the brake adjustment was changed to remove the drum, adjust the brakes until the drum will just fit over the brakes. After the wheel is installed it will be necessary to complete the adjustment. See "Brake Adjustment" later in this chapter. If a front wheel was removed, tighten the wheel bearing adjusting nut to 17–25 ft. lbs. while rotating the wheel. This will seat the bearing. Loosen the adjusting nut 1/2 turn, then retighten it to 10–15 ft. lbs.

Brake Shoe
REMOVAL

NOTE: *If you are not thoroughly familiar with the procedures involved in brake replacement, only disassemble and assemble one side at a time, leaving the other wheel intact as a reference.*

1. Remove the brake drum. See the inspection procedure.

2. Place the hollow end of a brake spring service tool (available at auto parts stores) on the brake shoe anchor pin and twist it to disengage one of the brake retracting springs. Repeat this oepration to remove the other spring.

CAUTION: *Be careful that the springs do not slip off the tool during removal, as they could cause personal injury.*

3. Reach behind the brake backing plate and place a finger on the end of one of the brake hold-down spring mounting pins. Using a pair of pliers, grasp the washer on the top of the hold-down spring that corresponds to the pin that you are holding. Push down on the pliers and turn them 90° to align the slot in the washer with the head on the spring mounting pin. Remove the spring and washer and repeat this operation on the hold-down spring on the other brake shoe.

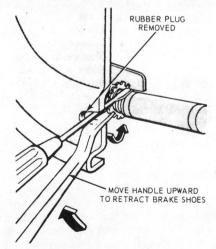

RUBBER PLUG REMOVED

MOVE HANDLE UPWARD TO RETRACT BRAKE SHOES

Backing off brake adjusting starwheel

4. Place the tip of a screwdriver on the top of the brake adjusting screw and move the screwdriver upward to lift up on the brake adjusting lever. When there is enough slack in the automatic adjuster cable, disconnect the loop on the top of the cable from the anchor. Grasp the top of each brake shoe and move it outward to disengage it from the wheel cylinder (and parking brake link on rear wheels). When the brake shoes are clear, lift them from the backing plate. Twist the shoes slightly and the automatic adjuster assembly will disassemble itself.

5. If you are working on rear brakes, grasp the end of the brake cable spring with a pair of pliers and, using the brake lever as a fulcrum, pull the end of the spring away from the lever. Disengage the cable from the brake lever.

INSTALLATION

1. If you are working on the rear brakes, the brake cable must be connected to the secondary brake shoe before the shoe is installed on the backing plate. To do this, first transfer the parking brake lever from the old secondary shoe to the new one. This is accomplished by spreading the bottom of the horseshoe clip and disengaging the lever. Position the lever on the new secondary shoe and install the spring washer and the horseshoe clip. Close the bottom of the clip after installing it. Grasp the metal tip of the parking brake cable with a pair of pliers. Position a pair of side cutter pliers on the end of the cable coil spring and, using the plier as a fulcrum, pull the coil spring back with the side cutters. Position the cable in the parking brake lever.

2. Apply a *light* coating of high-temperature grease to the brake shoe contact points on the backing plate. Position the primary brake shoe on the front of the backing plate and install the hold-down spring and washer over the mounting pin. Install the secondary shoe on the rear of the backing plate.

3. If working on the rear brakes, install the parking brake link between the notch in the primary brake shoe and the notch in the parking brake lever.

4. Install the automatic adjuster cable loop end on the anchor pin. Make sure the crimped side of the loop faces the backing plate.

5. Install the return spring in the primary brake shoe and, using the tapered end of the brake spring service tool, slide the top of the spring onto the anchor pin.

CAUTION: *Be careful to make sure that the spring does not slip off the tool during installation, as it could cause injury.*

6. Install the automatic adjuster cable guide in the secondary brake shoe, making sure the flared hole in the cable guide is inside the hole in the brake shoe. Fit the cable into the groove in the top of the cable guide.

7. Install the secondary shoe return spring through the hole in the cable guide and the brake shoe. Using the brake spring tool, slide the top of the spring onto the anchor pin.

8. Clean the threads on the adjusting screw and apply a light coating of high-temperature grease to the threads. Screw the adjuster closed, then open it one-half turn.

9. Install the adjusting screw between the brake shoes with the star wheel nearest to the secondary shoe. Make sure the star wheel is in a position that is accessible from the adjusting slot in the backing plate.

10. Install the short hooked end of the automatic adjuster spring in the proper hole in the primary brake shoe.

11. Connect the hooked end of the automatic adjuster cable and the free end of the automatic adjuster spring in the slot in the top of the automatic adjuster lever.

12. Pull the automatic adjuster lever (the lever will pull the cable and spring with it) downward and to the left and engage the pivot hook of the lever in the hole in the secondary brake shoe.

13. Check the entire brake assembly to make sure that everything is installed properly. Make sure that the shoes engage the wheel cylinder properly and are flush on the anchor pin. Make sure that the automatic adjuster cable is flush on the anchor pin and in the slot on the back of the cable guide. Make sure that the adjusting lever rests on the adjusting screw star wheel. Pull upward on the adjusting cable until the adjusting lever is free of the star wheel, then release the cable. The adjusting lever should snap back into place on the adjusting screw star wheel and turn the wheel one tooth.

14. Expand the brake adjusting screw until the brake drum will just fit over the brake shoes.

15. Install the wheel and drum and adjust the brakes. See "Brake Adjustment."

DRUM BRAKE ADJUSTMENT

1. Raise the car and support it with safety stands.

2. Remove the rubber plug from the adjusting slot on the backing plate (if so equipped).

3. Insert a brake adjusting spoon into the slot and engage the lowest possible tooth on the star wheel. Move the end of the brake spoon downward to move the star wheel upward and expand the adjusting screw. Repeat this operation until the brakes lock the wheel.

4. Insert a small screwdriver or piece of firm wire (coat-hanger wire) into the adjusting slot

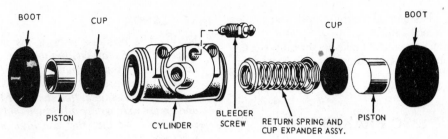

Wheel cylinder disassembled

and push the automatic adjuster lever out and free of the star wheel on the adjusting screw.

5. Holding the adjusting lever out of the way, engage the topmost tooth possible on the star wheel with a brake adjusting spoon. Move the end of the adjusting spoon upward to move the adjusting screw star wheel downward and contract the adjusting screw. Back off the adjusting screw star wheel until the wheel spins freely with a minimum of drag. Keep track of the number of turns the star wheel is backed off.

6. Repeat this operation for the other side. When backing off the brakes on the other side, the adjusting lever must be backed off the same number of turns to prevent side-to-side brake pull.

7. Repeat this operation on the other set of brakes (front or rear).

8. When all four brakes are adjusted, make several stops, while backing the car, to equalize all of the wheels.

9. Road-test the car.

Wheel Cylinders

OVERHAUL

Since the travel of the pistons in the wheel cylinder changes when new brake shoes are installed, it is possible for previously good wheel cylinders to start leaking after new brakes are installed. Therefore, to save yourself the expense of having to replace new brakes that become saturated with brake fluid and the aggravation of having to take everything apart again, it is strongly recommended that wheel cylinders be rebuilt every time new brake shoes are installed. This is especially true on high-mileage cars.

1. Remove the brakes.

2. Place a bucket or old newspapers under the brake backing plate to catch the brake fluid that will run out of the wheel cylinder.

3. Remove the boots from the ends of the wheel cylinders.

4. Push one piston toward the center of the cylinder to force the opposite piston and cup out the other end of the cylinder. Reach in the open end of the cylinder and push the spring, cup, and piston out of the cylinder.

5. Remove the bleeder screw from the rear of the cylinder, on the back of the backing plate.

6. Inspect the inside of the wheel cylinder. If it is scored in any way, the cylinder must be honed with a wheel cylinder hone or fine emery paper, and finished with crocus cloth if emery paper is used. If the inside of the cylinder is excessively worn, the cylinder will have to be replaced, as only 0.003 in. of material can be removed from the cylinder walls. When honing or cleaning the wheel cylinders, keep a small amount of brake fluid in the cylinder to serve as a lubricant.

7. Clean any foreign matter from the pistons. The sides of the pistons must be smooth for the wheel cylinders to operate properly.

8. Clean the cylinder bore with alcohol and a lint-free rag. Pull the rag through the bore several times to remove all foreign matter and dry the cylinder.

9. Install the bleeder screw and the return spring in the cylinder.

10. Coat new cylinder cups with new brake fluid and install them in the cylinder. Make sure that they are square in the bore or they will leak.

11. Install the pistons in the cylinder after coating them with new brake fluid.

12. Coat the insides of the boots with new brake fluid and install them on the cylinder. Install the brakes.

REPLACEMENT

1. Remove the brake shoes.

2. On rear brakes, loosen the brake line on the rear of the cylinder but do not pull the line away from the cylinder or it may bend.

3. On front brakes, disconnect the metal brake line from the rubber brake hose where they join in the wheel well. Pull off the horseshoe clip that attaches the rubber brake hose to the underbody of the car. Loosen the hose at the cylinder, then turn the whole brake hose to remove it from the wheel cylinder.

4. Remove the bolts and lockwashers that attach the wheel cylinder to the backing plate and remove the cylinder.

5. Position the new wheel cylinder on the

backing plate and install the cylinder attaching bolts and lockwashers.

6. Attach the metal brake line or rubber hose by reversing the procedure given in Steps 2 or 3.

7. Install the brakes.

FRONT DISC BRAKES

INSPECTION

1. Raise the vehicle until the wheel and tire clear the floor. Place safety stands under the vehicle.

2. Remove the wheel cover. Remove the wheel and tire from the hub and disc.

3. Visually inspect the shoe and lining assemblies. If the lining material has worn to a thickness of 0.030 in. or less, or if the lining is contaminated with brake fluid, replace all pad assemblies on both front wheels. Make all thickness measurements across the thinnest section of the pad assembly. A slight taper on a used lining should be considered normal.

4. To check disc run-out, tighten the wheel bearing adjusting nut to eliminate end-play. Check to make sure the disc can still be rotated.

5. Hand-spin the disc and visually check for run-out. If the disc appears to be out of round or if it wobbles, it needs to be machined or replaced. When the run-out check is finished, loosen the wheel bearing adjusting nut and re-tighten to specifications, in order to prevent bearing damage.

6. Visually check the disc for scoring. Minor scores can be removed with a fine emery cloth. If it is excessively scored, it must be machined or replaced.

7. The caliper should be visually checked. If excess leakage is evident, the caliper should be replaced.

8. Install the wheel and hub assembly.

Hub and Disc

REMOVAL

1. Raise and safely support the vehicle. Remove the wheel.

2. Remove the caliper. Slide the caliper assembly away from the disc and suspend it with a wire loop. It is not necessary to disconnect the brake line.

3. Remove the grease cap from the hub. Remove the cotter pin, nut lock, adjusting nut, and flat washer from the spindle.

4. Remove the outer wheel bearing cone and roller assmbly from the hub.

5. Remove the hub and disc assembly from the spindle.

INSTALLATION

NOTE: *If a new disc is being installed, remove the protective coating with carburetor degreaser. If the original disc is being installed, make sure that the grease in the hub is clean and adequate, that the inner bearing and grease retainer are lubricated and in good condition, and that the disc breaking surfaces are clean.*

1. Install the hub and disc assembly on the spindle.

2. Lubricate the outer bearing and install the thrust washer and adjusting nut.

3. Adjust the wheel bearing as outlined in the "Wheel Bearing Adjustment" section.

4. Install the nut lock, cotter pin, and grease cap.

5. Install the caliper assembly.

6. Install the wheel and tire assembly and torque the nuts to 75–110 ft. lbs.

7. Lower the vehicle and road-test it.

Kelsey-Hayes Single-Piston, Floating-Caliper Disc Brakes— 1971 Models

PAD REPLACEMENT

1. Raise and safely support the vehicle. Remove the front wheel.

2. Remove the lockwires from the two mounting bolts and lift the caliper away from the disc.

3. Remove the retaining clips with a screwdriver and slide the outboard pad and retaining pins out of the caliper. Remove the inboard pad.

4. Slide the new inboard pad into the caliper so that the tabs are between the retaining clips and anchor plate and the backing plate lies flush against the piston.

5. Insert the outboard pad retaining pins into the outboard pad and position them in the caliper.

NOTE: *Stabilizer, insulators, pad clips, and pins should always be replaced when the disc pads are replaced.*

6. Hold the retaining pins in place (one at a time) with a short drift pin or dowel and install the retaining clips.

7. Slide the caliper assembly over the disc and align the mounting bolt holes.

8. Install the lower bolt finger-tight. Install the upper bolt and torque to specification. Torque the lower bolt to specification. Safety-wire both bolts. Upper bolt torque: 45–60 ft. lbs. Lower bolt torque: 45–60 ft. lbs.

CAUTION: *Do not deviate from this procedure. The alignment of the anchor plate depends on the proper sequence of bolt installation.*

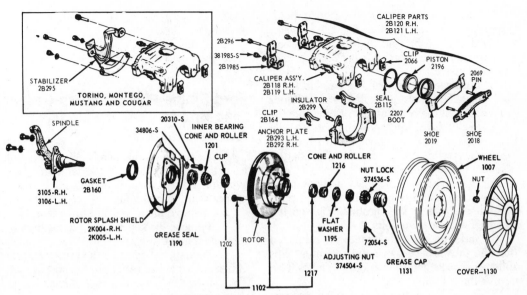

1971 floating caliper front disc brake

9. Check the brake fluid level and pump the brake pedal to seat the linings against the disc. Replace the wheels and road-test the car.

CALIPER ASSEMBLY SERVICE

1. Raise and safely support the vehicle. Remove the front wheels.

2. Disconnect and plug the brake line.

3. Remove the lockwires from the two caliper mounting bolts and remove the bolt. Lift the caliper off the disc.

4. Remove and discard the locating pin insulators. Replace all rubber parts at reassembly.

5. Remove the retaining clips with a screwdriver and slide the outboard pad and retaining pins out of the caliper. Remove the inboard pad. Loosen the bleed screw and drain the brake fluid.

6. Remove the two small bolts and caliper stabilizers.

7. Remove the inboard pad retaining clips and bolts.

8. Clean and inspect all parts, and reinstall on the anchor plate. Do not tighten the stabilizer bolts at this time.

9. Remove the piston by applying compressed air to the fluid inlet hole. Use care to prevent the piston from popping out of control.

CAUTION: *Do not attempt to catch the piston with the hand. Use folded towels to cushion it.*

10. Remove the piston boot. Inspect the piston for scoring, pitting, or corrosion. The piston must be replaced if there is any visible damage or wear.

11. Remove the piston seal from the cylinder bore. *Do not use any metal tools for this operation.*

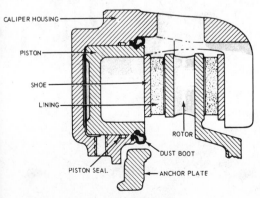

Floating caliper—sectional view

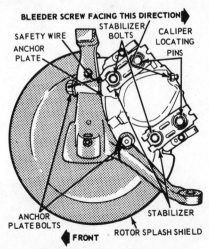

Floating caliper installed—inboard view

12. Clean the caliper with fresh brake fluid. Inspect the cylinder bore for damage or wear. Light defects can be removed by rotating crocus cloth around the bore. (Do not use any other type of abrasive.)

13. Lubricate all new rubber parts in brake fluid. Install the piston seal in the cylinder groove. Install the boot into its piston groove.

14. Install the piston, open end out, into the bore while working the boot around the outside of the piston. Make sure that the boot lip is seated in the piston groove.

15. Slide the anchor plate assembly onto the caliper housing and reinstall the locating pins. Tighten the pins to specification. Tighten the stabilizer anchor plate bolts.

16. Slide the inboard pad into the caliper so that the tabs are between the retaining clips and anchor plate and the backing plate lies flush against the piston.

17. Insert the outboard pad retaining pins into the outboard pad and position them in the caliper.

18. Hold the retaining pins in place (one at a time) with a short drift pin or dowel and install the retaining clips.

19. Slide the caliper assembly over the disc and align the mounting bolt holes.

20. Install the lower bolt finger-tight. Install the upper bolt and torque to specification. Torque the lower bolt to specification. Safety-wire both bolts.

CAUTION: *Do not deviate from this procedure. The alignment of the anchor plate depends on the proper sequence of bolt installation.*

21. Connect the brake line and bleed the brakes (see "Brake Bleeding").

22. Install the front wheels, recheck the brake fluid level, and road-test the car.

Ford Single-Piston Sliding-Caliper Disc Brakes 1972–79 Models

PAD REPLACEMENT

1. Remove approximately ⅔ of the fluid from the rear reservoir of the tandem master cylinder. Raise and support the vehicle, taking proper safety precautions.

2. Remove the wheel and tire assembly.

3. Remove the key retaining screw from the caliper retaining key.

4. Slide the retaining key and support spring either inward or outward from the anchor plate. To remove the key and spring, a hammer and drift may be used, taking care not to damage the key in the process.

5. Lift the caliper assembly away from the anchor plate by pushing the caliper downward against the anchor plate and rotating the upper end upward out of the anchor plate. Be careful not to stretch or twist the flexible brake hose.

6. Remove the inner shoe and lining assembly from the anchor plate. The inner shoe antirattle clip may become displaced at this time and should be repositioned on the anchor plate. Lightly tap on the outer shoe and lining assembly to free it from the caliper.

7. Clean the caliper, anchor plate, and disc assemblies, and inspect them for brake fluid leakage, excessive wear or signs of damage.

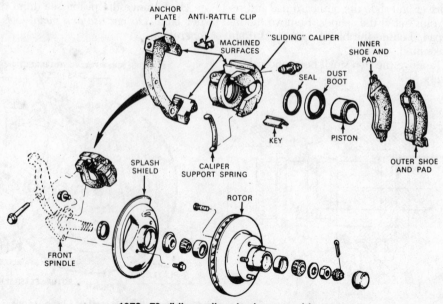

1972–79 sliding caliper brake assembly

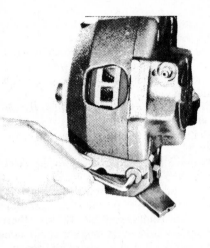

1

1. Front caliper removal

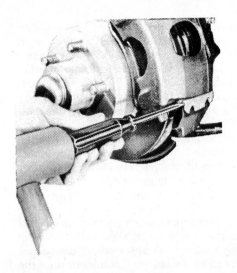

2

2. Remove the caliper retaining screw. Drive the caliper screw and support spring inward or outward.

3

3. Remove the key and caliper support spring.

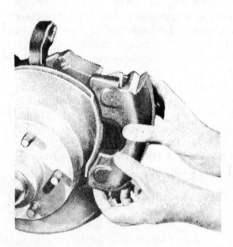

4

4. Push the caliper downward and work the upper end off the disc.

Replace the pads if either of them are worn to within 1/32 in. of the rivet heads.

8. To install new pads, use a 4 in. C-clamp and a block of wood 1¾ in. × 1 in. and approximately ¾ in. thick to seat the caliper hydraulic piston in its bore. This must be done in order to provide clearance for the caliper to fit over the rotor when new linings are installed.

9. At this point, the antirattle clip should be in its place on the lower inner brake shoe support of the anchor plate with the pigtail of the clip toward the inside of the anchor plate. Position the inner brake shoe and lining assembly on the anchor plate with the pad toward the disc.

10. Install the outer brake shoe with the lower flange ends against the caliper leg abutments and the brake shoe upper flanges over

the shoulders on the caliper legs. The shoe is installed correctly when its flanges fit snugly against the machined surfaces of the shoulders.

11. Remove the C-clamp used to seat the caliper piston in its bore. The piston will remain seated.

12. Position the caliper housing lower V-groove on the anchor place lower abutment surface.

13. Pivot the caliper housing upward toward the disc until the outer edge of the piston dust boot is about ¼ in. from the upper edge of the inboard pad.

14. In order to prevent pinching of the dust boot between the piston and the inboard pad

during installation of the caliper, place a clean piece of thin cardboard between the inboard pad and the lower half of the piston dust boot.

15. Rotate the caliper housing toward the disc until a slight resistance is felt. At this point, pull the cardboard downward toward the disc centerline while rotating the caliper over the disc. Then remove the cardboard and complete the rotation of the caliper down over the disc.

16. Slide the caliper up against the upper abutment surfaces of the anchor plate and center the caliper over the lower anchor plate abutment.

17. Position the caliper support spring and key in the key slot and slide them into the opening between the lower end of the caliper and the lower anchor plate abutment until the key semicircular slot is centered over the retaining screw threaded hole in the anchor plate.

18. Install the key retaining screw and torque to 12–16 ft. lbs.

19. Check the fluid level in the master cylinder and fill as necessary. Install the reservoir cover. Depress the brake pedal several times to properly seat the caliper and pads. Check for leakage around the caliper and flexible brake hose.

20. Install the wheel and tire assembly and torque the nuts to 70–115 ft. lbs. Install the wheel cover.

21. Lower the car. Make sure that you obtain a firm brake pedal and then road-test the car for proper brake operation.

CALIPER ASSEMBLY SERVICE

1. Raise the vehicle and place jackstands underneath.

2. Remove the wheel and tire assembly.

3. Disconnect the flexible brake hose from the caliper. To disconnect the hose, loosen the tube fitting which connects the end of the hose to the brake tube at its bracket on the frame. Remove the horseshoe clip from the hose and bracket, disengage the hose, and plug the end. Then unscrew the entire hose assembly from the caliper.

4. Remove the key retaining screw from the caliper retaining key.

5. Slide the retaining key and support spring either inward or outward from the anchor plate. To remove the key and spring, a hammer and drift may be used, taking care not to damage the key in the process.

6. Lift the caliper assembly away from the anchor plate by pushing the caliper downward against the anchor plate and rotating the upper end upward out of the anchor plate.

7. Remove the piston by applying compressed air to the fluid inlet port with a rubber-

tipped nozzle. Place a towel or thick cloth over the piston before applying air pressure to prevent damage to the piston. If the piston is seized in the bore and cannot be forced from the caliper, lightly tap around the outisde of the caliper while applying air pressure.

CAUTION: *Do not attempt to catch the piston with your hand.*

8. Remove the dust boot from the caliper assembly.

9. Remove the piston seal from the cylinder and discard it.

10. Clean all metal parts with isopropyl alcohol or a suitable non-petroleum solvent and dry them with compressed air. Be sure there is no foreign material in the bore or component parts. Inspect the piston and bore for excessive wear or damage. Replace the piston if it is pitted, scored, or if the chrome plating is wearing off.

11. Lubricate all new rubber parts in brake fluid. Install the piston seal in the cylinder groove, being careful not to twist it. Install the dust boot by setting the flange squarely in the outer groove of the bore.

12. Coat the piston with brake fluid and install it in the bore. Work the dust boot around the outside of the piston, making sure that the boot lip is seated in the piston groove.

13. Install the caliper as outlined in Steps 12–18 in the sliding caliper "Shoe and Lining Replacement" procedure.

14. Thread the flexible brake hose and gasket onto the caliper fitting. Torque the fitting to 12–20 ft. lbs. Place the upper end of the flexible brake hose in its bracket and install the horsehoe clip. Remove the plug from the brake tube and connect the tube to the hose. Torque the tube fitting nut to 10–15 ft. lbs.

15. Bleed the brake system as outlined in the "Brake Bleeding" section.

16. Check the fluid level in the master cylinder and fill as necessary. Install the reservoir cover. Depress the brake pedal several times to properly seat the caliper and shoes. Check for leakage around the caliper and the flexible brake hose.

17. Install the wheel and tire assembly and torque the nuts to 70–115 ft. lbs. Install the wheel cover.

18. Lower the car. Make sure that you obtain a firm brake pedal and then roadtest the car for proper brake operation.

Ford Single Piston Sliding Caliper Disc Brakes

PAD REPLACEMENT

1. Remove the master cylinder cap, and check the fluid level in the primary (large) res-

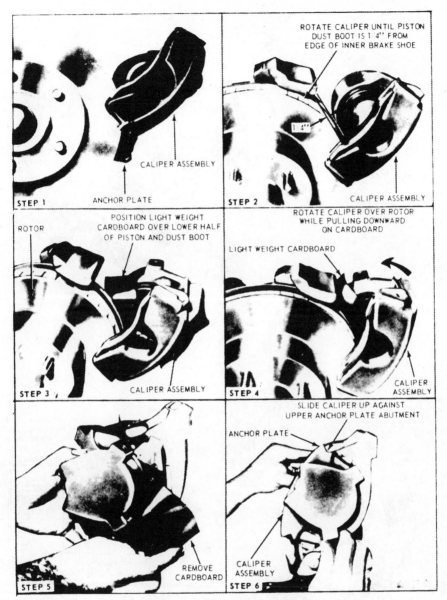

STEP 1 — CALIPER ASSEMBLY / ANCHOR PLATE

STEP 2 — ROTATE CALIPER UNTIL PISTON DUST BOOT IS 1 4'' FROM EDGE OF INNER BRAKE SHOE / 1 4'' / CALIPER ASSEMBLY

STEP 3 — ROTOR / POSITION LIGHT WEIGHT CARDBOARD OVER LOWER HALF OF PISTON AND DUST BOOT / CALIPER ASSEMBLY

STEP 4 — ROTATE CALIPER OVER ROTOR WHILE PULLING DOWNWARD ON CARDBOARD / LIGHT WEIGHT CARDBOARD / CALIPER ASSEMBLY

STEP 5 — REMOVE CARDBOARD

STEP 6 — SLIDE CALIPER UP AGAINST UPPER ANCHOR PLATE ABUTMENT / ANCHOR PLATE / CALIPER ASSEMBLY

Installing the caliper assembly on 1972–79 models

ervoir. Remove brake fluid until the reservoir is half full. Discard this fluid.

2. Raise and safely support the vehicle. Remove the wheel and tire assembly from the hub. Be careful to avoid damage to or interference with the caliper splash shield or bleeder screw fitting.

3. Remove the caliper locating pins.

4. Lift the caliper assembly from the integral spindle/anchor plate and rotor. Remove the outer shoe from the caliper assembly on Continental and Mark VII models slip shoe down the caliper leg until clip is disengaged.

5. Remove the inner shoe and lining assembly. On Continental and Mark VII models, pull shoe straight out of piston. This could re-

quire a force as high as 20–30 lbs. Inspect both rotor braking surfaces. Minor scoring or build-up of lining material does not require machining or replacement of the rotor.

6. Suspend the caliper inside the fender housing with a wire hooked through the outer leg hole of the caliper. Be careful not to damage the caliper or stretch the brake hose.

7. Remove and discard the plastic sleeves that are located inside the caliper locating pin insulators. These parts must not be reused.

8. Remove and discard the caliper locating insulators. These parts must not be reused.

9. Use a 4 inch C-clamp and a block of wood 2¾ inch x 1 inch and approximately ¾ inch thick to seat the caliper hydraulic piston in its

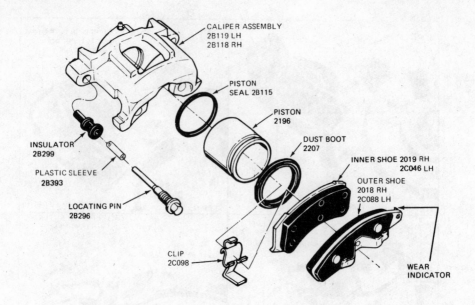

PIN SLIDER CALIPER ASSEMBLY—DISASSEMBLED
RH SIDE SHOWN

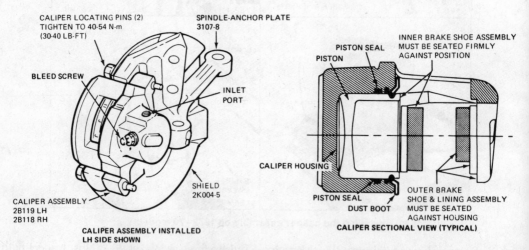

Front disc brake components from 1980—except Continental

bore. This must be done to provide clearance for the caliper assembly to fit over the rotor when installed. Remove the C-clamp from the caliper (the caliper piston will remain seated in its bore).

CAUTION: *On Continental and Mark VII models, the piston is made of phenolic material and must not be seated in bore by applying C-clamp directly to the piston.*

10. Install new locating pin insulators and plastic sleeves in the caliper housing. Do not use sharp-edged tool to insert insulators in the caliper housing. Check to see if both insulator flanges straddle the housing holes and if the plastic sleeves are bottomed in the insulators as well as slipped under the upper lip.

11. Install the correct inner shoe and lining assembly in the caliper piston. All vehicles, except the Continental and Mark VII have a separate anti-rattle clip and insulator that must be installed to the inner shoe and lining prior to their assembly to the caliper. The inner shoes are marked LH or RH and must be installed in the proper caliper. Also, care should be taken not to bend the anti-rattle clips too far in the piston or distortion and rattles can result.

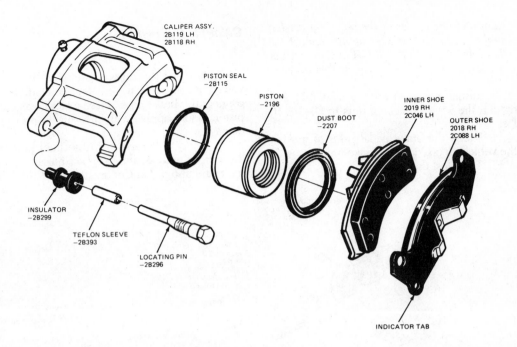

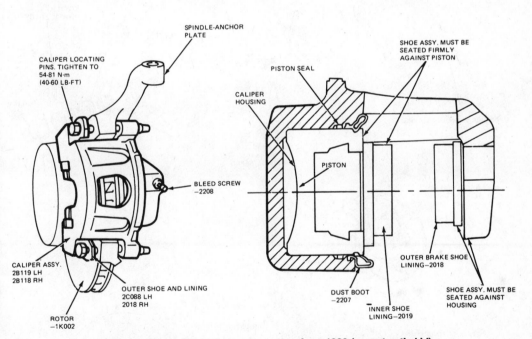

Continental front disc brake components—from 1980 (except anti-skid)

Inner shoe installation on Continental and Mark VII models is accomplished by holding each end of the shoe, making sure it is square with the piston, and pushing the shoe in firmly until the clip snaps in position. Do not allow shoe or clip tangs to cock during installation to avoid bending clip.

12. Install the correct outer brake shoe and lining assembly (RH/LH), making sure that the

clip and/or buttons located on the shoe are properly seated. The outer shoe can be identified as right-hand or left-hand by the wear indicator which must always be installed toward the front of the vehicle or by a LH or RH mark. Refill master cylinder.

WARNING: *Make certain that two round torque buttons on all vehicles, except Continental and Mark VII models, are seated sol-*

*idly in the two holes of the outer caliper leg
and that the shoe is held tightly against the
housing by the spring clip. If buttons are not
seated, a temporary loss of brakes may occur.*

13. Install the wheel and tire assembly, and
tighten the wheel attaching nuts to 80–105 ft.
lbs.

14. Pump the brake pedal prior to moving
the vehicle to position the brake linings.

15. Road test the vehicle.

CALIPER OVERHAUL

1. Remove the caliper assembly from the
vehicle as outlined in Pad Replacement. Disconnect the brake hose. Place a cloth over the
piston before applying air pressure to prevent
damage to the piston.

2. Apply air pressure to the fluid port in
the caliper with a rubber-tipped nozzle to remove the piston. On Continental and Mark VII

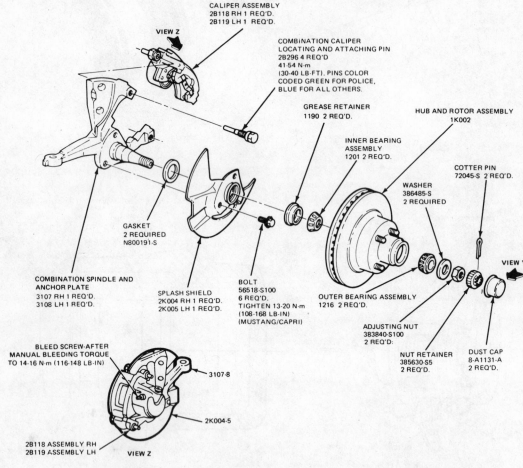

CALIPER ASSEMBLY
2B118 RH 1 REQ'D.
2B119 LH 1 REQ'D.

VIEW Z

COMBINATION CALIPER
LOCATING AND ATTACHING PIN
2B296 4 REQ'D
41-54 N·m
(30-40 LB-FT). PINS COLOR
CODED GREEN FOR POLICE,
BLUE FOR ALL OTHERS.

GREASE RETAINER
1190 2 REQ'D.

HUB AND ROTOR ASSEMBLY
1K002

INNER BEARING
ASSEMBLY
1201 2 REQ'D.

COTTER PIN
72045-S 2 REQ'D.

WASHER
386485-S
2 REQUIRED

VIEW Y

GASKET
2 REQUIRED
N800191-S

COMBINATION SPINDLE AND
ANCHOR PLATE
3107 RH 1 REQ'D.
3108 LH 1 REQ'D.

SPLASH SHIELD
2K004 RH 1 REQ'D.
2K005 LH 1 REQ'D.

BOLT
56518-S100
6 REQ'D.
TIGHTEN 13-20 N·m
(108-168 LB-IN)
(MUSTANG/CAPRI)

OUTER BEARING ASSEMBLY
1216 2 REQ'D.

ADJUSTING NUT
383840-S100
2 REQ'D.

NUT RETAINER
385630-S5
2 REQ'D.

DUST CAP
8-A1131-A
2 REQ'D.

BLEED SCREW-AFTER
MANUAL BLEEDING TORQUE
TO 14-16 N·m (116-148 LB-IN)

3107-8

2K004-5

2B118 ASSEMBLY RH
2B119 ASSEMBLY LH

VIEW Z

BEARING ADJUSTMENT

TIGHTEN ADJUSTING NUT A WHILE ROTATING HUB
AND ROTOR ASSEMBLY TO 24-33 N·m (17-25 LB-FT).
BACK OFF ADJUSTING NUT 1/2 TURN. RETIGHTEN
TO 10-15 LB-IN (FINGERTIGHT). SELECTIVELY
POSITION NUT RETAINER B ON ADJUSTING NUT SO
THAT A SET OF SLOTS ARE IN LINE WITH COTTER
PIN HOLE. ADJUSTING NUT MUST NOT BE ROTATED
IN THIS OPERATION. LOCK ADJUSTING NUT AND
NUT RETAINER WITH COTTER PIN C.

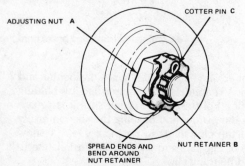

ADJUSTING NUT A

COTTER PIN C

NUT RETAINER B

SPREAD ENDS AND
BEND AROUND
NUT RETAINER

VIEW Y

Caliper, splash shield and rotor from 1980—except Continental

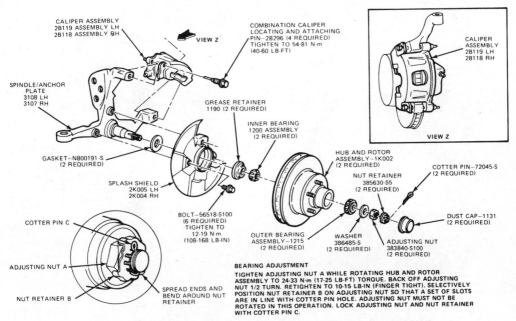

BEARING ADJUSTMENT

TIGHTEN ADJUSTING NUT A WHILE ROTATING HUB AND ROTOR ASSEMBLY TO 24-33 N·m (17-25 LB-FT) TORQUE. BACK OFF ADJUSTING NUT 1/2 TURN. RETIGHTEN TO 10-15 LB-IN (FINGER TIGHT). SELECTIVELY POSITION NUT RETAINER B ON ADJUSTING NUT SO THAT A SET OF SLOTS ARE IN LINE WITH COTTER PIN HOLE. ADJUSTING NUT MUST NOT BE ROTATED IN THIS OPERATION. LOCK ADJUSTING NUT AND NUT RETAINER WITH COTTER PIN C.

Continental caliper, splash shield and rotor from 1980 (except anti-skid)

models, use layers of shop towels to cushion possible impact of the phenolic piston against the caliper iron when piston comes out of the piston bore. Do not use a screwdriver or similar tool to pry piston out of the bore, damage to the phenolic piston may result. If the piston is seized and cannot be forced from the caliper, tap lightly around the piston while applying air pressure. Use care because the piston can develop considerable force from pressure build-up.

3. Remove the udst boot from the caliper assembly.

4. Remove the rubber piston seal from the cylinder, and discard it.

5. Clean all metal parts and phenolic piston with isopropyl alcohol. Then, clean out and dry the grooves and passageways with compressed air. Make sure that caliper bore and component parts are thoroughly clean.

6. Check the cylinder bore and piston for damage or excessive wear. Replace the piston

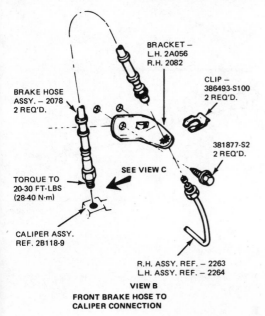

VIEW B
FRONT BRAKE HOSE TO CALIPER CONNECTION

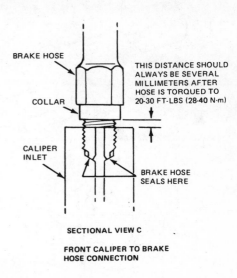

SECTIONAL VIEW C

FRONT CALIPER TO BRAKE HOSE CONNECTION

Hydraulic connections on all except Continental

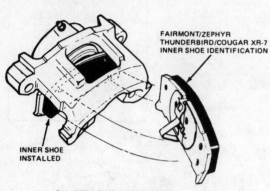

FAIRMONT/ZEPHYR
THUNDERBIRD/COUGAR XR-7
INNER SHOE IDENTIFICATION

INNER SHOE
INSTALLED

R.H. INNER SHOE INSTALLATION

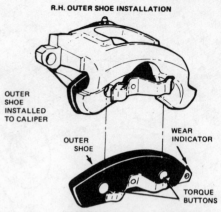

R.H. OUTER SHOE INSTALLATION

OUTER
SHOE
INSTALLED
TO CALIPER

OUTER
SHOE

WEAR
INDICATOR

TORQUE
BUTTONS

WARNING: OUTER SHOE TORQUE BUTTONS
MUST BE SOLIDLY SEATED IN CALIPER
HOLES OR TEMPORARY LOSS OF BRAKES
MAY OCCUR.

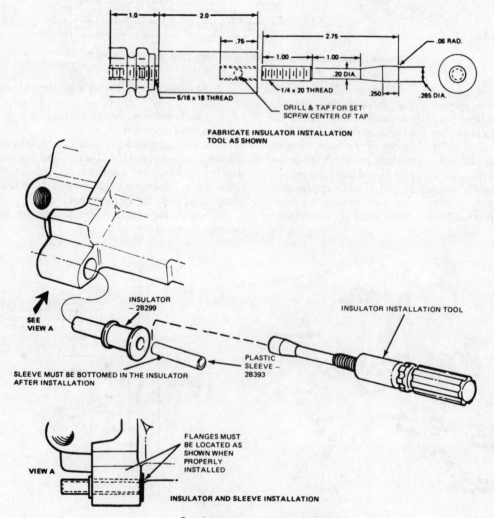

FABRICATE INSULATOR INSTALLATION
TOOL AS SHOWN

Servicing the pin-slider caliper

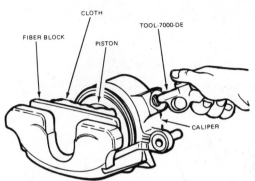

Removing the piston from the caliper with compressed air

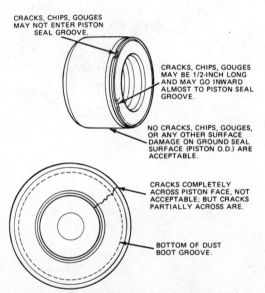

CRACKS, CHIPS, GOUGES MAY NOT ENTER PISTON SEAL GROOVE.

CRACKS, CHIPS, GOUGES MAY BE 1/2-INCH LONG AND MAY GO INWARD ALMOST TO PISTON SEAL GROOVE.

NO CRACKS, CHIPS, GOUGES, OR ANY OTHER SURFACE DAMAGE ON GROUND SEAL SURFACE (PISTON O.D.) ARE ACCEPTABLE.

CRACKS COMPLETELY ACROSS PISTON FACE, NOT ACCEPTABLE; BUT CRACKS PARTIALLY ACROSS ARE.

BOTTOM OF DUST BOOT GROOVE.

Checking piston surface for irregularities

if it is pitted, scored, corroded, or the plating is worn off. Do not replace phenolic piston cosmetic surface irregularities or small chips between the piston boot groove and shoe face.

7. Apply a film of clean brake fluid to the new caliper piston seal, and install it in the cylinder bore. Be sure the seal does not become twisted but is firmly seated in the groove.

8. Install a new dust boot by setting the flange squarely in the outer groove of the caliper bore.

9. Coat the piston with brake fluid, and install the piston in the cylinder bore. Be sure to use a wood block or other flat stock when installing the piston back into the piston bore. Never apply C-clamp directly to a phenolic piston, and be sure pistons are not cocked. Spread the dust boot over the piston as it is installed. Seat the dust boot in the piston groove.

10. Install the caliper over the rotor as outlined.

REAR DISC BRAKES

Caliper
REMOVAL AND INSTALLATION
Versailles

1. Raise the car and install jackstands. Remove the rear wheels.

2. Remove the brake line from the caliper. Disconnect the hose bracket from the axle spring seat and remove the hollow retaining bolt used for connecting the hose fitting to the caliper, if so equipped. Unhook the parking brake cable.

3. Remove the retaining screw from the caliper retaining key.

4. Tap the retaining key and support spring from the caliper, using a hammer and a drift pin of some sort. Don't use excessive force. The key should slide out easily.

5. Rotate the caliper assembly up and away from the anchor plate and the rotor. It may be necessary to scrape away the rust buildup on the rotor edge in order to gain enough clearance to remove the caliper. Remove the caliper. If the caliper still cannot be removed, loosen the caliper end retainer one-half turn, after removing the retaining screw and caliper parking brake lever.

NOTE: *Turning the retainer more than one-half turn could cause internal fluid leaks on the caliper, which would make caliper rebuilding necessary.*

6. If the end retainer was loosened in order to remove the caliper, perform the following:

a. Install the caliper on the anchor plate and secure it with the key, but do not install the pads.

b. Torque the end retainer to 75–95 ft. lb.

c. Install the caliper parking brake lever with the arm pointing rearward and down. Tighten the lever retaining screw to 16–22 ft. lb. Check for free rotation of the lever.

d. Remove the caliper from the anchor plate

7. Make sure that the antirattle clip is correctly positioned in the lower inner brake pad support and that the clip loop is facing the inside of the anchor plate.

8. Place the inner brake pad on the anchor plate. Install the outer brake pad in the caliper.

9. Position the bottom of the caliper against the anchor plate lower abutment surface. Rotate the caliper housing until it is completely over the disc. Be careful not to damage the dust boot.

10. Slide the caliper outward until the inner pad is seated firmly against the disc. Measure

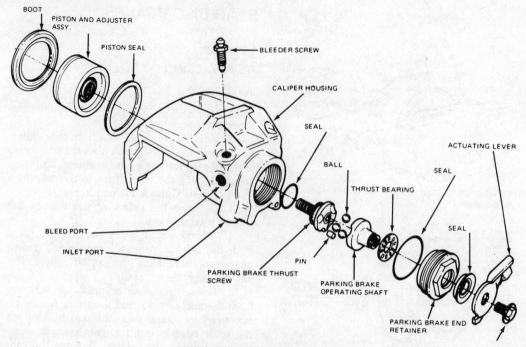

Versailles rear disc brake caliper

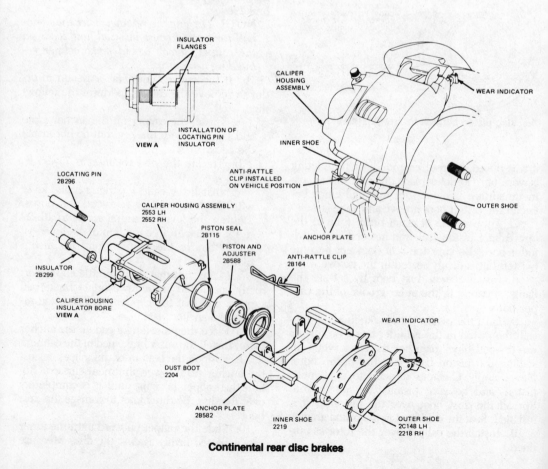

Continental rear disc brakes

the outer pad-to-disc clearance. It should be 1/16 inch or less. If it is more, you will need a special tool (available from your Ford dealer) which is used to adjust the piston outward until the correct clearance is obtained.

11. Using the special tool, adjust the caliper piston outward if this needs to be done.

NOTE: *See the pad replacement section for instructions on how to use the special tool. Because of the parking brake assembly, pad-to-rotor clearance is critical. If piston clearance is more than 1/16 inch, the adjuster may pull out the piston when the brakes are applied, causing adjuster failure.*

12. Center the caliper over the anchor plate and install the retaining spring and key. Install the setscrew and tighten it to 12–16 ft. lb.

13. Attach the parking brake cable. Attach the brake line.

14. Bleed the brake system. Adjust the parking brake cable if necessary. Pump the brake a number of times to bring the pedal back up to normal.

15. Reinstall the wheels and lower the car. Check the brake pedal to make sure it is firm, then road test the car.

Continental and Mark VII

1. Raise the vehicle, and install safety stands. Block both front wheels if a jack is used.

2. Remove the wheel and tire assembly from the axle. Use care to avoid damage or interference with the splash shield.

3. Disconnect the parking brake cable from the lever. Use care to avoid kinking or cutting the cable or return spring.

4. Remove the caliper locating pins.

5. Lift the caliper assembly away from the anchor plate by pushing the caliper upward toward the anchor plate, and then rotate the lower end out of the anchor plate.

6. If insufficient clearance between the caliper and shoe and lining assemblies prevents removal of the caliper, it is necessary to loosen the caliper end retainer 1/2 turn, maximum, to allow the piston to be forced back into its bore. To loosen the end retainer, remove the parking brake lever, then mark or scribe the end retainer and caliper housing to be sure that the end retainer is not loosened more than 1/2 turn. Force the piston back in its bore, and then remove the caliper.

CAUTION: *If the retainer must be loosened more than 1/2 turn, the seal between the thrust screw and the housing may be broken, and brake fluid may leak into the parking brake mechanism chamber. In this case, the end retainer must be removed, and the internal parts cleaned and lubricated; refer to Caliper Overhaul.*

7. Remove the outer shoe and lining assembly from the anchor plate. Mark shoe for identification if it is to be reinstalled.

8. Remove the two rotor retainer nuts and the rotor from the axle shaft.

9. Remove the inner brake shoe and lining assembly from the anchor plate. Mark shoe for identification if it is to be reinstalled.

10. Remove anti-rattle clip from anchor plate.

11. Remove the flexible hose from the caliper by removing the hollow retaining bolt that connects the hose fitting to the caliper.

12. Clean the caliper, anchor plate, and rotor assemblies and inspect for signs of brake fluid leakage, excessive wear, or damage. The caliper must be inspected for leakage both in the piston boot area and at the operating shaft seal area. Lightly sand or wire brush any rust or corrosion from the caliper and anchor plate sliding surfaces as well as the outer and inner brake shoe abutment surfaces. Inspect the brake shoes for wear. If either lining is worn to within 1/8 inch of the shoe surface, both shoe and lining assemblies must be replaced using the shoe and lining removal procedures.

13. If the end retainer has been loosened only 1/2 turn, reinstall the caliper in the anchor plate without shoe and lining assemblies. Tighten the end retainer to 75–96 ft. lb. Install the parking brake lever on its keyed spline. The lever arm must point down and rearward. The parking brake cable will then pass freely under the axle. Tighten the retainer screw to 16–22 ft. lb. The parking brake lever must rotate freely after tightening the retainer screw. Remove the caliper from the anchor plate.

14. If new shoe and lining assemblies are to be installed, the piston must be screwed back into the caliper bore, using Tool T75P-2588-B or equivalent to provide installation clearance. This tool requires a slight modification for use on Continental rear disc brakes. This modification will not prevent using the tool on prior year applications. New tools purchased from the Special Service Tool catalog under the T75P-2588-B number will already be modified. Remove the rotor, and install the caliper, less shoe and lining assemblies, in the anchor plate. While holding the shaft, rotate the tool handle counterclockwise until the tool is seated firmly against the piston. Now, loosen the handle about 1/4 turn. While holding the handle, rotate the tool shaft clockwise until the piston is fully bottomed in its bore; the piston will continue to turn even after it becomes bottomed. When there is no further inward movement of the piston and the tool handle is rotated until there is a firm seating force, the piston is bottomed. Remove the tool and the caliper from the anchor plate.

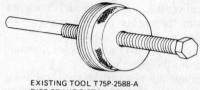

EXISTING TOOL T75P-2588-A
DISC BRAKE PISTON REMOVER
(DOES NOT REQUIRE MODIFICATION)

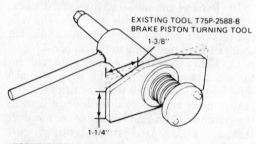

EXISTING TOOL T75P-2588-B
BRAKE PISTON TURNING TOOL
1-3/8"

1-1/4"

MODIFY TOOL BY REMOVING
METAL AS INDICATED BY
DOTTED LINES

Special tools needed for servicing the rear disc brake caliper

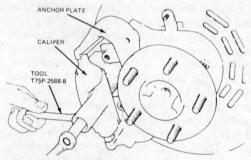

ANCHOR PLATE

CALIPER

TOOL
T75P-2588-B

Adjusting the piston depth

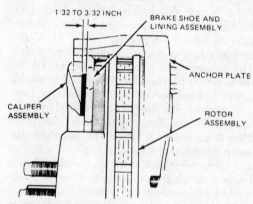

1/32 TO 3/32 INCH

BRAKE SHOE AND
LINING ASSEMBLY

ANCHOR PLATE

CALIPER
ASSEMBLY

ROTOR
ASSEMBLY

Checking lining clearance

15. Lubricate anchor plate sliding ways with lithium or silicone grease. Use only specified grease because a lower temperature type of lubricant may melt and contaminate the brake pads. Use care to prevent any lubricant from getting on the braking surface.

16. Install the anti-rattle clip on the lower rail of the anchor plate.

17. Install inner brake shoe and lining assembly on the anchor plate with the lining toward the rotor.

18. Be sure shoes are installed in their original positions as marked for identification before removal.

19. Install rotor and two retainer nuts.

20. Install the correct hand outer brake shoe and lining assembly on the anchor plate with the lining toward the rotor and wear indicator toward the upper portion of the brake.

21. Install the flexible hose by placing a new washer on each side of the fitting outlet and inserting the attaching bolt through the washers and fitting. Tighten to 20–30 ft. lb.

22. Position the upper tab of the caliper housing on the anchor plate upper abutment surface.

23. Rotate the caliper housing until it is completely over the rotor. Use care so that the piston dust boot is not damaged.

24. Piston Position Adjustment: Pull the caliper outboard until the inner shoe and lining is firmly seated against the rotor, and measure the clearance between the outer shoe and caliper. The clearance must be 1/32 inch to 3/32 inch. If it is not, remove the caliper, then readjust the piston to obtain required gap. Follow the procedure given in Step 13, and rotate the shaft counterclockwise to narrow gap and clockwise to widen gap (1/4 turn of the piston moves it approximately 1/16-inch).

CAUTION: *A clearance greater than 3/32-inch may allow the adjuster to be pulled out of the piston when the service brake is applied. This will cause the parking brake mechanism to fail to adjust. It is then necessary to replace the piston/adjuster assembly following the procedures under Overhaul.*

25. Lubricate locating pins and inside of insulator with silicone grease.

26. Add one drop of Loctite® E0AC-19554-A or equivalent to locating pin threads.

27. Install the locating pins through caliper insulators and into the anchor plate; the pins must be hand inserted and hand started. Tighten to 29–37 ft. lb.

28. Connect the parking brake cable to the lever on the caliper.

29. Bleed the brake system. Replace rubber bleed screw cap after bleeding.

30. Fill the master cylinder as required to within 1/8 inch of the top of the reservoir.

31. Caliper Adjustment: With the engine running, pump the service brake lightly (approximatley 14 lbs. pedal effort) about 40 times. Allow at least one second between pedal applications. As an alternative, with the engine Off, pump the service brake lightly (approximatley 87 lbs. pedal effort) about 30 times. Now check

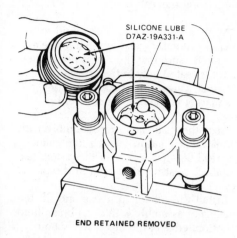

END RETAINED REMOVED

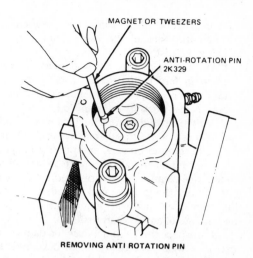

REMOVING ANTI ROTATION PIN

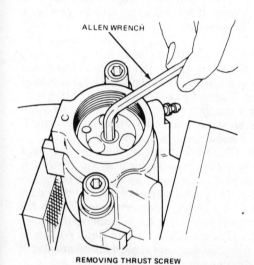

REMOVING THRUST SCREW

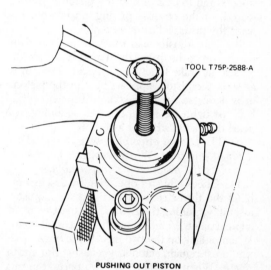

PUSHING OUT PISTON

Servicing the caliper assembly

the parking brake for excessive travel or very light effort. In either case, repeat pumping the service brake, or if necessary, check the parking brake cable for proper tension. The caliper levers must return to the Off position when the parking brake is released.

32. Install the wheel and tire assembly. Tighten the wheel lug nuts. Install the wheel cover. Remove the safety stands, and lower the vehicle.

33. Be sure a firm brake pedal application is obtained, and then road test for proper brake operation, including parking brakes.

OVERHAUL

All Models

1. Remove the caliper assembly from the vehicle as outlined.

2. Remove the caliper and retainer.

3. Lift out the operating shaft, thrust bearing, and balls.

4. Remove the thrust screw anti-rotation pin with a magnet or tweezers.

NOTE: *Some anti-rotation pins may be difficult to remove with a magnet or tweezers. In that case, use the following procedure.*

a. Adjust the piston out from the caliper bore using the modified piston adjusting tool. The piston should protrude from the housing at least one inch.

b. Push the piston back into the caliper housing with the adjusting tool. With the tool in position on the caliper, hold the tool shaft in place, and rotate the handle counterclockwise until the thrust screw clears the anti-rotation pin. Remove the thrust screw and the anti-rotation pin.

5. Remove the thrust screw by rotating it counterclockwise with a ¼ inch allen wrench.

6. Remove the piston adjuster assembly by

installing Tool T75P-2588-A or equivalent through the back of the caliper housing and pushing the piston out.

CAUTION: *Use care not to damage the polished surface in the thrust screw bore, and do not press or attempt to move the adjuster can. It is a press fit in the piston.*

7. Remove and discard the piston seal, boot, thrust screw C-ring seal, end retainer O-ring seal, end retainer lip seal, and pin insulators.

8. Clean all metal parts with isopropyl alcohol. Use clean, dry, compressed air to clean out and dry the grooves and passages. Be sure the caliper bore and component parts are completely free of any foreign material.

9. Inspect the caliper bores for damage or excessive wear. The thrust screw bore must be smooth and free of pits. If the piston is pitted, scored, or the chrome plating is worn off, replace the piston/adjuster assembly.

10. The adjuster can must be bottomed in the piston to be properly seated and provide consistent brake function. If the adjuster can is loose in the piston, appears high in the piston, or is damaged, or if brake adjustment is regularly too tight, too loose, or nonfunctioning, replace the piston/adjuster assembly.

NOTE: *Do not attempt to service the adjuster at any time. When service is necessary, replace the piston/adjuster assembly.*

11. Check adjuster operation by first assembling the thrust screw into the piston/adjuster assembly, pulling the two pieces apart by hand approximately ¼ inch, and then releasing them. When pulling on the two pieces, the brass drive ring must remain stationary, causing the nut to rotate. When releasing the two parts, the nut must remain stationary, and the drive ring must rotate. If the action of the components does not follow this pattern, replace the piston/adjuster assembly.

12. Inspect ball pockets, threads, grooves, and bearing surfaces of the thrust screw and operating shaft for wear, pitting, or brinnelling. Inspect balls and anti-rotation pin for wear, brinnelling, or pitting. Replace operating shaft, balls, thrust screw, and anti-rotation pin if any of these parts are worn or damaged. A polished appearance on the ball paths is acceptable if there is no sign of wear into the surface.

13. Inspect the thrust bearing for corrosion, pitting, or wear. Replace if necessary.

14. Inspect the bearing surface of the end plug for wear or brinnelling. Replace if necessary. A polished appearance on the bearing surface is acceptable if there is no sign of wear into the surface.

15. Inspect the lever for damage. Replace if necessary.

16. Lightly sand or wire brush any rust or corrosion from the caliper housing insulator bores.

17. Apply a coat of clean brake fluid to the new caliper piston seal, and install it in the cylinder bore. Be sure that the seal is not twisted and that it is seated fully in the groove.

18. Install a new dust boot by seating the flange squarely in the outer groove of the caliper bore.

19. Coat the piston/adjuster assembly with clean brake fluid, and install it in the cylinder bore. Spread the dust boot over the piston, like it is installed. Seat the dust boot in the piston groove.

20. Install the caliper in a vise and fill the piston/adjuster assembly with clean brake fluid to the bottom edge of the thrust screw bore.

21. Coat a new thrust screw O-ring seal with clean brake fluid, and install it in the groove in the thrust screw.

22. Install the thrust screw by turning it into the piston/adjuster assembly with a ¼ inch allen wrench until the top surface of the thrust screw is flush with the bottom of the threaded bore. Use care to avoid cutting the O-ring seal. Index the thrust screw, so that the notches on the thrust screw and caliper housing are aligned. Then install the anti-rotation pin.

NOTE: *The thrust screw and operating shaft are not interchangeable from side to side because of the ramp direction in the ball pockets. The pocket surface of the operating shaft and the thrust screw are stamped with the proper letter (R or L), indicating part usage.*

23. Place a ball in each of three pockets of the thrust screw, and apply a liberal amount of silicone grease on all components in the parking brake mechanism.

24. Install the operating shaft on the balls.

25. Coat the thrust bearing with silicone grease and install it on the operating shaft.

26. Install a new lip seal and O-ring on the end retainer.

27. Coat the O-ring seal and lip seal with a light film of silicone grease, and install the end retainer in the caliper. Hold the operating shaft firmly seated against the internal mechanism while installing the end retainer to prevent mislocation of the balls. If the lip seal is pushed out of position, reset the seal. Tighten the end retainer to 75–95 ft. lb.

28. Install the parking brake lever on its keyed spline. The lever arm must point down and rearward. The parking brake cable will then pass freely under the axle. Tighten the lever retaining screw to 16–22 ft. lb. The parking brake lever must rotate freely after tightening.

29. Arrange the caliper in a vise and bottom the piston with modified Tool T75P-2588-B.

30. Install new pin insulators in the caliper

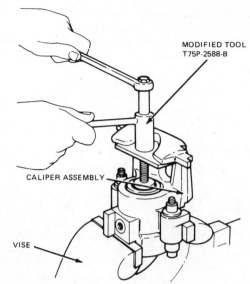

Bottoming the piston in the caliper

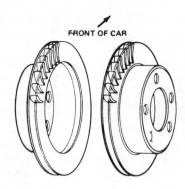

FRONT OF CAR

LEFT REAR ROTOR   RIGHT REAR ROTOR

Versailles rear rotor

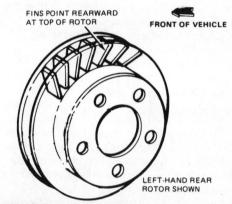

FINS POINT REARWARD
AT TOP OF ROTOR   FRONT OF VEHICLE

LEFT-HAND REAR
ROTOR SHOWN

1982 Continental rear rotor

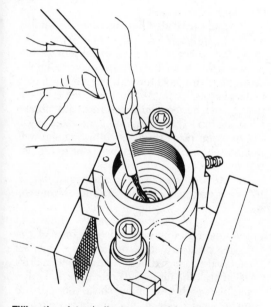

Filling the piston/adjuster assembly with clean fluid

housing. Check to see if both insulator flanges straddle the housing holes.

31. Install the caliper on the vehicle.

Disc Brake Pads

REMOVAL AND INSTALLATION

All Models

1. Remove the caliper as outlined earlier. In this case, however, it is not necessary to disconnect the brake line. Simply wire the caliper to the frame to prevent the brake line from breaking.

2. Remove the pads and inspect them. If they

are worn to within ⅛ inch of the shoe surface, they must be replaced. Do not replace pads on just one side of the car. Uneven braking will result.

3. To install new pads, remove the disc and install the caliper without the pads. Use only the key to retain the caliper.

4. Seat the special tool firmly against the piston by holding the shaft and rotating the tool handle.

5. Loosen the handle one-quarter turn. Hold the handle and rotate the tool shaft clockwise until the caliper piston bottoms in the bore. It will continue to turn after it bottoms.

6. Rotate the handle until the piston is firmly seated.

7. Remove the caliper and install the disc.

8. Place the new inner brake pad on the anchor plate. Place the new outer pad in the caliper.

9. Reinstall the caliper according to the directions given earlier.

Brake Discs

REMOVAL AND INSTALLATION

1. Raise the car and support it. Remove the wheels.

2. Remove the caliper, as outlined earlier.

3. Remove the retaining bolts and remove the disc from the axle.

4. Inspect the disc for excessive rust, scoring or pitting. A certain amount of rust on the edge of the disc is normal. Refer to the specifications chart and measure the thickness of the disc, using a micrometer. If the disc is below specifications, replace it.

5. Reinstall the discs, keeping in mind that the two sides are not interchangeable. The words "left" and "right" are cast into the inner surface of the raised section of the disc. Proper reinstallation of the discs is important, since the cooling vanes cast into the disc must face in the direction of forward rotation on versailles, and opposite forward rotation on 1982 Continental.

6. Reinstall the caliper.

7. Install the wheels and lower the car.

Front Wheel Bearings

ADJUSTMENT

The front wheels each rotate on a set of opposed, tapered roller bearings as shown in the accompanying illustration. The grease retainer at the inside of the hub prevents lubricant from leaking into the brake drum.

Adjustment of the wheel bearings is accomplished as follows: Lift the car so that the wheel and tire are clear of the ground, then remove the grease cap and remove excess grease from the end of the spindle. Remove the cotter pin and nut lock shown in the illustration. Rotate the wheel, hub and drum assembly while tightening the adjusting nut to 17–25 ft. lbs. in order to seat the bearings. Back off the adjusting nut one half turn, then retighten the adjusting nut to 10–15 in. lbs. *(inch-pounds)* on models with disc brakes. 5–7 ft. lbs. on drum brake models. Locate the nut lock on the adjusting nut so that the castellations on the lock are lined up with the cotter pin hole in the spindle. Install a new cotter pin, bending the ends of the cotter pin around the castellated

flange of the nut lock. Check the front wheel for proper rotation, then install the grease cap. If the wheel still does not rotate properly, inspect and clean or replace the wheel bearings and cups.

REMOVAL, REPACKING, AND INSTALLATION

Drum Brakes

The procedure for cleaning, replacing and adjusting front wheel bearings on vehicles equipped with self-adjusting drum brakes is as follows:

1. Taking proper safety precautions, raise the car until the wheel and tire clear the floor. Install jackstands under the lower control arms.

2. Remove the wheel cover. Remove the grease cap from the hub. Then remove the cotter pin, nut lock, adjusting nut, and flat washer from the spindle. Remove the outer bearing cone and roller assembly.

3. Pull the wheel, hub and drum assembly off the spindle. When encountering a brake drum that will not come off, disengage the adjusting lever from the adjusting screw by inserting a narrow tool through the adjusting hole in the carrier plate. While the lever is disengaged, back off the adjusting screw with a brake adjusting tool. The self-adjusting mechanism will not function properly if the adjusting screw is burred, chipped, or otherwise damaged in the process, so exercise extreme care.

4. Remove the grease retainer and the inner bearing cone and roller assembly from the hub.

5. Clean all grease off from the inner and outer bearing cups with solvent. Inspect the cups for pits, scratches, or excessive wear. If the cups are damaged, remove them with a drift.

6. Clean the inner and outer cone and roller assemblies with solvent and shake them dry. If the cone and roller assemblies show excessive wear or damage, replace them with the bearing cups as a unit.

7. Clean the spindle and the inside of the

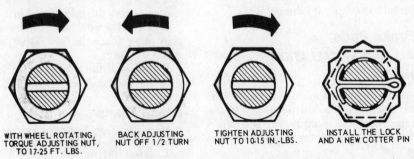

WITH WHEEL ROTATING, TORQUE ADJUSTING NUT, TO 17-25 FT. LBS.

BACK ADJUSTING NUT OFF 1/2 TURN

TIGHTEN ADJUSTING NUT TO 10-15 IN.-LBS.

INSTALL THE LOCK AND A NEW COTTER PIN

Front wheel bearing adjusting sequence

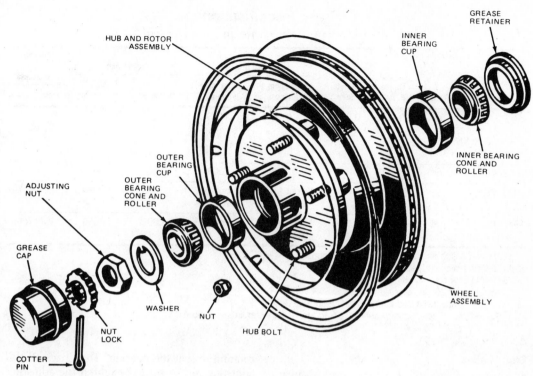

Front hub disassembled

hub with solvent to thoroughly remove all old grease.

8. Covering the spindle with a clean cloth, brush all loose dirt and dust from the brake assembly. Remove the cloth carefully so as to not get dirt on the spindle.

9. If the inner and/or outer bearing cups were removed, install the replacement cups on the hub. Be sure that the cups seat properly in the hub.

10. It is imperative that all old grease be removed from the bearings and surrounding surfaces before repacking. The new lithium-base grease is not compatible with the sodium base grease used in the past.

11. Work as much grease as possible between the rollers and cages in the cone and roller assemblies. Lubricate the cone surfaces with grease.

12. Position the inner bearing cone and roller assembly in the inner cup. Grease retainers require a light film of grease on the lips before installation Make sure that the retainer is properly seated.

13. Install the wheel, hub, and drum assembly on the wheel spindle. To prevent damage to the grease retainer and spindle threads, keep the hub centered on the spindle.

14. Install the outer bearing cone and roller assembly and the flat washer on the spindle. Install the adjusting nut.

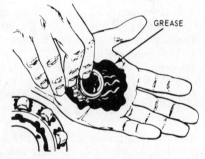

Packing bearings

15. Adjust the wheel bearings by tightening the adjusting nut to 17–25 ft. lbs. with the wheel rotating to seat the bearing. Then back off the adjusting nut ¼ turn. Retighten the adjusting nut to 5–7 ft. lbs. Install the locknut so that the castellations are aligned with the cotter pin hole. Install the cotter pin. Bend the ends of the cotter pin around the castellations of the locknut to prevent interference with the radio static collector in the grease cap. Install the grease cap.

16. Remove the adjusting hole cover from the carrier plate and, from the carrier plate side, turn the adjusting screw star wheel upward with a brake adjusting tool. Expand the brake shoes until a slight drag is felt with the drum rotating. Replace the adjusting hole cover.

17. Install the wheel cover.

Brake Specifications

All measurements given are (in.) unless noted

Year	Model	Lug Nut Torque (ft. lbs.)	Master Cylinder Bore	Brake Disc		Brake Drum		Minimum Lining Thickness	
				Minimum Thickness	Maximum Run-Out	Diameter	Max. Wear Limit	Front	Rear
1971	all	70–155	0.9375 (disc) 1.0 (drum)	.875	.0007	10.0	10.060	2/32	2/32
1972–75	all	70–115	1.00	1.180	.003	10.0 ①	10.060 ②	1/32	2/32
1976–78	all	70–115	1.00	Front 1.100 Rear .895	Front .003 Rear .004	11.030	11.090	1/32	2/32
1979–85	all	70–115	1.00 ③	Front .972 ④ Rear .895	Front .003 Rear .004	11.030 ⑤	11.090	1/8	2/32

① 11.030 on police package cars, and all wagons
② 11.090 on police package cars, and all wagons
③ 1983 and later (exc. Continental) .875
   Continental 1.125
④ Exc. Continental 1983 and later: .810, Continental .972
⑤ 1983 and later: Exc. Continental—9.0 (Wagons 10.0), Wear limit: +.060

Disc Brakes

The procedure for cleaning, repacking, and adjusting front wheel bearings on vehicles equipped with disc brakes is as follows:

1. Taking proper safety precautions, raise the car until the wheel and tire clear the floor.

2. Remove the wheel cover. Remove the wheel and tire from the hub.

3. Remove the calper from the disc and wire it to the underbody to prevent damage to the brake hose. For floating-caliper brakes, follow Steps 3, 4, 5, and 6 under "Caliper Assembly Service."

4. Remove the grease cap from the hub, and the cotter pin, nut lock, adjusting nut, and flat washer from the spindle. Remove the outer bearing cone and roller assembly.

5. Pull the hub and disc assembly off the wheel spindle.

6. Remove and discard the old grease retainer. Remove the inner bearing cone and roller assembly from the hub.

7. Follow Steps 5–10 of the "Removal, Repacking, and Installation" procedure for "Drum Brakes" as previously outlined.

8. Install the hub and disc on the wheel spindle. To prevent damage to the grease retainer and spindle threads, keep the hub centered on the spindle.

9. Install the outer bearing cone and roller assembly and the flat washer on the spindle. Install the adjusting nut.

10. Adjust the wheel bearings by torquing the adjusting nut to 17–25 ft. lbs. with the wheel rotating to seat the bearing. Then back off the adjusting nut ½ turn. Retighten the adjusting nut to 10–15 in. lbs. Install the locknut so that the castellations are aligned with the cotter pin hole. Install the cotter pin. Bend the ends of the cotter pin around the castellations of the locknut to prevent interference with the radio static collector in the grease cap. Install the grease cap.

NOTE: *New bolts must be used when servicing floating caliper units. The upper bolt must be tightened first. For floating-caliper units, follow Steps 19, 20, and 21 under "Caliper Assembly Service." For sliding-caliper units, follow Steps 12–19 under "Shoe and Lining Replacement."*

11. Install the wheel and tire on the hub.

12. Install the wheel cover.

PARKING BRAKE

Checking and Adjusting
REAR DRUM BRAKES

The parking brake should be checked for proper operation every 12 months or 12,000 miles and adjusted whenever there is slack in the cables. A cable with too much slack will not hold a vehicle on an incline which presents a serious safety hazard. Usually, a rear brake adjustment will restore parking brake efficiency, but if the

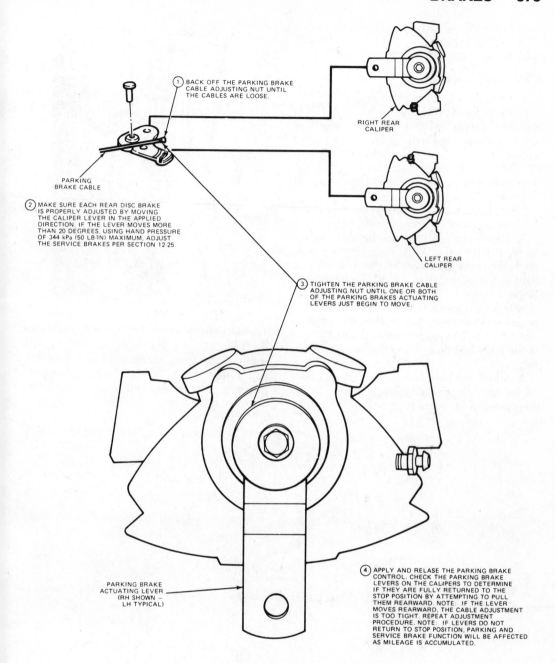

1. BACK OFF THE PARKING BRAKE CABLE ADJUSTING NUT UNTIL THE CABLES ARE LOOSE.

RIGHT REAR CALIPER

PARKING BRAKE CABLE

2. MAKE SURE EACH REAR DISC BRAKE IS PROPERLY ADJUSTED BY MOVING THE CALIPER LEVER IN THE APPLIED DIRECTION. IF THE LEVER MOVES MORE THAN 20 DEGREES, USING HAND PRESSURE OF 344 kPa (50 LB·IN) MAXIMUM, ADJUST THE SERVICE BRAKES PER SECTION 12·25.

LEFT REAR CALIPER

3. TIGHTEN THE PARKING BRAKE CABLE ADJUSTING NUT UNTIL ONE OR BOTH OF THE PARKING BRAKES ACTUATING LEVERS JUST BEGIN TO MOVE.

PARKING BRAKE ACTUATING LEVER (RH SHOWN — LH TYPICAL)

4. APPLY AND RELESE THE PARKING BRAKE CONTROL. CHECK THE PARKING BRAKE LEVERS ON THE CALIPERS TO DETERMINE IF THEY ARE FULLY RETURNED TO THE STOP POSITION BY ATTEMPTING TO PULL THEM REARWARD. NOTE: IF THE LEVER MOVES REARWARD, THE CABLE ADJUSTMENT IS TOO TIGHT. REPEAT ADJUSTMENT PROCEDURE. NOTE: IF LEVERS DO NOT RETURN TO STOP POSITION, PARKING AND SERVICE BRAKE FUNCTION WILL BE AFFECTED AS MILEAGE IS ACCUMULATED.

PARKING BRAKE ADJUSTMENT · REAR DISC BRAKE

Parking brake adjustment on models with rear disc brakes

cables appear loose or stretched when the parking brake is released, adjust as necessary.

The procedure for adjusting the parking brake on all pedal-actuated systems is as follows:

1. Fully release the parking brake.

2. Depress the parking brake pedal one notch from its normal released position. On vacuum release brakes, the first notch is approximately 2 in. of travel.

3. Taking proper safety precautions, raise the car and place the transmission in Neutral.

4. Loosen the equalizer locknut and turn the adjusting nut forward against the equalizer until moderate drag is felt when turning the rear wheels. Tighten the locknut.

5. Release the parking brake, making sure that the brake shoes return to the fully released position.

6. Lower the car and apply the parking brake. Under normal conditions, the third notch will hold the car if the brake is adjusted properly.

REAR DISC BRAKES

1. Fully release the parking brake.
2. Place the transmission in Neutral. If it is necessary to raise the car to reach the adjusting nut and observe the parking brake levers, use an axle hoist or a floor jack positioned beneath the differential. This is necessary so that the rear axle remains at the curb attitude, not stretching the parking brake cables.

CAUTION: *If you are raising the rear of the car only, block the front wheels.*

3. Locate the adjusting nut beneath the car on the driver's side. While observing the parking brake actuating levers on the rear calipers, tighten the adjusting nut until the levers just begin to move. Then, loosen the nut sufficiently for the levers to fully return to the stop position. The levers are in the stop position when a ¼ in. pin can be inserted past the side of the lever into the holes in the cast iron housing.

4. Check the operation of the parking brake. Make sure the actuating levers return to the stop position by attempting to pull them rear-

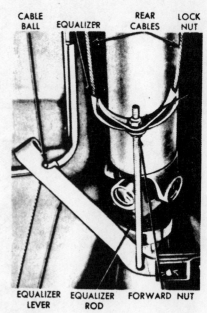

Typical parking brake linkage with rear drum brakes

ward. If the lever moves rearward, the cable adjustment is too tight, which will cause a dragging rear brake and consequent brake overheating and fade.

Troubleshooting

10

This section is designed to aid in the quick, accurate diagnosis of automotive problems. While automotive repairs can be made by many people, accurate troubleshooting is a rare skill for the amateur and professional alike.

In its simplest state, troubleshooting is an exercise in logic. It is essential to realize that an automobile is really composed of a series of systems. Some of these systems are interrelated; others are not. Automobiles operate within a framework of logical rules and physical laws, and the key to troubleshooting is a good understanding of all the automotive systems.

This section breaks the car or truck down into its component systems, allowing the problem to be isolated. The charts and diagnostic road maps list the most common problems and the most probable causes of trouble. Obviously it would be impossible to list every possible problem that could happen along with every possible cause, but it will locate MOST problems and eliminate a lot of unnecessary guesswork. The systematic format will locate problems within a given system, but, because many automotive systems are interrelated, the solution to your particular problem may be found in a number of systems on the car or truck.

USING THE TROUBLESHOOTING CHARTS

This book contains all of the specific information that the average do-it-yourself mechanic needs to repair and maintain his or her car or truck. The troubleshooting charts are designed to be used in conjunction with the specific procedures and information in the text. For instance, troubleshooting a point-type ignition system is fairly standard for all models, but you may be directed to the text to find procedures for troubleshooting an individual type of electronic ignition. You will also have to refer to the specification charts throughout the book for specifications applicable to your car or truck.

TOOLS AND EQUIPMENT

The tools illustrated in Chapter 1 (plus two more diagnostic pieces) will be adequate to troubleshoot most problems. The two other tools needed are a voltmeter and an ohmmeter. These can be purchased separately or in combination, known as a VOM meter.

In the event that other tools are required, they will be noted in the procedures.

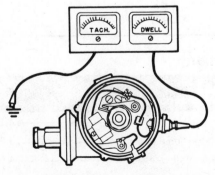

Tach-dwell hooked-up to distributor

Troubleshooting Engine Problems

See Chapters 2, 3, 4 for more information and service procedures.

Index to Systems

System	To Test	Group
Battery	Engine need not be running	1
Starting system	Engine need not be running	2
Primary electrical system	Engine need not be running	3
Secondary electrical system	Engine need not be running	4
Fuel system	Engine need not be running	5
Engine compression	Engine need not be running	6
Engine vacuum	Engine must be running	7
Secondary electrical system	Engine must be running	8
Valve train	Engine must be running	9
Exhaust system	Engine must be running	10
Cooling system	Engine must be running	11
Engine lubrication	Engine must be running	12

Index to Problems

Problem: Symptom	Begin at Specific Diagnosis, Number ____
Engine Won't Start:	
Starter doesn't turn	1.1, 2.1
Starter turns, engine doesn't	2.1
Starter turns engine very slowly	1.1, 2.4
Starter turns engine normally	3.1, 4.1
Starter turns engine very quickly	6.1
Engine fires intermittently	4.1
Engine fires consistently	5.1, 6.1
Engine Runs Poorly:	
Hard starting	3.1, 4.1, 5.1, 8.1
Rough idle	4.1, 5.1, 8.1
Stalling	3.1, 4.1, 5.1, 8.1
Engine dies at high speeds	4.1, 5.1
Hesitation (on acceleration from standing stop)	5.1, 8.1
Poor pickup	4.1, 5.1, 8.1
Lack of power	3.1, 4.1, 5.1, 8.1
Backfire through the carburetor	4.1, 8.1, 9.1
Backfire through the exhaust	4.1, 8.1, 9.1
Blue exhaust gases	6.1, 7.1
Black exhaust gases	5.1
Running on (after the ignition is shut off)	3.1, 8.1
Susceptible to moisture	4.1
Engine misfires under load	4.1, 7.1, 8.4, 9.1
Engine misfires at speed	4.1, 8.4
Engine misfires at idle	3.1, 4.1, 5.1, 7.1, 8.4

Sample Section

Test and Procedure	Results and Indications	Proceed to
4.1—Check for spark: Hold each spark plug wire approximately ¼″ from ground with gloves or a heavy, dry rag. Crank the engine and observe the spark.	→ If no spark is evident:	→**4.2**
	→ If spark is good in some cases:	→**4.3**
	→ If spark is good in all cases:	→**4.6**

Specific Diagnosis

This section is arranged so that following each test, instructions are given to proceed to another, until a problem is diagnosed.

Section 1—Battery

Test and Procedure	Results and Indications	Proceed to
1.1—Inspect the battery visually for case condition (corrosion, cracks) and water level.	If case is cracked, replace battery:	**1.4**
	If the case is intact, remove corrosion with a solution of baking soda and water (**CAUTION**: *do not get the solution into the battery*), and fill with water:	**1.2**

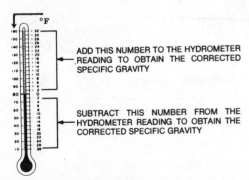

DIRT ON TOP OF BATTERY   PLUGGED VENT
CORROSION
LOOSE CABLE OR POSTS
CRACKS
LOW WATER LEVEL

Inspect the battery case

1.2—Check the battery cable connections: Insert a screwdriver between the battery post and the cable clamp. Turn the headlights on high beam, and observe them as the screwdriver is gently twisted to ensure good metal to metal contact.	If the lights brighten, remove and clean the clamp and post; coat the post with petroleum jelly, install and tighten the clamp:	**1.4**
	If no improvement is noted:	**1.3**

TESTING BATTERY CABLE CONNECTIONS USING A SCREWDRIVER

1.3—Test the state of charge of the battery using an individual cell tester or hydrometer.	If indicated, charge the battery. **NOTE:** *If no obvious reason exists for the low state of charge (i.e., battery age, prolonged storage), proceed to:*	**1.4**

°F

ADD THIS NUMBER TO THE HYDROMETER READING TO OBTAIN THE CORRECTED SPECIFIC GRAVITY

SUBTRACT THIS NUMBER FROM THE HYDROMETER READING TO OBTAIN THE CORRECTED SPECIFIC GRAVITY

Specific Gravity (@ 80° F.)

Minimum	Battery Charge
1.260	100% Charged
1.230	75% Charged
1.200	50% Charged
1.170	25% Charged
1.140	Very Little Power Left
1.110	Completely Discharged

The effects of temperature on battery specific gravity (left) and amount of battery charge in relation to specific gravity (right)

1.4—Visually inspect battery cables for cracking, bad connection to ground, or bad connection to starter.	If necessary, tighten connections or replace the cables:	**2.1**

Section 2—Starting System
See Chapter 3 for service procedures

Test and Procedure	Results and Indications	Proceed to
Note: Tests in Group 2 are performed with coil high tension lead disconnected to prevent accidental starting.		
2.1—Test the starter motor and solenoid: Connect a jumper from the battery post of the solenoid (or relay) to the starter post of the solenoid (or relay).	If starter turns the engine normally:	2.2
	If the starter buzzes, or turns the engine very slowly:	2.4
	If no response, replace the solenoid (or relay).	3.1
	If the starter turns, but the engine doesn't, ensure that the flywheel ring gear is intact. If the gear is undamaged, replace the starter drive.	3.1
2.2—Determine whether ignition override switches are functioning properly (clutch start switch, neutral safety switch), by connecting a jumper across the switch(es), and turning the ignition switch to "start".	If starter operates, adjust or replace switch:	3.1
	If the starter doesn't operate:	2.3
2.3—Check the ignition switch "start" position: Connect a 12V test lamp or voltmeter between the starter post of the solenoid (or relay) and ground. Turn the ignition switch to the "start" position, and jiggle the key.	If the lamp doesn't light or the meter needle doesn't move when the switch is turned, check the ignition switch for loose connections, cracked insulation, or broken wires. Repair or replace as necessary:	3.1
	If the lamp flickers or needle moves when the key is jiggled, replace the ignition switch.	3.3

Checking the ignition switch "start" position

STARTER RELAY (IF EQUIPPED)

2.4—Remove and bench test the starter, according to specifications in the engine electrical section.	If the starter does not meet specifications, repair or replace as needed:	3.1
	If the starter is operating properly:	2.5
2.5—Determine whether the engine can turn freely: Remove the spark plugs, and check for water in the cylinders. Check for water on the dipstick, or oil in the radiator. Attempt to turn the engine using an 18″ flex drive and socket on the crankshaft pulley nut or bolt.	If the engine will turn freely only with the spark plugs out, and hydrostatic lock (water in the cylinders) is ruled out, check valve timing:	9.2
	If engine will not turn freely, and it is known that the clutch and transmission are free, the engine must be disassembled for further evaluation:	Chapter 3

Section 3—Primary Electrical System

Test and Procedure	Results and Indications	Proceed to
3.1—Check the ignition switch "on" position: Connect a jumper wire between the distributor side of the coil and ground, and a 12V test lamp between the switch side of the coil and ground. Remove the high tension lead from the coil. Turn the ignition switch on and jiggle the key.	If the lamp lights:	**3.2**
	If the lamp flickers when the key is jiggled, replace the ignition switch:	**3.3**
	If the lamp doesn't light, check for loose or open connections. If none are found, remove the ignition switch and check for continuity. If the switch is faulty, replace it:	**3.3**

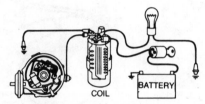

Checking the ignition switch "on" position

3.2—Check the ballast resistor or resistance wire for an open circuit, using an ohmmeter. See Chapter 3 for specific tests.	Replace the resistor or resistance wire if the resistance is zero. **NOTE:** *Some ignition systems have no ballast resistor.*	**3.3**

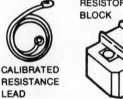 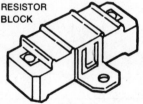

RESISTOR BLOCK

CALIBRATED RESISTANCE LEAD

Two types of resistors

3.3—On point-type ignition systems, visually inspect the breaker points for burning, pitting or excessive wear. Gray coloring of the point contact surfaces is normal. Rotate the crankshaft until the contact heel rests on a high point of the distributor cam and adjust the point gap to specifications. On electronic ignition models, remove the distributor cap and visually inspect the armature. Ensure that the armature pin is in place, and that the armature is on tight and rotates when the engine is cranked. Make sure there are no cracks, chips or rounded edges on the armature.	If the breaker points are intact, clean the contact surfaces with fine emery cloth, and adjust the point gap to specifications. If the points are worn, replace them. On electronic systems, replace any parts which appear defective. If condition persists:	**3.4**

Test and Procedure	Results and Indications	Proceed to
3.4—On point-type ignition systems, connect a dwell-meter between the distributor primary lead and ground. Crank the engine and observe the point dwell angle. On electronic ignition systems, conduct a stator (magnetic pickup assembly) test. See Chapter 3.	On point-type systems, adjust the dwell angle if necessary. **NOTE:** *Increasing the point gap decreases the dwell angle and vice-versa.*	**3.6**
	If the dwell meter shows little or no reading;	**3.5**
	On electronic ignition systems, if the stator is bad, replace the stator. If the stator is good, proceed to the other tests in Chapter 3.	

WIDE GAP   NARROW GAP

CLOSE   OPEN

NORMAL DWELL

SMALL DWELL

INSUFFICIENT DWELL

LARGE DWELL

EXCESSIVE DWELL

Dwell is a function of point gap

3.5—On the point-type ignition systems, check the condenser for short: connect an ohmeter across the condenser body and the pigtail lead.	If any reading other than infinite is noted, replace the condenser	**3.6**

OHMMETER

Checking the condenser for short

3.6—Test the coil primary resistance: On point-type ignition systems, connect an ohmmeter across the coil primary terminals, and read the resistance on the low scale. Note whether an external ballast resistor or resistance wire is used. On electronic ignition systems, test the coil primary resistance as in Chapter 3.	Point-type ignition coils utilizing ballast resistors or resistance wires should have approximately 1.0 ohms resistance. Coils with internal resistors should have approximately 4.0 ohms resistance. If values far from the above are noted, replace the coil.	**4.1**

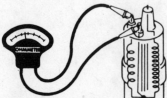

Check the coil primary resistance

Section 4—Secondary Electrical System

See Chapters 2–3 for service procedures

Test and Procedure	Results and Indications	Proceed to
4.1—Check for spark: Hold each spark plug wire approximately ¼″ from ground with gloves or a heavy, dry rag. Crank the engine, and observe the spark.	If no spark is evident:	**4.2**
	If spark is good in some cylinders:	**4.3**
	If spark is good in all cylinders:	**4.6**

Check for spark at the plugs

Test and Procedure	Results and Indications	Proceed to
4.2—Check for spark at the coil high tension lead: Remove the coil high tension lead from the distributor and position it approximately ¼″ from ground. Crank the engine and observe spark. **CAUTION:** *This test should not be performed on engines equipped with electronic ignition.*	If the spark is good and consistent:	**4.3**
	If the spark is good but intermittent, test the primary electrical system starting at 3.3:	**3.3**
	If the spark is weak or non-existent, replace the coil high tension lead, clean and tighten all connections and retest. If no improvement is noted:	**4.4**
4.3—Visually inspect the distributor cap and rotor for burned or corroded contacts, cracks, carbon tracks, or moisture. Also check the fit of the rotor on the distributor shaft (where applicable).	If moisture is present, dry thoroughly, and retest per 4.1:	**4.1**
	If burned or excessively corroded contacts, cracks, or carbon tracks are noted, replace the defective part(s) and retest per 4.1:	**4.1**
	If the rotor and cap appear intact, or are only slightly corroded, clean the contacts thoroughly (including the cap towers and spark plug wire ends) and retest per 4.1:	
	If the spark is good in all cases:	**4.6**
	If the spark is poor in all cases:	**4.5**

Inspect the distributor cap and rotor

Test and Procedure	Results and Indications	Proceed to
4.4—Check the coil secondary resistance: On point-type systems connect an ohmmeter across the distributor side of the coil and the coil tower. Read the resistance on the high scale of the ohmmeter. On electronic ignition systems, see Chapter 3 for specific tests.	The resistance of a satisfactory coil should be between 4,000 and 10,000 ohms. If resistance is considerably higher (i.e., 40,000 ohms) replace the coil and retest per 4.1. **NOTE: *This does not apply to high performance coils.***	

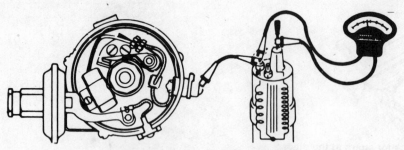

Testing the coil secondary resistance

4.5—Visually inspect the spark plug wires for cracking or brittleness. Ensure that no two wires are positioned so as to cause induction firing (adjacent and parallel). Remove each wire, one by one, and check resistance with an ohmmeter.	Replace any cracked or brittle wires. If any of the wires are defective, replace the entire set. Replace any wires with excessive resistance (over $8000\,\Omega$ per foot for suppression wire), and separate any wires that might cause induction firing.	**4.6**

Misfiring can be the result of spark plug leads to adjacent, consecutively firing cylinders running parallel and too close together

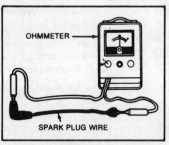

OHMMETER

SPARK PLUG WIRE

On point-type ignition systems, check the spark plug wires as shown. On electronic ignitions, do not remove the wire from the distributor cap terminal; instead, test through the cap

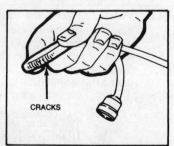

CRACKS

Spark plug wires can be checked visually by bending them in a loop over your finger. This will reveal any cracks, burned or broken insulation. Any wire with cracked insulation should be replaced

4.6—Remove the spark plugs, noting the cylinders from which they were removed, and evaluate according to the color photos in the middle of this book.	See following.	**See following.**

Test and Procedure	Results and Indications	Proceed to
4.7—Examine the location of all the plugs.	The following diagrams illustrate some of the conditions that the location of plugs will reveal.	**4.8**

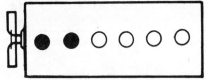

Two adjacent plugs are fouled in a 6-cylinder engine, 4-cylinder engine or either bank of a V-8. This is probably due to a blown head gasket between the two cylinders

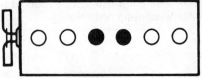

The two center plugs in a 6-cylinder engine are fouled. Raw fuel may be "boiled" out of the carburetor into the intake manifold after the engine is shut-off. Stop-start driving can also foul the center plugs, due to overly rich mixture. Proper float level, a new float needle and seat or use of an insulating spacer may help this problem

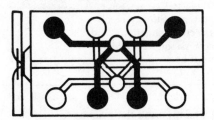

An unbalanced carburetor is indicated. Following the fuel flow on this particular design shows that the cylinders fed by the right-hand barrel are fouled from overly rich mixture, while the cylinders fed by the left-hand barrel are normal

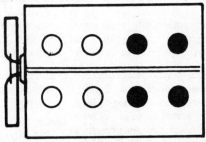

If the four rear plugs are overheated, a cooling system problem is suggested. A thorough cleaning of the cooling system may restore coolant circulation and cure the problem

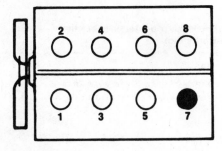

Finding one plug overheated may indicate an intake manifold leak near the affected cylinder. If the overheated plug is the second of two adjacent, consecutively firing plugs, it could be the result of ignition cross-firing. Separating the leads to these two plugs will eliminate cross-fire

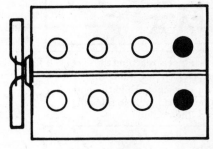

Occasionally, the two rear plugs in large, lightly used V-8's will become oil fouled. High oil consumption and smoky exhaust may also be noticed. It is probably due to plugged oil drain holes in the rear of the cylinder head, causing oil to be sucked in around the valve stems. This usually occurs in the rear cylinders first, because the engine slants that way

Test and Procedure	Results and Indications	Proceed to
4.8—Determine the static ignition timing. Using the crankshaft pulley timing marks as a guide, locate top dead center on the compression stroke of the number one cylinder.	The rotor should be pointing toward the No. 1 tower in the distributor cap, and, on electronic ignitions, the armature spoke for that cylinder should be lined up with the stator.	**4.8**
4.9—Check coil polarity: Connect a voltmeter negative lead to the coil high tension lead, and the positive lead to ground (**NOTE:** *Reverse the hook-up for positive ground systems*). Crank the engine momentarily. **Checking coil polarity**	If the voltmeter reads up-scale, the polarity is correct: If the voltmeter reads down-scale, reverse the coil polarity (switch the primary leads):	**5.1** **5.1**

Section 5—Fuel System
See Chapter 4 for service procedures

Test and Procedure	Results and Indications	Proceed to
5.1—Determine that the air filter is functioning efficiently: Hold paper elements up to a strong light, and attempt to see light through the filter.	Clean permanent air filters in solvent (or manufacturer's recommendation), and allow to dry. Replace paper elements through which light cannot be seen:	**5.2**
5.2—Determine whether a flooding condition exists: Flooding is identified by a strong gasoline odor, and excessive gasoline present in the throttle bore(s) of the carburetor.	If flooding is not evident: If flooding is evident, permit the gasoline to dry for a few moments and restart. If flooding doesn't recur: If flooding is persistent:	**5.3** **5.7** **5.5**

If the engine floods repeatedly, check the choke butterfly flap

5.3—Check that fuel is reaching the carburetor: Detach the fuel line at the carburetor inlet. Hold the end of the line in a cup (not styrofoam), and crank the engine.	If fuel flows smoothly: If fuel doesn't flow (**NOTE:** *Make sure that there is fuel in the tank*), or flows erratically:	**5.7** **5.4**

Check the fuel pump by disconnecting the output line (fuel pump-to-carburetor) at the carburetor and operating the starter briefly

CHILTON'S
AUTO BODY REPAIR TIPS

Tools and Materials • Step-by-Step Illustrated Procedures
How To Repair Dents, Scratches and Rust Holes
Spray Painting and Refinishing Tips

With a little practice, basic body repair procedures can be mastered by any do-it-yourself mechanic. The step-by-step repairs shown here can be applied to almost any type of auto body repair.

TOOLS & MATERIALS

You may already have basic tools, such as hammers and electric drills. Other tools unique to body repair — body hammers, grinding attachments, sanding blocks, dent puller, half-round plastic file and plastic spreaders — are relatively inexpensive and can be obtained wherever auto parts or auto body repair parts are sold. Portable air compressors and paint spray guns can be purchased or rented.

Auto Body Repair Kits

The best and most often used products are available to the do-it-yourselfer in kit form, from major manufacturers of auto body repair products. The same manufacturers also merchandise the individual products for use by pros.

Kits are available to make a wide variety of repairs, including holes, dents and scratches and fiberglass, and offer the advantage of buying the materials you'll need for the job. There is little waste or chance of materials going bad from not being used. Many kits may also contain basic body-working tools such as body files, sanding blocks and spreaders. Check the contents of the kit before buying your tools.

BODY REPAIR TIPS

Safety

Many of the products associated with auto body repair and refinishing contain toxic chemicals. Read all labels before opening containers and store them in a safe place and manner.

• Wear eye protection (safety goggles) when using power tools or when performing any operation that involves the removal of any type of material.

• Wear lung protection (disposable mask or respirator) when grinding, sanding or painting.

Sanding

1 Sand off paint before using a dent puller. When using a non-adhesive sanding disc, cover the back of the disc with an overlapping layer or two of masking tape and trim the edges. The disc will last considerably longer.

2 Use the circular motion of the sanding disc to grind *into* the edge of the repair. Grinding or sanding away from the jagged edge will only tear the sandpaper.

3 Use the palm of your hand flat on the panel to detect high and low spots. Do not use your fingertips. Slide your hand slowly back and forth.

WORKING WITH BODY FILLER

Mixing The Filler

Cleanliness and proper mixing and application are extremely important. Use a clean piece of plastic or glass or a disposable artist's palette to mix body filler.

1 Allow plenty of time and follow directions. No useful purpose will be served by adding more hardener to make it cure (set-up) faster. Less hardener means more curing time, but the mixture dries harder; more hardener means less curing time but a softer mixture.

2

2 Both the hardener and the filler should be thoroughly kneaded or stirred before mixing. Hardener should be a solid paste and dispense like thin toothpaste. Body filler should be smooth, and free of lumps or thick spots.

Getting the proper amount of hardener in the filler is the trickiest part of preparing the filler. Use the same amount of hardener in cold or warm weather. For contour filler (thick coats), a bead of hardener twice the diameter of the filler is about right. There's about a 15% margin on either side, but, if in doubt use less hardener.

2

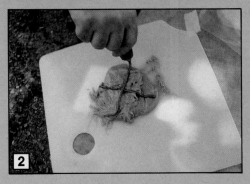

2

3 Mix the body filler and hardener by wiping across the mixing surface, picking the mixture up and wiping it again. Colder weather requires longer mixing times. Do not mix in a circular motion; this will trap air bubbles which will become holes in the cured filler.

3

Applying The Filler

1 For best results, filler should not be applied over 1/4" thick.

Apply the filler in several coats. Build it up to above the level of the repair surface so that it can be sanded or grated down.

The first coat of filler must be pressed on with a firm wiping motion.

Apply the filler in one direction only. Working the filler back and forth will either pull it off the metal or trap air bubbles.

REPAIRING DENTS

Before you start, take a few minutes to study the damaged area. Try to visualize the shape of the panel before it was damaged. If the damage is on the left fender, look at the right fender and use it as a guide. If there is access to the panel from behind, you can reshape it with a body hammer. If not, you'll have to use a dent puller. Go slowly and work the metal a little at a time. Get the panel as straight as possible before applying filler.

1 This dent is typical of one that can be pulled out or hammered out from behind. Remove the headlight cover, headlight assembly and turn signal housing.

2 Drill a series of holes ½ the size of the end of the dent puller along the stress line. Make some trial pulls and assess the results. If necessary, drill more holes and try again. Do not hurry.

3 If possible, use a body hammer and block to shape the metal back to its original contours. Get the metal back as close to its original shape as possible. Don't depend on body filler to fill dents.

4 Using an 80-grit grinding disc on an electric drill, grind the paint from the surrounding area down to bare metal. Use a new grinding pad to prevent heat buildup that will warp metal.

5 The area should look like this when you're finished grinding. Knock the drill holes in and tape over small openings to keep plastic filler out.

6 Mix the body filler (see Body Repair Tips). Spread the body filler evenly over the entire area (see Body Repair Tips). Be sure to cover the area completely.

7 Let the body filler dry until the surface can just be scratched with your fingernail. Knock the high spots from the body filler with a body file ("Cheesegrater"). Check frequently with the palm of your hand for high and low spots.

8 Check to be sure that trim pieces that will be installed later will fit exactly. Sand the area with 40-grit paper.

9 If you wind up with low spots, you may have to apply another layer of filler.

10 Knock the high spots off with 40-grit paper. When you are satisfied with the contours of the repair, apply a thin coat of filler to cover pin holes and scratches.

11 Block sand the area with 40-grit paper to a smooth finish. Pay particular attention to body lines and ridges that must be well-defined.

12 Sand the area with 400 paper and then finish with a scuff pad. The finished repair is ready for priming and painting (see Painting Tips).

Materials and photos courtesy of Ritt Jones Auto Body, Prospect Park, PA.

REPAIRING RUST HOLES

There are many ways to repair rust holes. The fiberglass cloth kit shown here is one of the most cost efficient for the owner because it provides a strong repair that resists cracking and moisture and is relatively easy to use. It can be used on large and small holes (with or without backing) and can be applied over contoured areas. Remember, however, that short of replacing an entire panel, no repair is a guarantee that the rust will not return.

1 Remove any trim that will be in the way. Clean away all loose debris. Cut away all the rusted metal. But be sure to leave enough metal to retain the contour or body shape.

2 Grind away all traces of rust with a 24-grit grinding disc. Be sure to grind back 3-4 inches from the edge of the hole down to bare metal and be sure all traces of paint, primer and rust are removed.

3 Block sand the area with 80 or 100 grit sandpaper to get a clear, shiny surface and feathered paint edge. Tap the edges of the hole inward with a ball peen hammer.

4 If you are going to use release film, cut a piece about 2-3″ larger than the area you have sanded. Place the film over the repair and mark the sanded area on the film. Avoid any unnecessary wrinkling of the film.

5 Cut 2 pieces of fiberglass matte to match the shape of the repair. One piece should be about 1″ smaller than the sanded area and the second piece should be 1″ smaller than the first. Mix enough filler and hardener to saturate the fiberglass material (see Body Repair Tips).

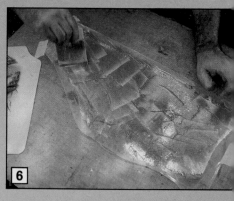

6 Lay the release sheet on a flat sur face and spread an even layer o filler, large enough to cover the repai Lay the smaller piece of fiberglass cloth in the center of the sheet and spread another layer of filler over the fiberglas cloth. Repeat the operation for the larger piece of cloth.

7 Place the repair material over th repair area, with the release film fac ing outward. Use a spreader and wor from the center outward to smooth the material, following the body contours Be sure to remove all air bubbles.

8 Wait until the repair has dried tack free and peel off the release sheet The ideal working temperature is 60° 90° F. Cooler or warmer temperatures o high humidity may require additiona curing time. Wait longer, if in doubt.

9

Sand and feather-edge the entire area. The initial sanding can be done with a sanding disc on an electric drill if care is used. Finish the sanding with a block sander. Low spots can be filled with body filler; this may require several applications.

10

10 When the filler can just be scratched with a fingernail, knock the high spots down with a body file and smooth the entire area with 80-grit. Feather the filled areas into the surrounding areas.

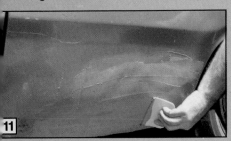

11

11 When the area is sanded smooth, mix some topcoat and hardener and apply it directly with a spreader. This will give a smooth finish and prevent the glass matte from showing through the paint.

12

12 Block sand the topcoat smooth with finishing sandpaper (200 grit), and 400 grit. The repair is ready for masking, priming and painting (see Painting Tips).

Materials and photos courtesy Marson Corporation, Chelsea, Massachusetts

PAINTING TIPS

Preparation

1 SANDING — Use a 400 or 600 grit wet or dry sandpaper. Wet-sand the area with a 1/4 sheet of sandpaper soaked in clean water. Keep the paper wet while sanding. Sand the area until the repaired area tapers into the original finish.

2 CLEANING — Wash the area to be painted thoroughly with water and a clean rag. Rinse it thoroughly and wipe the surface dry until you're sure it's completely free of dirt, dust, fingerprints, wax, detergent or other foreign matter.

3 MASKING — Protect any areas you don't want to overspray by covering them with masking tape and newspaper. Be careful not get fingerprints on the area to be painted.

4 PRIMING — All exposed metal should be primed before painting. Primer protects the metal and provides an excellent surface for paint adhesion. When the primer is dry, wet-sand the area again with 600 grit wet-sandpaper. Clean the area again after sanding.

4

Painting Techniques

Paint applied from either a spray gun or a spray can (for small areas) will provide good results. Experiment on an old piece of metal to get the right combination before you begin painting.

SPRAYING VISCOSITY (SPRAY GUN ONLY) — Paint should be thinned to spraying viscosity according to the directions on the can. Use only the recommended thinner or reducer and the same amount of reduction regardless of temperature.

AIR PRESSURE (SPRAY GUN ONLY) — This is extremely important. Be sure you are using the proper recommended pressure.

TEMPERATURE — The surface to be painted should be approximately the same temperature as the surrounding air. Applying warm paint to a cold surface, or vice versa, will completely upset the paint characteristics.

THICKNESS — Spray with smooth strokes. In general, the thicker the coat of paint, the longer the drying time. Apply several thin coats about 30 seconds apart. The paint should remain wet long enough to flow out and no longer; heavier coats will only produce sags or wrinkles. Spray a light (fog) coat, followed by heavier color coats.

DISTANCE — The ideal spraying distance is 8"-12" from the gun or can to the surface. Shorter distances will produce ripples, while greater distances will result in orange peel, dry film and poor color match and loss of material due to overspray.

OVERLAPPING — The gun or can should be kept at right angles to the surface at all times. Work to a wet edge at an even speed, using a 50% overlap and direct the center of the spray at the lower or nearest edge of the previous stroke.

RUBBING OUT (BLENDING) FRESH PAINT — Let the paint dry thoroughly. Runs or imperfections can be sanded out, primed and repainted.

Don't be in too big a hurry to remove the masking. This only produces paint ridges. When the finish has dried for at least a week, apply a small amount of fine grade rubbing compound with a clean, wet cloth. Use lots of water and blend the new paint with the surrounding area.

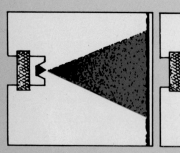

WRONG

Thin coat. Stroke too fast, not enough overlap, gun too far away.

CORRECT

Medium coat. Proper distance, good stroke, proper overlap.

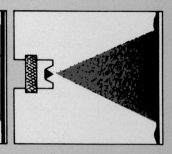

WRONG

Heavy coat. Stroke too slow, too much overlap, gun too close.

Test and Procedure	Results and Indications	Proceed to
5.4—Test the fuel pump: Disconnect all fuel lines from the fuel pump. Hold a finger over the input fitting, crank the engine (with electric pump, turn the ignition or pump on); and feel for suction.	If suction is evident, blow out the fuel line to the tank with low pressure compressed air until bubbling is heard from the fuel filler neck. Also blow out the carburetor fuel line (both ends disconnected):	**5.7**
	If no suction is evident, replace or repair the fuel pump: **NOTE**: *Repeated oil fouling of the spark plugs, or a no-start condition, could be the result of a ruptured vacuum booster pump diaphragm, through which oil or gasoline is being drawn into the intake manifold (where applicable).*	**5.7**
5.5—Occasionally, small specks of dirt will clog the small jets and orifices in the carburetor. With the engine cold, hold a flat piece of wood or similar material over the carburetor, where possible, and crank the engine.	If the engine starts, but runs roughly the engine is probably not run enough. If the engine won't start:	**5.9**
5.6—Check the needle and seat: Tap the carburetor in the area of the needle and seat.	If flooding stops, a gasoline additive (e.g., Gumout) will often cure the problem:	**5.7**
	If flooding continues, check the fuel pump for excessive pressure at the carburetor (according to specifications). If the pressure is normal, the needle and seat must be removed and checked, and/or the float level adjusted:	**5.7**
5.7—Test the accelerator pump by looking into the throttle bores while operating the throttle.	If the accelerator pump appears to be operating normally:	**5.8**
	If the accelerator pump is not operating, the pump must be reconditioned. Where possible, service the pump with the carburetor(s) installed on the engine. If necessary, remove the carburetor. Prior to removal:	**5.8**

Check for gas at the carburetor by looking down the carburetor throat while someone moves the accelerator

Test and Procedure	Results and Indications	Proceed to
5.8—Determine whether the carburetor main fuel system is functioning: Spray a commercial starting fluid into the carburetor while attempting to start the engine.	If the engine starts, runs for a few seconds, and dies:	**5.9**
	If the engine doesn't start:	**6.1**

Test and Procedure	Results and Indications	Proceed to
5.9—Uncommon fuel system malfunctions: See below:	If the problem is solved:	6.1
	If the problem remains, remove and recondition the carburetor.	

Condition	Indication	Test	Prevailing Weather Conditions	Remedy
Vapor lock	Engine will not restart shortly after running.	Cool the components of the fuel system until the engine starts. Vapor lock can be cured faster by draping a wet cloth over a mechanical fuel pump.	Hot to very hot	Ensure that the exhaust manifold heat control valve is operating. Check with the vehicle manufacturer for the recommended solution to vapor lock on the model in question.
Carburetor icing	Engine will not idle, stalls at low speeds.	Visually inspect the throttle plate area of the throttle bores for frost.	High humidity, 32–40° F.	Ensure that the exhaust manifold heat control valve is operating, and that the intake manifold heat riser is not blocked.
Water in the fuel	Engine sputters and stalls; may not start.	Pump a small amount of fuel into a glass jar. Allow to stand, and inspect for droplets or a layer of water.	High humidity, extreme temperature changes.	For droplets, use one or two cans of commercial gas line anti-freeze. For a layer of water, the tank must be drained, and the fuel lines blown out with compressed air.

Section 6—Engine Compression
See Chapter 3 for service procedures

6.1—Test engine compression: Remove all spark plugs. Block the throttle wide open. Insert a compression gauge into a spark plug port, crank the engine to obtain the maximum reading, and record.	If compression is within limits on all cylinders:	7.1
	If gauge reading is extremely low on all cylinders:	6.2
	If gauge reading is low on one or two cylinders: (If gauge readings are identical and low on two or more adjacent cylinders, the head gasket must be replaced.)	6.2

Checking compression

6.2—Test engine compression (wet): Squirt approximately 30 cc. of engine oil into each cylinder, and retest per 6.1.	If the readings improve, worn or cracked rings or broken pistons are indicated:	See Chapter 3
	If the readings do not improve, burned or excessively carboned valves or a jumped timing chain are indicated:	7.1
	NOTE: *A jumped timing chain is often indicated by difficult cranking.*	

Section 7—Engine Vacuum
See Chapter 3 for service procedures

Test and Procedure	Results and Indications	Proceed to
7.1—Attach a vacuum gauge to the intake manifold beyond the throttle plate. Start the engine, and observe the action of the needle over the range of engine speeds.	See below.	**See below**

INDICATION: normal engine in good condition

Proceed to: 8.1

Normal engine
Gauge reading: steady, from 17–22 in./Hg.

INDICATION: sticking valves or ignition miss

Proceed to: 9.1, 8.3

Sticking valves
Gauge reading: intermittent fluctuation at idle

INDICATION: late ignition or valve timing, low compression, stuck throttle valve, leaking carburetor or manifold gasket

Proceed to: 6.1

Incorrect valve timing
Gauge reading: low (10–15 in./Hg) but steady

INDICATION: improper carburetor adjustment or minor intake leak.

Proceed to: 7.2

Carburetor requires adjustment
Gauge reading: drifting needle

INDICATION: ignition miss, blown cylinder head gasket, leaking valve or weak valve spring

Proceed to: 8.3, 6.1

Blown head gasket
Gauge reading: needle fluctuates as engine speed increases

INDICATION: burnt valve or faulty valve clearance. Needle will fall when defective valve operates

Proceed to: 9.1

Burnt or leaking valves
Gauge reading: steady needle, but drops regularly

INDICATION: choked muffler, excessive back pressure in system

Proceed to: 10.1

Clogged exhaust system
Gauge reading: gradual drop in reading at idle

INDICATION: worn valve guides

Proceed to: 9.1

Worn valve guides
Gauge reading: needle vibrates excessively at idle, but steadies as engine speed increases

---

White pointer = steady gauge hand | Black pointer = fluctuating gauge hand

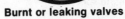

Test and Procedure	Results and Indications	Proceed to
7.2—Attach a vacuum gauge per 7.1, and test for an intake manifold leak. Squirt a small amount of oil around the intake manifold gaskets, carburetor gaskets, plugs and fittings. Observe the action of the vacuum gauge.	If the reading improves, replace the indicated gasket, or seal the indicated fitting or plug:	**8.1**
	If the reading remains low:	**7.3**
7.3—Test all vacuum hoses and accessories for leaks as described in 7.2. Also check the carburetor body (dashpots, automatic choke mechanism, throttle shafts) for leaks in the same manner.	If the reading improves, service or replace the offending part(s):	**8.1**
	If the reading remains low:	**6.1**

Section 8—Secondary Electrical System
See Chapter 2 for service procedures

Test and Procedure	Results and Indications	Proceed to
8.1—Remove the distributor cap and check to make sure that the rotor turns when the engine is cranked. Visually inspect the distributor components.	Clean, tighten or replace any components which appear defective.	**8.2**
8.2—Connect a timing light (per manufacturer's recommendation) and check the dynamic ignition timing. Disconnect and plug the vacuum hose(s) to the distributor if specified, start the engine, and observe the timing marks at the specified engine speed.	If the timing is not correct, adjust to specifications by rotating the distributor in the engine: (Advance timing by rotating distributor opposite normal direction of rotor rotation, retard timing by rotating distributor in same direction as rotor rotation.)	**8.3**
8.3—Check the operation of the distributor advance mechanism(s): To test the mechanical advance, disconnect the vacuum lines from the distributor advance unit and observe the timing marks with a timing light as the engine speed is increased from idle. If the mark moves smoothly, without hesitation, it may be assumed that the mechanical advance is functioning properly. To test vacuum advance and/or retard systems, alternately crimp and release the vacuum line, and observe the timing mark for movement. If movement is noted, the system is operating.	If the systems are functioning:	**8.4**
	If the systems are not functioning, remove the distributor, and test on a distributor tester:	**8.4**
8.4—Locate an ignition miss: With the engine running, remove each spark plug wire, one at a time, until one is found that doesn't cause the engine to roughen and slow down.	When the missing cylinder is identified:	**4.1**

Section 9—Valve Train
See Chapter 3 for service procedures

Test and Procedure	Results and Indications	Proceed to
9.1—Evaluate the valve train: Remove the valve cover, and ensure that the valves are adjusted to specifications. A mechanic's stethoscope may be used to aid in the diagnosis of the valve train. By pushing the probe on or near push rods or rockers, valve noise often can be isolated. A timing light also may be used to diagnose valve problems. Connect the light according to manufacturer's recommendations, and start the engine. Vary the firing moment of the light by increasing the engine speed (and therefore the ignition advance), and moving the trigger from cylinder to cylinder. Observe the movement of each valve.	Sticking valves or erratic valve train motion can be observed with the timing light. The cylinder head must be disassembled for repairs.	**See Chapter 3**
9.2—Check the valve timing: Locate top dead center of the No. 1 piston, and install a degree wheel or tape on the crankshaft pulley or damper with zero corresponding to an index mark on the engine. Rotate the crankshaft in its direction of rotation, and observe the opening of the No. 1 cylinder intake valve. The opening should correspond with the correct mark on the degree wheel according to specifications.	If the timing is not correct, the timing cover must be removed for further investigation.	**See Chapter 3**

Section 10—Exhaust System

Test and Procedure	Results and Indications	Proceed to
10.1—Determine whether the exhaust manifold heat control valve is operating: Operate the valve by hand to determine whether it is free to move. If the valve is free, run the engine to operating temperature and observe the action of the valve, to ensure that it is opening.	If the valve sticks, spray it with a suitable solvent, open and close the valve to free it, and retest. If the valve functions properly: If the valve does not free, or does not operate, replace the valve:	**10.2** **10.2**
10.2—Ensure that there are no exhaust restrictions: Visually inspect the exhaust system for kinks, dents, or crushing. Also note that gases are flowing freely from the tailpipe at all engine speeds, indicating no restriction in the muffler or resonator.	Replace any damaged portion of the system:	**11.1**

Section 11—Cooling System
See Chapter 3 for service procedures

Test and Procedure	Results and Indications	Proceed to
11.1—Visually inspect the fan belt for glazing, cracks, and fraying, and replace if necessary. Tighten the belt so that the longest span has approximately ½″ play at its mid-point under thumb pressure (see Chapter 1).	Replace or tighten the fan belt as necessary:	**11.2**

Checking belt tension

Test and Procedure	Results and Indications	Proceed to
11.2—Check the fluid level of the cooling system.	If full or slightly low, fill as necessary:	**11.5**
	If extremely low:	**11.3**
11.3—Visually inspect the external portions of the cooling system (radiator, radiator hoses, thermostat elbow, water pump seals, heater hoses, etc.) for leaks. If none are found, pressurize the cooling system to 14–15 psi.	If cooling system holds the pressure:	**11.5**
	If cooling system loses pressure rapidly, reinspect external parts of the system for leaks under pressure. If none are found, check dipstick for coolant in crankcase. If no coolant is present, but pressure loss continues:	**11.4**
	If coolant is evident in crankcase, remove cylinder head(s), and check gasket(s). If gaskets are intact, block and cylinder head(s) should be checked for cracks or holes.	
	If the gasket(s) is blown, replace, and purge the crankcase of coolant:	**12.6**
	NOTE: *Occasionally, due to atmospheric and driving conditions, condensation of water can occur in the crankcase. This causes the oil to appear milky white. To remedy, run the engine until hot, and change the oil and oil filter.*	
11.4—Check for combustion leaks into the cooling system: Pressurize the cooling system as above. Start the engine, and observe the pressure gauge. If the needle fluctuates, remove each spark plug wire, one at a time, noting which cylinder(s) reduce or eliminate the fluctuation.	Cylinders which reduce or eliminate the fluctuation, when the spark plug wire is removed, are leaking into the cooling system. Replace the head gasket on the affected cylinder bank(s).	

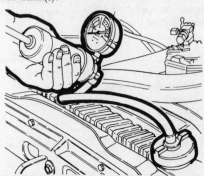

Pressurizing the cooling system

Test and Procedure	Results and Indications	Proceed to
11.5—Check the radiator pressure cap: Attach a radiator pressure tester to the radiator cap (wet the seal prior to installation). Quickly pump up the pressure, noting the point at which the cap releases.	If the cap releases within ± 1 psi of the specified rating, it is operating properly:	**11.6**
	If the cap releases at more than ± 1 psi of the specified rating, it should be replaced:	**11.6**

Checking radiator pressure cap

Test and Procedure	Results and Indications	Proceed to
11.6—Test the thermostat: Start the engine cold, remove the radiator cap, and insert a thermometer into the radiator. Allow the engine to idle. After a short while, there will be a sudden, rapid increase in coolant temperature. The temperature at which this sharp rise stops is the thermostat opening temperature.	If the thermostat opens at or about the specified temperature:	**11.7**
	If the temperature doesn't increase: (If the temperature increases slowly and gradually, replace the thermostat.)	**11.7**
11.7—Check the water pump: Remove the thermostat elbow and the thermostat, disconnect the coil high tension lead (to prevent starting), and crank the engine momentarily.	If coolant flows, replace the thermostat and retest per 11.6:	**11.6**
	If coolant doesn't flow, reverse flush the cooling system to alleviate any blockage that might exist. If system is not blocked, and coolant will not flow, replace the water pump.	

Section 12—Lubrication
See Chapter 3 for service procedures

Test and Procedure	Results and Indications	Proceed to
12.1—Check the oil pressure gauge or warning light: If the gauge shows low pressure, or the light is on for no obvious reason, remove the oil pressure sender. Install an accurate oil pressure gauge and run the engine momentarily.	If oil pressure builds normally, run engine for a few moments to determine that it is functioning normally, and replace the sender.	—
	If the pressure remains low:	**12.2**
	If the pressure surges:	**12.3**
	If the oil pressure is zero:	**12.3**
12.2—Visually inspect the oil: If the oil is watery or very thin, milky, or foamy, replace the oil and oil filter.	If the oil is normal:	**12.3**
	If after replacing oil the pressure remains low:	**12.3**
	If after replacing oil the pressure becomes normal:	—

Test and Procedure	Results and Indications	Proceed to
12.3—Inspect the oil pressure relief valve and spring, to ensure that it is not sticking or stuck. Remove and thoroughly clean the valve, spring, and the valve body.	If the oil pressure improves: If no improvement is noted:	— **12.4**
12.4—Check to ensure that the oil pump is not cavitating (sucking air instead of oil): See that the crankcase is neither over nor underfull, and that the pickup in the sump is in the proper position and free from sludge.	Fill or drain the crankcase to the proper capacity, and clean the pickup screen in solvent if necessary. If no improvement is noted:	**12.5**
12.5—Inspect the oil pump drive and the oil pump:	If the pump drive or the oil pump appear to be defective, service as necessary and retest per 12.1: If the pump drive and pump appear to be operating normally, the engine should be disassembled to determine where blockage exists:	**12.1** **See Chapter 3**
12.6—Purge the engine of ethylene glycol coolant: Completely drain the crankcase and the oil filter. Obtain a commercial butyl cellosolve base solvent, designated for this purpose, and follow the instructions precisely. Following this, install a new oil filter and refill the crankcase with the proper weight oil. The next oil and filter change should follow shortly thereafter (1000 miles).		

TROUBLESHOOTING EMISSION CONTROL SYSTEMS

See Chapter 4 for procedures applicable to individual emission control systems used on specific combinations of engine/transmission/model.

TROUBLESHOOTING THE CARBURETOR
See Chapter 4 for service procedures

Carburetor problems cannot be effectively isolated unless all other engine systems (particularly ignition and emission) are functioning properly and the engine is properly tuned.

Condition	Possible Cause
Engine cranks, but does not start	1. Improper starting procedure 2. No fuel in tank 3. Clogged fuel line or filter 4. Defective fuel pump 5. Choke valve not closing properly 6. Engine flooded 7. Choke valve not unloading 8. Throttle linkage not making full travel 9. Stuck needle or float 10. Leaking float needle or seat 11. Improper float adjustment
Engine stalls	1. Improperly adjusted idle speed or mixture **Engine hot** 2. Improperly adjusted dashpot 3. Defective or improperly adjusted solenoid 4. Incorrect fuel level in fuel bowl 5. Fuel pump pressure too high 6. Leaking float needle seat 7. Secondary throttle valve stuck open 8. Air or fuel leaks 9. Idle air bleeds plugged or missing 10. Idle passages plugged **Engine Cold** 11. Incorrectly adjusted choke 12. Improperly adjusted fast idle speed 13. Air leaks 14. Plugged idle or idle air passages 15. Stuck choke valve or binding linkage 16. Stuck secondary throttle valves 17. Engine flooding—high fuel level 18. Leaking or misaligned float
Engine hesitates on acceleration	1. Clogged fuel filter 2. Leaking fuel pump diaphragm 3. Low fuel pump pressure 4. Secondary throttle valves stuck, bent or misadjusted 5. Sticking or binding air valve 6. Defective accelerator pump 7. Vacuum leaks 8. Clogged air filter 9. Incorrect choke adjustment (engine cold)
Engine feels sluggish or flat on acceleration	1. Improperly adjusted idle speed or mixture 2. Clogged fuel filter 3. Defective accelerator pump 4. Dirty, plugged or incorrect main metering jets 5. Bent or sticking main metering rods 6. Sticking throttle valves 7. Stuck heat riser 8. Binding or stuck air valve 9. Dirty, plugged or incorrect secondary jets 10. Bent or sticking secondary metering rods. 11. Throttle body or manifold heat passages plugged 12. Improperly adjusted choke or choke vacuum break.
Carburetor floods	1. Defective fuel pump. Pressure too high. 2. Stuck choke valve 3. Dirty, worn or damaged float or needle valve/seat 4. Incorrect float/fuel level 5. Leaking float bowl

Condition	Possible Cause
Engine idles roughly and stalls	1. Incorrect idle speed 2. Clogged fuel filter 3. Dirt in fuel system or carburetor 4. Loose carburetor screws or attaching bolts 5. Broken carburetor gaskets 6. Air leaks 7. Dirty carburetor 8. Worn idle mixture needles 9. Throttle valves stuck open 10. Incorrectly adjusted float or fuel level 11. Clogged air filter
Engine runs unevenly or surges	1. Defective fuel pump 2. Dirty or clogged fuel filter 3. Plugged, loose or incorrect main metering jets or rods 4. Air leaks 5. Bent or sticking main metering rods 6. Stuck power piston 7. Incorrect float adjustment 8. Incorrect idle speed or mixture 9. Dirty or plugged idle system passages 10. Hard, brittle or broken gaskets 11. Loose attaching or mounting screws 12. Stuck or misaligned secondary throttle valves
Poor fuel economy	1. Poor driving habits 2. Stuck choke valve 3. Binding choke linkage 4. Stuck heat riser 5. Incorrect idle mixture 6. Defective accelerator pump 7. Air leaks 8. Plugged, loose or incorrect main metering jets 9. Improperly adjusted float or fuel level 10. Bent, misaligned or fuel-clogged float 11. Leaking float needle seat 12. Fuel leak 13. Accelerator pump discharge ball not seating properly 14. Incorrect main jets
Engine lacks high speed performance or power	1. Incorrect throttle linkage adjustment 2. Stuck or binding power piston 3. Defective accelerator pump 4. Air leaks 5. Incorrect float setting or fuel level 6. Dirty, plugged, worn or incorrect main metering jets or rods 7. Binding or sticking air valve 8. Brittle or cracked gaskets 9. Bent, incorrect or improperly adjusted secondary metering rods 10. Clogged fuel filter 11. Clogged air filter 12. Defective fuel pump

TROUBLESHOOTING FUEL INJECTION PROBLEMS

Each fuel injection system has its own unique components and test procedures, for which it is impossible to generalize. Refer to Chapter 4 of this Repair & Tune-Up Guide for specific test and repair procedures, if the vehicle is equipped with fuel injection.

TROUBLESHOOTING ELECTRICAL PROBLEMS

See Chapter 5 for service procedures

For any electrical system to operate, it must make a complete circuit. This simply means that the power flow from the battery must make a complete circle. When an electrical component is operating, power flows from the battery to the component, passes through the component causing it to perform its function (lighting a light bulb), and then returns to the battery through the ground of the circuit. This ground is usually (but not always) the metal part of the car or truck on which the electrical component is mounted.

Perhaps the easiest way to visualize this is to think of connecting a light bulb with two wires attached to it to the battery. If one of the two wires attached to the light bulb were attached to the negative post of the battery and the other were attached to the positive post of the battery, you would have a complete circuit. Current from the battery would flow to the light bulb, causing it to light, and return to the negative post of the battery.

The normal automotive circuit differs from this simple example in two ways. First, instead of having a return wire from the bulb to the battery, the light bulb returns the current to the battery through the chassis of the vehicle. Since the negative battery cable is attached to the chassis and the chassis is made of electrically conductive metal, the chassis of the vehicle can serve as a ground wire to complete the circuit. Secondly, most automotive circuits contain switches to turn components on and off as required.

Every complete circuit from a power source must include a component which is using the power from the power source. If you were to disconnect the light bulb from the wires and touch the two wires together (don't do this) the power supply wire to the component would be grounded before the normal ground connection for the circuit.

Because grounding a wire from a power source makes a complete circuit—less the required component to use the power—this phenomenon is called a short circuit. Common causes are: broken insulation (exposing the metal wire to a metal part of the car or truck), or a shorted switch.

Some electrical components which require a large amount of current to operate also have a relay in their circuit. Since these circuits carry a large amount of current, the thickness of the wire in the circuit (gauge size) is also greater. If this large wire were connected from the component to the control switch on the instrument panel, and then back to the component, a voltage drop would occur in the circuit. To prevent this potential drop in voltage, an electromagnetic switch (relay) is used. The large wires in the circuit are connected from the battery to one side of the relay, and from the opposite side of the relay to the component. The relay is normally open, preventing current from passing through the circuit. An additional, smaller, wire is connected from the relay to the control switch for the circuit. When the control switch is turned on, it grounds the smaller wire from the relay and completes the circuit. This closes the relay and allows current to flow from the battery to the component. The horn, headlight, and starter circuits are three which use relays.

It is possible for larger surges of current to pass through the electrical system of your car or truck. If this surge of current were to reach an electrical component, it could burn it out. To prevent this, fuses, circuit breakers or fusible links are connected into the current supply wires of most of the major electrical systems. When an electrical current of excessive power passes through the component's fuse, the fuse blows out and breaks the circuit, saving the component from destruction.

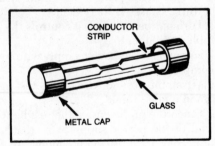

Typical automotive fuse

A circuit breaker is basically a self-repairing fuse. The circuit breaker opens the circuit the same way a fuse does. However, when either the short is removed from the circuit or the surge subsides, the circuit breaker resets itself and does not have to be replaced as a fuse does.

A fuse link is a wire that acts as a fuse. It is normally connected between the starter relay and the main wiring harness. This connection is usually under the hood. The fuse link (if installed) protects all the

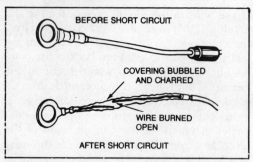

BEFORE SHORT CIRCUIT

COVERING BUBBLED AND CHARRED

WIRE BURNED OPEN

AFTER SHORT CIRCUIT

Most fusible links show a charred, melted insulation when they burn out

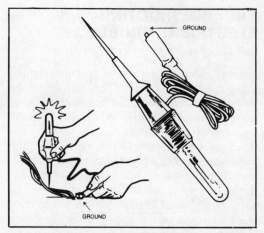

GROUND

GROUND

The test light will show the presence of current when touched to a hot wire and grounded at the other end

chassis electrical components, and is the probable cause of trouble when none of the electrical components function, unless the battery is disconnected or dead.

Electrical problems generally fall into one of three areas:

1. The component that is not functioning is not receiving current.

2. The component itself is not functioning.

3. The component is not properly grounded.

The electrical system can be checked with a test light and a jumper wire. A test light is a device that looks like a pointed screwdriver with a wire attached to it and has a light bulb in its handle. A jumper wire is a piece of insulated wire with an alligator clip attached to each end.

If a component is not working, you must follow a systematic plan to determine which of the three causes is the villain.

1. Turn on the switch that controls the inoperable component.

2. Disconnect the power supply wire from the component.

3. Attach the ground wire on the test light to a good metal ground.

4. Touch the probe end of the test light to the end of the power supply wire that was disconnected from the component. If the component is receiving current, the test light will go on.

NOTE: *Some components work only when the ignition switch is turned on.*

If the test light does not go on, then the problem is in the circuit between the battery and the component. This includes all the switches, fuses, and relays in the system. Follow the wire that runs back to the battery. The problem is an open circuit between the battery and the component. If the fuse is blown and, when replaced, immediately blows again, there is a short circuit in the system which must be located and repaired. If there is a switch in the system, bypass it with a jumper wire. This is done by connecting one end of the jumper wire to the power supply wire into the switch and the other end of the jumper wire to the wire coming out of the switch. If the test light lights with the jumper wire installed, the switch or whatever was bypassed is defective.

NOTE: *Never substitute the jumper wire for the component, since it is required to use the power from the power source.*

5. If the bulb in the test light goes on, then the current is getting to the component that is not working. This eliminates the first of the three possible causes. Connect the power supply wire and connect a jumper wire from the component to a good metal ground. Do this with the switch which controls the component turned on, and also the ignition switch turned on if it is required for the component to work. If the component works with the jumper wire installed, then it has a bad ground. This is usually caused by the metal area on which the component mounts to the chassis being coated with some type of foreign matter.

6. If neither test located the source of the trouble, then the component itself is defective. Remember that for any electrical system to work, all connections must be clean and tight.

Troubleshooting Basic Turn Signal and Flasher Problems
See Chapter 5 for service procedures

Most problems in the turn signals or flasher system can be reduced to defective flashers or bulbs, which are easily replaced. Occasionally, the turn signal switch will prove defective.

F = Front   R = Rear   ● = Lights off   ○ = Lights on

Condition		Possible Cause
Turn signals light, but do not flash	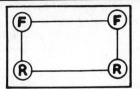	Defective flasher
No turn signals light on either side	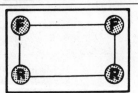	Blown fuse. Replace if defective. Defective flasher. Check by substitution. Open circuit, short circuit or poor ground.
Both turn signals on one side don't work	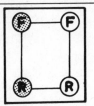	Bad bulbs. Bad ground in both (or either) housings.
One turn signal light on one side doesn't work	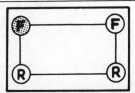	Defective bulb. Corrosion in socket. Clean contacts. Poor ground at socket.
Turn signal flashes too fast or too slowly	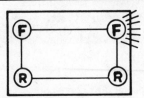	Check any bulb on the side flashing too fast. A heavy-duty bulb is probably installed in place of a regular bulb. Check the bulb flashing too slowly. A standard bulb was probably installed in place of a heavy-duty bulb. Loose connections or corrosion at the bulb socket.
Indicator lights don't work in either direction		Check if the turn signals are working. Check the dash indicator lights. Check the flasher by substitution.
One indicator light doesn't light		On systems with one dash indicator: See if the lights work on the same side. Often the filaments have been reversed in systems combining stoplights with taillights and turn signals. Check the flasher by substitution. On systems with two indicators: Check the bulbs on the same side. Check the indicator light bulb. Check the flasher by substitution.

Troubleshooting Lighting Problems
See Chapter 5 for service procedures

Condition	Possible Cause
One or more lights don't work, but others do	1. Defective bulb(s) 2. Blown fuse(s) 3. Dirty fuse clips or light sockets 4. Poor ground circuit
Lights burn out quickly	1. Incorrect voltage regulator setting or defective regulator 2. Poor battery/alternator connections
Lights go dim	1. Low/discharged battery 2. Alternator not charging 3. Corroded sockets or connections 4. Low voltage output
Lights flicker	1. Loose connection 2. Poor ground. (Run ground wire from light housing to frame) 3. Circuit breaker operating (short circuit)
Lights "flare"—Some flare is normal on acceleration—If excessive, see "Lights Burn Out Quickly"	High voltage setting
Lights glare—approaching drivers are blinded	1. Lights adjusted too high 2. Rear springs or shocks sagging 3. Rear tires soft

Troubleshooting Dash Gauge Problems
Most problems can be traced to a defective sending unit or faulty wiring. Occasionally, the gauge itself is at fault. See Chapter 5 for service procedures.

Condition	Possible Cause
COOLANT TEMPERATURE GAUGE	
Gauge reads erratically or not at all	1. Loose or dirty connections 2. Defective sending unit. 3. Defective gauge. To test a bi-metal gauge, remove the wire from the sending unit. Ground the wire for an instant. If the gauge registers, replace the sending unit. To test a magnetic gauge, disconnect the wire at the sending unit. With ignition ON gauge should register COLD. Ground the wire; gauge should register HOT.
AMMETER GAUGE—TURN HEADLIGHTS ON (DO NOT START ENGINE). NOTE REACTION	
Ammeter shows charge Ammeter shows discharge Ammeter does not move	1. Connections reversed on gauge 2. Ammeter is OK 3. Loose connections or faulty wiring 4. Defective gauge

Condition	Possible Cause

OIL PRESSURE GAUGE

| Gauge does not register or is inaccurate | 1. On mechanical gauge, Bourdon tube may be bent or kinked.
2. Low oil pressure. Remove sending unit. Idle the engine briefly. If no oil flows from sending unit hole, problem is in engine.
3. Defective gauge. Remove the wire from the sending unit and ground it for an instant with the ignition ON. A good gauge will go to the top of the scale.
4. Defective wiring. Check the wiring to the gauge. If it's OK and the gauge doesn't register when grounded, replace the gauge.
5. Defective sending unit. |

ALL GAUGES

All gauges do not operate	1. Blown fuse
	2. Defective instrument regulator
All gauges read low or erratically	3. Defective or dirty instrument voltage regulator
All gauges pegged	4. Loss of ground between instrument voltage regulator and frame
	5. Defective instrument regulator

WARNING LIGHTS

Light(s) do not come on when ignition is ON, but engine is not started	1. Defective bulb 2. Defective wire 3. Defective sending unit. Disconnect the wire from the sending unit and ground it. Replace the sending unit if the light comes on with the ignition ON.
Light comes on with engine running	4. Problem in individual system 5. Defective sending unit

Troubleshooting Clutch Problems

It is false economy to replace individual clutch components. The pressure plate, clutch plate and throwout bearing should be replaced as a set, and the flywheel face inspected, whenever the clutch is overhauled. See Chapter 6 for service procedures.

Condition	Possible Cause
Clutch chatter	1. Grease on driven plate (disc) facing 2. Binding clutch linkage or cable 3. Loose, damaged facings on driven plate (disc) 4. Engine mounts loose 5. Incorrect height adjustment of pressure plate release levers 6. Clutch housing or housing to transmission adapter misalignment 7. Loose driven plate hub
Clutch grabbing	1. Oil, grease on driven plate (disc) facing 2. Broken pressure plate 3. Warped or binding driven plate. Driven plate binding on clutch shaft
Clutch slips	1. Lack of lubrication in clutch linkage or cable (linkage or cable binds, causes incomplete engagement) 2. Incorrect pedal, or linkage adjustment 3. Broken pressure plate springs 4. Weak pressure plate springs 5. Grease on driven plate facings (disc)

Troubleshooting Clutch Problems (cont.)

Condition	Possible Cause
Incomplete clutch release	1. Incorrect pedal or linkage adjustment or linkage or cable binding 2. Incorrect height adjustment on pressure plate release levers 3. Loose, broken facings on driven plate (disc) 4. Bent, dished, warped driven plate caused by overheating
Grinding, whirring grating noise when pedal is depressed	1. Worn or defective throwout bearing 2. Starter drive teeth contacting flywheel ring gear teeth. Look for milled or polished teeth on ring gear.
Squeal, howl, trumpeting noise when pedal is being released (occurs during first inch to inch and one-half of pedal travel)	Pilot bushing worn or lack of lubricant. If bushing appears OK, polish bushing with emery cloth, soak lube wick in oil, lube bushing with oil, apply film of chassis grease to clutch shaft pilot hub, reassemble. NOTE: Bushing wear may be due to misalignment of clutch housing or housing to transmission adapter
Vibration or clutch pedal pulsation with clutch disengaged (pedal fully depressed)	1. Worn or defective engine transmission mounts 2. Flywheel run out. (Flywheel run out at face not to exceed 0.005″) 3. Damaged or defective clutch components

Troubleshooting Manual Transmission Problems
See Chapter 6 for service procedures

Condition	Possible Cause
Transmission jumps out of gear	1. Misalignment of transmission case or clutch housing. 2. Worn pilot bearing in crankshaft. 3. Bent transmission shaft. 4. Worn high speed sliding gear. 5. Worn teeth or end-play in clutch shaft. 6. Insufficient spring tension on shifter rail plunger. 7. Bent or loose shifter fork. 8. Gears not engaging completely. 9. Loose or worn bearings on clutch shaft or mainshaft. 10. Worn gear teeth. 11. Worn or damaged detent balls.
Transmission sticks in gear	1. Clutch not releasing fully. 2. Burred or battered teeth on clutch shaft, or sliding sleeve. 3. Burred or battered transmission mainshaft. 4. Frozen synchronizing clutch. 5. Stuck shifter rail plunger. 6. Gearshift lever twisting and binding shifter rail. 7. Battered teeth on high speed sliding gear or on sleeve. 8. Improper lubrication, or lack of lubrication. 9. Corroded transmission parts. 10. Defective mainshaft pilot bearing. 11. Locked gear bearings will give same effect as stuck in gear.
Transmission gears will not synchronize	1. Binding pilot bearing on mainshaft, will synchronize in high gear only. 2. Clutch not releasing fully. 3. Detent spring weak or broken. 4. Weak or broken springs under balls in sliding gear sleeve. 5. Binding bearing on clutch shaft, or binding countershaft. 6. Binding pilot bearing in crankshaft. 7. Badly worn gear teeth. 8. Improper lubrication. 9. Constant mesh gear not turning freely on transmission mainshaft. Will synchronize in that gear only.

Condition	Possible Cause
Gears spinning when shifting into gear from neutral	1. Clutch not releasing fully. 2. In some cases an extremely light lubricant in transmission will cause gears to continue to spin for a short time after clutch is released. 3. Binding pilot bearing in crankshaft.
Transmission noisy in all gears	1. Insufficient lubricant, or improper lubricant. 2. Worn countergear bearings. 3. Worn or damaged main drive gear or countergear. 4. Damaged main drive gear or mainshaft bearings. 5. Worn or damaged countergear anti-lash plate.
Transmission noisy in neutral only	1. Damaged main drive gear bearing. 2. Damaged or loose mainshaft pilot bearing. 3. Worn or damaged countergear anti-lash plate. 4. Worn countergear bearings.
Transmission noisy in one gear only	1. Damaged or worn constant mesh gears. 2. Worn or damaged countergear bearings. 3. Damaged or worn synchronizer.
Transmission noisy in reverse only	1. Worn or damaged reverse idler gear or idler bushing. 2. Worn or damaged mainshaft reverse gear. 3. Worn or damaged reverse countergear. 4. Damaged shift mechanism.

TROUBLESHOOTING AUTOMATIC TRANSMISSION PROBLEMS

Keeping alert to changes in the operating characteristics of the transmission (changing shift points, noises, etc.) can prevent small problems from becoming large ones. If the problem cannot be traced to loose bolts, fluid level, misadjusted linkage, clogged filters or similar problems, you should probably seek professional service.

Transmission Fluid Indications

The appearance and odor of the transmission fluid can give valuable clues to the overall condition of the transmission. Always note the appearance of the fluid when you check the fluid level or change the fluid. Rub a small amount of fluid between your fingers to feel for grit and smell the fluid on the dipstick.

If the fluid appears:	It indicates:
Clear and red colored	Normal operation
Discolored (extremely dark red or brownish) or smells burned	Band or clutch pack failure, usually caused by an overheated transmission. Hauling very heavy loads with insufficient power or failure to change the fluid often result in overheating. Do not confuse this appearance with newer fluids that have a darker red color and a strong odor (though not a burned odor).
Foamy or aerated (light in color and full of bubbles)	1. The level is too high (gear train is churning oil) 2. An internal air leak (air is mixing with the fluid). Have the transmission checked professionally.
Solid residue in the fluid	Defective bands, clutch pack or bearings. Bits of band material or metal abrasives are clinging to the dipstick. Have the transmission checked professionally.
Varnish coating on the dipstick	The transmission fluid is overheating

TROUBLESHOOTING DRIVE AXLE PROBLEMS

First, determine when the noise is most noticeable.

Drive Noise: Produced under vehicle acceleration.

Coast Noise: Produced while coasting with a closed throttle.

Float Noise: Occurs while maintaining constant speed (just enough to keep speed constant) on a level road.

External Noise Elimination

It is advisable to make a thorough road test to determine whether the noise originates in the rear axle or whether it originates from the tires, engine, transmission, wheel bearings or road surface. Noise originating from other places cannot be corrected by servicing the rear axle.

ROAD NOISE

Brick or rough surfaced concrete roads produce noises that seem to come from the rear axle. Road noise is usually identical in Drive or Coast and driving on a different type of road will tell whether the road is the problem.

TIRE NOISE

Tire noise can be mistaken as rear axle noise, even though the tires on the front are at fault. Snow tread and mud tread tires or tires worn unevenly will frequently cause vibrations which seem to originate elsewhere; *temporarily, and for test purposes only,* inflate the tires to 40–50 lbs. This will significantly alter the noise produced by the tires, but will not alter noise from the rear axle. Noises from the rear axle will normally cease at speeds below 30 mph on coast, while tire noise will continue at lower tone as speed is decreased. The rear axle noise will usually change from drive conditions to coast conditions, while tire noise will not. Do not forget to lower the tire pressure to normal after the test is complete.

ENGINE/TRANSMISSION NOISE

Determine at what speed the noise is most pronounced, then stop in a quiet place. With the transmission in Neutral, run the engine through speeds corresponding to road speeds where the noise was noticed. Noises produced with the vehicle standing still are coming from the engine or transmission.

FRONT WHEEL BEARINGS

Front wheel bearing noises, sometimes confused with rear axle noises, will not change when comparing drive and coast conditions. While holding the speed steady, lightly apply the footbrake. This will often cause wheel bearing noise to lessen, as some of the weight is taken off the bearing. Front wheel bearings are easily checked by jacking up the wheels and spinning the wheels. Shaking the wheels will also determine if the wheel bearings are excessively loose.

REAR AXLE NOISES

Eliminating other possible sources can narrow the cause to the rear axle, which normally produces noise from worn gears or bearings. Gear noises tend to peak in a narrow speed range, while bearing noises will usually vary in pitch with engine speeds.

Noise Diagnosis

The Noise Is:	Most Probably Produced By:
1. Identical under Drive or Coast	Road surface, tires or front wheel bearings
2. Different depending on road surface	Road surface or tires
3. Lower as speed is lowered	Tires
4. Similar when standing or moving	Engine or transmission
5. A vibration	Unbalanced tires, rear wheel bearing, unbalanced driveshaft or worn U-joint
6. A knock or click about every two tire revolutions	Rear wheel bearing
7. Most pronounced on turns	Damaged differential gears
8. A steady low-pitched whirring or scraping, starting at low speeds	Damaged or worn pinion bearing
9. A chattering vibration on turns	Wrong differential lubricant or worn clutch plates (limited slip rear axle)
10. Noticed only in Drive, Coast or Float conditions	Worn ring gear and/or pinion gear

Troubleshooting Steering & Suspension Problems

Condition	Possible Cause
Hard steering (wheel is hard to turn)	1. Improper tire pressure 2. Loose or glazed pump drive belt 3. Low or incorrect fluid 4. Loose, bent or poorly lubricated front end parts 5. Improper front end alignment (excessive caster) 6. Bind in steering column or linkage 7. Kinked hydraulic hose 8. Air in hydraulic system 9. Low pump output or leaks in system 10. Obstruction in lines 11. Pump valves sticking or out of adjustment 12. Incorrect wheel alignment
Loose steering (too much play in steering wheel)	1. Loose wheel bearings 2. Faulty shocks 3. Worn linkage or suspension components 4. Loose steering gear mounting or linkage points 5. Steering mechanism worn or improperly adjusted 6. Valve spool improperly adjusted 7. Worn ball joints, tie-rod ends, etc.
Veers or wanders (pulls to one side with hands off steering wheel)	1. Improper tire pressure 2. Improper front end alignment 3. Dragging or improperly adjusted brakes 4. Bent frame 5. Improper rear end alignment 6. Faulty shocks or springs 7. Loose or bent front end components 8. Play in Pitman arm 9. Steering gear mountings loose 10. Loose wheel bearings 11. Binding Pitman arm 12. Spool valve sticking or improperly adjusted 13. Worn ball joints
Wheel oscillation or vibration transmitted through steering wheel	1. Low or uneven tire pressure 2. Loose wheel bearings 3. Improper front end alignment 4. Bent spindle 5. Worn, bent or broken front end components 6. Tires out of round or out of balance 7. Excessive lateral runout in disc brake rotor 8. Loose or bent shock absorber or strut
Noises (see also "Troubleshooting Drive Axle Problems")	1. Loose belts 2. Low fluid, air in system 3. Foreign matter in system 4. Improper lubrication 5. Interference or chafing in linkage 6. Steering gear mountings loose 7. Incorrect adjustment or wear in gear box 8. Faulty valves or wear in pump 9. Kinked hydraulic lines 10. Worn wheel bearings
Poor return of steering	1. Over-inflated tires 2. Improperly aligned front end (excessive caster) 3. Binding in steering column 4. No lubrication in front end 5. Steering gear adjusted too tight
Uneven tire wear (see "How To Read Tire Wear")	1. Incorrect tire pressure 2. Improperly aligned front end 3. Tires out-of-balance 4. Bent or worn suspension parts

HOW TO READ TIRE WEAR

The way your tires wear is a good indicator of other parts of the suspension. Abnormal wear patterns are often caused by the need for simple tire maintenance, or for front end alignment.

Excessive wear at the center of the tread indicates that the air pressure in the tire is consistently too high. The tire is riding on the center of the tread and wearing it prematurely. Occasionally, this wear pattern can result from outrageously wide tires on narrow rims. The cure for this is to replace either the tires or the wheels.

This type of wear usually results from consistent under-inflation. When a tire is under-inflated, there is too much contact with the road by the outer treads, which wear prematurely. When this type of wear occurs, and the tire pressure is known to be consistently correct, a bent or worn steering component or the need for wheel alignment could be indicated.

Feathering is a condition when the edge of each tread rib develops a slightly rounded edge on one side and a sharp edge on the other. By running your hand over the tire, you can usually feel the sharper edges before you'll be able to see them. The most common causes of feathering are incorrect toe-in setting or deteriorated bushings in the front suspension.

When an inner or outer rib wears faster than the rest of the tire, the need for wheel alignment is indicated. There is excessive camber in the front suspension, causing the wheel to lean too much putting excessive load on one side of the tire. Misalignment could also be due to sagging springs, worn ball joints, or worn control arm bushings. Be sure the vehicle is loaded the way it's normally driven when you have the wheels aligned.

Cups or scalloped dips appearing around the edge of the tread almost always indicate worn (sometimes bent) suspension parts. Adjustment of wheel alignment alone will seldom cure the problem. Any worn component that connects the wheel to the suspension can cause this type of wear. Occasionally, wheels that are out of balance will wear like this, but wheel imbalance usually shows up as bald spots between the outside edges and center of the tread.

Second-rib wear is usually found only in radial tires, and appears where the steel belts end in relation to the tread. It can be kept to a minimum by paying careful attention to tire pressure and frequently rotating the tires. This is often considered normal wear but excessive amounts indicate that the tires are too wide for the wheels.

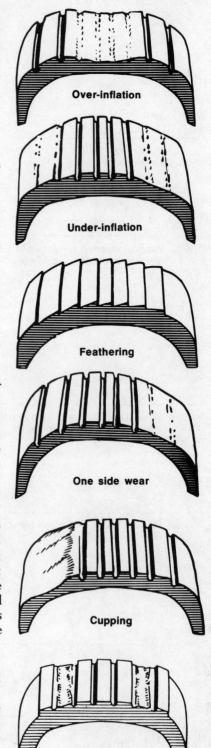

Over-inflation

Under-inflation

Feathering

One side wear

Cupping

Second-rib wear

Troubleshooting Disc Brake Problems

Condition	Possible Cause
Noise—groan—brake noise emanating when slowly releasing brakes (creep-groan)	Not detrimental to function of disc brakes—no corrective action required. (This noise may be eliminated by slightly increasing or decreasing brake pedal efforts.)
Rattle—brake noise or rattle emanating at low speeds on rough roads, (front wheels only).	1. Shoe anti-rattle spring missing or not properly positioned. 2. Excessive clearance between shoe and caliper. 3. Soft or broken caliper seals. 4. Deformed or misaligned disc. 5. Loose caliper.
Scraping	1. Mounting bolts too long. 2. Loose wheel bearings. 3. Bent, loose, or misaligned splash shield.
Front brakes heat up during driving and fail to release	1. Operator riding brake pedal. 2. Stop light switch improperly adjusted. 3. Sticking pedal linkage. 4. Frozen or seized piston. 5. Residual pressure valve in master cylinder. 6. Power brake malfunction. 7. Proportioning valve malfunction.
Leaky brake caliper	1. Damaged or worn caliper piston seal. 2. Scores or corrosion on surface of cylinder bore.
Grabbing or uneven brake action— Brakes pull to one side	1. Causes listed under "Brakes Pull". 2. Power brake malfunction. 3. Low fluid level in master cylinder. 4. Air in hydraulic system. 5. Brake fluid, oil or grease on linings. 6. Unmatched linings. 7. Distorted brake pads. 8. Frozen or seized pistons. 9. Incorrect tire pressure. 10. Front end out of alignment. 11. Broken rear spring. 12. Brake caliper pistons sticking. 13. Restricted hose or line. 14. Caliper not in proper alignment to braking disc. 15. Stuck or malfunctioning metering valve. 16. Soft or broken caliper seals. 17. Loose caliper.
Brake pedal can be depressed without braking effect	1. Air in hydraulic system or improper bleeding procedure. 2. Leak past primary cup in master cylinder. 3. Leak in system. 4. Rear brakes out of adjustment. 5. Bleeder screw open.
Excessive pedal travel	1. Air, leak, or insufficient fluid in system or caliper. 2. Warped or excessively tapered shoe and lining assembly. 3. Excessive disc runout. 4. Rear brake adjustment required. 5. Loose wheel bearing adjustment. 6. Damaged caliper piston seal. 7. Improper brake fluid (boil). 8. Power brake malfunction. 9. Weak or soft hoses.

Troubleshooting Disc Brake Problems (cont.)

Condition	Possible Cause
Brake roughness or chatter (pedal pumping)	1. Excessive thickness variation of braking disc. 2. Excessive lateral runout of braking disc. 3. Rear brake drums out-of-round. 4. Excessive front bearing clearance.
Excessive pedal effort	1. Brake fluid, oil or grease on linings. 2. Incorrect lining. 3. Frozen or seized pistons. 4. Power brake malfunction. 5. Kinked or collapsed hose or line. 6. Stuck metering valve. 7. Scored caliper or master cylinder bore. 8. Seized caliper pistons.
Brake pedal fades (pedal travel increases with foot on brake)	1. Rough master cylinder or caliper bore. 2. Loose or broken hydraulic lines/connections. 3. Air in hydraulic system. 4. Fluid level low. 5. Weak or soft hoses. 6. Inferior quality brake shoes or fluid. 7. Worn master cylinder piston cups or seals.

Troubleshooting Drum Brakes

Condition	Possible Cause
Pedal goes to floor	1. Fluid low in reservoir. 2. Air in hydraulic system. 3. Improperly adjusted brake. 4. Leaking wheel cylinders. 5. Loose or broken brake lines. 6. Leaking or worn master cylinder. 7. Excessively worn brake lining.
Spongy brake pedal	1. Air in hydraulic system. 2. Improper brake fluid (low boiling point). 3. Excessively worn or cracked brake drums. 4. Broken pedal pivot bushing.
Brakes pulling	1. Contaminated lining. 2. Front end out of alignment. 3. Incorrect brake adjustment. 4. Unmatched brake lining. 5. Brake drums out of round. 6. Brake shoes distorted. 7. Restricted brake hose or line. 8. Broken rear spring. 9. Worn brake linings. 10. Uneven lining wear. 11. Glazed brake lining. 12. Excessive brake lining dust. 13. Heat spotted brake drums. 14. Weak brake return springs. 15. Faulty automatic adjusters. 16. Low or incorrect tire pressure.

Condition	Possible Cause
Squealing brakes	1. Glazed brake lining. 2. Saturated brake lining. 3. Weak or broken brake shoe retaining spring. 4. Broken or weak brake shoe return spring. 5. Incorrect brake lining. 6. Distorted brake shoes. 7. Bent support plate. 8. Dust in brakes or scored brake drums. 9. Linings worn below limit. 10. Uneven brake lining wear. 11. Heat spotted brake drums.
Chirping brakes	1. Out of round drum or eccentric axle flange pilot.
Dragging brakes	1. Incorrect wheel or parking brake adjustment. 2. Parking brakes engaged or improperly adjusted. 3. Weak or broken brake shoe return spring. 4. Brake pedal binding. 5. Master cylinder cup sticking. 6. Obstructed master cylinder relief port. 7. Saturated brake lining. 8. Bent or out of round brake drum. 9. Contaminated or improper brake fluid. 10. Sticking wheel cylinder pistons. 11. Driver riding brake pedal. 12. Defective proportioning valve. 13. Insufficient brake shoe lubricant.
Hard pedal	1. Brake booster inoperative. 2. Incorrect brake lining. 3. Restricted brake line or hose. 4. Frozen brake pedal linkage. 5. Stuck wheel cylinder. 6. Binding pedal linkage. 7. Faulty proportioning valve.
Wheel locks	1. Contaminated brake lining. 2. Loose or torn brake lining. 3. Wheel cylinder cups sticking. 4. Incorrect wheel bearing adjustment. 5. Faulty proportioning valve.
Brakes fade (high speed)	1. Incorrect lining. 2. Overheated brake drums. 3. Incorrect brake fluid (low boiling temperature). 4. Saturated brake lining. 5. Leak in hydraulic system. 6. Faulty automatic adjusters.
Pedal pulsates	1. Bent or out of round brake drum.
Brake chatter and shoe knock	1. Out of round brake drum. 2. Loose support plate. 3. Bent support plate. 4. Distorted brake shoes. 5. Machine grooves in contact face of brake drum (Shoe Knock). 6. Contaminated brake lining. 7. Missing or loose components. 8. Incorrect lining material. 9. Out-of-round brake drums. 10. Heat spotted or scored brake drums. 11. Out-of-balance wheels.

Troubleshooting Drum Brakes (cont.)

Condition	Possible Cause
Brakes do not self adjust	1. Adjuster screw frozen in thread. 2. Adjuster screw corroded at thrust washer. 3. Adjuster lever does not engage star wheel. 4. Adjuster installed on wrong wheel.
Brake light glows	1. Leak in the hydraulic system. 2. Air in the system. 3. Improperly adjusted master cylinder pushrod. 4. Uneven lining wear. 5. Failure to center combination valve or proportioning valve.

Mechanic's Data

General Conversion Table

Multiply By	To Convert	To	
LENGTH			
2.54	Inches	Centimeters	.3937
25.4	Inches	Millimeters	.03937
30.48	Feet	Centimeters	.0328
.304	Feet	Meters	3.28
.914	Yards	Meters	1.094
1.609	Miles	Kilometers	.621
VOLUME			
.473	Pints	Liters	2.11
.946	Quarts	Liters	1.06
3.785	Gallons	Liters	.264
.016	Cubic inches	Liters	61.02
16.39	Cubic inches	Cubic cms.	.061
28.3	Cubic feet	Liters	.0353
MASS (Weight)			
28.35	Ounces	Grams	.035
.4536	Pounds	Kilograms	2.20
—	To obtain	From	Multiply by

Multiply By	To Convert	To	
AREA			
.645	Square inches	Square cms.	.155
.836	Square yds.	Square meters	1.196
FORCE			
4.448	Pounds	Newtons	.225
.138	Ft./lbs.	Kilogram/meters	7.23
1.36	Ft./lbs.	Newton-meters	.737
.112	In./lbs.	Newton-meters	8.844
PRESSURE			
.068	Psi	Atmospheres	14.7
6.89	Psi	Kilopascals	.145
OTHER			
1.104	Horsepower (DIN)	Horsepower (SAE)	.9861
.746	Horsepower (SAE)	Kilowatts (KW)	1.34
1.60	Mph	Km/h	.625
.425	Mpg	Km/1	2.35
—	To obtain	From	Multiply by

Tap Drill Sizes

National Coarse or U.S.S.

Screw & Tap Size	Threads Per Inch	Use Drill Number
No. 5	40	39
No. 6	32	36
No. 8	32	29
No. 10	24	25
No. 12	24	17
1/4	20	8
5/16	18	F
3/8	16	5/16
7/16	14	U
1/2	13	27/64
9/16	12	31/64
5/8	11	17/32
3/4	10	21/32
7/8	9	49/64

National Coarse or U.S.S.

Screw & Tap Size	Threads Per Inch	Use Drill Number
1	8	7/8
1 1/8	7	63/64
1 1/4	7	1 7/64
1 1/2	6	1 11/32

National Fine or S.A.E.

Screw & Tap Size	Threads Per Inch	Use Drill Number
No. 5	44	37
No. 6	40	33
No. 8	36	29
No. 10	32	21

National Fine or S.A.E.

Screw & Tap Size	Threads Per Inch	Use Drill Number
No. 12	28	15
1/4	28	3
6/16	24	1
3/8	24	Q
7/16	20	W
1/2	20	29/64
9/16	18	33/64
5/8	18	37/64
3/4	16	11/16
7/8	14	13/16
1 1/8	12	1 3/64
1 1/4	12	1 11/64
1 1/2	12	1 27/64

Drill Sizes In Decimal Equivalents

Inch	Decimal	Wire	mm	Inch	Decimal	Wire	mm	Inch	Decimal	Wire & Letter	mm	Inch	Decimal	Letter	mm	Inch	Decimal	mm
1/64	.0156		.39		.0730	49			.1614		4.1		.2717		6.9		.4331	11.0
	.0157		.4		.0748		1.9		.1654		4.2		.2720	I		7/16	.4375	11.11
	.0160	78			.0760	48			.1660	19			.2756		7.0		.4528	11.5
	.0165		.42		.0768		1.95		.1673		4.25		.2770	J		29/64	.4531	11.51
	.0173		.44	5/64	.0781		1.98		.1693		4.3		.2795		7.1	15/32	.4688	11.90
	.0177		.45		.0785	47			.1695	18			.2810	K			.4724	12.0
	.0180	77			.0787		2.0	11/64	.1719		4.36	9/32	.2812		7.14	31/64	.4844	12.30
	.0181		.46		.0807		2.05		.1730	17			.2835		7.2		.4921	12.5
	.0189		.48		.0810	46			.1732		4.4		.2854		7.25	1/2	.5000	12.70
	.0197		.5		.0820	45			.1770	16			.2874		7.3		.5118	13.0
	.0200	76			.0827		2.1		.1772		4.5		.2900	L		33/64	.5156	13.09
	.0210	75			.0846		2.15		.1800	15			.2913		7.4	17/32	.5312	13.49
	.0217		.55		.0860	44			.1811		4.6		.2950	M			.5315	13.5
	.0225	74			.0866		2.2		.1820	14			.2953		7.5	35/64	.5469	13.89
	.0236		.6		.0886		2.25		.1850	13		19/64	.2969		7.54		.5512	14.0
	.0240	73			.0890	43			.1850		4.7		.2992		7.6	9/16	.5625	14.28
	.0250	72			.0906		2.3		.1870		4.75		.3020	N			.5709	14.5
	.0256		.65		.0925		2.35	3/16	.1875		4.76		.3031		7.7	37/64	.5781	14.68
	.0260	71			.0935	42			.1890		4.8		.3051		7.75		.5906	15.0
	.0276		.7	3/32	.0938		2.38		.1890	12			.3071		7.8	19/32	.5938	15.08
	.0280	70			.0945		2.4		.1910	11			.3110		7.9	39/64	.6094	15.47
	.0292	69			.0960	41			.1929		4.9	5/16	.3125		7.93		.6102	15.5
	.0295		.75		.0965		2.45		.1935	10			.3150		8.0	5/8	.6250	15.87
	.0310	68			.0980	40			.1960	9			.3160	O			.6299	16.0
1/32	.0312		.79		.0981		2.5		.1969		5.0		.3189		8.1	41/64	.6406	16.27
	.0315		.8		.0995	39			.1990	8			.3228		8.2		.6496	16.5
	.0320	67			.1015	38			.2008		5.1		.3230	P		21/32	.6562	16.66
	.0330	66			.1024		2.6		.2010	7			.3248		8.25		.6693	17.0
	.0335		.85		.1040	37		13/64	.2031		5.16		.3268		8.3	43/64	.6719	17.06
	.0350	65			.1063		2.7		.2040	6		21/64	.3281		8.33	11/16	.6875	17.46
	.0354		.9		.1065	36			.2047		5.2		.3307		8.4		.6890	17.5
	.0360	64			.1083		2.75		.2055	5			.3320	Q		45/64	.7031	17.85
	.0370	63		7/64	.1094		2.77		.2067		5.25		.3346		8.5		.7087	18.0
	.0374		.95		.1100	35			.2087		5.3		.3386		8.6	23/32	.7188	18.25
	.0380	62			.1102		2.8		.2090	4			.3390	R			.7283	18.5
	.0390	61			.1110	34			.2126		5.4		.3425		8.7	47/64	.7344	18.65
	.0394		1.0		.1130	33			.2130	3		11/32	.3438		8.73		.7480	19.0
	.0400	60			.1142		2.9		.2165		5.5		.3445		8.75	3/4	.7500	19.05
	.0410	59			.1160	32		7/32	.2188		5.55		.3465		8.8	49/64	.7656	19.44
	.0413		1.05		.1181		3.0		.2205		5.6		.3480	S			.7677	19.5
	.0420	58			.1200	31			.2210	2			.3504		8.9	25/32	.7812	19.84
	.0430	57			.1220		3.1		.2244		5.7		.3543		9.0		.7874	20.0
	.0433		1.1	1/8	.1250		3.17		.2264		5.75		.3580	T		51/64	.7969	20.24
	.0453		1.15		.1260		3.2		.2280	1			.3583		9.1		.8071	20.5
	.0465	56			.1280		3.25		.2283		5.8	23/64	.3594		9.12	13/16	.8125	20.63
3/64	.0469		1.19		.1285	30			.2323		5.9		.3622		9.2		.8268	21.0
	.0472		1.2		.1299		3.3		.2340	A			.3642		9.25	53/64	.8281	21.03
	.0492		1.25		.1339		3.4	15/64	.2344		5.95		.3661		9.3	27/32	.8438	21.43
	.0512		1.3		.1360	29			.2362		6.0		.3680	U			.8465	21.5
	.0520	55			.1378		3.5		.2380	B			.3701		9.4	55/64	.8594	21.82
	.0531		1.35		.1405	28			.2402		6.1		.3740		9.5		.8661	22.0
	.0550	54		9/64	.1406		3.57		.2420	C		3/8	.3750		9.52	7/8	.8750	22.22
	.0551		1.4		.1417		3.6		.2441		6.2		.3770	V			.8858	22.5
	.0571		1.45		.1440	27			.2460	D			.3780		9.6	57/64	.8906	22.62
	.0591		1.5		.1457		3.7		.2461		6.25		.3819		9.7		.9055	23.0
	.0595	53			.1470	26			.2480		6.3		.3839		9.75	29/32	.9062	23.01
	.0610		1.55		.1476		3.75	1/4	.2500	E	6.35		.3858		9.8	59/64	.9219	23.41
1/16	.0625		1.59		.1495	25			.2520		6.		.3860	W			.9252	23.5
	.0630		1.6		.1496		3.8		.2559		6.5		.3898		9.9	15/16	.9375	23.81
	.0635	52			.1520	24			.2570	F		25/64	.3906		9.92		.9449	24.0
	.0650		1.65		.1535		3.9		.2598		6.6		.3937		10.0	61/64	.9531	24.2
	.0669		1.7		.1540	23			.2610	G			.3970	X			.9646	24.5
	.0670	51		5/32	.1562		3.96		.2638		6.7		.4040	Y		31/32	.9688	24.6
	.0689		1.75		.1570	22		17/64	.2656		6.74	13/32	.4062		10.31		.9843	25.0
	.0700	50			.1575		4.0		.2657		6.75		.4130	Z		63/64	.9844	25.0
	.0709		1.8		.1590	21			.2660	H			.4134		10.5	1	1.0000	25.4
	.0728		1.85		.1610	20			.2677		6.8	27/64	.4219		10.71			

Index

Chilton's Repair & Tune-Up Guides

The Complete line covers domestic cars, imports, trucks, vans, RV's and 4-wheel drive vehicles.

RTUG Title	Part No.
AMC 1975-82	7199
Covers all U.S. and Canadian models	
Aspen/Volare 1976-80	6637
Covers all U.S. and Canadian models	
Audi 1970-73	5902
Covers all U.S. and Canadian models.	
Audi 4000/5000 1978-81	7028
Covers all U.S. and Canadian models including turbocharged and diesel engines	
Barracuda/Challenger 1965-72	5807
Covers all U.S. and Canadian models	
Blazer/Jimmy 1969-82	6931
Covers all U.S. and Canadian 2- and 4-wheel drive models, including diesel engines	
BMW 1970-82	6844
Covers U.S. and Canadian models	
Buick/Olds/Pontiac 1975-85	7308
Covers all U.S. and Canadian full size rear wheel drive models	
Cadillac 1967-84	7462
Covers all U.S. and Canadian rear wheel drive models	
Camaro 1967-81	6735
Covers all U.S. and Canadian models	
Camaro 1982-85	7317
Covers all U.S. and Canadian models	
Capri 1970-77	6695
Covers all U.S. and Canadian models	
Caravan/Voyager 1984-85	7482
Covers all U.S. and Canadian models	
Century/Regal 1975-85	7307
Covers all U.S. and Canadian rear wheel drive models, including turbocharged engines	
Champ/Arrow/Sapporo 1978-83	7041
Covers all U.S. and Canadian models	
Chevette/1000 1976-86	6836
Covers all U.S. and Canadian models	
Chevrolet 1968-85	7135
Covers all U.S. and Canadian models	
Chevrolet 1968-79 Spanish	7082
Chevrolet/GMC Pick-Ups 1970-82 Spanish	7468
Chevrolet/GMC Pick-Ups and Suburban 1970-86	6936
Covers all U.S. and Canadian 1/2, 3/4 and 1 ton models, including 4-wheel drive and diesel engines	
Chevrolet LUV 1972-81	6815
Covers all U.S. and Canadian models	
Chevrolet Mid-Size 1964-86	6840
Covers all U.S. and Canadian models of 1964-77 Chevelle, Malibu and Malibu SS; 1974-77 Laguna; 1978-85 Malibu; 1970-86 Monte Carlo; 1964-84 El Camino, including diesel engines	
Chevrolet Nova 1986	7658
Covers all U.S. and Canadian models	
Chevy/GMC Vans 1967-84	6930
Covers all U.S. and Canadian models of 1/2, 3/4, and 1 ton vans, cutaways, and motor home chassis, including diesel engines	
Chevy S-10 Blazer/GMC S-15 Jimmy 1982-85	7383
Covers all U.S. and Canadian models	
Chevy S-10/GMC S-15 Pick-Ups 1982-85	7310
Covers all U.S. and Canadian models	
Chevy II/Nova 1962-79	6841
Covers all U.S. and Canadian models	
Chrysler K- and E-Car 1981-85	7163
Covers all U.S. and Canadian front wheel drive models	
Colt/Challenger/Vista/Conquest 1971-85	7037
Covers all U.S. and Canadian models	
Corolla/Carina/Tercel/Starlet 1970-85	7036
Corona/Cressida/Crown/Mk.II/Camry/Van 1970-84	7044
Covers all U.S. and Canadian models	

RTUG Title	Part No.
Corvair 1960-69	6691
Covers all U.S. and Canadian models	
Corvette 1953-62	6576
Covers all U.S. and Canadian models	
Corvette 1963-84	6843
Covers all U.S. and Canadian models	
Cutlass 1970-85	6933
Covers all U.S. and Canadian models	
Dart/Demon 1968-76	6324
Covers all U.S. and Canadian models	
Datsun 1961-72	5790
Covers all U.S. and Canadian models of Nissan Patrol; 1500, 1600 and 2000 sports cars; Pick-Ups; 410, 411, 510, 1200 and 240Z	
Datsun 1973-80 Spanish	7083
Datsun/Nissan F-10, 310, Stanza, Pulsar 1977-86	7196
Covers all U.S. and Canadian models	
Datsun/Nissan Pick-Ups 1970-84	6816
Covers all U.S. and Canadian models	
Datsun/Nissan Z & ZX 1970-86	6932
Covers all U.S. and Canadian models	
Datsun/Nissan 1200, 210, Sentra 1973-86	7197
Covers all U.S. and Canadian models	
Datsun/Nissan 200SX, 510, 610, 710, 810, Maxima 1973-84	7170
Covers all U.S. and Canadian models	
Dodge 1968-77	6554
Covers all U.S. and Canadian models	
Dodge Charger 1967-70	6486
Covers all U.S. and Canadian models	
Dodge/Plymouth Trucks 1967-84	7459
Covers all 1/2, 3/4, and 1 ton 2- and 4-wheel drive U.S. and Canadian models, including diesel engines	
Dodge/Plymouth Vans 1967-84	6934
Covers all 1/2, 3/4, and 1 ton U.S. and Canadian models of vans, cutaways and motor home chassis	
D-50/Arrow Pick-Up 1979-81	7032
Covers all U.S. and Canadian models	
Fairlane/Torino 1962-75	6320
Covers all U.S. and Canadian models	
Fairmont/Zephyr 1978-83	6965
Covers all U.S. and Canadian models	
Fiat 1969-81	7042
Covers all U.S. and Canadian models	
Fiesta 1978-80	6846
Covers all U.S. and Canadian models	
Firebird 1967-81	5996
Covers all U.S. and Canadian models	
Firebird 1982-85	7345
Covers all U.S. and Canadian models	
Ford 1968-79 Spanish	7084
Ford Bronco 1966-83	7140
Covers all U.S. and Canadian models	
Ford Bronco II 1984	7408
Covers all U.S. and Canadian models	
Ford Courier 1972-82	6983
Covers all U.S. and Canadian models	
Ford/Mercury Front Wheel Drive 1981-85	7055
Covers all U.S. and Canadian models Escort, EXP, Tempo, Lynx, LN-7 and Topaz	
Ford/Mercury/Lincoln 1968-85	6842
Covers all U.S. and Canadian models of FORD Country Sedan, Country Squire, Crown Victoria, Custom, Custom 500, Galaxie 500, LTD through 1982, Ranch Wagon, and XL; MERCURY Colony Park, Commuter, Marquis through 1982, Gran Marquis, Monterey and Park Lane; LINCOLN Continental and Towne Car	
Ford/Mercury/Lincoln Mid-Size 1971-85	6696
Covers all U.S. and Canadian models of FORD Elite, 1983-85 LTD, 1977-79 LTD II, Ranchero, Torino, Gran Torino, 1977-85 Thunderbird; MERCURY 1972-85 Cougar,	

continued on next page

RTUG Title	Part No.
1983-85 Marquis, Montego, 1980-85 XR-7; LINCOLN 1982-85 Continental, 1984-85 Mark VII, 1978-80 Versailles	
Ford Pick-Ups 1965-86	6913
Covers all ½, ¾ and 1 ton, 2- and 4-wheel drive U.S. and Canadian pick-up, chassis cab and camper models, including diesel engines	
Ford Pick-Ups 1965-82 Spanish	7469
Ford Ranger 1983-84	7338
Covers all U.S. and Canadian models	
Ford Vans 1961-86	6849
Covers all U.S. and Canadian ½, ¾ and 1 ton van and cutaway chassis models, including diesel engines	
GM A-Body 1982-85	7309
Covers all front wheel drive U.S. and Canadian models of BUICK Century, CHEVROLET Celebrity, OLDSMOBILE Cutlass Ciera and PONTIAC 6000	
GM C-Body 1985	7587
Covers all front wheel drive U.S. and Canadian models of BUICK Electra Park Avenue and Electra T-Type, CADILLAC Fleetwood and deVille, OLDSMOBILE 98 Regency and Regency Brougham	
GM J-Car 1982-85	7059
Covers all U.S. and Canadian models of BUICK Skyhawk, CHEVROLET Cavalier, CADILLAC Cimarron, OLDSMOBILE Firenza and PONTIAC 2000 and Sunbird	
GM N-Body 1985-86	7657
Covers all U.S. and Canadian models of front wheel drive BUICK Somerset and Skylark, OLDSMOBILE Calais, and PONTIAC Grand Am	
GM X-Body 1980-85	7049
Covers all U.S. and Canadian models of BUICK Skylark, CHEVROLET Citation, OLDSMOBILE Omega and PONTIAC Phoenix	
GM Subcompact 1971-80	6935
Covers all U.S. and Canadian models of BUICK Skyhawk (1975-80), CHEVROLET Vega and Monza, OLDSMOBILE Starfire, and PONTIAC Astre and 1975-80 Sunbird	
Granada/Monarch 1975-82	6937
Covers all U.S. and Canadian models	
Honda 1973-84	6980
Covers all U.S. and Canadian models	
International Scout 1967-73	5912
Covers all U.S. and Canadian models	
Jeep 1945-87	6817
Covers all U.S. and Canadian CJ-2A, CJ-3A, CJ-3B, CJ-5, CJ-6, CJ-7, Scrambler and Wrangler models	
Jeep Wagoneer, Commando, Cherokee, Truck 1957-86	6739
Covers all U.S. and Canadian models of Wagoneer, Cherokee, Grand Wagoneer, Jeepster, Jeepster Commando, J-100, J-200, J-300, J-10, J20, FC-150 and FC-170	
Laser/Daytona 1984-85	7563
Covers all U.S. and Canadian models	
Maverick/Comet 1970-77	6634
Covers all U.S. and Canadian models	
Mazda 1971-84	6981
Covers all U.S. and Canadian models of RX-2, RX-3, RX-4, 808, 1300, 1600, Cosmo, GLC and 626	
Mazda Pick-Ups 1972-86	7659
Covers all U.S. and Canadian models	
Mercedes-Benz 1959-70	6065
Covers all U.S. and Canadian models	
Mereceds-Benz 1968-73	5907
Covers all U.S. and Canadian models	

RTUG Title	Part No.
Mercedes-Benz 1974-84	6809
Covers all U.S. and Canadian models	
Mitsubishi, Cordia, Tredia, Starion, Galant 1983-85	7583
Covers all U.S. and Canadian models	
MG 1961-81	6780
Covers all U.S. and Canadian models	
Mustang/Capri/Merkur 1979-85	6963
Covers all U.S. and Canadian models	
Mustang/Cougar 1965-73	6542
Covers all U.S. and Canadian models	
Mustang II 1974-78	6812
Covers all U.S. and Canadian models	
Omni/Horizon/Rampage 1978-84	6845
Covers all U.S. and Canadian models of DODGE omni, Miser, 024, Charger 2.2; PLYMOUTH Horizon, Miser, TC3, TC3 Tourismo; Rampage	
Opel 1971-75	6575
Covers all U.S. and Canadian models	
Peugeot 1970-74	5982
Covers all U.S. and Canadian models	
Pinto/Bobcat 1971-80	7027
Covers all U.S. and Canadian models	
Plymouth 1968-76	6552
Covers all U.S. and Canadian models	
Pontiac Fiero 1984-85	7571
Covers all U.S. and Canadian models	
Pontiac Mid-Size 1974-83	7346
Covers all U.S. and Canadian models of Ventura, Grand Am, LeMans, Grand LeMans, GTO, Phoenix, and Grand Prix	
Porsche 924/928 1976-81	7048
Covers all U.S. and Canadian models	
Renault 1975-85	7165
Covers all U.S. and Canadian models	
Roadrunner/Satellite/Belvedere/GTX 1968-73	5821
Covers all U.S. and Canadian models	
RX-7 1979-81	7031
Covers all U.S. and Canadian models	
SAAB 99 1969-75	5988
Covers all U.S. and Canadian models	
SAAB 900 1979-85	7572
Covers all U.S. and Canadian models	
Snowmobiles 1976-80	6978
Covers Arctic Cat, John Deere, Kawasaki, Polaris, Ski-Doo and Yamaha	
Subaru 1970-84	6982
Covers all U.S. and Canadian models	
Tempest/GTO/LeMans 1968-73	5905
Covers all U.S. and Canadian models	
Toyota 1966-70	5795
Covers all U.S. and Canadian models of Corona, MkII, Corolla, Crown, Land Cruiser, Stout and Hi-Lux	
Toyota 1970-79 Spanish	7467
Toyota Celica/Supra 1971-85	7043
Covers all U.S. and Canadian models	
Toyota Trucks 1970-85	7035
Covers all U.S. and Canadian models of pick-ups, Land Cruiser and 4Runner	
Valiant/Duster 1968-76	6326
Covers all U.S. and Canadian models	
Volvo 1956-69	6529
Covers all U.S. and Canadian models	
Volvo 1970-83	7040
Covers all U.S. and Canadian models	
VW Front Wheel Drive 1974-85	6962
Covers all U.S. and Canadian models	
VW 1949-71	5796
Covers all U.S. and Canadian models	
VW 1970-79 Spanish	7081
VW 1970-81	6837
Covers all U.S. and Canadian Beetles, Karmann Ghia, Fastback, Squareback, Vans, 411 and 412	

Chilton's Repair & Tune-Up Guides are available at your local retailer or by mailing a check or money order for **$13.95** plus **$3.25** to cover postage and handling to:

**Chilton Book Company
Dept. DM
Radnor, PA 19089**

NOTE: When ordering be sure to include your name & address, book part No. & title.